INTRODUCTIONS A
ON THE MEGILLOTH

CONTENTS OF THE COMMENTARY SECTION

INTRODUCTIONS

RUTH

Hebrew Witnesses

This edition of Ruth in the *Biblia Hebraica Quinta* is entirely based upon recent photographs – films and color transparencies – of folios 421–423r of EBP. I B 19a "Leningradensis" of the Russian National Library in St. Petersburg, Russia (i.e., M^L). In addition, two major Tiberian manuscripts have been collated, the Aleppo Codex, and Cambridge, Univ. Libr. Add. Ms. 1753.

The Masoretic Text of Ruth in M^L has been very well preserved. In fact, there is only one case in which a textual corruption could be defended, namely in 4:4 with regard to the reading יִגְאַל.

The description of the *sətumôt* and *pətuhôt* in the three major Tiberian manuscripts can be extremely brief. M^L presents only one *pətuhâ* found between 4:17 and 4:18 and so do M^A and M^Y.

As to the apparatus, the Qumran evidence from 2Q has been cited according to the edition of M. Baillet, J.T. Milik, and R. de Vaux, O.P., *Les "petites grottes" de Qumrân* (DJD III; Oxford: Clarendon Press, 1962), plates XIV and XV, whereas the 4Q evidence is quoted from E. Ulrich, F.M. Cross, J.A. Fitzmyer, P.W. Flint, S. Metso, C.M. Murphy, C. Niccum, P.W. Skehan, E. Tov, and J. Trebolle Barrera, *Qumran Cave 4. XI Psalms to Chronicles* (DJD XVI; Oxford: Clarendon Press, 2000), 187–94 and Plate XXIV.

Sometimes, the Qumran evidence is so fragmentary that almost nothing can be concluded, e.g., in 2:23. Where it can be deciphered, it frequently supports M (1:14; 2:14; 2:20; 3:7). Occasionally, the Qumran materials support versional evidence over against M, as 2QRuth^b in 3:14, and, perhaps, 4QRuth^a in the case of 1:9. In some very rare cases, a plus is found which is not shared by any witness, e.g., the reading שם of 2QRuth^b in 3:15.

Greek Witnesses

With regard to the Greek evidence, use has been made of the Larger Cambridge edition by A.E. Brooke and N. McLean, *Joshua, Judges and Ruth* (Vol. 1, pt. 4 of *The Old Testament in Greek*; ed. A.E. Brooke and N. McLean; Cambridge: Cambridge University Press, 1917) 887–97, of Alfred Rahlfs's manual edition: *Septuaginta* (9th ed.; Stuttgart: Deutsche Bibelstiftung, 1979), and especially of Alfred Rahlfs's *Das Buch Ruth griechisch als Probe einer kritischen Handausgabe der Septuaginta* (Stuttgart: Württembergische Bibelanstalt, 1922). Rahlfs's epoch-making *Studie über den griechischen Text des Buches Ruth* (Berlin: Weidmann, 1923) has, of course, carefully been consulted, and the recensions he distinguished have occasionally been cited in the apparatus. In addition, thanks to the permission given by the Septuagint Committee of the Akademie der Wissenschaften in Göttingen, it has been possible to consult final collations and the last stage research done in the Göttinger Septuaginta-Unternehmen. The *sigla* used in this edition are those of Göttingen, and the *sigla* of the larger Cambridge edition have been converted according to the conversion tables published in Sidney Jellicoe, *The Septuagint and Modern Study* (Oxford: Clarendon Press, 1968), 362–69.

With the possible exception of 2:7, G must have used a *Vorlage* very close to M. Most differences can be easily explained by the desire of the translator to produce a receptor language text which could be well understood. Towards that aim, certain information has been made explicit (e.g., in 1:14; 4:7, 8) whereas other information has been left implicit because of a certain redundancy (e.g., in 1:2 and 4:16). Out of the same concern, the chronological order of the base text has sometimes been changed (e.g., in 1:5), or a contextual assimilation (2:19) or harmonization (4:14) has taken place. As far as figurative speech is concerned, the use of euphemism (1:12) and synecdoche (4:10) can be observed.

Finally, for the Hexaplaric evidence, the edition of F. Field, *Origenis Hexaplorum quae supersunt* (Oxford: Oxford University Press, 1875; repr., Hildesheim: Georg Olms, 1964) has been used and a comparison with the edition of Bernardus de Montfaucon, *Hexaplorum Origenis quae supersunt* (Paris: Ludovicus Guerin, 1713) has been made. In fact, the available material is extremely limited: one case of σ' in chapter 3, two cases of α' and three of σ' in chapter 4.

Latin Witnesses

As to the Latin sources, for the Old Latin, use has been made of the only manuscript of Ruth (Madrid, Bibl. Univ. 31, fol. 80v–81v; severely damaged during the Spanish civil war) according to the publications of S. Berger, "Notice sur quelques textes latins inédits de l'Ancien Testament," *Notices et extraits des manuscrits de la Bibliothèque Nationale et autres bibliothèques*, XXXIV/2 (Paris: Institut national de France, 1893) 122–26 and J. Cantera Ortiz de Urbina, *Vetus Latina – Rut: studio crítico de la version Latina prejeronomiana de Libro de Rut* (Textos y estudios del Seminario Filologico Cardenal Cisneros 4; Madrid and Barcelona: Seminario Filologico Cardenal Cisneros, 1965). In view of several shortcomings of the editions, it has been very helpful to consult the critical review of Cantera's edition by W. Baars ("Vetus Latina"), as well as the evaluation made by Rahlfs (*Studie*, 124–34).

The Old Latin sometimes has an independent reading, as can be seen in 1:3 and 2:23. It remarkably supports M without aligning with any known Greek evidence in at least four cases (2:14; 3:7; 4:8, 11). In these cases it always agrees with T, and in two cases with either V or S.

For the Vulgate, the edition of the Benedictine fathers of S. Girolamo in Rome, F.A. Gasquet, et al., eds., *Libri Iosue Iudicum Ruth* (vol. 4 of *Biblia Sacra iuxta Latinam Vulgatam Versionem*; Rome: Libreria Editrice Vaticana, 1939) has been the textual base, and the fourth edition of R. Weber, *Biblia Sacra iuxta Vulgatam Versionem* (2 vols.; 4th rev. ed.; Stuttgart: Deutsche Bibelgesellschaft, 1994) has been consulted.

V normally is a most reliable witness of M, and its deviations can frequently be explained by translational reasons. The lack of certain precise grammatical distinctions in Latin is at the base of the occasional use of the characterization "indeterminate" (e.g., in 2:6 and 4:4). In many cases in which V deviates from M, it is joined by G and S (e.g., 1:6, 8, 21; 2:21).

Syriac and Aramaic Witnesses

In the absence of a critical edition of Ruth by the Peshitta Institute in Leiden, the Syriac base for this edition has been the Codex Ambrosianus, which is quoted according to the photolithographic edition of A.M. Ceriani, *Translatio Syra Pescitto Veteris Testamenti* (Milan: J.B. Pogliani, 1883) 213–214r. The editions of the Dominicans of Mosul, *Biblia Sacra iuxta Versionem Simplicem quae dicitur Pschitta* (3 vols.; Mosul: Typis Fratrum Praedicatorum, 1887), and of the Syriac Bible of S. Lee (1826; repr., London: United Bible Societies, 1979) have also been used.

Although an important number of coincidences between readings of G and S occur, the translator of S apparently did not use G in any consistent way. There are many instances in which S stands alone in providing a syntactic facilitation (e.g., 1:1), a cultural assimilation (e.g., 1:8) or in leaving some information in the base text implicit (e.g., 1:1). For more details concerning the specific character of S, see Gerleman, *Ruth/Hohelied* (BKAT, 18/1; Neukirchen-Vluyn: Neukirchener, 1965), 3–4.

For the Syro-Hexapla, P. de Lagarde's edition in *Bibliothecae Syriacae* (Göttingen: Horstmann, 1892) 186–90 has been consulted. However, the Syro-Hexapla has been of special importance for the reconstruction of the history of the text of G, since it is a very literal translation of the Hexaplaric G-text by Paul of Tella, which in addition has preserved the Aristarchian signs.

Regarding the Targum, special use has been made of manuscript Urbinas Ebr. 1 of the Vatican Library, dated 1294. The editions of A. Sperber, *The Hagiographa* (vol. IVA of *The Bible in Aramaic*; Leiden: Brill, 1968), P. de Lagarde, *Hagiographa Chaldaice* (Leipzig: Teubner, 1873), and E. Levine, *The Aramaic Version of Ruth* (Rome: Biblical Institute Press, 1973), have also been consulted.

Whatever the time of origin of T may have been, its underlying Hebrew text is clearly that which is known to us from M. It is further characterized by much additional material which makes it twice as long as M. The additional material can sometimes be characterized as explicit information (3:11, 14; 4:7) and sometimes as a midrash (1:9).

Concluding Remarks

I would like to express my special thanks to Dr. U. Quast, the editor of Ruth in the Göttingen Septuagint, for all the valuable information he has provided, to Prof. Yohanan Goldman for his thorough revision of earlier drafts of this text, and to the other members of the editorial committee for their inspiring team contribution. I am also greatly indebted to Prof. A. Dotan for his improvements of the Masorah and to Prof. Peter W. Flint for having made available to me the final text of 4QRuth[a] and 4QRuth[b] before the appearance of the *editio princeps*.

CANTICLES

Hebrew Witnesses

For the *Masoretic Text* three mss. have been collated, viz., the Leningradensis (M^L = Russian National Library, EBP. I B 19a), fols. 423r–425r; the Aleppo Codex (M^A), pp. 587 f., and Cambridge, Univ. Libr. Ms. Add. 1753 (M^Y), pp. 98v–100v. M^A includes only 1:1–3:11 (בנות ציון). The differences with M^L concern only details of vocalization and plene/defective writing.

The text of Canticles is well preserved. There are only a few cases where textual corruption is likely, viz., 4:12 (גל); 7:7 (last word); 7:10 (last two words). In a few cases, more or less plausible emendations have been suggested, e.g., 1:5 (שלמה); 1:7 (כטעיה). In some other cases a translation problem may well be the result of a lack of knowledge of the literary background of the verse rather than textual corruption. A notable case is 6:12, which has puzzled translators as early as the Septuagint.

The following cases are not registered in the apparatus: M^A (as far as it goes) and M^Y differ from M^L in plene/defective writing: 2:14 השמיעני, 15 שעלים (2x); לחיין 13, עובר 5:5; רמנים 13, לבבתני 9 הגברים 4 שפתותיך 4:3; צאנה 11, מר 3:6; לערגות 6:2; יבזו 8:1; השמיעני 13. M^Y has החחים in 2:2.

The following differences in vocalization have not been included in the apparatus. M^L has a *ḥaṭep̄ sᵊgôl* instead of *šᵊwâ* in שֶׁשְּׁזַפְתַנִי in 1:6 (M^A and M^Y), and *ḥaṭep̄ pataḥ* instead of *pataḥ* in הַחֲלֹנות in 2:9 (M^A and M^Y). M^A has a *ḥaṭep̄ pataḥ* instead of *šᵊwâ* in תעוררו in 2:7, in ואסובבה in 3:2, and in הסבבים in 3:3.

In some cases a *dāḡeš*, a *ḥîreq*, or an accent cannot be discerned in M^L. Although an omission remains a possibility, more likely this is caused by surface damage in the manuscript. A *dāḡeš* is involved in כָּתְלֵנוּ, 2:9, הִנֵּה, 2:11, in the פ of אַרְפֶּנּוּ, 3:4, in מִגְדְּלֹות, 5:13, and in the שׁ of הַשּׁוּלַמִּית, 7:1, a *ḥîreq* in שָׁדַיִךְ, 4:5, and שְׁלָחַיִךְ, 4:13, and an accent in שֶׁמָּצָאתִי, 3:4. In הִנָּךְ, 4:1, the accent is not wholly clear. It seems to be a *mahpak̠*, rather than a *mûnaḥ* as in BHS. M^Y is not clear at this point.

In M^L at 4:1 the left end stroke of the last consonant of מבעד looks very much like a ר. There is, however, a fluidity in the distinctive traits of the two consonants, ד and ר. In this case, the letter is a bit damaged at the right curve/corner, which makes it impossible to be sure if it is a scribal error.

With respect to Mp, in 8:8 לאחתנו has a circellus without corresponding Mp-note; in 1:17; 5:3(?), 4 there is a Mp-note without circellus.

I gratefully acknowledge that for the analysis of some difficult details of the M-text, I had available the notes prepared by D. Barthélemy for *CTAT* (cited as *CTAT*, 5, *ad loc.*). I am indebted to Professor Adrian Schenker, Fribourg, for his help in clarifying the Mp-note at 5:7.

M^L, M^A, and M^Y agree in the division of the text in *parašiyyôt*, except for 4:11/12, where, in contrast to M^L, M^Y has a running text. They differ in that M^L and M^A have, with only few exceptions, *sᵊtumôt*, and M^Y with four exceptions *pᵊtuḥôt*, as is clear from the following tabular form. For the method of indicating the two types of *parašiyyôt*, see Yeivin, *Tiberian Masorah*, 40 f.

	M^L	M^A	M^Y
1:4-5	ס	פ	פ
1:8-9	ס	פ	ס
1:14-15	ס	ס	ס
2:7-8	ס	ס	ס
2:13-14	ס	ס	פ
2:14-15	ס	ס	פ
2:17–3:1	ס	ס	פ
3:5-6	ס	ס	פ
3:8-9	ס	ס	פ
3:11–4:1	ס		פ
4:7-8	ס		פ
4:11-12	ס		>
5:1-2	ס		פ
6:3-4	ס		פ
6:9-10	ס		ס
6:10-11	ס		פ
7:11-12	ס		פ
8:4-5	ס		פ
8:7-8	ס		פ
8:10-11	פ		פ

As far as the *Dead Sea Scrolls* from Qumran are concerned, the following fragments of Canticles have been found:

- 4QCant^a, one fragment, made up of smaller pieces, with part of two columns, covering in fragmentary form 3:7–4:6 (col. i); 4:7 and 6:11?–7:7 (col. ii)
- 4QCant^b, three fragments, covering in fragmentary form (1) 2:9–3:2; (2) 3:5, 9-11; 4:1b-3, 8-11a; (3) 4:14–5:1
- 4QCant^c, a scrap with a few letters and one full word (אחוזי; written plene) from 3:7-8
- 6QCant, a fragment with part of two columns, covering in fragmentary form 1:1-7.

These texts have been published in the microfiche edition by E. Tov, with the collaboration of S.J. Pfann, *The Dead Sea Scrolls on Microfiche* (Leiden: Brill, 1993). 4QCant^a is found on PAM 41.300 and 43.097 (fiche 24 and 65); 4QCant^b is found on PAM 40.604 (fiche 13 (fragment 1)), 41.277 (fiche 23 (fragment 1)), 43.093 (fiche 65 (the three fragments)), the last one also containing 4QCant^c. 6QCant is found on PAM 42.943 (fiche 60), in a very clear text, and on PAM 41.510 (fiche 29), the latter, however, being less sharp.

In his article "Qumranica I: Zu unveröffentlichten Handschriften aus Höhle 4 von Qumran" (*ZAW* 106 [1994]: 307–22), G.W. Nebe has given a list of the deviations of 4QCant^{a,b} from M. The fragments were edited and discussed in detail by E. Tov, in "Three Manuscripts (Abbreviated Texts?) of Canticum from Qumran Cave 4" (*JSS* 46 [1995]: 88–111). In some cases he gives a different reading from those of Nebe and in other cases a variant reading where Nebe's list has none. Tov is also the editor of 4QCant^{a,b} in E. Ulrich, F.M. Cross, J.A. Fitzmyer, P.W. Flint, S.

Metso, C.M. Murphy, C. Niccum, P.W. Skehan, E. Tov and J. Trebolle Barrera, *Qumran Cave 4: XI, Psalms to Chronicles* (DJD XVI; Oxford: Clarendon, 2000). I am very grateful to him for making available to me the text which he had prepared for DJD before its publication and allowing me to use it for the present edition.

Both 4QCant[a] and 4QCant[b] have a text which, as Tov has demonstrated, has intentionally been shortened: 4QCant[a] lacks 4:8–6:10, 4QCant[b] 3:6-8; 4:4-7; 4QCant[b] ends with 5:1. The text of 4QCant[a] is closer to M than that of 4QCant[b]; the first differs from M a few times over plene/defective writing. It has no obvious mistakes. 4QCant[b] has five cases of defective writing over against plene in M and seven cases of plene writing over against defective in M. There are five errors, for which see at 2:13, 15; 3:1 (twice); 4:8. Tov lists twelve cases of Aramaic influence, for which see at 2:17; 4:8, 10, 16 (where מגדיו has been read as מן גדיו).

The fragments from Cave 6 have been published and described by M. Baillet in M. Baillet, J.T. Milik and R. de Vaux, *Les "petites grottes" de Qumrân* (DJD III; Oxford: Clarendon, 1962). 6QCant has, apart from the variants listed in the apparatus, three orthographic differences with M (1:5 ירושלים; 1:6 שמוני and נוטרה).

Greek Witnesses

For the *Septuagint* (G), use has been made of A. Rahlfs, ed., *Septuaginta* (2 vols.; 9th ed.; Stuttgart: Deutsche Bibelstiftung, 1979). G's *Vorlage* must have been a Hebrew text which hardly differed from M. Its translation can be characterized as literal, if not sometimes slavish. In some cases the Hebrew was misunderstood, as in the rendering "breasts" instead of "love" (as V) in 1:2, 4; 4:10; 7:13, in the rendering "as doves" in 1:10 (cp. V: "as a dove"), and in translating לצמתך, 4:1, 3; 6:7, with "your silence", as does S; see commentary. Some geographical names were not understood as such in 2:1 (Sharon); 4:8 (Amana); 6:4 (Tirzah), and 7:1 (Mahanaim); cp. other witnesses. There are some pluses, which can be explained as assimilation to other places in Canticles, e.g., in 1:3, 4; 2:9, 10. It is possible that these assimilations had already taken place in the Hebrew of G's *Vorlage*. Some changes are of a stylistic nature, such as the addition of "what" in 1:10 (also σ'). This is especially true with respect to the addition/omission of the copula/conjunction. Where G differs from M in this respect it is joined by V (e.g., 2:12 [וקול]), by S (e.g., 2:14 [השמיעיני]), or by both (e.g., 2:13 [והגפנים]). There is no reason to consider these cases text-critical in nature and, moreover, no difference in meaning is involved. Consequently, these cases have not been included in the apparatus. For some other deviations from the Hebrew it is difficult to adduce a specific cause, as "they drew you" for "draw me" in 1:4. For a detailed survey of the character of G-Canticles see Gerleman, *Ruth/Hohelied*, 77–82.

D. Barthélemy thinks that the G-text of Canticles has undergone some influence of the *kaige* recension (*Les devanciers*, 33, 49). Following this lead, M. Harl, "La version LXX", has made further research ("un sondage limité," p. 120) in the relation between the lexical choices of G and those attributed to θ'. Her plausible conclusion is that G-Canticles is very close to θ'. She even thinks it possible that Theodotion was the author of the G-text, and later on undertook a limited revision which resulted in a few θ'-readings which differ from G (p. 119). She emphasizes the number of transcriptions in G, a feature characteristic for the *kaige*-Theodotion revision.

For the *Hexaplaric* witnesses, use has been made of F. Field, *Origenis Hexaplorum quae supersunt* (2 vols.; Oxford: Oxford University Press, 1875; repr., Hildesheim: Georg Olms, 1964). The relation of α', θ', and σ' to their *Vorlage* may well be reflected in the number of variant readings registered in the apparatus of this edition: σ' has the greatest number, viz., twenty-three, α' has fifteen, whereas θ' has only four, viz., 1:6 (the three actually constitute one variant reading) and 8:13, not counting 6:4 and 7:1 (the first). "Like-the-Seventy" readings have not been included in the apparatus. For M. Harl's view concerning θ' see above under G.

In ten cases a reading in the apparatus has been taken from Field's "Auctarium" at the end of the first volume; this has not been mentioned in the apparatus. These cases are 1:8 (ε'); 4:1 (concerns αἱ of α'); 4:6 (σ'); 4:8 (σ'; both occurrences); 7:1 (ε'; second occurrence); 7:7 (σ'); 7:13 (αλ'); 8:4 (α'); 8:5 (σ'; second occurrence).

Latin Witnesses

Since the edition of the *Old Latin* text of Canticles by P. Sabatier in his *Bibliorum Sacrorum Latinae versiones antiquae, seu Vetus Italica* (2d ed.; Paris: F. Didot), vol. 2 (1743), addenda in vol. 3 (1749), xi–xiii, much more material has been discovered. A new comprehensive edition of the text is being prepared by E. Schulz-Flügel for the edition of the Old Latin Text under the auspices of the Vetus Latina Institute, Beuron. In addition to Sabatier's edition, use has been made of the following three text editions:

(1) E. Schulz-Flügel, *Gregorius Eliberritanus. Epithalamium sive Explanatio in Canticis Canticorum* (Aus der Geschichte der lateinischen Bibel 26; Freiburg: Herder, 1994), which gives the La-lemma text, which Gregory of Elvira used in his commentary on Canticles;

(2) D. De Bruyne, "Les anciennes versions latines du Cantique des Cantiques" (*RBén* 38 [1962]: 97–122), which includes an edition of the text of Salzbourg, Abbey of St. Peter, Ms. IX 16 (= S, later on referred to as ms. 169), within the apparatus the variant readings of another ms., viz., Graz, University Library, *fol.* 167 (= G, later on referred to as ms. 170); both mss. had been discovered by De Bruyne;

(3) A. Vaccari, *Cantici Canticorum vetus latina translatio a S. Hieronymo ad graecum textum hexaplarem emendata* (Rome: Edizioni di Storia e Letteratura, 1959), which gives the text of the Hexaplaric revision of the La-text by Jerome. This text has been preserved as the lemma text in Epiphanius Scholasticus's translation of the Greek commentary on Canticles by Philo of Carpasia, Cyprus.

Moreover, Dr. Schulz-Flügel very kindly made available to me her survey of readings in the Ambrosius material with all variant readings. I am very grateful for her permission to make use of this material and other notes. I also received from her the lemma-text used by Jerome in his translation of Origen's homilies as excerpted by her from its edition by W.A. Baehrens in GCS 33 (1925) which very much facilitated use of the edition.

The La-texts show a great deal of variety. Yet the apparatus lists only a very limited number of La-readings that might presuppose a Greek *Vorlage* not preserved elsewhere.

In the apparatus the abbreviation "La" indicates the reading of Sabatier and any or all of the later texts mentioned above. This implies that the symbol "La" leaves open the possibility that one or more of the other texts support the competing reading of G. A few times a reading registered in the apparatus or the commentary differs from that given by Sabatier; in that case, the witness is listed as La^{Ep} for the text of Epiphanius as edited by Vaccari, as La^{Ambr} for a reading of Ambrosius, as La^{169} for a reading of ms. 169 as edited by De Bruyne, or as La^{Hie} for Jerome's lemma text.

For an introduction to the La-texts, see E. Schulz-Flügel's "Einleitung" to her (forthcoming) edition of the La-text in *Vetus Latina* 10/3, *Canticum Canticorum* (Freiburg 1992–).

For the *Vulgate* (V), use has been made of F.A. Gasquet, et al., eds., *Libri Salomonis* (vol. 11 in *Biblia Sacra iuxta Latinam Vulgatam Versionem*; Rome: Libreria Editrice Vaticana, 1957). In a few cases V's *Vorlage* may have differed from M (see esp. at 4:12 and 7:10), but in general deviating renderings can be explained as misunderstandings of the Hebrew, or stylistic variations. To the latter category belong the cases of added or omitted copula/conjunction, for which see under G. In this respect, V may stand alone, join G or S (e.g., 3:8 [מלמדי]) or both. V may agree with one or more other versions in a misunderstanding of the Hebrew. Notable cases are the translation of "breasts" instead of "love" in 1:2 and elsewhere, and the derivation of "Tirza" from the root רצה in 6:4.

Syriac and Aramaic Witnesses

The *Peshitta* text of Canticles has been edited in volume II, 5, of the Leiden Peshitta by J.A. Emerton and D.J. Lane ("Song of Songs." In *Proverbs, Wisdom of Solomon, Ecclesiastes, Song of Songs* [ed. A.A. DiLella, J.A. Emerton and D.J. Lane; vol. II/5 of *The Old Testament in Syriac, According to the Peshitta Version*; Leiden: Brill, 1979]). In my article "The Peshitta Text of Song of Songs," I have argued that in seven cases the reading relegated by the editors to the apparatus would merit to have been adopted in the text instead, and that in all other cases the readings in the apparatus are no real challenge to those adopted in the text. The seven cases have no bearing on the variant readings registered in the present edition. For a detailed treatment of the S-text, see the just-mentioned article.

What has been said about G holds good for S as well. It is a faithful translation of the Hebrew. The translator, however, aimed at idiomatic Syriac, which led him to deviate from a strict adherence to the Hebrew. Especially in the use of the copula, the translator often deviates from the Hebrew. For cases involving copula/conjunction, see under G and V. In a number of cases, the Syriac differs from the Hebrew over the number, by adding or omitting *seyame*. Where S stands alone in this regard, it has not been recorded. Some examples are: 1:7 (עדרי), 1:8 (בעקבי; משכנות), and 1:9 (ברכבי), where S has no *seyame*, 2:2 (כשושנה), and 4:5 (צביה), where S has *seyame*.

In some cases the translator apparently did not understand the Hebrew and just made the best of it. This was the case with respect to some proper names, e.g., "Sharon" in 2:1, translated as ܫܪܘܢ, "cypress," and "Tirzah" in 6:4, translated as ܪܓܬܐ, "desire" (cp. the other versions). Another example is ברח, 8:14, "flee, haste away," for which S has the ill-fitting ܘܟܕ ܐܬܐ, "and when he came." Sometimes S agrees with G against the Hebrew, the most notable example being לצמתך in 4:1, 3; 6:7, for which see commentary; other examples are נחרו in 1:6, which is derived from the root חרה by all witnesses (see commentary), and "Tirzah," 6:4, mentioned above. There is, however, no reason to assume dependency of S on G. It is clear that S is independent from G in 4:1, since in that same verse the translator, to whom שגלשו was not clear, did not follow G, but translated "which came up" (see commentary). For more details concerning the character of S, see G. Gerleman, *Ruth/Hohelied*, 82 f., and W.C. van Wyk, "The Peshitta," 181 – 89.

The *Targum* of Canticles is a prime example of the allegorical interpretation of this book. Verse by verse, it applies the text of Canticles to the history of Israel from the Exodus until the coming of the messianic era. It highlights God's dealing with his people and Israel's response. Sometimes it is possible to find a direct translation of one or more Hebrew words. In other cases, it is possible to discern which of two readings is presupposed in T's freer text. In both these cases, the Targum has been adduced as "T". In most cases T remains silent on the Hebrew text-critical point at issue. Therefore it is not included in the regular witnesses, and no *argumentum e silentio* is allowed. Where relevant, use has been made of A. Sperber's *The Hagiographa* (vol. IVA in *The Bible in Aramaic*; Leiden: Brill, 1968).

Concluding Remarks

In accordance with editorial guidelines, no reference is made in the apparatus to the early editions ("Ed/Edd" in *BHK*, *BHS*) of the Hebrew Bible and to Hebrew mss. listed in the collections of Kennicott and de Rossi ("Ms/Mss" in *BHK*, *BHS*). Neither are conjectural emendations proposed as in *BHS*, e.g., at 1:3 and 3:10. The Cairo Geniza material has also been excluded because none has been published by the time work on this edition was completed. In July 1995, I had the opportunity to see the many Canticles fragments preserved at the Cambridge University Library and compare a good number of them with M and with each other. This examination made clear that these fragments are in no way homogeneous. They differ among themselves in the form of writing, orthography (especially in plene/defective writing), presence/absence of vocalization, the vocalization itself, and – in a few cases – in text.

In the apparatus of *BHS*, 6QCant was taken into account. In the present edition, the 4QCant-fragments are also included.

Finally, I am very much indebted to my colleague Professor Arie van der Kooij for rekeyboarding my entire text, prepared with a DOS-program, into the DEP-program developed for this edition. In the process we had stimulating and helpful discussions on various points of form and contents. I am grateful for the corrections and suggestions made by the members of the editorial committee during the review process.

QOHELETH

Hebrew Witnesses

The Masoretic Text of Qoheleth presented in this edition is that of EBP. I B 19a in the Russian National Library of St. Petersburg (M^L). The ms. is described more fully in the general introduction. The text of Qoheleth follows the Song of Songs on folio 425r and ends on folio 429v.

Two other Masoretic manuscripts of the Tiberian type were collated: Ms. EBP. II B 34 in the Russian National Library of St. Petersburg (= Firkovich II. 34), its siglum in this edition is M^{L34}; and Cambridge Univ. Libr. Add. Ms. 1753, whose siglum in this edition is M^Y.

The differences in the division of the text into sections are represented in the following table (פ = open section; ס = closed section; > = no division):

	M^L	M^{L34}	M^Y
1:11-12	פ	ס	ס
3:1-2	ס	פ	ס
4:16-17	>	ס	>
9:10-11	ס	ס	>
11:8-9	>	ס	>

In all three mss., as well as in the mss. and lists consulted by C.D. Ginsburg (*Introduction*, 59–60), the book is made up of four *sədarîm* that begin in 1:1; 3:13; 7:1 and 9:7, respectively.

Cave 4 at Qumran contained the Hebrew fragments of two mss. of the book.

a. 4QQoh[a]

The fragments of this ms. preserve parts of Qoh 5:13-17; 6:3-8, 12; 7:1-10, 19-20. A first evaluation of three fragments was published by J. Muilenburg ("Qohelet Scroll," 20–28), who dates the ms. from the middle of the second century B.C.E. F.M. Cross proposes more or less the same date, 175–150. E. Ulrich edited the fragments in 1992 (Ulrich, "Ezra and Qohelet"). The edition of Ulrich in DJD XVI (E. Ulrich, F.M. Cross, J.A. Fitzmyer, P.W. Flint, S. Metso, C.M. Murphy, C. Niccum, P.W. Skehan, E. Tov and J. Trebolle Barrera, eds., *Qumran Cave 4: XI, Psalms to Chronicles* [DJD XVI; Oxford: Clarendon, 2000]) is the main source for readings in the apparatus.

b. 4QQoh[b]

This ms. is preserved in only two small fragments containing parts of Qoh 1:10-14. The plates of the Palestine Archeological Museum (43.090, 42.005, 42.635) were published in 1991 by R. Eisenmann and J. Robinson, and in 1993 in microfiche edition by E. Tov (Tov/Pfann, *Microfiche*). They were examined by E. Ulrich, who described the text and the variants of all the fragments and dated 4QQoh[b] from the middle of the first century B.C.E. (Ulrich, "Ezra and Qohelet," 148–49) W. Nebe contributed further analysis of the text, and compiled an index of published photographs for each ms. ("Qumranica I," 312–13). For this ms. too the reference edition is DJD XVI.

Only those Qumran variants that are considered more or less certain figure in the critical apparatus. Orthographical differences are not considered. 4QQoh[a] reflects a rather fluid textual transmission. Twelve times M and G are in agreement against it. In one place it supports G against M indirectly (6:4 הלך = G πορεύεται, opposite to M ילך) and in another place directly (7:19 תעזר = G βοηθήσει, opposite to M תעז).

This ms. already shows a tendency to soften Qoheleth's criticisms of professional sages (כמה יותר 6:8; תעזר 7:19). However in one or two places, the ms. seems to have preserved an early form (e.g., הלך 6:4; בית 7:4).

Greek Witnesses

Since Qoheleth has not yet appeared in the Göttingen Edition, the base text for the Old Greek text is A. Rahlfs, *Septuaginta* (2 vols.; 9th ed.; Stuttgart: Deutsche Bibelstiftung, 1979), 2:238–60. In those places where Rahlfs's edition appeared questionable, the following editions were consulted: H.B. Swete, The *Old Testament in Greek* (3 vols.; 4th ed.; Cambridge: Cambridge University Press, 1909–1922; repr., Cambridge: Cambridge University Press, 1930) 2:480–505; R. Holmes and J. Parsons, *Vetus Testamentum Graecum cum variis lectionibus* (5 vols. in 4; Oxford: Clarendon, 1798, 1827); and B.J. Diebner and R. Kasser, *Hamburger Papyrus Bil 1* (Geneva: P. Cramer, 1989).

Rahlfs's edition, in spite of its undeniable achievements, is not always reliable. The Greek translation of Qoheleth is very literal, and it appears that Rahlfs's guiding principle was to opt as often as possible for the Greek witness closest to the Masoretic text. For Rahlfs this would have been the most likely representative of an early Greek that was both very literal and close to the proto-Masoretic text. However, in spite of its literalism, G clearly attests a *Vorlage* different from that of the Masoretic text. I have thus proposed emendations in Rahlfs's text more than forty times, on the basis of its own critical apparatus and the editions already mentioned. The text of the Hamburg papyrus diglot offers a text very close to that of Vaticanus and, in our view, only rarely provides significant data concerning the ancient Greek.

Rahlfs's selection of a Greek text closest to the Masoretic Text typically results from his retroversion of the *"vetus latina"* of Qoheleth. The Latin text that he uses is actually a translation produced by Jerome for his commentary. Jerome clearly states that this Latin translation was made from a Hebrew text, and that the Greek, which is close to it, often served as a guide so that he would "not stray too far from the Hebrew": *"nullius auctoritatem secutus sum; sed de hebraeo transferens, magis me septuaginta interpretum consuetudini coaptavi, in his dumtaxat, quae non multum ab Hebraicis discrepabant"* (Jerome, "Commentarius in Ecclesiasten," 249). Because Jerome followed the proto-Masoretic text when he translated, against all witnesses of the Greek tradition, we can be fairly certain that he does not attest an earlier form of the Greek, but of the proto-Masoretic text.

There was neither time nor the mandate to collate all the known witnesses of the Greek of Qoheleth. Since Joseph Ziegler had done a collation, I settled for a quick survey of his collations for those cases where I had questioned the readings of Rahlfs. This was possible during a brief visit to Göttingen. The critical edition of the Greek text of Qoheleth has been assigned by the Göttingen Institute to Prof. Peter Gentry. Although the acknowledgments have been reserved for the end of this introduction, I would like to express my gratitude here for the warm welcome I received at the Septuagint Institute at Göttingen.

The Hexaplaric witnesses were consulted in F. Field's collation, *Origenis Hexaplorum quae supersunt* (2 vols.; Oxford: Oxford University Press, 1875; repr., Hildesheim: Georg Olms, 1964) 2:380–405, supplemented by the Auctarium, published as an appendix, 25–27.

Latin Witnesses

The Vulgate text is read in the major critical edition prepared by Benedictine monks of the San Girolamo Abbey in Rome (F.A. Gasquet, et al., eds., *Biblia Sacra iuxta Latinam Vulgatam Versionem* [18 vols.; Rome: Libreria Editrice Vaticana, 1926–1996]). Ecclesiastes is found in the volume XI published in 1957.

The translation of Qoheleth in the Vulgate is flexible in its choice of equivalents. In the matter of word order, it could be characterized as a free translation. Jerome also avoids "unnecessary" repetitions. If a word is translated once so that it is clearly represented in the Latin phrase, the word is not repeated as in the Hebrew. For example, the poetic repetition of the Hebrew שמש in 1:5a survives in the lemma of Jerome's commentary: *oritur sol et occidit sol*, but not in his translation: *oritur sol et occidit*. Such a distinction occurs again at the end of v. 6 where רוח is not translated the second time in V: *et in circulos suos regreditur*, whereas it is in the commentary: *et in circulos suos revertitur spiritus*. The Vulgate of Qoh is, in fact, the result of considerable exegetical work (Lanza, "Le tre versioni").The influence of Symmachus is even greater than generally acknowledged today, and merits a study of its own.

Since our apparatus is intended to adduce variants that reflect a Hebrew original, the text read by Jerome must be checked regularly against the literal translation he produced in his commentary. The textual witness of V has value when it is confirmed by the lemma in Jerome's commentary, or when the variants of V are not of a semantic or stylistic nature (variants in gender, number, voice, etc.).

The lemmata of Jerome's commentary, produced about a decade before the Vulgate, were consulted in the edition by M. Adriaen (Jerome, "Commentarius in Ecclesiasten," in *S. Hieronymi Presbyteri Opera I* [ed. M. Adriaen; CCSL 72; Turnhout: Brepols, 1959]). The text of the lemmata is systematically presented in the apparatus to redress the balance of the variable witness of the Vulgate in the question of the Hebrew text read by Jerome.

Syriac Witnesses

The Syriac text of Qoh was consulted in the edition of D.J. Lane, ed., "Qoheleth," in *Proverbs, Wisdom of Solomon, Ecclesiastes, Song of Songs* (ed. A.A. DiLella, J.A. Emerton and D.J. Lane; vol. II/5 of *The Old Testament in Syriac, according to the Peshitta Version*, Leiden: Brill, 1979). The editor provides a synthesis of the manuscript evidence for the Syriac version (Lane, "Peshitta text").

As is often the case, the Syriac version contains variants of widely varying quality. Aside from the great liberty taken with regard to word order and the logical order of the text, S exhibits numerous assimilations to the Greek text. But at times, there is also a strong probability that S attests a Hebrew original different from the other witnesses. Thus, it seems reasonable to view S as a potential witness to an early Hebrew text, a witness that deserves as much critical consideration as the other great witnesses to the Hebrew Bible.

The Targum

The text of the Targum of Qoheleth was consulted in A. Sperber's edition, *The Hagiographa* (vol. IVA of *The Bible in Aramaic*; Leiden: Brill, 1968), whose base text is British Museum ms. Or 2375. This text was collated with three mss. from the Western tradition: 1., Urbinas ebr. 1, Vatican Library; 2., Erfurt 3 (=Berlin Staatsbibliothek Or. fol. 1213); 3., The ms. of Alfonso de Zamora edited by L.D. Merino (*Targum de Qohelet: Edición Príncipe del Ms. Villa-Amil n. 5 de Alfonso de Zamora* [Madrid: C.S.I.C., 1987]). Very close to the latter ms. is the one edited, translated and annotated by M. Taradach and J. Ferrer (*Un Targum de Qohéleth: ms M-2 de Salamanca: editio princeps: texte araméen, traduction et commentaire critique* [Geneva: Labor et Fides 1998]).

The choice of a text for the Targum is often difficult. Taradach and Ferrer believe it is still not possible to produce a true critical edition of the Targum of Qoheleth.

Acknowledgments

I would especially like to thank Prof. Adrian Schenker for his advice and assistance, as well as Prof. Jan de Waard and his wife Tine de Waard for reviewing the Masoretic notes; Prof. Piet Dirksen for his responses to my questions concerning the Syriac tradition; Prof. David Talshir of Ben Gurion University for his thoughtful responses to my philological questions; and Prof. Françoise Vinel, who willingly engaged in dialogue on the nature of the Greek translation.

I would also like to express my gratitude to Prof. Anneli Aejmelaeus, who allowed me to consult the collation notebooks of Joseph Ziegler in Göttingen, and to Drs. Udo Quast and Detlef Frankel for their availability and their gracious welcome there. Dr. Quast very kindly introduced me to the unique idiom of Ziegler's notebooks and at times consulted certain microfilms himself. Prof. Peter Gentry, charged with the critical edition of Ecclesiastes by the Göttingen Institute, very kindly responded by courier to some of the difficult questions that arose concerning the Greek text. It goes without saying that the entire responsibility for the textual choices in the present edition lies with me.

LAMENTATIONS

Hebrew Witnesses

The Hebrew Text and the Masorah of Lamentations printed in BHQ are based on the color transparencies of folios 430a–432b of EBP. I B 19a in the Russian National Library at St. Petersburg, made by Bruce and Kenneth Zuckerman for the Ancient Biblical Manuscript Center of Claremont, CA (USA). Thanks to the high quality of these photographs, the text can be clearly discerned even in two places (Lam 3:43 and 4:14 on fol. 431b and fol. 432a in the upper part of the middle columns) where the legibility is affected by a larger dark brown discoloring.

Unfortunately, Lamentations is among the lost parts of the Aleppo Codex. The two other Tiberian manuscripts collated are fol. 105a–107b of the Cambridge

Univ. Libr. Add. Ms. 1753 (M^Y), and fol. 156b–162b of the ms. EBP. II B 34 of
the Russian National Library in St. Petersburg (M^{L34}). These were collated from
microfilms. M^{L34} has several *lacunae*, one of them in Lamentations, where the text
is partly damaged in Lam 4 and breaks off after הָטְמְאוּ in Lam 5:7.

The use of *sətumôt* and *pətuhôt* in M^L, M^Y and M^{L34} is identical in Lam 1, 2
and 4, where all three of them use a *sətumâ* after each verse and a *pətuhâ* at the
end of each chapter. In Lam 3, however, M^L has a *sətumâ* only after each group of
three verses, while M^Y and M^{L34} use the same pattern as in Lam 1, 2 and 4; all
three manuscripts have a *pətuhâ* after Lam 3:66. Disagreements about the presence
or absence of *sətumôt* in chap. 3 that depart from these patterns are treated in the
apparatus. In Lam 5, M^Y has *sətumôt* between all verses from vv. 1/2 to vv. 17/18,
a *pətuhâ* between vv. 18/19 and no further paragraphs in vv. 19-22; M^L also has a
pətuhâ between vv. 18/19, but no further paragraphs throughout the chapter, which
agrees with M^{L34} as far as that ms. is preserved.

Among the biblical texts from Qumran, there are fragments of four different
copies of Lamentations (3QLam, 4QLam, 5QLam^a and 5QLam^b), which are cited
according to DJD III (95, 174–78 and pl. X, XXXVIII) and DJD XVI (229–37
and pl. XXVII–XXVIII). In addition, use has been made of the relevant photographs in E. Tov with the collaboration of S.J. Pfann, eds., *The Dead Sea Scrolls
on Microfiche* (Leiden: E. J. Brill, 1993). The remains of 3QLam exhibit fragmentary text from Lam 1:1-12 and 3:53-62 without any variation in relation to M.
However, from the fragments of 3QLam it can be concluded that each verse in
Lam 1, as well as each group of three verses in Lam 3, was written in one single
line, which means that the layout of this ms. obviously reflected the poetical form
of these acrostic poems. 5QLam^a and 5QLam^b) exhibit fragmentary text from Lam
4:5–5:17. Apart from merely orthographic and morphological differences to M,
there are five textual variants which are recorded in our critical apparatus on 4:14,
15, 17 and 5:1, 3. The most significant fragment of Lamentations from Qumran is
4QLam, which preserves text from Lam 1:1-18 and a small piece from 2:5. In spite
of many obvious errors and the general carelessness of the scribe, 4QLam preserves a number of most valuable readings, which must simply be ascribed to the
antiquity of the ms. (cf. Cross, DJD XVI, 230). Of particular note is Lam 1:7,
where the evidence from 4QLam offers a text critical solution for a problem which
earlier could be treated only by means of literary criticism.

Greek Witnesses

The Septuagint and the Hexaplaric witnesses are cited from the edition of Lamentations by J. Ziegler, "Threni," in *Ieremias, Baruch, Threni, Epistula Ieremiae* (ed.
J. Ziegler; vol. XV of *Septuaginta: Vetus Testamentum Graecum* [Göttingen: Vandenhoeck & Ruprecht, 1957], 467–94).

The Septuagint of Lamentations is in general a very literal and sometimes even
slavish translation of M. The translator mostly rendered his *Vorlage* mechanically
word by word "with a surprising disregard for context and coherence" (Albrektson,
Studies, 208), sometimes deriving Hebrew words from a wrong root or mistaking
one Hebrew word for another (e.g., 1:4, 18; 2:15; 3:5, 16) and sometimes analyz-
ing forms incorrectly (1:9; 2:11; 5:4) or misunderstanding the Hebrew syntax (e.g.,
2:10, 20). "The translation as a whole must have made a strange impression on a
Greek reader who did not have access to the original. In some places it was doubt-

less unintelligible" (Albrektson, *Studies*, 208). Although the Greek version of Lamentations is not a "good translation," it is valuable for textual criticism, because the *verbatim* translation technique makes it comparatively easy to determine the consonantal text of a Hebrew *Vorlage*, which was almost identical with M. However, one must be aware that in some cases there are also examples of deviation from the Hebrew, e.g., by changing or adding a pronoun (1:12; 2:3, 4, 16; 3:57) or by a free rendering (2:2, 19; 4:1); but these cases are frequently translational and do not necessarily presuppose a different Hebrew *Vorlage*.

D. Barthélemy has pointed to the fact that the "Septuagint" of Lamentations uses regularly καί γε for גַּם (1:8; 2:9; 3:8; 4:3, 15, 21) and thus exhibits characteristics of the *kaige* recension. In addition, it can be observed that among the Hexaplaric witnesses for Lamentations there is not a single variant attributed to Theodotion. Both aspects together lead to the conclusion that the "Septuagint" of Lamentations might actually be the text of Theodotion's translation.

Latin Witnesses

For the Old Latin, use has been made of the edition by P. Sabatier, ed., *Bibliorum Sacrorum Latinae versiones antiquae seu Vetus Italica* (3 vols.; 2d ed.; Paris: F. Didot, 1751), 2:723–33. In a few cases (1:9; 2:16; 5:5) the Old Latin seemingly has an independent reading, and in another few cases it supports M either with the western tradition of T (1:11) or with Hexaplaric witnesses and V (3:22, 44).

The Vulgate is cited according to the S. Girolamo edition, F.A. Gasquet, et al., eds., *Biblia Sacra iuxta Latinam Vulgatam Versionem* (18 vols.; Rome: Libreria Editrice Vaticana, 1926–1996), 14:285–307. V normally agrees with M. Deviations from the Hebrew are mostly translational.

Syriac and Aramaic Witnesses

Since the edition by the Peshitta Institute in Leiden is not yet available, the Syriac translation of Lamentations is cited according to the thorough edition by B. Albrektson, *Studies in the Text and Theology of the Book of Lamentations with a Critical Edition of the Peshitta Text* (Lund: C.W.K. Gleerup, 1963), 41–54. Although Albrektson's edition is "in principle eclectic," it does "in fact disagree with A [i.e., Codex Ambrosianus, which is used as the base text for the Leiden edition] in only very few passages" (Albrektson, *Studies*, 32). The Syriac translator rendered faithfully a Hebrew text which was more or less identical to M. In contrast to the Greek translator, his main objective was "to produce a clear and and plausible meaning" and therefore "loyalty to the details in the original must usually give way to the demand for clarity and coherence" (Albrektson, *Studies*, 211). This causes frequent additions of a ܘ or a suffix, an explanatory or simplifying tendency, and a comparatively poor vocabulary. These are characteristics of the Peshitta of Lamentations. It is obvious that normally these minor additions and alterations in S are translational and do not point to a different Hebrew *Vorlage*.

The tradition of the Targum of Lamentations is divided into two branches: the Western Text (WT) and the Yemenite Text (Yem). WT is represented by the manuscript Urbinas Ebr. 1 of the Vatican Library and in the edition by P. de Lagarde. Yem is mainly represented in the critical edition by A. van der Heide, *The Yemenite Tradition of the Targum of Lamentations: Critical Text and Analysis of the Variant Readings* (Leiden: Brill, 1981). While WT is longer than Yem and exhibits many textual differences among the manuscripts, Yem is easily recognized as a distinct tradition, which "is in all probability a text revised on the basis of WT . . . with the aim of achieving a closer resemblance to MT" (van der Heide, *Yemenite Tradition*, 35). It is obvious "that WT must be examined if we are interested in the exegetical nature of TgLam" (Brady, *Rabbinic Targum*, 142), because in this respect the text of Yem "is somewhat inferior to the Western Text" (van der Heide, *Yemenite Tradition*, 3). But it seems that as a witness for the Hebrew Text, Yem is to be preferred. Thus the readings of T in the critical apparatus of Lam are normally cited according to van der Heide, *Yemenite Tradition*, 3*–55*. Significant variant readings of the WT are occasionally added either as T* or T^Mss (according to the edition of de Lagarde) or as T^U (if cited according to a microfilm of ms. Urbinas Ebr. 1).

In general, the Targum of Lamentations is a remarkably literal rendering of the Hebrew. There is, however, an expansive theological prologue at the beginning, and exegetical amplifications occur throughout the translation.

It is impossible to conclude without an expression of deep gratitude towards the editorial committee of BHQ, and especially towards Stephen Pisano, Adrian Schenker, and Richard Weis for all their patience, counsel, and encouragement during my work on this edition of Lamentations.

ESTHER

The textual history of the Book of Esther shows considerable fluidity, not so much in the Hebrew tradition as in the versions, in particular the Greek and the Aramaic ones. In the present edition only a selection of the major variants and differences from this broad and variegated tradition history can be presented.

Hebrew Witnesses

In the Codex Leningradensis (M^L, EBP. I B 19a in the Russian National Library) the Book of Esther is presented on folios 432v–437v. This base text has been compared with two Tiberian Masoretic manuscripts, namely Cambridge Univ. Libr. Add. Ms. 1753 (M^Y) and St. Petersburg EBP. II B 34 (M^L34). The latter has two major lacunae (from 1:1 to 1:22 [וישלח] and from 8:7 [ולמרדכי] to 9:15 [שלשׁ]) and in some instances is hardly legible (due to faded writing or black spots). A few references to Sassoon 1053 (M^S1) have been made as a secondary resource, when its text is legible. On the other hand, in this edition variant readings in C.D. Ginsburg, *Tenak*, IV: 612–30, and in early editions of the Hebrew Bible ("Ed/Edd" in *BHK*, *BHS*), as well as differences between the "Westerners" and the "Easterners" ("Occ" resp. "Or" in *BHK*, *BHS*), and variants in the collections of Kennicott and de Rossi ("Ms/Mss" in *BHK*, *BHS*) have not been made part of the material of the textual comparison except for some references in the Commentary on the Apparatus. Hebrew Esther fragments from the Cairo Genizah are also not collated since the value and date (before 1000 C.E.) of possible witnesses could not be clearly identified (cp. Davis, *Taylor-Schechter Old Series, passim*; *BHS* has in this respect 15 references, at 2:3, 8, 13; 3:9; 4:1, 10, 11, 13, 14; 5:2; 7:9; 8:2, 9 [twice]; 9:27). There are no Hebrew fragments for the Book of Esther among the Qumran materials (on some Aramaic ones see below).

On the whole, the Hebrew text of the Book of Esther as found in the base text of M^L is a stabilized text where no emendation seems to be needed, and the comparison of it with M^Y and M^{L34}, (partly also M^{S1}) shows no major but only minor, mainly orthographic, differences. This edition introduces corrections in relation to both *BHK* and *BHS* in the diplomatic rendering of M^L as the base text in 1:4 where M^L combines כבוד and מלכותו with a *maqqep̄*, and in 5:14 where M^L lacks *maqqep̄* between אל and המשתה. In 9:31 it corrects *BHS* by reading אֶת־, as has *BHK*.

The division of the Masoretic text in *parašiyyôṯ* (cp. Yeivin, *Tiberian Masorah*, §74; Oesch, *Petucha und Setuma*), expressed by *səṯumôṯ* (ס) and *pəṯuḥôṯ* (פ), varies among the three Tiberian manuscripts as shown in the following table:

	M^L	M^Y	M^{L34}
1:9-10	ס	ס	
1:12-13	>	ס	
1:15-16	ס	פ	
1:22–2:1	פ	פ	פ
2:4-5	ס	פ	פ
2:20-21	ס	ס	ס
2:23–3:1	פ	פ	פ
3:7-8	ס	ס	ס
3:15–4:1	פ	ס	פ
4:12-13	פ	פ	פ
4:17–5:1	ס	ס	ס
5:2-3	ס	>	ס
5:14–6:1	פ	ס	פ
7:4-5	ס	ס	ס
7:8-9	ס	ס	ס
7:10–8:1	פ	פ	פ
8:2-3	פ	ס	פ
8:6-7	ס	ס	ס
8:14-15	פ	ס	
9:4-5	פ	>	
9:9-10	>	ס	
9:11-12	ס	>	
9:19-20	פ	ס	פ
9:28-29	ס	ס	ס
9:32–10:1	פ	ס	פ

Greek Witnesses

The Hebrew base text of M^L is compared with the rich evidence of the ancient versions, among which the Greek ones enjoy a prominent place, not least because of their great complexity and their unique divided character. Specific to the Greek book of Esther are its two main text forms that are conspicuously different. In addition, Josephus, in his telling of the Esther story, presents a third form (*Ant* xi: 184–296). The most-witnessed Greek form, the traditional Septuagint text recovered in 37 manuscripts (the uncial manuscripts A B S V, 32 minuscule manuscripts and the Chester Beatty Papyrus 967), has been called the B-text (because of ms. B), whereas the other form, attested by 4 minuscule manuscripts (19, 93, 108, 319), is called the Alpha-text (AT). In the Göttingen Septuagint (R. Hanhart, ed. *Esther* [vol. VIII/3 of *Septuaginta: Vetus Testamentum Graecum*; 2d ed.; Göttingen: Vandenhoeck & Ruprecht, 1983]) the two text forms are respectively called the *o'*-text and the *L*-text. In the present edition, however, for which the Göttingen Septuagint is the primary reference source, the *o'*-text is called G (Old Greek) and the *L*-text G^{AT} (without any identification with the "Lucianic" recension). In recent research the Alpha-text has attracted considerable attention. The scholarly discussion may be divided mainly into two groups. The first group regards the Alpha-text as a translation from a hitherto unknown Hebrew *Vorlage* that is different from the MT (cp. Torrey, "Older Book;" Moore, "Greek Witness;" Clines, *The Esther Scroll*; Fox, *Redaction*; Jobes, *Alpha-Text*), whereas the second group regards it as more probably a revision of the Septuagint text (Hanhart, *Esther*; De Troyer, *End*). E. Tov, presenting a compromise, holds that the Alpha-text is a recension from the Septuagint towards a Hebrew text that is different from the MT (Tov, "The 'Lucianic' Text"). In this much debated situation it is presumed here that the G^{AT} text is a redaction of the G text. Therefore variant readings from G^{AT} will not be recorded systematically in the critical apparatus, but typically will be entered for cases generated by variant readings in other witnesses.

Textual expansions are characteristic of both G and G^{AT}. With some minor variations, they have six longer additions, commonly called A–F. In G, A precedes 1:1; B follows 3:13; C comes after 4:17 and D follows C until 5:1; E follows 8:12; F is an epilogue following 10:3. In his Latin translation Jerome placed them all at the end of the book (see Vulgate 10:4–16:24). These Greek expansions, however, will not be an object for textual documentation or discussion on this occasion, since they are not found in the Hebrew tradition and seem not to be of direct relevance to the M text. Besides these six major pluses and numerous minor ones, G is characterized by many minuses in comparison with M (Paton, *Esther*, 33f., states that "there is scarcely a verse from which one or more words of M are not deleted"). In view of the fact that G and especially G^{AT} are considerably shorter than the M text, not only the complex inner relationship of G and G^{AT}, but also their respective relation to the frequently redundant M text, in particular with regard to the question of a possibly pre-Masoretic Hebrew text of Esther, have been a matter of intricate dispute in modern textual research.

Latin Witnesses

Compared with the Greek, as well as the Aramaic traditions, the Latin text tradition, in spite of its main division into the Old Latin form (La) and Jerome's translation, the Vulgate (V), appears to be substantially more standardized, like the Syriac tradition. For V in particular, its relation to the M text is closer. With the present lack of a new Vetus Latina edition of the Book of Esther, from the Vetus Latina Institute at Beuron, the primary reference source in the present edition for the Old Latin version is P. Sabatier, ed., *Bibliorum Sacrorum Latinae versiones antiquae, seu Vetus Italica* (3 vols.; 2d ed.; Paris: F. Didot, 1751). For the Vulgate the primary source is the edition of San Girolamo of Rome, F.A. Gasquet, et al., eds., *Biblia Sacra iuxta Latinam Vulgatam Versionem* (18 vols.; Rome: Libreria Editrice Vaticana, 1926–1996), and secondarily R. Weber, ed., *Biblia Sacra iuxta vulgatam versionem* (2 vols.; 2d rev. ed.; Stuttgart: Württembergische Bibelanstalt, 1975).

Syriac and Aramaic Witnesses

The *Syriac text tradition* in the form of Peshitta (S) presents to a high degree a standard text that shows relatively few deviations from M. There are, however, interesting inner Syriac variants among major manuscripts now collated by the Peshitta Institute at Leiden. There are also distinctive differences between the Codex Ambrosianus B21 Inferiore, which the Peshitta Institute has made the base text for its forthcoming edition of the Syriac Esther text, and the Lee edition of the Syriac Bible (1823), based on the London Polyglot of 1657 and much used in earlier research; at Esth 1:1; 5:11; 9:14 *BHK* and *BHS* seem to reflect readings from this edition, see further Paton, *Esther*, 16–18; Dirksen, "Lee's Editions," and Dirksen, "Urmia Edition." Since the new edition of the Syriac Esther from the Institute at Leiden has not yet appeared, the base reference source of the present edition is the Codex Ambrosianus (A.M. Ceriani, ed., *Translatio Syra Pescitto Veteris Testamenti ex codice Ambrosiano sec. fere VI* [Milan: J.B. Pogliani, 1876–1883]), for which the Peshitta Institute has the siglum 7a1.

The *Aramaic text tradition* of the Targums (T) to Esther is conspicuously divided, but in a manner quite different from the Greek. In comparison with the Masoretic text, the targumic tradition is remarkably more expansive and paraphrastic. According to E. Levine, the Targums were tripartite, and he summarizes: "In fact, there are three basic targums to Esther: the ostensibly literal translation (found in the Antwerp Polyglot), the more paraphrastic and expansive Targum Rishon (found in the London Polyglot), and the Targum Sheni, in which the amount of midrashim and digressive addenda greatly exceeds the amount of actual translation, making it more of a midrash than a targum" (Levine, *Targum*, 117). R. Kasher and M.I. Klein, in a recent study on targumic material to Esther from the Cairo Genizah ("New Fragments") attest the targumic textual pluriformity although not as definitely as does Levine. (The Cairo Genizah fragments reproduced and commented by Kasher and Klein are: T-S B 12.32 for Esth 1:2, T-S AS 70.72 for 5:7-9; 6:13–7:4, T-S B 11.52 and T-S B 12.21 for 5:10–7:5.) Similarly, A. Sperber in his edition (*The Hagiographa* [vol. IVA of *The Bible in Aramaic*; Leiden: Brill, 1968], 169–205, reprinting BM Or. 2375) not only presents Targum Rishon (I) and Sheni (II) but also some material "not found there at all" (p. vii), which he marked as "n."

The focus of the present edition is on the shorter text of Targum Rishon (T^R) because it generally seems to be of greater relevance to the Masoretic text than the much more expansive Targum Sheni (T^{Sh}) although there are cases where Targum Sheni comes closer to M than Targum Rishon does. Normally reference is made to Targum Sheni when it deviates specifically from Targum Rishon in some way that has reference to M. The main source for the text of T^R in the present edition is B. Grossfeld, ed., *The First Targum to Esther: According to the MS Paris Hebrew 110 of the Bibliothèque Nationale* (New York: Sepher-Hermon, 1983), with critical apparatus, translation and commentaries. For T[Sh] it is B. Grossfeld, ed., *The Targum Sheni to the Book of Esther: A Critical Edition Based on MS. Sassoon 282 with Critical Apparatus* (New York: Sepher-Hermon, 1994). These have been supplemented with B. Grossfeld, *The Two Targums of Esther: Translated, with Apparatus and Notes* (ArBib 18; Collegeville, Minn.: Liturgical, 1991), where the translation of Targum Rishon is based on Madrid 116-Z40 (Ms. Villa-Amil No. 5) and the translation of Targum Sheni on Sassoon 282. This latter manuscript is also the base text of the translation of B. Ego in her recent study on *Targum Scheni zu Ester* (TSAJ 54; Tübingen: J. C. B. Mohr, 1996). Finally, there are some Esther related fragments extant from Qumran Cave 4 (4Q550[a–e], described as "Aramaic Proto-Esther" by J.T. Milik, "Les modèles araméens," but cf. S. White Crawford, "Has Esther been Found;" as well as J.J. Collins and D.A. Green, "Tales from the Persian Court."

NOTES ON THE MASORAH PARVA

RUTH

‏וַיִּשְׂאוּ‎ ‏מֹג‎ – *Com.:* Cf. Ginsburg, 2, ‏ג‎, §§ 401a and 401b.

‏בְּשָׂדֵה‎ ‏ב כתב ה‎ – *Com.:* The reference is only to Ruth. The other instance is 4:3.

‏כַלֹּתֶיהָ‎ ‏ב חד מל‎ – *Com.:* This Mp is not correct in so far as M^L is concerned, in which both cases are defective, but it does agree with, for example, the text of M^A.

‏שֹׁבְנָה‎ ‏ב בנתי בנתי‎ Twice (followed by) ‏בנתי‎: Ruth 1:11; 1:12. – *Com.:* The total number of instances is therefore three. Cf. also Mp Ruth 1:11; 1:12.

‏וַתֹּאמַרְנָה־לָּהּ‎ ‏ה בטע‎ – *Com.:* Cf. Yeivin, *Tiberian Massorah,* § 216; and also Weil, § 3661.

‏לַאֲנָשִׁים:‎ ‏ו‎ – *Com.:* For *waw* being an error for *zayin*, see Ginsburg, 1, ‏א‎, § 926.

‏עִמֵּךְ‎ ‏ה וחד ועמך‎ Five times, and once ‏ועמך‎ (Isa 60:21).

‏יַפְרִיד‎ ‏ב ובין עצומים‎ Twice: Prov 18:18.

‏בָּאֵנָה‎ ‏ב‎ Twice (in the book). – *Com.:* A third occurrence is found in Jer 8:7.

‏קְרֶאןָ‎ ‏ל חס‎ – *Com.:* ‏קראן‎ occurring only here, the Mp is equal to ‏ל וחס‎.

‏הָרֵע‎ ‏ד וחד ושב והרע‎ Four times and once ‏והרע‎: Josh 24:20.

‏מֵעִם יְהֹוָה‎ ‏ט‎ – *Com.:* This Mp does not take into account the three cases in 1 Kings. Cf. Weil, § 3417.

‏נֶחָמְתָּנִי‎ ‏ל וחד עזרתני‎ Once (like this) and once (preceded by a conjunction): Ps 86:17.

‏וַתֵּשֶׁב‎ ‏יב‎ – *Com.:* Cf. Weil, § 140.

‏נַעֲרוֹתָיו‎ ‏ב מל‎ – *Com.:* ‏נערותיו‎ occurring only here and in Ruth 3:2, the Mp is equal to ‏ב ומל‎.

‏בְּשָׂדֶה‎ ‏ה רפ‎ – *Com.:* See Mm on the same word in 2:8.

‏וַתֵּשֶׁב‎ ‏יב‎ – *Com.:* Cf. Weil, § 140.

‏בַּלָּט‎ ‏ב בכת‎ – *Com.:* The placing of the *circellus* is in error in M^L. The Mp should refer to ‏וַתָּבֹא‎ as is shown by the Mp in M^A.

‏כְּנָפֶךָ‎ ‏ל חס למערב‎ – *Com.:* Westerners read ‏כנפך‎ defective (see Yeivin, *Tiberian Masorah*, §153).

‏בְּרוּכָה‎ ‏ל וחד וברוכה‎ 1 Sam 25:33

‏דָּל‎ ‏יב‎ – *Com.:* See Ginsburg, 4, ‏ד‎, §163.

‏יִגְאָל‎ ‏ל וכול שום ברנש‎ – *Com.:* In all other occurrences, a personal name: Num 13:7; 2 Sam 23:36 and 1 Chr 3:22.

‏הֲבִי‎ ‏ל בטע‎ – *Com.:* There are no other occurrences of this verbal form with a different accent.

‏וְכָל־הָעָם‎ ‏ג באמצ פסוק‎ – *Com.:* Cf. Frensdorff, *Massorah,* 142; and also Ginsburg, 2, ‏ס‎, § 265.

‏לְכִלְיוֹן וּמַחְלוֹן‎ ‏ל וכול קרי חלוף‎ Once and everywhere else read in the reversed order (Ruth 1:2; 1:5).

‏אֵשֶׁת מַחְלוֹן‎ ‏ל ושאר אשת המת‎ Once (like this) and otherwise Ruth 4:5.

15 וְהָיָה לָךְ   ל   – *Com.:* Once, namely in the Writings. According to Weil (§ 2431), the other case is Isa 60:19.

17 עוֹבֵד   ב מל׳ למערב   – *Com.:* Westerners read עובד plene (see Yeivin, *Tiberian Masorah*, §153).

CANTICLES

1:2 מִנְּשִׁיקוֹת   נשיקות ונעתרות וחד ל   – *Com.:* For the reference ונעתרות נשיקות, see Prov 27:6.

4 חֲדָרָיו   וחדריו וחד ל   – *Com.:* For the reference וחדריו, see 1 Chr 28:11.

7 שֶׁאָהֲבָה   ב   – *Com.:* "Twice" must be a mistake since this form occurs five times, viz. here and in 3:1, 2, 3, 4.

8 אִם־לֹא   פסוק רא ח   – *Com.:* Not included are the occurrences in Job, viz. 17:2; 22:20; 30:25; 31:20, 31, 36.

15 הִנָּךְ   בסיפ ל   – *Com.:* Either this is an error, since the word occurs four times in Canticles (twice here and twice in 4:1), or it refers to this word with the accent *mahpak*; in the other three occurrences, the word has a different accent.

16 יָפֶה דוֹדִי   ה   – *Com.:* Although the circellus seems to be over the combination of two words, the number "five" must refer to יפה only (2 Sam 14:25; Ezek 31:9; Cant 1:16; Qoh 3:11; 5:17).

17 רַחִיטֵנוּ   רהיטנו ק   – *Com.:* There is no circellus.

2:4 הֱבִיאַנִי   ה   – *Com.:* This must be a mistake for "four times," as Mp has correctly at 1:4. M^A has "four times." Cp. Mm at 1:4.

9 הַחַלּוֹנוֹת   חס ג   – *Com.:* "Three times" must be a mistake since there are four occurences of the defective form; see Mm.

10 וְאָמַר לִי   אדבר מה ב   – *Com.:* For the reference מה אדבר, see Isa 38:15.

13 לֵכִי   קר לך ל   – *Com.:* There is a dot over לך, but no dot is discernible over (the *resh* of) קר.

3:4 שֶׁהֲבֵיאתִיו   ל   – *Com.:* The first person perfect *hifil* with this form of the third person singular masculine suffix occurs five times (cp. Mp in *BHS*): Gen 43:9; Num 14:24; 1 Sam 1:22; Isa 48:15; Cant 3:4, but only in the last verse with ב. In the other places the form is הביאתיו.

5 תָּעִירוּ   ב   – *Com.:* The circellus is above the ת. If indeed this is meant, then "twice" is a mistake since the form occurs three times, viz., here and in 2:7 and 8:4. "Twice" would be correct if the circellus refers to the combination אִם־תָּעִירוּ, which occurs here and in 2:7. In 8:4 we have the combination מַה־תָּעִירוּ with the circellus over the *maqqep̄*, and the Mp "once." M^A and M^Y have no Mp at 3:5.

8 מְלֻמְּדֵי   ל   – *Com.:* This must be a mistake since the word occurs also in 1 Chr 25:7, though with a different accent; cp. Mm. M^A and M^Y have "twice", although in M^A there is at best only a trace of a circellus visible over מלמדי.

4:1 מִבַּעַד   ב   – *Com.:* "Twice" must be a mistake since the word, in the same combination with לצמתך, occurs three times, viz. here, in v. 3 and 6:7. In neither of the latter two places is there a Mp.

לְצַמָּתֵךְ   ב   – *Com.:* See previous comment.

2 הָרְחֵצָה   ל   – *Com.:* The word also occurs in the same expression in 6:6, where Mp has correctly "twice."

3 כְּפֶ֣לַח הָרִמּוֹן֙ ג· – *Com.:* The circellus is positioned over the space between the two words. Since this combination occurs only twice (here and 6:7), the circellus probably belongs to כפלח, which does occur three times (here, 6:7 and Job 41:16).

4 דָּוִיד֒ ה מל – *Com.:* The plene writing occurs five times outside the Dodekapropheton, Ezra, Nehemiah, and Chronicles, viz., 1 Kgs 3:14; 11:4, 36; Ezek 34:22; Cant 4:4.

6 אֶל־הַר וכל כרמל הכרמל כות יֹו Sixteen times and all occurrences with "Karmel/the Karmel" likewise. – *Com.:* The combination with "Karmel" (without the article) does not occur.

9 לְבָבְתִּ֖נִי ב וחס – *Com.:* This does not hold good for M^L, where the second occurrence in the same verse is plene. In M^Y both occurrences are defective.

   מִצַּוְּרֹנָ֑יִךְ: ב חס א בליש Twice defective, once in this form. – *Com.:* The dot on the ב is lacking. The defective form, without א, occurs here and in Neh 3:5. Only here does the word occur in the form צַוְּרֹן.

10 טֹבוּ אֹהָלֶ֖יךָ ב – *Com.:* The reference, אהליך, is to Num 24:5. The circellus is over the ב, but although the form טבו occurs twice, the circellus should probably have been over מה־טבו as in the same expression in Num 24:5, where Mp refers to Cant 4:10.

11 נֹ֫פֶת יֹא ראש פסו נון וסוף נון – *Com.:* See Mm.

13 פַּרְדֵּ֣ס ל וחד שומר הפרדס – *Com.:* For the reference שומר הפרדס, see Neh 2:8 (with defective שמר).

15 מַעְיַ֣ן דֹ – *Com.:* "Four times" refers to the construct form (with *patah*).

3 אֵיכָ֤כָה ב בטע – *Com.:* There is no clear circellus. There may be a trace of a circellus over the ה.

4 הֲמ֖וּ ל – *Com.:* No circellus can be discerned.

5 וְאֶצְבְּעֹתַי֙ ל וחד אצבעתי – *Com.:* For the reference אצבעתי, see Ps 144:1 (with the word written plene). Mp is divided over the right margin of the third column (ל) and the left margin.

7 הִכּ֜וּנִי ג· – *Com.:* Either this is an error, since the form occurs twice, here and in Prov 23:35, or it includes Gen 34:30 with והכוני.

   הַחֹמֽוֹת: ז כתב Seven times (thus) written. – *Com.:* The word seems to have the most complicated Masoretic tradition in Canticles. The plural form, including the occurrences without article and with a preposition, occurs fourteen times. In M^L the word is written as חומת four times: 2 Kgs 25:10; Jer 51:12; Lam 2:7; Neh 2:13; three times the form is חומות: Isa 26:1; Ps 51:20; 2 Chr 8:5); the remaining seven places, with the form חמות, are Jer 1:18; 39:8; 51:58; 52:14; Ezek 26:4; Neh 4:1; Cant 5:7. These seven places must be referred to by Mp at Cant 5:7, which means that the note ז כתב must be understood as ז כת כן, seven times thus written, as at Jer 39:8; 52:14 (cp. 51:12 with Mp as ד כת כן). A different Masorah in M^L sorts out the cases where the word is a plural form to distinguish it from the singular form חומת, viz., at Ezek 26:4: חמות: eight times, 2 Kgs 25:10; Isa 26:1; Ezek 26:4; Neh 2:13; 4:1; Lam 2:7; Ps 51:20; 2 Chr 8:5, and all of Jeremiah likewise, except for three, Jer 15:20; 49:27; 51:44. In this list, Cant 5:7 should have been included, which would bring the total number of plural forms outside Jeremiah to nine. The number "eight" is also mentioned in a Mp-note, besides Ezek 26:4, at 2 Kgs 25:10; Ps 51:20 (with the addition: "and all of Jeremiah likewise, except for three"); Lam 2:7; Neh 4:1. See Ginsburg, 4, ח, § 69.

9   דּוֹדֶ֫ךָ‎¹ ב‎ – *Com.:* Either the note refers to this verse only, or is a mistake, since the word occurs four times, twice here, and twice in 6:1. Another possibility is that the circellus, over first ד, is misplaced and actually refers to the combination מַה־דּוֹדֵךְ, which occurs twice in this verse.

    דּוֹדֶ֫ךָ‎² ג מל֤ בסיפ‎ – *Com.:* This must be a mistake for "four times"; see previous comment. At 6:1 Mp has correctly "four times."

11 כָּעוֹרֵֽב׃ כערב וחד ל‎ – *Com.:* For the reference כערב, "as Oreb," see Ps 83:12.

14 סַפִּירִֽים׃ בספירים וחד ל‎ – *Com.:* For the reference בספירים, see Isa 54:11.

15 כָּֽאֲרָזִֽים׃ כארזים וחד ל‎ – *Com.:* For the reference כֲארזים, see Num 24:6.

6:4 נָאוָ֫ה ה‎ – *Com.:* If this is not an error, it must include 1:5, where this word occurs with copula; at that place Mp has "once."

6 מַתְאִימֹ֫ות ומל ל‎ – *Com.:* This must be a mistake since this word occurs also at 4:1, where Mp gives "twice and plene."

10 שָׁ֫חַר ז‎ – *Com.:* This form (*qameṣ*; no article) occurs, however, eight times, viz. Isa 8:20; 14:12; Ps 57:9; 108:3; 139:9; Job 3:9; 41:10; Cant 6:10. Ginsburg (2:617–18) gives two lists, §§ 332 and 333, one: four times (the first four references), one: eight times (all references).

    כַּנִּדְגָּלֹֽות׃ ל‎ – *Com.:* It should be "twice," since the word also occurs in v. 4, where Mp has correctly "twice."

11 הָרִמֹּנִֽים׃ חס בכת ל‎ – *Com.:* In 7:13 the form occurs plene.

7:1 תֶּחֱזוּ ל‎ – *Com.:* The same form also occurs in Isa 30:10, though without accent. "Once" may be an error for "once in the book" as given by Weil in *BHS*.

5 עַל־שַׁעַר ב‎ – *Com.:* In M^L the circellus is over שׁ, but there is virtually no space for a circellus above the *maqqep̄*, where it belongs in view of the number "twice" (here and 2 Chr 26:9).

13 דֹּדָי ב‎ – *Com.:* The word with this suffix, however, occurs only here.

8:7 יֽוּכְלוּ יֹא‎ – *Com.:* This number ("eleven times") includes the two occurrences where the form is defective, viz., Josh 7:12; Ps 18:39. Apart from these eleven instances, the form occurs with different vowels in Jer 5:22; 20:11; Ps 21:12. – *Com.:* M^L has a circellus over the word, but there is no Mp-note. The form אֲחֹתֵ֫נוּ occurs three times defective, viz. here, in Gen 34:14 (Mp: ג) and in Gen 24:60, where Mp has "four times", including Gen 34:31, where the word is written plene. The four places are listed in Mm at Gen 34:14.

11 לַנֹּטְרִים ל‎ – *Com.:* This occurrence (with *pataḥ*) is to be distinguished from v. 12, where we have לְנטרים.

12 הָאֶ֫לֶף ג‎ – *Com.:* Josh 18:28 is not included; see Mm.

QOHELETH

1:7 שֶׁהַנְּחָלִים ל‎ – *Com.:* The word lacks a corresponding circellus above it in M^L.

12 קֹהֶ֫לֶת ה‎ – *Com.:* In fact, the word occurs *six times* in the book: 1:1, 2, 12; 7:27; 12:9, 10, and once more with the article in 12:8. The Mp "five times" occurs at 1:12 and 12:10. In 1:1, the word is found in a cstr. chain, so is perhaps excluded from this counting, unless the Masorah records an old form with the article in 7:27, which therefore would be excluded; see the apparatus there.

15 מְעֻוָּת ל‎ – *Com.:* An erasure appears under the ל of this Mp.

8 וְהַמְּדִינוֹת למדינות וחד ומל ל Only once, and plene, and once with the preposition ל (Esth 2:18).

0 אָצַלְתִּי מֵהֶם ל – *Com.:* There is no certainty about the circellus for this Mp. What is found between these two words might be a spot. Ben Ḥayyim's Masorah attests such a note with a circellus on the *maqqēp̄* of the following לֹא־מנעתי "Once, and once ולא מנעתי."

1 בְּיוֹם אשמתו יִתְּנֶנּוּ ב Twice (with) Lev 5:24.

4 מִיַּד הָאֱלֹהִים בליש ד The expression (the hand of God) occurs four times. – *Com.:* In the Masorah finalis of Ben Ḥayyim's edition a list states "There are three occurrences of יד האלהים (instead of the much more frequent יד ה') and their references are: 1 Sam 4:8; 5:11; 2 Chr 30:12; and all Qohelet likewise"; these are Qoh 2:24; 9:1; see Ginsburg, 4, י, §87. This makes five and not four. Thus, the Mp in M^L is most probably a corruption for "five" (alteration of ה to ד), the five including the occurrences with the preposition מן (1 Sam 4:8; Qoh 2:24) or בְּ־ (Qoh 9:1) as well as without a preposition, hence the wording בליש indicating "similar forms."

6 זֶה הֶבֶל בסוף פסוק ג – *Com.:* M^L has only one circellus on these two words, which is a contradiction of the content of the note itself, which includes the last two words of the verse. See the commentary on the Mm for the last four words of the verse.

4 כִּי כָל־אֲשֶׁר יַעֲשֶׂה מכל התעבות ב Twice (with) Lev 18:29.

6 הָרֶשַׁע: ל Once pausal form.

2 בַּמֶּה ל Unique with prep. vocalized šǝwâ.

2 אֶת־הַמֵּתִים וחד את החיים ואת המתים ל Once, and once ואת המתים (Ruth 2:20).

9 הַשְּׁנַיִם ב יעמדו Twice (with) Qoh 4:12.

0 לַהֲקִימוֹ: ולהקימו וחד ל – *Com.:* The Mp seems to be wrong. Actually there are two occurrences of להקימו: Qoh 4:10; 2 Sam 12:17. Mandelkern does not indicate any occurrence with a cj. attached to this word. Ginsburg, 2, ק, §143 found a list with the two verses above. The ו is probably due to a scribal error in the process of transmission.

1 לִפְנֵי הָאֱלֹהִים ו Six times (outside the book).

יהיו ימיו מְעַטִּים: ב Twice (with) Ps 109:8.

6 אֲחָדִים וּדְבָרִים ב Twice (with) Gen 11:1.

8 הוּא ק הִיא – *Com.:* The circellus for this *qǝrê* is lacking in M^L.

0 רָאִית ק ראות – *Com.:* The circellus for this *qǝrê* is lacking in M^L.

2 כי למועד שָׁמוּר ב Twice (with) 1 Sam 9:24.

5 לָרוּחַ: ג Three times with *pataḥ*. – *Com.:* The Mp protects the three occurrences with the article. Because of the ה its wording should probably be: "Three times with *qames*"; the occurrences are in Ezek 5:2; Job 28:25; Qoh 5:15.

6 וָקֶצֶף: בזיון וקצף ב Twice (with) Esth 1:18. – *Com.:* There is a circellus on ורבה, but no Mp note.

3 וּלימים וְשָׁנִים ב Twice (with) Gen 1:14.

6 לא אני לפניו וְטוֹבָה ב Twice: Qoh 6:6; Esth 8:5.

0 חצי הספ מַה פ – *Com.:* The second half of the book begins at 6:10. Some confusion is introduced in M^L, due to the fact that this note has been written below the *qǝrê* note on שהתקיף of v. 10.

9 וְנָתוֹן יז – *Com.:* The Mp in M^L mistakenly has "seventeen" instead of "seven"; a contamination from the preceding note on רשע.

לְרַע בֹ – *Com.:* As a matter of fact there are three occurrences of לְרַע with *pataḥ* - the form appears in Jer 7:6; 25:7, and the Mp on Jer 25:7 gives "three times"; see Ginsburg, 2, ר, §380.

11 פִּתְגָּם בֹ ונשמע Twice (with) Esth 1:20.

9:6 גַּם יֹב יחיד דרא פסֹ אית בהון מן גֹ גֹ מלין קרחיֹ Twelve unusual verses whose first word is one of a series of three without conjunction.

10:3 כְּשֶׁהַסָּכָל ה יתיר – *Com.:* On the left side of the column the Mp states: "unique," and, in accordance with the *qərê* found in other mss., this Mp note on the right side of the column says: "the ה is superfluous."

17 בַשְׁתִּי: ל וכול ערב כות בֹ מ א Unique and all the woof is similar except one. – *Com.:* The Mp means: "this sequence of consonants and vowels בשתי is unique in Qoh as well as in the whole Bible with that meaning (from the root שתה drink). And all other occurrences of this sequence of letters where this word (= "warp") forms a pair with ערב (= "woof") are identical in vocalization, except in Lev 13:48," where there is no article. All these occurrences can be found in Lev 13:49, 51, 53, 57; compare Frensdorff, *Ochlah*, §49.

18 יִדְלָף ל וחד ואת ידלף Unique and once ואת ידלף (Gen 22:22).

11:4 יִקְצֹור: – *Com.:* In M[L] the Mp note for this circellus was left out. In the Aleppo Codex a Mp has גֹ מל "three times plene" at Isa 17:5. In fact, this word is written plene in Isa 17:5; Prov 22:8 and Qoh 11:4; see Ginsburg, 2, ק, §236.

5 הַמְּלֵאָה בֹ – *Com.:* This Mp is wrongly placed on Qoh 11:5. There are three occurrences of המלאה in the Bible; see the list edited by Ginsburg, 2, מ, §403. The note "twice" found here probably belongs to the two other occurrences - Deut 22:9; Amos 2:13 - where the מ does not have the *dageš*.

8 יִחְיֶה יֹח וכל חיו יחיה כותה Eighteen times and every occurrence of חיו יחיה is identical.

שָׁבָא שבא־מחלפ There is a variant tradition with a *maqqep̄*.

9 וּבְמַרְאֵי ל וכת Unique and written (י).

12:2 תֶחְשַׁךְ ל וחד ותחשך הארץ Unique and once with cj. (Exod 10:15).

5 בַּשּׁוּק בֹ Twice (in the book).

14 וְאִם־רָע: בֹ בקול יי אלהינו אם־טֹוב Twice (with) Jer 42:6.

LAMENTATIONS

1:1 יֹ – *Com.:* אֵיכָה occurs seventeen times in the Bible so that יֹ is here probably a scribal error instead of יֹז "seventeen times." See, for example, the Mp in the margin of 2:1; 4:1, 2 and Weil, §1095.

וַהֲנָחָה לַמְּדִינוֹת ל ומל וחד והנחה למדינות בַּמְּדִינֹות Once plene and once וַהֲנָחָה לַמְּדִינוֹת (Esth 2:18).

2 בָּלוֹ ה כתוֹ Five times written with ו (at the end).

3 וּמֶרֶב בֹ ימים יפקדו Twice, (here and in) Isa 24:22.

7 מַחֲמֻדֶּיהָ ל וכת Unique, that is (in this) orthography.

עֹוזֵר ו – *Com.:* This note refers to the sequence וְאֵין עֹוזֵר (see M[Y] and cp. Weil, §2129). The correct Mp with עֹוזֵר would be ה מל as e.g. in M[Y]. Thus in M[L] either the circellus is misplaced or the first circellus and the second note together have been omitted by mistake.

8 הָיְתָה דֹ Four times (vocalized with) *qames* (in the second syllable).

0   בַּקָּהָל   דָגֵש ד   Four times (with preposition בּ and) *dageš*.

1   מַחֲמוּדֵּיהֶם   וּ יתיר   – *Com.:* The circellus is lacking in M[L] but obviously the note refers to מַחֲמוּדֵּיהֶם. The written consonants mean מַחֲמוּדֵּיהֶם (cp. 1:7 and see Bauer/Leander, *Grammatik*, §493z҃) while the reading tradition is מַחֲמַדֵּיהֶם.

2   הוֹגָה   ג   – *Com.:* הוֹגָה occurs three times with ה *rapê*: twice plene (Lam 1:12; 3:32) and once defective (2 Sam 20:13). Further there is one הוֹגָהּ with *mappîq* in Lam 1:5. See Ginsburg, 4, י, §74.

5   סֶלָה   ב   Twice. – *Com.:* Probably a part of the note has been omitted. Its meaning seems to be "twice, once with ה (Lam 1:15) and once with א (סִלָּא 2 Kgs 12:21)"; see Weil in *BHS*.

8   מָרִיתִי   ב מנהון בס   (Three times) two of them in this book. – *Com.:* The beginning of the note is missing and the numeral "two" lacks the usual superscript dot in M[L]. The three references of מריתי are: Isa 50:5; Lam 1:18; Lam 1:20.

9   וְיָשִׁיבוּ   ג   – *Com.:* Twice plene (here and in Isa 41:28) and once defective (Deut 1:22).

0   מָרִיתִי   ב ואנכי   Twice, (here and in) Isa 50:5. – *Com.:* Cp. 1:18. This Mp is either incomplete or wrong. There are three מָרִיתִי in the Hebrew Bible, two of them in the book of Lam (1:18 and 1:20) and one in Isa 50:5.

1   וְיִהְיוּ   יא   – *Com.:* ויהיו occurs eleven times with י *rapê*, i.e., vocalized וְיִהְיוּ (with *šəwâ* at the beginning) instead of וַיִּהְיוּ (with *patah* and subsequent *dageš forte*); see Weil, §417 and Ognibeni, *ʾOklah*, §18F.

   כָּמוֹנִי׃   ל חס   Unique defective (in the book). – *Com.:* In opposition to this Mp the text of M[L] (and likewise M[L34]4) is written plene here, while the orthography in M[Y] is indeed defective.

2   עַל כָּל־פְּשָׁעָי   ל   Unique (as sequence of words).

1   אֵיכָה   יז פסוק   (One of) seventeen verses (containing the word אֵיכָה).

2   בִּלַּע   ב רא פסוק המות   Twice at the beginning of a verse, (here and in) Isa 25:8.

4   מַחֲמַדֵּי   ב והמתי   Twice, (here and in) Hos 9:16.

6   שַׁבּוֹ   ל כת שׂ   Unique written with שׂ (instead of ס).

   מוֹעֵד וְשַׁבָּת   ב חס   – *Com.:* This note is obviously in error, since there is neither anything "defective" nor does this sequence occur "twice." In M[Y] the note "twice" (without the characterisation "defective") is connected with וְשַׁבָּת alone which indeed occurs only here and in Isa 1:13.

   וְכֹהֵן׃   ב חד ראש פסו וחד סוף פסוק   Twice, once at the beginning of a verse (Lev 22:11) and the other at the end of a verse (Lam 2:6).

2   לְאִמֹּתָם   ל וחד לְאַמֹּתָם   Unique, and one לְאַמֹּתָם (Gen 25:16).

4   נְבִיאַיִךְ   כול מל   – *Com.:* Since this form is unique the note either refers to all forms of נביא in the book of Lam or it originally read ל ומל "unique and that plene" as suggested by Weil in *BHS*.

7   וַיִּשְׂמַח   ל וחד ושמח   Unique, and one וְשָׂמַח (Prov 27:11) .

8   צָעַק   ב אל המלך   Twice, (here and in) 1 Kgs 20:39.

9   נֹכַח פְּנֵי   ל   – *Com.:* Possibly the meaning is "unique in this book" (cp. Weil in *BHS*) since there is a אֶל־נֹכַח פְּנֵי in Num 19:4. There are also various examples of the sequence with suffixes: Jer 17:16; Ezek 14:3, 4, 7.

   אֲדֹנָי   יד כת כן   Fourteen times spelled like this (in the book).

0   עוֹלְלְתָּ   כול חס   – *Com.:* Presumably a mistake since the text is against the note. The form עוֹלַלְתָּ occurs also in 1:22. Thus the correct meaning of the note might perhaps be "always plene (in this book)."

עֲלָלֵי   כּוֹל חֹס   – *Com.:* The note seems unclear since according to M^L this form is unique.

ז בלשון נביאיה וְנָבִיא: – *Com.:* There are only six occurrences of this form including Lam 2:20 and Dan 9:24. The seventh case is probably וְנָבָא in Ps 90:12 (cp. Weil's Mp at Ps 90:12 in *BHS*). Note however that this form (cj. + 1st c. pl. fut. *hifil* from בוא√) is morphologically completely different from the noun "prophet." Note further that strictly speaking neither Lam 2:20 nor Dan 9:24 nor Ps 90:12 are part of the "Prophets."

22   יֹא   כְיוֹם   – *Com.:* The note refers to the eleven occurrences of כִּיוֹם beginning with the prep. כ and *šəwâ*; see Ognibeni, *ʾOklah*, §14B.

ב   וְרַבִּיתִי   – *Com.:* This Mp is in error. The form וְרַבִּיתִי is unique in the Hebrew Bible (see M^Y and *BHS*).

י   אֹיְבֵי   – *Com.:* There are only seven occurrences of this form. Possibly י was written by mistake instead of ז; cp. Weil in *BHS*.

3:1   ל   רָאָה עֳנִי   – *Com.:* The circellus might be misplaced in M^L. In *BHS* this Mp is attached only to עֳנִי, which is unique in the book of Lam.

2   ל   וַיֵּלַךְ   Unique (in this vocalization).

5   ל   רֹאשׁ וּתְלָאָה: – *Com.:* The circellus might be misplaced. In M^Y (and in *BHS*) this note is attached to וּתְלָאָה only.

6   ב   בְּמַחֲשַׁכִּים   – *Com.:* Since this form occurs also in Pss 88:7 and 143:3, Mp either is in error or has the meaning: "There are 2 *other* occurrences." See Mm.

10   ק אריֹ   אַרְיֵה   – *Com.:* The lemma lacks a circellus in M^L.

11   כּוֹל חֹס שָׁמֵם: Always defective (in this form). – *Com.:* The word was originally written plene in M^L but the ו has been erased.

12   ל וכֹת א   כְּמַטְּרָא   Unique (with the preposition כ) and written with א.

14   ד חֹס בכתֹי   שָׂחֹק   – *Com.:* This note is not in accordance with the text of M^L because in the Writings there are only three cases of שְׂחֹק in defective spelling in that manuscript (Job 12:4, Qoh 7:6, Lam 3:14). The controversial case seems to be בִּשְׂחוֹק in Prov 14:13 where the reading of M^L is plene while the Mp states "three times defective in this or similar forms." M^Y, on the other hand, is in accordance with that latter Mp and consequently also with the note in Lam 3:14 because this ms. reads בִּשְׂחֹק (defective) in Prov 14:13 and there are in fact two other cases of שְׂחֹק with defective spelling and a preceding preposition in the Hebrew Bible (Jer 48:26, 39).

16   ל וכֹת   וַיִּגְרֵס   Unique, and written (like this, i.e., with ס).

17   ב לא נשׁיתי   נָשִׁיתִי   Twice, (here and in) Jer 15:10.

19   בּ   זָכָר־   Twice with *qameṣ (qatan)*. – *Com.:* The meaning of the note is probably that only twice in the Writings, here and in Ps 25:7, the form זָכָר־ is not followed by either אֲנִי, זֹאת or נָא. A third case might have been Ps 119:49, but the vocalization in M^L is זְכֹר־ there.

בּ   וְרֹאשׁ:   Twice with *qameṣ* (i.e., preformative וְ).

32   גׁ   הוֹגָה   – *Com.:* See Mp commentary on הוגה in 1:12.

33   גׁ   וַיּוּגֶּה   – *Com.:* Probably an error, since the form וַיְּגֶּה (יגה√ *piel*) is unique in the Hebrew Bible. Perhaps the error was caused by its nearness to הוֹגָה in v. 32, which indeed occurs "three times" in Lam.

41   ו   נִשָּׂא   – *Com.:* The note includes four cases of נִשָּׂא which are all different grammatical forms (*qal* in Lam 3:41; *nifal* in 2 Sam 19:43; *piel* in 1 Kgs 9:11; *nifal* ptc. in Isa 2:12), and two cases of נִסָּה (Gen 22:1; 1 Sam 17:39).

ל   כַּפָּיִם   – *Com.:* In M^L it is not quite clear whether the circellus is between

‎אֶל־ and כַּפִּים or over the כ of כַּפִּים. In M^Y the circellus is clearly over כַּפִּים only. This pausal form with *qameṣ* is unique within Lam and even within the Writings. However, there is one other כַּפִּים in Hag 1:11, but with *sillûq* instead of *zaqep̄*.

סָחִי   שַׁחִי   ל וחד שחי   Unique, and one שְׁחִי (Isa 51:23).

עֵינִי   וֹמֹל   ל — *Com.*: The circellus is misplaced in M^L. Obviously the note refers to the subsequent lemma עוֹלְלָה.

לְרַוְחָתִי לְשַׁוְעָתִי: ל — *Com.*: In opposition to M^L the circellus is placed with לְרַוְחָתִי in M^Y and with לְשַׁוְעָתִי in *BHS* while M^{L34} repeats the note with both lemmata.

אֲדֹנָי   כֵּן כת יֹד   Fourteen times spelled like this (in the book).

מִשְׁפָּטִי   יֹו — *Com.*: Including one וּמִשְׁפָּטִי (Isa 51:4) and one לְמִשְׁפָּטִי (Ps 35:23).

שְׁמֵי יְהֹוָה: ל וחד שמי יהוה   Unique (in this vocalization), and one שְׁמִי יהוה (Jer 16:21).

כַּי עֵנִים   כיעינים ק — *Com.*: The lemma lacks a circellus in M^L.

לְמַעֲדַנִּים   מַעֲדַנִּים וַיִּתֵּן   ל וחד ויתן מעדנים   Unique (with preposition) and one וְיִתֵּן מַעֲדַנִּים (Prov 29:17).

אַשְׁפְּתוֹת: — *Com.*: The word has a circellus in M^L, but lacks a note. *BHK* assigns a ב̇ – although it is written on the right margin of the *subsequent* line – to אַשְׁפְּתוֹת. As to the assignment *BHS* follows *BHK*, but corrects "twice" into "once." Obviously neither editor could determine another reference for that ב̇. The ב̇ however refers to נִגְאָלוּ (4:14) in the neighboring column. Although the word נִגְאָלוּ is affected by a dark brown discoloring in the ms., its circellus is still clearly visible in the color transparency.

שֶׁהֶם   ב הרהיבוני   Twice, (here and in) Cant 6:5.

יָבֹא   ב חס בס — *Com.*: The form יָבֹא is unique in the book of Lam. Obviously "in the book" means "in the *məḡillôṯ*" (cp. Cant 4:16).

זְקֵנִים   וזקנים ק — *Com.*: There is neither a circellus nor an additional *šûreq* with the lemma in M^L while M^Y has a circellus as well as the vocalization זְקֵנִים. M^{L34} has the reading וּזְקֵנִים in the text (without any Masoretic note).

קְצֵינוּ   ב̇   Twice (in this verse).

מָשִׁחַ   ל וכול שמואל כות ב מ א   (This form) occurs only here and always in the books of Samuel with one exception (2 Sam 1:21).

יֹשַׁבְתִּי   יושבת ק — *Com.*: The lemma lacks a circellus in M^L.

הַבִּיט   הביטה ק — *Com.*: The lemma lacks a circellus in M^L.

לֹא   ולא ק — *Com.*: The lemma lacks a circellus in M^L.

אֵינָם   ואינם ק — *Com.*: The lemma lacks a circellus in M^L.

אֲנַחְנוּ   ואנחנו ק — *Com.*: The lemma lacks a circellus in M^L.

פְּרָק   ב וחס ואין מציל   Twice, and that defective, Ps 7:3.

כַּתַּנּוּר   ל   Unique (with *mûnaḥ*).

זַלְעָפוֹת   ל וחד זלעפות   Unique and one זַלְעָפוֹת (Ps 11:6).

טְחוֹן   ל וחד טחון   Unique and one טָחוֹן (Deut 9:21).

לְאָבֶל   ל וכת כן   Unique and spelled like this. – *Com.*: לְאָבֶל occurs four times in the Bible (an identical form in 2 Sam 19:13 and further with different accents in Amos 8:10 and Job 30:31). Obviously the circellus is misplaced in M^L. The note belongs to the subsequent מְחֹלֵנוּ which is in fact unique and and should be written defective (cp. M^Y where the note reads ל והס). It seems that in M^L the *mater lectionis* first was written, but then has been erased.

18 שׁוּעָלִים ב מל – *Com.:* The note is not in accordance with the text of M^L, since שׁוּעָלִים is also written plene in Judg 15:4 and twice in Cant 2:15.

ESTHER

1:1 הַמֶּלֶךְ ג – *Com.:* M^L indicates two occurrences with article, here and Jer 22:11, and one without article, Jer 33:21.

שֶׁבַע וְעֶשְׂרִים ג – *Com.:* This Mp concerns the whole figure 127 although there is only one circellus in M^L (between the figures 7 and 20).

2 בַּיָּמִים הָהֵם ב – *Com.:* Twice in the book, the other occurrence is at 2:21.

כְּשֶׁבֶת | ב – *Com.:* In M^L שבת is constructed with כ only here and in two instances it is combined with ב: Judg 11:26; Ezek 38:14. The Mp indication of two occurrences may be due to a variant reading with כ also in Judg 11:26 (cf. Ginsburg, 4, י, §654).

3 בִּשְׁנַת שָׁלוֹשׁ לְמָלְכוֹ ב – *Com.:* The Mp indicates "twice"; the other instance is 2 Chr 17:7, but there the first word is preceded by ו.

10 בִּזְתָא – *Com.:* Circellus, but ל is lacking in the margin.

14 רִאשֹׁנָה י חס בכתי – *Com.:* The adverb ראשנה resp. ראשונה occurs ten times when also the abnormal form ראישנה (Josh 21:10) is included.

16 כִּי עַל־כָּל־הַשָּׂרִים ד וחד מעל כל השרים – *Com.:* This Mp of M^L is not correct since this is the only occurrence, besides a variant with prep. מן in Esth 3:1. However, the combination of על and השרים occurs four times (Zeph 1:8; Esth 1:16; 3:1; 5:11).

2:3 תַּמְרוּקֵיהֶן: ל וחס – *Com.:* The Mp is contrary to the plene written form of M^L.

4 תִּיטַב ל וחד ותיטב Once, and once ותיטב (Esth 2:9).

9 וַתִּיטַב ל וחד אשר תיטב Once, and once אשר תיטב (Esth 2:4).

תַּמְרוּקֶיהָ ל ומל – *Com.:* Cf. the Mp comment on the lemma at v. 3.

18 לַמְּדִינוֹת ל וחד במדינות Once, and once במדינות (Lam 1:1).

19 יֹשֵׁב ל חס בסיפ – *Com.:* This Mp is in conflict with M^L since in 2:21 a second case of defectively written ישב occurs.

20 וְאֶת־מַאֲמַר ל וחד את מאמר Once, and once את מאמר (Esth 1:15).

עֹשָׂה ו Six times with *qames*.

3:2 יִשְׁתַּחֲוֶה: ג וחד ואשתחוה Three times, and once with ואשתחוה (Gen 24:48).

5 וַיִּמָּלֵא ז – *Com.:* The Mp ז is incorrect, opposed by the Mm: Six times (so also in M^Y and M^{L34}); cf. Weil, §1907.

6 וַיִּבֶז ב הבכרה Twice: Gen 25:34.

מַלְכוּת אֲחַשְׁוֵרוֹשׁ ל – *Com.:* This Mp is in error, מלכות אחשורוש occurring a second time in 9:30.

7 נִיסָן ב Twice with *qames*.

8 וְלַמֶּלֶךְ ב·ליהוה Twice: 1 Chr 29:20.

10 צֹרֵר כול חס All (occurrences in Esther) defectively written.

12 כְּכָל־אֲשֶׁר־צִוָּה ג בכת – *Com.:* The Mp is erroneous: ככל־אשר־צוה (with double *linea maqqep̄*) does not occur "three times" (nor "four times", *BHS*) but twice: Esth 3:12; 8:9; with only the second *maqqep̄* it occurs five times (Josh 4:10; 2 Kgs 11:9; 16:16; Jer 35:18; 2 Chr 23:8).

אֲחַשְׁוֵרֹשׁ ד חס – *Com.:* The ו of the plene writing has been erased.

4 פַּתְשֶׁגֶן   ב בסיפ – *Com.*: This Mp is in error, פתשגן occurring three times in the book: 3:14; 4:8 and 8:13.

2 וַיָּבֹא   כּוּל סיפֹ מל ב מֹ חס   In the whole book written plene, except for ⟨two⟩ written defectively (5:5; 7:1).

4 וַתְּבוֹאֶינָה   ל מֹל – *Com.*: M^L does not indicate the *kəṯîḇ-qərê* phenomenon, as does M^{L34}.

5 וְעַל־מַה־זֶּה: ל וחד על מה זה אתה מבקש   Once, and once על מה זה (Neh 2:4).

7 קָרֵהוּ   גֹ – *Com.*: The Mp of M^L indicates "three" occurrences, besides Esth 6:13 it may include also the form with a preceding ו, i.e., Gen 44:29.

1 וְאִשָּׁה   ד בטע – *Com.*: This Mp is in error, ואשה occurs 22 times; in M^L only two of these cases have the accent *pazer*, here and in Lev 15:25.

2 לְמָרְדֳּכָי   – *Com.*: M^L has here the unique form לְמָרְדֳּכָי for which it has circellus and the Mp ל זק קמֹ, but the circellus and Mp is misplaced over מרדכי in v. 13 (but so not in *BHK*; *BHS*).

3 מָרְדֳּכַי   ל זק קמֹ – *Com.*: M^L has erroneously combined circellus and the Mp ל זק קמֹ, which actually belongs to the unique form לְמָרְדֳּכָי in v. 12, with the ordinary form of מרדכי here.

4 רֶוַח   ל וחד ורוח   Once, and once ורוח (Gen 32:17).

1 בְּבֵית הַמַּלְכוּת   ה זוגין מֹ ב ב מיחד בבית וחד בית   Five pairs of two (and) two particular (expressions), (once) בבית and once בית.

2 וַתִּגַּע   – *Com.*: M^L has no circellus over this lemma that occurs twice (the other instance is 1 Kgs 6:27), nor has M^{L34}. On the other hand, M^L has the circellus for the Mp ב over the following word בראש, which occurs thirty-five times. Its placing of circellus may therefore be erroneous; see the next lemma. *BHK^3* follows M^L, whereas *BHS* has corrected the indication of the Mp, referring ב to ותגע and, like M^{L34}, the Mp לֹה to בראש. Cf. Weil, § 2840.

  בְּרֹאשׁ   ב – *Com.*: M^L has placed the circellus for the Mp over this lemma, that occurs thirty-five times, instead of over the preceding lemma ותגע which in fact occurs twice; cf. Weil, § 2840; see the comment on the preceding lemma.

7 וּבְקָשָׁתִי: ל וחד ולעשות את בקשתי   Once, and once ולעשות את בקשתי (Esth 5:8).

9 וְלֹא־קָם   ב נביא עוד   Twice: Deut 34:10.

2 אוֹתִי   ה בסיפֹ – *Com.*: אותי occurs thirty times plene, five times in the Writings and once in Esther (cf. Weil, § 1238 א).

.9 וְהִרְכִּיבֻהוּ   ל וכֹת   Once, and (thus) written.

  הַסּוּס   ו – *Com.*: The form הסוס occurs five times in the Writings (Pss 33:17; 147:10; Esth 6:9, 10, 11). In addition, there is the preceding והסוס in this verse, occurring once.

0 תַּפֵּל   ל וחד ותפל   Once, and once ותפל (Dan 8:10).

:4 הַצָּר   גֹ בֹ   Three times, twice with *qames*.

5 מְלָאוֹ   ל – *Com.*: The circellus seems to be lacking, or there is a slight remnant of it above א, or perhaps after ו.

8 חָפוּ   ב – *Com.*: The Mp ב of M^L may be erroneous since the form חפו also occurs in 2 Sam 15:30 and Jer 14:4 (cf. Weil, § 2535).

:3 הָמָן הָאֲגָגִי   ל חס בן המדתא   One (instance) lacking בן המדתא.

6 בִּמְדִינוֹת   ל וחד שרתי במדינות   Once, and once with the vocalization בְּמְדִינוֹת (Lam 1:1).

.9 וּמִשְׁלוֹחַ   ב וחס – *Com.*: The Mp is in conflict with the text; here and in 9:22 M^L has plene writing, without ו also in Isa 11:14.

20 הַקְּרוֹבִים   ה מל֓   – *Com.:* In spite of the fact that the Masoretes put the circellus on the preceding אֲחַשְׁוֵרוֹשׁ, that in plene form occurs twenty-eight times, this Mp goes with the following הקרובים, occurring plene in the form קרובים in Isa 33:13; Ezek 23:5; 42;13 and in the form הקרובים in Esth 9:20 and 1 Chr 12:14. Cf. Frensdorff, *Massorah*, 171.

22 וּמִשְׁלֹוחַ   ב וחס֓   – *Com.:* The Mp is erroneous; see the comment at v. 19.

27 יַעֲבֹור   י מל֓   – *Com.:* The Mp of M^L is in conflict with the text, the plene writing occurring seven times (Isa 31:9; 40:27; 41:3; Ps 148:6; Job 14:5; Esth 1:19; 9:27).

31 קַיֵּם   ב֓   Twice with *paṭaḥ*: Esth 9:32.

NOTES ON THE MASORAH MAGNA

RUTH

1 Two verses unusual and unique in the Hebrew Bible: ויהי רעב בארץ twice with these accents: Gen 12:10; Ruth 1:1.

0 ⟨ותאמרנה־לה⟩: Eight times with the accent, and their references are: Gen 8:18; Num 28:26; Jer 2:31; Ezek 7:25; 2 Kgs 9:2; Ezek 11:18; 2 Chr 20:8; Ruth 1:10. And twice identically: Dan 4:9; 4:18. – *Com.*: In M^L one of the eight references, ובאת שמה (2 Kgs 9:2), has no *maqqep̄*, hence its accent is a *ṭip̄ḥâ*, not a *mâyəlâ*. Consequently there are only seven occurrences with the peculiar accent *mâyəlâ contra* this Mm.

1 לאנשים: Six times *pataḥ*, and their references are: 1 Sam 4:9 (twice in it); 1 Sam 25:11; 2 Kgs 4:40; Jer 29:6; Ruth 1:11; and once: 2 Sam 3:20. – *Com.*: Ezek 23:40 is not mentioned.

6 אל אשר: Five times, and their references are: Exod 32:34; Num 33:54; Ezek 1:12; 42:14; Ruth 1:16. And their opposite, אשר אל, six times: Exod 28:26 and its double (39:19); Jer 36:23; Ezek 8:14; 41:12; 40:44. – *Com.*: In the second list, Ezek 42:13 and Ezek 47:16 are not mentioned, no doubt because the Hebrew *Vorlage* which was used read על.

עמך: Five times, and their references are: Num 5:21; Ezek 26:11; Nah 3:13; Ps 45:11; Ruth 1:16.

9 ותהם: Three times: 1 Sam 4:5; 1 Kgs 1:45; Ruth 1:19.

4 קוצרים: Four times plene: Ruth 2:4, and the three following verses. – *Com.*: This Mm is erroneous as to the text of M^L, הקוצרים being the fifth case of plene writing in 2:14.

8 הלוא: Nine times plene in the Writings, and their references are: Ruth 2:8; 2:9; Ps 139:21; Prov 14:22; Esth 10:2 in the scroll of Esther; Ezra 9:14; Neh 5:9; 13:18; 13:26.

בשדה: Five times *rap̄ê*, and their references are: Num 20:17; 21:22; Isa 5:8; Ruth 2:8; 2:22. – *Com.*: *Rap̄ê* seems to refer to the absence of a *dāḡeš* in the שׂ as a result of the indefinite use of the noun.

2 ותהי: Fourteen times, and their references are: Num 23:10; 1 Sam 18:17; 18:21, twice there פלשתים, 2 Kgs 19:25; Isa 37:26; 1 Kgs 1:2; Isa 30:8; Job 21:2; 13:5; 6:10; Ruth 2:12 ⟨Gen 24:51; Lev 15:24⟩.

0 ⟨אשר לא־עזב חסדו⟩: The first case in the Pentateuch: Gen 24:27; the second in Ruth: Ruth 2:20.

4 וידעת: Seven times, and their references are: Isa 49:23; 60:16; Ezek 16:62; 22:16; Hos 2:22; Zech 2:15; ⟨Ruth 3:4⟩.

5 ⟨ ⟩: These are pronounced and not written: Judg 20:13; 2 Sam 8:3; 18:20; 16:23; 2 Kgs 19:37; 19:31; Jer 31:38; 50:29; Ezek 9:11; Ruth 3:5; 3:17.

7 בלט: Four times, once with superfluous א, and their references are: Judg 4:21; 1 Sam 18:22; 24:5; Ruth 3:7.

8 בחצי הלילה: Three times, and their references are: Exod 12:29; Judg 16:3; Ruth 3:8.

12 ⟨אם⟩: These are written and not pronounced, and their references are: 2 Kgs 5:18; Jer 38:16; 51:3; Ezek 48:16; 2 Sam 15:21; Jer 39:12. – *Com.:* The reference to Ezek 48:16 is an allusion. This Mm follows without separation mark the Mm on אנכי in 3:13.

13 אנכי: Eight times with the accent on the נ, and their references are: Gen 3:10; Exod 4:10; Judg 17:9; 1 Sam 30:13; 9:21; Amos 7:14; 2 Sam 3:8; Ruth 3:13. And always with *zaqep̄* and *ʾatnaḥ*. And *sôp̄ pasûq* like this except for . . . – *Com.:* This Mm is followed without separation mark by the Mm on אם in 3:12. Because of its incompleteness, it is unclear to which text the sentence at the end refers. Weil (§1571) considers *zaqep̄* to be erroneous and the sentence to refer to Job 33:9, where the accent is on י.

15 וישת: Six times, and their references are: Gen 30:40; 48:14; Num 24:1; 1 Sam 2:8; 2 Sam 22:12; Ruth 3:15.

4:4 זולתך: Twice, and their references are: Isa 64:3; Ruth 4:4.

7 וזאת: Sixteen times at the beginning of a verse, and their references are: Exod 25:3; Lev 7:1; 7:11; 6:7; Deut 4:44; 6:1; Lev 15:3; Num 4:19; 4:31; 6:13; Deut 33:1; 33:7; Jer 44:29; Mal 2:13; Zech 14:12; Ruth 4:7. – *Com.:* Two errors in this Mm: תהיגה in the reference to Zech 14:12 for תהיה, and לפני in Ruth 4:7 for לפנים.

11 שתיהם: Twice: Ruth 1:19; 4:11.

14 ויקרא: Twice: Gen 48:16; Ruth 4:14.

17 עובד: Twice plene: Ruth 4:17; 4:21, and everywhere in Chronicles like this, except for עבד אדם.

Masorah finalis: The number of verses in the book is eighty-five.

CANTICLES

1:3 לריח: Sixteen times, and their references are: Exod 29:25; 29:41 from Exodus; Lev 2:12; 3:16; 4:31; 8:21; 8:28; 17:6; Num 15:24; 18:17; 28:6; 28:27; 29:2; ⟨29:6⟩; Ezek 16:19; Cant 1:3. – *Com.:* Num 28:27 is referred to by בכורים, which occurs in v. 26. Num 29:2 is thematically referred to by ראש שנה; cp. Weil, §574. The note "from Exodus" is to distinguish the reference Exod 29:41 from Num 28:8. The reference Num 29:6 has dropped out.

4 הביאני: Four times, and their references are: Deut 9:4; Ezek 40:2; Cant 1:4; 2:4. – *Com.:* Although this note is placed between those concerning 1:14 and 2:3, it probably does not refer to 2:4 since at that verse Mp has incorrectly "five times"; at 1:4 it has correctly "four times."

10 נאוו: Twice: Isa 52:7; Cant 1:10.

14 אשכל: Five times defective, and their references are: Gen 14:13; 14:24; Num 13:23; Deut 1:24; Cant 1:14.

2:3 ופריו: Twice, and their references are: Cant 2:3; Isa 14:29. – *Com.:* Mm has erroneously מתוך instead of מתוק.

6 לראשי: Four times: 1 Sam 28:2; Jonah 2:6; Ps 140:8; Cant 2:6 the first of it. – *Com.:* The remark "the first of it" must refer to the first occurrence of שמאלו in Canticles; the second occurrence is in 8:3.

9 החלנות: Three times defective, and their references are: Ezek 40:25; 41:16; Cant

2:9. – *Com.:* The defective form occurs also in Ezek 41:16, though without the article.

4 בֶּחָגוֵי: Three times: Cant 2:14; Obad 3; Jer 49:16.

◖ בַּלֵּילוֹת: Four times, and their references are: Cant 3:1; Pss 92:3; 134:1; Cant 3:8. – *Com.:* In the second reference, בְּלֵיוֹת is an error for בַּלֵּילוֹת.

2 אֲקוּמָה: Three times: 2 Sam 3:21; Job 19:18; Cant 3:2.

7 גִּבֹּרִים: Seven times defective: Josh 10:2; 1 Sam 2:4; 2 Sam 1:25; 17:8; Zech 10:5; Prov 21:22; Cant 3:7. – *Com.:* For 2 Sam 1:25, Mm gives אֵיךְ נָפְלוּ גִבֹּרִים דִּיהוֹנָתָן, the latter word being an addition to M^L. This reference is applied by Weil, § 3633, to 2 Sam 1:19; in that place, however, גִבּוֹרִים is written plene, in contrast to 2 Sam 1:25. Most probably, the addition "of Jonathan" is meant to distinguish v. 25, which mentions Jonathan (as does v. 26), from v. 27, which begins with the same words. Mm has left out of account 2 Sam 23:9, where M$^{L(ket)}$ gives גִבֹּרִים, M$^{L(qere)}$ adding the article.

8 מְלֻמְּדֵי: Twice: 1 Chr 25:7; Cant 3:8. – *Com.:* The reference שִׁיר בֵּית יהוה may have been influenced by 1 Chr 25:6, where this expression occurs; 1 Chr 25:7 has שִׁיר לַיהוה.

◖0 עַמּוּדָיו: Four times plene: Exod 36:38; 40:18; Num 4:31; Cant 3:10.

4 תָּלוּי: Three times, and their references are: Deut 21:23; 2 Sam 18:10; Cant 4:4.

◖9 (בְּאַחַד:) These are the places where ת is read but not written, and their references are: 2 Sam 12:24 (וַיִּקְרָא); 20:23 (הַכְּרִי); 23:8 (אֶחָד); 2 Kgs 24:14 (עֲשָׂרָה); 25:17 (אַמָּה); Isa 66:17 (אַחַד); Jer 49:25 (תְּהִלָּה); 52:21 (קוֹמָה); Qoh 12:6 (יֵרָחֵק); 2 Chr 11:18 (בֵּן); Cant 4:9 (בְּאַחַד) the first occurrence in the verse.

1 (נֹפֶת:) Eleven times a verse begins with נ and ends with נ, and their references are: Lev 13:9; Num 32:32; Deut 18:15; Jer 50:8; 1 Chr 12:2; Pss 46:5; 77:21; 78:12; Cant 4:11; Prov 7:17; 20:27.

1 דֹּדִים: Four times, three times defective and once plene, and their references are: Ezek 16:8; 23:17; Prov 7:18; Cant 5:1 the last plene.

2 יָשֵׁנָה: Twice, once plene and once defective: plene in 1 Kgs 3:20; (defective in) Cant 5:2. For the Eastern Masoretes, both are defective. – *Com.:* M^L has defective writing also in the first place.

3 כֻּתָּנְתִּי: Twice: Job 30:18; Cant 5:3. – *Com.:* In the first reference, כְּפִי is erroneously written as בְּפִי.

5 מוֹר: Three times plene in the book, and their references are: 5:5 twice in the verse; 5:13.

◖2 לִלְקֹט וְלַלְקֹט: Three times: Exod 16:27; Ruth 2:8; Cant 6:2. – *Com.:* The form with copula occurs in Cant 6:2, the form without it in the other two verses.

8 שְׁמֵנִים: Twice defective: 2 Chr 2:17; Cant 6:8. And the whole Scripture likewise, except for six occurrences in plene writing.

9 בָּרָה: Five times written with ה, and their references are: Judg 7:24 (twice); Ps 19:9; Cant 6:9; 6:10, and all occurrences where the word refers to eating likewise, e.g., 2 Sam 13:10; Job 39:13.

וַיְאַשְּׁרוּהָ: Twice: Cant 6:9; Prov 31:28.

12 מַרְכְּבוֹת: Four times: Exod 15:4; 2 Kgs 23:11; Isa 22:18; Cant 6:12. – *Com.:* The word (without copula or suffix) is written defective in Exod 15:4 and plene in the other three places.

11 וְעָלַי: Five times, and their references are: 2 Sam 15:4; 18:11; 1 Kgs 2:15; Cant 7:11; Ezra 7:28.

13 נִרְאֶה: Three times: Isa 5:19; Jer 5:12; 42:14; Ps 36:10; Cant 7:13, and once וְנִרְאֶה

1 Sam 10:14. – *Com.:* Mm gives "three times," but correctly lists five places. 1 Sam 10:14 has וַיֵּרָאֶה. Mandelkern, *Concordantiae*, gives another four places with וְנִרְאָה.

8:1 יְבוּזוּ: Three times, once defective and twice plene, and their references are: Cant 8:1; 8:7; Prov 6:30. – *Com.:* In M^L all places have plene writing. M^Y has the defective writing for Cant 8:1.

8 אֲחֹתֵינוּ: Four times, three times defective and once plene: Gen 24:60; 34:14; 34:31; Cant 8:8. – *Com.:* In deviation from all references, the lemma has both ו and י. The plene writing (with ו) occurs in Gen 34:31.

12 הָאָלֶף: Four times, and their references are: Exod 38:28; Josh 18:28 the second; Cant 8:12; 1 Sam 17:18. – *Com.:* Mp gives "three times," not counting Josh 18:28, where the word is not a numeral but (part of) a proper name; cp. Ginsburg (4, א, § 724). This latter reference is followed by "the second," which probably means that Mm reads הָאָלֶף as an independent name, the second in the verse, and not as part of the name Zela Haeleph (= Zela, 2 Sam 21:14); cp. G^A (Σηλαλέφ).

Masorah finalis: (Sum of the verses in this book:) 117.

QOHELETH

1:5 וְזָרַח: Three times, and their references are: Deut 33:2; Isa 58:10; Qoh 1:5.

6 סֹבֵב: Defective in Gen 2:11 and in the second occurrence of the verse in Qoh 1:6.

8 מִשְּׁמֹעַ: Four times defective, and their references are: Isa 21:3; 33:15; Prov 28:9; Qoh 1:8. – *Com.:* The first reference of the Mm is to Isa 21:3 (מִשְּׁמֹעַ) נַעֲוֵיתִי, but it has suffered a spontaneous contamination from Ps 38:7 נַעֲוֵיתִי שַׁחֹתִי.

9 שֶׁהָיָה: Three times: Qoh 1:9; 2:18; 8:7.

11 זִכְרוֹן: Three times, and their references are: Lev 23:24; Qoh 1:11; 2:16.

2:2 וּלְשִׂמְחָה: Three times, and their references are: Judg 16:23; Zech 8:19; Qoh 2:2.

6 בְּרֵכוֹת: Twice: Cant 7:5; Qoh 2:6.

7 וָצֹאן: Four times, and their references are: Lev 27:32; Num 22:40; 2 Chr 31:6; Qoh 2:7. – *Com.:* The scribe of the Mm seems to have erroneously written יְצֹאו instead of וָצֹאן. The verse in 2 Chr is referred to as "the one of Hezekiah."

8 שָׁרִים: Five times, and their references are: Pss 68:26; 87:7; 2 Sam 19:36; 1 Kgs 10:12; Qoh 2:8; 2 Chr 35:25.

(וְתַעֲנֻגֹת) There are two similar words whose form is defective in the Bible: Mic 2:9; Qoh 2:8. – *Com.:* The Mm seems to protect an old defective form – with *qibbûṣ* under the ג, as in Mic 2:9, against the present text of M^L in Qoh 2:8.

9 עָמְדָה: Four times, and their references are: Gen 30:9; 2 Kgs 13:6; Ps 26:12; Qoh 2:9.

13 אֲנִי: Six times in the book (with *qameṣ*), and their references are: 2:13, 14, 24; 5:17; 8:12; 9:16.

16 זִכְרוֹן: Three times, and their references are: Lev 23:24; Qoh 1:11; 2:16.

17 אֶת הַחַיִּים: Three times: Deut 30:15; Ruth 2:20; Qoh 2:17.

18 עָמָל: Five times in the book, and their references are: Qoh 2:18, 2:22; 3:9; 4:8; 9:9. – *Com.:* The second reference to 2:22 was mistakenly written by the copyist of the Masorah as מֶה הֹיֶה instead of מַה הֹוֶה.

26 (לָאָדָם) In the whole book with *qameṣ* (under the preposition), except for two: 2:26, 2:21.

זה הבל ורעות רוח: Three times at the end of a verse: Qoh 2:26; 4:4; 6:9.

3 לרפא: Twice, once defective and once plene, and their references are: Hos 5:13; Qoh 3:3.

לרפא: Twice, once defective and once plene: Hos 5:13; Qoh 3:3. – *Com.:* This translation is for the Mm note at the bottom of folio 426a, its doublet is at the top of the same folio.

9 העשה: defective in the Western tradition, plene in the Eastern tradition.

1 יָפֶה: Five times: 2 Sam 14:25; ⟨Ezek 31:9⟩; Qoh 3:11; 5:17; Cant 1:16.

4 וממנו: Twice: Qoh 3:14; Dan 8:11.

5 והאלהים: Seven times: Gen 22:1; Exod 19:19; 21:13; 1 Chr 28:3; 2 Chr 13:15; Qoh 3:14; 3:15.

6 ומקום: Three times, and their references are: Isa 60:13; Ps 26:8; Qoh 3:16.

ומקום: Three times: Isa 60:13; Ps 26:8; Qoh 3:16. – *Com.:* This is the translation of the Mm note at the top of folio 426b. Its doublet is at the bottom of the same folio.

8 ולראות: Three times: Qoh 3:18; 5:17; 8:16.

המה להם: Twice, and their references are: 1 Kgs 14:23; Qoh 3:18.

9 ומותר האדם מן הבהמה אָין: No other occurrence with *qameṣ* under a *zaqep̄*, but there is one with *pataḥ*: Gen 2:5.

0 אל מקום אחד: Three times, and their references are: Gen 1:9; Qoh 3:20; 6:6. – *Com.:* The third reference of the Mm (Qoh 6:6) has suffered an interpolation of two words (שהם בהמה) from the list on ולראות (3:18).

8 ולמי: Three times: Gen 32:18; 1 Sam 9:20; Qoh 4:8.

4 למלך: Three times, and their references are: 1 Kgs 2:15; 6:1; Qoh 4:14.

7 יודעים: Four times plene, and their references are: Qoh 4:17; 9:5 twice in it; 2 Chr 2:7.

1 כי האלהים: Six times, and their references are: Gen 45:8; 1 Sam 10:7; 1 Chr 17:2; Qoh 5:1; 5:19; Neh 12:43.

3 תאחר: Four times, and their references are: Exod 22:28; Deut 23:22; Isa 46:13; Qoh 5:3; and three times תאַחַר.

8 (היא) Five similar cases where it is written היא but read הוא; and their references are: Ps 73:16; Qoh 5:8; Job 31:11; 1 Kgs 17:15; 1 Chr 29:16.

9 גם זה הבל: Three times, and their references are: Qoh 2:19; 5:9; 7:6; 8:10. – *Com.:* ג of the Mm in M^L is an error for ד.

7 חיו: Four times defective, and their references are: 2 Sam 18:18; 2 Kgs 25:30; Jer 52:33; Qoh 5:17.

1 יש רעה: Its first occurrence is Qoh 5:12, the second one 6:1.

ורבה: Four times, and their references are: Exod 23:29; Isa 6:12; Hos 9:7; Qoh 6:1.

על האדם: Three times, and their references are: Gen 2:21; 2:16; Qoh 6:1. And every על הארץ ועל הבהמה is similar. – *Com.:* The scribe of the Mm mistakenly wrote . . . וכול על הארץ instead of . . . וכול על האדם; see Ginsburg, 2, ע, §390; Weil, §15.

5 לזה: Three times, and their references are: Qoh 6:5; 1 Sam 21:12; 25:21.

6 ואלו: Twice: Qoh 6:6; Esth 7:4.

0 ולא יוכל: Four times with *pataḥ* and once with *qameṣ,* and their references are: Exod 10:5; Jer 44:22; Qoh 6:10; Isa 16:12, the last one with *qameṣ*. – *Com.:* There is an inner contradiction in the Mm resulting from a slight alteration. The Mm must be understood as follows: there are four verses with this sequence; the one in Isaiah is distinguished by *qameṣ* under the כ; See Weil, §2268.

12 כצל: Five times with *dageš*, and their references are: 1 Chr 29:15; Job 14:2; 17:7; Qoh 8:13; 6:12.

7:23 הז: Ten times, and their references are: 2 Kgs 6:19; Ezek 40:45; Hos 7:16; Ps 132:12; Qoh 5:15; 9:13; 2:24; 5:18; 7:23; 2:2. – *Com.:* The second reference (Ezek 40:45) is given a cj. as if the scribe had read or recalled the first word of Ezek 40:46. The third and fourth (Hos 7:16; Ps 132:12) are written זו; see the Mp commentary at 2:2.

נסיתי: Twice: 1 Sam 17:39; Qoh 7:23.

28 ולא מצאתי: Five times: Deut 22:14; 1 Sam 29:3; Ps 69:21; Ezek 22:30; the first occurrence in Qoh 7:28.

8:1 (ישנא) 2 Kgs 25:29; Ps 127:2; Qoh 8:1; Lam 4:1 are written with א.

2 (שמור) In the Western tradition שמור is written plene and in the Eastern tradition defective.

שבועת: Five times, and their references are: Exod 22:10; Num 30:14; 2 Sam 21:7; 1 Kgs 2:43; Qoh 8:2; and once with cj. in Zech 8:17.

5 שומר: Ten times plene, and their references are: 1 Sam 17:22; Pss 121:4; 127:1; 145:20; Prov 10:17; 22:5; Neh 9:32; Qoh 8:5; 1 Chr 7:32; 2 Chr 34:22. – *Com.:* The ninth reference (1 Chr 7:32) is וחבר immediately followed by two letters דו which could be an alteration of הו marking the beginning of the next word: הוליד, a phenomenon of abbreviation of words which occurs from time to time in the lists. Weil (§ 3634) restores this word. Or it may be a careless writing of די indicating Chronicles (דברי הימים).

9 באדם: Four times, and their references are: Lev 13:9; 22:5; Qoh 8:9; Prov 23:28; and once with cj. in Prov 28:2.

12 חטא: Three times defective, and their references are: Isa 1:4; Qoh 8:12; 9:2.

13 מלפני אלהים: Twice: 2 Chr 34:27; Qoh 8:13.

17 וראיתי: Twelve times, and their references are: Exod 12:13; 1 Sam 19:3; Ezek 37:8; Qoh 2:13; 3:22; 4:4; 8:17; Esth 8:6 twice in it; Ezek 41:8; Dan 10:7; 12:5.

9:2 ולרשע: Twice: Ps 50:16; Qoh 9:2.

3 הז: Three times with this accentuation at the beginning of a verse: Exod 30:13; Josh 9:12; Qoh 9:3; and once וזה in Ezra 7:11.

7 רצה: Twice, and their references are: Qoh 9:7; 1 Chr 28:4. – *Com.:* The copyist has written רצה האלהים as his lemma, while only רצה is involved in this Mm. Moreover, he made a nice slip of the pen in giving as the first reference כי כבד פה (Exod 4:10) instead of כי כבר of Qoh 9:7 (!); see Weil, § 3715.

10 מעשֶׂה: Ten times, and their references are: Num 31:51; Isa 3:24; 19:15; 29:16; 2 Chr 16:14; 31:21; Job 33:17; Qoh 8:9; 9:10; 12:14.

14 ובא אליה: Twice, and their references are: Deut 22:13; Qoh 9:14.

וסבב: Three times, and their references are: 1 Sam 7:16; 2 Chr 33:14; Qoh 9:14. – *Com.:* In the *sîman* for 1 Sam 7:16, the copyist has written ביתאל without a *maqqep̄* or a space.

מצודים: Twice and plene, and their references are: Qoh 9:14; 7:26.

10:3 הלך: Four times defective: Qoh 1:4; 9:10; 10:3; 12:5. – *Com.:* The last reference (Qoh 12:5) presents two variations against the text: 1) עולמו, written plene in the text, is quoted defectively in the Mm; 2) the preposition אל of the text has been quoted על in the Mm.

4 תנח: Three times: Qoh 7:18; 10:4; 11:6; and once ותנח in Gen 39:16.

11 בלוא: Six times plene, and their references are: Isa 55:1 twice in it; Isa 55:2 twice in it; Jer 2:11; Qoh 10:11.

) במשפט: Eight times with *dageš* (article): Lev 19:15; 19:35; ⟨Deut 1:17⟩; Isa 5:16; Pss 1:5; 25:9; Prov 18:5; Qoh 11:9; and so in the whole book of Job, except Job 14:3. – *Com.:* The first reference is the same for the two verses of Leviticus 19. A separation mark :o: has also been inserted between the last reference and the final sentence.

ß הראות: Four times, and their references are: Deut 4:3; 11:7; 3:21; Qoh 12:3.
הראות: Four times: Deut 4:3; 11:7; 3:21; Qoh 12:3.
בארבות: Twice: 1 Kgs 4:10; Qoh 12:3.

ł וסגרו: Twice: Qoh 12:4; Isa 24:22; and once (without cj.) in Jer 13:19.

❚ נתנו: Six times, and their references are: Lev 10:14; Ezek 31:14; 32:29; 35:12; 32:23; Qoh 12:11.

ß ואת מצותיו: Three times, and their references are: Deut 4:40; 13:5; Qoh 12:13.
Masorah finalis: (Sum of the verses in this book:) 222.

LAMENTATIONS

❚ בדד: Eight times, and their references are: Lev 13:46; Deut 32:12; 33:28; Isa 27:10; Jer 49:31; 15:17; Lam 1:1; ⟨Lam 3:28⟩. – *Com.:* Probably a scribe omitted ישב (Lam 3:28) after he had written ישבה (Lam 1:1). See the correct list in Jer 15:17 (M^L fol. 254a); Weil, § 2544; Ginsburg, 4, ב, § 49.

5 ⟨מן בת:⟩ Eight times words are written as two but pronounced as one, and their references are: Judg 16:25; 1 Sam 9:1; Isa 9:6; 1 Sam 24:9; Isa 44:24; 2 Chr 34:6; Lam 1:6; 4:3. – *Com.:* There are two orthographic particularities in this Mm: The lemma for Isa 44:24 is erroneously spelled מאתו instead of the correct form מאתי. The reference בחרבותיהם (2 Chr 34:6) is written plene while the *qərê* בחרבתיהם as well as the *kətîb* בחר בתיהם in 2 Chr 34:6 are defective.

ß היתה: Four times (with this vocalization), and their references are: Isa 14:24; 2 Chr 15:19; Isa 64:9; Lam 1:8.

0 בקהל: Four times with a *dageš* (with the ק), and their references are: Judg 21:5; 2 Chr 30:17; Job 30:28; Lam 1:10. – *Com.:* According to M^L there is no עליה in Judg 21:5. Probably it has been added erroneously to the *sîman*.

3 עצמתי: Five times defective in spelling, and their references are: Gen 50:25 and its companion (i.e., Exod 13:19); 1 Kgs 13:31; Jer 20:9; Lam 1:13. – *Com.:* The lemma of the Mm lacks the prep. בְ because the subsequent list comprises all cases of עַצְמֹתַי irrespective of the prepositions. The first *sîman* is written plene whereas in the text of M^L at Gen 50:25 the lemma is written defective. The *sîman* for 1 Kgs 13:31 erroneously reads הניחו את עצמתיכם instead of הניחו את עצמתי. Cf. Weil, § 3723.

שוממה: Three times, twice defective and once plene, and their references are: 2 Sam 13:20; Isa 54:1; Lam 1:13. – *Com.:* There is a contradiction in the Mm here. Although שוממה is said to occur twice defective and once plene, the word is spelled once defective (2 Sam 13:20) and twice plene (Isa 54:1; Lam 1:13) in the *sîmanîm*. The case in question seems to be Lam 1:13. The lemma at the beginning of the note and the *sîman* have שוממה, while the text of M^L now reads שְׁמֵמָה. But obviously the original reading was שׁוֹמֵמָה in accordance with the *sîman* and also, e.g., with the text of M^Y. The erasure of the ו and the remains of the uppermost part of that letter are still clearly visible in the photograph of M^L. However, according to the corrected text of M^L, the plene spelling of the last *sîman* is wrong; cf. Weil, § 3724 and Ginsburg, 4, שׁ, § 690. In accordance with Mm and the corrected text of M^L, Mp must be interpreted as "twice (defective)."

דוה: Three times, and their references are: Lev 20:18; Isa 30:22; Lam 1:13. – *Com.:* ואשה at the beginning of the *sîman* for Lev 20:18 is obviously an error; read ואישׁ. Cf. Weil, § 778.

17 בידיה: Three times, and their references are: Exod 35:25; Prov 14:1; Lam 1:17.

21 שׁמעו: Three times at the beginning of a verse: Exod 15:14; Jer 46:12; Lam 1:21. – *Com.:* In Exod 15:14 the text of M^L reads עַמִּים יִרְגָּזוּן. The reading גוים of the *sîman* is probably influenced by the following reference to Jer 46:12.

2:1 ולא זכר: Three times, and their references are: Gen 40:23; 2 Chr 24:22; Lam 2:1.

5 תאניה ואניה: Twice: Isa 29:2; Lam 2:5.

6 מעדו: Three times written defective in the respective various forms and their references are: Lev 23:44; Deut 31:10; Lam 2:6. And (in the Pentateuch) בְּמֹעֲדוֹ is always written (defective) like them, with two exceptions plene: Num 9:2; Num 28:2. – *Com.:* In M^L there is neither a circellus nor a Mp with this lemma. In opposition to the Mm the scribe of M^L's consonantal text has written the lemma plene, while the defective spelling in M^Y and M^{L34} aligns precisely with the note (cf. also Ginsburg, 2, מ, § 157). In Num 9:3 the scribe of M^L has written במועדו plene as well, although according to the Mm under consideration the plene spelling is required solely in Num 9:2 and in Num 28:2. "Two exceptions" obviously refers to the Pentateuch only (cf. Weil, § 3727), since there is a third case of plene spelling in Hos 2:11 (cf. Weil, § 3003).

7 מזבחו: Three times, and their references are: Judg 6:32; Judg 6:31; Lam 2:7.

14 ויחזו: Twice, and their references are: Exod 24:11; Lam 2:14.

15 ⟨וינעו:⟩ Three times defective in various forms (of the *hifîl*): Num 32:13; Amos 9:9; Lam 2:15. – *Com.:* In M^L the word was originally written plene but י has been erased.

משוש: Four times, and their references are: Isa 32:13; 66:10; 65:18; Lam 2:15. – *Com.:* The *sîman* for Isa 32:13 is not quite correct since it omits כָּל.

17 עשה: Twice at the beginning of a verse: Ps 104:19; Lam 2:17.

19 קומי: Four times at the beginning of a verse: Isa 60:1; [?]; Mic 4:13; Lam 2:19. – *Com.:* The *sîman* ובאי cannot be identified. Probably it originated by error from שאי (Gen 21:18) which one would expect here.

Ginsburg, 2, ק, § 121 records a variant version of this Mm, which lists only three references, "one from the Torah, one from the Prophets and one from the Writings"; Mic 4:13 is missing in that version, possibly due to a defective spelling.

3:6 במחשכים: Three times: Pss 143:3; 88:7; Lam 3:6. – *Com.:* "Three times" (ג) has been added above the line apparently by the same hand.

7 גדר: Three times, and their references are: Job 19:8; Lam 3:9; 3:7.

8 שתם: Twice, one written with ס and one written with שׂ: 2 Chr 32:30; Lam 3:8.

9 נתיבותי: Twice, one plene: Job 19:8; Lam 3:9.

10 במסתרים: Three times *rāp̄ê* (i.e. the מ without *dageš*), and their references are: Ps 17:12; Lam 3:10; Jer 13:17. – *Com.:* The list contains the three cases with *šəwâ* under the prep. בּ, as opposed to three cases with *patah*. Cf. Ognibeni, *ʾOklah*, § 303; Ginsburg, 4, מ, § 601 and § 602. אורב is written plene in the *sîman* for Lam 3:10 while the writing in the text is defective.

וֹהטוב: Four times and their references are: Deut 6:18; 2 Kgs 20:3; and its companion (Isa 38:3); Lam 3:38.

עד יהוה: Four times, and their references are: Deut 4:30; 30:2; Isa 19:22; Hos 14:2; Lam 3:40. – *Com.:* "Four times" in the Mm is obviously a scribal error, because subsequently five references are given. The Mp correctly notes "five times". The *sîman* for Lam 3:40 differs from the text of M[L] by reading לבבנו (from v. 41?) instead of דרכינו.

לבבנו: Four times and those defective: Deut 1:28; Josh 2:11; 1 Kgs 8:58; Lam 3:41. – *Com.:* The *sîman* for 1 Kgs 8:58 seems to be incomplete; it should correctly read לבבנו אליו. Probably the mistake originated by confusion with the similar wording לבבנו אל in the *sîman* for Lam 3:41.

נחנו: Three times with *paṯaḥ:* Num 32:32; Lam 3:42; Gen 42:11. – *Com.:* In the text of M[L] the word occurs only twice with *paṯaḥ:* Num 32:32; Lam 3:42. In the third case, Gen 42:11, it is written with *qames* (i.e. in pausal form).

סכותה: Three times, once defective and twice plene, and their references are: Ps 140:8; Lam 3:43; 3:44. – *Com.:* Mm does not agree with the text of M[L], since it obviously requires plene writing not only in Lam 3:44 but also in 3:43 (cf. the spelling of the *sîman* and the fact that the reading in Ps 140:8 is the one which is defective). However, in the text of M[L] סַכֹּתָה is written defective in 3:43 whereas the text of M[Y], writing סַכּוֹתָה plene in 3:43 and 3:44, is in accordance with the note. On the other hand M[L34] has in both of these cases the defective spelling. Apparently we are dealing with different orthographic traditions, which were not yet standardized.

וירא: Three times and their references are: 1 Sam 24:16; Jer 23:18; Lam 3:50.

תשיב: Ten times, and their references are: Gen 24:6; Deut 24:13; ⟨Judg 5:29⟩; 2 Kgs 18:24; Isa 36:9; 58:13; Pss 89:44; 74:11; Job 15:13; Lam 3:64. – *Com.:* This list collects the ten occurrences of תָּשִׁיב *hifil* in order to avoid confusion with תָּשׁוּב *qal* (cf. Ognibeni, *ʾOklah*, § 3G).

חשך: Four times, and their mnemonic is: The sun troubles the black tent.

חשך: Four times, and their references are: Isa 5:30; Isa 13:10; Job 18:6; Lam 4:8. – *Com.:* There are two different Mm notes with this lemma. The first is an Aramaic mnemonic for the four occurrences, the second gives the usual Hebrew references, i.e., it lists the four occurrences of חָשַׁךְ with שׂ (as opposed to the seven occurrences with שׁ; see Ognibeni, *ʾOklah*, §§ 270–271).

יוכלו: Eleven times and their references are: Josh 7:12; Ps 18:39; 2 Sam 17:17; Isa 56:10; Jer 1:19; 15:20; 6:10; Hos 8:5; Lam 4:14; Jer 11:11; Cant 8:7. – *Com.:* In Josh 7:12 and in Ps 18:39 (against the spelling of the *sîmanîn*) the lemma is written defective (יְכְלוּ) in the text of M[L]; likewise אויביהם in Josh 7:12.

⟨עודינה:⟩ These are the cases in which ה is written, but ו is read; and their references are: Lev 21:5; Deut 21:7; 1 Kgs 22:49; Jer 2:15; 2 Kgs 24:10; [Ezek 37:22]; Jer 50:6; Ezek 23:43; Jer 22:6; Ezek 35:12; Ps 73:2; Job 16:16; Lam 4:17; ⟨Dan 3:29⟩. – *Com.:* The list seems to be damaged in at least one case, since the *sîman* והיה is not significant in this context. A longer version of the list, given in the Mm at Lev 21:5, suggests that והיה most probably represents an original יהיה (Ezek 37:22); cf. Weil, § 782 and Ginsburg, 1, ה, § 49). Beyond the thirteen references according to the version in M[L], Ginsburg's version as well as the list at Lev 21:5 include שלה (Dan 3:29) as a fourteenth case. At Lev 21:5 the the total number of cases is indicated as הֹי "fifteen," although only fourteen references are given. Among these surprisingly היה (Jer 50:6) is missing while הזהירה (2 Kgs 6:10) has been added, although it differs significantly from the other cases, because in all these instances the *kəṯîḇ* reads sg. while the *qərê* is in the pl. Frensdorff, *Ochlah*, §113 has a list, which differs slightly from Ginsburg's as to the sequence of the *sîmanîm*, but comprises the same fourteen cases. "By fixing the number at fourteen, the design of this Massorah is to militate against the Eastern recension, which has עוֹדֵינוּ the plural as the textual reading in Lament 4 17, and no *Keri*" (Ginsburg, 4, ה, §49). Note in this respect that in the Mm at Lev 21:5 the *sîman* for Lam 4:17 reads עודינו (which is obviously a contradiction to the intention of the list).

יושע: Twice defective, and their references are: Job 22:29; Lam 4:17. – *Com.*: Despite the instruction "defective" יושיע is written plene in the *sîman* for Job 22:29.

5:6 נתנו: Three times with *dageš*, two of them with *pataḥ* and one with *qames*, and their references are: Ezek 27:19; 1 Chr 29:14; Lam 5:6; and one ונתנו in Gen 34:16. – *Com.*: "With *dageš*" refers to the third consonant. The case with *qames* is in Ezek 27:19.

21 ⟨יהוה:⟩ Westerners write השיבנו יהוה whereas Easterners write אדני; and in two (other) cases it is *vice versa*. – *Com.*: The references of these "two (other) cases" are not found in the common lists of variations and thus cannot be determined precisely. Variation between the Tetragrammaton and אדני is not surprising. Among the Masoretic mss. of Lam this phenomenon can be observed for example in 2:18, 19 (see the apparatus there; cp. further the variants of 4QLam in 1:15, 17, 18).

ונשובה: Seven times and their references are: Gen 22:5; Num 14:4; 1 Sam 9:5; Jer 46:16; Hos 6:1; Lam 3:40; 5:21; in Jer 46:16 is written ונשבה. – *Com.*: Obviously this Mm presupposes in v. 21 the reading of the *qərê*. The concluding remark about the defective spelling in Jer 46:16 does agree with the consonantal text of M^L. According to Ginsburg's version of this Mm (Ginsburg, 2, ש, §201) in Jer 46:16 should be written וְנָשׁוּב, which is, however, the *kəṯîḇ* in Lam 5:21 in M^L and also according to the version of the list recorded by Ognibeni (*ᵓOklah*, §3K).

22 מאוס: Three times, and their references are: Isa 7:15; 7:16; [7:16]; ⟨Lam 5:22⟩ and one סחי ומאוס (Lam 3:45). The first and the last (of these four cases) are written plene, the two cases in the middle (are written defective). – *Com.*: כי בטרם (Isa 7:16) is repeated erroneously in place of the *sîman* for Lam 5:22 (see Weil, §2229). In the second phrase of this Mm the final word חס is lacking.
Masorah finalis: (Sum of the verses in this book:) 154.

ESTHER

1:1 ויהי בימי: Five times, and their references are: Jer 1:3; Isa 7:1; Gen 14:1; Ruth 1:1; Esth 1:1, and once ויהי רעב בימי 2 Sam 21:1.

5 קטן הקטן: Five times with *qames*, and their references are: Gen 27:42; 1 Sam 16:11; 2 Sam 9:12; 1 Chr 12:15; Esth 1:5, and like them all (occurrences) at the *ᵓatnaḥ* or at the *sôp pasûq*. – *Com.*: The *sîman* for Esth 1:5 is ובמלאות although the text has ובמלאת.

6 אחוז: Four times, and once ואחוז, and their references are: Num 31:30; Esth 1:6;

1 Chr 24:6, and there three times. – *Com.:* In all other cases than Esth 1:6 the form is defectively written.

9 ושתי המלכה: Four times, and their references are: Esth 1:9; 1:11; 1:16; 1:17. – *Com.:* The לה in the second *sîman* is a dittography.

6 מדינות המלך אחשורוש: Four times, and their references are: Esth 1:16; 8:12; 9:2; 9:20.

8 והיום הזה: Twice, and their references are: 2 Sam 18:20; Esth 1:18.

וקצף: Twice, and their references are: Esth 1:18; Qoh 5:16.

0 וכל הנשים: Three times, and their references are: Exod 35:26; Jer 44:15; Esth 1:20; once in the Law, once in the Prophets, once in the Writings.

1 נגזר: Three times, and their references are: Isa 53:8; 2 Chr 26:21; Esth 2:1.

5 ⟨בֶּן⟩: Lev 1:5; 24:10; Isa 8:2; Esth 2:5; Neh 6:18; ⟨1 Chr 9:21⟩. – *Com.:* The Mm has an unusual form: the lemma, number of cases, and introduction to the *sîmanîm* are lacking. It gives five cases; the sixth, 1 Chr 9:21, is lacking. Neh 6:18 has the erroneous יברכיהו instead of the correct ברכיה.

6 ירושלים: Four times plene (לים–), and their references are: Jer 26:18; 2 Chr 25:1; Esth 2:6; 1 Chr 3:5; and once (ירושלימה) 2 Chr 32:9. – *Com.:* For Jer 26:18 the Aramaic plural ending of עי is used although the text of M^L has the Hebrew ending. The defective writing בירושלם in the *sîman* for 1 Chr 3:5 is an error.

הגלה: Twice defectively written, and their references are: 1 Chr 5:22; Esth 2:6.

1 יום וים: Twice: Esth 2:11; 3:4.

2 בשמן: Six times *rapê* (i.e. without article): Num 28:5; Exod 29:40; Num 35:25; Pss 89:21; 92:11; Esth 2:12.

3 באה: Eleven times with accent at א, and their references are: Gen 29:6; 37:25; 1 Sam 25:19; Isa 66:18; Jer 10:22; Jonah 1:3; ⟨Mic 4:8⟩; Zech 14:18; Prov 13:12; Esth 2:13; 2:14; and so always in Kings and Ezekiel, with two exceptions (1 Kgs 2:28; Ezek 7:7).

8 משאת ומשאת והמשאת: Five times in (this) form: Jer 6:1; Zeph 3:18; Esth 2:18; Jer 40:5; Judg 20:40; and once בשאת (Lev 13:10).

0 עשה: Six times with *qameṣ*: Deut 20:20; Pss 148:8; 118:16; 118:15; Qoh 2:2; Esth 2:20.

3 ויכתב: Three times in the book, and their references are: Esth 2:23; 3:12; 8:9.

1 ⟨?⟩ – *Com.:* The first Mm on M^L's fol. 434r, that starts with 3:1, is misplaced. It consists of two lines that should be read separately since they represent two distinct notes:

1. כל תהלים ואיוב ומשלי וחומשה ודניאל: All Psalms, and Job, and Proverbs, and Pentateuch, and Daniel.

2. יש הבל שנים בפסוק: There is a vanity, twice in the verse.

The first note seems to be a fragment of some other note. The second one is an independent Masorah that may belong to Qoh 8:14, where both יש and הבל occur twice in the verse.

2 ישתחוה: Three times: 2 Sam 15:32; Esth 3:2; 2 Chr 25:14.

5 וימלא: Six times, and their references are: Exod 7:25; 1 Kgs 7:14; Ezek 10:4; 2 Kgs 10:21; Esth 3:5; 5:9.

8 ישנו: Four times, and their references are: Deut 29:14; 1 Sam 14:39; 23:23; Esth 3:8.

1 ויאמר המלך להמן: Twice: Esth 3:11; 6:10. – *Com.:* This Mm occurs twice, first on fol. 434r, lower margin, second on fol. 434v, upper margin, but there וסימנה is added after בֿ and, as for Esth 6:10, ואת הסוס is added after הלבוש.

ויאמר המלך להמן: Twice, and their references are: Esth 3:11; 6:10.

נתון: Three times and plene, and their references are: 2 Chr 1:12; Neh 13:4; Esth 3:11. – *Com.:* This Mm on fol. 434r, lower margin, is repeated on fol. 434v, upper margin, but there the first instance (2 Chr 1:12) ends with והמדע and the second instance (Neh 13:4) starts with נתון. This is the form in Weil, § 3753; Ognibeni, *’Oklah,* § 5N.

נתון: Three times, plene, and their references are: 2 Chr 1:12; Neh 13:4; Esth 3:11.

12 בשלשה עשר יום בו: Twice: Esth 3:12; 9:1. – *Com.:* The first word of the Mm is in the text of M^L written plene (בשלושה).

13 לבוז: Three times, and their references are: 2 Chr 20:25; Esth 3:13; 8:11.

4:1 ומרדכי: Twice at the beginning of a verse: Esth 4:1; ⟨8:15⟩. – *Com.:* Both in Mp and in Mm two instances are indicated, but in the Mm only one is presented (Esth 4:1).

3 יצע: Twice: Esth 4:3; Isa 14:11.

5 על מרדכי: Twice: Esth 4:5; 5:9.

11 יקרא: Twenty-one times, and their references are: Gen 2:23; 17:5; 21:12; 35:10; 21:12; Num 23:3; Deut 3:13; 22:6; 1 Sam 9:9; Isa 1:26; 4:1; 14:20; 32:5; 31:4; 35:8; 56:7; 54:5; 62:4; 62:12; Jer 19:6; Prov 16:21; Esth 4:11. – *Com.:* As for the references of the Mm, there are twenty-two lemmata, but Gen 21:12 is cited twice (cf. Weil, § 17).

נקראתי: Twice: 2 Sam 1:6; Esth 4:11. – *Com.:* Mm has written נקראתי also for 2 Sam 1:6, although the verb form there is written נקריתי. In addition, M^L has in 2 Sam 1:6 the Mp: ב̇ חד כת̇ יוד וחד כת̇ א.

שלשים: Twice plene in the Writings, and their references are: 2 Chr 16:12; Esth 4:11.

16 ובכן: Twice: Esth 4:16; Qoh 8:10. – *Com.:* The Mm occurs twice, first on fol. 434v and second on fol. 435r, both in the lower margin; the second instance is without the last word קבורים. See the next Mm.

ובכן: Twice: Esth 4:16; Qoh 8:10.

5:1 ה̇ זוגין: Five pairs of two (and) two particular (expressions), once בבית and once בית, and their references are: Exod 12:29; Jer 37:16; 2 Kgs 15:5; 2 Chr 26:21; Prov 3:33; Mic 6:10; Qoh 7:4; 7:2; Esth 5:1; 1:9.

5 מהרו: Four times: Gen 45:9; Judg 9:48; 2 Sam 15:14; Esth 5:5, and three times: Isa 49:17; 2 Chr 24:5; Ps 106:13. – *Com.:* The first four cases are for the pointing מַהרו and the last three for מְהרו.

⟨ויבא⟩: All ויבא in the book are plene with the exception of two, and their references are: Esth 5:5; 7:1.

8 ומחר: Six times, and their references are: Exod 19:10; 2 Sam 11:12; 1 Sam 28:19; Josh 22:18; Esth 5:8; Prov 3:28.

9 וכראות: Twice: 1 Sam 17:55; Esth 5:9; and once ובראות: 2 Chr 12:7. – *Com.:* The Mm is rendered twice, once on the upper and once on the lower margin on fol. 435r, and in the last case with the addition וסימנהון; see the next Mm.

וכראות: Twice, and their references are: 1 Sam 17:55; Esth 5:9; and once ובראות: 2 Chr 12:7.

10 ויתאפק: Twice: Gen 43:31; Esth 5:10.

14 אמר למלך: Twice: Jer 13:18; Esth 5:14. – *Com.:* This Mm has its text reference on fol. 435r of M^L but is written on fol. 435v, upper margin.

ובא: Twice in this form of (the verb) "to come": Esth 5:14; Jer 17:27. – *Com.:*

The reference text is on M^L fol. 435r but the Mm to it is on fol. 435v, upper margin.

וימצא: Seven times, and their references are: Gen 44:12; Esth 6:2; Ezra 10:18; 1 Chr 26:31; Esth 2:23; 2 Chr 15:15; 15:4. – *Com.*: The reference text is on M^L fol. 435r but the Mm to it is on fol. 435v, upper margin. As for 2 Chr 15:4 the text of M^L reads ויבקשהו whereas the *sîman* for it reads ויבקשוהו.

לתלות: Twice, and their references are: Esth 6:4; Ezek 15:3.

יותר: Seven times with plene form, and their references are: Exod 16:19; 1 Sam 15:15; Qoh 7:16; 2 Sam 8:4 and its companion (1 Chr 18:4); Qoh 6:8; Esth 6:6.

ונתון: Seven times: Gen 41:43; Ezek 23:46; Isa 37:19; Jer 37:21; Qoh 8:9; Esth 2:3; 6:9. – *Com.*: There is an error in the reference to Qoh 8:9: אל לבי should be את לבי, and there is an addition: דקהלת.

⟨**על־יד**⟩: In the whole Esther scroll (it is written) אל יד except for one על יד: Esth 6:9; and (thus) in the whole Scripture except for five times אל יד.

יעשה לאיש: ⟨Three times:⟩ Deut 25:9; Esth 6:9, and its companion (6:11). – *Com.*: As for Deut 25:9, Mm has left out לאיש between יעשה and אשר, and instead of בית אחיו, it has בית אביו.

הצר: Three times, once with *paṭaḥ*, and twice with *qameṣ*, and their references are: Num 10:9; Zech 8:10; Esth 7:4.

מי הוא זה: Three times, and their references are: Jer 30:21; Ps 24:10; Esth 7:5.

חרבונא: Twice, once written with א and once written with ה, and their references are: Esth 1:10 written (א); 7:9.

ויתלו: Twice: 2 Sam 4:12; Esth 7:10, and once: ויתלו: Esth 5:14 (וְיִתְלוּ).

⟨**היהודיים**⟩: Written six times יהודיים with two י and read יהודים, and their references are: Esth 4:7; 8:1; 8:13; 8:7; 9:18 at the beginning of the verse; 9:15; and they occur (all) in one book (i.e., Esther).

ותוסף: Three times plene, and their references are: 1 Sam 19:8; Ezek 23:14; Esth 8:3.

וטובה: Twice: Qoh 6:6; Esth 8:5.

ברעה: Twice, and their references are: Esth 8:6; Neh 13:7.

שבע ועשרים ומאה: Three times: Esth 1:1; 8:9; 9:30.

האחשתרנים: Twice, and their references are: Esth 8:10; 8:14. – *Com.*: The ב in בשם is lacking in the *sîman* of Esth 8:10. It may be regarded as haplography with the last letter of ויכתב.

ולעמד: Three times, and their references are: Num 16:9; 1 Chr 23:30; Esth 8:11.

ולהיות: Twice, and their references are: 2 Chr 29:11; Esth 8:13.

⟨**אורה**⟩: Our ancestors did six things in those days (of trouble): great mourning, and fasting, and weeping, and lament, sackcloth, and ashes. When the Almighty, blessed be He, turned this around for them (they did) six things in place of (these) six: light, and gladness, and joy, and honor, feasting, and holiday, and sending of presents one to another.

ויקר: Twice, and their references are: Esth 8:16; Ezek 22:25; and every Aramaic occurrence of the expression (ויקרה, ויקרא, ויקר) is like these.

⟨**והאחשדרפנים**⟩: Three words are counted in the Scripture that each have eleven letters, and their references are: Ezek 20:44; 16:47; Esth 9:3. – *Com.*: The ר in והאחשדרפנים is lacking in the *sîman* for Esth 9:3.

עשי: Sixteen times written with י, and their references are: Exod 35:35; Isa 19:10; Mal 3:15; 1 Chr 22:15; 2 Chr 26:13; 34:10, second (occurrence of the word) in the verse; 34:17; 24:13; 1 Chr 27:26; Pss 103:20; 103:21; 107:23; Prov 12:22;

Neh 13:10; Esth 3:9; 9:3; and from 2 Kgs 12:7 to the end of the book (of Kings) (the form is always) like this (עשׂי). – *Com.:* The Mm protects the pl. cstr. ptc. against the sg. ptc. M[L] has no Mp here.

17　וׁעשׂה: Three times, and the references are: Jer 44:25; Ezek 23:48; Esth 9:17; and its companion (Esth 9:18). – *Com.:* This Mm says "three times" but gives four *sîmanîm*. The reference to Ezek 23:48 is erroneous (cf. Weil, § 2710). In the *sîman* for Esth 9:17 is משׁתה written twice.

20　רׁחוקים: Seven times plene, and their references are: Josh 9:22; Judg 18:7; Isa 33:13; 46:12; Zech 6:15; Esth 9:20; Neh 4:13.

22　כׁימים: Four times, and their references are: Deut 1:46; 10:10; Zech 8:11; Esth 9:22.

26　⟨על כן⟩: 1 Sam 5:5; Gen 32:33; Isa 5:25; 16:9; Esth 9:26. – *Com.:* The Mm is following directly after the Mm on לימים of this verse, probably due to the over-lapping (i.e., double use) of the particle על כן. Above the word ידרכו is יאכלו written with smaller letters (cf. Weil, § 3781).

　　לׁימים: Five times, and their references are: Judg 17:10; 2 Sam 14:26; Ezek 22:14; Dan 10:14; Esth 9:26. – *Com.:* This Mm has no marker of the end (:o:). See the Mm on the preceding על כן.

28　וׁימי: Twice: Deut 11:21; Esth 9:28.

29　⟨הפרים⟩: From "and Queen Esther wrote" (i.e., 9:29) to the end of the book פרים is defectively written and the rest plene. – *Com.:* This Mm of M[L] is not in accordance with the text of M[L] since 9:29 has the plene form (הפורים) whereas the defectively written form occurs twice in 9:31-32.

30　אל כל היהודים: Three times, and their references are: Jer 44:1; Esth 9:20; and its companion (Esth 9:30).

10:2　וׁכל מעשה: Three times, and their references are: Num 31:20; Mic 6:16; Esth 10:2.

　　Masorah finalis: (Sum of the verses in this book:) 168. – *Com.:* With minor differences M[Y] and M[L34] have a longer final Masorah, and the number is said to be קֹסֿז (167).

COMMENTARIES ON THE CRITICAL APPARATUS

RUTH

1 בִּימֵי שְׁפֹט הַשֹּׁפְטִים   Campbell (*Ruth*, 50) is no doubt right in his judgment that some of the ancient versions considered the syntactical combinations of M as redundant. S and G solved this redundancy each in their own way. A vocalization שֹׁפֵט could be the base of T נְגוֹד, found in the Polyglots of Antwerp and Paris and in the Urbinas Ebr. 1. It could also explain the reading *iudicis* in La and the reading (*unius*) *iudicis* in V. Rahlfs (*Studie*, 130) supposes that the reading of La has been taken from V and that *iudicis iudicum* in La combines the readings of V and G.

2 וַיִּהְיוּ־   T has been taken here as support for M since it maintains the verb. The unique specification "they became royal adjutants" probably reflects an attempt to round out the Hebrew phrase "and they were there".
It seems likely that both S and V give a correct translation of the component of meaning of היה in this context; therefore no dependency of S and V upon 4QRuth^a was constructed, although elsewhere ישׁב is rendered by the same Syriac verb. S has an identical rendering of the two Hebrew verbs in vv. 2 and 4, but V prefers stylistic variation: *morabantur* and *manseruntque*. 4QRuth^a looks like an assimilation to 1:4, especially since G clearly supports the *lectio difficilior* of M. A question mark seems nevertheless necessary.

5 מִשְּׁנֵי יְלָדֶיהָ וּמֵאִישָׁהּ:   The chronological order of events has been restored by G and S. The chiastic order of M should be preferred. It is confirmed by 4QRuth^a.

7 בַּדֶּרֶךְ   Verse 7b is lacking as a whole in some editions of T, whereas it is present in Urbinas Ebr. 1 and in all other manuscripts. The absence in some editions may be due to homoioteleuton, the scribe's eye having moved from the final ה in עִמָּהּ to the final ה of יְהוּדָה (so Campbell, *Ruth*, 60).

9 לָכֶם   According to Sperber's edition: אגר שלים. Urbinas Ebr. 1 reads אגר טב שׁלים, "a good, full reward." The whole sentence reads: "full reward for the kindness you have done me. (And in that reward . . .)." Levine (*Aramaic Version*, 51) correctly considers this information as a "significant midrashic addition." Therefore the evaluation of T differs from that of S and G^L. The Lucianic character of the reading is clear since it is attested by 54, 75, 82, 106, 134, 344 314, and 93. The reading of 106 has been provided here on the authority of Rahlfs (*Studie*, 80, note 1).

קוֹלָן   V is the only version which explicitly says that only the two young women are weeping, not all three of them. The same statement could be present in 4QRuth^a if the ם- suffix reflects an old feminine dual (Campbell, *Ruth*, 65, 66). The Hebrew syntax, especially in the beginning of verse 10, is certainly in favor of such an interpretation. Because of the speculative character of the dual presupposition, the reading of 4QRuth^a has not been preferred.

12 לֵכְן   Because of the defective writing of the imperative (without final ה), some Greek manuscripts vocalized the consonantal text as לָכֵן. S has a tendency to leave repeated information implicit. The asyndetic addition of a second verb of

movement is certainly original, since the two verbs occur in 8 and 12 in a chiastic order.

הַלַּיְלָה   The Hebrew base for λελαϊκωμένην was already noted by J.G. Scharfenberg (*Animadversiones*, 87) in 1781. Although unattested, the Greek reading
could be due to θ' (Thornhill, "Greek Text," 239). συλλαβεῖν in σ' can hardly
be based upon חלילה and it seems to render the Hebrew idiom as such. It may
have influenced V: (*hac nocte*) *concipere*.

14   לַחֲמוֹתָהּ   According to Houbigant, M abbreviated the original text since all the
versions agree regarding the same extra information. This is, however, not the
case. The apparatus clearly shows that the versions glossed in different ways.
For T the gloss in the Antwerp polyglot and in the different manuscripts used
by Levine has been provided in the apparatus (there is no gloss in the London
polyglot nor in the Masoretic Bibles). The differences between the versions
make it abundantly clear that each version wanted to make explicit in its own
way what the "kissing of the mother-in-law" meant. They easily found the clues
in the immediate context as Buxtorf (*Anticritica*, 691) already suspected. For all
these reasons, *CTAT* (1:130) considers M as the earliest attainable text which is,
moreover, supported by 4QRuth[b].

15   שׁוּבִי   G has the extra information δή καὶ σύ. The fact that δή is lacking in G[75]
should not be stressed. The group to which this manuscript belongs has δή.
Moreover, G[75] has many scribal errors (Rahlfs, *Studie*, 66, note 2). The absence
of δή from La and other ancient versions such as Ethiopic, Armenian, and Sahi-
dic should not be underlined either. For it may have been very difficult for
translators to render a particle like δή into the receptor language (Rahlfs, *Studie*,
56, note 5). *CTAT* (1:130) also notes that V respects the austerity of M, the
manuscript Laudianus with its addition *et tu* after *vade* being the only exception.
T does the same at this point, but it presents the extra information ולדחלתיך
*לות עמיך, "to your people and to your gods," at the end of the verse.

19   וַתֵּהֹם   The general interpretational tendency of the versions makes it tempting to
evaluate G with Gerleman (*Ruth/Hohelied*, 17) likewise as interpretational. On
the other hand, lexicographical considerations make the shift of root as proposed by Ehrlich (*Randglossen*, 7:22) and Joüon (*Ruth*, 43) attractive. This is a
borderline case which could be eliminated if G also is considered as interpretational. Are we the victims of our modern lexicography?

21   עָנָה   The immediate context is certainly not unfavorable to the *piel* meaning "afflict" of the root ענה[II], and the selection of such a meaning by G V and S is
therefore not surprising. ענה[II], however, as has been stated in recent research
(*CTAT*, 1:131; Sasson, *Ruth*, 35; Campbell, *Ruth*, 77; Hubbard, *Ruth*, 126f.; de
Waard/Nida, *Handbook*, 83), is always constructed with the accusative of the
afflicted and never with the preposition בְּ, as is the case with the *qal* meaning
"testify" of ענה[I]. Even though a divine agent never figures as "testifier" (Myers,
Literary Form, 22), the vocalization of M should nevertheless be retained. The
construction with the preposition בְּ seems to express contrary evidence, whereas
the construction with לְ would present favorable evidence.

2:7   עַתָּה   See commentary on זֶה שִׁבְתָּהּ הַבַּיִת.

זֶה שִׁבְתָּהּ הַבַּיִת   The precise meaning of M will probably never be known. If one
does not want to consider ἐν τῷ ἀγρῷ of G as a rendering of הבית in the sense
of Akkadian *bītu* or Arabic *bayt* as suggested by Weippert ("Kommentar zu
Ruth," 272, n. 8), one of the possible explanations is that G had a *Vorlage* with-

out הבית or that the translator considered it to be a dittography. G made explicit what it considered to be the right location. It is important to note that, apart from the transposition of ἐν τῷ ἀγρῷ and μικρόν in the Lucianic recension (Rahlfs, *Studie*, 81), there is no evidence of any variant reading in any Greek manuscript. According to its exegesis of the source text, G also provided precision with regard to time by replacing וְעַד־עַתָּה with καὶ ἕως ἑσπέρας. Rahlfs's R group has here ἕως νῦν τοῦτο (Rahlfs, *Studie*, 109), which is not surprising since one of the main characteristics of this recension is its frequent agreement with M. In addition, G has vocalized שבתה as שָׁבְתָה and has performed a negative transformation. Although V shares with G this negative transformation, it renders הבית, and it seems to have read שָׁבָה *reversa est*. The diversity of the text traditions probably only shows different attempts to make sense out of a difficult text (*CTAT*, 1:131).

A possible interpretation of M would seem to be the one given by Zimolong ("Ruth 2.7," 158) who retouches the Hebrew accentuation by taking זֶה with the preceding עַתָּה and who takes שִׁבְתָּה הַבַּיִת as an apposition of זֶה. מְעָט would then refer to the small quantity Ruth as an inexperienced gleaner had gathered. He has taken up again the millenary exegesis of Yefet ben Eli, probably without knowing this (*CTAT*, 1:132). As a result, M could be paraphrased as follows: "She has come and stayed since this morning. And until now, the time for her to sit down at home, it is little she has gathered."

לְעֵת Because of the stronger disjunctive accent on הָאֹכֶל, M takes לְעֵת as the time setting of Boaz's utterance (Joüon, *Ruth*, 57–58), and it ascribes these words to the narrator. Only such a division does justice to the time lapse between verses 13 and 14 and to the staging of the story (Campbell, *Ruth*, 102). G, however, provides a different syntactical division of the Hebrew text by making ἤδη ὥρα τοῦ φαγεῖν part of the speech of Boaz. The different renderings of La (*hora manducandi . . .*) and of V (*quando hora . . . fuerit*) also testify to such a syntactical division of the text. As to Greek text traditions, some manuscripts belonging to Rahlfs's R group read τῇ δὴ ὥρα and others, mainly Lucianic, τῇ ὥρα, adopting therefore the syntactical division of M.

וַיִּצְבָּט־ The *hapax legomenon* וַיִּצְבָּט of M is now clearly supported by 2QRuth^a. The question marks following the evaluation are only meant to warn against the drawing of hasty conclusions. The typical Septuagint verb and neologism (Lust, *Lexicon*, 83b) βουνίζω, "to heap up," is further only used by G in Ruth 2:16 for the rendering of הַצְּבָתִים: βεβουνισμένων. Did the translator ignore the meaning of both *hapax legomena* and did he link them with forms of צבר as the most similar item in his lexical stock (*CTAT*, 1:132)? Or did the translator (a) consider ט and ת as alternate spellings; (b) analogous to Ugaritic *mṣbṭm*, "tongs," understand the Hebrew verb to mean "he took with tongs for her," generically understood as "passing over," (c) translationally mark quantity (to heap up) because of the grammatical object ἄλφιτον and because of the fact that Ruth was entirely satisfied? The first presupposition is certainly easier, but nothing is more complex than translational processes. Although the rendering of V *congessit polentam sibi*, "she heaped up barley for herself (!)" causes further complications, it is not to be excluded that the translation *congessit* stems from G.

וַתֵּרֶא Two manuscripts of M (Kenn. 18 and 109) read וַתַּרְא אֶת־, providing a causative followed by the sign of the direct object, which makes "mother-in-law" the first of a double accusative. The same textual understanding is found in V and S. The two manuscripts are Ashkenazi type, dating from late thirteenth to early fourteenth century, and they have a weak authority (*CTAT*, 1:133). Moreover, the preservation of the same grammatical subject of the two preceding verbs וַתִּשָּׂא and וַתָּבוֹא is certainly syntactically facilitating. On the other hand, in M the sign of the direct object only figures before "what she had gleaned" taking "mother-in-law" as the grammatical subject of the verb under discussion. M further has the support of G and T. The vocalization of M should therefore be preferred (Joüon, *Ruth*, 62; Campbell, *Ruth*, 104–5).

19 אֵת אֲשֶׁר־עָשְׂתָה עִמּוֹ   In 2QRuth[a] there is a lacuna between עשתה and שם but the space is sufficient for עמו ותאמר.

21 הַמּוֹאָבִיָּה   On the photographs of 2QRuth[a] (fragment IV, 5 of plate XIV in DJD III), only the left part of the upper vertical stroke of the ה of המואביה is visible. Not only this textual support, but also the use of the literary device of the so-called "inclusio of identity" (Gow, *Ruth*, 124), is in favor of the reading of M. The extra information πρὸς τὴν πενθερὰν αὐτῆς in G is not based upon a *Vorlage* אֶל־חֲמוֹתָה (Joüon, *Ruth*, 65), but it is the result of the application of a translation technique of making participants explicit. S either shows dependence upon G, or has independently used the same technique.

23 לְלַקֵּט   ללוט is the primitive reading of 2QRuth[a]. To the left of the incomplete *waw*, a trace of an added ק may be visible, a correction which would produce the infinitive qal reading ללקוט with the same meaning as the infinitive piel reading of M.

וַתֵּשֶׁב אֶת־   2QRuth[a] has only been cited here in order to point out to the user of the apparatus that some fragmentary text exists. So fragmentary, that only the upper stroke of the initial ו of ותשב can be detected on the photographs (fragment VI, 5 of plate XIV in DJD III). Even in the (theoretical) case of more completeness, the text would have remained indecisive with regard to the vocalization of the verb. Only the use of the preposition would have been decisive.

Two manuscripts de Rossi (379 and the first hand of 495) have the reading וַתָּשָׁב, which seems to have been followed by V, *(postquam autem) reversa est*. The characterization "shift of meaning" has been used to characterize these secondary readings. They certainly intend to create smoother transitions. The sentence in M could be taken as sequential to the preceding one (Campbell, *Ruth*, 108–9) or as contemporaneous with it (Sasson, *Ruth*, 62).

3:12 כִּי אִם   For syntactic and semantic reasons, כי אם has to be considered as an accidental dittography of the preceding (נם)כי אמ.

14 וַיֹּאמֶר   The two preceding verbs have Ruth as the agent to obtain a more logical sequence. S also made Ruth the grammatical subject of the utterance with the implication of further shifts: "she said to him, 'Nobody should know that I came to you on the threshing floor.'" S therefore made a syntactical assimilation. There can be no doubt that the subject is Boaz as it has been explicitly stated in G V. It is more difficult to know to whom the utterance in M is addressed. In T Boaz is speaking "to his servant" and in the midrash *Ruth Rab.* II, 1 "to his foreman." A number of manuscripts of the Hexaplaric (!) family (Rahlfs, *Studie*, 67–71) have Boaz addressing Ruth: καὶ εἶπεν αὐτῇ (19, 108, 426), καὶ εἶπεν Βόος αὐτῇ (376), καὶ εἶπεν αὐτῇ Βόος (58). V has Boaz implicitly addressing Ruth with implied further shifts: *et dixit Booz, cave ne quis noverit quod huc veneris*. Another midrash (*Ruth Rab.* VII, 1) has Boaz praying to God: " . . .

may it be your will that it not be known that the woman came to the threshing floor." All these different interpretations clearly show that M is the oldest attainable text and that the utterance should most probably be understood as a monologue: "he thought to himself."

וַיָּבֹא   The reading of M with Boaz as grammatical subject is found in M^A, M^Y, and M^L, as well as in the editions of Ben Ḥayyim and Minḥat Shay. On the other hand, more than forty manuscripts of M have the reading with the feminine preformative וַתָּבֹא, making Ruth the implied subject.

The reading of G καὶ εἰσῆλθεν is grammatically, of course, indeterminate with regard to the agent. However, the fact that G starts the discourse immediately following with καὶ 'Ρούθ εἰσῆλθεν shows that the intended subject of the verb is here the same as that of the preceding aorists, namely Boaz, as it has been explicitly stated in 3:4. Only a part of the Lucianic recension makes Ruth explicit in the text. V and S by their feminine forms express the same reading.

יִגְאַל   Question marks following the evaluations express continued uncertainties. As observed in *CTAT* (1:134), the reading of M is witnessed by its best representatives: M^A, M^L, and the editions of Ben Ḥayyim and Minḥat Shay. It is also protected by a Mp of manuscript Paris BN Hébreu 3, which refers for this sequence to Lev 27:20 and which protects this sequence against the *nifal* reading יִגָּאֵל found three times (Lev 25:30, 54; Lev 27:27).

In contrast with two Arabic Jewish versions of Ruth, published by M. Peritz, which read תִגְאַל, Saadya in his commentary on Ps 4:4 quotes in the first instance Ruth 4:4 as an authority for his thesis that Hebrew can use the third person for the first and the second and vice versa. As additional proof he cites Mic 7:19 and Ps 81:17. Ibn Ezra (par. 120), on the other hand, retaining the third person, interprets: "if no redeemer redeems it," supported in this by Yefet ben Eli who states that Boaz addresses himself to the elders. This interpretation which is also found in Midrash Rabbah, has recently been taken up again by Sasson: "But, should he decide not to redeem it (added Boaz as he addressed the elders before turning back to the redeemer) . . . " (*Ruth*, 103 and 118).

Although one may not want to take away the vestiges of a vivid impression, the weight of more than fifty manuscripts of M followed by at least two versions in favor of the reading תִגְאַל is, of course, impressive. One can therefore understand the text correction proposed in *CTAT* (1:134). It remains nevertheless impossible to explain the origin of M. As Rudolph (*Ruth/Hohes Lied/Klagelieder*, 59) has already stated, it is difficult to explain M as a scribal error. Moreover, it is not impossible that V *tibi displicet (hoc)* and T (למפרוק) רעותך deal in a similar way with the difficulty of M.

וּמֵאֵת   Several proposals with regard to this issue have been made. It has been suggested to maintain M and to consider the מ as enclitic. On the other hand, it has been proposed to simply delete the מ or to read, following V, גַּם אֶת־, considering therefore the ו of M as an error for the ג. A variant of the last suggestion is the proposed reading וְגַם אֶת־, which entirely harmonizes with the reading found in 4:10. The last two proposals are facilitating assimilations.

Without going into all the details of this *crux interpretum*, the ambiguity of certain textual witnesses should be noted. Although G through its rendering καὶ παρά confirms the reading וּמֵאֵת of M, it also confirms through its double translation καὶ αὐτήν the interpretation of V. The same applies to T. In spite of the equalization מן ידא דנעמי ומן ידא דרות, T also states: "you must acquire her by levirate marriage," a significant midrashic addition which to a high degree confirms the same interpretation.

It seems therefore that the problems are largely interpretational. As remarked in *CTAT* (1:135), one wonders whether the use of distinct prepositions in M, מְיַּד and מֵאֵת, does not reflect the distinct relations both women have with regard to the transaction. Through the purchase, the patrimony no longer is in the hands of Naomi, but it does not enter into the possession of the buyer. In pursuance of levirate rights, the purchase takes place on behalf of Ruth and in her name. It may therefore well be that V, in spite of its translational treatment, has correctly understood M as already Buxtorf (*Anticritica*, 760) suspected. And the same could apply to all the versions.

11   וְהַזְּקֵנִים עֵדִים   G reads καὶ εἴποσαν (εἶπαν) πᾶς ὁ λαὸς οἱ ἐν τῇ πύλῃ Μάρτυρες. καὶ οἱ πρεσβύτεροι εἴποσαν (εἶπαν) . . . . In other words, it gives different functions to the two different groups. It has all the people in the gate perform as witnesses, and it has only the elders pronounce the blessing.

For Joüon (*Ruth*, 89) G is based upon an original Hebrew text which could have run as follows: ויאמר כל־העם אשר בשער עדים והזקנים אמרו. M would be a condensed text. His major argument is that it is very difficult to understand how ordinary people could formulate such poetic wishes and such sophisticated allusions.

It is, however, exactly such a reasoning which could have led to the Greek translator's interpretation of M. Mainly two arguments favor M: (1) in the three instances in this chapter (4:9 and 11) in which the people and the elders interfere, they act together; (2) the order of the two groups in verse 9 has been reversed in verse 11, and several other examples could be given of an intentional chiastic arrangement of participants.

By its inversion, S assimilates the order of participants to that of verse 9. In addition, S amplifies M by providing, like G, each group with a verb of saying. Unlike G, however, S has the two groups act in concert.

CANTICLES

1:3   שֶׁמֶן תּוּרַק   תורק as a verbal form is a feminine imperfect *hofal* of ריק, "(which) is emptied/poured out." The feminine form is, however, not congruent with the masculine subject. Many exegetes, therefore, emend the text to the participle מוּרַק, which seems to be presupposed in G, ⟨α'⟩, ⟨ε'⟩, V (v. 2), and T. The reading of S could have been occasioned by this Hebrew form, or otherwise is a guess. In 6QCant there is no שמן; instead of it only the letter מ is certain, a ר is probable. On the basis of available space, Baillet (DJD III, 113) has conjecturally reconstructed the text as מרן\קחת מורקה, "an aromatic mixture poured out," a reading which does not help to explain the text of M. A conjectural emendation is תמרוק, "cosmetic treatment" (Esth 2:3, 9, 12); so Rudolph (*Ruth/Hohes Lied/Klagelieder*, 122) and F. Horst (apparatus *BHS*). It has also been suggested that תורק may not be a verb form at all, but has a meaning which can no longer be established, so that we should translate "Turaq-oil."

4   אַחֲרֶיךָ   In the accentuation of M, אחריך is connected with the following: "draw me, we will hurry after you." Since this would refer to a third person besides

the two lovers, this accentuation is usually ignored, the translation being: "draw me behind you, let us hurry." This latter reading may be supported by 6QCant, that is in Baillet's reconstruction (DJD III, 113), who on the basis of letter count assumes a space after אחריך. The same division holds good for ⟨ε'⟩ with "you have drawn me after you. I hasten to the scent of your perfumes." Field (*Origenis Hexaplorum*, 2:411) gives it also for ⟨α'⟩, although his source, Syh, is indeterminate (ܠܒܬܪܟ ܓܪܬܢܝ). In T אחריך seems to do double duty in the rendering גְּגִידְנָא בתרך ונהי רהטין בתר אורח טובך, "We have been drawn (*or:* draw us) after you and (we) hurry after your good path." V (v. 3; *trahe me post te curremus*) and S ("draw me after you we will hurry") are indeterminate in this respect. The three main G-manuscripts all have "they drew you," but differ among themselves in the text division. G^A (text Rahlfs) has it as an independent sentence; G^B connects it with the preceding and has a caesura after it: "the maidens loved you, they drew you near," for which compare La^{Ambr} and La^{169}: "dilexerunt te et adtraxerunt te"; G^S connects it with the following: "They drew you behind you . . . we will run."

מֵישָׁרִים אֲהֵבוּךָ:   In מישרים אהבוך the first word must be meant adverbially: "rightly do they love you," in which the subject can hardly be other than "the maidens" of the previous verse. The versions, however, have interpreted the word differently. G has εὐθύτης ἠγάπησέν σε, "righteousness loves you"; ⟨α'⟩ has εὐθεῖαι ἠγάπησάν σε, "righteous (women) love you"; ⟨σ'⟩ gives εὐθεῖς εἰσιν οἱ ἀγαπῶντές σε, "righteous are those who love you", to which V (v. 3) may be compared with *recti diligunt te*. The translation of ⟨ε'⟩ seems to be a guess: ἀληθὴς ἡ σοφία σου, "true is your wisdom." The מ has been translated as a preposition, "more than," by S with ܡܢ ܬܪܝܨܐ ܪܚܡܬܟ, "and (we commemorate) more than the righteous your love." 6QCant supports M in the first word, though not in the second with מישרים אהובים, "those who are rightly loved ."(?)

5   בָּנוֹת   With respect to בנתי, Baillet (DJD III, 113) hesitates between a copying mistake and an archaic form with defective writing and *hîreq compaginis*.

שְׁלֹמֹה: "Solomon" is unchallenged in all ancient versions, including T. Yet it is thought by many scholars that the word should be read as "Salma," a tribe of Arab nomads referred to, e.g., in Targ Gen 15:19; this then would be in parallelism to "Kedar": "like the tents of Kedar and like the tent-curtains of Salma." Scholars who retain the Masoretic vocalization assume that "Kedar" connects with "black" and "Solomon's curtains" with "beautiful". See for detailed treatment *CTAT*, 5, *ad loc*. This parallelism of relations (black-Kedar/beautiful-Solomon's curtains) also holds if ונאוה is translated "*and* beautiful" (Ettien, "Translating," esp. 224–26).

6   נִחֲרוּ־   In the source of Field (*Origenis Hexaplorum*, 2:412), the quotation involved is attributed to σ' but according to Field it is actually the reading of θ'. This is indeed likely since this reading, a third singular form instead of a plural form, is in conformity with the singular "son" and with the following "he put," as θ' has. It agrees with the other ancient witnesses in translating the Hebrew with "to fight": G ἐμαχέσαντο, σ' διεμαχέσαντο, V (v. 5) *pugnaverunt*, S ܐܬܟܬܫܘ. Salkind (*Die Peschitta*, 19) thinks that S has translated נלחמו; also the verb used by G is nine times the translation of נלחם. Yet it is not likely that all versions have made the same reading mistake. More probably the Hebrew word has not been recognized as a *piel* form of נחר, "to snort," but has been inter-

preted as the *nifal* of חרה, נֶחֱרוּ, "to be angry (with)," although in that case this is the only place where "to be angry" has been rendered as "to fight (against)."

שָׁמֹנִי   For θ'*, see the preceding comment. Over against this reading, 6QCant supports M with the unambiguous שמוני. σ' has κατεστάθην, "I have been set as . . . ," which reflects M with the subject understood as the impersonal "they."

7   כְּעֹטְיָה   The Hebrew form is a feminine participle of עטה, "to be veiled." It is difficult to understand what this would refer to, and many commentators emend to כטעיה, with a reference to S, which has ܐܝܟ ܛܥܝܬܐ, "as a wandering woman." This is generally taken to reflect a participle of טעה, "to wander"; this root occurs only once in the Bible in a *hifil* form, "to make wander," Ezek 13:10, and is considered to be a parallel form of תעה. The same form may account for σ', V, and T ("Let me know . . . why they [Israel] are exiled [מטלטלין]"). As the reading of α', Syh gives ܕܫܒܝܩܬܐ, "a woman who has been sent away", which also is best explained as a rendering of כטעיה. On the other hand, M is supported by 6QCant, in which the first two letters of the word – the rest is not preserved – are כע, at least in Baillet's reconstruction (DJD III, 113). The microfiche does not show a clear ע. The only thing which is sure is that the second letter is not a ט. Also G (ὡς περιβαλλομένη) reflects M.

8   צְאִי־לָךְ   σ' has two Greek verbs "go out (aor. ptc.) and go." It is also quoted in Syh with a repeated ܐܙܠܝ, which may reflect an additional σύ. Whether this is the case or not, the second verb indicates that לך has been rendered as a verb "go," as is also the case in V (v. 7; *egredere et abi*). Also for α', Syh gives a variant reading: ܠܟܝ ܐܘ ܦܘܩܝ, which seems like a double translation of לך. Although the variant reading would make good sense, there is no reason to challenge M's text. Cp. 2:10.

11   תּוֹרֵי   The Hebrew תורי refers to strings (of pearls?), and has been so understood by ε' (στρεπτοῦ fort. στρεπτούς), V (v. 10; *murenulas*) and S (ܓܕܘܠܐ). σ' has περίβλεπτα, "respected things," which may have resulted from a misunderstanding of the Hebrew as derived from the verb ראה (Schleusner, *Thesaurus*, 4:288); cp. 1 Chr 17:17, where G renders כתור with ὡς ὅρασις. The same misunderstanding may account for G with ὁμοιώματα, the singular form of which renders תאר in Judg 8:18 (Gerleman, *Ruth/Hohelied*, 105).

17   רַחִיטֵנוּ   The Hebrew רחיט occurs only here. The *qərê* רהיט does not occur in biblical Hebrew, but in later Hebrew refers to beams of a house (see *HALAT*, 1114 and Jastrow, *Dictionary*, 1454). It is difficult to say whether the versions have known this word, or translated the Hebrew (whichever of the two readings was in their *Vorlage*) on the basis of the context. The word is translated "our ceilings" in G (φατνώματα ἡμῶν), σ' (αἱ φατνώσεις), V (v. 16; *laquearia nostra*), "beams" in S (ܩܪܝܬܐ) and T (שירתוהי). Syh gives as the rendering of ε' ܩܢܘܦ, "lathes" (?; the meaning is not certain; see Field, *Origenis Hexaplorum*, 2:413).

2:4   וְדִגְלוֹ   Only T seems to have understood ודגלו as a substantive with "the order (טיקס) of his commandments." It has been read as a plural imperative by G (keeping up with the imperative at the beginning of the verse) and S: "set love upon me," and as a singular perfect by α' and V (*ordinavit*). The reading of σ', a plural imperative, "heap up," may derive from a reading ודגרו. The Aramaic verb דגר means "to heap up" (and "to brood"); in the Bible it occurs twice with the meaning "to hatch," or, according to some "to gather," viz. Isa 34:15; Jer 17:11. Schleusner (*Thesaurus*, 2:492) mentions this possibility, but thinks it more likely that σ' is based upon a military meaning of the imperative דִּגְלוּ, since warriors gather together when the banner is raised.

7 הָאֲהֻבָה   Four times V translates אהבה, with "beloved," viz., in 2:7; 3:5; 8:4 (*dilecta[m]*) and in 7:7 (v. 6; *carissima*). In the latter case, V is joined by σ' and S (ܪܚܝܡܬܐ). We cannot be certain whether this rendering is due to a reading of the *Vorlage* as אהבה or to the understanding of "love" as an *abstractum pro concreto*. In 7:7 the meaning is clearly "beloved," but there is no reason to emend MT as is done, e.g., by Horst (apparatus *BHS*) and Würthwein ("Das Hohelied," 64) since "love" can be understood as *abstractum pro concreto*. A number of scholars, e.g., Barthélemy, think that this interpretation holds good for the other three places as well. For a detailed treatment, see *CTAT*, 5, *ad loc.*

10 עֲנָה   Field (*Origenis Hexaplorum*, 2:415) gives φθεγξάλενος as the translation of σ' for עָנָה. This must be an error for φθεγξάμενος, aorist ptc. of φθέγγομαι, which translates עָנָה also in Jer 51:14 (G 28:14); Hab 2:1; Ps 119:172 (Hatch/Redpath, *Concordance*, 2:1429)

לָךְ¹   לך¹ is certainly a *dativus ethicus*, because it cannot be vocalized as a feminine imperative and the imperative "go" occurs later in the verse. G has erroneously read it as an imperative of הלך; the rendering of V, "hurry," probably presupposes the same misunderstanding. 4QCant^b has no vocalization, but there is no reason to doubt that it aligns with M.

11 הַסְּתָו   The word סְתָו, "winter", has no ו of itself. The insertion of a ו in M^L(qere) must be meant to protect the pronunciation of the ו as a consonant instead of as a long ô. This feature occurs also elsewhere in M^L; see Revell, "Leningrad Codex," xxxviii–xxxix. M^A and M^Y have the same reading as M^L(ket) (without ו), but do not mark it as a *kətîb-qərê* issue.

13 הַתְּאֵנָה   The reading of 4QCant^b, התנאה, may well be an erroneous metathesis, cp. 3:1. Tov (DJD XVI, 212), mentions also the possibility, which he seems to favor, that this spelling points to the pronunciation *tena* with an א inserted secondarily in the wrong position.

לְכִי   As in v. 10, the form under discussion must be a *dativus ethicus*, לך. G has misunderstood it as an imperative. V has no explicit equivalent, which may be taken as implicitly supporting the M^qere.

14 הַמַּדְרֵגָה   The reading of 4QCant^b is not listed by Tov (DJD XVI, 212) as an error but considered as an example of phonetic interchange of ר and ל. It is hard to explain G's translation other than as a guess. With respect to S (ܕܣܘܓܐ), it is suggested by Salkind (*Die Peschitta*, 23) that it presupposes מגדרה, "fence." This word, however, does not occur in Hebrew or Aramaic. Yet, Salkind may be right in that S has been led by the root גדר; ܣܘܓܐ is the rendering for גדר, "wall," in Num 22:24; Isa 5:5; Mic 7:11; Ps 62:4; 80:13. The same holds good for V. *Maceria*, "fence," renders גדר in the places just mentioned, plus in Hos 2:8 (where S uses the verb ܣܘܓ, "to fence in," "to enclose").

וּמַרְאֵיךְ   The vocalization וּמַרְאֵיךְ is strange because (1) it is in contrast to מַרְאַיִךְ earlier in this verse and (2) it does not accord with the consonants. Neither in M^L nor in M^A (M^Y insuf.) is this point a *kətîb-qərê* issue, although some commentaries refer to it as such, e.g., Rudolph (*Ruth/Hohes Lied/Klagelieder*, 133) and Krinetzki (*Kommentar*, 104), and compare *HALAT*, 596, *s.v.* מַרְאֶה, and apparatus *BHS*. Instead, Mp considers the form as written plene, which would be a very unusual case at least. Perhaps the suffix -*ayik* was understood as a plural suffix and as such incompatible with the singular predicate. For the suffix in מַרְאַיִךְ as a singular suffix, see Gesenius/Kautzsch (*Grammatik*, §93*ss*) and Joüon/Muraoka (*Grammar*, §96C*e*). There is no reason to assume that the word should be vocalized differently from the same word earlier in the verse. Many KR mss. have adapted the consonants to the vocalization and read וּמרְאךָ.

15   שׁוּעָלִים[2]   The omission of this word in 4QCant^b is based on letter count (DJD XVI, 212).

17 **v 17**   The text of 4QCant^b seems to be shorter. Tov (DJD XVI, 212) thinks that the lacking words are אוֹ לְעֹפֶר הָאַיָּלִים.

    וְנָסוּ   In the first apparatus of *BHK³*, here and at 4:6, it is suggested that behind the rendering of σ', V, and S is Hebrew ונטו. A reading mistake is possible for each individual witness. It is, however, unlikely that the same mistake has occurred at both places in three versions. More likely, the translation was meant as an idiomatic rendering of ונסו, perhaps under the influence of a few other places with a comparable translation in connection with shadows, as a rendering of Hebrew נטה, viz. Jer 6:4 (S ܚܛ), Ps 102:12 (V *declinaverunt*; cp. Hbrs *inclinati sunt*; S ܚܛ), 109:23 (V *declinat*; cp. Hbrs *inclinatur*; S ܚܛ); for none of these places is σ' available. It is to be noted that at 4:6 also α' (or σ' ?) has κλιθῶσιν, which has not been recorded in *BHK³*. For 2:17, the reading of α' has not been preserved. Only here does G use κινέω to render נוס.

    הָרֵי בָתֶר: The word בתר has been a problem for the translators. It has been transcribed by ⟨α'⟩ (Βαθήρ [or βιθήρ, Field, *Origenis Hexaplorum*, Auctarium]), ⟨σ'⟩ (τοῦ βαιθήρ [or βαθθάρ, Field, *Origenis Hexaplorum*, Auctarium]), and V (Bether); it seems to have been understood as derived from בתר, "to cut" (Gen 15:10) by G ([ὄρη] κοιλωμάτων, "[mountains] of ravines") and ⟨ε'⟩ (διχοτομη-μάτων, "[mountains] of parts"). It has been understood as referring to spices by θ' ([τὰ ὄρη] θυμιαμάτων, "[the mountains] of perfumes"), S ("[mountains] of spices," as in 8:14) and probably also by ζ' (μαλαβάθρων; Field, *Origenis Hexaplorum*, Auctarium).

4:1 לְצַמָּתֵךְ   There can be no doubt that the Hebrew word (צמה) refers to the veil covering the face. The rendering of the ancient witnesses is, however, difficult to interpret. G has (ἐκτὸς) τῆς σιωπήσεώς σου, "outside your silence." Schleusner (*Thesaurus*, 5:56f.) thinks that "silence" renders "veil" since a veil calls for silence. This, though reflecting the meaning of the Hebrew, would not be a correct translation of the Hebrew word since "silence" is not a normal equivalent of "veil." The question remains what led the translator to "silence," a question which holds good also for S (ܫܬܩܟܝ), which elsewhere betrays no influence from G and therefore has probably independently arrived at the same translation. It is usually assumed that both versions (or three if θ' reflects an independent choice) derive the word from the root צמת, with the (supposed) meaning "to make silent." The same is the case in v. 3 and 6:7. None of the renderings reflects a textual variant. The translations of ε', (ἀπὸ πλήθους) τοῦ κάλλους σου, "(from the abundance of) your beauty," and of V, *quod intrinsecus latet*, "what is hidden inside," seem to be guesses. In v. 3 and 6:7, σ' has correctly translated with καλύμματι, whereas in 6:7, V (v. 6) has made a meaningful guess with *(absque) occultis tuis*.

    שֶׁגָּלְשׁוּ   The Hebrew verb גלשׁ occurs only here and in the same expression in 6:5. Its meaning is uncertain and must be guessed on the basis of the context. V and S (ܕܣܠܩ) render "which go up," which might reflect the reading שֶׁעָלוּ (cp. Schleusner, *Thesaurus*, 1:365). G's reading suggests שֶׁנִּגְלוּ (cp. Schleusner, ibid.)

or שֶׁנָּגְלוּ. In 6:5 G^{A,B} has αἳ ἀνεφάνησαν, "which appeared" (cp. σ' at 4:1), par-
allelled by V (v. 5), with *quae apparuerunt*; G^S has ἀνέβησαν [assim. v. 6?],
and S has again ܕܣܩ. The La-witnesses differ among themselves. La^{Ambr} (*quae
revelatae sunt*) renders G. La^{169} has *quae respexerunt*, whereas La^{Ep} has the
same reading as V. With respect to La^{Ep} it is to be noted that Vaccari's edition
gives *quae*, but that the only manuscript available for La^{Ep} has *qui*, which either
refers back to *greges* (plural, as G), or is a mistake. (Dr. E. Schulz-Flügel kindly
communicated this observation to me.)

וּמִדְבָּרֵיךְ   The consonantal text points to a plural form, מדברַיך, whereas the vocalization is that of a singular. The reason for this was probably the singular
predicate נאוה; cp. מראַיך in 2:14. It is actually a case of *kǝtîb-qǝrê* although it
is not represented as such, at least not in M^L (M^A is not extant, M^Y insuf.). Mp
only notes that this form occurs only once. 4QCant^b has the consonantal text of
a singular form. The versions also seem to presuppose a singular with the translation "speech" (G ἡ λαλιά σου, V *eloquium tuum*, S ܘܡܡܠܠܟܝ).

רַקָּתֵךְ   For Masoretic רקתך, 4QCant^a certainly has another reading. Nebe
("Qumranica I", 310) gives מרקנתך, "grün-gelbes Aussehen (?)"; Tov (DJD
XVI, 202) reads מזקנתך, a reading which is confirmed by a check of the microfiche. The word is unknown, but must be related to זקן and somehow refer to
the chin.

אַתְּ^1 and אַתְּ^2   Tov (DJD XVI, 216) thinks the reading of 4QCant^b may be a
hypercorrection by the scribe, who explained אתי as the Aramaic 2 f. sg. pronoun and changed it to Hebrew את. G, V, and S read the same consonantal text
as M, but presuppose a different vocalization (אַתִּי). The variant reading makes
good sense, but so does M. An important point is the structure which one assumes. For a treatment of the problem, see *CTAT*, 5, *ad loc.*

מִלְּבָנוֹן^1 and מִלְּבָנוֹן^2   In M^L, to judge from the facsimile edition and the color
transparencies, the ל in מִלְּבָנוֹן^2 seems to have a *ḥîreq* instead of a *šǝwâ*.

מֵרֹאשׁ שְׂנִיר וְחֶרְמוֹן   The homoioteleuton occurs only in the text of 4QCant^b (וֹן–),
which suggests that the reading אמנון occured in its *Vorlage*. The missing text
may have been supplied in the margin (DJD XVI, 216).

גַּל   גַּל means "heap of stones"; in the meaning "wave" it occurs only in the plural. Neither meaning is applicable here. Repetition is one of the literary devices
in Canticles; cp., e.g., v. 1, 8, 9, 10 (Gerleman, *Ruth/Hohelied*, 159). Most commentators assume an original גן. Both meaning and the reading of the versions
make this a very likely assumption indeed. The reading גן occurs also in a great
number of KR mss., probably a case of assimilation rather than an authentic
textual tradition. For a detailed discussion of the case, see *CTAT*, 5, *ad loc.*

חֶלְבֵּי to אָכַלְתִּי   Only the first clause (. . . אכלתי) is legible in 4QCant^b. It is
preceded and followed by lost text. In Tov's reconstruction (DJD XVI, 217–18),
the second clause (. . . שתיתי) had its place, not in the second, but in the first
open space.

דּוֹדִים: The Leiden Peshitta has erroneously ܪܚܡ, without *seyame*.

מֵרְבָבָה: Syh has in the text ܪܒܘܬܐ, and refers in the margin to α'-σ'-θ' with "as
the Seventy." For ε' however, it gives explicitly a plural form, which suggests
that the G-text referred to was supposed to have a singular: ἀπὸ μυριάδος (so
Field, *Origenis Hexaplorum*, 2:419). La presupposes a singular with *ex/de de-
cem mil(l)ibus* or *a multitudine* (La^{169}). La^{Ep} has *ex multis milibus*, which is
probably an adaptation to G.

13　מִגְדְּלוֹת מֶרְקָחִים　G and T seem to have vocalized the first word as a participle *piel* מְגַדְּלוֹת: G has φύουσαι, "making grow," whereas T has מרביא, "bringing forth" in "The two tables of the Law (. . .) bring forth fine things as a garden brings forth spices." V has *consitae a pigmentariis,* "sown by pigment merchants," which probably derives from the same reading, but is a freer rendering occasioned by the fact that the second word was read as מֶרְקָחִים. The variant reading מְגַדְּלוֹת is accepted, e.g., by Würthwein ("Das Hohelied," 57). Some scholars connect "towers" not with "beds of spices" but with "his cheeks" and understand the word as referring to a perfumed decoration, worn on the head. See further *CTAT,* 5, *ad loc.*

6:6　בָּהֶם:　V. 6b is parallel to 4:2, and v. 7 to 4:3b. G has the text of 4:3a in between. Technically this plus may be considered as either following 6b or preceding 7a. The second possibility seems to be the choice of Rahlfs, who has this plus as v. 7a, whereas Swete has it as part of v. 6. The apparatus follows Swete in this on the basis of the consideration that an assimilation comes after a common text, rather than preceding it.

10　כַּנִּדְגָּלוֹת:　S translates here ܐܟܘܬܗ. According to Salkind (*Die Peschitta*, 35 f.), however, S translates here ܪܒܘܬܐ, "ten thousands," since from 5:10 the translator understood that the number of warriors under one flag was ten thousand. However, Salkind made use of Lee's 1823 edition, which in many instances represents a younger text tradition. The reading "ten thousands" comes up only in 10c1[c] and 12a1*fam.* The reading of the ancient mss., without doubt the older one, is ܪܘܪܒܬܐ, "great deeds, great ladies, princesses." This rendering is independent from 5:10 and is easily understood as being based on the root גדל, just as that of ε' ("as women made great") and ζ' ("among [ἐν < בְּ?] women made great"). The rendering of σ', μετὰ στίφους, "as columns," probably presupposes the same military understanding as that of G, V, T. The rendering of αλ' seems to be derived from the root גלה.

12　שָׂמַתְנִי　σ' and V (v. 11; [*anima mea*] *conturbavit me*) seem to have the same understanding of the text: "[my soul] has confused me." But how did they read it? Some scholars, e.g., Tournay ("Les chariots," 290), think that this translation presupposes שַׂמַּתְנִי, from the verb שׂמם. The only merit of this suggestion seems to be the lack of a plausible alternative since (a) the Hebrew verb in the *qal* is only used as intransitive, "to be desolated, appalled," and (b) its meaning is strongly negative, and even if one assumes an unusual transitive use here, hardly covers the element of confusion in a more positive sense. Garbini (*Cantico*, 98, 160) reads שממתני as a *qal* form with a transitive sense and the unusual meaning "to snatch away": "*mi ha rapito il carro . . . .*"

　　עַמִּי־נָדִיב:　The versions do nothing to solve the meaning of the Hebrew, but only testify to the riddle it poses. It is translated as a proper name, "Aminadab," by G and V (v. 11); α', ⟨θ'⟩, and S, translating נדיב, have "my (α' ⟨θ'⟩; for α' see Field, *Origenis Hexaplorum*, Auctarium) willing people," whereas σ' and ε', doing the same, have "leading people."

7:1　הַשּׁוּלַמִּית　The Hexaplaric witnesses have tried to find a meaning in the word. α' and ε' in rendering "living in peace" were guided by the root שׁלם; σ' rendered "the spoliated," which probably goes back to the root שׁלל (Schleusner, *Thesaurus*, 5:64 f.). The same holds good for α' and σ' in the second occurrence (בשולמית).

　　שׁוּבִי שׁוּבִי[2]　The omission in 4QCant[a] is based on letter count. Since practically

the whole line is illegible, it is not certain whether the omission concerns the
first or the second occurrence of שׁובי שׁובי (DJD XVI, 204).

בַּשּׁוּלַמִּית   See comment at הַשּׁוּלַמִּית.

כִּמְחֹלַת הַמַּחֲנָיִם: Already the ancient witnesses did not understand this expression. ε' ("going past as a chorus of the camps"), and S have rendered כמחלת as
a singular, whereas G, σ', and V have translated it as a plural. G, ε', and S,
moreover, have expanded the phrase with a participle "going/going past/going
down." In σ' ἐν looks like a translation of the preposition בּ (ex כּ), followed by
τρώσεσι, "wounds," which seems to presuppose a derivation from the root חלל
(Schleusner, *Thesaurus*, 5:350; cp. σ' at Ezek 30:11 and Ps 77:11). All witnesses
have rendered מחנים as "camps," rather than as the name of a city. This holds
good also for T, with "the camps (משׁריתא) of Israel and Judah."

5 בְּרֵכוֹת   The preposition "as" is sometimes added for stylistic reasons in translation; see v. 3 and 5:11, 14. In this case, however, the preposition may have
dropped out in M through haplography, although certainty is impossible. It is to
be noted that כּ is used in the other comparisons in vv. 5 and 6. On these
grounds, a number of exegetes emend the Hebrew, e.g., F. Horst (apparatus
BHS) and Rudolph (*Ruth/Hohes Lied/Klagelieder*, 169).

7 אַהֲבָה   Field (*Origenis Hexaplorum*, 2:422) quotes ἀγαπητή as the reading of
αλ'. In a footnote he states that this must be σ'. In his Auctarium to *Origenis
Hexaplorum*, Field quotes from another source as the reading of σ' ἀγάπη. See
also the comment at 2:7.

בַּתַּעֲנוּגִים: The Hebrew "in delights" hardly makes sense. G supports M with ἐν
τρυφαῖς (+ σου) as do σ' ([ἀγαπητὴ] ἐν σπατάλαις, "[loved one] in delights";
cp. preceding comment), and V (v. 6; [*carissima*] *in deliciis*). α' agrees with S
(ܒܬ ܦܘܢܩܐ) in "daughter of delights" (cp. Mic 1:16; 2:9). This reading gives a
much better sense and presupposes only haplography of ת in the Hebrew text.
The emendation is accepted among others by Würthwein ("Das Hohelied," 64),
Gerleman, (*Ruth/Hohelied*, 202) and Barthélemy (*CTAT*, 5, *ad loc.*). "Daughter
of delights" is then in apposition to אהבה, "love," used as *abstractum pro concreto* for "loved one."

0 שִׂפְתֵי יְשֵׁנִים: שׂפתי has been read as שׂפתי, "my lips," by G and S. All witnesses,
except T, have "*and* teeth," reading the copula instead of the י, S having moreover the suffix: "my teeth." T seems to presuppose M with "the dead were re-
sembling a sleeping man." Some commentators think the Masoretic text can be
translated as it is, e.g., Gerleman (*Ruth/Hohelied*, 203) and Keel (*Das Hohelied*,
232), but their (different) interpretations are less than convincing. Many commentators, therefore, emend the text on the basis of the versions. Since in coor-
dinated nouns the possessive suffix has to be added to each of them (Gesenius/
Kautzsch, *Grammatik*, §135m), the second word must be emended to וִשֵׁנַי (e.g.,
Rudolph, *Ruth/Hohes Lied/Klagelieder*, 174, and Horst, apparatus *BHS*). The מ
is explained as enclitic by, e.g., Murphy (*Song of Songs*, 184). There are, however, no certain examples of enclitic מ after a possessive suffix; the few examples of Hummel ("Enclitic *Mem*," 99–100) are hypothetical. Besides the above
emendation, the first word is emended to בשׂפתי by Rudolph (*Ruth/Hohes
Lied/Klagelieder*, 174). Because the verb occurs only here, it is, however, impossible to establish whether it is transitive or intransitive.

3 אם   That the lack of a *maqqep̄* in M^L is a copyist's error and not on purpose is
clear from the fact that אם has no accent.

8:2 תְּלַמְּדֵנִי   The variant reading of G and S actually consists of an addition and an omission. After "to the house of my mother," the two witnesses have added "and to the chamber of her who bore me" in assimilation to 3:4, after which תלמדני was left untranslated. Syh has combined G and M by adding to G's translation between asterisk and obelos ܐܠܦܬܢܝ, "you have taught me." The addition occurs also in four codices; see Field (*Origenis Hexaplorum*, 2:422). La follows G, except La[Ambr], which also combines the two readings: *et in secretum eius quae concepit me docebis me.*

מִיַּיִן הָרֶקַח   In M הרקח, "spice," must be understood as in apposition to "wine," "wine, that is spice," meaning "spiced wine." G has a genitive construction which seems to presuppose מִיֵּין הָרֶקַח. σ' has . . . ἠρτυμένου, "(from) spiced (wine)," V *ex vino condito* (same meaning), and S "from my sweet wine." σ' and V could have both resulted from reading the text as a genitive construction and from reading it in conformity with M. S, with "my wine," must have read the second word as in apposition.

5 יְלָדַתְךָ:   G, σ', V read the Hebrew as a participle. S has the ambiguous ܝܠܕܬܟܝ (with 2 f. sg. sfx.), which can be both perfect and participle. The early Peshitta-mss leave this case undecided: 6h13 has no vocalization; 7a1 and 8a1 have probably a perfect, whereas 9c1 has a participle. The three editions, Lee, Urmia and Mosul, all have a participle. In spite of the reading of the versions, it remains very doubtful whether the Hebrew form should be emended to a participle, as in the apparatus of *BHS*, since the result is a repetition of the previous clause and a tautology (Rudolph, *Ruth/Hohes Lied/Klagelieder*, 180). M has a meaningful sequel to the previous clause: "was in labor . . . was in labor, bore you."

6 שַׁלְהֶבֶתְיָה: Mishael ben Uzziel mentions this case as one of the eight cases where the text of Ben Naftali differs from that of Ben Asher: שלהבת־יה (Lipschütz, "Kitāb al-Khilaf," 16).

13 הַיּוֹשֶׁבֶת   Both the י and the ו have a dot. A likely explanation is that the first dot is the original *ḥolem*, and that when the ו, which is certainly secondary, was added later on together with its own dot, the first dot was not deleted. Alternatively, the first dot (*ḥolem*) was mechanically and erroneously added when the *šûreq* was inserted. As it is now, no *dāḡeš* in the י can be discerned. It is, however, a likely assumption that this *dāḡeš* was later on covered by the ו. For the place of the *dāḡeš* in a י, compare, e.g., on the same page of M[L] שֶׁיַּעֲמֹל (Qoh 1:2) and שֶׁיִּהְיוּ (Qoh 1:11).

QOHELETH

1:1 מֶלֶךְ בִּירוּשָׁלָ͏ִם: M is supported by Syh, which has "Israel" (present in G) under obelos. ירושלם is supported by G, where Ἰσραήλ seems to be a facilitation, inspired by (but not identical to) v. 12, where ἐπὶ Ἰσραήλ translates על ישראל. On a strictly textual basis, M is to be retained.

2 קֹהֶלֶת   In the seven occurrences of the name קהלת (1:1, 2, 12; 7:27; 12:8, 9, 10), G reads the article only three times (1:2; 7:27; 12:8), always in the expression אמר הקהלת. G is supported by M in 12:8, and indirectly in 7:27 (אמרה קהלת). In 1:2, where the proto-M text omitted the article (אמר קהלת), an as-

similation to 1:1 (דברי קהלת) is far more likely than an assimilation to 7:27 or 12:8 in G, which is a very literalistic version regarding the presence or absence of the article – G Qoh shows no reluctance to translate the term without the article.

‎3 עֲמָלֹו   The word עמל usually appears in this context with the 3 sg. sfx. (2:22, 24; 3:13; 4:8; 5:14, 17, 18; 8:15), which explains the presence of the sfx. here too in M as an assimilation to the usual form. Aquila's reading without the sfx. is supported by S, which everywhere else attests the sfx. found in M (also with the 1 sg. sfx.: 2:10, 18, 19; comp. 2:20 where S supports M כל־העמל without sfx.). The original form should be either בכל־עמל or, better, בכל־העמל (see 2:20).

הַשָּׁמֶשׁ:   In the Leiden edition of S, D.J. Lane, according to the general rules of the edition, edits "under the sun" with the great majority of the Syriac witnesses against Codex Ambrosianus, in which "under the sky" is said to be an error "by assimilation to familiar or nearby phrases" ("Qoheleth," iv); similarly in 1:13. But the "familiar form" which is also the nearest one (v. 9) is "under the sun," and this expression is even more frequent in S than in M. In M there are 27 occurrences of "under the sun" against three of "under the sky," in the Codex Ambrosianus the figures are 28 against two (not counting 'pluses' like 3:9), and in the rest of the Syriac tradition "under the sun" has pervaded the whole book. That tendency in the scribal transmission is a clear feature of the Syriac tradition; it is also attested in v. 13 by a large majority of Syriac witnesses, alongside a number of Masoretic mss., T, V (see there). We can conclude that it is the other Syriac mss. that assimilate to the more familiar "under the sun" in this case. Conversely, it is difficult, if not impossible, to say that the Codex Ambrosianus assimilates; this early ms. attests an original reading that cannot be said to be under the influence of M or G here.

From the text transmission standpoint, "under the sky" is clearly the *lectio difficilior,* while "under the sun" assimilates to the frequent form and is probably conditioned by the context of v. 5, as is the case with some witnesses in v. 13 in relation to v. 14. On literary grounds, a case can be made in favour of "under the sky"; see the development of v. 4.

5 וְזָרַח   There are two variations on this word, with respect to the conjunction and to the verbal form (perfect vs. participle). The cj., attested in M and G, introduces circularity in the thought and fits the poetic expression of vv. 5-6, meaning that what is described is already iteration. Conversely its omission (V Hie[lem] S) seems to be a facilitation, as does its addition before זוֹרֵחַ in T and Jerome's *Vorlage* of v. 5b. The cj. with the first word must be kept, with M and G. It might be the cause of vocalizing the verb as pf. in M and ⟨α'⟩, but the ptc. is supported by G, which translates most ptc. in vv. 5-7 with the present, except for the one at the end of v. 5 for obvious stylistic reasons. The ptc. is also supported by ⟨σ'⟩ V and S, in so far as the diacritical points of Codex Ambrosianus are reliable. A good translation of our preferred reading is to be found in KJV: "The sun also ariseth, and the sun goeth down."

שׁוֹאֵף   All witnesses support M. Jerome reports a Hebrew *soeph.* G ἕλκει for שאף *desire* is attested in other books of the Greek Bible showing a rather literal translation (Jer 14:6; Ps 119:131). The α' revision, εἰσπνεῖ, is most probably inspired by the expression ἄνεμον ἑλκύειν in Jer 2:24; 14:6. The interpretation by σ'-θ', "to return," is quoted in Jerome's commentary as *recurrit;* it becomes *revertitur* in V, and is also found in S ܗܦܟ. Such an interpretation is influenced by v. 7 and might be based on an "equivalence" established between Hebrew שאף and the Aramaic ptc. תאב, thus eliminating the subjective notion of desire in order to avoid the common ancient Near Eastern personification of the sun in its journey. Both texts of T clearly reflect M. As to Graetz's suggestion (*Kohélet*, 56) to emend to שב || אף זורח, it is contradicted by all the witnesses although it would have been an easier text. The *zaqep̄ qaṭan* should be placed on this word as supported by all the versions as well as Rashi and Ibn Ezra; see also Wickes, *Accentuation*, 141. The interpretation of T's text שחיף in Jacob Ben Ḥayyim's edition is also found in ms. 110 of BN Paris; in most other mss., the text has been facilitated with a simple transcription of the Hebrew (שאיף).

10 יֵשׁ דָּבָר שֶׁיֹּאמַר G ὃς λαλήσει καὶ ἐρεῖ may be no more than an interpretation of what is found in M, with יש being interpreted as the mark of eventuality (ὃς λαλήσει καὶ ἐρεῖ may be read as a conditional sentence: "If somebody speaks, and says . . ."; see Kühner/Blass/Gerth, *Grammatik*, 2:441) and the relative of שיאמר being logically anticipated. S follows G. We are confronted here with two revisions of G assigned to σ'. One is transmitted by Jerome, who can be trusted: *Putasne est qui possit dicere;* "as if he had read: ἆρα ἔστι τις ὃς ἐρεῖ," says Field. The σ' text, as is very often the case, is the base for V: *nec valet quisquam dicere*. The other text, assigned (wrongly) to σ', edited by Nobilius and Field, is far more literal and resembles Aquila's style: ἆρα ἔστι τι ὃ ἐρεῖ τις (where ἔστι τι stands for יש דבר). It is not surprising to find an equivalent of this in the literalistic translation of Jerome's commentary, written ten years before, *estne verbum de quo dicatur.*

The first text of σ' quoted above seems to be a stylistic revision of the second one, as Symmachus often tries to do with Aquila's renderings.

Although the vocalization of דבר as a ptc. cannot be entirely ruled out (see G S), there is no clear evidence of such a variant reading, which would be bad Hebrew, in any case. M is not only the *lectio difficilior* here, but preserves the basic double meaning of דָּבָר on which Qoheleth seems to build his device (see v. 8).

הָיָה[2] The pl. in G T and Jerome's works may be translational, as in 1:16; 2:7a, 9 and 4:16. It is to be noted, however, that in most cases the sg. may just as well be a theologically motivated change – here, because of the possible misinterpretation of לעולמים, and in 4:16 as a subsequent adaptation to 1:10. In 1:16, "all (the kings) who were before me over Jerusalem" may have raised a problem in regard to the pseudepigraphy of the book, with 2:9 being a subsequent adaptation to 1:16. Regarding the note of *BHS*, which recommends reading the pl. with some Masoretic mss., it must be noted that only ms. 17 of Kennicott attests such a plural (a ms. dated by Kennicott to the mid-thirteenth century), and de Rossi, who strives to find some support for the pl., finds only two or three medieval liturgical mss. and the first hand of two others (187, 386), the last being uncertain. All these are late mss., not representative enough of the Masoretic tradition.

13 הַשָּׁמָיִם The assimilation of תחת השמים to the usual תחת השמש is attested here by some Masoretic mss., T, and a correction of the Sinaiticus. It was already a fact in Jerome's *Vorlage* – V as well as the lemma of his commentary support it against M and G. This phenomenon of assimilation, reinforced here by the

proximity of v. 14, is even more conspicuous in the Syriac tradition; see our comment on 1:3 הַשֶּׁמֶשׁ.

הוּא | The reading assigned to σ' in the margin of Syh (ܗܘ ܕܝܢ ܗܘ ܗܘܝܘ ܕܒܪ) probably renders the pronoun of M. Field expresses surprise at the first pronoun; the repetition most likely points toward the possibility of interpreting the pronoun in the text of M as both copula and demonstrative.

אֱלֹהִים   G Qoh is careful in translating the article, including the case of אלהים. There are 40 occurrences of the word in M, 42 in G, and only four divergences between them, where G attests the article against M in 1:13; 3:10; 7:18; 8:13. Thus, G might reflect a *Vorlage* with a *slight* tendency to implement the determiner before אלהים. But its omission here (M) has theological consequences: 1:13 is the first mention of God in the book, and אלהים without the article appears as a proper name. This might be a correction stressing Qoheleth's faith in God and personal relationship with him, in a context where people not acquainted with paradoxical thought could see a kind of philosophical relativism. It is to be noted that the parallelism האדם // האלהים of G's *Vorlage* is superior. Omission of the article in M might reflect the same correction in 7:18 for the "god" a man fears. The two other similar divergences ה/אלהים are 3:10, a parallel to 1:13, and 8:13, the exact counterpart of 7:18. Note that in three other places G agrees with M in omitting the determiner in the construct chains מתת אלהים (3:13; 5:18), שבועת אלהים (8:2).

4 שֶׁנַּעֲשׂוּ   The tendency to replace the relative אשר by -ש is attested in 4QQohᵃ 7:19, 20, where M has, respectively, אשר היו and אשר יעשה. Though in 4QQohᵃ 7:19, 20, the relative ש is separated from what follows by a small lacuna, it can be clearly distinguished since it begins a column, so there could be no א before it; see DJD XVI, 225–26.

5 לִתְקֹן   According to Driver ("Problems," 225): "All the ancient Vss and the parallel verb, as well as the context, demand a passive rather than an intransitive form of the verb; hence לְתֻקַּן (Graetz) or לְהִתָּקֵן (Siegfried) have been proposed." Driver suggests that the *pual* inf. cstr. לְתֻקַּן has been missed by the Masoretes. However, the use of this verb is peculiar to Qoh in biblical Hebrew, and its two other occurrences are *piel* (7:13; 12:9), so that a *pual* form would have been more easily read and preserved than the intransitive *qal* here. Thus, the *qal* would clearly be the *lectio difficilior*. Moreover, while "missing" the *pual,* the Masoretes would have chosen a *nifal* rather than the *qal,* which is attested only here. So the *qal* of M must be an old tradition. And strict parallelism is not so much to be expected in Qoh as to impose a strictly passive form here (parallel to לְהִמָּנוֹת). M can be understood as a stative verb (BDB) and translated with KJV: "That which is crooked cannot be made straight," or NEB: "What is crooked cannot become straight."

לְהִמָּנוֹת: M, supported by G, is quoted in a midrashic narrative about Hillel: "Bar He He said to Hillel : that word להמנות, it should be להמלות" (*b.Hag.* 9b). In this verse the root חסר seems to call for מלא, as in the sentence of *b.Ber.* 16b: המקום ימלא חסרונך "May God fill your lack." But precisely for that reason, it is difficult to imagine how the verb מלא (even if the inf. is written המלות), which is so fitting here, would have generated מנות of M. The weight of the witnesses as well as the logic of scribal alteration clearly favor M. On the other hand, the weight of M G is partly counterbalanced by the agreement between σ' and S; and the form להמנות as it has always been interpreted, although it gives some meaning, is not satisfactory. The logic of the context as well as the development of the themes חסר and מלא in Qoh (1:7-8; 6:2, 7) call for מלא, which could have occurred without א – for confusion of ל״א and ל״ה in late biblical Hebrew, see GKC, § 75 *nn-rr*. Strangely enough, there is a complement to the verb in the reading assigned to θ' in Syh: ܠܚܘܫܒܢܐ ܡܣܬܚܒܘ; the same is true in σ' ἀναπληρῶσαι ἀριθμόν, where the conflated form suggests that the hesitation between the two readings is rather old.

16   הִגְדַּלְתִּי   There are three occurrences of the verb גדל in the book: 1:16; 2:4, 9. G Qoh probably translates a *qal* of גדל here, as in 2:9; compare 2:4, where the *hifil* has been translated with the active voice of μεγαλύνω. The assimilation to 2:9 was tempting and facilitates the text; moreover, the content of v. 16 requires the reading of M which is *difficilior* and provides a better literary unit.

  עַל־יְרוּשָׁלַ͏ִם   The text with the prep. ב (G V S) could be an assimilation to 2:7, 9 (see also 1:1, 12), but the text with על (M) might be intended to ensure the attribution of the book to Solomon in late transmission, with 1:1 referring either to the direct son of David or to any other descendant of the lineage of David. Numerous medieval Masoretic mss. agree with the variant of G.

17   וָדַעַת   דעת must be understood as a second complement of the verb לדעת, and the *zaqep* should be moved from חכמה to דעת. If דעת were an inf. cstr. it should be introduced with ל, parallel to the preceding לדעת חכמה (any other construction with the two following words makes odd Hebrew). T has this complement after the following הוללות of M. For the meaning of the sentence, see the next case.

  הוֹלֵלוֹת   There are five occurrences of הוללות in the Hebrew Bible, all in Qoh: 1:17; 2:12; 7:25; 9:3; 10:13. In M only 10:13 is vocalized sg. הוֹלֵלוּת, which is probably the original abstract form of the noun making up a hendiadys with סִכְלוּת (1:17; 2:12; 7:25; 10:13). The plural endings in 2:12 and 7:25 follow the same interpretation as in 1:17 (see hereafter). G supports the sg. everywhere else, hesitating mainly between παραφορά "derangement of mind, madness," and περιφορά, "error, deviation" – a hesitation that might originate in the scribal transmission. Qoh 1:17 is the only place where G does follow M's pl., for the sake of interpretation. In effect, it was difficult to accept that Qoheleth had "applied his heart" to madness and stupidity as well as to wisdom and knowledge. In M the pl. was enough to lead the reader to a meaning other than "madness." Breaking with the preceding sg. of חכמה ודעת, the pl. הוללות may refer to attitudes or actions explored by Qoheleth. A second intervention was substituting שׁ for ס in the following word, which allowed reading שׂכלות "understanding" (cf. G S T) instead of סכלות "stupidity," which is the usual form (2:3, 12, 13; 7:25; 10:1, 13). In 1:17, G παραβολάς and ἐπιστήμην reflect precisely these two features of M; the pair of words has been changed to a positive meaning. This means that שׂכלות, translated ἐπιστήμη instead of ἀφροσύνη, may have been present already in the Hebrew model of G. As to the rendering of הוללות by παραβολάς, it may be noted that it forms an inclusio on this theme with G 12:9.

The hypothesis presented by Gordis (*Koheleth – The Man*, 202) that ΠΑΡΑΒΟΛΑΣ would be an inner-Greek corruption of ΠΑΡΑΦΟΡΑΣ: (1) is graphically unlikely; (2) ignores the fact that הוללות plural is an exception in G Qoh; (3) ignores the agreement between M שׂכלות and G ἐπιστήμη; (4) and finally, ignores the literary inclusio made by this word in G Qoh (1:17–12:9). These features clearly support an interpretative work of the translator along the same lines as M.

T* is quoted according to Zamora-Salamanca and Urbinas Ebr. 1 against Sperber (הולהולתא). T interprets הוללות as חולחולתא דמלכותא "political maneuvering," which is another midrashic attempt to understand הוללות וסכלות in a positive way. It is interesting to note that in 9:3, where the word is applied to the perversion of humankind, T gives only חולחולתא, a translation suggesting the same line of semantic interpretation as the Greek rendering περιφέρεια. Here T moves this "political maneuvering" between wisdom and knowledge, the two preceding words in the text. The source of the targumic interpretation is Rabbi Hanina bar Pappa in *Midr. Qoh.* 1, §11, on Qoh 2:12. In M the pl. of 1:17 has pervaded the other occurrences in the book, 2:12; 7:25; 9:3, with the exception of 10:13, where the sg. is protected by the sg. adjective רעה.

Against the conjunctive accent of M under ודעת, the text is best translated: "I applied my heart to know wisdom and knowledge, madness and folly" (see NEB).

וְשִׂכְלוּת   See the commentary on the preceding word הוללות.

יָדַעְתִּי   The G text of B 998 S with the pronoun (> A) most probably reflects a Hebrew *Vorlage*. The presence of the pronoun in other Greek mss. makes G nearer to M. If Old Greek does have the pronoun, the question is: Which one is the older Hebrew text, the one with the missing pronoun (= M) or the one with the pronoun following the verb (= G*)? Both are possible. On one hand, omission is more expected in this context than addition, which speaks against M. On the other hand, addition (= G) may result from assimilation to the nearby verse 2:1. The cj. found in V S is a spontaneous facilitation. As for T, after moving הוללות, interpreted as "political maneuvering," between חכמה ודעת, it interprets שכלות ידעתי as a unit, with the sense of "I found out to know that . . ." T places a cj. on the finite verb of M, as V and S do, but this might well be part of the targumic reworking of the verse.

2   מְהוֹלָל   Instead of מהולל, S read מה הללו "what are these?" with the pl. demonstrative of Mishnaic Hebrew (Segal, *Mishnaic Hebrew*, 41). T "mockery" reflects a substantive.

3   תַּרְתִּי בְלִבִּי לִמְשׁוֹךְ בַּיֵּין   Without any support, Rahlfs edits a text in harmony with M, κατεσκεψάμην ἐν καρδία μου τοῦ ἑλκῦσαι εἰς οἶνον. Rahlfs relied on Klostermann's conjectural reconstruction (*De libri Coheleth*, 58), only adding to Klostermann's conjecture an article before the infinitive. With this addition of Rahlfs, the reconstruction closely resembles the style of G Qoh, which uses an article to render the prep. ל before an inf. cstr. Among the witnesses of G, only 998 with ελκυσε *could* be an alteration of ελκυσαι (= α'), as suggested by the editors of the papyrus (influenced by Klostermann-Rahlfs, they also conjecture κατεσκεψάμην ἐν in the preceding lacuna). Whatever the origin of the altered form (ελκυσε) in 998, it is doubtful that this witness represents Old Greek here, in that it lacks the article before the infinitive, which would be the normal rendering in G Qoh for the infinitive complement with preposition ל. The conjecture of the editors of 998 for the lacuna is unnecessary: the scribe may have read [κατεσκεψάμην εἰ ἡ] before καρδία μου ἔλκυσε, this last word being understood as an aorist without the augment, under the influence of the following one, and having the same grammatical subject: (καρδία μου) ὡδήγησεν. This reading gave the whole phrase a coherent meaning. Such a defective aorist without aug-

ment occurs sometimes in late Greek, and is not very surprising for a verb as unstable as ἑλκύω/ἕλκω.

Regarding G, ὡς οἶνον is supported by θ' according to Syh; a Hebrew model introducing the simile כיין (instead of ביין M S T Hie) might have been the source of G's text. The rest of G, except the cj. at the beginning of the verse, would then be a subsequent interpretation, and not a witness for a textual variant: "And I examined my heart (to know) if it will draw *like* wine (my flesh)." The cj. is also attested in the revised text attributed to α'-σ': καὶ ἐνοήθην, as well as in θ' according to Syh (καὶ διενοήθην). V *abstrahere a vino* (= למשוך מיין) is contextual and hyper-interpretation. In his commentary, Jerome points out the opposition between משך and נהג and translates: *consideravi in corde meo ut traherem in vino carnem meam, et cor meum deduxit me in sapientiam*. Notwithstanding the moralizing aspect of so sharp a contrast, the point is important for the interpretation and has been recognized by Hitzig (*Prediger Salomo's,* 136), an assiduous reader of Jerome.

M is supported by the versions, particularly the form בלבי (ἐν τῇ καρδίᾳ μου α'-σ' θ' Hie), and has been adopted by most commentators from the nineteenth century until now. משך is easily understood with the figurative meaning "to draw, attract, stimulate." Mishnaic usage, mentioned by Delitzsch (*Hoheslied und Koheleth*), developed the meaning "rejoice (attract the heart)" (*b.Hag.* 14a), which is also how S understood it (ܡܣܒ *pael*): "to make cheerful, to delight." The meaning of M is: "I explored with my heart, rejoicing (drawing) my flesh with wine, while my heart behaved in wisdom." Through this paradoxical attitude, the wise can search even folly (סכלות): "and seizing hold of folly . . ." to discern what is good to do (end of verse).

נֹהֵג   V *(ut animum meum) transferrem (ad sapientiam)*, is an interpretation similar to that of σ' ἵνα (τὴν καρδίαν μου) μεταγάγω (εἰς σοφίαν). G's aorist follows upon the interpretation it presents in v. 3a; see apparatus commentary above. S is given without diacritical points in the Leiden text, but it is to be noted that Codex Ambrosianus, as well as the Lee edition, have a diacritical point indicating a ptc. M is *difficilior* and may be considered to have good literary value. As mentioned in BDB the semantic value is probably that of late Hebrew: "Yet my heart behaving in wisdom (= keeping wisdom)." The various renditions of the versions all resemble a "dynamic equivalent" translation.

בְּסִכְלוּת   All the known witnesses of G attest ἐπ' εὐφροσύνῃ, but this last word is specialized in G Qoh for Hebrew שמחה (2:1, 2, 10, 26; 5:19; 7:4; 8:15; 9:7). Thus, ἐπ' εὐφροσύνῃ is probably an inner corruption of ἐπ' ἀφροσύνῃ, as edited by Rahlfs, who relies on the Latin translation in Jerome's commentary. McNeile (*An Introduction*, 157) quotes some passages that exhibit precisely the same confusion between the two words in some Greek mss. of Qoh. S ܒܣܘܟܠܬܢܘܬܐ, "with prudence, intelligence," is an interpretation similar to the one found in M at 1:17. Codex Ambrosianus of S attests the same interpretation again in 2:12, where it could also be the original Peshitta (against Leiden's edition). T* בשטות עולימיא is taken from ms. Zamora, edited by Diez Merino, and Urbinas Ebr. 1. Sperber has שעת עולימיא.

4   מַעֲשַׂי   Against G, there is no attestation of מעשה sg. + 1 sg. sfx. in the Hebrew Bible. Out of 21 occurrences of the word in M Qoh, twenty are read in G as substantives; of these, only five divergences from M are found (2:4; 5:5; 7:13; 8:17 [first]; 11:5), which means that G is as literalist in its rendition of this

word as in the rest of its translation. Moreover, the same word מַעֲשֵׂי was recognized by G at v. 11 as pl. + 1 sg. sfx.

M seems *facilior* here: (1) It is the currently attested form; (2) It alludes to all Solomon's deeds detailed in the following verses; (3) There is no reason why the literalist Greek translator should have transformed the common pl. into a sg. The text of G with the sg. + 1 sg. sfx. could express, instead of the magnificence of deeds, the increasing grandeur in action; compare הגדלתי (. . .) חכמה in 1:16; see Lauha, *Kohelet*, 47. Nevertheless, this reading remains a bit strange to the ear of the Bible reader and this is why it has not been proposed as a preferred reading in the apparatus.

7   קָנִיתִי   Like several medieval Hebrew mss., S has assimilated to the beginning of vv. 5, 6, 8, as well as to the complement found twice in v. 7: היה לי.

  וּבְנֵי־בַיִת הָיָה לִי   The adverb הרבה, which occurs in 7b, seems superfluous there, where the final clause: "more than any who were before me in Jerusalem," suffices to express the great quantity of flocks and herds he possessed. Conversely, it seems to be necessary in 7a, where it would apply to the slaves and their children born in the house, a reality known in wealthy families. This explains why Jerome, who states in his commentary that his text reads v. 7a without the adverb, nevertheless moves the adverb to the end of v. 7a in V. It also explains why S attests the adverb in both places.

  הָיָה   The pl. of the verb is a natural facilitation in this context. If it had been the original text, there should have been no reason for a later scribe to introduce the sg. here. According to Gordis: "the masculine singular verb is either used in neuter fashion (. . .) or is the result of attraction to בית" (*Koheleth – The Man*, 207); see GKC, §145*u*.

  מִכֹּל שֶׁהָיוּ   As indicated in *BHS,* several medieval Hebrew mss. attest a sg. here, but the Tiberian text is supported by all the ancient versions and is to be preferred.

8   וְזָהָב   In the Greek tradition, B 998 A attest a second גם before זהב. The omission of a second καί γε would be expected in the Greek tradition, and conversely, its addition would be rather unexpected. Thus, these witnesses probably represent the Old Greek. The omission of גם in the pre-Masoretic tradition *might* be a spontaneous assimilation to the parallel pairs of words in the verse. The case, however, remains uncertain.

  וּסְגֻלַּת   Although the pl. could be translational, the weight of the witnesses supporting the pl. deserves consideration, particularly in view of the *hapax* this pl. would represent in the Bible, where סגלה is always sg. (Exod 19:5; Deut 7:6; 14:2; 26:18; Mal 3:17; Ps 134:4; Qoh 2:8; 1 Chr 29:3). α' οὐσίας with the meaning "riches, estates" is most probably accusative pl. in that position in the sentence; cp. Jerome: *et substantias*. σ' πεκούλια supports a pl. as well. The only version against the pl. would be S, where the difference depends solely on the *seyame* (diacritical points for pl.).

  שָׁדָּה וְשִׁדּוֹת: Both words שדה ושדות are attested in the entire tradition of the text. The only potential variant is a pl. of the first word, which is found in σ' (*mensarum species et appositiones*), S (ܟܣܘܬܐ) and Jerome (lemma: *ministros vini et ministras;* V: *scyphos et urceos*). The pl. suggests that a מ instead of a ה was read in שדה – i.e., שדם ושדות, echoing שרים ושרות a few words before. The interpretation of the versions relies on the Aramaic meaning ("pour out") of שדא: "cups" α' Hie; "channels" for baths T; "channels" for gardens S, although

the last word of S is rather enigmatic. S reads the two words: ܫ̈ܩܝܬܐ ܘܫܩܝܬܐ.
The first one presents no difficulty, meaning either *irrigatio* or *canalis*. For the
second one, Brockelmann (*Lexicon Syriacum,* 385a) offers *pocillatrix,* which is
feminine for "cup-bearer," but it can be suspected that he does so only to get a
meaning for Qoh 2:8, which he cites. Similarly, Payne Smith, *Thesaurus,* vol.
II, col. 4281, cites Qoh 2:8 with the following translation: *pincernae et propina-
trices,* and notes that Gabriel Sionita's interpretation derived from שדא, like G.
The best interpretation of S seems to be that the first word ܫܩܝܬܐ has its ordinary value of "channel, irrigation"; and the second word ܫܩܝܬܐ is to be understood as a f. pl. pass. ptc. of ܫܩܐ meaning here "irrigated land."

As Hitzig (*Prediger Salomo's,* 138) points out, the preceding תַּעֲנוּגֹת, which
probably includes what is spoken about here, means "the delights of love," as in
Cant 7:7 and elsewhere. Moreover, the Bible has a clear tradition about King
Solomon's search for women (1 Kgs 11:3; Cant 6:8), and love's pleasures have
not yet been mentioned in Qoh. So it is probable that these two words refer to
the women loved by Solomon. Salmon Ben Yeruham sees here a synecdoche of
שַׁד "breast" meaning "young woman"; see Barthélemy, *CTAT,* 5, *ad loc.,* and
the vocalization known by Jerome: *sadda et saddot.* For the relationship of the
word to the semantic field of love in semitic languages, see *HALAT* and E. Bons
("Verständnis eines Hapaxlegomenons"). Ibn Ezra reads the words as pertaining
to the root שדד and understands "women prisoners of war." In line with this, it
must be noted that, although textual tradition is unified on שרים ושרות, these
two words fall under suspicion. So, following Ibn Ezra's etymology, the original
reading could have been: "I acquired princes and princesses (שרים ושרות) and
the delights of the sons of men: prisoners of war male and female" – retaining
the m. pl. for the first word with σ', S, and V.

10   מִכָּל[2]   Under the influence of the two preceding prepositions, M assimilates to
the second מכל עמלי, where it is correct.

11   וּבֶעָמָל   σ' is probably not a variant reading but a stylistic harmonization whose
verb is not attested in what has survived of Symmachus' text.

12   וְהוֹלֵלוֹת   In the Greek tradition, B 998 gives παραφορά for הוֹלֵלוֹת, as does A in
7:25. A Theodotionic revised text attests καὶ παρεφέρετο for ויתהלל in 1 Sam
21:14; see Barthélemy (*Études,* 223).

מֶה הָאָדָם   Taking over a suggestion by Budde, *BHS* suggests reading מה יעשה
האדם, inserting a verb in order to facilitate the second part of v. 12b. There is
no need for such a conjecture. The question is: "what is the man . . . ?" which
means: "what is his value?", as rightly analysed by Gordis (*Koheleth – The
Man,* 211), who quotes parallels.

Rahlfs includes the article with the Hexaplaric and minority text of Codex Venetus, bringing G nearer to M, but B 998 S A Complutensis and the majority of
Greek mss. have no article, so G probably did not read an article in its source
text, the translator being very careful to render the presence or absence of deter-
miners. V *quid est inquam homo* translates σ' τί δὲ ὁ ἄνθρωπος (where δέ is
for the initial כִּי). G*'s *Vorlage* probably resulted from a haplography of ה.

הַמֶּלֶךְ   G βουλῆς interprets מלך as Aramaic מְלַךְ "counsel" (cf. Dan 4:24). It is
followed by σ', who seems to give the word the intellectual meaning: παρακο-
λουθέω βουλῇ. As for S, rather than a conflation of M and G (so Euringer, *Der
Masorahtext,* 48), it is an interpretation of the entire half-verse: "who is the
man who will go after the king in judgment, still more with His Maker?" A

similar line of interpretation is represented in T: "what is the profit for a man to pray after the sentence of the King?"

כְּבָר   This word occurs nine times in Qoh and is regularly translated in G and S (except 9:7), so that its absence in these versions is probably indicative of a Hebrew source text without it. Jerome's commentary, *ante (factorem suum),* might be a spatial interpretation of כבר on the basis of some Greek text.

עָשׂוּהוּ:   In view of the question, "what is the man who will come after the king?", the two forms of the answer offered in the witnesses are defensible: "What he has been made already" (M), or: "what he (the king) has made him" (עָשָׂהוּ see V S). The feminine pronoun in G is only a translational adaptation to βουλή, but the verb has been read as sg., as in Hie V and S. While both answers are defensible, M עשוהו might be a theological correction of עָשָׂהוּ, which could appear too strong a warrant for a human subject: only God could make man (7:29). That's why early interpretations understood God as the implicit subject of עשה. This is true of S, Hier and *Midr. Qoh.,* which says: "The Holy One Blessed Be He and his council made him." The verse is best understood if one considers the context. At first, all that Qoheleth had done (עשה vv. 4-9) gave him some pleasure (v. 10), but in the end was shown to be "vanity and chasing the wind" (v. 11); even what he has done (עשה) as a genitor does not satisfy his quest (v. 12). So he turned to consider wisdom and madness, but wisdom, in its turn, appeared to be devoid of any superiority over madness (vv. 13-16), so that Qoheleth came to hate all he had done in wisdom, which he is going to leave to the "man coming after [him]" (vv. 17-18). The development is marked by a progressive parallelism of the themes between action (4-9) and wisdom (13-16) with two respective conclusions which are strongly parallel (11-12 // 17-18). This supports the interpretation of 12b in the light of 18b. T* is read in Urbinas Ebr. 1 and Zamora (Sperber has לי instead of ליה). The meaning of this half verse is either: "For what is the (value of the) man who will come after the king but what he has made him already?" or: "For what is the (value of the) man who will come after the king but what he has already been made?"

3 כִּיתְרוֹן   The vocalization of M^L כִּיתְרוֹן, with a *meteg* after the *hîreq* is supported by M^{L34} and M^Y as well as the Ben Hayyim edition and is most probably the older text against the variant presented in the apparatus of *BHS* : כְּיִתְרוֹן; see GKC, § 24e.

5 אָז   It is often claimed that V and S do not translate אז; but they have made the preceding sentence conditional, introduced by if (*si,* ܐܢ), which may be an elegant way of translating by anticipating the אז of the apodosis. The mss. of G are divided; the omission in part of the tradition could be due to the moving of ἐγώ from the end of the question to the beginning of the subsequent reflection, as Rahlfs himself has it. But the word is confirmed by Jerome in his commentary *(tunc),* which does justice to the text of G, reading it with its own different division of the passage: *Et ut quid sapiens factus sum ego? Tunc abundanter locutus sum in corde meo.* The word אז and the following יותר are lacking in Jerome's lemma, but he himself affirms that what he reads in G (including these two words) is a translation of what he reads in M, only with a different division. So the words are well attested in the early transmission.

אז was a central difficulty in this text; however, it could be given a temporal nuance associated with its logical value: "at that time," i.e., "when I shall arrive at the end of life, like the fool, why shall I have become wiser (than he)?" יותר

is well attested in late Hebrew with such a value. The division of G's *Vorlage* is the one transmitted by Jerome, ending the question at אָנִי and beginning a subsequent reflection with אָז יוֹתֵר דִּבַּרְתִּי. This division goes with the omission of the cj. in (וְ)דִבַּרְתִּי, as attested in G. M seems to be preferable, since יוֹתֵר used adverbially with verb דבר is rather odd; especially in Qoh, where יוֹתֵר is most frequently attested (seven of nine occurrences in the Bible).

הֶבֶל: There are two clues that this 'plus' of G is a later gloss in the transmission of G.

1. G Qoh nowhere uses περίσσευμα as an equivalent for יוֹתֵר or יִתְרוֹן, nor does the rest of the Greek Bible. περισσεία is consistently used for יִתְרוֹן and twice for יוֹתֵר understood as a substantive (6:8; 7:11); elsewhere the translation is περισσός, most often as adverbial accusative.

2. The gloss has two different locations in the ancient mss. of G: in B 998 it is inserted at the end of the verse, as it is in Syriac, while in S A it is found before ὅτι καί γε τοῦτο ματαιότης, as it is in the translation of G by Jerome. The text of the gloss in G Qoh is probably inspired by Luke 6:45; Matt 12:45.

22 כִּי מֶה־הֹוֶה With ὅτι τί γίνεται, Rahlfs brings G near to M by adding τί with one ms. of the 12th century (157) where, according to Holmes-Parsons, it is an addition written in different smaller characters. So G* is to be read without the interrogative: ὅτι γίνεται. G and all ancient witnesses alike have interpreted הֹוֶה as a verbal form of הָיָה. For G the subject of this verb is the content of v. 21: "and great evil (is) (v. 22) since it happens to man in all his labor and the project of his heart." In the other text form (= M) the insertion of מֶה is a facilitation. Though ignoring the meaning of the word, G indirectly witnesses a consonantal text, without מֶה, which makes sense. One should probably vocalize הַוָּה, a word which evokes mainly a desire that is vain and leads to emptiness and corruption (see Ps 55:12), all themes fitting the context (vv. 21, 23) and restoring a strong parallelism with v. 23. A possible translation: "For it is vain desire (emptiness) for a man in all his trouble and project of his heart!" Ambition and projects allow no rest to the heart, even during sleep (v. 23). V *quid enim proderit* is inspired by σ' ὅτι γὰρ περιγέγονεν, except for the interpretation of מה as interrogative.

23 עִנְיָנוֹ Although Jerome shows much hesitation about the right translation of this word (*occupatio, adflictio, distentio, sollicitudo, cura superflua* – a double translation with *adflictio* in 2:26), he usually keeps to the sg. for עִנְיָן in his source text. This in his first translation (the lemma of his commentary) as well as in V. Thus, the pl. in his two translations might reflect a variant reading here (עִנְיָנָיו). It must be noted, however, that he makes an exception when translating *curas* in V 5:2.

24 שֶׁיֹּאכַל Hitzig (*Prediger Salomo's*, 143–44) suggests that a מ has fallen away in the transmission of the text attested by M. G* εἰ μή is supported by a majority of mss. and has been changed into πλήν in hexaplaric mss. Omission of εἰ μή, preferred by Rahlfs, is found in B 998 S. The preferred reading is not only supported by G* S Hie T, but by the parallel expression in 3:22. Although formally *difficilior*, M might be the result of an accident by haplography (-מֶשּׁ being unusual), unless it is the result of an intentional change meant to correct the harsh affirmation that "there is nothing good in man but to eat and drink." The change of the preceding בָּאָדָם into לָאָדָם in the *Vorlage* of G was probably caused by the same difficulty in face of such an affirmation. The original text

might be understood: "there is nothing good in being human but to eat and
drink."

The suggestion by Barthélemy in *CTAT*, 5, *ad loc.*, to read M: "It depends not
on man that he eats and drinks," is interesting but it does not fit the placement
of טוב, and 3:12, which he invokes as evidence, is instead a counterproof to his
proposition for 2:24. V *comedere* echoes σ' (τοῦ) φαγεῖν, but both witnesses
provide no clear evidence for the case.

5 יָחוּשׁ   Rahlfs prefers the Origenian text found in Syh (ܚܘܣ), which is a revised
text and corresponds to a reading assigned to α'-σ' in Syh: (ὡσαύτως) φείσεται
(ܚܘܣ ܢܚܣ). It must be noted that the Greek text read by Origen was already a
mixed form of G and its revisions (Jellicoe, *The Septuagint*, 145). Moreover,
when confronted with variant readings he considered as corruptions, Origen often took from the revisions what he considered to be Old Greek (Swete, *Introduction*, 69; Barthélemy, *Études*, 208). Thus, the Origenian text preferred by
Rahlfs here, similar to the one attributed to α', is most probably a revision of G.
All the direct witnesses of the Greek tradition read πίεται. Regarding the lemma of Jerome: *(quis) parcet,* it is taken from α'-σ' in order to translate יחוש as
another form for יחוס, taking שׂ/שׁ as an equivalent of ס.

Late Hebrew borrows from the Aramaic language a sense of חוּשׁ "to perceive,
to feel." Ben Yehudah in his *Dictionary* (1475b) classifies Qoh 2:25 as the oldest attested occurrence with this meaning; a meaning which makes sense here,
though the Aramaic value was more general (see Ps 141:1). G "to drink" is
probably a contextual interpretation of this meaning (compare v. 24). Modern
philology has found a related Akkadian root *hašāšu* meaning "to rejoice"; cf. V
deliciis affluere. One can either translate: "For who can eat and have pleasure,
if not (coming) from Him?" or: "Who can eat and have any feeling if not from
Him?" For the last word, see the next case.

מִמֶּנִּי: The sfx. here must refer to God; see the end of v. 24. A 1 sg. sfx. referring
to Qoheleth himself fits neither the context nor the usage of חוץ which can
hardly mean "more." With almost all commentators, it is to be read מִמֶּנּוּ –
against Barthélemy in *CTAT*, 5, *ad loc.*, who interprets: "There is no gourmet
nor sensualist but me" as a justification of the affirmation of M at v. 24a: "there
is no good for man to eat and drink."

3 לַהֲרוֹג   The conjectures להרוס and להדוף (Galling) presented in *BHS* have no
support among the witnesses, all of which support M. Moreover, it is quite natural to set "to kill" and "to heal" in opposition, רפא being used for the healing
of wounds (e.g., 2 Kgs 8:29) as well as of illnesses. S spontaneously rendered
רפא with ܐܚܝ "to restore life."

6 עֵת לְבַקֵּשׁ   The text in M G V is *difficilior* and makes sense. S transposes "a time
to search" after "a time to lose," attempting to create some logic: one must lose
something before he looks for it. Such freedom in changing the word order is a
clear tendency of the Syriac Bible.

0 אֱלֹהִים   See the apparatus commentary at 1:13.

1 אֶת־הַכֹּל   The witnesses of G are split, but it is striking that the ones with the
article have it before σύμπαντα, which is not the normal use in G Qoh (see
7:15; 10:19; 11:5); this is the reason Rahlfs conjectures σὺν τὰ πάντα. See also
the apparatus and the commentary on the following word (עָשָׂה).

עָשָׂה   A large majority of Greek witnesses attest the relative ἅ; the relative ὅσα
is attested in 998 261. The witnesses omitting the relative are the first hand of

Codex Sinaiticus and a few minuscules. The relative is to be seriously considered as the original Greek here, against Rahlfs. All the more so if the article before the preceding word was missing in the original Greek; see the apparatus. The source text of G may have had את כל אשר עשה יפה בעתו instead of את הכל עשה יפה בעתו attested in M. It is not easy to determine which text is prior, although G is somewhat *difficilior,* and proto-M might be a theological shift.

12 בָּם   The complement בָּם (M G S T) refers to all that God has made (v. 11a), in which the best thing is to rejoice rather than to explore the whys and wherefores of it (v. 11b). The pl. sfx. is for a singular collective; see GKC, §135*p.* T understands the sfx. as referring to אדם in v. 10, as does S (ܒܗܘܢ) which provides a pl. sfx. on the last word of the verse: *in their lives* (ܒܚܝܝܗܘܢ). Several commentators have followed the solution of S T, although it is an assimilation to 2:24 (Siegfried, *Prediger und Hoheslied*, 41). בחייו at the end is best understood as impersonal: "in one's life," as for הולדו in 7:1 (Gordis, *Koheleth – The Man*, 257).

13 הָאָדָם   Rahlfs edits the text of Codex Vaticanus, bringing G in harmony with M as he so often does. For further discussion, see the apparatus and the commentary at 5:18.

16 הַצֶּדֶק   As noted by Ehrlich (*Randglossen*, 7:67), the parallelism in M is flat: "the place for judgement, there the wickedness, and the place for justice, there the wickedness." Regarding the first member of the parallelism, Qoheleth has surely seen "wickedness" (רֶשַׁע) in the tribunal (M), but in the second half the thought goes on to the cause: this happens where the wicked has taken the place of the righteous, that is, the place of the judge. The second member has been corrected in the making of the proto-M text in order to avoid having the judge (who should be צדיק) be declared "wicked" (רָשָׁע). This is one of a number of places where M attests a revision to soften Qoheleth's criticisms addressed to the "wise" and the "righteous" (e.g., 7:19: 8:1). Thus, the second half is to be read with G. Conversely, in G's source text or its Greek translation, רֶשַׁע in the first member of the parallelism has been wrongly read רָשָׁע by assimilation to the second member, where the opposition is between the righteous and the wicked. M is to be kept in the first member with V S, but corrected in the second member with G: δίκαιος and ἀσεβής. Literally, the verse reads: "Moreover I saw under the sun: in the place of the judgement, there the wickedness and in the place of the righteous, there the wicked."

הָרֶשַׁע: Most mss. of G offer εὐσεβής. Only Complutensis, Aldine, and Grabe have ἀσεβής. It seems that outside these editions ἀσεβής is scarcely attested in the mss.; nevertheless, this is a most common confusion in the Greek manuscript tradition. See further comments on the preceding case הַצֶּדֶק.

17 שָׁם: Horst in *BHK* proposed reading a ptc. שֹׁמֵר, and in *BHS* מֵשִׂם. Some scholars, following Houbigant, read the ptc. שָׂם "he sets." Many conjectures have been offered to correct or interpret the text; for an examination of the conjectures, see Hertzberg, *Der Prediger*, 100–101. Vilchez Lindez (*Eclesiastés*, 250) interprets the word as a substantive for the sake of the parallelism, but this does not fit the introductory preposition על. From the text critical standpoint, there is no way to change the text here, as all the versions agree on this word, and no satisfying conjecture has been proposed as yet.

The comment by Jerome shows that he understands the adverb שם as referring to the world to come, as does T "every deed in that world will be judged there."

Supported by all the witnesses, שָׁם must be understood with Jerome and T as an echo of the two שָׁמָּה of v. 16: "be that as it may, there is a place where justice will be made." A critical edition of G should move ἐκεῖ to the end of v. 17, instead of the beginning of v. 18 as in Rahlfs' edition.

3 לְבָרָם   Irwin ("Eccles. 3:18," 298–99), in view of the context, suggests reading לִבְרָאָם "that he created them." Preceded by a passage on social inequalities, and an affirmition of cosmic universal retribution, "as the cosmic wheel of Fate slowly turns," Qoheleth would now affirm the "bestial nature" of the human species. Irwin cites Ewald's *Syntax* to read ולראות as a continuation of לברם. It must be noted that M may mean לברם, as well, so that it could be more an interpretational problem than a textual case; see the commentary on the next case ולראות.

וְלִרְאֹת   ולראות may be read as a consecutive infinitive used for a finite verb (GKC, §113z, and §114p for the ו of consecution). Such an infinitive comes after a finite verb, so that ולראות is the natural continuation of אמרתי. As noted in GKC: "In most examples of this kind . . . the infinitive with ל virtually depends on an idea of intention (. . .) which is contained in what has preceded." Here Qoheleth, thinking about the human condition (אמרתי בלבי) is led to see (ולראות) "that they are beasts."

Regarding the preceding לברם, it is often proposed to read it as the inf. cstr. of ברר "to test," with a 3 m. pl. sfx. But the idea of testing does not fit the context. It is back in vv. 10-11 that one finds a kind of "test" for human beings. Moreover, that precise semantic value of ברר is not attested elsewhere (*HALAT*, 155). Conversely, ברא + sfx., treated here as a ל"ה verb, is no surprise in a late Hebrew text. Reading ברא with S, we have in M a text that coheres well literarily with what follows. Qoheleth gives a strongly sceptical statement about the particular destiny of humanity among living creatures: "In spite of what is narrated about their creation by God, they are, like beasts, fated to die."

The syntactic function of the infinitive phrase לברם האלהים may be understood in two ways: (1) As a complement depending on a *verbum dicendi* (GKC, §157, n. 2) – although the general rule is to have כי or אשר introducing a dependent clause after verbs like אמר – : "I thought in my heart, about the children of Adam, that God created them, but I saw that they, too, are beasts." (2) As an apposition to על דברת בני האדם (infinitive clauses in apposition: Judg 8:1aβ; Jer 35:8; with inf. abs.: Deut 15:2a; 2 Kgs 19:29aα, see König, *Lehrgebäude* II, 2, §400): "I thought in my heart about the children of Adam – [about] their creation by God – and I saw that they, too, are beasts."

In the versions, where לברם was translated with a finite verb, ולראות became its continuation and it was necessary to vocalize this new verb as *hifil*, with God as subject, since keeping the *qal* would have meant that God had something to discover in his creatures. Most probably all the difficulties in the passage originated in the interpretation of ולראות.

הֵמָּה לָהֶם: G seems to translate גם להם. The text of M, המה להם, is either an alteration of גם להם through dittography: (ב)המה המה להם or a conscious development in order to give a moral perspective to the harsh statement that they are "beasts to each other." G is *difficilior* – it is hard to imagine why it would have been introduced into the text if it is not the original reading. In view of the context, the preposition of להם is to be understood as a ל *relationis,* as suggested by McNeile (*An Introduction,* 64), introducing the meaning: "even in their own estimation." Although human beings apparently have the advantage of raising questions, exploring and thinking, even to themselves they appear to be animals (v. 18), because they are going to die (v. 19), returning to dust like all other creatures (v. 20), and who knows what happens to the spirit of man (v. 21)? That is all they know about their life (v. 22). The transfer of the last word to the next verse in S is probably a late misunderstanding attached to the corruption of the first word of v. 19 (see next case). Both words of the lemma are given in T in the midst of a long paraphrasis.

19　כִּי   The witnesses of G are divided: B and a few mss. have a very suspect negation οὐ, A C Complutensis and others omit the word, mss. S V, followed by a good number of minuscules and Aldine, attest ὡς. The Origenian text according to Syh, chosen by Rahlfs, has ὅτι (= M). Ὡς is the most probable text of G, though uncertain as long as we do not have a larger apparatus and a better critical text of Greek Qoheleth. This last reading reflects a Hebrew כמקרה, assimilating to כמות of the second part of the verse. The omission of ὡς in some mss. of G is probably due to the reading of καί γε αὐτοῖς from v. 18 at the beginning of v. 19. V idcirco could be an interpretation from G ὡς as well as from M כי, though Jerome does not normally render the Hebrew כי with idcirco (in the lemma of his comm., Jerome translates quia = כי). Syriac ܡܛܠ "comes" is a corruption of ܡܛܐ (McNeile, An Introduction, 141) due to the moving of ܠܗܘܢ "to them" from the end of v. 18 to the beginning of v. 19: "to them comes . . ." Originally S probably supported M.

מִקְרֶה   מקרה has the clear meaning of "fate, destiny" throughout the book (2:14; 3:19; 9:2, 3). So it cannot be read as a predicate of בני־האדם and הבהמה in its first two occurrences in this verse, whatever the gymnastics of some scholars to save the absolute state suggested by the Masoretic vocalization. A construct state with səḡôl is not totally out of the question. Though T ארעון could be in the abs. as well as in the cstr. state, the choice of the targumist ("what meets, what happens to") makes it clear that מקרה has been read as a construct.

Siegfried (Prediger und Hoheslied, 43) suggests that we have here an attempt by the Masoretes to introduce the idea of chance through the vocalization, which was their only possibility to intervene. It is a fact that in v. 21 the vocalization of העלה and הירדת by the Masoretes betrays a theological correction of a passage, which some superficial readers could misunderstand as being heterodox to the revelation. Such a fear is already reflected in the late form attested by M for the third occurrence of מקרה in the verse, where M has introduced a cj. before the word. The Masoretic tradition, following in the footsteps of proto-M changes, endeavours to ensure the correct reading of the passage: the common fate of human and animal in the face of life and death is relative to their ignorance of when death comes: "chance is humankind and chance is beast and one common fate . . ." See, along the same lines, the omission of the cj. at the beginning of v. 21 and our comment there.

וּמִקְרֶה[1]   The Targum reading in Sperber, וארום, is an error repeating the first word of the verse instead of the second. The correct text is found in Ben Ḥayyim and ms. Zamora (Díez Merino's edition). For the preferred reading, see the commentary on the first occurrence of מקרה in the verse.

וּמִקְרֶה[2]   See the commentary on the first occurrence of מקרה in the verse.

וּמוֹתַר   This is the only occurrence of מותר in Qoh (elsewhere: Prov 14:23;

21:5). G καὶ τί ἐπερίσσευσεν read: וּמַה־יּוֹתֵר (see 6:8, 11), so too σ' καὶ τί πλέον.

מִי   The omission of the cj. in proto-M creates a separation between v. 20 and v. 21. One may suspect this is a theological revision in line with the Masoretic vocalization of the following הָעֹלָה and הַיֹּרֶדֶת. The cj. introduces a question related to v. 20: "everything is from the earth and goes back to the earth, and who knows what the future will be for the spirit of humans?" Though this is a question addressing human knowledge, it has been slightly corrected in proto-M and M in order that it might not be misunderstood by biased readers as addressing the fate and responsibility of humans before their creator after life (cf. vv. 17-18). For the whole passage in M, see the apparatus commentary on 3:19 מִקְרֶה.

הָעֹלָה   As pointed out in GKC, §100m, the Masoretic vocalization is a theological correction. The same remark goes for הַיֹּרֶדֶת of M, although Gordis argues that this is the trace of "a tendency to vocalize the interrogative *He* with full vowels and dageš" (*Koheleth – The Man*, 228).

הַיֹּרֶדֶת   See the commentary on העלה in this verse.

וּמָיֵד   The lemma of Jerome *et in manibus* is original and reflects a Hebrew reading. It is tempting to adopt it, but the weight of the witnesses supporting the *lectio difficilior* recommends restraint. The cj. in S and T has been moved elsewhere in the sentence.

וְשַׁבֵּחַ   Ehrlich (*Randglossen*, 7:69) considers ושבח to be a scribal error for ושבחתי *piel* as is reflected in the versions. But M may be read as an inf. abs. consecutive for a finite verb; references for such inf. abs. with a pronoun subject are to be found in GKC, §113gg. Such a consecutive infinitive can be understood as a perfect, as the versions do, which would mean there is no real variant here. If there is a real variant – pf. in G σ' Hie S T V – it should be considered an assimilation to v. 1. M has been read as a verbal adjective by Abraham Ibn Ezra and David Qimḥi (*Mikhlol*, 58b); Gesenius (*Thesaurus*², 1352b) sees in it an equivalent of the ptc., and Davidson (*Lexicon*, 697a) classifies it as a late form of the *piel* ptc. – with the dropping of preformative מ – Davidson quotes a few occurrences of the *pual* ptc. with the aphaeresis of מ (*Lexicon*, Table of Paradigms, X. 6). Whatever the choice of the translators or their Hebrew source, there is no ground to emend M. The context recommends translating with a present tense what is most probably an infinitive absolute; see GKC, §113ff; and for more extensive comment on this case, see Isaksson, *Studies*, 63–64; Schoors, *The Preacher Sought*, 178.

עָמָל   G had העמל in its *Vorlage,* since it is very faithful in rendering the determiner (compare the following ἀνδρείαν).

חִבֵּק   The aorist of G might be a gnomic aorist, frequent in proverbs; see Blass/Debrunner/Rehkopf, *Grammatik*, §333. Thus, it is very uncertain that there is a real variant reading here.

וְאֹכֵל   The case is the same as for חבק three words before; see the apparatus commentary. Though the form of S is indeterminate in the edition of Leiden, the diacritical point in Codex Ambrosianus and, above all, the context with the ptc. translation of חבק before, show clearly that S reads as M does. As for T, it renders the following logic: "he does not work (during the summer), then he will not eat (during the winter)."

בְּשָׂרוֹ:   As Prof. Adrian Schenker kindly suggested to me, the pl. of G, followed by Jerome, might be due to the distinction between the general meaning of σάρξ sg. in the Greek Bible and flesh as such. The plural could be inspired by ancient Greek literature, and particularly Homer, who almost always uses the word in the plural and uses it with this very concrete meaning. See Spicq, *Theological Lexicon*, σάρξ.

6 נַחַת   The apparent triteness of such a comparison: "Better one handful of rest than both fists full of toil," has lead some critics to emend it by adding a cj. before נחת and עמל (Ehrlich, *Randglossen*, 7:70). But G and S clearly support M. Regarding σ' μετὰ ἀναπαύσεως, it is a probable interpretation of the word as adverbial accusative. V *cum requie* is, as so often, a Latin translation of σ'. T בהניות נפש "in tranquillity of soul" (literally "in pleasure of soul") follows the same line of interpretation and, contrary to what is suggested in *BHS*, no cj. is supposed by T. According to Gordis (*Koheleth – The Man*, 231), "the two words are undoubtedly adverbial accusatives," the first one meaning "through ease" and the second "through exertion," so they do not need to be emended. Another view of the verse may be gained from נחת, meaning "satisfaction," as pointed out by Gordis himself about 6:5. It is not necessary to work out a logical parallelism; the comparison is between the man satisfied with little and the one always unsatisfied in עמל, "longing for wind," like the jealous of v. 4; this is always עמל in the worst meaning for Qoh. The verse would run this way: "Better one handful of satisfaction than two handfuls of toil," which offers a good continuation of v. 4.

8 וְאָח   The omission of γε as edited by Rahlfs is poorly supported. Most probably the translator read גם בן (ו)גם אח אין לו, because he translates either גם or וגם with καί γε.

10 יִפֹּלוּ   The *lectio difficilior* beyond any doubt is the pl. It is probable that the group of old Syriac mss. retain the original, with some probability. A few Greek mss. of the Holmes-Parsons collation (106, 147, 157, 159) and Aldine have the facilitating sg. too, as do the translations of Jerome.

וְאִילוֹ   The word אי meaning אוי is found in 10:16 (אי לך) and was read here by G V S, as well as by the Masoretes. Some medieval lexicographers, basing their work on M, have recognized it in the Masoretic vocalization (but not the targumist!). The probable error here is only in the merging of the two words in the consonantal text of M.

11 וּלְאֶחָד   G read והאחד. M with ולאחד assimilates to -ל וחם, which precedes. Although G read, incorrectly, a substantive in the preceding member, it had no reason to transform the prep., nor had its source text. V *unus* is purely stylistic and equivalent to *et unus* of Jerome's lemma.

12 יִתְקְפוֹ   There are two occurrences of תקף in Qoh (4:12; 6:10). Here, it is sometimes proposed to understand "to attack" (Rashi, Knobel), but this meaning is not attested with certainty in the Hebrew Bible, and Qoh 6:10 points to the meaning "to prevail over" (*HALAT*, 1644a), as σ' and V interpret here. M vocalizes יתקפו as 3 m. sg. impf. + 3 m. sg. sfx. (= יתקפהו, see GKC, § 60d). The suggestion by Gordis (*Koheleth – The Man*, 232 f.) to read the sfx. in יתקפו as an anticipation of the complement האחד, as in Aramaic, blurs the idea of the "man alone," and makes the sfx. in נגדו ambiguous. The reader who wants to keep M should read the sfx. in יתקפו and נגדו as referring to the same person: "If (some-)one prevails over him, the two will stand for him." It must be said,

however, that in view of the whole verse, as well as of the parallelism with v. 11, this interpretation of M is the less satisfying solution.

It has been suggested to read יתקפו as a 3 pl. with an indefinite subject ("they"): "If they prevail over the loner, two will stand for him." This might well be the origin of M; it gives a better text, and the end of the verse is also better introduced, with the meaning: "two may help where the one is helpless, and three (the threefold cord) are even stronger." Nevertheless, the sg. without sfx., as attested in G, fits the parallelism with v. 11 better and introduces the conclusion nicely. In that form of the text, there are two verbs in v. 12a with two opposite subjects: האחד subject of תקף and השנים subject of עמד, and the same opposition of "one" vs. "two," already present in v. 11, appears here: "If one becomes strong (or prevails), two will stand in front of him." Still better than this equilibrium of strength are the three together (v. 12b): "and the three-fold cord is not quickly broken." One can notice the chiastic structure reinforcing the parallelism between 11 and 12a: a. to lie; b. the two; c. the one; d. to get warm – d'. to get strong; c'. the one; b'. the two; a'. to stand. In V *si quispiam preavaluerit contra unum,* the last word renders the sfx. in יתקפו and *quispiam* renders האחד.

4   מבית הסורים   All traditions seem to have read הָסוּרִים as an equivalent for הָאֲס-ורים, except T, which interprets הַסוּרִים, probably with a word play on the root סור "to turn aside" (from God), which is in line with the Midrash tradition about Abraham's family; see Knobel, "Targum of Qohelet," 33. The elision of the א is presupposed by the Masoretic vocalization of the article; see GKC, §35d. The text remains difficult in terms of the parallelism with v. 14b. See the interesting hypothesis by Dahood, "Qoheleth," 356f.: "to go forth from between the entrails"; and the apparatus commentary on the next case. The double translation of V represents the two interpretations attested in Greek: δεσμίων and δεσμῶν. T גניסת "family" is read in Urbinas Ebr. 1, this word has undergone two corruptions: phonetic גניזת (Sperber) and graphic גניבת (Zamora - Salamanca).

יָצָא   G read the impf. because it relates the verb to the poor lad who, being wise, will get out of prison and accede to kingship, though he was born poor during the kingship of the old and foolish king – the sfx. in במלכותו relating to the foolish king. Though it gives some logic to the passage, the interpretation of G, as well as the current explanation of M, are probably facilitating solutions, all based on reading בית האסורים in the preceding words. In fact, this interpretation depends upon understanding כי גם as equivalent to גם כי, for which GKC, §160b, and BDB, 169b indicate only Qoh 4:14. In addition, the sfx. of מלכותו remains rather unnatural and ambiguous in this interpretation. Verse 14 most probably refers to the old king and his birth as equal to the one of the poor lad: "for he went out of the (womb?) for even in his kingship he was born deprived (as well as the poor)"; see the possible interpretation of בית הסורים as a reference to the (filthy?) womb of birth according to Y. Yadin ("DSD 4:20," 42, n. 23) and the proposal of Dahood ("Qoheleth," 356f.): "to go forth from between the entrails." If this is correct, M has rightly preserved the pf. for יצא, but the Masoretic vocalization of הסורים is due to a misunderstanding of the word in a part of the ancient Jewish tradition.

7   רַגְלְךָ   G has the sg. πόδα σου, but the correct text is probably τὸν πόδα σου;

see Ziegler, "Gebrauch des Artikels," 84 (note by D. Fraenkel). The sg. is to be kept, with M^qere and the versions.

כַּאֲשֶׁר   There is some hesitation in the transmission of באשר and כאשר in Qoh. M and G agree in reading באשר in 3:9 and כאשר in 5:3, 14; 8:7; 9:2b. But in 4:17; 8:16; 11:5 (and probably 9:2a), G has read באשר (ἐν ᾧ , ἐν οἷς) against כאשר in M; conversely in 7:2; 8:4, M reads באשר against כאשר, attested in G (καθότι, καθώς).

מִתֵּת   A reading מַתַּת is reflected in G ὑπὲρ δόμα, its recensions (α' θ') δόμα, and Hie^lem *donum,* though G supposes מְמַתַּת which, if not an interpretation of what is found in M, could be a conflated reading. The proposal in BHS to add a word to M, טוֹב מִתֵּת, is unjustified: (1) It is supported only by S though it would be the easier reading, and there would have been no ground for its disappearing from the other witnesses; (2) The inf. abs. קרוב may well be understood, with σ' (ἔγγιζε), as imperative, parallel and consequent to שְׁמֹר in v. 17aα: "Guard your steps as you go to the house of God and draw near to listen rather than to offer the sacrifice of fools" (NASB); see Gordis, *Koheleth – The Man,* 237, who also submits the hypothesis that קרוב means "praiseworthy." The unusual order of the words might underline that it is not giving a sacrifice in itself which is bad but the way it is offered: מתת הכסילים זבח.

5:2   הַחֲלוֹם   Though S T attest the emphatic state, it is not possible to deduce with certainty that they read the article. Jerome, in his rather literal translation for his commentary, has the sg. *somnium,* then in V the pl. *somnia.* As for σ', its translation is not literal enough to be a firm witness for the absence of the article.

עִנְיָן   Rahlfs considers G πειρασμοῦ as a corruption from περισπασμοῦ, with Grabe. It is a fact that πειρασμός in LXX ordinarily translates נסה, as for example in the portions of Ben Sira which have been recovered in Hebrew. And it is true that the mss. of G Qoh tend to alter περισπασμός into πειρασμός (A in 3:10; 4:8; 8:16 and S in 5:13). The revision assigned to σ': ἀνομία, translates עוון (as does σ' in the book of Psalms), which is graphically close to ענין. V *curas* probably translates ענין, as in 2:26; so does *sollicitudo* of Jerome's lemma in his commentary of the book, here and in 2:26. T gives the usual equivalence for this word in T Qoh: גוון "manner," better attested in Zamora than in Sperber. Supported by G (as restored by Grabe) V Hie S T, M (understood as in 1:13) fits the context perfectly and can be translated as in KJV "(the mutitude of) business." It is to be noted that V and T attest a pl. here, which is unusual for both but probably due to the context: ברב ענין !

3   אֵת   G σὺ οὖν is unanimously attested in the Greek mss. Klostermann (*De libri Coheleth,* 44) emended it to σύν. That interesting emendation was picked up in Rahlfs edition, making G a support to M's text, but it is improbable that CYN, so frequent in G Qoh, would have become CY OYN; the contrary would be expected. As McNeile (*An Introduction,* 139) points out, the particle οὖν is foreign to G Qoh, so that CY OYN of G *might* be the alteration of a conflate reading: CY CYN, rendering the two spellings of את (pronoun and accusative particle). McNeile explains G as a corruption of the simple CYN. α' read the subject pronoun, and θ' seems to have read the accusative particle: ὅσα (= את אשר), though this is a case where confusion may have occurred easily and early in the transmission of the Greek witnesses. T -ד ית ואנת clearly attests the pronoun; it seems to translate the accusative particle too, but this may be a purely translational feature. There is an old hesitation between the two vocalizations, and

both are possible original readings. My preference is for the pronoun, however, (1) it is *lectio difficilior;* (2) it has a good literary value; and (3) it is easy to see how the pronoun could become the particle in the process of transmission, particularly if it was written without the *mater lectionis.*

5   הַמַּלְאָךְ   It seems to Euringer (*Der Masorahtext*, 67) that M ("angel") is *difficilior* and that G is the traditional interpretation of M. But one could argue with McNeile (*An Introduction*, 68) that "the alteration to המלאך may have been made from fear of irreverence."

לָמָה   In G Qoh ἵνα + subjunctive is used three times for translating Hebrew שֶׁ + impf. (3:14; 5:14; 7:14). In 7:17 למה has been interpreted as equivalent for the classical פֶן, as here in 5:5. Such an interpretation is probably due to the influence of the Aramaic use of דילמא / דילמה (also מא as part of שמא; see Segal, *Mishnaic Hebrew*, 475). Gordis (*Koheleth – The Man*, 239) thinks that already in Qoh the word is used as a conjunction like פֶן (he refers to 7:16, 17).

6   כִּי אֶת־   Among the witnesses of Greek, G* ὅτι σύ is attested by B 998 S Syh and a majority of medieval mss., against V A C, a number of medieval mss., and the Aldine and Alcala editions. The simplest way to understand the verse is to read the two parts introduced by כי as oppositional: "In the multitude of dreams, and vanities and words, just fear God." Gordis (*Koheleth – The Man*, 239f.) suggests understanding ברב with a concessive value of the preposition ב, as in Ps 94:19. Although that value is not attested elsewhere in Qoh, the solution is satisfying and requires no emendation. The vocalization אַתָּ in G V S clarifies the opposition, but is not necessary. V *tu vero* renders כִּי אַתָּ, with an adversative value for כי, while the lemma in Jerome's commentary confirms that value of כי but not the pronoun: *sed Deum time.* σ' ἀλλὰ τόν gives כי its adversative value and keeps the translation of G for the accusative particle.

8   בְּכֹל   In his edition of G, Rahlfs chooses the first hand of V, a strongly Hexaplaric ms., against all the witnesses of G he knows, bringing G in harmony with M.
As noted by Barthélemy in *CTAT*, 5, *ad loc.*, עבד *nifal* always refers to the working of the land in the Hebrew Bible (Deut 21:4; Ezek 36:9, 34). Thus G can be read: "And the benefit of a land, above all, is a king to a cultivated ground"; for על־כל meaning "above all," see Pss 95:3; 96:4; 97:9. M can be understood: "And the benefit of the land in everything is a king to a cultivated ground." The two readings are very close. However, the text transmitted by M conveys the idea of a general well-being coming to a land with a king and cultivated ground. The text as reflected in G gives a more contrasted expression between the powers of a commercial culture, which produces administration and all kinds of social strata with their iniquities (v. 7), and what is best "above all" for a land, a society living from agriculture and having a king at its head. V *insuper universae* seems to align with G, but V is very free, and Jerome reads like M in his commentary.

הִיא   The syntax of G and θ' makes it most probable that these witnesses have read the masculine pronoun.

9   לֹא תְבוּאָה   A. *The text of G*: The negation לא does not appear in G. Instead, two main readings are attested in the tradition: (1) a majority of mss. read αὐτοῦ, (2) B S* V* and Syh as well as a number of medieval mss. attest αὐτῶν. The pl. form is the *lectio difficilior* and is, nevertheless, well attested. The sg. posed a temptation to copyists, as a harmonization to the rest of the verse. So Rahlfs, here, follows a sound principle in choosing αὐτῶν. The translator probably read

neither לֹא nor לוֹא as preposition + sfx., but rather the pl. sfx. in בהמונם. The preposition בְּ before הָמוֹן is not a dittography, as suggested in *BHS;* it is supported by the textual agreement of M and G (two different texts here!), and by the analogy of חפץ ב־ and חשק ב־ noted by Hitzig (*Prediger Salomo's*, 162).

B. An attempt at reconstructing a possible original: Gordis (*Koheleth – The Man*, 241) has tried to solve the difficulty by vocalizing the following word: לֹא תְבוֹאֶה "it will not come to him" (direct accusative with בוֹא). But הָמוֹן occurs 90 times in the Hebrew Bible, always as a masculine except in the controversial Job 31:34 cited by Gordis, which is, in any case, outside the semantic field of "wealth, abundance." So the feminine verb posited by Gordis would not agree with its subject. Moreover, the meaning "it will not come to him" (הָמוֹן) does not fit the context very well, which speaks of the lack of satisfaction in *actually* hoarding wealth. Someone in antiquity anticipated Gordis, trying to make something of the verb בוֹא: καὶ τίς ἠγάπησε δῶρα ἐν πλήθει οὐκ ἐλεύσεται (Field, *Origenis Hexaplorum*, Auctarium:25). See also the interpretation of this verb in the double translation of T: "he has no praise in the world to come . . . for he does not deserve the reward of the produce to eat"; first interpretation is "to come" and the second "the reward"; see Knobel, "Targum of Qohelet," 35.

M is not satisfying, nor is G, but G might be an indirect witness of a better text, if the מ it attests at the end of בהמונם came from the beginning of the following word תבואה. The meaning of that text, reflected in a corrupted form in G, would be: "(He that loves money will never be satisfied with money) and the one who loves wealth more than the harvest, this too is vanity." In such a parallelism, there is a wordplay between שבע of the first stichos and תבואה in the second, alluding to the product of the soil as giving satisfaction as opposed to the accumulation of wealth. The verse echoes the criticisms of vv. 7-8, where agriculture is perceived as the proper road to prosperity, against the cruel commercial system of the מדינה. Moreover, it prepares for what follows: "better to be among those who just receive and eat than among the producers of riches" (vv. 10-11).

10 הַטּוֹבָה   The weight of the witnesses fully supports a Hebrew source of G without the article. Moreover, there is an α' text with the article transmitted as a variant of G (see Field, *Origenis Hexaplorum*, Auctarium:25).

כִּי אִם־   Rahlfs' text ὅτι ἀλλ᾿ ἤ is witnessed by a corrector of Codex Sinaiticus, as well as V 253, which are hexaplaric mss. The translation of כי אם elsewhere in Qoh is either: εἰ μή (3:12; 8:15), or ὅτι ἐάν (4:10; 11:8) when כי is read as a cj. on its own followed by a conditional sentence. Thus, ὅτι ἀλλ᾿ ἤ in 5:10 is not the Old Greek, but rather a late evolution of G inspired by a revised text. G* ὅτι ἀρχή interprets the second word of כי אם as אֵם "point of departure" (cf. Ezek 21:26). σ' εἰ μὴ μόνον is a reinforced translation of M.

רְאִית   The *qərê* רְאוּת is a *hapax* and could be the *lectio difficilior,* but it is more probably a late Masoretic alteration of רְאוֹת – attested by G θ' V Hie^lem T – under the double influence of the *kətîb* it corrects, which is a noun, and the substantive כשרון in the first part of the phrase. The *kətîb* is the cstr. of the noun רְאָיָה, an attested substantive in post-biblical Hebrew. As such, the *kətîb* seems more credible than the *qərê* (so Ehrlich, *Randglossen*, 7:76). Nevertheless, the substantive remains an easier text, harmonizing with כשרון. The inf. cstr. ראות seems to be the *lectio difficilior* within v. 10b and echoes the first inf. cstr. in v. 10a רבות. It is an echo which gets support from the two words with 3 f. sfx.

(אוכליה and לבעליה) in the two central stichoi of the verse producing a chiastic play on forms and sounds and establishing a relationship between "multiply" (רַבּוֹת) and "look at" (רְאוֹת). It is Qoheleth's conclusion that striving for riches is mainly due to jealousy and greed (see 4:4). σ' and S, both with a substantive, could align with the qərê as well as the kətîb.

◀ הָעֹבֵד   Although S ܦܠܚܐ might be interpreted as the noun "servant," the choice of ܦܠܚ "to cultivate, plough, work," a root used in 5:8 for the "cultivated field," points to a reading of the ptc., as in M; otherwise, the translator would have chosen the root ܥܒܕ as he does elsewhere to translate the "servant-slave" (2:7; 7:21; 9:1; 10:7). Though G is supported by σ'-θ' according to the margin of Syh, there is a Greek reading supporting M: τοῦ δουλεύοντος in two Hexaplaric mss., V and 253.

The discourse is about possession without enjoyment. For the servant or slave (G) who has no riches, whatever he receives to eat, his sleep is free from worry; in contrast, the rich man, even if he eats his fill, will not sleep. In the proto-M text, it is the "working man" (ptc.), a man who is not excluded from working for money, who is allowed to enjoy his sleep. M offers a possible spiritualizing of the passage too, introducing with the "worker" a religious nuance exploited by the targumist.

וְהַשָּׂבָע לֶעָשִׁיר   G read וְהַשָּׂבֵעַ לְ(הֶ)עָשִׁיר. The adjective שָׂבֵעַ (= G) does not occur elsewhere in Qoh, nor does the substantive read by M σ' V S. Probably G misunderstood the rather rare form of the noun, which fits here in view of the second half of the verse where G = M. Regarding the second word, the reading in G of an inf. cstr. with the elided ה (comp. 5:5aα) is a consequence of that first error. In M the ל before עשיר is genitive.

2 רָעָה חוֹלָה   σ' Hie[lem] V and S ignored the adjectival value of the ptc. חולה and read it as a substantive, making רעה an adjective that qualifies חולה. G ἀρρωστία renders חֳלִי in 5:16; 6:2, but it is also given for M חולה in 5:15. Whatever G read in its Vorlage (חֳלִי or חולה), רעה was not there – as it is clear from v. 15, where G had no difficulty giving רעה the adjectival value before חולה. There are two ways of looking at G: (1) Its Vorlage attested חֳלִי; (2) the translator interpreted חולה as a substantive, as σ', Jerome and S did afterwards. In both cases the text witnessed by G is difficilior, and the insertion of רעה in the proto-M text is easily explained by harmonization with v. 15, possibly under the influence of the parallel in 10:5. The word חֳלִי must be understood here as in Qoh 6:2, where it is found in the same context of a man not willing (here) or not able (there) to take pleasure from his riches; see at 6:2 the proposal of RSV, NASB "affliction," and Gordis (Koheleth – The Man, 160), who translates: "plague." The word probably intends to show that there is a kind of sickness in running after riches, but a sickness that is also to be seen as an affliction, a plague on a human.

4 כַּאֲשֶׁר   Muilenburg ("Qoheleth Scroll," 27) considered 4QQoh[a] כיא a variant for כאשר (G καθώς), as did Horst in BHS and Ulrich (DJD XVI, 222–23). But Nebe ("Qumranica I," 312) is probably right in viewing כיא as a "plus" at the beginning of the verse.

שֶׁיֵּלֵךְ   Since Euringer (Der Masorahtext, 72), it has been assumed that T agrees with G and S. The non-midrashic parts of T, however, show that this is not the case (italics hereafter are for midrashic parts): "Behold: as he came out of the womb of his mother naked without merit nor anything good so will he return and go *to his tomb void of merit*, behold: as he came (M כשבא) *into this world* and any[-thing] (M ומאומה) *good reward* he will not receive (M לא ישא) for his labor (בעמלו) to carry (M שילך) *with him in the world he is going as a merit* in his hand (M בידו)." It may be that T has provided a second translation in the midrashic part with "*he is going*." But that double translation is based on a wordplay in which עמלו is replaced by עלמו and *hifil* vocalization in שילך by *qal* vocalization. As for σ' ὃ συναπελεύσεται, it seems to insist on the relationship between the relative שׁ־ and עמלו, reading that last word probably as the subject of שֶׁיֵּלֵךְ. M is supported by a parallel of הלך *hifil* with the same meaning in 10:20. V *et nihil auferet secum de labore suo* seems to be a free stylistic reduction, with *auferet secum* rendering both לא ישא and שילך בידו.

15 **כָּל־עֻמַּת**   About this case, David Qimḥi says in his *Sefer Ha-Shorashim*, 271: "כל has been bound to עמת as in Aramaic כל קבל דנה (Dan 2:12; Ezra 7:17) and right is the explanation of Gaon Ibn Ghiyyat that לעמת may not occur without the ל. . . the כ is the one of comparison and the ל the one of לעמת, and it should have been one single word: כלעמת." For the opinion of Ibn Ghiyyat quoted by Qimḥi, see Qafih, חמש מגילות, p. רכו. McNeile (*An Introduction*, 70–71) and Gordis (*Koheleth – The Man*, 243) agree with Qimḥi. But Hertzberg (*Der Prediger*, 129) rightly points out that עמת already conveys the idea of comparison, and that would make a double comparison in one expression. The literalistic text of G seems to translate כִּי לְעֻמַּת, and is supported by S and the lemma of Jerome. M might derive from that form by a misreading of כיל(עמת) becoming כול(עמת).

16 **בַּחֹשֶׁךְ יֹאכֵל**   Hitzig (*Prediger Salomo's*, 164) deems that mourning has no place in this verse. He suggests reading כל ימיו as an object complement of אכל, meaning: "he consumes all his days in darkness." It is simpler, however, to read כל ימיו as an accusative of time as in 2:23. Ibn Ezra has a simple explanation of M: "During the daylight he does not eat, but only in darkness, and that is because he is so busy in his work to get money that he does not eat before nightfall and he is full with vexation and sickness." Yefet ben Ely already offered the same interpretation, adding that, being avaricious, he saves on the oil (Vajda, *Deux commentaires karaïtes*, 170). However, it must be noted that אכל may have a broader significance; see v. 18!

Rahlfs omits the second ἐν (πένθει) with Codex Venetus, a strongly Hexaplaric ms. The evidence for the Greek tradition indicates that most probably this second ἐν is part of G*, and the translator found ובאבל in its *Vorlage*. S has the word in a doublet, probably taken from G; see its text in the commentary on the next case. At first ובאבל appears to be a facilitation of the text witnessed by M Hie[lem] V T. But, a harmonization of the ideas in the proto-M is not to be excluded. Twice "mourning" occurs in the book: 7:2, 4. There, "mourning" is clearly related to the wise man who does not frequent the banqueting house, but the "house of mourning." Thus, "mourning" could have appeared to the revisers of the proto-M text as inapt for the sadness and irritation of the foolish businessman, who, instead, receives his due as in 7:2, that is, eating.

וְכָעַס   M vocalization *weQatal* after יאכל is a syntactical facilitation. The anacoluthon is not so rude as it is sometimes argued. The series of 16b concludes the whole unit of vv. 9-16, where the hoarder is described: others take advantage of his work, not he, and finally: "(15b) What profit has he in toiling for the wind? (16) And what is more, all his days are in darkness and mourning and much

vexation, and sickness and wrath!" That is all his gain from his toil for the
wind, the result of his way of life; so Podechard, *L'Ecclésiaste*, 351. A similar
interpretation is also possible if one reads with M the preceding word (יאכל);
see KJV and NASB. S has doublets here, translating: "and in much vexation
+(and in anger and in mourning)+ and in sickness and anger." The reading
ובנסיס "and in grief/trouble" in T* is from mss. Zamora and Salamanca; Sperber's ms. reads: ובנכסין, a word present in M and T of v. 18 and added in T of
v. 17, which might have influenced the corruption of an original בנססין. Urbinas Ebr. 1 has: ובכנס. The preposition supplied by all the versions except G is
translational.

וְחָלְיוֹ   The final ו is considered by Rashi as superfluous. It might have appeared
from dittography of the following cj. All the versions except G supply a preposition for the sake of translation, as was also the case with the preceding word.

8 הָאָדָם   G ὁ ἄνθρωπος, as edited by Rahlfs, is taken from two Hexaplaric mss., V
and 253. G* read a text without the article. The situation is similar to 3:13
where Old Greek is not Rahlfs' text but the one without the article. At first
sight, the article of M is *lectio difficilior,* particularly in view of the following
relative clause in 3:13 and 5:18. However, the problem is probably a literary
one and this double variation of 3:13; 5:18 should be approached with a look at
7:2, where G no longer reflects the article before אדם.

9 מַעֲנֶה   M is difficult in view of the semantic value of ענה in Qoh: "to be preoccu-
pied with," here *hifil*; a complement must be supplied. V reads בשמחה instead
of the cstr. בשמחת and made of לבו the direct complement of מענה: *eo quod
Deus occupet deliciis cor eius.* He had already done this in the lemma of his
commentary, where he follows the order witnessed by M: *occupat in laetitia
cor eius.* G witnesses a pronoun as complement: ὁ θεὸς περισπᾷ αὐτόν (=
מענהו). The text of G is very satisfying; it is consistent with the value of ענה in
Qoh and has the best literary value in the context. With Podechard (*L'Ecclésiaste*, 353s.), Wildeboer (*Prediger*, 142), and most contemporary critics, the
verse must be understood: "*God keeps him occupied with the gladness of his
heart,* so that he is not worried about the other days of his life" (v. 19a; cp.
5:16; 6:3); 19a concludes on the theme of v. 17 and 19b on the theme of v. 18.
The omission of the sfx. in the pre-M text is easy to understand: there are only
three other occurrences of ענה *hifil* in the Hebrew Bible (1 Kgs 8:35 // 2 Chr
6:26 & Prov 15:1) and their meaning is "to answer," against some 60 forms
vocalized *piel* in M. Thus, the omission was probably a spontaneous reaction to
the reading of the ptc. as *piel* ("to afflict") with sfx. (see Isa 60:14; Zeph 3:19),
which would be odd in this context of joy.

4 יֵלֵךְ   The pf. is recommended by the parallelism with v. 5 and supported by the
Qumran text (הלך), whose clear tendency to plene writings would have probably produced הולך if a ptc. was to be read (see DJD XVI, 223–24). G vocalized הָלֵךְ in preparation for the impf. at the end of the verse (יכסה); the impf.
ילך in M is probably in the same line of facilitation.

5 יָדַע נַחַת   The division between verb and noun is attested by M G S Hie^lem and
fits the structure of the following sentence: נחת לזה מזה "satisfaction to this one
more than to that one." V *neque cognovit distantiam* is probably inspired by σ'
οὐκ ἐπειράθη διαφορᾶς. In Syh's margin the accusative ἀνάπαυσιν is assigned
to the revisers, which means the substantive has been read as object complement of the verb.

נֵחָת   The form נוחת in 4QQoh[a] is difficult to explain. A similar form, understood as a construct name, is found in Sirach Hebrew 30:17, where the context expresses the same ideas as here; see Qoh 6:6 too. However this does not help much with the meaning of the orthography in 4QQoh[a].

8   כִּי מַה־יּוֹתֵר   According to Field, θ' α' σ' support the interrogative pronoun of M. The tradition of G is split between the attestation and the omission of τίς in ὅτι (τίς) περισσεία. However, the asterisk with attribution to α' θ' within the text of Syh points to an original Greek without the interrogative. This is reinforced by the fact that its omission in S is probably due to the influence of G*. Nevertheless, a final decision will have to be made when a critical edition of G Qoh is published. Probably 4QQoh[a] כמה יותר is an attempt to give an advantage to the חכם, rather than a "Phoenician spelling in the omission of the *mater lectionis*" (Muilenburg, "Qoheleth Scroll," 25). In 7:19, 4QQoh[a] attests another variant reading by which wisdom is given an advantage (עזר instead of עזז).

מַה־לֶּעָנִי   Except in 2:15, a late gloss, διότι does not occur elsewhere in G Qoh. It might be explained as an interpretation of מה ל-, analogous to the interpretation of למה with a final meaning: ἵνα τί; see 2:15; 5:5 comm.; 7:16, 17. In that case, διότι should be read as a direct interrogative. It must be noted, however, that in a marginal note of Syh, α' and θ' are described as being "like the Septuagint"; now in Syh, G is presented as διὰ τί (ܡܛܠ ܡܢܐ). If this was the correct form of G, the interpetation of מה ל- as causal is probable (למה). S ܠܡܢܐ could reflect either Greek form. To sum up, no actual divergent text is attested here, except for the conjunction in σ', V and T, which is a facilitation in syntax and underlines the parallelism with the preceding stichos. T* is Urbinas Ebr. 1, Zamora and Salamanca, to which the editions of Sperber and Ben Ḥayyim only add גברא before עניא.

9   מֵהֲלָךְ־   σ' ὁδεύειν (Jerome quotes σ' as *ambulare*) and V *desiderare* both support the inf. of M, as does S ܡܗܠܟܐ, a substantive equivalent to "going, wandering." G ὑπὲρ πορευόμενον ψυχῇ read the ptc. of הלך (to avoid the idea of a soul's wandering?); it is supported by Hie[lem] *super ambulantem in anima,* which might reflect Old Latin here, as it does in a few instances.

10   שֶׁהַתִּקִּיף   Gordis (*Koheleth – The Man*, 253) considers the *kᵊtîb* as a conflation of two forms: שתקיף and התקיף. It may also be a relative followed by תקף *hifil,* the *qal* of which was used in 4:12, but the *hifil* form of this root is unknown in the Bible. The versions probably read the *qᵊrê,* unless they read עם התקיף, which is not directly attested. The article in G probably renders the relative ש; cf. שהיה 1:9 or שנעשה 1:14.

12   כַּצֵּל   The verb עשה (כ/בצל) means "to spend time," see Gordis, *Koheleth – The Man*, 254. Hertzberg chooses the text witnessed by G (*Der Prediger*, 138–39), ἐν σκιᾷ. He points out that "in the shadow" makes an interesting opposition to "under the sun." From a text critical standpoint, the text witnessed by G (= בצל) is clearly *difficilior,* and its alteration to כצל was very tempting, as an assimilation to M Qoh 8:13, which recalls verses like Pss 102:12; 109:23; 144:4; Job 14:2; 1 Chr 29:15, all concerned with the days of humans passing fast away. But here, in Qoh 6:12, the theme related to the expression (see the following relative as well as the first part of the verse) is not the shortness of life but the *ignorance* of the human, who will never know what comes after his own life under the sun – and though they are under the sun, humans nevertheless spend their time in the shadow of ignorance.

T* כטללא is taken from Zamora and Ben Ḥayyim; Urbinas Ebr. 1 has כטולא (same value) and Sperber a corrupted בטילא. In Qoh 8:13, טללא is the form attested by all these witnesses (Ben Ḥayyim טלל).

1 הֻלְּדוֹ:   The sfx. of M *seems* to be attested in 4QQohª (DJD XVI, 223). It is attested in numerous Greek mss., and absent in B 998 S*, about ten minuscules, and Aldine. Its omission seems required and could be secondary, but Syh clearly assigns the pronoun to α' and gives it an asterisk (ܕ‍ܠܗ‍) in its text, which tends to prove that Origen already knew a form of G without the sfx. Moreover, its absence in S might result from the influence of G. V has no pronoun, but it is a free translation; in his lemma for the commentary Jerome has: *nativitatis eius.* T speaks of the "day in which a wicked man is born," but T also supplies a subject in the preceding member (the day in which *a man* dies). As Gordis suggests (*Koheleth – The Man*, 257), the sfx. may be understood as an expression of an impersonal subject: "the day of one's birth" – cf. 8:16bβ, where אדם is also present in the preceding verse. The sfx. of M is *lectio difficilior*. On the other hand, it might have arisen from a kind of stylistic harmonization with the end of v. 2 speaking of the "living."

2 מִלֶּכֶת   ῞Οτι has no equivalent in M; G usually renders the מ of comparison with ὑπέρ + accusative. The translator seems to have read a *Vorlage* מִשֶּׁלֶכֶת; see 3:22, where מֵאֲשֶׁר has a comparative value. Jerome (V Hie) has not repeated *ire,* most probably for stylistic reasons, though his lemma is ordinarily very literal.

   סוֹף כָּל־   From what appears in the photograph PAM 43092, the inversion of the two words כול and סוף is almost certain in 4QQohª, with a ס clearly legible after כול; so Ulrich (DJD XVI, 223, 225). The variant is described by Wilhelm Nebe ("Qumranica I," 312). At the end of the preceding word, the letter ה appears, הו]א[, which points to a rather careless copy at this point.

   יִתֵּן   The bulk of Greek mss. attests the complement ἀγαθόν but Rahlfs again brings G in harmony with M, choosing Syh, even though Syh is often mixed with revisions toward M. As to the "Old Latin" Rahlfs quotes in his apparatus, it is Jerome's lemma translating the proto-M text when it departs too much from G (see Introduction). V *cogitat* translates the last three Hebrew words: יתן אל לבו under the influence of σ' *respiciet ad mentem,* quoted in Jerome's comm. G's model: טוב אל לבו (יתן) may be an interpretation derived from the following verse, particularly v. 3b.

   On the other hand, if this text was original it might have been a problem: "let the living give Good to his heart; Good is anger . . .," so that a voluntary omission of טוב in proto-M is a fair possibility. The case is to be decided on literary grounds.

5 מֵאִישׁ שֹׁמֵעַ   The variant reading from 4QQohª (col. 2 line 19) is pointed out by Ulrich. The supralinear insertion of שׁ in 4QQohª is the correction of the erroneous למוע; see DJD XVI, 223–24.

6 כִּי   A majority of Greek mss. supports the omission of ὅτι, including B 998 and S.

   הַכְּסִיל   The reading assigned to σ' in the margin of Syh, with a pl. ptc.: ܕܠܐ ܪܕ‍ܐ "who are undisciplined," seems to be an error, since τῶν ἀπαιδεύτων already translates the preceding הסירים, understood as related to the root סור or סרר. The text of σ' given by Nobilius in Greek and Jerome in Latin indicates the reading of a sg. in the second part of v. 6a, though it does seem a rather strange version from the hand of Symmachus: διὰ γὰρ φωνῶν ἀπαιδεύτων ἐν δεσμωτηρίῳ γίνεταί τις; see Field, *Origenis Hexaplorum*, 2:392, n. 14.

7 וְיְאַבֵּד   The present tense in G* may interpret the gnomic value of the impf. in this proverb. Rahlfs has chosen the classical form ἀπόλλυσι with Codex Vaticanus instead of ἀπολλύει attested in the rest of the tradition; but the clear tendency in Septuagint Greek is to alter these forms toward the ω verbs; ἀπολλύμενος in v. 16 is not counterproof, for the medio-passive forms were more protected against that tendency; see Helbing, *Grammatik*, 107, who must nevertheless be corrected on Qoh 7:7, where he has inverted the witnesses.

Regarding the text of 4QQoh^a, Muilenburg conjectured the last two letters of his proposal יעוה, with a good parallel in Prov 12:8. Ulrich (DJD XVI, 225) agrees with this view.

מַתָּנָה: σ' quoted by Jerome clearly supports M: *et perdit cor MATTHANA (donum)*. Jerome says that the Hebrew word and its interpretation *(donum)* are both part of the σ' text. This line of interpretation understands the verse in the following way: "Surely extortion drives a wise man crazy and a gift (bribe) destroys the heart." But the composition of the second member is irregular in several ways compared to the first one. The verb's inflection is masculine with a feminine subject (GKC, §145o), and the complement introduced with אֵת lies between verb and subject. Each of these features may be found in the Hebrew Bible but they are rather irregular language; and here they join together to disturb the parallelism. Moreover, in this odd construction, the complement לֵב introduced by the accusative particle lacks a determiner. Most probably the interpretation of מתנה as "gift (bribe)," making it the subject of יאבד, results from ignorance of a rare word, assimilating the verse to passages like Exod 23:8; Deut 16:19 about the effect of a bribe on the wise.

A clearer line of interpretation makes the last word of the verse a determinative of לֵב, with two possibilities attested in ancient Jewish traditions.

1. G, which according to Jerome is supported by α' θ', read the root מתן with the meaning "strength, vigor": τὴν καρδίαν εὐτονίας αὐτοῦ. Given the transliteration MATTHANA found in the σ' text quoted by Jerome, it is probable that the consonants were actually already מתנה but were read by α' θ' as מָתְנָה "his vigor." From this derives V *robur (cordis) illius*. While the dual of מֹתֶן is specifically for "loins," the sg. could be understood as "vigor"; see in Deut 33:11, where strength and loins are parallel; cf. Ezek 21:11; Job 40:16; Nah 2:2. McNeile (*An Introduction*, 161) and Driver ("Problems," 230) suggest vocalizing thus. The meaning of the verse would then be: "Extortion makes the wise man crazy and ruins his vigorous heart." The reading εὐγενεία in some Greek mss. is most probably a late correction of ΕΥΓΟΝΙΑ, which is itself a slight graphic corruption of ΕΥΤΟΝΙΑ, as already recognized in Migne's edition of Jerome's commentary (PL 23:1062b).

2. A second way of reading מתנה as qualifying לֵב is found in *Midr. Qoh.*, where it is said: "ויאבד לב מתנה, it is written מתונה, if Moses had kept calm . . ." (Euringer and later McNeile wrongly interpret מתונה as "rebellion"). In *BHK*[2], S.R. Driver suggested, in the same vein: לֵב מַתְנִים, referring to *Pirke Avot* I, 1: הוו מתונים בדין "be circumspect when judging." This would mean that a defective spelling מַתְנָם was corrupted to the present מתנה, which, though possible, is not easy to accept. In any case, the syntax as well as semantics of both ancient Jewish interpretations point to an original root מתן rather than נתן,

and the cstr. chain solves the three irregularities of syntax mentioned above, regarding the last four words of M.

Other possiblities along these lines are:

1. Keeping the vocalization of *Midr. Qoh.* and reading the adjective לֵב מַתְנֶה "a restrained (calm) heart," which supposes an exceptional feminine of לֵב as in Prov 12:25.

2. Conjecturing an original מְתָנָה "poise, self control," as an analogous antonym of מְהֵרָה "haste, speed" – and the possible source of the eventual מתינה (hence מתונה in Midrash) resulting from the preference for words of the type מְתִינָה in late Hebrew (Barth, *Nominalbildung*, 137, 85 f.), where מתינה means "patience, self control." The difficulty here is the absence of a determiner in the cstr. chain after the accusative particle, though this is a possible origin of the alteration of the passage.

3. Finally, it cannot be entirely ruled out that מַתְנָה in M might mean something other than "gift"; for example, a meaning related to a sentence like יתן אל לבו of v. 2b, which is near to the well known שׂום לב "pay attention" (with the same difficulty as above due to the absence of the article). In that case the cstr. chain would mean: "an attentive, a cautious heart"; see NJPS translation: "and destroy the prudence of the cautious."

) מֶחְכְּמָה V *stulta est* may translate M לֹא מחכמה, but it could also be a translation of G. The same may be said of σ' and Hie[lem]; the ב of בחכמה witnessed by G could be read as having a sociative value (instrumental). Indeed, if G were not so literal in Qoh, one could consider this case as a matter of exegesis rather than text criticism, but G Qoh is to be taken as reflecting a Hebrew *Vorlage* in such cases.

2 בְּצֵל בְּצֵל and בְּצֵל   Three forms are witnessed: (1) בצל . . . כצל in G; (2) כצל . . . כצל in σ' V; (3) בצל . . . בצל in M. Literally, S could represent צל . . . כצל, but it probably renders a text like the one of σ' V (2). In G, αὐτῆς, which determines ἐν σκιᾷ, could be from a dittography in בצל(ה) החכמה. M is the smoothest text, and Rashi gives the most obvious explanation of it: "anyone who gets in the shadow of wisdom, gets in the shadow of money, because wisdom causes riches to come." But this appears to be somewhat inconsistent with v. 11, to which v. 12a should offer a parallel. If wisdom is good *with an estate,* one can deduce that wisdom is not automatically a source of riches. It has been suggested that the two prepositions of M be read as ב *essentiae* in this way: "while shadow is the wisdom, shadow is the money," meaning: "wisdom is protection just as money is protection" (Hitzig, *Prediger Salomo's,* 173). Not only would this be a very odd example of ב *essentiae,* but it would require at least a cj. before the second one in order to eliminate the ambiguity in which each assertion may be predicate to the other, and to avoid the simplest reading of the Hebrew (like Rashi's one). For that same reason, Ibn Ezra's interpretation of M is not acceptable: "So will the wise man find refuge in the shadow of wisdom and the shadow of money." M is rather to be discarded here.

There are two ways of looking at the history of the text.

1. The text read by σ' V (כצל . . . כצל) has been corrected by copyists who did not tolerate such an equivalence between "protection of wisdom" and "protection of money." The first step might have been to read the first comparative particle as the preposition ב, giving priority to wisdom as the real protection (= G). The second step would have been the harmonization of the second preposi-

tion (= M); this is the view of McNeile (*An Introduction*, 145–46). The original text (= σ') would mean either: "Good is wisdom with an heritage . . . (12) For protection of wisdom is like protection of money . . . (see Gen 18:25)"; or: "for protection of money is like protection of wisdom (see Hos 4:9)." But this hypothesis depends on a parallel relationship between נחלה "estate" and כסף "money," which is rather questionable in the thought of Qoheleth, for whom money is the opposite of a sound relationship to the land.

2. The text of G is original and has been harmonized in two different ways in the process of its scribal transmission (either with ב or כ), through ignorance of the pregnant construction with כ. The phrase means: "Good is wisdom with a heritage . . . (25) for (being) in the protection of wisdom is like (to be) in the protection of money, and the advantage of knowledge is: wisdom will preserve the life of its owner."

In favor of this text form, one must recall the contrast in 5:8-9 between the search for money and the satisfaction found in the produce of the earth. By נחלה is very probably meant here an estate, landed property. There would be, then, an opposition between נחלה "property, estate" and כסף "money," the search for which never brings humans peace; see 5:9. For the wise man with an estate, there is no need to look for money (v. 11), "for to be in the shadow of wisdom (not only) is like being in the shadow of money, but wisdom has the advantage of giving life to its owner." For the pregnant construction of כ, see GKC, §118*s-x*, n. 2; Waltke/O'Connor, *Hebrew Syntax*, 11.2.9.

13   מַעֲשֵׂה   For the translation of this word in G Qoh, see the commentary on 2:4. Among the five divergences between M and G mentioned there, are the three occurrences of מעשה האלהים in which G reads מעשה pl.: 7:13; 8:17; 11:5. σ' and Jerome probably depend on G here.

14   הֱיֵה   α' and θ' are attested as "like Septuagint" in Syh.

וּבְיוֹם רָעָה רְאֵה   Variations in the versions are mainly around the meaning and, consequently, the place assigned to the imperative of ראה. σ', quoted in Jerome, makes the "day of unhappiness" the direct complement of ראה: *diem vero malum intuere*. This is not a variant reading, as can be seen from 3:22, where σ' translates ב- ראה with a direct complement (θεάσασθαι τὰ ἐσόμενα). V *et malam diem praecave* also makes it a direct complement and interprets ראה as "foresee in order to take measures," a possible meaning but out of place here. S, "and in the day of unhappiness take care of yourself (*lit.* your soul)," is also an interpretation of רְאֵה. T has a different division in order to interpret the verb. First the targumist makes of the bad day another good day, as long as the man goes on doing good in reaction to the good days given by the Lord; then he places רְאֵה as an introduction to what follows (v. 14bα): "On the day that the Lord does good to you, you also be good and do good to every one so that the evil day does not come upon you. See and consider . . ." (Knobel's translation). Rahlfs brings the text of G in line with M by using a retroversion of Syh. As for G*, it attests the verb twice: καὶ ἴδε ἐν ἡμέρᾳ κακίας. ἴδε . . . "and consider to be satisfied in the bad day. Look . . . " If M is original, it is not easy to understand why the verb would have then been placed where it stands in its first occurrence in the text witnessed by G. Conversely, if its original place was before יום as in G's text, it is easy to understand why it would have been repeated before v. 14bα. Thus, the history of the text may be represented as follows: in the syntagm וּרְאֵה בְיוֹם רָעָה the verb, which was not easy to understand, has been attracted to v. 14bα in order to provide an introduction for the motivation of v. 14a and a simple meaning of ראה. The result of this change in word order is the text form found in M: even with the ʾaṭnaḥ, it remains like a Greek ὅτι, so to speak, at the beginning of what follows. G* has a conflated form, having first the original and its repetition at the end of the syntagm. Not going so far as Lauha (*Kohelet*, 169), who interprets רְאֵה in 9.9 as meaning "to enjoy," one must follow him in recognizing an adjacent meaning of the verb: "be satisfied with," "be content with," I would say: "consider being content with," as, for example, in 9:9, where Qoh encourages contentment in the life shared with the wife one loves, or has loved. In the same way here, there could be an allusion to the sequence of good days followed by bad days (see context). Perhaps 8:16 is to be understood along the same line; there the meaning *might* be "one does not consider indulging oneself with sleep" (שנה בעיניו איננו ראה).

אֶת־ B 998 Aldine Sixtine attest the accusative particle of M against almost all the other witnesses of G. Rahlfs, again, chooses the text closest to M. The particle (M) emphasizes the meaning, i.e., "even *that one* as this one has God created". S is indeterminate since it does not usually render the accusative particle in Qoh (1:13, 14; 2:3; etc.). T* is given according to Urbinas Ebr. 1, Zamora and Ben Ḥayyim. The ms. edited by Sperber has a corruption יתבין for ית דין.

8 אַל־תְּנַּח All Greek mss. attest μὴ μιανῃς. Although it is tempting to judge it as resulting from a dittography altering MHANHC into MHMHANHC, then transformed through itacism in MHMIANHC (so Euringer, *Der Masorahtext*, 86), it is striking that the extant witnesses of G attest neither the intermediary (MHMHANHC) nor the supposed original MHANHC, which appears in the margin of ms. 161, and is assigned to θ' in Syh, according to Field. G might translate a *corrupted* form of תניח (cf. 2 Chr 29:19, where הזניח is translated μιαίνω). G, as edited by Rahlfs, is taken from θ' in Field and allegedly supported by the "Old Latin," i.e., Jerome's translation of proto-M whenever he considered G to depart too much from his Hebrew text (see Introduction, Greek Witnesses, §§ 2–3).

9 תָּעֹז M reads עזז *qal*, followed with the complement לחכם; this is unusual and it is doubtful whether the meaning "to strengthen" required in the context belongs to the semantic field of the root (cf. חזק). BDB's proposal "wisdom is strong for the wise (more than ten governors!)" is no more satisfying. Moreover, it is certainly not the intention of Qoheleth in this context to present a boasting praise of the power of wisdom; even if one allows for a later development, surely the root עזז would not have been used for praising wisdom. What precedes (vv. 16-18a) is about the dangers of making oneself too much of a righteous and wise man, and what follows (v. 20) goes on about the impossibility of being a perfectly righteous human. Verse 19 is part of that context in which the themes of righteousness and wisdom are intertwined. In v. 19 the warning to the disciples of wisdom is that it makes the wise man trust too much in himself, makes him bolder even than any political power (ten governors = ten *archontes*, the totality of power in Hellenistic cities? see Gordis, *Koheleth – The Man*, 269). The original verse, with the vocalization *hifil* proposed here in the apparatus, can be understood so: "Wisdom makes bold (haughty, self assured) the wise more than ten governors who were in the city." The only certain attestations of עזז for the meaning "to make audacious" are *hifil* (Prov 7:13; 21:29). In these occurrences the *hifil* is transitive, both with an object complement פנים, but the

verb is also found in the *hofal* for a man in Ben Sira (10:12). The ל before חכם is an accusative marker. The only other attestation of the root in Qoh is עז פנים (8:1), where the meaning "boldness, haughtiness" is quite clear. Although the *qal* vocalization is also given a meaning *trotzen*, adjacent to "make bold," in *HALAT,* 764b for Ps 9:20, there it could mean "to prevail" as usual (so BDB). In M, α' and S the *qal* vocalization is rather an attempt to soften a too sharp warning about wisdom. In the source of 4QQoh[a] and G, it was felt necessary to go farther, and תעז was transformed into תעזר with the intent of protecting the value of wisdom, which "helps the wise human more than ten governors . . .". Such a tendency to protect the wise man is attested in 4QQoh[a] at the beginning of 6:8 (see comm.). These accommodations of the text of Qoheleth, protecting the governors as well as the wise, seem to ignore that the teaching of Qoh is a warning for disciples of wisdom.

21 אֲשֶׁר יְדַבֵּרוּ   As shown by the lemma in his commentary, *quos loquentur,* the text of Jerome in V, *qui dicuntur,* is a stylistic adaptation for the impersonal subject, inspired by σ' τοῖς λαλουμένοις. In view of the second part of the verse, the short text (M σ' Hie[lem] V) is not only *difficilior,* but a better literary one. Though ἀσεβεῖς has been chosen here as probable G*, only a critical edition of the text of G will make clear whether this is the original text.

22 יָדַע   In its present state, G is a conflation of two translations: ὅτι πλειστάκις πονηρεύσεταί σε | καὶ καθόδους πολλὰς κακώσει (καρδίαν σου). As McNeile rightly analyzes (*An Introduction,* 163), the second translation is probably the nearest to G Qoh (which has strong ties to Aquila's version), while the first one resembles the version of σ', ὅτι πρὸς πλεονάκις καιροῦ πονηρεύσεται (καρδία σου), falsely attributed to α' as Field points out. The intrusion of the complement σε in the first version might have appeared in relation to κακώσει of the second one. As a side note, the word καρδία, read as an accusative in most Greek mss., seems to be an error due to the occurrence of that form in the preceding verse; the nominative preserved in B is probably the original reading. In any case, in this double text, the verb in the source text is twice read with ר, perhaps under the influence of v. 20. The future in these Greek translations shows that the variant reading touches only the ד/ר confusion. The best text for T seems to be ידיע בלבבך attested in Urbinas Ebr. 1, Zamora-Salamanca. Sperber's text: יידע לבך might be an alteration of it; both, however, support M in reading the ד in the verb.

23 רְחוֹקָה   In G V Hie[lem], there is a verbal form here, as proposed in our preferred reading. In that form of the text, wisdom, the subject of the verb, is presented as going away from a man trying to get it (אמרתי אחכמה), fleeing beyond any access to it. This reading implies a different division, with the phrase beginning at v. 23bβ going till the end of v. 24a. For an overall view of the passage, see the next cases in v. 24 (מה־שהיה and ימצאנו).

24 מַה־שֶׁהָיָה   G ὑπὲρ ὃ ἦν is supported by V, where *multo magis quam erat* aims to alleviate the repetition of the root רחק. G seems to present the *lectio difficilior* here, translating משהיה, in which שהיה means anything that has ever come into existence, cf. 3:15, 20; 4:3; 6:10.

In the text witnessed by M, the preceding רחוק and the following עמק have been read as predicate adjectives of מה־שהיה, whereas they are to be read as adverbs; v. 24a is a clarification of the last sentence in v. 23: והיא | רחוק משהיה רחקה ממני (= G). The whole might be translated: "(23) I thought, 'I shall get

wisdom', but it fled away from me, (24) farther than any reality . . ." The subject חכמה is present through a wordplay in the cohortative אחכמה. The emer-
gence of M 24a might have been caused by the reading of what could be termed
an anaphoric omission in v. 24b: "and the deepest who can discover it?"
Seemingly, S read: מכל מה שהיה (ܡܢ ܟܠ ܡܕܡ ܕܗܘܐ), the word רחוק being
transposed after this.

וְעָמֹק | עָמֹק   G, supported by Hie[lem] *et alta profunditas*, seems to have read
וְעָמֹק עֹמֶק. This could be a syntactic facilitation meant to provide a clear referent for the m. sfx. at the end of the following verb; see the next case.

יִמְצָאֶנּוּ:   The f. sfx. is attested in G's tradition by Syh, the first hand of S, a
majority of medieval mss., and the Aldine edition. The understanding of G in v.
24b depends upon a decision about the gender of this sfx. The m. sfx., well
attested in the ancient mss., would refer to the עֹמֶק: "and mysterious is the
depth, who can find it?" Alternatively, the f. sfx. would refer to wisdom: "(wisdom) fled away farther than any reality, and mysterious is the depth! who can
find her (wisdom)?" In both cases, the idea is similar to what is expressed in
Job 11:7-8 (cf. Prov 25:3; Jer 31:37). In M, v. 24b is quite in harmony with 24a
and can easily be read as in NASB: "What has been is remote and exceedingly
mysterious. Who can discover it?" It seems that the m. sfx. at the end of the
verse has caused both the reading of M in v. 24a (רחוק instead of רחקה) and
the appearance of the substantive (עֹמֶק instead of עָמֹק) in G's *Vorlage* of v.
24b, in each case in order to provide a clear referent for the sfx. I suggest adopting G for v. 23bβ-24a, and M in v. 24b, which results in the following text: "I
decided to get wisdom, but it fled away from me farther than any reality; and
the deepest who can find it?" This means that one never finds the foundations
of reality, one never finds the ultimate wisdom and the world remains hermeti-
cally sealed to human understanding (cf. 3:11).

5   וְלִבִּי   As noted by Euringer (*Der Masorahtext*, 89), the *lectio difficilior* found in
M is supported by the best witnesses and could not be derived from the easy
and ordinary בלבי. The interpretation by σ', followed by Jerome in V, was probably in the air, as shown by the tendency in the Masoretic medieval mss. to alter
ו to ב.

וְהַסִּכְלוּת הוֹלֵלוֹת: The last four words of the verse may be read along two main
lines: (1) as a series of complements of ולדעת; (2) as two nominal sentences
explaining the content of ולדעת.
1. The first line of interpretation we find in G, which read three complements
of ולדעת, the first two words being a cstr. chain and forming the first complement, and the last two words the other two complements. The reading of the
first two words as a cstr. chain is probably due to the absence of a cj. between
them (רשע כסל). S follows the same interpretation, "the wickedness of the
fool"; as does T, "the retribution of the fault of the fool." G's translation re-
verses the usual logic of the cstr. chain (a reversal attested elsewhere in the
Bible), and addresses "the folly of ungodliness": (τοῦ γνῶναι) ἀσεβοῦς ἀφροσύνην (the first word is a neuter adjective with a substantive function: τὸ ἀσε-
βές).
Jerome, like M, has not read a cj. between the last two words, and he goes on
with a second cstr. chain: (*et ut cognoscerem*) *impietatem stulti et imprudentium
errorem* (lemma). In doing so, Jerome potentially supports G regarding the absence of an article in ו(ה)סכלות.

2. This article in M betrays the intention of reading both series of two words as two verbless clauses, which is the second line of interpretation: "to know: wickedness is stupidity and the foolishness is madness" (so Podechard, *L'Ecclésiaste*, and Gordis, *Koheleth – The Man*). But this gives the last clause a flat and odd content; moreover, as pointed out by Ehrlich (*Randglossen*, 7:85), it anticipates the results of the search which is only announced here (cf. v. 26). The article of M makes clear that Qoheleth, as any good חכם, did indeed find that wickedness *is* folly and folly *is* wildness; see comm. on 1:17.

I propose to follow Ehrlich in reading the four last words of the verse as four different object complements of ולדעת (so Hertzberg, *Der Prediger*, 137). The first two (רשע כסל) may possibly be a cstr. chain (G S), though an article before כסל would better fit such a construction.

The α' text presented here is found in the next verse in some Hexaplaric mss. and the hand of a corrector of Codex Sinaiticus. Though also reading a verbless clause, it omits the article before the third word: καὶ ἀφροσύνην πλάνας. For the last word of the verse, Field gives a text ascribed to σ', ἔννοιαν θορυβώδη, which suggests the absence of a cj. before the last word (= M). T according to Sperber Urbinas Ebr. 1 and Salamanca has no cj., like M; ms. Zamora alone has it, which is probably a spontaneous alteration.

The sg. הוֹלֵלוּת preferred here is discussed in 1:17 and 2:12. Here it is suported by G σ' V Hie[lem] S.

26　וּמוֹצֵא אֲנִי　　Rahlfs' edition of G, καὶ εὑρίσκω ἐγώ, must be corrected on two points:

1. In καὶ εὑρίσκω ἐγὼ αὐτήν, the pronoun αὐτήν is attested by the whole tradition. The Old Latin invoked by Rahlfs is the translation of the proto-M text by Jerome in the lemma of his commentary (see Introduction).

2. It is followed by καὶ ἐρῶ in a minority of mss., among which are B S* 998 and a few others. However, this is probably Old Greek, because it is not an easy form in the context and nevertheless resembles the literalistic approach of G Qoh. Moreover, it has been deliberately corrected by a reviser to καὶ εἶπον, as attested in the text of mss. V 253 637 S[cor] (εἶπα), which are among the best witnesses of the hexaplaric text of G.

The *Vorlage* of G may be conjectured as: ומוצא אני אתה ואמר. The last word is either a new introduction to vv. 26-28 after a complement אתה, referring to wisdom, was added to the verb מצא or, what is more probable, this new verb resulted from a dittography of the following word מר, as suggested by McNeile (*An Introduction*, 163): מרומר(א)אניורמ. In that case, only the א must be supplied. Once this second verb was added, the first one received a complement (אתה).

The ptc. of M is supported by the present tense in G and Jerome's lemma, against the pf. in V S T, so M is to be kept.

אֲסוּרִים יָדֶיהָ　　Rahlfs, δεσμοὶ χεῖρες αὐτῆς, has taken the lemma of Jerome as a witness of Old Latin, though it is most often a translation by Jerome of the proto-M text, especially when G departs from it, as Jerome himself states clearly in his introduction; see my remarks in the introduction. In almost all the extant witnesses of G, including Syh, G reads δεσμὸς εἰς χεῖρας αὐτῆς. The revised Greek is partly attested in σ', αἱ χεῖρες, and entirely in the specific group of Hexaplaric mss.: δεσμοὶ αἱ χεῖρες αὐτῆς. G* probably read אסור בי דיה. The accusative of movement (εἰς χεῖρας) is a way, within the limits of a literalist translation, to express that such a woman sees herself bound, the chain

cast upon her hands, so that she cannot act. It is noticeable that S and T attest
the same type of interpretation. S "She has bound her hands from what is good"
is based on a double translation of טוב at the beginning of v. 26b in M, ܛܒ,
meaning first "(away) from what is good," and second "the one who is good"
before God etc.; cf. 7:18a – this Peshitta text was kindly clarified for me by Dr.
Piet Dirksen. T has the same kind of interpretation: "Her hands are tied so that
she cannot do anything."

I see two ways of looking at the variations between the witnesses here.

1. The *Hebrew source* of M σ' ⟨α'⟩ V T is an assimilation of the sg. אָסוּר to the
preceding plurals through alteration of the following ב into a final ם at the end
of אסור.

2. The *Vorlage* of G misinterpreted the final ם of אסורם (written defectively) as
a preposition; so McNeile (*An Introduction*, 146).

The sg./pl. alternation could speak in favor of G's Hebrew source: a woman
(sg.) who is *snares* (pl.), whose heart (sg.) is *nets* (pl.), a bond (sg.) is *in her
hands* (pl.). But M has the clear advantage of the alliterations integrated in an
ongoing metaphor: she *is* snares, her heart nets and her hands chains. The support σ' brings to M's text is limited to the extant partial reading αἱ χεῖρες.

7 אָמְרָה קֹהֶלֶת   See commentary on קהלת at 1:2.

8 אָדָם   Rahlfs has no support for the omission of the cj. except the "Old Latin,"
i.e., the translation of the proto-M text by Jerome (see Introduction).

4 מִי כְּהֶחָכָם   α' τίς ὧδε σοφός and V *quis talis ut sapiens* both read: מי כה חכם.
According to Field's restoration, σ' read the same, translating: τίς οὕτως σοφός.
However, the syntax of the verse recommends keeping the rather unusual use of
the article after the preposition as in M, a use which seems to be a feature of
late Biblical Hebrew (GKC, §35*n*). The article is attested by M Hie^[lem] and S. As
to T, "Who is the wise who can stand against the wisdom of the Lord?," it
could be an interpretation of that particular use of the article of M, i.e., "the
Wise" *par excellence* is the Lord (cf. *b. Ber.* 10a). As suggested by Klostermann
(*De libri Coheleth*, 60) and then analysed by Euringer (*Der Masorahtext*,
93-94), what is now found in the mss. of G is probably a corruption of an original
ΤΙCΩΔΕ(CΟΦΟC) assimilated to the following ΤΙΣ ΟΙΔΕΝ. The plural
σοφούς perhaps stemmed from ΟΙΔΕ in this reading.

וְעֹז   All the versions read an adjective here, with a substantive value as in Ps
59:4. They make it the subject of ישנא, with פניו being read either as the *nomen
rectum* of עז (G S T) or the object complement (V Hie) of ישנא. In M the subject of the verb is the cstr. chain עז פניו, echoing חכמת אדם of the first stichos.
It must be noted that "boldness" or "arrogance" is the semantic value in late
Hebrew for the whole expression עז פנים – *per se* עז means "strength" in biblical as well as late Hebrew. So M should be translated: "The wisdom of a human
illuminates his face and his arrogance will be changed."

In view of what is presently found in the witnesses, it seems preferable to read
the adjective of the versions and understand: "The wisdom of a human illuminates his face but the arrogant will change his face." The "changing of the face"
is to be understood as a revelation of internal feelings, as in Sir 13:25: לב אנוש
ישנא פניו אם לטוב ואם לרע. So the text would mean: "Wisdom illuminates the
face of a human but the arrogant will give himself away." This is a good introduction to the following verses, whose theme is the delicate relation of the wise
to power.

Another explanation of the text of M has been proposed by Allgeier (*Prediger*, 5–6), who thinks that the odd אֲנִי at the beginning of the next verse is an alteration of a sfx. at the end of v. 1. In that case, the original text would read: וְעֹז פָּנָיו יְשַׁנָּאֶנּוּ "but his arrogance will alter him (i.e., his countenance)." In this line, the verb שׂנא should be understood as an Aramaism: it is quite often used in that language with the meaning of "alter," in connection with the human face. See Dan 5:6, 9, 10; 7:28, or the Targum on Deut 34:7, where it is said that the splendor of the glorious face of Moses had not been changed. This is a rather good solution too. The main objection to it is that it does not explain the disappearance of the sfx. נוּ in the *Vorlage* of G, where אֲנִי is not attested. This last objection cannot easily be answered, due to the fact that the sfx. would pose no difficulty and that the proposition of Allgeier, followed by Horst in *BHS*, implies in the transmission of proto-M a dittography of א followed by the creation of the rather odd אֲנִי in the following sentence. For the variant readings of יְשֻׁנֶּא, see the next case. T* וחציף אפין is found in Urbinas Ebr. 1, Zamora-Salamanca; Sperber has וחצון אפין, an alteration probably deriving from the late form חצוף.

יְשֻׁנֶּא: The verb שנה is written with א, as indicated in the Mm. The interchange of verbs ל"ה and ל"א is a frequent phenomenon in late Hebrew. It is noteworthy that in the two extant Hebrew verses in which Ben Sira attests the expression "change one's face," including the verse mentioned in the preceding case, the verb is also written with א (12:18; 13:25). (See, however, in the preceding case the possibility of reading the verb with its Aramaic nuances.) This א caused G and S to read "to be hated" from שׂנא. The Alcuin and Sixto-Clementine texts of V offer *commutabit*, which is also the lemma of Jerome's commentary; it might be the original Vulgate. As for the *pual* vocalization of M, it is bound up with the reading of עֹז פָּנָיו as subject. According to Gordis (*Koheleth – The Man*, 277), the meaning would be: "and the insolence of the face will be disguised," but the Hebrew content of the passage does not allow for such an interpretation – it is the whole expression עֹז פָּנִים that means "insolence," The simplest and most significant text, although *difficilior* from the point of view of textual transmission, is יְשֻׁנֶּא as Jerome has it; see the meaning and translation above in the commentary on עֹז. T interprets M, with: "(all) his ways are changed from good to evil"; some T mss. omit "all."

2 אֲנִי   Contrary to what is suggested by S.R. Driver in *BHK* and F. Horst in *BHS*, the versions offer no clear attestation of את instead of אֲנִי. G would probably have translated את with σύν, as it usually does in Qoh when the complement introduced by את differs from the subject of the verb. Moreover, the presence of את would require an article in the cstr. chain, something like: את פי המלך. On the other hand, there is no fully satisfactory interpretation of M אֲנִי; at best, see Gordis (*Koheleth – The Man*, 277–78), who interprets it as meaning: "I declare," which is along the same line as the attempt by σ' ἐγὼ παραινῶ. The word disturbs the sequence of ideas from v. 1 to vv. 2-4, but it must be recognized that the process of text transmission which led to the appearance of אֲנִי remains difficult to explain (see the hypothesis hereafter). Hitzig (*Prediger Salomo's*, 182) suggests keeping it and reading שְׁמֹר (instead of M impv.), as in V *ego os regis observo et preacepta iuramenti Dei*. However, there is a theological intention in that translation. Jerome considers this passage as one of the biblical attestations for "the unity of Reign of the Father and the Son," who

would be the divine king spoken of, parallel to God in the second part of the verse. This interpretation seems to Christianize an ancient Jewish tradition about the passage. In the Jerusalem Talmud, *y.Sanh.* 21b: Rabbi Yossi Be R. Bun says: "שמור מלך פי אני as for myself (אני) the mouth of the King of Kings I will observe (אשמור), who said to me at Sinaï: 'I am the Lord your God,' and (will observe) the word (ועל דברת): 'You will have no other gods'." According to *Midr. Qoh.* Rabbi Levy says: "As for myself (אני), the mouth of the King of Kings, the Holy Blessed Be He, I will observe (אשמור), that mouth which said, 'I am the Lord your God'." It must be noted that שמור written plene (which Mp confirms as occidental orthography) could be read inf. abs., suiting the syntactical relation of אני with שמור according to the Midrash (אני אשמור).

In this interpretation might lie the explanation for the introduction of אני at the beginning of v. 2. Whatever the meaning of the "oath of God(s)" in the second half of the verse, it has certainly been viewed as concerning the God of Israel. And it was necessary to separate the exhortation אל תבהל (M v. 3) from the "oath of God" (M v. 2); otherwise it could be read as a recommendation not to hurry/worry about (or because of) the oath of God when the king has spoken. Introducing אני as the subject of the inf. abs. שמור standing for a finite verb solved the problem. In this way M v. 3 could be read as a new sentence: a recommendation to the disciple of wisdom addressed by the subject (אני) of the whole of v. 2. This is how Symmachus understood it. Such an interpretation of v. 2 is reflected clearly in the Jewish ancient tradition. The Masoretic tradition would preserve the original vocalization of the impv. שמור within a late corrected text with אני. See a proposal for the translation of vv. 2-3 in the commentary on אל־תבהל (v. 3, next case).

3   אַל־תִּבָּהֵל   Except for Jerome, the versions differ from M in dividing the text. This divergence may have resulted from misunderstanding the rare construction: אל תבהל מפניו תלך, in which a finite verb replaces an inf. complement, see GKC, §120*a*, *g*. The attachment of אל תבהל to the end of v. 2b was known outside G and interpreted in ancient Jewish traditions as a recommendation not to hurry in pronouncing the name of God (T) or in transgressing the Torah (σ'). A good translation of M is the one by Jerome: *ne festines recedere a facie eius* ("Do not hurry to go out of his presence"), a warning against the temptation to get out of the service of the king (to stay in the face of the king is to serve him; see Dhorme, *L'emploi métaphorique*, 48). In fact, v. 3 is part of the same unit with v. 2; v. 2b is a causal clause and v. 3aα the main clause. So the whole sentence reads: "Observe the commandment of the king, and because of the oath of God, do not hurry to get out of his service; do not stand in a bad case, for he does whatever he pleases." The "oath of God" is the divine commitment to establish the king as *persona sacra;* see Hertzberg, *Der Prediger*, 164. For the value of kingship in Qoh, see the comm. on 5:8.

4   דְּבַר   The Greek tradition is diverse in its attestation of an equivalent for the consonants דבר. Rahlfs chose the nearest form to M, attested in the Hexaplaric mss.: καθὼς λαλεῖ βασιλεὺς ἐξουσιάζων. In A C S^{cor} and about thirty medieval mss., λαλεῖ appears at the end of v. 4a: καθὼς βασιλεὺς ἐξουσιάζων λαλεῖ, which points to a hesitation about placing the word in a pre-existing text. In B 998 S*, plus around twenty medieval mss., Aldine, Sixtine, and Complutensis editions, there is no equivalent for דבר. Moreover, a note in Syh states that Origen did not introduce a translation of that word in his text (Syh's text ܪܡܠܠ

was probably taken from S), which means Origen found a text of G without the word. In Syh, Theodotion's text is said to be "like the Septuagint," which Field interprets according to the text attested in Syh (= λαλεῖ). It is uncertain however if this marginal note bears also on the place of the word within the verse. Does G reflect an omission in its *Vorlage* to protect the "word of the king," which in M is easily related to the דבר רע of v. 3 (cf. v. 5 too)? M may be translated, with Gordis: "inasmuch as the king's word is power."

שִׁלְטוֹן   The text of G S T seems to translate שליט as in v. 8. σ' ἐξουσιαστικὸν εἶναι seems to be an interpretation of שלטון (דבר מלך); so, too, V *potestate plenus est* and Hie^lem *potestatem habens*. In V, Jerome translated *(sermo) illius* instead of *regis,* maybe in order to confirm his interpretation of v. 2, where the king is the Son and God the Father. In the text of V the complement *illius* may refer to the king as well as to God of v. 2.

5   יָדַע²   The reading of M is a harmonization with the following vv. 6-7. The difficulty of the version is the *apparent* contradiction between v. 5, in which Qoheleth says the wise heart knows the proper time and procedure, while in vv. 6-7 he says that although there is a proper time and a procedure for everything, man never knows what will happen.

7   כִּי כַּאֲשֶׁר יִהְיֶה   S "and what will be after him," and σ' (τίς) γὰρ τὰ ἐσόμενα (ἀναγγελεῖ αὐτῷ) could translate: כי אשר יהיה. V *et ventura* is inspired by σ', although Jerome insists in his commentary that his lemma is a literal translation. M is clearly *difficilior* and a good text.

   T* ארום בעידן דיהא is quoted according to Urbinas Ebr. 1, BN Paris 110, Zamora, M² Salamanca. Sperber offers ארום דיהא.

8   הַמָּוֶת   Rahlfs offers the Origenian text on the basis of Codex Venetus; the great majority of mss. omit the article.

   בַּמִּלְחָמָה   Rahlfs has no witness for omitting ἡμέρα in G; the Old Latin invoked in his apparatus is the lemma of Jerome, who most often translates proto-M when G diverges from M (see the Introduction). It is difficult to decide what the best text is here. In view of the absence of an article in יום מות in G and the only clearly attested meaning for משלחת (Ps 78:49), G leads to a Hebrew model with a rather expressive sequence: "there is no power in the day of death and no deputation in the day of war." The second יום might have been omitted (= M) to avoid the parallelism with the first one. But its insertion (= G) might also be an assimilation to the preceding expression, particularly if משלחת was hard to understand.

9   לְרַע לוֹ:   The verb of G S T Hie^lem might well be an interpretation – and even a correct one – of what is found in M, whose meaning could be ambiguous, as the interpretation by σ' shows: εἰς κακὸν ἑαυτοῦ. A strong case may be made for such an interpretation in view of Qoheleth's perception of life. There is no explicit reading for θ', which is characterized "like Septuagint" in Syh.

10   קְבֻרִים וָבָאוּ   G εἰς τάφους εἰσαχθέντας reflects קְבָרִים instead of קְבֻרִים, followed by יבאו instead of ובאו – vocalized either *qal* יָבֹאוּ or *hofal* יָבָאוּ written defectively. It must be noted that G read קברים pl., so that the frequently suggested transposition of the final מ to the beginning of ובאו is, in fact, not supported by G. In G as well as in M, the consonants קברים result from a faulty reading of קרבים. This may be concluded from the fact that a confusion between קבר and קרב, though not directly attested, accounts for all the difficulties of interpretation and syntax in the verse, as Serrano has shown ("(Eccl 8, 10),"

168–70). The emendation קְרֵבִים, suggested first by Rudolph, relies on a plausible confusion and has a strong capacity to explain the genesis of the extant forms. It has been accepted by Driver ("Problems," 230), Hertzberg (*Der Prediger*, 167, 170), Loretz (*Gotteswort*, 166), Galling ("Prediger," 111), Lauha (*Kohelet*, 155–56), Crenshaw (*Ecclesiastes*, 153–54), Michel (*Eigenart*, 220), and Vilchez Lindez (*Eclesiastés*, 343). For the liturgical meaning of קרב, a good attestation is found in Qoh 4:17, where Qoheleth recommends prudence in approaching God (see 5:1, as well). The corruption here is probably tied to the theme of the preceding verses, opposing the time before and after death.

As for the verb יבאו, it begins a new subdivision in the verse (see the commentary on יהלכו). V's translation of ובאו *etiam cum adviverent* is derived from σ' καὶ ὅποτε περιῆσαν, which is an attempt to solve the problem of this corrupted text. However we have not the equivalent of σ' for the first word (קברים). A reading attributed to α', καὶ ἦλθον, seems to support M. For the meaning of the whole verse, see the commentary hereafter on וישתכחו.

וּמִמְּקוֹם קָדוֹשׁ   No ms. of G supports the Rahlfs text. As often, he quotes as Old Latin the translation of proto-M by Jerome (see Introduction). It is to be noted that the Hexaplaric readings as well as the Origenian text mss. have no conjunction. For the preferred reading proposed here, see the commentary on the next word.

יְהַלֵּכוּ   Nowhere does הלך *piel* mean "to go out," a meaning often proposed here. Qoheleth probably meant "to walk in," and the alteration of the preposition ב in ובמקדש is easily explained in view of the preceding scribal error involving קרבים. If the wicked are not entering the sanctuary (קרבים) but are brought to the grave (קברים), they can no longer be brought *into* the sanctuary. That is why the original ובמקדש has been altered to וממקום (G), connecting this to the verb יהלכו which follows – and so imposing an alien meaning on this verb. In G and M, an attempt to make a clear separation between the wicked dead and the sanctuary may be observed. In the proto-M text, a cj. was read instead of the י in יבאו (G): ובאו (M). In the *Vorlage* of G, this same phenomenon transpired with יהלכו (M) becoming והלכו (G) – Rahlfs omits the cj., and, in fact, chooses the Origenian text, but the large majority of the Greek mss. attest the cj. καί here.

The history of the text can be traced in two main stages: (1) A confusion between קרבים and קברים led to the alteration of ובמקדש into וממקדש (G); (2) Interpreting that form, G then read והלכו, leaving וממקדש in an erratic position (which gave rise to the insertion of ἐπορεύθησαν after καὶ ἐκ τοῦ ἁγίου by a corrector of Codex Sinaiticus). The proto-Masoretic text avoided this by reading ובאו instead of יבאו, thus integrating וממקדש within the second phrase, and adding מקום for the sake of enlarging the concept of "sanctuary" (perhaps "synagogue" was meant; see Gordis, *Koheleth – The Man* 286). See the meaning of the original verse hereafter in the commentary on וישתכחו. σ' ἀναστρέφομαι is attested as an equivalent of הלך *piel* in Ps 55:15.

וְיִשְׁתַּכְּחוּ   The preferred text here is attested by G α' σ' V Hie^lem and fits perfectly the suggested restored form of the words 4-6 in the verse (see apparatus and comments), which would go like this: יבאו ובמקדש יהלכו וישתבחו בעיר אשר ובכן ראיתי רשעים קרבים ‖ כן עשו and can be translated: "And I have seen wicked men approaching (God); they come and walk in the sanctuary and thereafter they pride themselves for acting so." For קרבים, the nuance of "offering a sacrifice" is probably also understood – the liturgical meaning of "approaching" is attested in Qoh 4:17. A slightly different form is also possible and can be perceived in the restored form above: יבאו במקדש והלכו וישתבחו בעיר (the cj. before מקדש is omitted in the revised Greek and והלכו is supported by G). M וישתכחו is evidently due to קברים.

11   מַעֲשֵׂה הָרָעָה   G S read the prep. מן + cstr. pl. ptc.: מֵעֹשֵׂי. Jerome (V Hie[lem]), though reading ב instead of מ, implicitly attests that form: *contra malos*. The reading of these versions gives good sense too; however, that form might be an assimilation to vv. 11b-12a. M (מעשה) may be understood with NASB: "Because the sentence against an evil deed is not executed quickly." In T, רשיעיא "the evildoers" is implemented in the framework of the paraphrasis of the whole context. The accent in M seems wrong and פתגם מעשה הרעה must be read as a cstr. chain meaning "the judgment of the evil deed," which is indirectly supported by the versions. For the accent on פתגם, Wickes (*Accentuation*, 139, n. 21) suggests to read a *ṭəḇîr* instead of *zaqep̄*, with a few Masoretic mss. For the qameṣ in פתגם, a loan word from the Persian, see Gordis, *Koheleth – The Man*, 286.

12   עֹשֶׂה   Targum יעביד is equivalent to the present in the context of its interpretation: "And in the time that the sinner will do evil one hundred years"; see Knobel's translation: "When the sinner does evil one hundred years," which is correct. Though one is tempted to read S as a pf., the diacritical points in Codex Ambrosianus point toward a ptc.

        מְאַת   M מאת is probably a construct form of מאה "hundred." According to Gordis (*Koheleth – The Man*, 287), it could as well be "an archaic absolute . . . and modify רע which it follows for the sake of emphasis." The revisers of G, with ἀπέθανεν, most probably interpreted מאת as related to מות. The alteration of מאת into מאז in G's *Vorlage* is also responsible for the following reading καὶ ἀπὸ μακρότητος (= וּמֵאֹרֶךְ); see next case.

        וּמַאֲרִיךְ   The meaning of M מאריך is "prolonging one's life," as in 7:15, and its subject is the same as for the two preceding ptc. The complement לֹ is a dative of interest *(dativus commodi),* so that there is no need to introduce an elliptical subject, as σ' has done: μακροθυμίας γενομένης (αὐτῷ). V, *et per patientiam sustentatur,* is inspired by σ'.

        לֹ   The "Old Latin" invoked by Rahlfs to support his editing αὐτῷ for G, not only goes against all the Greek evidence, but is a translation of the proto-M text by Jerome! (See Introduction.) The pl. complement read by G* in its *Vorlage* (להם) is an assimilation to the second part of the verse.

13   כַּצֵּל   Jerome's quotation of Symmachus (given in his commentary on the preceding verse) seems to omit this word, *neque longo supererit tempore*. However this translation may have translated what is found in M. The preposition ב reflected in G is also found in G 6:12, where I suggested it is the best reading. Here M is to be preferred as it appears to be *difficilior* though making sense.

17   הָאָדָם[1]   On a literary level, this case could be related to the same variation in 3:13: 5:18: 7:2. The Aramaic use of the emphatic versus absolute state precludes classifying S and T, though S has the emphatic state here and T an absolute.

9:1   וְלָבוּר   M וְלָבוּר is taken to be a unique ע׳׳י variation of ברר introduced with a somewhat rare syntactic form (so Gordis, *Koheleth – The Man*, 289). As Hertzberg rightly points out (*Der Prediger*, 171), even with the meaning "to exam-

ine," which is rather uncertain, ברר would not fit the context: "what is described here is not examination but facts which are established." As a matter of
fact, the semantic value "to test, to prove," from which "examine" would be
derived, is itself only a questionable hypothesis in order to explain לברם in
Qoh 3:18; see the commentary there.

For G καὶ καρδία μου σὺν πᾶν εἶδεν τοῦτο, a *Vorlage* ולבי ראה את כל זה is
often suggested. An alleged haplography in the sequence את זה אה would be responsible for the appearance of M ולבור את. It must be noted, however, that
there is no reason for the very literalistic G Qoh to translate ראה between את
כל and זה. The only witness for the above suggested *Vorlage* is S "and my heart
saw all this" (ܘܠܒܝ ܚܙܐ ܫܘܝ ܗܠܝܢ). σ' is an interpretation of M and is presented
by Jerome with the same syntax in Hie^lem and V.

הַכֹּל לִפְנֵיהֶם: הַכֹּל   At the end of the verse, an original הבל (= ματαιότης in G)
has been written הכל in the early transmission of M, under the influence of
הכל, which occurs two words before. Consequently, this new הכל was read as
the beginning of v. 2. S has a conflate reading (M + G). The division found in
σ' makes good sense. In his first and literalistic translation Jerome (Hie^lem)
omitted the last word.

2 כַּאֲשֶׁר לְכֹּל   On the difficulty in transmitting באשר vs. כאשר in Qoh, see the
comm. on 4:17. Here, in M 9:2a הכל כאשר לכל, the word כאשר has become
the obligatory reading; see the commentary on the preceding case. As for G ἐν
τοῖς πᾶσιν, it is probably an inner corruption through haplography from EN
OIC TOIC ΠΑCIN; cf. McNeile, *An Introduction*, 149. In the lemma of his
commentary, Jerome follows G. The reading באשר is more probable than כאשר
in connecting the verse beginning here with the preceding verse ending with
הבל; see the preceding case.

לְטוֹב   The "plus" of the versions is late, while there would be no reason for the
omission of ולרע after לטוב. This last word itself *might* have appeared as an
erroneous reading of לטהור, so that the original text would be without לטוב (so
BHS); see Vilchez Lindez, *Eclesiastés*, 350. The word, however, is attested in
all the witnesses and makes no particular problem. It is clearly beyond the scope
of text criticism to omit it on the basis of what a "balanced" parallelism should
be in our view; compare the threefold series in vv. 6a, 12a, for example.

3 וְהוֹלֵלוֹת   The text of σ' given by Field (*Origenis Hexaplorum*, Auctarium) is a
genitive and should be understood as a second complement: ἐπληρώθη πονή-
ρου καὶ αὐθαδείας. This form is supported by the citation of σ' by Jerome in
his commentary: *repletur malitia et procacitate*. Syriac has a "plus," for it renders ܡܦܘܩܐ ܚܒܘܬܐ, but this is a probable assimilation to the end of 10:13. G
σ' V S T all support this reading of an abstract word sg. For the preferred reading, see commentary at 1:17 and 2:12.

וְאַחֲרָיו   M is *difficilior* and quite understandable. Gordis (*Koheleth – The Man*,
228) quotes a number of occurrences with the meaning "afterwards" (3:22;
6:12; 7:14; 9:3; Jer 51:46) and concludes that it "is best taken as an adverb with
petrified suffix, like יַחְדָו (so also Levy)." This seems to be the interpretation of
Jerome in his lemma as well as in V: *et post haec*. σ' and S read: ואחריתם "and
their end (is to the dead)." The ms. of T edited by Sperber as ובתר סופיהי is
either a literalist translation of אחריו or a slight corruption of ובתר סופוהי attested in Urbinas Ebr. 1.

4 יְבֻהַר   The versions support the *qərê,* as does G, though with an active conjuga-

tion (κοινωνεῖ). G is followed by Hie[lem] *communicet*. σ' τίς γὰρ εἰς ἀεὶ διατε-
λέσει ζῶν continues with the same vocabulary used at the end of the preceding
verse: τὰ δὲ τελευτεῖα αὐτῶν εἰς νεκρούς, but it reflects the basic idea of
being "united with life" (חבר); V, which most often depends on σ', is similar:
nemo est qui semper vivat. The *zaqep qatan* is to be removed; see Wickes, *Accentuation*, 74.

9   אֲשֶׁר² to הֶבְלֶךָ²   S attests the shortest form of the verse, without v. 9aβ. That part
is attested in G, but in a dubious way: (1) τὰς δοθείσας for אשר נתן, as indicated by McNeile (*An Introduction*, 150), is "foreign to the style of the translation"; (2) the translation of the last three words (כל ימי הבלך) πάσας (τὰς)
ἡμέρας ματαιότητός σου is omitted in Codex Alexandrinus and part of the
medieval mss.; and they are imported (in the nominative) from the Aquila version in the text of B and 998.

The omission in S and in G or their *Vorlage* might have resulted from an accidental parablepsis due to homoioteleuton, but on the other hand that part of the
verse is rather redundant.

כָּל יְמֵי הֶבְלֶךָ   Codex Alexandrinus and a majority of witnesses of the Greek tradition do not have these words, which in Codex Vaticanus (first hand) and 998
seem to have been imported from the Aquila version; see McNeile, *An Introduction*, 150.

10 בְּכֹחֲךָ   As in the versions, this word must be joined to the following, and a disjunctive accent should be placed on the word before (לעשות; see Wickes, *Accentuation*, 139). The reading of G seems better, meaning "as much as you
can."

12 הָאֲחֻזּוֹת   The text of M[L] is confirmed by M[L34] and M[Y], as well as by Jacob Ben
Hayyim's edition. None of them attests the secondary gemination of ז indicated
in *BHS* apparatus.

14 מְצוֹדִים   Plural מצודים occurs only twice in the Masoretic Bible: Qoh 7:26; 9:14.
In the first instance it probably refers to an instrument for catching a prey (see
vv. 26-27). Singular מצוד is found at Job 19:6, where Job says God has sur-
rounded him with His מצוד, and Prov 12:12, where no clear semantic value can
be assigned to the word, although "venison" appears as a possible field of
meaning for the context. On the basis of Qoh 7:26 and Prov 12:12, צוד is more
likely to be the root family of מצוד, which does not fit Qoh 9:14. That is why
M מצודים is often corrected here to מצורים (see BDB quoting Winckler), מצור
being the ordinary word for "siege" and "siege works." This is what the versions read: S ܩܠܡܘܣ (derived from Greek χαράκωμα) aligning either with G
χάραξ "palisaded camp, entrenchments," (cf. Deut 20:20, where מצור in a similar context is translated χαράκωσις in G and ܡܠܘܣ in S) or with Hie[lem] *ma-
chinam*, i.e., "siege engine," a meaning Ephrem ascribes to this Syriac word
(see Payne Smith, *Thesaurus*, col. 3643). The two Masoretic mss. indicated in
BHS have no Masorah and are of poor textual value.

McNeile (*An Introduction*, 80) suggests that a ר/ד confusion leading to M could
be due to the proximity of מצודה in 9:12, which is understandable if a rare m.
pl. of מצור was found here instead of the pl. of מצורה (Isa 29:3; 2 Chr 11:11;
12:4; 21:3). The verb בנה probably reinforced the tendency to read a word related to the root מצד, though בנה is also found with מצור in Deut 20:20. Regarding V *munitiones*, it could have read as M with ד; compare Jer 48:41; Ps
31:4 (and prob. מצדי in Ps 116:3), as well as with σ' ἀποτείχισμα, which LSJ,

222a, translate "lines of blockade." Finally the variation between sg. (σ' Hie[lem]) and pl. (G V S) should be noted.

▌ זְבוּבֵי מָוֶת   All the witnesses have read the pl., except T, where the "flies of death" are interpreted as "the evil inclination at the gate of the heart which is like the fly causing death" (cf. the old Hellenistic image about keeping the heart like the spider). McNeile (*An Introduction*, 165) suggests that G μυῖαι θανατοῦσαι "killing flies," is an inner Greek corruption of μυῖαι θανάτου σαπ(ριουσιν), the ending (θανατου)σαι being a dittography from σαπ. However, it might just as well be the same interpretation as found in T: "flies who bring death." Other interpretations of M are to be found in σ', which inverts the cstr. chain and reads "the death of the flies," and in V *muscae morientes* "dying flies." So there is most probably no variant reading for these two words.

יַבְאִישׁ   The sg. of M is attested only by σ' and T among the versions. In the source text of M, the ו of the pl. might have been read as the first י of יביע, which is unattested in the ancient versions. T in Urbinas Ebr. 1 and Zamora-Salamanca offers the *afel* sg. ptc. of סרי "to make stink, to corrupt" – the interpretation found in G S and σ' – while Sperber's edition offers מסר "to hand over." For the preferred reading, see the commentary on the next word.

יַבִּיעַ   This word is not attested in the versions; even the revision of σ' does not transmit any trace of it. S ܪܝܚܐ depends on G σκευασία and is inspired by the preceding ܡܢ ܚܕ (9:18), so it cannot be taken as a trace of גביע in this rather loose rendering, as it is sometimes suggested. The hypothesis that σκευασία, unused elsewhere in the Greek Bible, could be an alteration of the frequent σκεῦος which appears even in the preceding verse is most improbable. It should be at least a conscious correction pervading all the witnesses. But the word σκεῦος itself is so improbable as original Greek that such a correction has no basis at all. Nevertheless, it is regularly proposed, so that it is worth mentioning the objections to such a hypothesis. First, σκεῦος would translate not M יביע, but גביע, and one would need to explain how גביע, which could fit in the verse, was altered to the difficult יביע, which is either out of place or a semantic *hapax* in the Hebrew Bible. Second, one would need to explain why גביע was translated σκεῦος when it is never translated so elsewhere in the Greek Bible. Its equivalent is τὸ κόνδυ in Gen 44:2, 12, 16, 17; ὁ κρατήρ in Exod 25:31, 33, 34; and τὸ κεράμιον in Jer 42:5. The revisions, whose language is related to G Qoh (sometimes considered as "proto-Aquila"), offer σκύφος in these different books for α' and σ' (Gen 44:2; Exod 25:31, 34; Jer 42(35):5).

שֶׁמֶן רוֹקֵחַ   It is striking that σκευασία, here present in G Qoh, is attributed to θ' in Ezek 24:10 where M attests מרקחה. Now the last word in G is ἥδυσμα, which never translates the root רקח but is a regular equivalent for Hebrew בשם (once for סַמִּים in Exod 30:34). So G leads to a quite divergent Hebrew *Vorlage* vis-à-vis M. Its text may have read, more or less: זבובי מות יבאישו מרקחת שמן בשם "Dead flies make smelly the preparation of perfumed oil."

This might be indirectly confirmed by the text of σ', where ἔλαιον () μυρεψοῦ probably renders רוקח () שמן. The ptc. רוֹקֵחַ occurs five times in the Bible (Exod 30:25, 35; 37:29; 1 Chr 9:30; Qoh 10:1) and twice in Ben Sira (38:7; 49:1), always translated μυρεψός. Revising G Qoh 10:1, σ' restores the ptc. found in M and returns the word to the place it occupies there, for the sake of semantic coherence. Nevertheless, like G, it translates another word after שמן: εὐῶδες. Very likely σ' εὐῶδες and G ἡδύσματος translate a word that is absent in M. Now the regular equivalent for G ἥδυσμα, בֹּשֶׂם, is equally a possible source for σ' εὐῶδες. The word בֹּשֶׂם, which means "*aromata*," sometimes has the semantic value "smell, good smell," particularly when it determines another word. For example, it is translated εὐῶδες twice in Exod 30:23 in the expressions קְנְמָן־בֹּשֶׂם and קְנֵה־בֹשֶׂם. It must be said that in G Qoh and σ', a double translation for (מ)רוקח is improbable.

It is difficult to decide whether G's potential model, זבובי מות יבאיש ימרקחת שמן בשם, or M is superior. Though M seems corrupted, it is not easy to determine the history of its text form. The frequently suggested hypothesis that the *hifil* of נבע means "to ferment" posits an unknown semantic extension of a root whose value is otherwise clear: "to flow, to flow out, to spring." Moreover, such a semantic extension needs the confirmation of pharmacologists that a dead fly may actually make oil to ferment.

מְעַט to יְקָר   Except for the cj. before מכבוד, the lemma of Jerome's commentary fully supports M: *Pretiosa est super sapientiam et gloriam stultitia parva.* The same is true of T: "and how much more beautiful and precious than the wisdom of the sages and the riches of the rich men is a man whose stupidity is little and slight." This interpretation respects the known value of יקר in Hebrew (Podechard, *L'Ecclésiaste*, 425) and is perfectly in line with the thought of Qoheleth about wisdom. The same interpretation is also found in S, where ملم is attested at the end of the verse (= מעט of M), and the equivalent of רב (found in G) is placed with ומכבוד. So S runs: "More precious than wisdom and much glory a little folly." The reading of מעט at the end of the verse is also confirmed in a text assigned to σ' in Syh: κἂν μικρά. In V, מעט is read בעט and moved before סכלות, which supposes some liberty on the part of Jerome with a text similar to M (cp. his commentary lemma above). In the source text of G, the word רב was read at the end of the verse (dittography of לב?) and מעט moved to determine חכמה: "A little wisdom is more precious than the glory of much stupidity." For a good, though dated, *status quaestionis,* see Podechard (ibid.).

3   וְאָמַר לַכֹּל   McNeile (*An Introduction*, 165) suggests that G καὶ ἃ λογιεῖται πάντα is a corruption of an original καὶ λέγει τὰ πάντα, but this is rather improbable. The relative is also attested in S, which reflects the interpretation of G: مهل دmحsحد "and whatever he thinks." Possibly the relative marker אשר (or שׁ) dropped out by haplography, but the relative in G could just as well be interpretive.

The text of σ' *suspicatur de omnibus* followed by Jerome supports M, except that אמר is read as present. The absence of a cj. in the σ' reading might be due to the history of transmission of the Hexaplaric readings. In V the absence of the cj. is stylistic, as its presence in the lemma of Jerome shows.

5   שֶׁיֹּצֵא   The Masoretes vocalize this word as a f. ptc. related to the preceding word כשגגה. In this reading, the כ is to be understood as asseverative (Gordis, *Koheleth – The Man*, 309). The Masoretic vocalization and a great number of commentators understood vv. 6-7 as the content of that "inadvertence" (שגגה). However, it is questionable to characterize what is described in vv. 6-7 as "an inadvertence of the ruler," and the sentence is abstruse in its form if one follows the Masoretic vocalization: "an inadvertence coming from before the ruler." Moreover, the meaning "emanating from, coming from before," often proposed for explaining the vocalization of M, is contradicted by the use of מלפני in the

Hebrew Bible. That particular meaning "coming from before," "emanating from," is specialized when fire, wrath, etc., emanate from God. Otherwise, יצא מלפני means "to leave the presence of somebody" (cf. Gen 4:16; 41:16; 47:10; Num 17:24; Esth 8:15, etc.), which fits the discourse here perfectly: "There is an evil which I have seen under the sun: indeed, the inadvertence of leaving the presence of the ruler" (cf. v. 4) or literally: "the inadvertence that someone leaves the presence of the ruler."

V relates *egrediens* to *malum* (רעה) at the beginning of the verse, supporting M for the ptc., though making כשגגה an adverbial complement: *malum . . . quasi per errorem egrediens.* This understanding is already found in σ': κακόν ἐν ἀγνοία ἐξελθόν, whose text is presented independently from V in the apparatus since his ptc. is aorist. The text edited by Rahlfs with a relative pronoun is taken over from a minority group among the Greek mss.

0 לֹא־ The negation is found in the following sentence of T "and that generation does *not* pray before the Lord." See Knobel's translation ("Targum of Qohelet," 49, n. 14) with the explanation by R. Ammi, quoted in *b.Taʿan.* 7b., that לא פנים is understood as not praying before the Lord as a result of corruption.

הַכְשִׁיר All the versions have interpreted the root כשר here. σ' ὁ γοργευσάμενος is consistent with its rendering of כשרון in 2:21; 4:4 γοργότης "vivacity, briskness, impetuosity," and G in these passages has ἀνδρεία "courage." In 4:4 V has *industria,* as here. The important textual variation splits the versions between a masculine qualifier on one hand: "the strong, courageous one" (ἀνδρεῖος G) or "the brisk" (γοργευσάμενος σ' and pl. of ܚܝܠܬܢ in S), and a feminine abstract noun, on the other: "courage, strength" (*industria* V, *fortitudo* Hie[lem] and אכשרות T). The first group reads הַכָּשֵׁר and the second הַכּשֵׁר, two late Hebrew words. M *qərê* has the inf. abs. while the *kəṯîb* seems to read an inf. cstr.

1 הַנָּחָשׁ G is *difficilior,* an article being spontaneously added in M. Moreover, G reflects better assonance. The text of Rahlfs betrays once again the tendency to choose the text nearest to M, with a minority of greek witnesses. Regarding S, the emphatic state cannot be considered as the sure sign of a determiner in its source text. The pl. of T is interpretation.

4 לֹא־ Though *BHS* indicates several mss. with a cj. here, none of the ancient versions attests such a cj.

יָדַע S could be a pf., influenced by G, but more likely a ptc. in light of its complement ܡܐ ܕܗܘܐ ("Humans don't know what has been"). The present tense in V Hie[lem] might be an interpretation of M as a gnomic impf.; see the preceding verb, where the present *multiplicat* is also given for ירבה. It is to be noted, however, that this first verb is read as a present in all the versions, though a doubt persists about G πληθυνει, depending on where the accent is placed. Only σ' translated with a future there.

שֶׁיִּהְיֶה The versions might reflect a contextual exegesis, opposing the unknown past here to the unknown future in the following part of the verse: "what a human does not know is what is outside his own life *before* and after his days"; see also σ' τὰ προγενόμενα and V *(quod) ante se fuerit.* M opposes the future within the individual's lifetime to the future after the individual's lifetime. This might be an attempt to correct the verse in view of this: surely a man should know something of what happened before, particularly when told in the Holy Scriptures; see the Masorah commentary on 1:9 שיהיה.

Regarding the *dāḡeš* in the שׁ, M^L34 and M^Y fall in agreement with the majority in attesting the *dāḡeš*.

15   עֲמַל הַכְּסִילִים תְּיַגְּעֶנּוּ   עמל is masculine, but the verb יגע is feminine in M; moreover, the sfx. of the verb is sg. but it must refer to כסילים, which is pl. The attempts to justify M on a grammatical level are not convincing (Gordis, *Koheleth – The Man*, 314). The conjecture by Ehrlich (*Randglossen*, 7:99) proposed in our apparatus is the most probable, although the versions derive more or less from the same corrupted text as M. *If* the מ of מתי was read as the plural ending of כסיל, then it would have been rather natural to supply a י in כסילים and omit the one in מתי. It should be noted that this restored text fits well as a conclusion to the preceding verses, particularly the unit of vv. 12-15: "(14) the fool multiplies words, a human does not know . . . (15) when will the labor of the fool weary him? he who [even] does not know how to go to the city!" Knowing nothing, the fool speaks and speaks, because the effort he makes to get knowledge (עמל) does not wear him out; for this meaning of עמל see 8:17. As Hertzberg points out (*Der Prediger*, 195–96), the text conjectured by Ehrlich says clearly what M, which is corrupted, says vaguely; see his valuable *status quaestionis*. Notice that ייגענו is attested in the Babylonian tradition edited by G. Miletto (*L'Antico Testamento*), but this is a late harmonization between subject and verb.

17   בָּשְׂתִּי: G and Jerome read the root בשׂת, while M and S read the root שׁתה; see the Masorah commentary.

19   וְיַיִן יְשַׂמַּח   Field retroverts the text assigned to θ' in Syh (ܘܚܡܪܐ ܕܢܚܕܐ) as καὶ οἶνος τοῦ εὐφρανθῆναι, but ⟨θ'⟩ could just as well attest the accusative οἶνον, complement of ποιοῦσιν, as in G. In fact, the accusative is more probable than the nominative in view of the following infinitive of purpose retroverted by Field. As in M, the revision of ⟨θ'⟩ omits G καὶ ἔλαιον. If this is the case, θ' presents the first stage of alteration of this verse by reading לחם ויין as two successive complements of עֹשִׂים and the following verb as a final infinitive (translated τοῦ εὐφρανθῆναι). The alteration of ישמח to לשמח was easy and tempting, once the two words were read as accusatives. This seems to be a facilitation, giving to שׂחוק a positive nuance.

The positive interpretation of the verse, on the basis of Qoh 9:7-8 and Ps 104:15, has then led part of the tradition to a second alteration in which ושמן was inserted after ויין, attested in some Greek mss. (S B 998) and in Syriac; the placement of the word itself betrays a gloss.

M is the best text here, and the other witnesses only follow a route of harmonization with 9:7f. As Rashi indicates, עשה לחם means have a banquet (Dan 5:1; Gen 26:30); but it is important to remember that שׂחוק has a negative connotation in Qoh (Qoh 7:3, 6), and the following statement on money could be rather negative in the thought of Qoheleth.

20   הַכְּנָפָּיִם   For the expression בעל הכנפים of M, ⟨σ'⟩ presents τὸ πτερωτόν according to Field's retroversion from Syh ܦܪܚܬܐ. S with ܦܪܚܬܐ "bird" remains indeterminate as to the presence or absence of the article. ⟨α'⟩ καὶ ὁ κυριεύων πτέρυγος supposes the reading of the article, the word in M being read as a class name. V *et qui habet pinnas*; Hie^lem *et habens pennas* translates as ⟨θ'⟩ καὶ ὁ ἔχων πτέρυγας, but Latin is of necessity uncertain with regard to the article in the source text.

11:3   יְהוּא: The versions read a verbal form and M must be understood as a verbal

form too. Gordis (*Koheleth – The Man*, 320 f.) suggests that this might be a conflation of הוא and יהיה in order to preserve the two forms in the Masoretic
tradition. Possibly the unusual א at the end of this ל"ה verb (יהיא for יהיה) has
caused the hesitation in the tradition of the text.

5 אֵינְךָ יוֹדֵעַ At the end of the preceding verse, G read the three following words:
באשר אין יודע. An argument may be made in favor of G's *Vorlage,* which can
be divided in this way (regardless of internal variant readings):
v. 4 "He who watches the wind will not sow and he who looks at the clouds
will not reap, for he does not know."
v. 5 "Just as the path of the spirit in the bones inside the womb of the pregnant
woman, so you cannot know the deeds of God who creates all things."
In such a text, the logic of v. 5 runs from מה דרך to ככה, giving מה the excla-
mative value it acquires in late Hebrew and Aramaic for constructing comparative clauses. Though ordinarily the apodosis is introduced by אף, this text
should be considered as *difficilior* and of good literary value, which might have
elicited a change in the tradition of proto-M.

כַּעֲצָמִים V *et qua ratione (conpingantur ossa)* reflects the prep. כ of M – compare: *et sicut ossa* of Hie^lem. S "in the same way (a pregnant woman . . .)"
seems as well to interpret the preposition of M. T "(Just as you don't know how
the breath of the spirit of life goes) into the body of a young embryo . . ." reads,
or interprets: בעצמים.
Though not strongly supported by the textual witnesses, the preposition ב offers
a far better text, particularly in view of what has been said about the division of
G between vv. 4 and 5. Gordis reads the preposition ב (*Koheleth – The Man,*
322) and quotes biblical texts attesting the use of 'bones' pl. to refer to the
entire organism. The alteration of the preposition might be an intentional change
for theological motives, if it was felt improper to view the bones as the way for
the Spirit of God in man. For a translation, see our commentary on the preceding case.

9 בְּדַרְכֵי לִבְּךָ וּבְמַרְאֵי Most of the Greek witnesses reflect an "orthodox gloss"
(McNeile, *An Introduction,* 167): ἐν ὁδοῖς καρδίας σου ἄμωμος καὶ μὴ ἐν
ὁράσει, adding "blameless" after "the ways of your heart " and a negation before "the sight," creating the following text: "walk in the ways of your heart
blameless and not in the sight of your eyes." In any case, this must be regarded
as Old Greek, probably reflecting a Hebrew *Vorlage* in view of the very literalistic approach of G Qoh. Rahlfs presents as G the proto-M text via the lemma
of Jerome, characterized as "Old Latin." The word ἄμωμος is under obelos in
Syh. M is supported by V S T and the three revisions of G according to Syh,
where α'-σ'-θ' are characterized as being "like G." It is not surprising to find a
warning in T's translation: "walk in humility in the ways of your heart and be
careful in the sight of your eyes."

וּבְמַרְאֵי The Mp note seems to consider the י as a purely orthographic matter
and it may be that the Masoretes have vocalized a *qərê* מַרְאֶה here. All the
versions support the sg. Whether the י reflects a purely orthographic matter or a
plural is difficult to say. It is to be noted, however, that the pl. would be *difficilior* in all respects: it is an exception and it is more provocative in this context
than the sg. The only nuance that should be brought to this judgement is the fact
that the י balances the parallelism with the preceding words: בדרכי לבך.

1 בּוֹרְאֶיךָ The meaning of this word is "creator," singular, and has been under-

stood as such by the versions (τοῦ κτίσαντός σε; V *creatoris tui;* S ܠܒܪܝܟ); the pl. in M could be analogous to the pl. of אדון or בעל when spoken of God (compare Isa 54:5; Ps 149:2; Job 35:10; see GKC, §124*k*) unless it is merely a matter of late Hebrew orthography; see Gordis, *Koheleth – The Man*, 330 and GKC, §93*ss.*

4 וְסֻגְּרוּ The passive of M is better. A reading ascribed to α', καὶ κλεισθήσονται, supports M (see Field, *Origenis Hexaplorum*, 2:403, n. 13), though this reading was erroneously transmitted in some mss. in the place of the next α' reading καὶ κλιθήσονται (revising G καὶ ταπεινωθήσονται for וישחו) because of the similarity between the two readings.

וְיָקוּם The pl. in some mss. of G and in V may be an assimilation to the context. For this word and the next two, M is supported by all the versions and produces a nice antithesis with v. 4bβ between "stand up" and "bow down" as well as between the sound from outside and the lowering of human capacity to sing - whatever the meaning of בנות השיר is. So there is no textual basis nor literary need for emendation here; for interpretations see Gordis, *Koheleth – The Man*, 333–34.

5 יִרָאוּ Though it is sometimes proposed to emend the pl. to a sg., with S, the weight of the witnesses (M G σ' Hie^lem V) in favor of the *difficilior* pl. makes such an emendation very uncertain.

וְיָנֵאץ With the exception of σ', all the versions support the reading recommended by the Masorah: the *hifil* of נצץ "to blossom," וְיָנֵץ. The Mp states that the א is superfluous. Jerome remained puzzled by what he found in σ' *et obdormiet (vigilans);* see Field, *Origenis Hexaplorum*, 2:403, n. 16. It seems that σ' read as the subject of this verb a ptc. form of the following word השקד (= "the watchman"). If so, he might have vocalized the verb so: (הַשֹּׁקֵד) וְיָנֵץ, interpreting this as the disregard of the sentry, and consequently his falling asleep. See the commentary by Levy quoted in Gordis, *Koheleth – The Man*, 335.

וְיִסְתַּבֵּל It seems that G tried to render the verb in such a way that neither סכל nor סבל would be excluded. The verb παχύνω means "to make thick" or "to grow fat," with the nuance "to daze, to dull," well attested in the *Koine;* see Bauer, *Wörterbuch*, 1286 f. Thus, the passive of παχύνω may translate סכל *hitpael.* On the other hand, the choice of παχύνω allows understanding something like "to grow heavy" (= become a burden) on the basis of סבל *hitpael.* V *inpinguabitur* "will grow fat" reflects G (perhaps from Old Latin), and so, perhaps, does S (ܡܣܓܐ) ܘܢܣܓܐ "and (the locust) will abound" within a quite different interpretation of the verse. T ויתנפחון "and (your ankles) will be swollen" probably means "under the burden" interpreting וְיסתבל; a meaning "ankles" for Hebrew חגב was known in the time of Jerome, according to his own commentary. M ויסתבל is the only sure attested form, except in some medieval mss. of M where the error ויסתכל is found. M ויסתבל is to be kept and understood as: "the grasshopper will become a burden for itself" (instead of carrying any burden, the back [or the man himself] becomes a burden to himself); see Gordis, *Koheleth – The Man*, 335.

וְתָפֵר Σκεδάννυμι is regularly used in LXX for פרר *hifil* (cf. Gen 17:14), maybe on the basis of etymological ties to the root σχιζ (cf. Latin *scindo;* see Chantraine, *Dictionnaire étymologique*, 1012). The interpreters probably intended to introduce a correlation between "breaking the covenant" and "scatter." The verb, here, was read as *hofal* (וְתֻפַּר) by G and σ', who renders פרר *hifil* with διαλύειν in the Psalms (cf. Pss 32:10; 84:5; 88:34). The *hofal* is recommended here because the *hifil* (M) is transitive. G σ' are supported for the passive by Hie[lem] and V *et dissipabitur* (= G) and S, where a double translation gives first "be scattered" (= G) and then "cease" (= σ'). α' καρπεύσει read either the shortened form of the ל"ה verb: וְתֵפֶר (GKC, §75p), or, less probably, וְתִפְרֶה through dittography of the following ה. The verb read by α' is apparently recommended by its subject (אביונה = caperberry), but this would ignore the paradoxical logic of the passage: something in man is broken in his old age (appetite or sexual desire, according to the Jewish tradition, from the root אבה in אביונה).

5 יֵרָחֵק   The *qərê* יֵרָתֵק "be bound" is not attested in the *nifal* elsewhere, and the privative value it is often supposed to have here ("be loosened") is only known for *piel* verbs. In his *Thesaurus*[2], Gesenius adopted the view of Pfannkuche (1794), emending the *qərê* יֵרָתֵק in יִנָּתֵק, which fits the context and is confirmed by σ' κόπτω passive "to be cut," followed by Hie[lem] and V *rumpatur* and S نلܦܣܡ "will be cut." It must be recognized that ינתק is rather easy and makes its corruption into ירתק a bit enigmatic at first sight, but the reason for the alteration might be the reading of the negation in עד אשר לא meaning "before," as in Aramaic עד דלא; i.e., the negation has no negative value. Reading the negation as such would have meant "before not being torn away," so that it is understandable that such a reading might have undergone a correction toward a near form "before not being tied" (לא ירתק). The *kətîb* is a slight and easy alteration of the *qərê* from ירתק to ירחק "move away," by a scribe who correctly understood עד אשר לא. G ἀνατραπῇ might be an interpretation of the *kətîb* vocalized *nifal* (ירחק); an inner corruption from ΑΝΑΡΡΑΓΗ to ΑΝΑ-ΤΡΑΠΗ (= ינתק) as suggested by McNeile (*An Introduction*, 168) is less probable. T "your tongue becomes dumb" probably renders the *qərê* "be bound."

וְתָרֻץ   There are a few cases in M of the impf. of a ע"ע verb being erroneously vocalized as ע"ו (ירון Prov 29:6; ירוץ Isa 42:4, which is to be read יָרֹץ with G), and the witness of α' ⟨θ'⟩ (καὶ δράμῃ) and Jerome (*et recurrat*) shows this is already an early interpretation of these consonants here. But a passive is required, i.e., the *nifal* of רצץ, supported by G and σ' (καὶ θλασθῇ) as well as by S (ܘܢܬܪܥ); cf. Ezek 29:7. T* רעיעא (pass. ptc. of רעע "to break") is quoted according to Urbinas Ebr. 1; Zamora-Salamanca attest a later form of it: רעועא; Sperber has רעותא.

וְנָרֹץ   All the extant witnesses agree in reading two different verbs in v. 6a (ותרוץ) and v. 6b (M ונרוץ), once רוץ "to run" and once רצץ "to crush," but there is a variation among the witnesses as to where each of these roots belongs. M, in which the idea of breaking was absent for the first two verbs of the verse in v. 6a, read רצץ in v. 6b, harmonizing with the preceding שבר. G read: וְיָרֻץ הגלגל אל הבור. The impf. seems better in this context, like all the verbs of vv. 6-7; moreover, the prep. אל supports such an interpretation: "and (before) the wheel (of life) runs down to the grave" (cf. v. 7) alluding to the wheel of the well or cistern falling in the depth. The whole verse, according to our textual choices, would read: "(Remember your Creator) before the silver cord is broken and the golden bowl is crushed and the pitcher by the well is shattered and the wheel runs down to the cistern (grave)."

7 וְיָשֹׁב   Against the proposal in *BHS,* it must be said that if וְיָשֵׁב had been the original reading, there is no apparent reason why the Masoretes should not have

vocalized it this way; even though a number of jussive vocalizations for the impf. are attested in the Hebrew Bible; see Schoors, *The Preacher Sought*, 28, and cf. GKC, §109*k,* Joüon/Muraoka, *Grammar,* §114*l.*

9 הָעָם   Rahlfs suggests a corruption of ΛΑΟΝ after it was misread ΑΝΟΝ as the abbreviation of ἄνθρωπον, but the reverse would be more probable. A case could be made for the text of G (= הָאדם) as the original reading.

וְאָזֵן וְחִקֵּר   This is the only *piel* of אזן, which is otherwise *hifil* in the Bible (41 times), meaning "to hear." The causative was nevertheless understood by Jerome *audire fecit,* and then in V *narrare,* while α' S and T understood "to listen to." The *Vorlage* of G read: וְאָזֵן יַחְקֹר "and the ear will explore," and G understood the following תקן as a substantive (κόσμιον = תֶּקֶן "the arrangement"). Consequently, it ended the verse after משלים (G transfers הרבה to the beginning of v. 10). That form of text was mainly generated by the difficulty of recognizing a verb in אזן, and the absence of a cj. before תקן. The most probable meaning for אָזֵן is the one suggested by modern scholarship in relation to מאזנים "scales": "to weigh" (consider, evaluate).

10 וְכָתוּב יֹשֶׁר   The reading assigned to α' according some witnesses is assigned to σ' in Syh; see Field, *Origenis Hexaplorum,* 2:404, n. 32; in the Auctarium, Field quotes a ms. assigning the same reading to both α' and σ' (*Origenis Hexaplorum,* Auctarium). This reading, followed by Jerome, read וְכָתַב active, with יֹשֶׁר as an adverb. S also read the verb this way, but followed by a substantive as in M: ܩܘܫܬܐ ܘܟܬܒ "and he wrote the truth." M and G attest a *textus difficilior,* with G reading these words of M a cstr. chain: καὶ γεγραμμένον εὐθύτητος. Gordis (*Koheleth – The Man,* 342–43) suggests reading the inf. abs.: וכתוב "either as an inf. consecutive ("and he wrote") or as the object of בקש, "and (he sought) to write honestly, words of truth"; see also Podechard, *L'Ecclésiaste,* 474. It is not excluded that α' σ' and Jerome read this vocalization. But M is supported by G, where the only difference is that כתוב is read as part of a cstr. chain. Against Podechard and Gordis, one might ask, how וכתוב could have been missed here and transformed into the difficult וכתוב, particularly in Qoh, where this use of the infinitive is a rather frequent syntactic feature. From a textual point of view, it is best to keep M and understand it as a testimony about the transcription of Qoheleth's words: "and what is written is exactness"; see Barthélemy *CTAT,* 5, *ad loc.*

13 נִשְׁמַע   In its text, Syh offers the impv. pl.: ἀκούετε; in its margin a similar reading is assigned to α' and θ', but this text reflected in Syh is an alteration of ἀκούεται, which is the revised Greek shown in the Origenian text chosen by Rahlfs in his edition, often too prompt to choose a text near to M. It is not rare to find in Syh a Septuagint text already revised. The probable form of G is the one edited by Swete and attested by the Greek codices Vaticanus, Alexandrinus, and Sinaiticus. V *audiamus* is a free interpretation of נשמע.

14 מַעֲשֶׂה   The main divergence in reading here is between the sg. – M G σ' Hie[lem] T – and the pl. – ⟨θ'⟩ V S. Another difference is the presence of an article attested in G. The sg. is best attested and must be kept; the pl. in some witnesses is due to the context. Retaining the article depends on the conclusions about the very specific use of the article in some verses of the book; on this see commentary at 5:18 האדם. The attribution to θ' of the reading τὰ ἔργα τοῦ ἀνθρώπου is rather suspect; it reflects a targumic clarification.

LAMENTATIONS

3 הִיא, G has no equivalent for **הִיא** and on the other hand twice adds αὐτῆς in the preceding line. This is unexpected given the general literalness of the Greek translation of Lam but it does not necessarily presuppose a different Hebrew text. Note that the first αὐτῆς has ÷ in G^O and is absent in ⟨α'⟩ and the second has ÷ at least in Syh and in one Greek manuscript. In Albrektson's opinion "the αὐτῆς of 1.3a is in fact a corruption of an original αὐτή = **הִיא** in 1.3b. . . . The resultant δουλείας αὐτῆς may then have influenced a scribe to add an αὐτῆς after ταπεινώσεως as well" (Albrektson, *Studies*, 57). An easier explanation might be that the double addition of αὐτῆς was caused by the very frequent presence of this possessive pronoun in the immediate context. The absence of an equivalent for **הִיא** may be an adjustment to the Greek style as it is an adjustment to the Latin style in V.

1:4 and 1:8, where **הִיא** is rendered literally by αὐτή in G and by *ipsa* in V, are different because here the pronouns are necessary to introduce a new subject, which is not the case in 1:3.

הַמְּצָרִים: The Greek translator seems to have misunderstood the pl. of the rare noun **מֵצַר** as a ptc. (Albrektson, *Studies*, 58). After that it was tempting to add an obj. as a part of the Greek tradition does. S reads sg., but since the consonants of the pl. would be the same, the original translation might have had *seyame*.

4 נּוּגוֹת ἀγόμεναι (G), διωκόμεναι (⟨α'⟩), and αἰχμάλωτοι (⟨σ'⟩ according to Field) seem to be efforts of the Greek translators to guess the meaning of the unique form **נּוּגוֹת** (*nifal* ptc. √**יגה**), which was unknown to them. Since ἄγειν is in several cases used as Greek equivalent for Hebrew **נהג**, they apparently derived **נּוּגוֹת** from √**נהג**, probably interpreting it as **נְהוּגוֹת**. V has *squalidus*, which means not only "dirty" but also figuratively "mourning" and therefore can be judged as a witness for M; cp. **מתאבלין** in T. M is not only the *lectio difficilior* but also fits perfectly in the context and the different Greek readings can be explained without presupposing a different Hebrew *Vorlage*. (See *CTAT*, 2:863–64; Albrektson, *Studies*, 58; Rudolph, "Text der Klagelieder," 101.)

6 וַיֵּצֵא The Greek tradition is divided here: One branch represented by G^{S*}, G^A, the Hexaplaric and the Lucianic tradition, aligns with M translating ἐξῆλθεν, "is departed." The other branch, represented mainly by G^B, has ἐξήρθη, "is taken away." It is very unlikely that this presupposes a Hebrew **וַיֻּצָּא** (*BHK, BHS*), a form which is nowhere attested in the Bible. It may rather be a scribal error for ἐξῆλθεν, or what we would like to suggest, a free translation in order to express that the beauty "is departed" not by itself but that God is the one who has taken it away. See Albrektson, *Studies*, 59, and Rudolph, "Text der Klagelieder," 101.

מִן בַּת־ M^{ket} is the more unusual orthography, so that it seems easier to explain how this form became contracted than vice versa.

7 זָכְרָה יְרוּשָׁלַם In 4QLam is found a remarkable textual variant for the first part of this verse. The variation was presumably triggered by the form **זכרה** which allows two different interpretations, namely, as 3 f. sg. pf. (cf. M) or as an emphatic m. sg. impv. (cf. 4QLam with the orthography **זכורה**). The alternate readings **ירושלם** and **יהוה** for the subj. correlate with the respective interpretations of the verb. Regardless of the fact that "Remember, YHWH, . . ." is a

frequent invocation of God (e.g., 3:19; 5:1; Pss 132:1; 137:7, etc. and the emphatic forms in Neh 5:19; 6:14; 13:14, 22, etc.), it represents within the context
of Lam 1 the *lectio difficilior*, while the reading "Jerusalem" is easily explained
as an assimilation to the context (cf. בַּת־צִיּוֹן in v. 6 and יְרוּשָׁלִַם in v. 8). Compare Cross, "Lamentations 1," 140, and DJD XVI, 232–33.

יְמֵי עָנְיָהּ וּמְרוּדֶיהָ   Besides the different subj. at the beginning of the verse the
text of 4QLam is also significantly shorter than M. This is of special interest
because within the context of Lam 1 the abnormal length of v. 7 is generally
noticed in M. Since the shorter version in 4QLam is nevertheless consistent it
hardly results from an accidental omission (as, e.g., in v. 10f.). An intentional
alteration by the scribe seems unlikely as well, because the amount of errors
and mistakes in 4QLam points to a certain negligence, or to "a sleepy scribe"
(Cross, "Lamentations 1," 139) who would hardly have "corrected" his *Vorlage*
in such an extensive way. Thus it seems most likely that the scribe of 4QLam
found this shorter version already in the manuscript from which he copied, i.e.,
4QLam has preserved in this case an earlier stage of the textual development
than the stage reflected by M and the ancient translations. The plus in M is
probably an amplification (perhaps under the influence of 3:19).

כֹּל to קֶדֶם.   According to M (which agrees with the *Vorlage* of the ancient versions), 1:7 is the only verse in this lament that consists not of three but of four
lines (cp. a similar case in 2:19). This raises form critical questions. Usually this
second (or alternatively the third; Kaiser, "Klagelieder," 125) line because of its
content is regarded as an addition (see *BHK, BHS*). There is, however, no text
critical evidence for this hypothesis. The shorter text of 4QLam rather suggests
that the second part of the first line in M is an amplification (perhaps influenced
by 3:19); see the preceding comment and cp. the reconstruction of the text by
Cross, "Lamentations 1," 140–41, and DJD XVI, 233; see further *CTAT*,
2:866–67, and Albrektson, *Studies*, 62–63.

מַחֲמֻדֶּיהָ   Both readings depend on their respective contexts: מַחֲמַדֶּיהָ only makes
sense with "Jerusalem" as the preceding subj. while מכאובנו (especially the 1 pl.
sfx.) closely attaches to the preceding invocation "Remember, YHWH, . . .".
Since there is apparently no direct link between the two readings, they probably
presuppose a third one as their origin. Cross ("Lamentations 1," 140 and DJD
XVI, 233) has determined מְרוּדֶיהָ as that original reading, from which both
variants depart and which is still preserved in M within the amplification in the
preceding colon. The original מְרוּדֶיהָ was corrupted by misreading into מַחֲמַ-
דֶּיהָ (cp. v. 10f.); in other manuscripts it was altered to מכאובנו (cp. vv. 12, 18)
either as a facilitation of the difficult מְרוּדֶיהָ or as a 'correction' of מַחֲמַדֶּיהָ.
The assumption that an original מְרוּדֶיהָ has been corrupted is indirectly confirmed by the fact that all ancient versions struggled with וּמְרוּדֶיהָ in the preceding line (see the apparatus on that case) and thus attest the tendency to interpret
or alter this rare word (similarly again in 3:19).

צָרִים   G aligns with 4QLam as to the presence of a 3 f. sg. sfx. Note, however,
that beyond this detail the rendering of the whole colon by G is much closer to
M than to 4QLam.

עַל   4QLam has either a variant reading (if the restored text reads עַל [כו]ל) or
perhaps simply a ditt., i.e., a mistake similar to that of v. 6, where the scribe
wrote לוא twice.

מִשְׁבַּתֶּהָ:   σ' (τῆς καταργήσεως αὐτῆς) is the only version that keeps close to M.

T has a free exegetical paraphrase of M: עַל דפסק טובה מבינהא, "because her good had ceased from her." ⟨α'⟩ (καθέδρᾳ αὐτῆς) obviously committed the same error as G. S (ܡܦܘܠܬܗ, "her collapse") from the lexical point of view aligns with 4QLam because both use the same root (שבר / ܢܦܠ). However, semantically it can be regarded as "a perfectly intelligible and on the whole satisfactory rendering of MT" (Albrektson, *Studies*, 61) as well. M is not only the *lectio difficilior* but obviously also the origin at least of the readings in G, ⟨α'⟩ and V.

3 לְנִידָה G V and T confirm that the text implies a form of √נוד, "move to and fro," "wander (as fugitives)," "become homeless," and thus the form לָנוּד (i.e., the inf. לָנוּד) found in 4QLam might well be the original reading. Whether the particular meaning here is really "'Kopfschütteln' als Ausdruck des Spotts" (Rudolph, "Text der Klagelieder," 102; cp. *HALAT*, 657) remains uncertain, since in Jer 18:16, for example, this mocking gesture is not only expressed by a derivative of נוד but has an additional בְּרֹאשׁוֹ; cp. Ps 44:15.
The difficult reading לְנִידָה in M can probably best be explained as a corruption which resulted from assimilation of לָנוּד to לְנִדָּה in v. 17 (cp. ⟨α'⟩ σ' S), as suggested by Cross: "The *he* of לָנדה is a dittograph of the subsequent *he* of היתה, and *waw* is confused with *yod*, as persistently in Late Hasmonean and Herodian Jewish Scripts" (DJD XVI, 233; cp. Cross, "Lamentations 1," 141). On the other hand, לָנוּד in 4QLam might be a facilitation of the difficult and confusing לְנידה.
S has for לְנִידָה or לָנוּד the same equivalent (ܨܥܪܐ, "contempt," "abhorrence") as for לְנִדָּה in 1:17. But this does not necessarily presuppose that the translator had in both cases לְנִדָּה in his Hebrew text. It rather shows that he regarded לְנִידָה or לָנוּד as a variant form of לְנִדָּה.
The reading of σ' is obviously a double translation which combines both interpretations: σίκχος is an equivalent for נִדָּה and ἀνάστατον, "driven away," is a rendering via √נוד (Rudolph, "Text der Klagelieder," 102). Note that Codex Marchalianus (Q) reads σίγχος ἀν., which might be either an orthographic variant of σίκχος ἀν. or a free interpretation (σίγχος = σκίγγος, "skink," "lizard"; LSJ, 1597 and 1610). ⟨α'⟩ has εἰς κεχωρισμένην, "to a separated one," which either can be a rendering via √נוד (cp. σ': ἀνάστατον) or is based on the reflection that a person in "contempt" (נִדָּה) becomes "a separated one."

9 וַתֵּרֶד The versions of ⟨α'⟩ (κατέβη) and S (ܘܢܚܬܬ) as well as ונפלת in T confirm the vocalization of M.

1 מְבַקְשִׁים The presence of a *dageš* in M^L cannot be determined with certainty. There is a very weak brownish dot which can be either the remnant of a *dageš* or just a discoloring of the material. Note, however, that neither M^L34 nor M^Y have a *dageš* with this lemma.

מַחֲמַדֵּיהֶם The versions show some variation but none of them really presupposes a Hebrew text which would be different from M. V uses the indefinite pronoun instead of the possessive pronoun, probably to put stress on the aspect that *all* precious things must be given away. On the other hand, the sg. of the noun in S (in contrast with the pl. used in vv. 7 and 10) might express that everybody gives his *most* precious thing, while the sg. in T is rather to be understood in a collective sense (cp. vv. 7 and 10) and thus in its meaning aligns with M. The sg. sfx. in G may presuppose a Hebrew *Vorlage* like 4QLam, but nevertheless the 3 f. sg. sfx. is an assimilation to מחמדיה in v. 10 and therefore

compared with the m. pl. sfx. in M a *lectio facilior* which has been corrected
e.g. by σ' (τὰ ἐπιθυμήματα αὐτῶν).

Cross, on the other hand, regards the readings of 4QLam (מחמדיה) and G (τὰ
ἐπιθυμήματα αὐτῆς) as the original text and interprets the accordance with
מחמדיה in v. 10 not as an assimilation, but as a repetition which is "characteristic of the poetic structure of this lament" (DJD XVI, 235, and also Cross,
"Lamentations 1," 143). This view, however, leaves the pl. sfx. in M and in
most of the versions unexplained.

נֶפֶשׁ   Note that 4QLam has also a 3 f. sg. sfx. in the preceding colon (מחמדיה
instead of מחמדיהם).

זוֹלְלָה: The m. ptc. in 4QLam indicates that the 1 sg. has been incorrectly interpreted as the "I" of the poet instead of personified Zion. The same phenomenon
recurs at שֹׁמֵמָה and דָּוָה in v. 13. See DJD XVI, 235f., and Cross, "Lamentations 1," 143.

12   לוֹא אֲלֵיכֶם   There are two different readings attributed to Symmachus in this
case: ὦ ὑμεῖς according to Syh and οὐ πρὸς ὑμᾶς according to Codex Marchalianus (Q). Thus M is confirmed directly by G σ' S and indirectly also by ⟨σ'⟩ V
T, which presuppose only a slightly different vocalization (לוּא instead of לוֹא).
The reading οἵ πρὸς ὑμᾶς which is found in the great majority of the Greek
manuscripts is indeterminate, because οἵ either could result from inner-Greek
corruption of an original οὐ which would presuppose a Hebrew לוֹא or represents the equivalent to a Hebrew לוּא which would align with ⟨σ'⟩ V T.
Albrektson proposes the following interpretation of the difficult Hebrew text:
"(It is) not for (or about) you." כל־עברי דרך is in his view idiomatic and
means "the man in the street," "everybody." "The meaning of the whole phrase
. . . would then be: (This is) not for (= nothing which concerns) ordinary people,
this does not happen to everybody" (Albrektson, *Studies*, 68–69). According to
Rudolph לוא אליכם is a marginal note, which accidentally was incorporated
into the text and replaced an original לְכוּ (Rudolph, "Text der Klagelieder,"
102–3), but there is no textual evidence in favor of this view.

אֲשֶׁר עוֹלַל לִי   σ' (ὡς ἐπεφυλλίσθην, "when I have been gleaned," i.e., "when I
have been dealt hardly") can be regarded as a rather literal rendering of M,
since the syntactic variation (obj. becomes subj.) is required by the passive of
the verb ἐπιφυλλίζω, which is, however, a standard equivalent for Hebrew עלל
(cp. G in 1:22, 2:20 and 3:51). G (ὃ ἐγενήθη) confirms the Masoretic vocalization of עוֹלַל as a pass. (*poal*), but has no equivalent for לִי. Possibly the translator regarded לִי as already included in the immediately preceding term ἄλγος
μου, "my pain" and intended to avoid the tautology "my pain which happened
to me." G^O, G^L and V have an equivalent for לִי, but seemingly presuppose the
vocalization עוֹלֵל (*poel*). However, the rendering of עוֹלַל as an active could
could also be a simplification of the *passivum divinum* (cp. S).

אֲשֶׁר הוֹגָה יְהוָה   Ziegler judged ἐταπείνωσέ με κύριος to be the original text of
G. This is convincing insofar as ταπεινόω is G's standard equivalent for יגה in
Lam (cp. Lam 1:5; 3:32, 33), but it should be noted that in this form the reading
is not attested by any Greek manuscript. Most of the manuscripts read φθεγξάμενος ἐν ἐμοὶ ἐταπείνωσέ με κύριος, which is a double translation: ἐταπείνωσέ με via √יגה (cp. S and T) and φθεγξάμενος ἐν ἐμοί via √הגה (cp. σ'
and V). G^O has ἐταπείνωσέ με in the first place and ÷ with με and with ἐν
ἐμοί.

Besides the lexical problem the ancient translations reflect syntactical difficulties. According to the Hebrew text, אֲשֶׁר probably relates to the preceding לִי
(Rudolph, "Text der Klagelieder," 103): ". . . me, whom the Lord has caused
trouble." G has no equivalent for אֲשֶׁר but starts an independent clause and adds
the obj. "me": "the Lord has humbled me." S has the cj. "and" instead of the
particle of relation and agrees with G in the rest. T relates אֲשֶׁר either to מַכְאֹבִי
or to the whole preceding line and adds also the obj. "me": ". . . (my pain) . . . ,
whereby YHWH has broken me." It is uncertain whether G, S and T had a 1 sg.
sfx. in their *Vorlage*, because both the addition of the the obj. "me" and the
different treatment of the particle of relation by the versions can also be explained as mere translational adjustments in order to solve the syntactical difficulties. Finally V (*ut locutus est Dominus*) and σ' (ἀνεκάλεσε κύριος) despite
their lexical error confirm the absence of a 1 sg. sfx. in the Hebrew text.

4QLam, on the other hand, reads הוגירני, "he frightened me" (√יגר *hifil*), which
probably results either from interpretation or corruption of הוגה. In a first step
perhaps a sfx. was added (cp. G S T), and in a second step a scribe changed the
root. But it is also possible to argue for the opposite. Since the unique form
הוגירני in 4QLam can be judged as the *lectio difficilior* here, it may be regarded
as the original reading, from which M (and the versions which depend on M)
emerged by corruption (assimilation to Lam 1:5; 3:32); see DJD XVI, 235 and
Cross, "Lamentations 1," 144. However, given the generally careless character
of 4QLam, we hesitate here to follow this view.

חֲרוֹן אַפּוֹ׃   4QLam (חרו[נו]) could be regarded as the *lectio difficilior* while M
has the expression in its usual form (cp. e.g. 4:11; Isa 13:13; Jer 4:26, etc.); see
DJD XVI, 235. But again we hesitate to follow 4QLam because of its frequent
inaccuracy in details. The equivalent reading ὀργῆς αὐτοῦ in the Greek minuscule 534 from the eleventh century does not seem weighty enough to confirm
4QLam.

3 וַיִּרְדֶּנָּה   M σ' V T and probably also ⟨α'⟩ (see Rudolph, "Text der Klagelieder,"
103) read a form of √רדה׀, "to dominate," but this makes the 3 f. sg. sfx. difficult in a context where Jerusalem occurs in the 1st person. The versions try to
resolve this difficulty by changing the sfx. from 3 f. sg. either into a 1 sg. referring to Jerusalem (σ' καὶ ἐπαίδευσέν με; V *et erudivit me*), or into a 3 pl. referring to "my bones" (⟨α'⟩ καὶ ἐλίκμησεν [or ἐπαίδευσεν? cf. Rudolph, "Text
der Klagelieder," 103] αὐτά) or "my fortified cities" (T paraphrases the beginning of the verse by "from heaven he sent fire into my fortified cities" and then
renders וירדנה by וכבש יתהון, "and he conquered them"). S (ܐܘܚܬܢܝ, "and made
me descend") aligns with σ' and V in changing the sfx. into 1 sg., but for the
vb. it presupposes a Hebrew √ירד *hifil* as does G (see below). Note that all
these versions, including G, regard YHWH as the subj.

In order to keep M it has been suggested to make אֵשׁ (which usually is f.!) the
subj. of וַיִּרְדֶּנָּה and to relate the 3 f. sg. sfx. to the pl. בְּעַצְמֹתַי. The meaning
would then be: "he sent fire into my bones, and it overcame them" (Driver,
"Hebrew Notes," 137; cp. ⟨α'⟩ T). Although this is syntactically not entirely impossible (see *CTAT*, 2:871), it remains rather uncertain.

G, which in Lam usually translates its Hebrew *Vorlage* very literally, suggests
an easier solution. The translator of G is the only one who agrees with M in the
3 sg. sfx. For the vb., however, he obviously read √ירד *hifil* (cp. S) and this
without the cj. Thus his *Vorlage* presumably read יוֹרִדֶנָּה and this reading in fact

might represent the original Hebrew text. 4QLam ("ויורידני or less likely
"ויורידנו", DJD XVI, 234) clearly confirms the reading of ירד√ *hifil* although the
sfx. remains uncertain: with 1 sg. sfx. it aligns with S and with 3 m. sg. it could
be a sub-variant of the original Hebrew reading with אֵשׁ treated as masculine
(see DJD XVI, 235 and Cross, "Lamentations 1," 145). The use of a *wayyiqtol*-
form in 4QLam seems to be a facilitation introduced by the scribe. This indicates that probably the uncommon (but not unique; cp., e.g., 1:14) use of a
yiqtol-form for the past has triggered the corruption of the original Hebrew text.
By a simple metathesis of י and ו an original יוֹרִדֶנָּה has been erroneously changed
into וירדנה.

Note finally that the original יוֹרִדֶנָּה is not only a perfect parallel with מִמָּרוֹם
שָׁלַח at the beginning of the verse, but also solves the syntactical or stylistic
problems and produces a well balanced parallelism: "from on high he sent fire,
into my bones he made it descend."

14   נִשְׂקַד   נִשְׂקַד (with the diacritical point on the left) is doubtless the classical Tiberian orthography which presumably has preserved the original reading. The
meaning of the Hebrew term נִשְׂקַד עֹל is unknown, but T* "the yoke has become heavy" possibly points in the right direction. The text of T* is preserved
in T^U: אֵתִיקָר נִיר מְרוֹדִי בִּידֵיה, "the yoke of my rebellion has become heavy
by/in his hand." Other mss. and the editions by van der Heide and Sperber read
אֵיתְקִיד נוּר, "the fire . . . has been lit," instead of אֵתִיקָר נִיר, "the yoke . . . has
become heavy." But this is very likely an inner-Aramaic corruption of T* and
therefore irrelevant for the evaluation of M.
G G^L V S (followed by a number of KR Hebrew manuscripts), interpreted the
unknown word perhaps as נִשְׂקַד (although a *nifal* of שׂקד√ occurs nowhere else
in the Bible) or related it in another way to שׁקד√, "to watch." Thus, apart from
the lexical error, all these versions confirm the consonants of M. All these versions are "simplifying attempts to explain a word which was no longer understood" (Albrektson, *Studies*, 74).
The reading נקשרה in 4QLam is probably due to a metathesis of שׂ and ק which
subsequently lead to a confusion of ד and ר. Vice versa, Cross departs from the
reading in 4QLam and regards נשקד in M as the corrupt reading of an "original" נקשׁר (DJD XVI, 236 and "Lamentations 1," 146) .

עֹל   4QLam uses in the same line for "yoke" the orthography עול. Thus it is
almost sure that על means the prep. עַל. The opposite argument that in 4QLam
the preceding נקשרה imposes the vocalization עֹל (DJD XVI, 236) seems less
convincing.

עָלוּ   M G V T regard "my sins" as the subj. of the two verbs יִשְׂתָּרְגוּ and עָלוּ.
4QLam and σ' read עָלוֹ or עוּלוֹ (sg. noun + 3 m. sg. sfx.). S wrongly takes עלו
(vocalized as a pl. noun with 3 m. sg. sfx.: עֻלָּו) as the subj. of יִשְׂתָּרְגוּ which
produces a rather strange sense. G^L is ambiguous: the reading might be either
an explication of a Hebrew עָלוֹ or an exegesis of the Masoretic term עָלוּ עַל
which evokes the metaphor of a yoke (see Albrektson, *Studies*, 74). It seems
probable that it could be both, i.e., a double translation of עלו.

16   vv 16-17   The alphabetical order of these verses in 4QLam is ע–פ while M has
פ–ע here. It is hardly possible to decide which sequence is the original one. For
further discussion see Cross, DJD XVI, 236 and "Lamentations 1," 148. Note
that in 2:16-17, 3:46-51 and 4:16-17 also, M has the order פ–ע, while G^L and S
transpose the verses and repeat the sequence ע–פ from 1:16-17.

עֵינִי | עֵינִי   עֵינִי   G V either depend on a *Vorlage* in which the second עֵינִי was lost by hapl., or they simply facilitate M in their translation. On the other hand, the single instance of pl. in G^{Mss} and S (the pl. is sure by the connection with a pl. ptc.) is rather a facilitating interpretation of M than a witness for only one עיני in the *Vorlage*. The expression ותרתין עיני, "and my two eyes," in T seems to be an interpreting paraphrase of M. σ' interpreted the repetition as an expression of intensity which he rendered by the adverb ἀδιαλείπτως (*CTAT*, 2:877). Thus, M seems to be confirmed not only by G^O, which has the second ὁ ὀφθαλ-μός μου under an asterisk, but indirectly also by σ', G^{Mss}, S and T. עיני in 4QLam is a pl. (clearly indicated by the pl. form of verb בכו) with 1 sg. sfx.. G^{Mss} (οἱ ὀφθαλμοί μου) and S (ﻣﺤﻨﻰ) align with 4QLam. Note, however, the different syntax: 4QLam takes עיני as the subj. of the first colon, while G^{Mss} and S align with the syntax of M. Cp. the comment on the preceding case.

7   לָֽהּ   The addition in 4QLam is composed of two elements (glosses?). מכול אוה-ביה is a quotation from Lam 1:2, where the preceding colon is almost identical with the second colon of Lam 1:17. Probably the scribe added it automatically because he knew the text by heart. The second element צדיק אתה יהוה appears to be a variant of the beginning of v. 18.

צִוָּה   The "extremely awkward, if not impossible" (DJD XVI, 237) reading of M might be judged as the *lectio difficilior* and is witnessed unanimously by the versions, but probably the reading of 4QLam nevertheless represents the origi-nal Hebrew text. In Ps 37:32 "צפה followed by the preposition *lĕ*- appears in one context where evil intent is meant"; according to 4QLam the construction in Lam 1:17 is more or less identical and "makes admirable sense" (DJD XVI, 237). The reading of M is perhaps an effort to avoid the anthropomorphism of the original text and thus seems to result from theological consideration rather than from a phonological or graphical error.

0   בַּבַּיִת כַּמָּֽוֶת: There is widespread discussion among scholars on the meaning of בַּבַּיִת כַּמָּֽוֶת. It has been argued that S (ﺭﺤﻤﻬﻣﺒﺤﺮﺩﻣ ﺭﺤﺒﻣﺤﻰ, "and in the house is death") and La (*et ab intus mors*) presuppose a different Hebrew text without the difficult prep. כְּ. But this is far from certain. G (which seemingly transposed the two Hebrew words: ὥσπερ θάνατος ἐν οἴκῳ), V (*et domi mors similis est*) and even the highly paraphrastic T (ומלגיו חרגת כפנא כמלאך דממונא על מותא, "and amidst the agony of starvation, like the angel who is appointed over death"), are clearly based on M. Thus, S and La might simply have preferred a clear and readable translation to a literal rendering of the Hebrew text. Perles ("Threni 1,20," 157–58) suggested the vocalization כְּמוּת = akkad. *kamû-tu*, "captivity." However, the easiest solution is to translate M as it stands: "in the house it is as death" (Gottwald, *Studies*, 9). Albrektson adds that כְּ may include other prepositions, e.g., בְּ (cp. *HALAT*, 433) without this being ex-pressed in writing and he translates: "in the house it (i.e. the situation) is as in the realm of death (in Sheol)" (Albrektson, *Studies*, 82).

2   לֹא   The asyndetic construction of the *kətîb* is the *lectio difficilior* and has sup-port from G. Thus it is the preferable reading here.

חֲלַל מַמְלָכָה   S probably does not presuppose a Hebrew חֲלָלֶיהָ (*BHK, BHS*), but is based on a different division of words. Instead of חלל ממלכה the translator (or his *Vorlage*) read חללם מלכה, and that vocalized as חַלְלָם מְלָכָה (see Al-brektson, *Studies*, 88f. and cp. the following case). He took both together with the following noun as an enumeration related to the verb הִגִּיעַ. The addition of a 3 f. sg. sfx. by the translator is not surprising, since he found this sfx. with two of the three nouns. For the reading of G, see comment on the following case.

מַמְלָכָה   S (ܟܠܚܡ) most likely read מִלְכָה, as the result of the first מ being connected with the preceding word (see above comment on חִלֵּל מַמְלָכָה) and the sfx. added according to the following וְשָׂרֶיהָ. Apart from the different division of words S may be regarded as a witness for the consonantal text of M. The Greek tradition has "her king" (G) or "her kings" (G^L βασιλεῖς αὐτῆς; G^B βασιλέας αὐτῆς) instead of the Hebrew "the kingdom." This might result from a hapl. of one מ, the remaining consonants being vocalised by the translators either מַלְכָּה or מִלְכָה (according with the following וְשָׂרֶיהָ). The different Greek readings might as well be inner-Greek corruptions of an original βασιλείαν αὐτῆς. However, it is surprising that even the Lucianic recension did not restore the abstract "kingdom," but changed only the concrete sg. "king" into the concrete pl. "kings." Therefore the easiest explanation is probably that the Greek translators did not have a different Hebrew *Vorlage*, but a particular interpretation of M. Perhaps they wanted to avoid the general formulation that God had desecrated the "kingdom" and therefore replaced the abstract by the concrete (influenced by the parallel וְשָׂרֶיהָ).

3   אָכְלָה סָבִיב: G probably read the last three consonants of אכלה twice, which resulted in אכלה כל הסביב. The reading ܐܝܕܘܗܝ, "his hands," in S is best explained as an inner-Syriac corruption of an original ܣܚܪܘܗܝ, "his surroundings," which would be a normal rendering of סביב or סביביו in S; cp., e.g., 1:17 (Albrektson, *Studies*, 90).

4   נִצָּב יְמִינוֹ   The reading חֵץ בִּימִינוֹ "an arrow in his right hand" has been suggested (Torczyner, "Anmerkungen," 403; see Rudolph, "Text der Klagelieder," 106; Kaiser, "Klagelieder," 130; cf. *BHS*), but all ancient versions support M, although G V S facilitate by using an active.

5   אַרְמְנוֹתֶיהָ   The reading אַרְמְנוֹתָיו (*BHK*) or אַרְמְנוֹתָו הִשְׁחַת (*BHS*; differ-div) has been suggested instead of M, but there are no supporting variants for this hypothesis. On the contrary, the 3 f. sg. sfx. is the *lectio difficilior*, which must not be altered here. It refers either to Jerusalem, because the "palaces" are primarily connected with the capital (Albrektson, *Studies*, 93), or else "Israel" is taken unusually as a feminine here (cp. 1 Sam 17:21; 2 Sam 24:9). G faithfully renders the different suffixes of M: τὰς βάρεις αὐτῆς and τὰ ὀχυρώματα αὐτοῦ.

6   וַיַּחְמֹס כַּגַּן   The Yemenite tradition of T reads בגנתא "in the garden" which seems to be a graphical error or a simplification of T*. The verb διεπέτασεν "has opened and spread out" (LSJ) in G* is usually regarded as a corruption of an original διέσπασεν "has torn down," which would correspond with ἐξέσπασεν of G^L, but there is no further textual evidence for this hypothesis. ὡς ἄμπελον is usually explained as based on a Hebrew כְּגֶפֶן instead of כַּגַּן (*BHK, BHS*), which could be an assimilation to Job 15:33 either by the translator or in his *Vorlage*. Note, however, that the Greek version of Job 15:33 has nothing in common with the Greek version of Lam 2:6. Therefore it might be an easier solution to regard ὡς ἄμπελον in Lam 2:6 as an allusion to Isa 1:8 and 5:5, where ἄμπελος is the equivalent of כֶּרֶם "vineyard." Note that the imagery of 2:6 is closely related to Isa 5:5. In this view G* need not be explained by supposing two errors (inner-Greek corruption of the verb and corruption of the

noun) but can be regarded as a free rendering of M in order to make allusion to Isa 5:5: "he has opened and spread out his dwelling like a vineyard (is opened and spread out)." For the syntax and translation of M, see Albrektson, *Studies*, 95 and *CTAT*, 2:883.

הִסְגִּיר   G and ⟨α'⟩ are probably based on a (mis)understanding of the subsequent בְּיַד as "by the hands of" instead of "into the hands of" (Albrektson, *Studies*, 99–100).

חָשַׁב   The Greek translator might have read erroneously either וַיֵּשֶׁב (this would explain the καί which has no equivalent in M) or הֵשֵׁב or הֵשִׁיב (a form which occurs in the subsequent line).

וַיַּאֲבֶל־   G V T seemingly read *qal* (וַיֶּאֱבַל "has been mourning") instead of *hifil* ("has caused to mourn") and consequently misunderstood the syntax by regarding the obj. חֵל as the subj. of the phrase. G^L renders the subsequent חֵל by δυνάμεις and therefore puts the verb into pl.

חֵל   While G V T and ⟨σ'⟩ give the correct meaning of the comparatively rare Hebrew חֵל, G^L and S have confused it with the more frequent חַיִל = חֵיל "power," "force," which they understood here in the sense of "military forces," "army." This explains why they both used pl. Besides that, S adds a 3 f. sg. sfx., which is most likely due to the translator.

אֻמְלָלוּ:   G V change the verb into sg. because they regard only חוֹמָה as its subj. and חֵל as the subj. of ויאבל (see above, comment on וַיַּאֲבֶל). S also regards חוֹמָה as the subj. of אֻמְלָלוּ, but leaves the verb and adjusts the noun by using pl. (+ 3 f. sg. sfx.). All these adjustments are due to the translators and do not presuppose a different Hebrew text.

אִבַּד וְשִׁבַּר   S uses pl., which means that "they" (i.e., the enemies) become the subj. instead of "he" (i.e., the Lord). This seems to confirm the Syriac manuscripts which point already at the beginning of the verse the verb ܐܠܒܚ as a *pael* ("they – i.e., the enemies – have caused to sink") and not as a *peal* ("they – i.e., the gates – have sunk"), which would correspond to M. Thus S probably regards "the enemies" as the subj. of the whole line. See Albrektson, *Studies*, 102–3. Finally, there is no text critical hint that one of these two verbs should be deleted (cf. *BHK, BHS*).

יָשְׁבוּ   The ptc. in T probably aligns with the present in M rather than with the past in G V S.

יְרוּשָׁלָ͏ִם: to הוֹרִידוּ   The Greek translator misunderstood the Hebrew syntax. He took רֹאשׁ in a figurative sense as "the leaders" (presumably he understood the form as an Aramaizing pl. or he read רֹאשֵׁם), and regarded the subj. בְּתוּלַת together with "the leaders" as the obj. of the clause: κατήγαγον εἰς γῆν ἀρχηγοὺς παρθένους Ἰερουσαλήμ "they have brought down to the ground the leaders, the maidens of Jerusalem." G^L "corrected" into ἀρχηγοὺς παρθένου θυγατρὸς Ἰερουσαλήμ "the leaders of the maiden Daughter of Zion," which (according to Rudolph, "Text der Klagelieder," 107) might presuppose a Hebrew רָאשֵׁי בְּתוּלַת בַּת יר' or simply is an assimilation to the context where combinations with בַּת־ occur several times (vv. 8, 10, 11, 13). La (*deduxerunt in terram principes, virgines Ierusalem*) aligns with G.

Apart from רֹאשׁ, which is freely rendered as a pl. "their heads" in V S and T^Mss, V and T^Mss exactly align with M. S also clearly reflects M, but surprisingly uses a 3 m. sg. for the verb (ܣܚܦ). In T all the text from חָגְרוּ to רֹאשׁ has been omitted, obviously by homtel., but rather in Aramaic (רישיהון – רישיהון)

than in Hebrew (רֹאשָׁם – רֹאשָׁן). T^{Mss}, however, have restored a complete translation of M.

13   מָה־אֲעִידֵךְ   G S T and also La (*quid testabor tibi*) give a more or less literal translation of M, which they obviously understood as a *hifil* of √עוד^{II}. Since this sense does not seem very satisfying it has been suggested to 'correct' M starting from V (*cui conparabo te*), which was assumed to presuppose a Hebrew אֶעֱרֹךְ or אֶעֱרוֹךְ (Meinhold, "Threni 2,13," 286; *BHK; BHS*). But this assumption is far from certain. It is much easier to understand V as a free (but probably correct) interpretation of מָה־אֲעִידֵךְ, parallel with the subsequent מָה אֲדַמֶּה־לָּךְ (see *CTAT*, 2:807 and Ehrlich, *Randglossen*, 7:37). Note, further, that possibly in Jer 49:19 the consonants יעידני (vocalized as a *hifil* of √יעד by the Masoretes parallel with Jer 50:44) originally also intended a *hifil* of √עוד with the meaning "dem Objekt gleichkommen, eigentlich dessen Duplikat bilden" (Ehrlich, *Randglossen*, 4:361) or "repeat = produce yet another case of, name a parallel to" (Albrektson, *Studies*, 108). ⟨σ'⟩ τί ἐξισώσω σοι, which seems to agree with V, is probably not a rendering of מָה־אֲעִידֵךְ as recorded in the Syrohexapla (Ceriani, *Fragmenta*; cp. *CTAT*, 2:805 f.) but of מָה אַשְׁוֶה־לָּךְ in the line below (Ziegler, *Jeremias, Baruch, Threni*; cp. Albrektson, *Studies*, 108 f. and *CTAT*, 2:885). Since the reading of M is seemingly confirmed by all ancient versions, the case has to be judged not as a textual problem but as a question of interpretation.

   מָה³ to וַאֲנַחֲמֵךְ   All Greek mss. (apart from a few insignificant variants) read τίς σώσει σε καὶ παρακαλέσει σε (= La *quis salvam te faciet, et quis consolabitur te*) which has been judged to presuppose a different Hebrew text (*BHK, BHS*). However, the Syh records (although erroneously attached to the preceding line) a σ'-reading (ܡܢܘ ܐܫܘܝܟܝ ܠܟܝ ܐܝܟ ܕܐܒܝܐܟܝ) which suggests an alternative explanation. Based on the retroversion ⟨σ'⟩ τί (ἐξ)ισώσω σοι ἵνα παρακαλέσω σε, Ziegler (following Katz) assumed τί ἰσώσω σοι καὶ παρακαλέσω σε to be the original Greek and regarded the reading τίς σώσει σε καὶ παρακαλέσει σε found in the manuscripts (and consequently in La, the daughter-version) simply as the result of an inner-Greek corruption. Barthélemy (*CTAT*, 2:885) follows Ziegler in principle but conjectures τίς ἰσώσει σε καὶ παρακαλέσει σε as the original text, a reading even closer to the corrupt version of the manuscripts but further from M. Presumably inner-Greek corruption spread from misreading τίς instead of τί ἰσ... which subsequently caused the form of verbs to be changed from the 1st into the 3rd person. Thus Ziegler's suggestion offers the most plausible link between M and G^{Mss}.

14   שְׁבִיתֵךְ   The reading שְׁבוּת occurs eighteen times and the reading שְׁבִית twice in the Hebrew Bible without a *qərê*. Further there are three cases of שְׁבוּת with the *qere* שְׁבִית and eight cases of שְׁבִית with the *qərê* שְׁבוּת. These changes reflect the uncertain morphology of the noun and its uncertain derivation either from שׁבה or from שׁוב. For bibliography and further discussion see *HALAT*, 1289–90; *THAT*, 2:887; *ThWAT*, 7:958–65.

In the present case, G obviously relates the noun to √שׁבה translating the phrase לְהָשִׁיב שְׁבוּתֵךְ/שׁביתך by τοῦ ἐπιστρέψαι αἰχμαλωσίαν σου. V and T, on the other hand, relate the noun to √שׁוב and translate *ut te ad paenitentiam provocarent* (V) and לאהדרותיך בתיובתא (T) "to turn you to repentance." One gets the impression that G read rather שביתך in its *Vorlage* while V and T read rather שְׁבוּתֵךְ. S combines both possibilities in a double translation ܕܬܗܦܟܝܢ ܘܐܗܦܟ ܫܒܝܬܟܝ "that you will repent and I will turn back your captivity." This clearly reflects the translator's uncertainty about the reading or interpretation of the noun. From a text critical point of view G indicates that the *kǝṯîḇ* שביתך is perhaps the earlier reading. But exegetically the *qǝrê* שְׁבוּתֵךְ is usually preferred in Lam 2:14, and the term שׁוּב שְׁבוּת understood as "restore to its former condition" (see Albrektson, *Studies*, 111).

5 שֶׁיֹּאמְרוּ to הָאָרֶץ: This phrase is often judged as too long, but since there is no textual evidence of a shorter text, emendations as suggested in *BHK* and *BHS* seem arbitrary.

כְּלִילַת יֹפִי   G misunderstood כְּלִילַת (from Hebrew כָּלִיל "perfect[ion]") in the sense of Aramaic כלילא or Syriac ܟܠܝܠܐ "crown," "wreath." ⟨α'⟩ (τελεία κάλλει) corrected the error and G^L added after στέφανος δόξης the explanation καλὴ εὐπρέπεια, which corresponds to M.

5 **vv 16-17**   Compare 1:16-17 and see comment there.

3 צָעֵק לְבֵּם   Various emendations have been suggested instead of M (see *BHK, BHS* and Albrektson, *Studies*, 116–18). From all these suggestions it is at least widely accepted among modern scholars to read impv. (צְעֵקִי) instead of pf. (צָעֵק). But since M is confirmed by all the ancient versions (without any variation worth mentioning), any emendation seems highly questionable (see *CTAT*, 2:887).

חוֹמַת   The syntax of this verse was obviously the main difficulty for the translators. G^O and T (explicating חוֹמַת as שׁוּר קִרְתָּא "city-wall") agree with M, taking "wall of the daughter of Zion" as the subj. of a new phrase. G and La also follow this syntax of M, but since they introduce the subj. in the pl., they have to adjust the subsequent verb (or vice versa?). G^L and V draw the term (in pl.) to the verb צָעֵק at the beginning of v. 18 (G^L ἐβόησε . . . τῶν τειχῶν; V *clamavit . . . super muros*) while S related it to the preceding אֲדֹנָי: ܡܪܐ ܕܫܘܪܐ "the Lord of the walls." Apart from their syntactical differences, all ancient versions agree in presupposing the consonants חומת which they vocalized either as a sg. (M G^O T) or as a pl. (G G^L La V S). Therefore, emendations such as חֵמִי or בְּתוּלַת (see *BHK, BHS*) are not justified.

בַּת־צִיּוֹן   Since the term בַּת־צִיּוֹן occurred already in 2:1, 4, 8, 10, 13 the reading of G appears to be the *lectio difficilior* here, while M and the other versions probably assimilated the term in v. 18 to the preceding occurrences adding בַּת by dittography of the preceding consonants –מת which look similar. The opposite, i.e., G as the result of haplography is also possible but seems less probable.

הוֹרִידִי   The pl. in G and La (*deducant*) is probably a mistake that followed from their reading of a pl. חוֹמֹת in the preceding line. See above, comment on חוֹמַת.

9 לְרֹאשׁ   Possibly G has transferred the pl. from the subsequent "watches" to "beginnings"; see comment on the following case.

אַשְׁמֻרוֹת   The reading εἰς ἀρχὰς φυλακῆς σου in G does not necessarily presuppose a different Hebrew *Vorlage* (e.g., Robinson in *BHK*: רֹאשֵׁי אַשְׁמְרֹתֶךָ). It might rather be a free translation of M (Rudolph, "Text der Klagelieder," 109: "anderes Stilgefühl, kein anderer Text"). "Even if the translation is generally extremely literal, one cannot presuppose that the translator was always fully consistent . . ." (Albrektson, *Studies*, 119). S and T also use a sg. as the equivalent for אַשְׁמֻרוֹת but in contrast to G such minor variation in number is quite frequent with them.

חוּצוֹת to הָעֲטוּפִים: The line is usually regarded as a later addition to the original text (perhaps based on 2:11-12). This seems reasonable, since v. 19 has four lines (cp. 1:7) while all the other verses in the chapter consist of only three. However, it should be noted that there is no textual evidence that would indicate an addition, i.e., the "addition" belongs to the development of the text prior to the state that can be reached by textual criticism.

20 עֹלְלֵי טִפֻּחִים   The full reading of G* transmitted in the Greek manuscripts is ἐπιφυλλίδα ἐποίησε μάγειρος φονευθήσονται νήπια θηλάζοντα μαστούς "the butcher has made a gleaning, infants suckling the breasts shall be killed." This is obviously a double translation, based on several misunderstandings: (1) ἐπιφυλλίδα ἐποίησε is an equivalent for the Hebrew verb עלל in Lam (cp. 1:22; 3:51), i.e., the translator erroneously regarded עֹלְלֵי as a form of this verb, which occurred already in the preceding line. (2) μάγειρος results from a phonological error (or perhaps lexical ignorance) via טַבָּח "cook," "butcher" instead of √טפח "to care for." (3) φονευθήσονται is a second effort at rendering טִפֻּחִים but based on the same error, i.e., relating the form to √טבח "to slaughter," "to kill," instead of √טפח (Albrektson, *Studies*, 121). Others regard φονευθήσονται as a second rendering of יֵהָרֵג in the following line, but this seems less convincing. (4) νήπια θηλάζοντα μαστούς is the second rendering of the Hebrew עֹלְלֵי, pleonastic but correct. Note, however, that G^O regards νήπια θηλάζοντα μαστούς as the equivalent of the whole lemma and has everything else including φονευθήσονται under ÷.

⟨α'⟩ (βρέφη παλαιστῆς) and V (*parvulos ad mensuram palmae*) also try to render M, but erroneously relate טִפֻּחִים to טֶפַח "hand-breadth." S (ܠܠܐ ܕܡܚܪܒܝܢ "children dashed in pieces") could be either a lexical error (perhaps an interpretation via the Aramaic meaning of טפח "strike," "knock") or an inner-Syriac corruption (see Albrektson, *Studies*, 121). T עולימיא דמתלפפין בסדינין "the children who are swathed in linen sheets") might be a free rendering of M. Conclusion: None of these versions really presupposes a different Hebrew text.

21 נָפְלוּ   The reading ἔπεσαν ἐν ῥομφαίᾳ, which is printed in Ziegler's edition as the equivalent of G for the Hebrew נָפְלוּ בָחָרֶב, is a mere conjecture entirely based on the reading ܢܦܠܘ ܒܚܪܒܐ in the margin of the Syrohexapla. The Greek manuscripts, on the other hand, almost unanimously read ἐπορεύθησαν ἐν αἰχμαλωσίᾳ ἐν ῥομφαια καὶ ἐν λιμῷ. Thus, the earliest Greek equivalent for נָפְלוּ which can be reached by means of textual criticism is ἐπορεύθησαν ἐν αἰχμαλωσίᾳ recorded in the apparatus as G*. For further discussion of this case see *CTAT*, 2:889 f. and Albrektson, *Studies*, 122 f.

3:5 רֹאשׁ   The reading ܡܪܘܕܐ "rebellion" in the Syriac manuscripts "is almost certainly an inner-Syriac corruption of ܡܪܝܪܐ 'bitterness'" (Albrektson, *Studies*, 131).

וּתְלָאָה: The Greek translator has taken ותלאה as a verb in 3 f. sg. impf., a lapse presumably triggered by his preceding misunderstanding of רֹאשׁ as κεφαλή (f.); see Albrektson, *Studies*, 131. The enigmatic reading ושלחו אצון which is found in the Yemenite tradition of T probably emerged by corruption from T*; see van der Heide, *Yemenite Tradition*, 87.

וּתְלָאָה: בְּמַחֲשַׁכִּים   The pattern of *saṯumôṯ* in M^L34 normally aligns with M^Y. The reason for the exception is obvious: The narrow columns of M^L34 have space for ten to twelve Hebrew characters. In the present case this created a problem for the scribe. If he would have left space for the *saṯumâ* behind וּתְלָאָה: he would have had to write בְּמַחֲשַׁכִּים הוֹשִׁיבַנִי (= fourteen characters) in the subse-

quent line (which would have been almost impossible). Thus he apparently preferred to drop the *sətumâ* and to squeeze בְּמַחֲשַׁכִּים: וּתְלָאֵה (= twelve characters)
in one line (which barely worked).

) בְּגָזִית   The reading of G possibly results from a different division of the line. The
translator separated בְּגָזִית from גָּדַר דְּרָכַי and joined it with the subsequent noun
נְתִיבֹתַי. Thus ἐνέφραξε τρίβους μου might be a somewhat paraphrastic rendering of גָּדַר . . . בְּגָזִית נְתִיבֹתַי (cp. Rudolph, "Text der Klagelieder," 110). On the
other hand, Albrektson regards ἐνέφραξε as an inner-Greek corruption of an
original ἐν φράξει = בְּגָזִית (Albrektson, *Studies*, 133).

The misreading of S might perhaps be due to a *Vorlage* that "was in places
illegible or at least difficult to read" (Albrektson, *Studies*, 134; cp. Lam 3:1).

◀ דְּרָכַי   The version of G is sometimes (e.g., Wiesmann, *Klagelieder*, 176) regarded as the result of a misreading (√רדף instead of √דרך). This assumption,
however, seems improbable for the beginning of a verse within the ד-stanza of
the lament. More likely the Greek translator misunderstood the syntactical relation between this and the subsequent Hebrew word regarding סוֹרֵר as an obj.
related to דְּרָכַי, which he took as a form of verb (probably as an inf.). The
meaning κατεδίωξεν "has pursued closely" was presumably derived from the
Aramaic √דרך "to overtake" (Albrektson, *Studies*, 135). Note that G also disre-
garded the 1 sg. sfx., which has been reintroduced by G^L (κατεδίωξέν με).

וַיְפַשְּׁחֵנִי   G* (καὶ κατέπαυσέ[ν] με "and has put an end to me") might render the
real meaning of this unique Hebrew word; cp. Akkad. *pašāhu* "to become quiet"
(*HALAT*, 921). G^L (καὶ διεσπάραξέ[ν] με "and has torn me to pieces"), V (*et
confregit me* "and has broken me"), S (ﺣﺴﺪ "has torn me to pieces") and T
(וּשְׁסַעֲנִי "and has torn me to pieces") obviously derive the meaning from Aramaic פשׁח "to split," "to tear off." It is, however, surprising that T does not use
the Aramaic פשׁח but the synonym שׁסע. Note that G^L, V, S (> cj.) and T confirm the reading of M as well as G* does; they only presuppose a different
meaning. The rendering καὶ ἐχώλανέ με "and has made me lame" by ⟨α'⟩ is
based on the Hebrew √פסח "to be lame." This rendering also witnesses to the
translator's interpretation of M rather than to a different Hebrew *Vorlage*.

The Greek reading καὶ κατέσπασέ με "and has pulled me down" which is
printed in Ziegler's edition is only found as a correction in one manuscript from
the thirteenth or fourteenth century while most manuscripts, including the best,
read καὶ κατέπαυσέ(ν) με (see above).

4 עַמִּי   The textual evidence is in favor of the reading עַמִּי. Note that the Mp protects M against the *səbîr* עַמִּים. However, the final decision between עַמִּי and
עַמִּים depends on the interpretation of Lam 3 either as an individual or as a
collective poem (Albrektson, *Studies* 137; *CTAT*, 2:894).

6 וַיִּגְרַס   ⟨σ'⟩ combines the different verbs used in G (καὶ ἐξέβαλεν) and ⟨α'⟩ ([καὶ]
ἐξετίναξεν), although they have approximately the same meaning.

הִכְפִּישַׁנִי   The exegesis behind the reading of G and V is probably connected with
Ps 102:10 and is also found in a midrash (see *CTAT*, 2:896).

8 מִיהוָה: ס זְכָר־   The scribe of M^Y deviated from his usual pattern (see the Introduction to Lamentations) and left out this and the following *sətumâ*, probably in
order to interrupt a series of four indented lines. If the scribe had kept these two
sətumôt, the sequence of indented lines would still have continued.

9 זְכָר־   זְכָר can be either impv. or inf. cstr. Within the context, the interpretation
as an inf. seems to be preferable. However, ⟨α'⟩ V S T interpret זְכָר as an impv.

according to its frequent use, e.g., in many psalms (Ps 25:6; 74:2, 18; 89:48 etc.). G (ἐμνήσθην "I have remembered") probably does not presuppose a Hebrew זכרתי (*BHK*), but appears to be a free rendering with זְכָר taken as an inf. Note that the Greek translator seemingly struggled with the interpretation of the verse (cp. the following cases and see Albrektson, *Studies*, 139–41) and his rendering remains "eine ungenaue Umschreibung des nicht ganz leichten Satzes" (Rudolph, "Text der Klagelieder," 111).

וּמְרוּדִי   It has been suggested to read וּמְרוּרִי or וּמְרוֹרַי "and my bitterness" instead of וּמְרוּדִי "and my wandering." The only textual evidence in favor of that reading is T according to the "western" tradition, which paraphrases ומה דאמרירו בי סנאי. But this simply seems to be a misreading (ר instead of ד) influenced by the context, i.e., the neighborhood of מְרוֹרִים (M) or מריר (T) in 3:15. S confirms M by reading ܘܡܪܘܕܝ, which can be regarded as a sort of transcription of M and can mean "and my chastisement" (√ܪܕܐ) as well as "and my rebellion" (√ܡܪܕ). The differences between M and the ancient versions testify to the translators' confusion of the roots רוד, רדד/רדה, מרד and מרר and to their special exegesis rather than to a different Hebrew *Vorlage*. Cp. at 1:7 the apparatus on וּמְרוּדֶיהָ and the comment on מַחֲמָדֶיהָ; for detailed discussion see *CTAT*, 2:864–66.

20 תִּזְכּוֹר   תִּזְכּוֹר can be either 3 f. sg. (subj. "my soul") or 2 m. sg. (addressed to God). The first possibility corresponds to the traditional interpretation represented by the ancient versions and followed by most of the modern exegetes. The second possibility, mainly represented in the rabbinic exegesis (see McCarthy, *Tiqqune Sopherim*, 122f.), seems less appropriate, because "the change from grief and sorrow to hope and confidence does not come until v. 21. It was probably under the influence of the note of hope in v. 21 that the rabbis began to interpret v. 20 likewise" (McCarthy, *Tiqqune Sopherim*, 123 n. 297 with reference to Wiesmann, *Klagelieder*, 179). Cp. the subsequent comments on תשיח and נפשי.

וְתָשִׁיחַ   There are two divergent readings attributed to σ' here, one in a Greek manuscript and the other in Syh (see *CTAT*, 2:900). G (καταδολεσχήσει "will talk") and σ' (προσλαλήσει "will talk to") presuppose a Hebrew וְתָשִׁיחַ (√שׂיח[II]), which obviously agrees with the *kətîb*. On the other hand, ⟨σ'⟩ (κατακάμπτεται "bends down") and T (ותצלי "inclines," "prays") align with the *qərê* וְתָשׁוֹחַ (√שׁחח). G[L] (τακήσεται "will melt") and V (*tabescet* "will melt") derive the word from the rare √שׁיח (*HALAT*, 1369), which regularly would have the form וְתָשִׁיחַ (= *kətîb*) but can probably also have the irregular form וְתָשׁוֹחַ (= *qərê*; see Bauer/Leander, *Grammatik*, §56h"). Thus G[L] and V do not contribute to the decision between *kətîb* and *qərê*.

In comparison with M[qere] וְתָשׁוֹחַ (a facilitation) and with וְתָשִׁיחַ (possibly a hybrid form), וְתָשִׁיחַ, which aligns with M[ket] G σ', seems to be the older, more difficult and therefore preferable reading. Note, however, that *CTAT*, 2:899–901 finally prefers M[qere].

In spite of their different interpretations all ancient versions except S agree in regarding the verb as a 3 sg. Thus the Hebrew form most likely is a 3 f. sg. (relating to נַפְשִׁי as the subj.) and not a 2 m. sg. as sometimes has been suggested (e.g. Albrektson, *Studies*, 142f.); cp. preceding comment on תִּזְכּוֹר. The whole phrase וְתָשִׁיחַ עָלַי נַפְשִׁי "my soul is talking about (or against?) me" probably means "I am soliloquizing about my destiny," which gives a good parallel with the preceding זָכוֹר תִּזְכּוֹר.

נַפְשִׁי: According to a *tiqqûn sôpərîm* the "original" reading was נַפְשֶׁךָ, but the authenticity of this *tiqqûn* is dubious; it probably emerged (as a further exegetical development in certain rabbinic circles) from interpreting the preceding verbs as 2 m. sg. (McCarthy, *Tiqqune Sopherim*, 120–23); cp. comment on תִּזְכּוֹר. Note that there are no traces of a reading נַפְשֶׁךָ in any ancient version.

2 תָמְנוּ   תָמְנוּ is an irregular 1 pl. (see Bauer/Leander, *Grammatik*, § 58p'; the regular form would be תַּמּוֹנוּ). Many exegetes prefer the emendation תָמּוּ (e.g. *BHK, BHS*), based on T, S and the 3 m. pl. in the parallel colon v. 22b. However, from the text critical point of view M is obviously the *lectio difficilior*. G unfortunately does not contribute to the solution of the question, because vv. 22-24 have been omitted by homtel. G^L aligns with M and the reading ἐξέλιπέν με found in G^{Mss} and G^O most probably results from inner-Greek corruption of an earlier ἐξελίπομεν, which is still preserved in G^L.

5 לְקֹוָו   M^L and M^Y do not have any Mp note here. In M^{L34} the reading לְקֹוָו is protected by the note ל' וכת. In many other manuscripts the consonants לקויו are added on the margin as the *qərê* (cp. *BHK²* and Weil's note in *BHS*), which implies that the *kətîb* was regarded as a sg. In fact, the parallelism with the following לְנֶפֶשׁ תִּדְרְשֶׁנּוּ is in favor of a sg., which is also found in S (ܠܢ ܕܡܣܟܐ ܠܗ "to somebody who waits for him"). Since קוה *qal* elsewhere occurs only as pl. ptc., the *qərê* probably represents an assimilation to the usual expression.

6 וְיָחִיל וְדֹומָם   Various emendations have been suggested: יוֹחִילוּ דוּמָם "that they should wait quietly;" הֹחִיל וִדֹמֹם "to tarry and be still" (based on ⟨α'⟩ ὑπομένειν καὶ ἡσυχάζειν and T which also uses inf.); וְיָחֵל וְדָמַם "and waits and is quiet" (based on G καὶ ὑπομενεῖ καὶ ἡσυχάσει); see Albrektson, *Studies*, 146–48. However, since the construction of M is difficult but by no means impossible, it is easier to regard the variation in the ancient versions as a result of the translators' efforts to facilitate the syntax. The reading ܒܫܪܪܐ "in truth" which is found in S results probably from an inner-Syriac corruption of an original ܒܫܬܩܐ (or ܒܫܬܩܐ) "in silence" which is recorded in the apparatus under the siglum S*. A possible translation of M might be "gut ist das Warten, und zwar still" (Gesenius, *Handwörterbuch*, 459, *s.v.* יָחִיל) which agrees with V *bonum est praestolari cum silentio*.

7 בִּנְעוּרָיו: The variant, which seemingly presupposes the prep. מִן, probably emerges from the idea that the Torah is the yoke which one has to carry from childhood; cp. also the variant of T in the preceding case.

2 הֹוגָה   Again ⟨σ'⟩ renders הוגה by ἐπήγαγε (via √נהג?) as in Lam 1:5; cp. further the comment on נּוּגוֹת in 1:4.

חֲסָדָיו: The pl. in S is not significant, because ܪܚܡܐ "mercy," "love" is used mostly in the pl. The pl. in M$^{L(qere)}$ M^Y M^{L34} can simply be an assimilation to the pl. in 3:22, or it may be a result of the theological consideration not to speak about the divine nature but about the divine acts; v. 33, however, suggests the former rather than the latter.

3 וַיֻּגֶּה   The vocalization וַיֹּגֶה (*hifil*) proposed in *BHK* would be an assimilation to the more frequent form, which is not justified.

6 רָאָה: εἶπε (G*; and consequently *dixit* in La) is the earliest Greek reading found in the manuscripts, but it seems very unlikely that this represents the original

Greek text. Based on the Hebrew text G^O and G^L have corrected εἶπε into εἶδε. Probably εἶδε was also the original Greek reading, which then had been corrupted into εἶπε under the influence of the subsequent εἶπε at the beginning of the next verse.

39   חָי גֶּבֶר   There is no textual evidence which would justify emendations such as, e.g., יְהִי גְבִיר (*BHS*; cp. Rudolph, "Text der Klagelieder," 113).

   חֲטָאוֹ:   While the sg. in M^ket and G underlines the fundamental phenomenon of sin (cp. 1:8), the pl. presumably reflects a more moralizing interpretation with the focus on the individual acts of failure. The weight of the witnesses and the correspondence with 1:8 suggest the sg. to be preferred.

40   נַחְפְּשָׂה and וְנַחְקֹרָה   G misunderstood both verbs as forms of 3 f. sg. pf. *nifal* and regarded דרכינו (vocalized as a sg. דְּרָכֵינוּ) as their subj.

   דְּרָכֵינוּ   The Greek translator regarded דרכינו as the subj. of the preceding and the following verb. Since he interpreted both verbs as 3 f. sg. pf. *nifal*, he consequently had to vocalize דרכינו as a sg. Cp. comment on the preceding case.

41   אֶל־¹   ⟨σ'⟩ (σύν) and V (*cum*) do not presuppose a different Hebrew text, but are a correct rendering of אֶל in the sense of "in addition to." See Albrektson, *Studies*, 154 and Gesenius, *Handwörterbuch*, 59 ("lasst uns unser Herz nebst den Händen erheben"). T has purification in mind (cp. *Lam. Rab.* III, 9) and gives a free exegetical paraphrase: ונדכי ידנא מגזילן "and let us clean our hands from robbery."

42   וּמָרִינוּ   The reading of G* ἡμαρτήσαμεν ἠσεβήσαμεν is found in the great majority of the Greek manuscripts as the equivalent for the Hebrew נַחְנוּ פָשַׁעְנוּ וּמָרִינוּ. The cj. was probably dropped by haplography of one of the two subsequent וּ. An additional καὶ παρεπικράναμεν in G^Mss appears to be an effort of correction which ended up in a double translation of וּמָרִינוּ. For further discussion of the variant Greek readings see Albrektson, *Studies*, 155f. S (ܘܡܪܝܢ) derived the form וּמָרִינוּ from √מרר instead of √מרה (as in 1:18) and added a 2 m. sg. sfx. Both result from the translator's activity and do not presuppose a different Hebrew text.

44   מֵעֲבוֹר   Although S uses the same root (ܥܒܪ) as M, the meaning is different. However, the translation ("you have removed our prayer" or "you have let our prayer pass by") reproduces freely but correctly the meaning of M ("so that no prayer can pass through").

45   סְחִי   None of the ancient versions with the exception of ⟨σ'⟩ gives a precise rendering of the *hapax legomenon* סְחִי "offscourings," "rubbish." The translators tried to guess the meaning either from the context (T) or by connecting it with similiar roots as שִׂיח (⟨α'⟩ G^L) and presumably נסח (V S). The rendering in T* (טלטולין ורטישין "homeless people and vagabonds" instead of the Hebrew סְחִי וּמָאוֹס "offscouring and refuse") corresponds to the midrashic comment תשימנו פסילאייא מאסייא בקרב העמים "you have made us loathsome outcasts among the nations" (*Lam. Rab.* III, 45). The origin of the reading καμ(μ)ύσαι με "to close my eyes" in G* is unclear. It is tempting to regard it as an inner-Greek corruption of an original κάμψαι με "to bend me down" (via √שחח; cp. Ziegler and Rudolph, "Text der Klagelieder," 113f.), but κάμψαι με is only the retranslation of a note in the margin of Syh and not attested in any Greek ms. The great majority of Greek mss. has the peculiar reading καμμύσαι με, which might somehow result from lexical ignorance.

46   **vv 46-51**   Compare 1:16-17 and see the comment there.

וָפַחַת   The reading καὶ βόθυνος "and pit," which Ziegler accepted in his edition as the reading of G, is a mere conjecture based on Isa 24:17 and Jer 48:43, where φόβος καὶ βόθυνος is the Greek equivalent of פַּחַד וָפַחַת (Schleusner, *Thesaurus*, I:574). The expression פַּחַד וָפַחַת seems to be a sort of proverb or a saying (cp. פַּחַד וָפַחַת וָפָח in Isa 24:17 and Jer 48:43), but it is surprising that none of the ancient versions gives a literal translation in Lam 3:47. Seemingly the translators regarded פַּחַד וָפַחַת as a hendiadys and thus did not render the second noun literally ("pitfall"), but used a synonym of the first noun instead (see Rudolph, "Text der Klagelieder," 114): καὶ θάμβος "and astonishment" (G^{Mss}) or καὶ τρόμος "and trembling" (G^L), וזיע "and trembling" (T). S (ܪܬܝܬܐ "and fright") probably aligns also with these versions, but cp. comment below on הַשֵּׁאת. G*, represented by the manuscripts G^B and G^A, reads θυμός "anger," "violence," which might be a free rendering or an effort to guess the meaning of פַּחַת (via √נפח?) rather than a synonym of פַּחַד. On the other hand, θυμός has been judged as a corruption of the assumed "original" βόθυνος (see Schleusner, "Curae criticae," 39, and Albrektson, *Studies*, 158f, and cp. Ziegler's note). However, there is no textual evidence for this, neither in the Greek nor in the Hexaplaric witnesses, although one would expect that an original βόθυνος had at least left some traces in the textual tradition. Albrektson nevertheless supports the conjecture, but this may result at least partly from an interest to confirm his hypothesis of the particular literalness of G in Lam. V uses *laqueus* = פַּח "snare," which is either due to a misreading of the Hebrew text (or a scribal error in the *Vorlage*) or perhaps to an assimilation to Isa 24:17 and Jer 48:43 by the translator.

הַשֵּׁאת   הַשֵּׁאת "devastation" is another *hapax legomenon* which caused difficulties for the translators. ἔπαρσις "elevation," "rising" (G ⟨α'⟩) and probably also ἔκστασις (G^L) and *vaticinatio* (V, cp. e.g. מַשָּׂא "saying") are derivations via √נשא. This corresponds with de Rossi's observation that some Hebrew manuscripts and editions read הַשֵּׁאת (de Rossi, *Scholia*, 130). Note that G and ⟨α'⟩ apparently have not regarded the preformative ה as an article. T (רתיתא "trembling") again uses a synonym for "fear". Surprisingly S reads now ܓܘܡܨܐ "pit" which would rather have been expected in v. 47a. This could be due either to a misreading (הַשַּׁחַת "pitfall" instead of הַשֵּׁאת; see Albrektson, *Studies*, 159) or to a transposition of פַּחַת and שֵׁאת (perhaps to obtain a climax: fear – fright – pitfall – crushing) by the translator. In the latter case ܪܬܝܬܐ "fright" would be the equivalent of שֵׁאת (cp. G^L and T) and ܓܘܡܨܐ "pit" would be an entirely adequate rendering of פַּחַת.

תִדְמֶה   Probably "the translator of G found it impossible to say of the eye that it was silent" (Albrektson, *Studies*, 160 following Schleusner, "Curae criticae," 40).

בְּנוֹת עִירִי: Rudolph, "Text der Klagelieder," 114 (cp. *BHS*) suggests transposing v. 51 from the end to the beginning of the ע-strophe, i.e., before v. 49. Then he concludes that עירי was a "verdorbene Doppelschreibung" of the subsequent עיני at the beginning of v. 49, and instead of the remaining מִכֹּל בְּנוֹת, he reads מִכֹּל בָּכוֹת "vor lauter Weinen." However, this suggestion seems rather arbitrary, since it is neither necessary to transpose v. 51, nor does any textual evidence exist which would support such an emendation.

עִירִי: ס צֹוד   Apparently M^{L34} had originally a *sǝtumâ* in this place, the beginning of v. 52 being written in a new line with the usual indent. However, the text of the preceding verse seems to have been originally shortened by accident. When later the scribe erased the shorter version and wrote the correct wording into the gap he needed all the space available. After having squeezed seventeen characters in one single line (the columns of M^{L34} usually have space for ten to twelve characters), he used the *sǝṭumâ*, i.e., the indent at the beginning of the subsequent line, for the final word עִירִי׃. Cp. a similar case in 3:5/6.

58 רִיבֵי   S has no *seyame* in the manuscripts, but "there is a slight possibility that the original Syriac translator intended ܪ.ܒܝ as plur." (Albrektson, *Studies*, 166).

גָּאַלְתָּ   V is either the result of a misreading (גָּאַל) by the translator or in his *Vorlage* (since ת and ה look very similar, a sort of haplography might occasionally have happened), or perhaps simply a free translation.

59 שָׁפְטָה   M (m. sg. impv. + paragogic הָ-) is the *lectio difficilior*. G and S are due rather to an assimilation to the pf. forms of the context than to a different *Vorlage* (e.g. *BHK, BHS:* שָׁפַטְתָּ; Rudolph, "Text der Klagelieder," 115: שָׁפַטָה as an orthographic variant; the latter would only presuppose a different vocalization of M, but this kind of assimilation is not attested in Biblical Hebrew).

65 תַּאֲלָתְךָ   It is difficult to say whether the versions missed the meaning of M or used euphemisms.

66 תִּרְדֹּף   Since σὺ αὐτούς at the beginning of v. 66 in G^{Mss} is obviously an inner-Greek corruption of an original (μόχθον) σου αὐτοῖς at the end of v. 65 (see G^O and Rudolph, "Text der Klagelieder," 116), there is no support for the emendation תִּרְדְּפֵם (*BHK, BHS*). Neither does the reading καταδιώξεις αὐτούς (G^O G^L) necessarily presuppose the presence of a Hebrew 3 m. pl. sfx. but may be judged as an explanation or an assimilation to the subsequent וְתַשְׁמִידֵם.

מִתַּחַת שְׁמֵי יְהוָה׃   Only T aligns with M, while G V S facilitate the syntax in order to avoid the difficulty that a verse which is addressed to the Lord (תִּרְדֹּף . . . . וְתַשְׁמִידֵם) at the same time mentions his name in the genitive ("the heavens of the Lord"). G and V thus interpret שְׁמֵי as an absolute state and יהוה as a vocative. S does the same, but also adds a 2 m. sg. sfx. ("your heavens, Lord;" cp. G^O τοῦ οὐρανοῦ ÷ σου ⊀ κύριε). G^L also has the vocative, but transposed it to the end of the first part of the verse. Note that the presence of the name יהוה is confirmed by all witnesses, i.e., all of them are based on M, which represents the *lectio difficilior*.

4:2 מַעֲשֵׂה   The pl. cstr. was probably already in G's *Vorlage*. De Rossi, *Scholia*, 130 found the reading מעשי also in two Hebrew mss. Compare the variants at כְּמַעֲשֵׂה in 3:64.

3 תַּנִּין   The *kǝtîb* תנין is ambiguous. It can be interpreted either as the sg. תַּנִּין "sea-monster," "snake" (cp. T), or as an irregular Aramaic pl. of the noun תַּן* "jackal," i.e., simply an orthographic variant of the usual form תַּנִּים (see Rudolph, "Text der Klagelieder," 117). The latter is not only suggested by the *qǝrê* but also required by the context (pl. form of the following vb.). The versions except T agree with the *qǝrê* as to the *interpretation*, but they necessarily remain indeterminate with regard to the *orthography* תנין or תנים. Note, that G (δράκοντες "dragons") seems to be related *semantically* with תַּנִּין sg. ("sea-monster," "snake") rather than with תַּנִּין / תַּנִּים pl. ("jackals"), but cp. Jer 9:10; Mic 1:8, where δράκοντες is used as an equivalent for hebr. תַּנִּים. Finally it is the pl. in G which is decisive here because it clearly indicates that the Greek translator understood תנין not as a sg. The orthography of the *kǝtîb* is supported particularly by the transliteration θανιν given in a note of the Syh and further

by the (mis)interpretation as a sg. תנינא(לְ) in T. In conclusion the ambiguous *kətîb* תנין seems to be the *lectio difficilor* while the *qərê* תַּנִּים is an initiative to eliminate the ambiguity.

כִּי עֵנִים   The usual term for "ostrich" in Biblical Hebrew is בַּת הַיַּעֲנָה (Lev 11:16), pl. בְּנוֹת יַעֲנָה (e.g. Isa 34:13 parallel with תַּנִּים). יְעֵנִים is probably the pl. of a noun יָעֵן* which occurs only here in the Bible. The defective spelling of the *qərê* seems preferable because it agrees perfectly with the consonants of the *kətîb* and the latter can easily be explained as the result of an erroneous division of words. Note that many KR manuscripts have the *qərê* (either defective or plene) as the only reading.

5 חָלוּ   In modern exegesis the form חָלוּ is usually derived from חול√ "turn" so that the colon has the meaning "and no hands were turned against her" (Albrektson, *Studies*, 180) or "o[hne] dass (Menschen)hände i[n] ihm (scil. Sodom) wüteten" (Gesenius, *Handwörterbuch*, 329). G (ἐπόνεσαν"were exhausted") and S (ܠܐܝ, "were weary") derive it from חלה√. Rudolph ("Text der Klagelieder," 117) agrees with this interpretation and reads at the end of the colon יְלָדִים instead of יָדָיִם: "ohne dass Kinder darin leiden mussten." σ' (ἐτρώσαν "have wounded/pierced") and V (*coeperunt* "have begun") seemingly related חָלוּ with חלל√. T does not give a translation but a very particular exegesis of the whole colon: ולא שריאו בה לאתנבאה נביאיא למהדר יתה בתיובתא "and no prophets remained in her to prophesy her, to turn her back in repentance."

7 נְזִירֶיהָ   The tempting conjecture נְעָרֶיהָ instead of M's נְזִירֶיהָ has no support from any textual witness. Being further the *lectio facilior*, this conjecture seems rather improbable. נְזִירֶיהָ is probably not used in its technical sense "Nazirite" here, but has the wider meaning "persons of high rank/singled out" as in Gen 49:26 and Deut 33:16 (see Albrektson, *Studies*, 180).

אָדְמוּ עֶצֶם מִפְּנִינִים   The main difficulty for the ancient translators was the rendering of עֶצֶם. σ' and T understand it in the sense of "body," "appearance," and take it as an adverbial accusative: "as to the appearance." This interpretation most probably meets the intention of M. S takes עֶצֶם as the subj. of אָדְמוּ and renders it by the pl. + sfx. "their bones." ⟨α'⟩ reads ὀστοῦν, "bone(s)." V chooses the free translation "ivory" (also departing from the meaning "bone"). G has no equivalent for עֶצֶם but it might be possible that the translator understood it in the sense of "they themselves" and regarded it as implicit in the vb. Note further that for the vb. all Greek manuscripts read either ἐτυρώθησαν "were made into cheese" or ἐπυρώθησαν "were burnt." However, both of these readings are most probably corruptions from an original ἐπυρρώθησαν "were ruddy," which Ziegler and Rahlfs have introduced as a conjecture in the text of their editions.

The rare noun פְּנִינִים "corals" has been interpreted as some kind of (precious) stone in G S and T, while σ' understood it in a wider sense (via פנה√) as τὰ περίβλεπτα "the admired (things)." Similarly the adj. *antiquo* in V might perhaps result from an interpretation of מִפְּנִינִים via פנה√ in a temporal sense (e.g., מִלְּפָנִים?, see *BHK*). All that "variation" in the versions results from lexical and syntactical difficulties in M and does not point to a different Hebrew *Vorlage*.

גִּזְרָתָם: Presumably none of the ancient translators knew the precise meaning of this word. G (τὸ ἀπόσπασμα αὐτῶν "their piece/part") obviously derived it from גזר√ and then translated very literally. σ' did the same, but used a pl. (τὰ μέλη αὐτῶν "their limbs"). G^L (τὸ εἶδος αὐτῶν "their form"), S (ܐܣܟܡܬܗܘܢ

"their body") and T (פרצופיהון "their faces") probably tried to guess the meaning from the context. V (*pulchriores* "they were more beautiful than . . .") used a free paraphrase.

8   יָבֵשׁ הָיָה   G seemingly regarded either "bones" or ναζιραῖοι (v. 7) as the subj. and therefore used pl. with the verbs here. V and S add a cj. as usual in cases of an asyndetic Hebrew construction.

9   שֶׁהֶם to שָׁדָיִ:   This line has often been regarded as corrupt. Various emendations have been suggested (see *BHK, BHS* and Rudolph, "Text der Klagelieder," 118) but none of the textual witnesses clearly presupposes a text different from M. For the interpretation of M, see e.g. Albrektson, *Studies*, 184.

   יָזוּבוּ   G's puzzling ἐπορεύθησαν (La *abierunt*; Syh ܐܙܠܘ) for the Hebrew יָזוּבוּ might result either from a misreading (יֵלֵכוּ instead of יָזוּבוּ; note that the orthography is defective – יָזֻבוּ – in M^Y and M^L34) or perhaps from an inner-Greek corruption (Albrektson, *Studies*, 184, suggests ἐπιρρεύσουσι or ἐπιρρεύσονται as the original reading). For the rest of the line G gives a very literal translation of M. Obviously, V S and T (which gives a longer paraphrase influenced by a midrashic explanation; see *Lam. Rab.* IV, 12) presuppose M.

10   לִבְרוֹת   בָּרוֹת can be regarded as a mixed form of inf. cstr. בְּרוֹת and the noun בָּרוּת (Gesenius, *Handwörterbuch*, 174). The ancient versions interpreted it as a noun, but this does not necessarily presuppose a different vocalization.

12   וּכֹל   Since the asyndetic construction confirmed by G is also the *lectio difficilior*, the *qərê* is to be preferred.

13   דָּם צַדִּיקִים: The adj. δίκαιον in all Greek manuscripts is usually judged as an inner-Greek corruption from an original δικαίων "of the righteous" (e.g., Ziegler), but it is surprising that this "correct" reading should not have survived in any manuscript. Or could the reading αἷμα δίκαιον possibly result from activity of Christian scribes who assimilated the Greek text to Matt 23:25? Compare comment on מְשִׁיחַ יְהוָה in 4:20. Note, finally, that the different word order in G* (αἷμα δίκαιον ἐν μέσῳ αὐτῆς) has been altered in G^O (ἐν μέσῳ αὐτῆς αἷμα δίκαιον) to agree with M.

14   עִוְרִים   G G^L and S possibly reflect ancient efforts of emendation. Since the fragmentary reading of 5QLam^a confirms at least that the word in question ended with the character ם, the addition of a 3 f. sg. sfx. in G and S is probably due to the translators.

   בְּלֹא   The variant readings in 5QLam^a (if not simply a mistake by the scribe) and S might result from the ambiguity of M, which can mean either "that one could not touch their garments" or "what they were not allowed (to touch), they touched with their clothes." 5QLam^a and S (which might have had a *Vorlage* similar to 5QLam^a) clarified the meaning in favor of the first possibility, which is syntactically easier. But the understanding intended by M is rather the latter, which fits better in the immediate context as well as in the context of the cultic rules of purity as far as we know them: ". . . in v. 14a the point is that the priests, who had shed the blood of the righteous are now themselves the blood-stained victims, and in [v. 14]b that those who had been anxious to keep all the cultic rules of purity cannot avoid contact with unclean things. This understanding of the passage gives a natural transition to the next verse . . ." (Albrektson, *Studies*, 187).

   יִגְּעוּ   The fragmentary reading of 5QLam^a can be completed either as ובג[עת] which would be syntactically difficult, or as יבג[דו] which would be difficult in this context. The editors of the fragment call our attention to the fact that there is a point below the ב which might indicate that the ב was written erroneously and should be erased. In this case the fragment would read יג[עו] in accordance with M. See DJD III, 175.

טָמֵא   G and T took טָמֵא for the obj. of the impv. סוּרוּ. T ("turn away from the unclean [sg.]"), however, kept to the sg. of M, while G used a pl. This could either result from the Greek translator's liberty, or it might indicate that he (in contrast with T) had a different reading in his *Vorlage*. The same is true for the pl. ptc. used in V (*polluti*) and for the pl. in S (ܐܒܝ̈ܐ). Unfortunately the picture remains unclear because G V and S have different syntactical interpretations of the Hebrew. If the translators of G V and S really had a different Hebrew *Vorlage*, its reading presumably was rather טמאו as found in 5QLam[a] than טְמֵאִים (*BHK, BHS*). However, M seems preferable in any case, because the pl. can be regarded as a stylistic facilitation.

קָרְאוּ לָמוֹ   These words are usually regarded as a gloss. However, their presence is confirmed by 5QLam[a] and by all ancient versions. G and S presuppose only the slightly different vocalization קְראוּ and G[L] (ἐκάλεσαν ἡμᾶς) read the pronoun as a 1 pl.

סוּרוּ סוּרוּ   It has been suggested to delete the second סוּרוּ as a dittography (*BHK, BHS*), but 5QLam[a] and the versions unanimously confirm the repetition.

אָמְרוּ בַּגּוֹיִם   Parallel to his interpretation of קָרְאוּ in the preceding line, the translator of G vocalized אִמְרוּ (impv.). Further there is no textual evidence that אָמְרוּ בַּגּוֹיִם (or at least אָמְרוּ; see Rudolph, "Text der Klagelieder," 119f.) should be a secondary addition (cp. קָרְאוּ לָמוֹ in the preceding line). *CTAT*, 2:912 introduces the distinction between "gloss" and "parenthesis," which indeed might be helpful in this and similar cases. Thus if אָמְרוּ בַּגּוֹיִם is not a gloss it still may be regarded as a parenthesis.

vv 16-17   Although 5QLam[a] is fragmentary it clearly shows לָגוּר (the end of v. 15) immediately followed by פֿנ. This indicates that the order of verses in the fragment agrees with M. Compare 1:16-17 and the comment there.

זְקֵנִים   From the text critical evidence it is in this case hardly possible to decide whether the cj. has been omitted (hapl) or added (ditt/facil-styl). However, there are other examples for a general tendency to smoothen the asyndetic style in Lamentations by adding conjunctions (see, e.g., 2:2, 21; 3:43; 5:3, 5, 7). Thus the addition is perhaps the more probable.

צָדוּ   The accent shows that צָדוּ was related to √צדה "be after," "destroy" by the Masoretes. ἠρημώθησαν in ⟨α´⟩ and הנון צדאן in T[Mss] (and perhaps also *lubricaverunt* in V) seemingly result from this Masoretic interpretation, while the other versions obviously related צָדוּ to √צוד "hunt." Note, however, Albrektson's remark (*Studies*, 192) that "it is doubtful whether it is really possible to distinguish clearly between the two roots." The reading of 5QLam[b] could be either צדו as in M, or צרו (via √צרר; cp. KR and Rudolph, "Text der Klagelieder," 120) which might result from assimilation to Job 18:7 and Prov 4:12 (see *CTAT*, 2:912).

מְשִׁיחַ יְהֹוָה   All Greek manuscripts have χριστὸς κύριος "Christ, the Lord," which is obviously a christological alteration of an original χριστὸς κυρίου "the anointed of the Lord." La and V accordingly read *Christus Dominus*. On the other hand, S (ܕܡܪܝܐ ܡܫܝܚܗ) and, of course, T (משיח ייי) correctly render the cstr. as intended by M.

בִּשְׁחִיתוֹתָם   Only S (ܒܚܒܝܠܗܘܢ "in their pit") gives the proper meaning of M; the sg. probably results from the translator's freedom. In the other versions the noun seemingly has been derived from the root שׁחת "corrupt," "spoil," "destroy," which produces a different meaning (e.g. G ἐν ταῖς διαφθοραῖς αὐτῶν "in their destructions") without presupposing a different Hebrew text. In G^Mss (ἐν ταῖς διαφθοραῖς ἡμῶν), La (*in interitu nostro*) and particularly in V (*in peccatis nostris*) the 1 pl. sfx. shows that the translators continued their christological interpretation from the preceding colon (see above, comment on מְשִׁיחַ יהוה); this means that most probably these readings do not presuppose a different Hebrew text.

21 יוֹשַׁבְתִּי   The archaic form of ptc. with a paragogic יִ- given by the *kǝṯîḇ* has been "corrected" into the usual one by the *qǝrê*. Nevertheless, the form of the *kǝṯîḇ* is justified and representing the *lectio difficilior* it may be regarded as the original reading. See Joüon/Muraoka, *Grammar*, § 93o.

בְּאֶרֶץ עוּץ   The reading ἐπὶ (τῆς) γῆς in G (without an equivalent for the Hebrew עוּץ) is probably the result of an omission caused by homtel. either in the Hebrew *Vorlage* or in the course of the transmission of the Greek text (see Albrektson, *Studies*, 194).

כּוֹס   The addition κυρίου in G may be either an allusion to Jer 25:15 ff., where הַכּוֹס מְיַד יהוה (v.17) as a symbol of judgment appears in context with the geographical names עוּץ (v. 20) and אֱדוֹם (v. 21), or perhaps another trace of reinterpretation by Christian scribes (assim-1 Cor 10:21, 11:27; cp. comment on מְשִׁיחַ יהוה in 4:20), but it could also simply result from an inner-Greek corruption (ditt. of the second half of the word ποτήριον; Albrektson, *Studies*, 194 f.).

תִּשְׁכְּרִי   The Syriac reading ܕܬܕܘܝܢ "so that you will be miserable" which is found in all manuscripts "is doubtless an error for ܕܬܪܘܝܢ so that you shall become drunk" (Albrektson, *Studies*, 195).

וְתִתְעָרִי: The meaning of M is "you will denude yourself"; cp. V (*nudaberis*) and with some freedom ⟨σ'⟩ (ἀσχημονήσεις). Thus it has been assumed that the reading καὶ ἀποχεεῖς in G might presuppose a Hebrew וּתְעָרִי, i.e., *piel* instead of the rare *hitpael*. But this is rather uncertain. The verb ערה can mean both "denude" and "pour out," and the Greek translator might simply have thought of the latter when he tried to interpret the rare *hitpael* form (see Albrektson, *Studies*, 195). The interpretation of T ותרוקני "and you will be poured out") aligns with G. S (ܘܬܬܛܪܦܝܢ) does probably not presupose a different Hebrew text, e.g., וְתִתְעֹרְרִי "and you will get excited" (*BHK*) or וְתֵעָפִי "and you will be exhausted" (Rudolph, "Text der Klagelieder," 120), since in Jer 25:27; 48:26 and 51:7 the Syriac translator uses the verb ܛܪܦ *ethpa*. "to indicate the effects of drunkenness . . . The Syriac verb here seems to mean 'reel, stagger in drunkenness', and this is probably the meaning intended by the translator of Lam. 4.21 too" (Albrektson, *Studies*, 195). Thus ܘܬܬܛܪܦܝܢ can most probably be regarded as a very free rendering or a guess at the meaning of M. La (*adhuc*) is enigmatic; it results perhaps from a damaged *Vorlage* (with ד in the place of ר: ותתעדי?).

5:1 הַבֵּיט   The *kǝṯîḇ* הַבֵּיט (cp. Ps 142:5) is an irregular plene writing of the m. sg. *hifil* impv. which which normally has the form הַבֵּט. The *qǝrê* הַבִּיטָה is a m. sg. *hifil* impv. + paragogic ה (Joüon/Muraoka, *Grammar*, § 48d). Although there is no difference in meaning, the irregular form הַבֵּיט (*kǝṯîḇ*) seems to be preferable as the *lectio difficilior*, while the *qǝrê* הַבִּיטָה might follow 3:63.

2 לְנָכְרִים: In the last syllable of this lemma 5QLam^a has an additional א written above the line; the editor of the fragment judges this longer form (לְנָכרִיאם) metrically more satisfying than M (DJD III, 175).

3 אֵין . Since the asyndetic construction reflected by the versions is also the *lectio difficilior*, the *kǝṯîḇ* is to be preferred.

4 מֵימֵ֫ינוּ The reading of G and its correction in G^{Mss} are combined in G^L and a few manuscripts: ὕδωρ ἡμῶν ἐν ἀργυρίῳ ἐπίομεν ἐξ ἡμερῶν ἡμῶν; G^O has the same but puts ἐξ ἡμερῶν ἡμῶν under ÷.

יָבֹאוּ: G^L V and also La (*accepimus*) simply changed the subj. of the phrase and then used an appropriate verb in order to facilitate the style. While none of these versions changed the meaning basically, ⟨σ'⟩ interpreted עֵצֵינוּ as "our trees" and obviously thought of gathering the fruits (see Rudolph, "Text der Klagelieder," 121).

5 עַל צַוָּארֵ֫נוּ M "upon our neck (we are pursued)" seems difficult. S wrongly connects עַל צַוָּארֵנוּ with יָבֹאוּ in v. 4. Among the commentators it is the common opinion that the difficulty of M in this place results from textual corruption. It has been suggested either to follow σ' ("a yoke is upon our neck, we are pursued") or to read עַל אַרְצֵנוּ ("in unserem eigenen Lande werden wir verfolgt," *BHS* = Rudolph, "Text der Klagelieder," 121 following Ehrlich, *Randglossen*, 7:53) instead of עַל צַוָּארֵנוּ. Note, however, that M is strongly supported by almost all ancient versions, while σ' may be either a double translation or result from dittography in a Hebrew text or simply shows the translator's interpretation of M (see comment on the following case). A possible interpretation of M could be, that the phrase expresses "the imminence of the danger and the persistency of the persecutors"; see Albrektson, *Studies*, 197f., referring to a parallel from the Latin.

נִרְדָּ֫פְנוּ The variation in V La T shows the translators' efforts to clarify the meaning of M. Note that all three of these renderings (without presupposing a different Hebrew *Vorlage*) basically align with the interpretation which ⟨σ'⟩ gives to this colon by adding ζυγός at the beginning (see comment on the preceding case and cp. Rudolph, "Text der Klagelieder," 121).

לֹא . The asyndetic construction of the *kǝṯîḇ*, being the *lectio difficilior* and confirmed by G and V, is to be preferred.

6 נָתַנּוּ G and S took מִצְרַיִם (S obviously read מִצְרִים) as the subj. and apparently read נָתְנוּ (3 m. pl.) instead of M's נָתַנּוּ (1 c. pl.). The sg. ἔδωκε in G does not necessarily presuppose a Hebrew נָתַן but might simply be a translational adjustment to the sg. Αἴγυπτος (Albrektson, *Studies*, 198).

7 אֵינָם . M^{ket} confirmed by G represents the *lectio difficilior* and is therefore to be preferred while M^{qere} seems to be a stylistic or syntactical facilitation. But there remains a certain possibility that M^{ket} could simply result from hapl. However, cp. the following case.

אֲנַ֫חְנוּ . Again the asyndetic construction of M^{ket} being the *lectio difficilior* and confirmed by G is to be preferred.

0 עוֹרֵ֫נוּ The reading of 5QLam^a is uncertain. The scribe first wrote the same consonants as in M (i.e., the sg. עורנ[.]ו), but seemingly the reading then was changed into the pl. (עורינ[.]ו) by adding a י above the line (DJD III, 175). One could imagine that the scribe first copied his *Vorlage* mechanically, but when he came to write the vb. (pl.!) he went back to the subj. and added the י. Many KR manuscripts also read עורינו. Note, however, that otherwise the pl. of עור is

עוֹרוּת. The pl. in S does not necessarily presuppose a pl. in the *Vorlage* but may rather be introduced by the translator who adjusted the number of the subj. to the pl. of the vb. (see KR). Vice versa G V La changed the vb. into sg. (see below, apparatus and comment on נִכְמָרוּ).

נִכְמָרוּ   The main difficulty in M is the lack of agreement between the subj. (עוּרֵנוּ, sg.) and the vb. (נכמרו, pl.). In order to solve this problem, the versions either change the subj. into a pl. (S) or the vb. into a sg. (G V La). Note, however, that these changes are translational adjustments which most probably do not presuppose a different Hebrew *Vorlage*. M is confirmed by 5QLam[a] and T. The reading ἐπελιώθη which is attributed to G by Ziegler is not directly attested by a Greek manuscript but suggested by La (*livida facta est*) and G[O] (ἐπελιώθη ÷ συνεσπάσθησαν ⌐). G[Mss] and S have a double translation using the second word as the vb. for the subsequent colon; note that S uses equivalents of the Greek words but in reverse order.

וְלִעָפוֹת   The omission of ע in 5QLam[a] may indicate a certain instability in the pronunciation of laryngals (DJD III, 175).

22   כִּי אִם‎   The versions use different cj. at the beginning of v. 22: V (*sed*) presumably aligns with the intention of M (כִּי אִם in the sense of "but"; see Joüon/Muraoka, *Grammar*, §173c; GKC, §163ab; Albrektson, *Studies*, 206f.; according to others כִּי אִם means here "es sei denn, dass," e.g., Rudolph, "Text der Klagelieder," 122, but compare the discussion in Albrektson, *Studies*, 206). G (ὅτι), La (*quia*), and S (ܡܛܠ ܕ) have a causal clause ("because . . .") which looks like the rendering of only כִּי. Note, however, that this could be simply the result of the translators' interpretation of M without presupposing a different Hebrew *Vorlage*. ⟨σ'⟩ (εἰ δέ) has a conditional clause, which indicates that אם was present in his *Vorlage*.

Note further that in connection with the subsequent consonants . . . מאסמאס the addition of אם "als Doppelschreibung der beiden folgenden Konsonanten" (Rudolph, *Ruth/Hohes Lied/Klagelieder*, 258) is not the only possibility. It could have been omitted by hapl (or by an err-phonol) as well, and this is perhaps even the more probable (see KR and cp. G La S). Considering all these aspects a conclusion about the original text remains uncertain. M might be preferable, being the *lectio difficilior*.

ESTHER

1:1   וַיְהִי בִּימֵי   Whereas the καὶ ἐγένετο of G and G[AT] attests the shorter text of M, its following plus μετὰ τοὺς λόγους τούτους relates to the preceding addition A and may have the purpose of moderating the abrupt starting of the verse in M. However, the *wayyiqtol* form ויהי as opening of a book without continuing a preceding narrative is not unusual (cf. Josh 1:1; Judg 1:1; 1 Sam 1:1; 2 Sam 1:1; Joüon/Muraoka, *Grammar*, §118e). The narrative proper begins in v. 3, with the pf. עשׂה, and everything between the *wayyiqtol* and the *qatal* forms gives a redundant presentation of the king as the principal figure.

וַאֲחַשְׁוֵרוֹשׁ[1]   The name אֲחַשְׁוֵרוֹשׁ occurs twenty-nine times in Esther, four times in the form אחשׁורשׁ (2:21; 3:12; 8:7,10), and elsewhere only twice (Dan 9:1; Ezra

4:6). G always has Ἀρταξέρξης in Esther. There is a dual tradition, represented by M G^{AT} V S T^R against G (cf. La and Jos, *Ant* xi.184ff.). (Cf. Paton, *Esther*, 51–54; Grossfeld, *First Targum*, 75; Moore, *Studies*, xxxvii–xliii).

הוּא אֲחַשְׁוֵרוֹשׁ   Due to the second ocurrence of the king's name, the complex syntax has caused some variation in the textual transmission. G brackets the latter half of the verse. G^{AT} and V omit the words. A later Syriac tradition has the addition "son of," attested by Lee, *Ketabe qaddishe* (based on the London Polyglot; see the Introduction; cf. Gerleman, *Esther*, 47); T^R and T^{Sh} have longer expansions (cf. Grossfeld, *Two Targums*, 28 f., 96–99).

שֶׁבַע וְעֶשְׂרִים וּמֵאָה   S (or part of the S tradition) reads 120 here. It may have assimilated with Dan 6:2, but in the identical instances in Esth 8:9 and 9:30 it has 127 (cf. Gerleman, *Esther*, 47).

2 | כְּשֶׁבֶת   Apparently two traditions existed for the understanding of the inf. construction כְּשֶׁבֶת (cf. Mp comm.), both of them using finite forms and both being interpretative. Against the ingressive of G stands the durative of V S and T^{Sh}; T^R which is strongly paraphrastic, is durative as well (cf. Grossfeld, *Two Targums*, 29; also Ego, *Targum Scheni*, 66ff.; Haupt, "Critical Notes," 103; Paton, *Esther*, 133; Moore, *Esther*, 5).

בְּשׁוּשַׁן הַבִּירָה: The τῇ πόλει of G (and G^{AT} in v. 5; cf. הָעִיר שׁוּשָׁן in 3:15; 8:15) may represent a general rendering of בִירה which in the first instance means "citadel," "acropolis" (*HALAT*, 119a); cf. *civitas* of V that otherwise has a unique cultural paraphrase.

3 | חֵיל   Although followed by a *paseq* חֵיל may be connected with the following (cf. *HALAT*, 299a), as in V, S and T^R; however, the position of the word seems to have been found obscure, being omitted by G and G^{AT}. The proposal of an insertion of וְשָׂרֵי or וְרָאשֵׁי before it (*BHS*), is questionable (cf. Bardtke, *Esther*, 273; Gerleman, *Esther*, 47). Cf. the comment on כָּל־חֵיל at 8:11.

הַפַּרְתְּמִים וְשָׂרֵי הַמְּדִינוֹת   The variants of the versions, especially G and S, may be generated by the redundant sequence of word pairs (cf. Striedl, "Untersuchung," 84f.; Moore, *Esther*, 5f.).

4 בְּהַרְאֹתוֹ   This inf. construction is translated in various ways. G, which differs from M also at the start of the verse, reads the sfx. of the inf. as indirect accusative and changes it into plural. But the inf. may express narrative continuation (not purpose) of the action of the king: "in his showing"/"and he showed" (cf. Paton, *Esther*, 135; Moore, *Esther*, 6).

אֶת־עֹשֶׁר כְּבוֹד־מַלְכוּתוֹ   The textual redundancy of M, and especially the syntactical position of כבוד, seems to have generated various facilitations, but M needs not to be emended (cf. Bardtke, *Esther*, 275).

יָמִים רַבִּים   As v. 4b has two different indications of time, one general ("many days") and another precise one ("180 days"), the double form may represent a conflation of two competing readings. Whereas the first one is omitted by G and G^{AT}, presumably for stylistic reasons, the second one is attested by all the other versions.

5 | וּבִמְלוֹאת   When M^L, like M^Y (in M^{L34} there is a *lacuna*), has the unusual inf. form מלואת, and no *qərê* (cf. Mandelkern, *Concordantiae*, 673), the complex case may be due to the fact that the usual qal inf. מְלֹאת (on the analogy of ל"ה verbs), when written plene, has resulted in a metathesis of the radicals א and ו (cf. GKC, §74h; Joüon/Muraoka, *Grammar*, §78j; also Gordis, *Biblical Text*, 154 and 202, n. 568).

שִׁבְעַת יָמִים   The variant "six" for "seven" in G may be theologically motivated and have "arisen out of regard for the Sabbath" (so Paton, *Esther*, 143 f.).

6 חוּר | כַּרְפַּס   This verse, replete with rare and technical words, is unconnected with the preceding. It starts with a series of nouns, which has generated many variants in the versions, not only as regards the technical terms but even syntactically, e.g. by adding predicates, in order to integrate its enumerating style into the narrative style of the context (cf. Paton, *Esther*, 138–40, 144–46; Fraenkel, "Bemerkungen," 84 f.). There are scarcely sufficient text historical grounds for emendations like reading תחת instead of חור (and deleting ותכלת) or transposing חור and כרפס (cf. *BHK*; *BHS*).

רִצְפַת בַּהַט־וָשֵׁשׁ וְדָר   In the last part of v. 6, omitted by T[Sh], there are many variants. T[R] is paraphrastically redundant, but this may not make the assumption of a deviating hebr. text form necessary or the reconstruction of a different M possible (cf. Paton, *Esther*, 146: "There is no reason to regard the text of either J [Jerome] L [Old Latin] or G S as superior to M").

10 לִמְהוּמָן   The textual transmission of the verse shows many variants in the versions, especially with regard to the names of the seven eunuchs, where G[AT] and T[Sh] leave out all the names and S reads the first name as a title ("eunuch"). On the problem of the Persian names see Millard, "Persian Names," and Moore, *Esther*, 8 f. (with reference to Gehman, "Persian Words," and Duchesne-Guillemin, "Les noms").

וַאֲבַגְתָא   S is unique in adding here an extra name, Teresh, as substitute for the first one read as a title (cf. Gerleman, *Esther*, 47).

13 יֹדְעֵי הָעִתִּים   In view of the stylistic redundancy of vv. 13-15 the abbreviations of G, G[AT] and V may be regarded as a syntactical facilitation (in v. 14 G has only three names, G[AT] none). An emendation הַדְּתִים (cf. Moore, *Esther*, 2, 9) may not be required (cf. Eissfeldt, "Rechtskundige und Richter," 31–33; Bardtke, *Esther*, 383 f.; *CTAT*, 1:576, with references to 1 Chr 12:33; 29:30).

14 וְהַקָּרֹב   G and G[AT] render a finite verb, which has motivated conjectures like וְהִקְרִיב / וְהַקְרֵב (cf. *HALAT*, 1058 f.) or הַקְרֵב (cf. 1 Kgs 5:7). These proposals may not be necessary, though a plural form seems to be supported (cf. Bardtke, *Esther*, 285; Moore, *Esther*, 2).

15 כְּדָת   As shown by the versions, the syntactical position of כדת has caused translational difficulties. Modern proposals have sought to overcome the difficulties, either by combining the word with the preceding, but without versional support (cf. *BHK*; Bardtke, *Esther*, 284f) or by omitting the word (cf. G[AT] V, also *BHS*, whereas S repeats the initial verb of v. 13), or by incorrectly explaining it as dittography of the three preceding consonants (Rudolph, "Textkritisches zum Estherbuch," 89). Nevertheless, the form of M may be retained and the position of the word possibly may be understood as emphatic (so Paton, *Esther*, 153) or resumptive, "after the long parenthetical expression of vss. 13b–14" (so Moore, *Esther*, 10).

16 מְמוּכָן   The *qərê* מְמוּכָן occurs as *kəṯîb* in vv. 14 and 21 and is supported by V (S) and T (cf. Gordis, *Biblical Text*, 157).

17 עַל־כָּל־הַנָּשִׁים   As for the prep. עַל there seems not to be any Masoretic support for a variation אֶל. The proposal to read אֶל instead of עַל (cf. Haupt, "Critical Notes," 111; Striedl, "Untersuchung," 77; *BHS*) is opposed by Paton (*Esther*, 159) and Gerleman (*Esther*, 47), who explain a mixing of עַל and אֶל as a late and Aramaic influenced phenomenon (cf. Brockelmann, *Hebräische Syntax*,

§108c). The interchange of אֶל and עַל may also be due to differences between the text transmission of Easterners versus Westerners, as is the case in 2:3; 2:14 and 3:9. The phenomenon is also to be seen at 4:5; 4:10 and 7:8.

8 | תֹּאמַרְנָה The problem of the word, within a syntactically difficult context, is the lack of an object. Some versions (G La V) have avoided a direct translation by a contextual interpretation (cf. Paton, *Esther*, 159; Gerleman, *Esther*, 47).

0 כִּי רַבָּה הִיא The syntactical position of the short sentence has obviously been felt difficult: it was omitted by G. The feminine form was preserved and referred to פתגם by T^R (interpreting פתגם as the f. גזירתא "decree") and to מלכות by S, that thereby supports M. It is more likely that the f. form may refer to "kingdom," in a concessive sense (cf. Haupt, "Critical Notes," 113; Gerleman, *Esther*, 69).

2 וּמְדַבֵּר כִּלְשׁוֹן עַמּוֹ: These three words are contextually difficult, and the versions have either omitted them or rendered them differently on the basis of M (cf. Paton, *Esther*, 162f.; Gordis, "Esther Narrative," 53, with reference to Neh 13:23-24; Gerleman, *Esther*, 69f., as well as *CTAT*, 1:577f.).

2 נַעֲרֵי־הַמֶּלֶךְ מְשָׁרְתָיו The occurrence of משרתיו along with נערי־המלך was not understood as a double phrase by V S, which differentiate them (*pueri : ministri*) and connect them by "and." In G, G^AT and La the two nouns seem to have been understood as synonyms and have been stylistically simplified. Although varying in form these witnesses may reflect a *Vorlage* like M, which is attested by T^R.

3 אֶל־יַד See the comment on עַל at 1:17.

הֵגָא The rendering of the name הגא, which most probably also occurs in vv. 8 (twice) and 15 (there in the form הֵגַי), shows some variety (also in M). G omits the name here and in v. 15. G reads Γαι in v. 8 and again in v. 14, where it renders שעשׁגז. T^Sh has שעשׁגז in v. 3 (and v. 14) but not in vv. 8 and 15 where it is like M (cf. Haupt, "Critical Notes," 114; Paton, *Esther*, 69; Moore, *Esther*, xlii, 15, 18; *HALAT*, 228).

6 מֶלֶךְ־יְהוּדָה to עִם־הַגֹּלָה M has in v. 6 a stylistic redundancy, with three אֲשֶׁר clauses. This was facilitated in various ways by the versions, to the greatest extent by G and G^AT. However, the question may be raised whether the Greek tradition had a shorter Hebrew *Vorlage* in relation to which the present M may be regarded as an expansion, motivated by the presentation of Mordecai as one of the principal characters of the book.

7 דֹּדוֹ When G adds the name Aminadab, it may be related to v. 15 and to 9:29, where G also reads 'Αμιναδάβ; but here the name of her father is in M אֲבִיחַיִל. This discrepancy may have caused the variants in La and V. The problem has been widely discussed in Jewish tradition (cf. Grossfeld, *First Targum*, 94f.; Gerleman, *Esther*, 78f.; Moore, *Esther*, xli–xliv).

לְקָחָהּ מָרְדֳּכַי לוֹ לְבַת: Whereas G^AT omits this part of the verse, G expands it in an explicit way that comes near to the expansion of T^R which may relate to a midrashic discussion as attested in *b.Meg.* 13a, where "house" is semantically paralleled to "wife." In this point T^Sh is as short as M (cf. Grossfeld, *First Targum*, 97f.; idem, *Two Targums*, 136; Gerleman, *Esther*, 72, 78f.).

8 הֵגַי See v. 15 and the comment at 2:3 (הֵגָא) (cf. Paton, *Esther*, 69).

9 לְטוֹב בֵּית הַנָּשִׁים: As indicated by the diverging versional renderings, this last part of the verse, especially the phrase לטוב, seems to have been difficult to understand (in S, 7a1* may have had ܠ). Although the versions mostly refer

the phrase to the treatment of the women, it may be more likely that it has a qualifying or superlative sense in relation to the following (cf. Joüon/Muraoka, *Grammar*, §141*e*; GKC, §§132*d*, 133*g*).

12 הֱיוֹת לָהּ כְּדָת הַנָּשִׁים   The whole verse has in M a redundant style that is attested by most versions. In view of this, the facilitating omission by G and the longer omission by G^AT (that in 2:10-23 only has parts of vv. 14, 17 and 18; cf. Jobes, *Alpha-Text*, 101) can hardly be an argument for deleting these lexemes (cf. *BHK*).

חֹדֶשׁ   The unique Syriac variant "days" for "months" (S mss. 7a1, 6f1, 10f1) is hard to explain (cf. Gerleman, *Esther*, 72).

13 וּבָזֶה   The divergence of readings may be motivated by a different syntactical understanding of the context. On the one hand, "by this"/"in this way" (M, S and T^Sh) resumes and continues the temporal clause of the preceding verse, whereas the apodosis follows in v. 13b. On the other hand, "then"/"at that very time" (G and T^R) makes v. 13a to be the apodosis of v. 12 (cf. Paton, *Esther*, 179–81; Moore, *Esther*, 23).

14 שֵׁנִי   The form and syntactic position of the lexeme, being "unrelated to the rest of the verse" (cf. Moore, *Esther*, 23), are difficult. With reference to G, Gerleman (*Esther*, 73) proposes the reading הַשֵּׁנִי, while Bardtke (*Esther*, 293) renews the proposal of Buhl: מִשְׁנֶה (cf. *BHK*; *BHS*); in either case it refers to the "house of women," which is also the common opinion.

אֶל־יַד   See the comment on עַל at 1:17.

שַׁעֲשְׁגַז   Obviously there was some uncertainty regarding this name, especially in the versions. G renders by Γαΐ (cf. הגי in v. 8) that it otherwise omits in v. 3 (הגא) and v. 15 (see the comment at v. 3); in addition, there are some inner-Greek variants, e.g., G^93 σασαγάζ (cf. Hanhart, *Esther*, 146). La, like G^AT and Jos, *Ant* xi.201, omits the name; both in V and S there are variants (cf. Gerleman, *Esther*, 73).

15 אֲבִיחַיִל   See the comment on דדו at v. 7, otherwise 9:29 (cf. Moore, *Esther*, 24).

18 וַיִּתֵּן מַשְׂאֵת כְּיַד הַמֶּלֶךְ:   This verse exhibits many variants, especially in G and S; the meaning of its last part seems to have been obscure. G, on the one hand, leaves it out, as does G^AT, which in addition omits the rest of the chapter. V, on the other hand, shows a redundant rendering of M, and so also T^R and T^Sh, although with paraphrastic additions. T^R lets the royal "gifts" be given to Esther; in this concentration on Esther it is similar to S that twice in the preceding context (vv. 17-18), unlike the other versions, has made Esther the subject of the verbs (cf. Gerleman, *Esther*, 73).

19 וּבְהִקָּבֵץ בְּתוּלוֹת שֵׁנִית   שֵׁנִית is an old *crux interpretum*. Referring to its omission in G, both *BHK* and *BHS* propose emendations; but the G variant may be understood as an evasion of a textual problem (cf. Paton, *Esther*, 186–88; Gerleman, *Esther*, 82f.). Moore (*Esther*, 29-30) reads *šōnôt* 'various (virgins)' instead of *šnyt*, but M is well attested by S and T^R, in the main also by T^Sh and V, and may be preferred, probably having the meaning "anew" (cf. *CTAT*, 1:578).

20 בְּאָמְנָה   The *hapax legomenon* אָמְנָה (of √אמןⁱⁱ) that may be understood as an abstract noun ("fosterage," cf. *DCH*, I:318) seems to have been an early *crux* that G omitted and S, perhaps theologically, related to the "faith" of Esther (cf. Gerleman, *Esther*, 73), whereas V, T^R and T^Sh, in a paraphrastic context, connected it with her upbringing in the house of Mordecai. The proposal to read אָמְנָה "her fostering" instead of אָמְנָה (cf. Driver, "Problems," 235, with refer-

ence to G V T; *BHS*; Moore, *Esther,* 30) is scarcely justified, and a reference to
G that omits it is unjustified.

◀ בִּגְתָ֖ן וָתֶ֑רֶשׁ   The names of the two eunuchs of the king are, with some minor
variations, attested by most versions including La. They are omitted by G, and
so also in 6:2, although some G^{Mss} in both instances have variants of the names
(cf. Hanhart, *Esther,* 148, 175; *BHK*; see the comment at 1:10; cf. Moore,
Esther, 30 f.).

◀ הָמָ֧ן בֶּֽן־הַמְּדָ֛תָא הָאֲגָגִ֖י   The names exhibit many variants, in particular within the
Greek tradition and especially as regards Βουγαῖον (cf. Hanhart, *Esther,* 148,
and especially Jobes, *Alpha-Text,* 124–28; *BHK*; *BHS*; see also at 8:5; 9:10, and
cf. 1:10; 9:24). On parallels between the amplified T^R text (and the more paraphrastic text of T^{Sh}) and Jewish midrash regarding Haman's genealogy, cf.
Grossfeld, *First Targum,* 110 f., 143 f.; idem, *Two Targums,* 51, 140–42, 211 (Table 10).

4 בְּאָמְרָ֥ם   See Gordis, *Biblical Text,* 144, 193 (also Ginsburg, *Tenak*). M$^{L(ket)}$ as
the preferable form is also argued for by Paton, *Esther,* 199; Haupt, "Critical
Notes," 125; cf. Bardtke, *Esther,* 314; Gerleman, *Esther,* 88.

5 וַיִּבֶז בְּעֵינָ֑יו   The divergent renderings of the versions may indicate that the *qal*
form ויבז was a *crux*. Since the *qal* usually is used transitively and the form
here is combined with בעיניו it has been proposed that the verb should be read
as *nifal* וַיִּבָּז, like at Ps 15:4 (cf. *BHK* and *BHS*). The form, however, seems first
of all to be related to the following inf. and may be retained as *qal* (cf. Bardtke,
Esther, 315).

עַם מָרְדֳּכָ֑י²   The lemma occurs twice in the verse and is in both instances
omitted by G, in the first case as part of G's omission of v. 6a; otherwise it is
generally attested by the versions. The proposal to read prep. עַם 'together with'
[Mordecai] instead of subst. עַם 'people' (*BHS*, with reference to G's omission;
cf. Moore, *Esther,* 37) may deprive the Hebrew narrative of a stylistic effect
(cf. Bardtke, *Esther,* 315, 317 f.).

7 וּמֵחֹ֕דֶשׁ לְחֹ֖דֶשׁ שְׁנֵים־עָשָׂ֑ר   The extant text of M represents a *crux interpretum*. As
לחדש, in analogy with מיום ליום, is to be combined with the preceding ומחדש,
the following numeral "twelve" seems to be unrelated. M is scarcely in original
order and is difficult to restore with certainty.
The oldest history of the text is divided. In G there are two additional elements.
First, G takes into this verse words from the end of v. 6, which otherwise was
omitted, and from v. 13 (ὥστε ἀπολέσαι ἐν μιᾷ ἡμέρᾳ τὸ γένος Μαρδοχαίου).
Second, it indicates an exact date of the annihilation of the Jews when it says
the "fourteenth" day of the month Adar (ἔπεσεν ὁ κλῆρος εἰς τὴν τεσσαρεσ-
καιδεκάτην τοῦ μηνός). By contrast G^{AT}, having the verse sequence: 5, 6, 8, 9,
11, 10, 7, 13, (B), 14, 15, says in v. 7 "the thirteenth day of the month Adar
Nisan." Finally, at 8:12 and 9:1 G agrees with M, having "thirteen." Contrary to
these witnesses that here use the name of the month and have a fixed day, other
witnesses only indicate, like M, the counted "twelfth" month, and these are S,
T^R and T^{Sh} as well as V, that otherwise seems to be dependent on G. Whereas
T^R, apparently on the basis of M, has a very long paraphrastic addition (cf.
Grossfeld, *Two Targums,* 52–54, 144), S and T^{Sh} have short texts which come
near M. After a punctuation mark, S repeats the noun "month" prefixed by the
preposition ܒ (ܒܝܪܚܐ). T^{Sh} facilitates M by linking ירחא and תרתי׳ עסרא
with ד.

It is assumed that in M some words are lacking by haplography due to a homoioteleuton of לחדש (cf. Haupt, "Critical Notes," 129; Delitzsch, *Lese- und
Schreibfehler*, § 92), and that the words may be restored by inserting them from
G and G[AT]. Many modern scholars have followed the proposal of Bertheau,
with partial reference to G: וַיִּפֹּל הַגּוֹרָל עַל־שְׁלוֹשָׁה עָשָׂר יוֹם לַחֹדֶשׁ, so also *BHK*
(with a similar text) and *BHS* (with a longer retroversion from G, but with
"thirteen"). Gerleman (*Esther*, 89) seems to have the shortest proposal, without
reference to G: וַיִּפֹּל הַגּוֹרָל עַל־חֹדֶשׁ.
Barthélemy (*CTAT*, 1:578–80) has questioned the use of G in this case, because
the additional elements in v. 7 and also its double tradition elsewhere about the
day of the event ("thirteen" as well as "fourteen") suggest that it has intentionally
created a different chronology from that of M. That is, G obviously has related the
Jewish counter-attack to the day before (thirteenth day, so in 8:12 and 9:1) the
royally prescribed Persian pogrom (on the fourteenth day, so in 3:7 and 3:18, as
well as in Addition B 6), whereas M relates both to "the thirteenth day of the
twelfth month." In conclusion, the syntax of M may be accepted in its present form
(as is found in *TOB*), or, understood as a brachylogy, where "עַד־חֹדֶשׁ" est sous-en-
tendu après "לַחֹדֶשׁ" (580; cf. Brockelmann, *Hebräische Syntax*, § 85e).
However, taking into account the fact that שְׁנֵים־עָשָׂר now is contextually unrelated and that therefore something might be missing, a restoration of a preferred
text may take its point of departure in the reading of S (cf. T[Sh]), where the noun
"month" is reiterated. This leads to the simplest solution, that a second לחדש
after the present one may have been left out by haplography, and thus may be
restored as the original reading: וּמֵחֹדֶשׁ לְחֹדֶשׁ לְחֹדֶשׁ שְׁנֵים־עָשָׂר, "and from
month to month, to (unto) the twelfth month (that is Adar)."

9 עַל־יְדֵי See the comment on עַל at 1:17.

10 בֶּן־הַמְּדָתָא הָאֲגָגִי צֹרֵר הַיְּהוּדִים: The long apposition to the name of Haman (cf.
v. 1) which is attested by V S and both Targums, is omitted in the Greek tradition; and in G, a variant on the sealing of the decrees against the Jews (σφραγί-
σαι κατὰ τῶν γεγραμμένων κατὰ τῶν Ἰουδαίων) is substituted.

12 אֲחַשְׁדַּרְפְּנֵי־הַמֶּלֶךְ There seems to have been some uncertainty regarding the exact meaning of this Persian loanword in M (also in 8:9; 9:3), whether it relates
to civil (so V T[R]) or military (so S) leaders. G and T[Sh] render it more generally
(cf. *HALAT*; Gerleman, *Esther*, 89).

13 וְנָשִׂים to לְהַשְׁמִיד With three verbs for "destroy" and a specification of the completeness of the annihilation of the Jews, M has an amplified style which G[AT]
has omitted entirely. G has considerably simplified by rendering three synonymous verbs by one (showing the same tendency with regard to synonyms as in
vv. 2 and 8 above; cf. Haupt, "Critical Notes," 131) and by omitting the specification. This may be a literary characteristic of the Greek tradition in the book;
and it seems to have influenced V (reducing the three verbs to two).

4:3 v 3 G[AT] has many cases of omissions and recasting in ch. 4 (cf. Hanhart, *Esther*,
156–61; Jobes, *Alpha-Text*, App. 1); and there seems to have been some am-
bivalence in the textual transmission, possibly of a facilitating character. As for
v. 3, there are elements of this verse at 4:1 of G[AT] (cf. Hanhart, *Esther*, 23,
157). In criticism of the proposal of transferring v. 3 to the end of 3:15 (cf.
Paton, *Esther*, 21; *BHK*; *BHS*, referring to G[AT]), see Bardtke, *Esther*, 329.

5 אֲשֶׁר הֶעֱמִיד In view of a dual textual tradition at this point, the main issue
seems to be the understanding of אֲשֶׁר. M and also V take it as object, whereby

the king is subject for the causative הֶעֱמִיד, but G S and T^Sh treat it as subject. In various ways these versions render the verb as an active form that corresponds to *qal* עָמַד. Haupt argues that הֶעֱמִיד could be intransitive as well (Haupt, "Critical Notes," 134). The motivation for this divided understanding may be an exegetical one: whether the king or the eunuch should be focused upon. The preference may be given to M, not to G S T^Sh (as is the case in *BHS*).

10 אֶל־מָרְדֳּכָי: See the comment on עַל at 1:17.

3 לְהִמָּלֵט בֵּית־הַמֶּלֶךְ   There has been some discussion on the understanding of בֵּית, not least in a syntactical sense. The variants may be regarded as efforts at meaningful renderings of a very brief M, which does not seem to need any emendation (cf. *BHS*; see further Paton, *Esther*, 224; Driver, "Problems," 235).

4 הִגַּעַתְּ לַמַּלְכוּת: In various ways, the versions seem to have aimed at explicit renderings of a concise Hebrew expression (cf. Haupt, "Critical Notes," 137 f.; also Dommershausen, *Estherrolle*, 73 f.).

6 וְאַל־תֹּאכֵלוּ   The reading without וֹ, which is attested by V and both Targums, may be stylistically motivated (cf. *BHK*; *BHS*; Bardtke, *Esther*, 328; see also the next comment).

וּבְכֵן   Generally, the versions have understood the M phrase temporally (cf. Haupt, "Critical Notes," 138 f.; not so Gerleman, *Esther*, 102). In three cases in this verse (וְאַל versus אַל; גַם versus וְגַם, as well as the understanding of וּבְכֵן, whether temporally or not) minor divergences in style and grammar exhibit some fluidity and translational freedom in the transmission of the text.

1 וַיְהִי | The two forms of addition D in G and in G^AT especially are not as clearly separated from their respective contexts as the other five additions (cf. Hanhart, *Esther*, 168–75; Jobes, *Alpha-Text*, App. 1; further Paton, *Esther*, 230 ff.; Moore, *Esther*, 54: "A Greek editor expanded vss. 1 and 2 into the sixteen dramatic verses of Addition D, the high point of the Greek Book of Esther").

מַלְכוּת   The brief text of M: ותלבש אסתר מלכות has caused the versions to make explicit renderings, mostly by filling in some word for "garment." Whether M, on the other hand, should be emended in the same way, either by adding לְבוּשׁ "garment," as in 6:8; 8:15 (cf. *BHS*), or the synonymous מַלְבּוּשׁ (cf. Rudolph, "Textkritisches zum Estherbuch," 89; Bardtke, *Esther*, 336), has been questioned. Haupt ("Critical Notes," 139) argues that it "is perhaps not necessary to insert" a word before מַלְכוּת, since this abstract noun "may mean *regalia*"; and similarly, Gerleman (*Esther*, 108) contends that the Hebrew expression is an elliptical one that the versions have filled in.

4·8 הַיּוֹם   See the next comment, at v. 8.

8 אֲשֶׁר to הַמֶּלֶךְ:   The meal that Esther prepares for the king and Haman has caused some confusion, both in v. 4 and here (cf. Paton, *Esther*, 235 ff.). Here, only T^Sh and V, with a minor deviation, attest M, while G, G^AT and S variously make explicit that a second meal will take place the next day; T^R does likewise in a unique way when it indicates "in the evening," probably meaning the start of the next day (cf. Grossfeld, *First Targum*, 147 f.; idem, *Two Targums*, 66). Whether M should be emended by the insertion of a מחר before ומחר that might have been omitted by haplography (cf. *BHK*; Bardtke, *Esther*, 336; Moore, *Esther*, 57) remains disputable (cf. Gerleman, *Esther*, 108).

1 כָּל־   The position of כֹל is conspicuously weak in the versions and is only attested by T^Sh (T^R has "all" at the end of the verse before "princes and servants";

cf. Grossfeld, *First Targum*, 151). According to Haupt, the particle "is impossible" in its context ("Critical Notes," 142), but see Gerleman (*Esther*, 111). See further the next two comments.

גִּדְּלוֹ   The use of the two different but semantically related verb forms גִּדְּלוֹ and נִשְּׂאוֹ has generated various stylistical facilitations in the versions; see the next comment.

עַל־הַשָּׂרִים וְעַבְדֵי הַמֶּלֶךְ:   The versional transmission of the stylistically redundant v. 11b exhibits some fluidity, as shown by the position of כל and by the presence of both גדלו and נשאו. At the end of the verse, G substitutes nouns with verbs ("to take precedence and bear chief rule in the kingdom"), and S repeats the prep. על.

13   יוֹשֵׁב בְּשַׁעַר הַמֶּלֶךְ:   As for Mordecai's "sitting in the King's gate" (cf. 2:19, 21; 5:9; 6:10, 12), there is a divided tendency, either to reduce, like G, or, more generally, to amplify in some way, like G^{AT} and T^R, so partly also S and T^{Sh}, whereas La does both.

14   לִפְנֵי הָמָן   The variant form בעיני, attested by S, may be regarded as harmonization since this form occurs more frequently than לפני, although the last form too, in the sense of "being preferable"/"please," is found elsewhere (Neh 2:5), to which ἀρέσκειν of G and G^{AT}, *placuit ei* of V and קדם of the Targums seem to give support.

6:1   נָדְדָה שְׁנַת   Against M, where "the king's sleep" is the subject of the verb, G (*the Lord*) and G^{AT} (*the Mighty One*) have made God the subject. M is attested by S, and indirectly by V, as well as by the Targums that, on the one hand, witness the syntax of M but, on the other hand, add a broad theological paraphrase on God's wonderful intervention. *BHS* adopts a proposal of Driver ("Problems," 238), who, with reference to G, reads נדדה as נָדַד ה', whereby ה' is taken to be an abbreviation of יהוה. However, this emendation is scarcely plausible, since ה' is not a likely abbreviation of the Tetragrammaton and since it is the general tendency of the Hebrew Esther to avoid the name of God.

4   לַחֲצַר   It has been suggested that due to haplography with the preceding word, the extant ל has lost an originally preceding א and should be read אֶל־, as *BHK* and *BHS* propose (cf. Haupt, "Critical Notes," 143; Gerleman, *Esther*, 114); but there is scarcely any versional evidence in its support.

6   בָּאִישׁ   The versions seem to support a reading with ל as prep. (cf. *BHS*), but ב may also be combined with the vb. עשה in the sense of "do with"/"happen to" (cf. *HALAT*, 844; *BHK*).

8   וַאֲשֶׁר to בְּרֹאשׁוֹ:   The last part of v. 8 represents an old *crux*. The main problem is the point of reference of the royal crown, i.e., on whose head it is to be placed (cf. Gerleman, *Esther*, 114–18). G and G^{AT} might have avoided a quandary by omitting it. In the other versions the crown is never referred to the horse but either to the king or to the man whom the king will honor. The last option seems to be favored by V and T^{Sh}, since they omit אשר. S with its temporal rendering of אשר may be influenced by T^R, which in a paraphrastic way refers it to the king and to his day of coronation. However, the versional variants, as well as modern proposals of emendation (cf. Haupt, "Critical Notes," 144; *BHK*; *BHS*), facilitate M, which might be enigmatic but not impossible (cf. Paton, *Esther*, 248 f.; Moore, *Esther*, 65).

9   וְהִלְבִּישׁוּ   When G and G^{AT} transform the pl. form of this and the following verbs into sg., it may be due to the preceding אִישׁ (see also v. 11). The pl. form of M

that has been retained by the Targums, may be meant to be impersonal (cf. Paton, *Esther,* 249, versus Haupt, "Critical Notes," 144 f., who emends to sg. and is followed by *BHK, BHS*, and also Bardtke, *Esther,* 344).

וְהִרְכִּיבֻהוּ   See the preceding comment on וְהִלְבִּישׁוּ.

וְקָרְאוּ   See the preceding comment on וְהִלְבִּישׁוּ.

חֲכָמָיו   While G^{AT} V and both Targums retain the difference of M between "friends" in v. 13a and "wise men"/"advisors" in v. 13b, G has οἱ φίλοι in both places (cf. 5:10, 14). S has the same. G has this rendering for חכמים at 1:13 also (cf. *CTAT*, 1:576), but there it is not followed by S. This word has G also for שׂרים in 1:3; 2:18; 3:1; 6:9. Thus, G exhibits not only contextual assimilation, but to some degree terminological standardization as well (which does not favor the proposals of *BHK* and *BHS*; cf. *CTAT*, 1:580).

וְתִנָּתֶן לָךְ   At this crucial point in the narrative, M has a redundant and symmetrical style which G, G^{AT}, La and S have facilitated to various degrees, but which both Targums, although witnessing to M, have expanded.

וְאִלוּ   When G, G^{AT} and V, perhaps due to lexical ignorance, omit the (Aramaic) conditional conjunction (cf. *HALAT*, 50; Brockelmann, *Hebräische Syntax*, §165d) and with various renderings refer the following to the preceding, they transform the syntax considerably, which has consequences for the rendering of the last sentence of the verse (see the next comment).

הַמֶּלֶךְ: to כִּי אֵין   As is evident from the varied interpretative renderings of the versions, this last clause seems particularly hard to understand (see also the comment on ואלו above). Paton (*Esther,* 258) states that it "is one of the most difficult in the book." On the other hand, Haupt ("Critical Notes," 148) contends that the "various renderings presuppose no different text," and that all "emendations proposed are unnecessary" (so also Bardtke, *Esther,* 351–55). *BHK* and *BHS* have some proposals for emending the text, but it does not seem possible to restore a variant proto-Masoretic form.

וַיֹּאמֶר^{1} to הַמַּלְכָּה   The problem of the double construction in M, with two occurrences of ויאמר, is solved by the versions in different ways. M may represent a conflation of two traditional readings (hyparchetypes), and most versions have facilitated the conflated text by abbreviating it in various ways (cf. Paton, *Esther,* 258). Only T^{R} and partially S come close to the redundant M form. The most deviant are G^{AT}, with its substitute ("was angry"), and T^{Sh}, with its insertion of an "interpreter" results in two different subjects for the two verbs. The versions may presuppose the extant M; whether some of them may represent a simpler M (as archetype) is hard to decide.

אֲשֶׁר־מְלָאוֹ לִבּוֹ   The unusual form מְלָאוֹ (transitive *qal* with sfx.) has led to various renderings that may have the character of "dynamic equivalence". The proposal מְלָא of *BHK* (cf. Haupt, "Critical Notes," 149) seems not to have versional support and is disputable (cf. *BHS*; Gerleman, *Esther,* 121).

אֵלָיו   For the proposal to read עָלָיו, attested by S and the Targums (*BHK; BHS*; cf. Haupt, "Critical Notes," 151), see the comment on על at 1:17.

עַל־   In view of the unanimous versional evidence, support for the proposal to read אל instead of על seems to be lacking (cf. *BHS*; Bardtke, *Esther,* 355), but see comment on על at 1:17.

חָפוּ:   Except for G, G^{AT} and V, the versions attest the form of M. Its impersonal sense may correspond to the pass. form in S and the Targums. Modern emendations that have been made on the basis of G (cf. *BHK; BHS*; Haupt, "Critical

Notes," 152; Paton, *Esther*, 267; Rudolph, "Textkritisches zum Estherbuch,"
90), do not seem to be grounded satisfactorily.

9   חַרְבוֹנָה   See the commentary on למהומן at 1:10; cf. Duchesne-Guillemin, "Les
noms," 275; Gehman, "Persian Words," 237; Millard, "Persian Names," 485.

דִּבֶּר־טוֹב עַל־   For this not uncommon phrase of M (cf. 1 Sam 25:30; Jer 32:42)
Haupt has, without any support of the versions, proposed to read גמל דָּבָר טוֹב
("Critical Notes," 153). This is noted by *BHK* and *BHS* although they prefer M.
Paton (*Esther*, 267) and Bardtke (*Esther*, 355) are opposed to the proposal.

8:1   מֶה הוּא־לָהּ:   The nominal clause of M (cf. Bardtke, *Esther*, 361) has mostly
received interpretative renderings among the versions. The variants do not seem
to presuppose a different Hebrew *Vorlage*.

5   מַחֲשֶׁבֶת הָמָן בֶּן־הַמְּדָתָא הָאֲגָגִי   The narrative style of the preceding context is
repetitive, and the versions have obviously felt that the inclusion of these appositions is difficult in the context, especially since they interrupt the syntactical
connection of הספרים and אשר. Except for the name of Haman, which is
needed as subject of the following כתב, the appositions have been left out. G,
G^{AT} (with a longer minus), La and V omitted them totally. S and the Targums
omitted some name elements. In V מחשבת etc. has been replaced by an interpretative substitute. See further the comments on המן בן־המדתא האגגי at 3:1
(cf. 9:10, 24).

הַיְּהוּדִים   The added כל in M^Y is attested by other M mss. (seven mss. registered
by Ginsburg, *Tenak*, thirty-six mss. in Kennicott and forty-one mss. in de Rossi) as well as by La, S and both Targums. V puts the lemma in apposition to
Haman (*et hostis Iudaeorum*; see the comment above).

6   יִמְצָא   The use of מצא in the sense of "happen"/"befall" is unique in the book.
Elsewhere this is expressed by the verb קרה (cf. 4:7; 6:13; Paton, *Esther*, 271).
Among the versions there is a division between the Greek and Latin tradition
that avoids the verb and the Aramaic-Syriac form that, in an interpretative context, attests M.

וְרָאִיתִי[2]   This second occurrence of the phrase in the verse has obviously been
seen as difficult by the versions. On the form וראיתי with cj. after impf. אוכל,
see GKC, §112*p;* Brockelmann, *Hebräische Syntax*, §143*a* (cf. Haupt, "Critical
Notes," 154; Gerleman, *Esther*, 126).

9   אֶל־הַיְּהוּדִים   When Haupt made the proposal to read על instead of אל and to
regard the last four words of the verse as a gloss, he referred to S ("Critical
Notes," 155f.; cf. *BHK*; *BHS*). His proposal is followed by Moore (*Esther*, 79f.),
but not by Paton (*Esther*, 272), Bardtke (*Esther*, 366), or Gerleman (*Esther*,
126). In the light of T^{Sh}, where על is not only connected with the Jews but also
with "the dignitaries of the king" as well as with "the princes and governors of
the king in the provinces," and so used four times in a row, the Syriac reading
ܠ, that also may mean "to"/"unto," seems to have lost some of its weight. See
the comment on על at 1:17.

10   הָאֲחַשְׁתְּרָנִים   The Persian loanword that occurs only here and in v. 14 as an attri-
butive to רכש has been rendered and interpreted variously; it most likely means
"royal" (cf. Paton, *Esther*, 277f.; Gerleman, *Esther*, 126–28; *HALAT*, 36).

11   כָּל־חֵיל   In view of the stylistically redundant M, the variants of V and S seem
to have combined את־כל with הצרים אתם. This may represent a stylistic facilitation, or may indicate a simpler proto-Masoretic form that did not have חיל

עם ומדינה (cf. the proposal of *BHK* and *BHS* to delete חיל). See the comment on חיל at 1:3.

3 וְלִהְיוֹת   There seem to be two different ways of understanding the syntactical position of the lexeme: either it is paralleled to the preceding לְהִנָּתֵן, as in M and G, or it is assimilated to the similar instance 3:14, where the word is without copula, as may be the case in V S T^R (cf. *BHK*; *BHS*). However, in 3:14 the "peoples" and not the "Jews," as here, are the subject.

4 הָאֲחַשְׁתְּרָנִים   See the comment on האחשתרנים at v. 10.

5 וְתַכְרִיךְ   The lexeme, which is a *hapax legomenon* noun of Aramaic origin (√כרך "enclose") meaning "mantle," is attested only by V and the Targums. It is read as a verb (pass. ptc.) by S: "enclosed, wrapped in." G and G^AT, possibly due to lexical ignorance, rendered as "a diadem."

7 מִתְיַהֲדִים   The lexeme is a denominative verb from יְהוּדִי and occurs only in *hitpael* and only here (but cf. 9:27). It may mean "to denote oneself as a Jew" or "to act as a Jew" (cf. *HALAT*, 376; Bardtke, *Esther*, 373, 376f.) and is rendered literally only by S. Elsewhere it is modified in some way: both Targums substitute it with the more general "converting" (becoming a proselyte); G specifies by adding the verb "circumcise" to the literal "judaize," while G^AT has only "circumcise." V has the widest variation: *plures alterius gentis et sectae eorum religioni et caerimoniis iungerentur*, "many of another people and way of life joined themselves to their worship and ceremonies."

1 בַּיּוֹם אֲשֶׁר   The lexemes and their context show translational fluidity. In G they have been transposed to the beginning of v. 2 (in connection with an omission in v. 1b). They have been omitted by G^AT, which also has a considerably shorter text than M in the rest of the chapter (cf. Jobes, *Alpha-Text*, App. 1) as well as by La, which omits vv. 1-2, and by S, probably for facilitating reasons. Only V and the Targums attest M.

3 וְעֹשֵׂי הַמְּלָאכָה   Whereas S and the Targums attest M with minor differences (so also V in an amplifying way), G uses a more general expression that also occurs in 3:9. G abbreviates the administrative terminology, not only here but also at the beginning of the verse, where it combines the first two titles. As for this fourth title, G^AT corresponds to G; but unlike G, it differentiates the first two titles.

   מְנַשְּׂאִים   As in 3:1 and 5:11, the *piel* form נשא, with a personal object, is used in the sense of "elevate, honor." This is so also unanimously, although with some minor variety, in the versions. Most modern commentators, however, translate "help, support" (cf. Paton, *Esther*, 283; Moore, *Esther*, 84; also *HALAT*, 686), but Levenson (*Esther*, 118f.) has "gave honor."

7 vv 7-9   As in 1:10 and 1:14, there are many variants in the forms of the names in the list. This may be taken as an example of the great fluidity in the textual transmission of the book of Esther, especially in the Greek tradition (cf. Hanhart, *Esther*, 198f.; Clines, *Esther Scroll*, 82, 86f.; also Haupt, "Critical Notes," 164–66, especially the synoptic overview, 164; Moore, *Esther*, 87; Bardtke, *Esther*, 378). See further the comment on למהומן at 1:10.

0 בֶּן־הַמְּדָתָא   There is some fluidity in the renderings of the name: for G, see Hanhart, *Esther*, 199; for G^AT, see Jobes, *Alpha-Text*, 124–28; the addition in S is the same as in 3:1, 10; 8:3, 5; 9:24. See the comment on the name at 3:1 and 8:5.

   וּבַבִּזָּה לֹא שָׁלְחוּ אֶת־יָדָם: It is somewhat surprising that G, perhaps assimilating

to 3:13, does not have a negative formulation as it has in the parallel occurrences of this phrase in vv. 15-16, and even more so as it also omits the preceding "they killed" (cf. Hanhart, *Esther*, 199). G[AT], which also omits "killed," has
an amplified formulation, but it lacks the parallel occurrences in vv. 15-16 (cf.
Jobes, *Alpha-Text,* 84).

12 וּמַה־[1] The sequence of three interrogative pronouns has made the position of
the middle one difficult since it is related both to what precedes and to what
follows. In relation to the preceding מה it begins something new that requires
an expression of transition, expressed by οὖν in G. It is related to the following
מה in that it introduces a double question. The same or similar double question
occurs also in 5:3, 6 and 7:2; and, being directly introduced, it has in these
instances the form: מה – וּמֶה. Both inner-Hebrew and versional variants may
have assimilated to this form. The syntax, however, is different in 9:12.

14 תָּלוּ: The variant תלו על־העץ supported by G[249] and T[Sh] should most likely be
regarded as a case of contextual harmonization with the end of the preceding
verse. In addition to 9:13 there are similar forms in 2:23; 6:4; 7:10; 8:7; 9:13;
9:25, where G has equivalent forms to the vb. תלה and in 6:4; 7:10; 8:7 (cf.
5:14 pass.) also has the phrase ἐπὶ τῷ ξύλῳ/τοῦ ξύλου. G[AT] lacks the whole
expression in all instances, with the exception of 6:4 where it reads ἵνα κρε-
μάσῃ τὸν Μαρδοχαῖον. The form of M is attested by V S (witnessed by S mss.
6f1, 7a1, 8a1, 10f1) and T[R]. When *BHK* and *BHS* refer to S for this addition, it
may be on the basis of the edition of Lee (or Urmia) that reads ܥܠ ܩܝܣܐ ܕܠܘܬܗ.

15 וּבַבִּזָּה לֹא שָׁלְחוּ אֶת־יָדָם: See the comment on the case at v. 10.

16 וְנוֹחַ Although the verb is attested by most versions, its contextual position has
been questioned. In relation to its occurrences in vv. 17 and 18, it has been
taken as an anticipation (cf. Paton, *Esther*, 291). It is lacking in G[AT] and V and
in the similar text of 8:11-12. Some emendations have been proposed (cf. *BHS*).
Both Rudolph ("Textkritisches zum Estherbuch," 90) and Driver ("Problems,"
237) have assumed that there has been a loss of מ by haplography and have
proposed וְנָחוֹם (*niphal* inf. abs. of נחם) "and avenged themselves" (Bardtke,
Esther, 386, 388). In spite of these arguments, the phrase נוח מאיביהם may be
another expression for being victorious, and the form of M may be retained (cf.
Moore, *Esther*, 85; Gerleman, *Esther*, 130; see also *HALAT*, 624b).

חֲמִשָּׁה וְשִׁבְעִים אֶלֶף On the differing numerals in the versions, cf. Haupt, "Critical Notes," 167; Moore, *Esther,* 89; Jobes, *Alpha-Text,* 121.

וּבַבִּזָּה לֹא שָׁלְחוּ אֶת־יָדָם: See the comment on the case at v. 10.

19 הַפְּרוֹזִים The word that represents the *kǝṯîb-qǝrê* phenomenon is contextually related in two different ways. First, it is in apposition to the preceding personal
noun "the Jews," which may coincide with its *kǝṯîb* form. Second, it is related
to the following cognate word פְּרָזוֹת that is the same as the *qǝrê* form of the
first word. The evidence in the versions is divided. There is a tendency to prefer
the *qǝrê* form (cf. Bardtke, *Esther*, 385–89; *HALAT*, 908f.), but in that case there
will be some overlapping between the two similar words. Gordis (*Biblical Text*,
126, 181, n. 229), referring to *b.Meg*. 19a, understands the *kǝṯîb* form as "a participle passive used actively" (פְּרוּזִים) in the sense of "dweller in hamlet" (cf.
Haupt, "Critical Notes," 168; Paton, *Esther*, 292).

22 כַּיָּמִים M may be retained; for the understanding of the preposition see GKC,
§118x (cf. Haupt, "Critical Notes," 169; Gerleman, *Esther*, 136).

3 וְקִבֵּ֖ל   On the incongruence of the verb and its subj. cf. Brockelmann, *Hebräische Syntax*, § 50a (Paton, *Esther*, 298). See the comment on וקבל at v. 27.

4 הָאֲגָגִ֖י   See the comment on the case at 3:1.

כָּל־   The position of כל is somewhat ambiguous, but in view of the stylistically redundant context M may be retained.

5 וּבְבֹאָהּ֩   As shown by the differences in the versions, the inf. cstr. form of M, with prep. and sfx., has been understood as ambiguous with regard to its syntactic reference. Whereas G^{AT} omits the verb, in G it refers to Haman, who is mentioned in the preceding. In most of the versions, however, it refers explicitly to Esther, who was not mentioned immediately before. In the contextual framework of vv. 24-25 which serve as motive clauses to v. 23, recapitulating what was previously narrated and stated, a neutral sense seems to be the most likely one (and that in pluperfect: "and when it had come before the king he said . . .": cf. Paton, *Esther*, 296; Bardtke, *Esther*, 390; Gerleman, *Esther*, 136).

עִם־הַסֵּ֖פֶר   The expression has obviously been difficult to understand and render (cf. Paton, *Esther*, 296, 299; Gerleman, *Esther*, 139). Taking into account the recapitulative character of its context (see the preceding comment on ובבאה), it may be relevant to consider it as a reference to 8:8 (cf. *CTAT*, 1:581).

6 פּוּרִים֙   There are many inner-Greek variants to Φρουραί; see Hanhart, *Esther*, 203 f. (cf. *BHK*). Jos, *Ant* xi.295, has Φρουρέας (Φρουραίους). Cf. Haupt, "Critical Notes," 171.

עַל־כֵּ֖ן²   Because of the double עַל־כֵּן and the following עַל, M has a syntactically complex form that has been treated by the versions with various kinds of simplification. The problem, however, may not be as much one of a strictly text critical character as of a literary one (cf. Haupt, "Critical Notes," 171).

7 וְקִבֵּ֣ל   The form, with subj. in pl., is the same as in v. 23 (but there without a qərê in pl.). As the inf. of V (*suscepere*) seems to indicate, the *kətîb* form may be vocalized as an inf. abs. קַבֵּ֖ל (cf. Paton, *Esther*, 299; Gordis, *Biblical Text*, 38, 97; also *BHK*; *BHS*).

וְלֹ֣א יַעֲב֔וֹר   The words seem to have a parenthetical character (cf. Gerleman, *Esther*, 137) but do not need to be transposed to the end of the verse and changed to plural (cf. Haupt, "Critical Notes," 172; *BHK*; *BHS*).

9 וַתִּכְתֹּ֨ב   The f. sg. verb form of M, with Esther as subject, is generally attested, with the exception of V, which has the verb in the plural due to treating "Mordecai the Jew" as part of the subject. That a part of the Hebrew text tradition has the first ת written large (so *editio Bombergiana* and Ginsburg, *Tenak*, unlike M^L, M^Y, M^{L34} as well as M^{S1}) may be understood as an accentuating of the sg. and f. form as related to Esther as the sole subject (cf. Yeivin, *Tiberian Masorah*, § 84; *CTAT*, 1:581 f.).

אֵֽת־כָּל־תֹּ֖קֶף   This syntactically difficult phrase has been a *crux*, both for the versions, whose renderings are varied, and for later interpreters (some of whose emendations are listed in *BHK* and *BHS*). The connection of the phrase with the initial verb seems clear; the function of את may possibly be that of *nota accusativi* (cf. Haupt, "Critical Notes," 172 f.; Gerleman, *Esther*, 137; Grossfeld, *Two Targums*, 88, n. 43; otherwise Moore, *Esther*, 95 f.).

10 וַיִּשְׁלַ֤ח   The form of M is well attested, apart from the Greek tradition that has omissions in this part of the chapter (G omits v. 30 and parts of v. 31, whereas G^{AT} lacks vv. 26-32 and La lacks vv. 30-32), and the plural form of V that

may have assimilated to the preceding verse. It may have an impersonal sense (cf. Haupt, "Critical Notes," 173; Paton, *Esther*, 302; Bardtke, *Esther*, 397).

31 וְאֶסְתֵּר הַמַּלְכָּה   Cf. the comment on וַתִּכְתֹּב at v. 29; *CTAT*, 1:581 f.

דִּבְרֵי הַצֹּמוֹת וְזַעֲקָתָם׃   This syntactically unrelated end of the verse has obviously caused difficulties and is rendered variously by the versions. The inclusion of the words that have some reference to 4:1, 3, 16 (cf. also Zech 7:5; 8:19) may be motivated by the fact that "fasting" and "lamentation" were not mentioned in the preceding vv. 20-22, or in vv. 23-28 (cf. Haupt, "Critical Notes," 173 f.; Paton, *Esther*, 301; Moore, *Esther*, 97 f.).

10:1 | אֲחַשְׁרֹשׁ   Of 29 occurrences of the name of the Persian king in the book of Esther, this *kǝtîb* form with double defective writing is unique. See the comment on the name at 1:1.

2 מָרְדֳּכַי   Regarding the obviously difficult relationship between the Persian king and Mordecai, there are two main tendencies in the textual variants: in the Greek tradition, the focus is upon the king, and Mordecai is omitted (G and G^AT). In the other versions, the interest, in various ways, is concentrated upon Mordecai (cf. Fox, *Redaction,* 77 f.). Haupt's syntactical understanding and proposal of transposition ("Critical Notes," 174, reiterated by *BHK* and *BHS*) can hardly do justice to this state of affairs.

3 וְגָדוֹל לַיְּהוּדִים   In view of the varied and somewhat interpretative renderings of the versions, it may not be necessary to renew Haupt's proposal to read בְּ/ instead of לְ/ ("Critical Notes," 175, reiterated by *BHK* and *BHS*; cf. Gerleman, *Esther*, 143).

וְרָצוּי לְרֹב אֶחָיו   At the end of the book, where the position and role of Mordecai is particularly important, the renderings of the versions, except for S, are very interpretive (cf. Paton, *Esther,* 304; Ego, *Targum Scheni,* 333).

זַרְעוֹ׃   On the relation of V's longer additions to those in G and G^AT, see Hanhart, *Esther*, 19 (also "Greek Witnesses" in the "Introduction" to the present edition).

WORKS CITED

Albrektson, *Studies*
> Albrektson, Bertil. *Studies in the Text and Theology of the Book of Lamentations with a Critical Edition of the Peshitta Text*. Studia theologica lundensia 21. Lund: C.W.K. Gleerup, 1963.

Allgeier, *Prediger*
> Allgeier, Arthur. *Das Buch des Predigers oder Koheleth*. Die Heilige Schrift des Alten Testaments 6/2. Bonn: Hanstein, 1925.

Baars, "Vetus Latina"
> Baars, W. "Vetus Latina: Estudio crítico de la version latina prejeronimiana del libro de Rut." *Vetus Testamentum* 18 (1968): 125–27.

Bardtke, "Neuere Arbeiten"
> Bardtke, Hans. "Neuere Arbeiten zum Estherbuch: Eine kritische Würdigung." *Ex Oriente Lux* 19 (1965/1966): 519–49.

Bardtke, *Esther*
> Bardtke, Hans. *Das Buch Esther*. Kommentar zum Alten Testament 17/5. Gütersloh: Gerd Mohn, 1963. (Bound together with Hertzberg, *Der Prediger*.)

Barth, *Nominalbildung*
> Barth, Jacob. *Die Nominalbildung in den semitischen Sprachen*. 2d ed. Leipzig: J.C. Hinrichs, 1894.

Barthélemy, *Études*
> Barthélemy, Dominique. *Études d'histoire du texte de l'Ancien Testament*. Orbis biblicus et orientalis 21. Fribourg: Éditions Universitaires; Göttingen: Vandenhoeck & Ruprecht, 1978.

Barthélemy, *Les devanciers*
> Barthélemy, Dominique. *Les devanciers d'Aquila*. Vetus Testamentum Supplements 10. Leiden: Brill, 1963.

Barton, *Ecclesiastes*
> Barton, George Aaron. *A Critical and Exegetical Commentary on the Book of Ecclesiastes*. International Critical Commentary 17. Edinburgh: T&T Clark, 1908.

Bauer, *Wörterbuch*
> Bauer, Walter. *Griechisch-Deutsches Wörterbuch zu den Schriften des Neuen Testaments und der frühchristlichen Literatur*. 6th rev. ed. Revised and edited by Viktor Reichmann, Kurt Aland and Barbara Aland. Berlin and New York: Walter de Gruyter, 1988.

Bauer/Leander, *Grammatik*
> Bauer, Hans, and Pontus Leander. *Historische Grammatik der hebräischen Sprache des Alten Testamentes*. Halle an der Saale: M. Niemeyer, 1918, 1922. Repr., Hildesheim: Georg Olms, 1965.

BDB
> Brown, Francis, S. R. Driver, and Charles A. Briggs. *A Hebrew and English Lexicon of the Old Testament with an Appendix Containing the Biblical Aramaic*. Oxford: Clarendon, 1907.

Beit-Arié/Sirat/Glatzer, *Codices Hebraicis Litteris Exarati*
  Beit-Arié, M., C. Sirat, and M. Glatzer. *Codices Hebraicis Litteris Exarati Quo Tempore Scripti Fuerint Exhibentes.* 3 vols. Monumenta Palaeographica Medii Aevi, Series Hebraica. Turnhout: Brepols, 1997–2002.
Beit-Arié, M., ed. *The Damascus Pentateuch.* Vol. 2 in *Early Hebrew Manuscripts in Facsimile.* Edited by M. Beit-Arié. Copenhagen: Rosenkilde & Bagger; Baltimore: Johns Hopkins University Press, 1982.
Ben-Yehudah, *Dictionary*
  Ben-Yehudah, Eliezer, and Naphtali Hertz Tur-Sinai. *Milon ha-lashon ha-'Ivrit ha-yeshanah veha-hadashah.* 17 vols. Berlin: Schöneberg, Langenscheidt; Jerusalem: Hemda & Ehud Benyehuda; New York and London: Thomas Yoseloff, 1908–1959. Repr., *A Complete Dictionary of Ancient and Modern Hebrew.* 8 vols. New York: Thomas Yoseloff, 1960.
Berger, "Quelques textes latins"
  Berger, Samuel. "Notice sur quelques textes latins inédits de l'Ancien Testament." Pages 122–26 in *Notices et extraits des manuscrits de la Bibliothque Nationale et autres bibliothèques,* XXXIV/2. Paris: Institut national de France, 1893.
Berges, *Klagelieder*
  Berges, Ulrich. *Klagelieder.* Herders theologischer Kommentar zum Alten Testament. Freiburg: Herder, 2002.
Bertheau, *Esra, Nechemia und Ester*
  Bertheau, Ernst. *Die Bücher Esra, Nechemia und Ester.* 2d ed. Revised by Victor Ryssel. Kurzgefasstes exegetisches Handbuch zum Alten Testament 17. Leipzig: S. Hirzel, 1887.
BHK
  Kittel, Rudolf, ed. *Biblia Hebraica.* (Ordinarily, this refers to the edition of 1937 [*BHK³*] and its subsequent revisions.)
BHK¹
  Kittel, Rudolf, ed. *Biblia Hebraica.* Leipzig: J. C. Hinrichs, 1905.
BHK²
  Kittel, Rudolf, ed. *Biblia Hebraica.* Leipzig: J. C. Hinrichs, 1913.
BHK³
  Kittel, Rudolf, ed. *Biblia Hebraica.* Stuttgart: Württembergische Bibelanstalt, 1937.
BHS
  Elliger, Karl, and Wilhelm Rudolph, eds. *Biblia Hebraica Stuttgartensia.* 5th ed. Stuttgart: Deutsche Bibelgesellschaft, 1997. (First edition: Stuttgart: Deutsche Bibelstiftung, 1977.)
Blass/Debrunner/Rehkopf, *Grammatik*
  Blass, Friedrich, Albert Debrunner and Friedrich Rehkopf. *Grammatik des neutestamentlichen Griechisch.* 16th ed. Göttingen: Vandenhoeck & Ruprecht, 1984.
Bons, "Verständnis eines Hapaxlegomenons"
  Bons, Eberhard. "*Šidda wᵊšiddot*: Überlegungen zum Verständnis eines Hapaxlegomenons." *Biblische Notizen* 36 (1987): 12–16.
Brady, *Rabbinic Targum*
  Brady, Christian M. M. *The Rabbinic Targum of Lamentations: Vindicating God.* Leiden and Boston: Brill, 2003.

Breuer, כתר ארם צובה

Breuer, M. כתר ארם צובה והנוסח המקובל של המקרא. Jerusalem: Mosad HaRav Kook, 1976.

Brockelmann, *Hebräische Syntax*

Brockelmann, Carl. *Hebräische Syntax*. Neukirchen: Neukirchener Verlag, 1956.

Brockelmann, *Lexicon Syriacum*

Brockelmann, Carl. *Lexicon Syriacum*. Halle: Max Niemeyer, 1928. Repr., Hildesheim: Georg Olms, 1995.

Brooke/McLean, *Joshua, Judges and Ruth*

Brooke, Alan England, and Norman McLean, eds. *Joshua, Judges and Ruth*. Vol. I, pt. 4 of *The Old Testament in Greek*. Edited by Alan England Brooke and Norman McLean. Cambridge: Cambridge University Press, 1917.

Brooke/McLean/Thackeray, *Esther, Judith, Tobit*

Brooke, Alan England, Norman McLean, and H. St. J. Thackeray, eds. *Esther, Judith, Tobit*. Vol. III, pt. 1 of *The Old Testament in Greek*. Edited by Alan England Brooke and Norman McLean. Cambridge: Cambridge University Press, 1940.

Buxtorf, *Anticritica*

Buxtorf, Johann, Jr. *Anticritica seu vindiciae veritatis hebraicae, adversus L. Cappelli criticam*. Basel: L. Regis, 1653.

Campbell, *Ruth*

Campbell, Edward F. *Ruth*. Anchor Bible 7. Garden City, New York: Doubleday, 1975.

Cantera Ortiz de Urbina *Vetus Latina*

Cantera Ortiz de Urbina, Jesus. *Vetus Latina-Rut: studio crítico de la version latina prejeronomiana del libro de Rut*. Textos y estudios del Seminario Filologico Cardenal Cisneros 4. Madrid and Barcelona: Seminario Filologico Cardenal Cisneros, 1965.

Cassuto, *Qeré-Ketib*

Cassuto, Philippe. *Qeré-Ketib et listes massorétiques dans le manuscrit B 19a*. Judentum und Umwelt 26. Frankfurt am Main: Peter Lang, 1989.

Ceriani, *Fragmenta*

Ceriani, Antonio Maria, ed. *Fragmenta latina Evangelii S. Lucae, Parvae Genesis et Assumptionis Mosis. Baruch, Threni et Epistola Jeremiae versionis syriacae Pauli Telensis*. Vol. I/1 in *Monumenta sacra et profana ex codicibus praesertim Bibliothecae Ambrosianae*. Milan: Bibliotheca Ambrosiana, 1861.

Ceriani, *Translatio Syra*

Ceriani, Antonio Maria, ed. *Translatio Syra Pescitto Veteris Testamenti: ex codice Ambrosiano sec. fere VI*. Milan: J.B. Pogliani, 1876–1883.

Chantraine, *Dictionnaire étymologique*

Chantraine, P. *Dictionnaire étymologique de la langue grecque: Histoire des mots*. Paris: Klincksieck, 1968–1980.

Clines, *Esther Scroll*

Clines, David J.A. *The Esther Scroll: The Story of the Story*. Journal for the Study of the Old Testament: Supplement Series 30. Sheffield: JSOT Press, 1984.

Collins/Green, "Tales from the Persian Court"
>   Collins, John J., and Deborah A. Green. "Tales from the Persian Court
>   (4Q550^{a-e})." Pages 39–50 in *Antikes Judentum und Frühes Christentum:
>   Festschrift für Hartmut Stegemann zum 65. Geburtstag.* Edited by Bernd
>   Kollmann, Wolfgang Reinbold, and Annette Steudel. Beihefte zur Zeitschrift
>   für die neutestamentliche Wissenschaft und die Kunde der älteren Kirche 97.
>   Berlin and New York: Walter de Gruyter, 1999.

Crenshaw, *Ecclesiastes*
>   Crenshaw, James. *Ecclesiastes: A Commentary.* Old Testament Library. Phi-
>   ladelphia: Westminster, 1987.

Cross, "Lamentations 1"
>   Cross, Frank Moore. "Studies in the Structure of Hebrew Verse: The Prosody
>   of Lamentations 1:1–22." Pages 129–55 in *The Word of the Lord Shall
>   Go Forth: Essays in Honor of David Noel Freedman in Celebration of his
>   Sixtieth Birthday.* Edited by Carol L. Meyers and Michael Patrick O'Connor.
>   Winona Lake, Ind.: Eisenbrauns, 1983.

CTAT
>   Barthélemy, Dominique. *Critique textuelle de l'Ancien Testament.* 3 vols.
>   Orbis biblicus et orientalis 50/1–3. Fribourg: Éditions Universitaires; Göttin-
>   gen: Vandenhoeck & Ruprecht, 1982, 1986, 1992. Handwritten notes on
>   Psalms and the Megillot to be published in forthcoming volumes (4 and 5) of
>   *CTAT.*

Dahood, "Qoheleth"
>   Dahood, Mitchell J. "Qoheleth and Northwest Semitic Philology." *Biblica*
>   43 (1962): 349–65.

Davidson, *Lexicon*
>   Davidson, Benjamin. *The Analytical Hebrew and Chaldee Lexicon.* London:
>   S. Bagster & Sons, 1848. Repr., Grand Rapids, Mich.: Zondervan, 1972.

Davis, *Taylor-Schechter Old Series*
>   Davis, Malcolm C. *Taylor-Schechter Old Series and Other Genizah Collec-
>   tions in the Cambridge University Library.* Volume 1 of *Hebrew Bible Manu-
>   scripts in the Cambridge Genizah Collections.* Cambridge: Cambridge Uni-
>   versity Library, 1978.

Day, *Three Faces*
>   Day, Linda. *Three Faces of a Queen: Characterization in the Books of
>   Esther.* Journal for the Study of the Old Testament: Supplement Series 186.
>   Sheffield: Sheffield Academic Press, 1995.

DCH
>   Clines, David J. A., ed. *The Dictionary of Classical Hebrew.* Sheffield: Shef-
>   field Academic Press, 1993–.

De Bruyne, "Les anciennes versions"
>   De Bruyne, Donatien. "Les anciennes versions latines du Cantique des Can-
>   tiques." *Revue Bénédictine* 38 (1926): 97–122.

de Rossi, *Scholia*
>   de Rossi, Giovanni Bernardo. *Scholia critica in V.T. libros seu supplementa
>   ad varias sacri textus lectiones.* Parma: Bodoni, 1798.

de Rossi, *Variae lectiones*
>   de Rossi, Giovanni Bernardo, ed. *Variae lectiones Veteris Testamenti.* 4 vols.
>   Parma: Bodoni, 1784–1788. Repr., Amsterdam: Philo, 1969–1970.

De Troyer, *End*

De Troyer, Kristin. *The End of the Alpha-Text of Esther: Translation and Narrative Technique in MT 8:1-17, LXX 8:1-17, and AT 7:14-41.* Septuagint and Cognate Studies Series 48. Atlanta: Scholars Press, 2000. Rev. trans. of *Het einde van de alpha-tekst van Esther.* Leuven: Peeters, 1997.

de Waard/Nida, *Handbook*

de Waard, Jan, and Eugene A. Nida. *A Translator's Handbook on the Book of Ruth.* 2d ed. New York: United Bible Societies, 1992.

Delitzsch, *Hoheslied und Koheleth*

Delitzsch, Franz. *Hoheslied und Koheleth.* Biblischer Commentar über das Alte Testament 4. Leipzig: Dörffling & Franke, 1875.

Delitzsch, *Lese- und Schreibfehler*

Delitzsch, Friedrich. *Die Lese- und Schreibfehler im Alten Testament.* Berlin: Walter de Gruyter, 1920.

Dhorme, *L'emploi métaphorique*

Dhorme, Edouard Paul. *L'emploi métaphorique des noms des parties du corps en hébreu et en akkadien.* Paris: Gabalda/V. Lecoffre, 1923.

Diebner, Jørg, and Rodolphe Kasser, eds. *Hamburger Papyrus Bil 1: Die alttestamentlichen Texte des papyrus bilinguis 1 der Staats- und Universitätsbibliothek Hamburg.* Geneva: P. Cramer, 1989.

Díez Merino, Luis. *Targum de Qoheleth: Edición Príncipe del Ms. Villa-Amil n. 5 de Alfonso de Zamora.* Madrid: CSIC, 1987.

Dirksen, "Lee's Editions"

Dirksen, Piet B. "Lee's Editions of the Syriac Old Testament and the Psalms, 1822–1826." Pages 63–71 in *In Quest of the Past: Studies on Israelite Religion, Literature, and Prophetism. Papers Read at the Joint British-Dutch Old Testament Conference Held at Elspeet, 1988.* Edited by Adam S. van der Woude. Oudtestamentische Studiën 26. Leiden: Brill, 1990.

Dirksen, "Song of Songs"

Dirksen, Piet B. "The Peshitta Text of Song of Songs." *Textus* 19 (1998): 171–81.

Dirksen, "Urmia Edition"

Dirksen, Piet B. "The Urmia Edition of the Peshitta: The Story behind the Text." *Textus* 18 (1995): 157–67.

DJD III

Baillet, Maurice, Jozef Tadeusz Milik, and Roland de Vaux. *Les "petites grottes" de Qumrân.* 2 vols. Discoveries in the Judean Desert III. Oxford: Clarendon, 1962.

DJD XVI

Ulrich, Eugene, Frank Moore Cross, Joseph A. Fitzmyer, Peter W. Flint, Sarianna Metso, Catherine M. Murphy, Curt Niccum, Patrick W. Skehan, Emanuel Tov, and Julio Trebolle Barrera. *Qumran Cave 4: XI, Psalms to Chronicles.* Discoveries in the Judean Desert XVI. Oxford: Clarendon, 2000.

Dommershausen, *Estherrolle*

Dommershausen, Werner. *Die Estherrolle: Stil und Ziel einer alttestamentlichen Schrift.* Stuttgarter Biblische Monographien 6. Stuttgart: Katholisches Bibelwerk, 1968.

Dotan, "Codex Or. 4445"

Dotan, Aron. "Reflections Towards a Critical Edition of Pentateuch Codex

Or. 4445." Pages 39–51 in *Estudios Masoréticos (X Congreso de la IOMS): En memoria de Harry M. Orlinsky*. Edited by E. Fernández Tejero and M. T. Ortega Monasterio. Madrid: Instituto de Filología del CSIC, 1993.

Driver, "Hebrew Notes"
  Driver, Godfrey Rolles. "Hebrew Notes on 'Song of Songs' and 'Lamentations'." Pages 134–46 in *Festschrift für Alfred Bertholet zum 80. Geburtstag*. Edited by Walter Baumgartner, et al. Tübingen: J.C.B. Mohr (Paul Siebeck), 1950.

Driver, "Problems"
  Driver, Godfrey Rolles. "Problems and Solutions." *Vetus Testamentum* 4 (1954): 225–45. Repr., pages 387–407 in *Studies in the Book of Esther*. Edited by Carey A. Moore. The Library of Biblical Studies. New York: KTAV, 1982.

Duchesne-Guillemin, "Les noms"
  Duchesne-Guillemin, Jacques. "Les noms des eunuques d'Assuérus." *Muséon* 66 (1953): 105–8. Repr., pages 273–76 in *Studies in the Book of Esther*. Edited by Carey A. Moore. The Library of Biblical Studies. New York: KTAV, 1982.

Ego, *Targum Scheni*
  Ego, Beate. *Targum Scheni zu Ester: Übersetzung, Kommentar und theologische Deutung*. Texte und Studien zum Antiken Judentum 54. Tübingen: J.C.B. Mohr (Paul Siebeck), 1996.

Ehrlich, *Randglossen*
  Ehrlich, Arnold B. *Randglossen zur hebräischen Bibel: Textkritisches, Sprachliches und Sachliches*. 7 vols. Leipzig: J.C. Hinrichs, 1908–1914. Repr. Hildesheim: Georg Olms, 1968.

Eissfeldt, "Rechtskundige und Richter"
  Eissfeldt, Otto. "Rechtskundige und Richter in Esther 1:13–22." Pages 164–66 in *Festschrift für Wilhelm Eilers*. Wiesbaden: Otto Harrassowitz, 1967. Repr., pages 31–33 in *Kleine Schriften*, vol. 5. Tübingen: J.C.B. Mohr, 1973.

Emerton, John Adney, and D. J. Lane, eds. "Song of Songs." In *Proverbs, Wisdom of Solomon, Ecclesiastes, Song of Songs*. Edited by Alexander A. DiLella, John Adney Emerton and D. J. Lane. Vol. II/5 of *The Old Testament in Syriac, According to the Peshitta Version*. Edited by The Peshitta Institute, Leiden. Leiden: Brill, 1979.

Ettien, "Translating"
  Ettien, Koffi Nda. "Translating the Term 'but' – Unsuspected Challenges." *The Bible Translator* 47 (1996): 218–26.

Euringer, *Der Masorahtext*
  Euringer, Sebastian. *Der Masorahtext des Koheleth kritisch untersucht*. Leipzig: J.C. Hinrichs, 1890.

Field, *Origenis Hexaplorum*
  Field, Frederick. *Origenis Hexaplorum quae supersunt*. 2 vols. Oxford: Clarendon, 1875. Repr., Hildesheim: Georg Olms, 1964.

Fox, *Redaction*
  Fox, Michael V. *The Redaction of the Books of Esther: On Reading Composite Texts*. Society of Biblical Literature Monograph Series 40. Atlanta: Scholars Press, 1991.

Fraenkel, "Bemerkungen"
    Fraenkel, M. "Bemerkungen zum hebräischen Wortschatz." *Hebrew Union College Annual* 31 (1960): 55–102.
Frensdorff, *Massorah*
    Frensdorff, Solomon. *Die Massora Magna: erster Theil, Massoretisches Wörterbuch.* Hannover: Cohen & Risch, 1876. Repr., New York: KTAV, 1968.
Frensdorff, *Ochlah*
    Frensdorff, Solomon. *Das Buch Ochlah W'ochlah (Massora).* Hannover: Hann'sche Hofbuchhandlung, 1864. Repr., New York: KTAV, 1968.
Galling, "Prediger"
    Galling, Kurt. "Der Prediger." In *Die fünf Megilloth,* by Ernst Würthwein, Kurt Galling, and Otto Plöger. Handbuch zum Alten Testament, erste Reihe 18. 2d rev. ed. Tübingen: J.C.B. Mohr, 1969.
Garbini, *Cantico*
    Garbini, Giovanni. *Cantico dei cantici: Testo, traduzione, note e commento.* Biblica, Testi e studi 2. Brescia: Paideia, 1992.
Gasquet, et al., *Biblia Sacra*
    Gasquet, Francis Aidan, et al., eds. *Biblia Sacra iuxta Latinam Vulgatam Versionem.* 18 vols. Rome: Libreria Editrice Vaticana, 1926–1996.
Gehman, "Persian Words"
    Gehman, Henry Snyder. "Notes on the Persian Words in the Book of Esther." *Journal of Biblical Literature* 43 (1924): 321–28.
Gerleman, *Esther*
    Gerleman, Gillis. *Esther.* Biblischer Kommentar: Altes Testament 21. Neukirchen-Vluyn: Neukirchener Verlag, 1973.
Gerleman, *Ruth/Hohelied*
    Gerleman, Gillis. *Ruth / Das Hohelied.* Biblischer Kommentar: Altes Testament 18. Neukirchen-Vluyn: Neukirchener Verlag, 1965.
Gesenius, *Handwörterbuch*
    Gesenius, Wilhelm. *Hebräisches und Aramäisches Handwörterbuch über das Alte Testament.* 18th ed. Edited by Rudolf Meyer, Herbert Donner, and Udo Rüterswörden. Heidelberg: Springer, 1987– .
Gesenius, *Thesaurus*[2]
    Gesenius, Wilhelm. *Thesaurus philologicus criticus linguae Hebraeae et Chaldaeae Veteris Testamenti.* Completed by Emil Roediger. 3 vols. 2d ed. Leipzig: Fr. Chr. Guil. Vogel, 1829–1842.
Gesenius/Kautzsch, *Grammatik*
    Gesenius, Wilhelm. *Hebräische Grammatik.* 26th ed. Edited and enlarged by Emil Friedrich Kautzsch. Leipzig: F.C.W. Vogel, 1896.
Ginsburg
    Ginsburg, Christian D. *The Massorah: Compiled from Manuscripts. Alphabetically and Lexically Arranged.* 4 vols. London, 1880–1905. Repr., New York: KTAV, 1975.
Ginsburg, *Introduction*
    Ginsburg, Christian D. *Introduction to the Massoretico-Critical Edition of the Hebrew Bible.* London: Trinitarian Bible Society, 1897. Repr., New York: KTAV, 1966.

Ginsburg, *Tenak*
>   Ginsburg, Christian D., ed. תורה נביאים וכתובים. 4 vols. London: British and Foreign Bible Society, 1926.

GKC
>   Gesenius, Wilhelm. *Gesenius' Hebrew Grammar*. 2d English edition. Edited and enlarged by Emil Friedrich Kautzsch. Translated by A. E. Cowley. Oxford: Clarendon, 1910. Repr., Oxford: Oxford University Press, 1946.

Goldman, "Book of Esther"
>   Goldman, S. "The Book of Esther." Pages 115–86 in *The Five Megilloth*. 2d ed. Edited by A. Cohn. The Soncino Books of the Bible. London: Soncino, 1952.

Gordis, "Esther Narrative"
>   Gordis, Robert. "Studies in the Esther Narrative." *Journal of Biblical Literature* 95 (1976): 43–58. Repr., pages 408–23 in *Studies in the Book of Esther*. Edited by Carey A. Moore. The Library of Biblical Studies. New York: KTAV, 1982.

Gordis, *Biblical Text*
>   Gordis, Robert. *The Biblical Text in the Making: A Study of the Kethib-Qere*. Philadelphia: Dropsie College, 1937.

Gordis, *Koheleth – The Man*
>   Gordis, Robert. *Koheleth – The Man and His World*. 2d ed. Texts and Studies of the Jewish Theological Seminary of America 19. New York: The Jewish Theological Seminary of America, 1955.

Gordis, *Megillat Esther*
>   Gordis, Robert. *Megillat Esther: The Masoretic Hebrew Text, with Introduction, New Translation and Commentary*. New York: Rabbinical Assembly, 1974.

Goshen-Gottstein, Moshe H., ed. *The Aleppo Codex. Volume 1, The Plates*. Jerusalem: Magnes, 1976.

Gottwald, *Studies*
>   Gottwald, Norman K. *Studies in the Book of Lamentations*. Studies in Biblical Theology 14. London: SCM, 1954.

Gow, *Ruth*
>   Gow, Murray D. *The Book of Ruth: Its Structure, Theme and Purpose*. Leicester: Apollos, 1992.

Graetz, *Kohélet*
>   Graetz, Heinrich H. *Kohélet oder der Salomonische Prediger übersetzt und kritisch erläutert*. Leipzig: C.F. Winter, 1871.

Grossfeld, *Concordance*
>   Grossfeld, Bernard. *Concordance of the First Targum to the Book of Esther*. Society of Biblical Literature Aramaic Studies 5. Chico, Calif.: Scholars Press, 1984.

Grossfeld, *First Targum*
>   Grossfeld, Bernard, ed. *The First Targum to Esther: According to the Ms Paris Hebrew 110 of the Bibliothèque Nationale*. New York: Sepher-Hermon, 1983.

Grossfeld, *Targum Sheni*
>   Grossfeld, Bernard, ed. *The Targum Sheni to the Book of Esther: A Critical*

Edition Based on MS Sassoon 282 with Critical Apparatus. New York: Sepher-Hermon, 1994.

Grossfeld, *Two Targums*
Grossfeld, Bernard. *The Two Targums of Esther: Translated, with Apparatus and Notes.* The Aramaic Bible 18. Collegeville, Minn.: Liturgical, 1991.

HALAT
Koehler, Ludwig, Walter Baumgartner, and Johann Jakob Stamm. *Hebräisches und Aramäisches Lexikon zum Alten Testament.* 5 vols. Leiden: Brill, 1967–1995.

Haller, *Megilloth*
Haller, Max. *Die fünf Megilloth: Ruth, Hoheslied, Klagelieder, Esther.* Handbuch zum Alten Testament, erste Reihe 18. Tübingen: J.C.B. Mohr (Paul Siebeck), 1940.

Hanhart, *Esther*
Hanhart, Robert, ed. *Esther.* Vol. VIII/3 of *Septuaginta: Vetus Testamentum Graecum auctoritate Academiae Scientiarum Gottingensis editum.* 2d ed. Göttingen: Vandenhoeck & Ruprecht, 1983.

Harkavy, Alexander, and H. L. Strack. *Catalog der hebräischen Bibelhandschriften der kaiserlichen öffentlichen Bibliothek.* 2 vols. St. Petersburg: C. Ricker; Leipzig: J. C. Hinrichs, 1875.

Harl, "La version LXX"
Harl, Marguerite. "La version LXX du Cantique des Cantiques et le groupe Kaige-Théodotion – quelques remarques lexicales." *Textus* 18 (1995): 101–20.

Hatch/Redpath, *Concordance*
Hatch, Edwin, and Henry A. Redpath. *A Concordance to the Septuagint and the Other Greek Versions of the Old Testament.* 2 vols. Oxford: Clarendon, 1897. Repr., Graz: Akademische Verlagsanstalt, 1975.

Haupt, "Critical Notes"
Haupt, Paul. "Critical Notes on Esther." *American Journal of Semitic Languages and Literature* 24 (1907–1908): 97–186. Repr., pages 1–90 in *Studies in the Book of Esther.* Edited by Carey A. Moore. The Library of Biblical Studies. New York: KTAV, 1982.

Helbing, *Grammatik*
Helbing, Robert. *Grammatik der Septuaginta: Laut- und Wortlehre.* 2d ed. Göttingen: Vandenhoeck & Ruprecht, 1979.

Hertzberg, *Der Prediger*
Hertzberg, Hans Wilhelm. *Der Prediger.* Kommentar zum Alten Testament 17/4. Gütersloh: Gerd Mohn, 1963. (Bound together with Bardtke, *Esther.*)

Hitzig, *Prediger Salomo's*
Hitzig, Ferdinand. *Der Prediger Salomo's.* Kurzgefasstes exegetisches Handbuch zum Alten Testament 7. Leipzig: Weidmann, 1847. (Bound together with Ernst Bertheau, *Die Sprüche Salomo's.*)

Holmes, Robert, and James Parsons, eds. *Vetus Testamentum Graecum cum variis lectionibus.* 5 vols. in 4. Oxford: Clarendon, 1798, 1827.

Houbigant, *Biblia Hebraica*
Houbigant, Charles François. *Biblia Hebraica cum notis criticis et versione latina ad notas criticas factas.* Paris: A. C. Briasson & L. Durand, 1753.

Hubbard, *Ruth*
    Hubbard, Robert L. *The Book of Ruth*. The New International Commentary
    on the Old Testament. Grand Rapids: Eerdmans, 1988.
Hummel. "Enclitic *Mem*"
    Hummel, Horace D. "Enclitic *Mem* in Early Northwest Semitic, Especially
    Hebrew." *Journal of Biblical Literature* 76 (1957): 85–107.
Ibn Ezra, *Sephat Jether*
    Ibn Ezra, Abraham ben Meir. *Sephat Jether*. Edited by G. H. Lippmann.
    Frankfurt: G. H. Lippmann, 1843.
Irwin, "Eccles. 3:18"
    Irwin, William Andrew. "Eccles. 3:18." *American Journal of Semitic Lan-
    guages and Literature* 56 (1939): 298–99.
Isaksson, *Studies*
    Isaksson, Bo. *Studies in the Language of Qohelet. With Special Emphasis on
    the Verbal System*. Studia semitica upsaliensia 10. Uppsala: Almqvist &
    Wiksell, 1987.
Jastrow, *Dictionary*
    Jastrow, Marcus. *A Dictionary of the Targumim, the Talmud Babli and
    Yerushalmi, and the Midrashic Literature*. 2 vols. London: Luzac; New
    York: G.P. Putnam, 1886–1903. Repr. New York: Pardes, 1950.
Jellicoe, *The Septuagint*
    Jellicoe, Sidney. *The Septuagint and Modern Study*. Oxford: Clarendon,
    1968.
Jerome, "Commentarius in Ecclesiasten"
    Jerome. "Commentarius in Ecclesiasten." Pages 249–361 in *S. Hieronymi
    Presbyteri Opera I*. Edited by Marcus Adriaen. Corpus Christianorum: Series
    Latina 72. Turnhout: Brepols, 1959.
Jobes, *Alpha-Text*
    Jobes, Karen H. *The Alpha-Text of Esther: Its Character and Relationship to
    the Masoretic Text*. Society of Biblical Literature Dissertation Series 153.
    Atlanta: Scholars Press, 1996.
Jos, *Ant*
    Josephus. *Jewish Antiquities*. Translated by Ralph Marcus, et al. Loeb Clas-
    sical Library. Cambridge, Mass.; Harvard University Press, 1930–1965.
Joüon, *Ruth*
    Joüon, Paul. *Ruth: Commentaire philologique et exégétique*. Rome: Ponti-
    fical Biblical Institute, 1953.
Joüon/Muraoka, *Grammar*
    Joüon, Paul. *A Grammar of Biblical Hebrew*. Translated and revised by
    Takamitsu Muraoka. 2 vols. Subsidia Biblica 14/1–2. Rome: Pontifical Bib-
    lical Institute, 1991.
Kahle, Paul. "The Hebrew Ben Asher Bible Manuscripts." *Vetus Testamentum* 1
    (1951): 161–67.
Kahle, Paul. *Die Masoreten des Westens*. 2 vols. Stuttgart: W. Kohlhammer, 1927–
    1930.
Kaiser, "Klagelieder"
    Kaiser, Otto. "Klagelieder." Pages 91–198 in *Das Hohelied, Klagelieder,
    Das Buch Ester*, by Otto Kaiser, Hans-Peter Müller and James Alfred

Loader. 4th rev. ed. Das Alte Testament Deutsch: Neues Göttinger Bibelwerk 16/2. Göttingen: Vandenhoeck & Ruprecht, 1992.

Kasher/Klein, "New Fragments"
Kasher, Rimon, and Michael L. Klein: "New Fragments of Targum to Esther from the Cairo Genizah." *Hebrew Union College Annual* 61 (1990): 89–124.

Keel, *Das Hohelied*
Keel, Othmar. *Das Hohelied*. Zürcher Bibelkommentare, AT 18. Zürich: Theologischer Verlag, 1986.

Kennicott, *Vetus Testamentum*
Kennicott, Benjamin, ed. *Vetus Testamentum Hebraicum cum variis lectionibus*. 2 vols. Oxford: Clarendon, 1776–1780.

Klostermann, *De libri Coheleth*
Klostermann, Erich. *De libri Coheleth versione Alexandrina*. Kiel: Schmidt & Klaunig, 1892.

Knobel, "Targum of Qohelet"
Knobel, Peter S. "The Targum of Qohelet: Translated, with a Critical Introduction, Apparatus, and Notes." Pages 1–60 in *The Targums of Job, Proverbs, Qohelet*. By Céline Mangan, John F. Healey and Peter S. Knobel. The Aramaic Bible 15. Collegeville, Minn.: Liturgical, 1991.

König, *Lehrgebäude*
König, Eduard. *Historisch-kritisches Lehrgebäude der hebräischen Sprache*. 2 vols. in 3. Leipzig: J.C. Hinrichs, 1881–1897. Repr., Hildesheim: Georg Olms, 1979.

Krinetzki, *Kommentar*
Krinetzki, Günter. *Kommentar zum Hohenlied: Bildsprache und theologische Botschaft*. Beiträge zur biblischen Exegese und Theologie 16. Frankfurt am Main: Peter Lang, 1981.

Kühner/Blass/Gerth, *Grammatik*
Kühner, Raphael, Friedrich Blass, and Bernhard Gerth. *Ausführliche Grammatik der Griechischen Sprache*. 4 vols. 3d ed. Leipzig: Hahnsche, 1890–1904.

Lagarde, *Bibliothecae syriacae*
Lagarde, Paul de. *Bibliothecae syriacae . . . quae ad philologiam sacram pertinent*. Göttingen: L. Horstmann, 1892.

Lagarde, *Hagiographa chaldaice*
Lagarde, Paul de. *Hagiographa chaldaice*. Leipzig: B.G. Teubner, 1873.

Lane, "Peshitta text"
Lane, D. J. "'*Lilies that fester . . .*': the Peshitta text of Qoheleth." *Vetus Testamentum* 29 (1979): 481–90.

Lane, "Qoheleth"
Lane, David J., ed. "Qoheleth." In *Proverbs, Wisdom of Solomon, Ecclesiastes, Song of Songs*. Edited by Alexander A. DiLella, John Adney Emerton and D. J. Lane. Vol. II/5 of *The Old Testament in Syriac, According to the Peshitta Version*. Edited by The Peshitta Institute, Leiden. Leiden: Brill, 1979.

Lanza, "Le tre versioni"
Lanza, S. "Le tre versioni geronimiane dell'Ecclesiaste." *Annali di storia dell'esegesi* 4 (1987): 87–108.

Lauha, *Kohelet*
> Lauha, Aarre. *Kohelet.* Biblischer Kommentar: Altes Testament 19. Neukirchen-Vluyn: Neukirchener Verlag, 1978.

Lee, *Ketabe qaddishe*
> Lee, Samuel. *Ketabe qaddishe: ketabe de diyatiqi 'attiq[t]a whedhata: Vetus Testamentum Syriace.* 1826. Repr., London: United Bible Societies, 1979.

Levenson, *Esther*
> Levenson, Jon D. *Esther: A Commentary.* Old Testament Library. Louisville: Westminster John Knox, 1997.

Levine, *Aramaic Version*
> Levine, Étan. *The Aramaic Version of Ruth.* Analecta biblica 58. Rome: Biblical Institute Press, 1973.

Levine, *Targum*
> Levine, Étan. *The Targum of the Five Megillot.* Jerusalem: Makor, 1977.

Lipschütz, "Kitāb al-Khilaf"
> Lipschütz, L. "Kitāb al-Khilaf: The Book of the Ḥillufim." *Textus* 4 (1964): 1–29.

Loretz, *Gotteswort*
> Loretz, Oswald. *Gotteswort und menschliche Erfahrung: Eine Auslegung der Bücher Jona, Rut, Hoheslied und Qohelet.* Freiburg: Herder, 1963.

LSJ
> Liddell, Henry George, and Robert Scott. *A Greek-English Lexicon.* Revised and augmented by Henry Stuart Jones. 9th ed. with supplement. Oxford: Clarendon, 1968.

Lust, *Lexicon*
> Lust, Johan, et al. *A Greek-English Lexicon of the Septuagint.* 2 vols. Stuttgart: Deutsche Bibelgesellschaft, 1992, 1996.

Mandelkern, *Concordantiae*
> Mandelkern, Solomon. *Veteris Testamenti Concordantiae Hebraicae atque Chaldaicae.* 9th ed. Tel-Aviv: Schocken, 1974.

Margoliouth, *Hebrew and Samaritan Manuscripts*
> Margoliouth, G. *Catalogue of the Hebrew and Samaritan Manuscripts in the British Museum.* 3 vols. London: British Museum, 1899–1915.

McCarthy, *Tiqqune Sopherim*
> McCarthy, Carmel. *The Tiqqune Sopherim and Other Theological Corrections in the Masoretic Text of the Old Testament.* Orbis biblicus et orientalis 36. Freiburg: Universitätsverlag; Göttingen: Vandenhoeck & Ruprecht, 1981.

McNeile, *An Introduction*
> McNeile, Alan Hugh. *An Introduction to Ecclesiastes: With notes and appendices.* Cambridge: Cambridge University Press, 1904.

Meinhold, "Threni 2,13"
> Meinhold, Johannes. "Threni 2,13." *Zeitschrift für die alttestamentliche Wissenschaft* 15 (1895): 286.

Michel, *Eigenart*
> Michel, Diethelm. *Untersuchungen zur Eigenart des Buches Qohelet.* Beihefte zur Zeitschrift für die alttestamentliche Wissenschaft 183. Berlin: Walter de Gruyter, 1989.

Miletto, *L'Antico Testamento*
> Miletto, Gianfranco. *L'Antico Testamento ebraico nella tradizione babilo-*

nese: i frammenti della Genizah. Quaderni di Henoch 3. Turin: S. Zamorani, 1992.

Milik, "Les modèles araméens"

Milik, Jozef Tadeusz. "Les modèles araméens du livre d'Esther dans la Grotte 4 de Qumrân." *Revue de Qumrân* 15 (1992): 321–406.

Millard, "Persian Names"

Millard, Alan R. "The Persian Names in Esther and the Reliability of the Hebrew Text," *Journal of Biblical Literature* 96 (1977): 481–88.

Montfaucon, *Hexaplorum Origenis*

Montfaucon, Bernard de. *Hexaplorum Origenis quae supersunt.* 2 vols. Paris: Ludovicus Guérin, 1713.

Moore, "Esther Revisited"

Moore, Carey A. "Esther Revisited Again: A Further Examination of Certain Esther Studies of the Past Ten Years." *Hebrew Annual Review* 7 (1983): 169–86.

Moore, "Greek Witness"

Moore, Carey A. "A Greek Witness to a Different Hebrew Text of Esther." *Zeitschrift für die alttestamentliche Wissenschaft* 79 (1967): 351–58.

Moore, *Esther*

Moore, Carey A. *Esther: Introduction, Translation, and Notes.* Anchor Bible 7B. Garden City, N.Y.: Doubleday, 1971.

Moore, *Studies*

Moore, Carey A., ed. *Studies in the Book of Esther.* The Library of Biblical Studies. New York: KTAV, 1982.

Muilenburg, "Qoheleth Scroll"

Muilenburg, James. "A Qoheleth Scroll from Qumran." *Bulletin of the American Schools of Oriental Research* 135 (1954): 20–28.

Murphy, *Song of Songs*

Murphy, Roland E. *The Song of Songs.* Hermeneia. Minneapolis: Fortress, 1990.

Myers, *Literary Form*

Myers, Jacob M. *The Linguistic and Literary Form of the Book of Ruth.* Leiden: Brill, 1955.

Nebe, "Qumranica I"

Nebe, G. Wilhelm. "Qumranica I: Zu unveröffentlichten Handschriften aus Höhle 4 von Qumran." *Zeitschrift für die alttestamentliche Wissenschaft* 106 (1994): 307–22.

Oesch, *Petucha und Setuma*

Oesch, Josef M. *Petucha und Setuma: Untersuchungen zu einer überlieferten Gliederung im hebräischen Text des Alten Testaments.* Orbis biblicus et orientalis 27. Freiburg: Universitätsverlag; Göttingen: Vandenhoeck & Ruprecht, 1979.

Ognibeni, *ʾOklah*

Ognibeni, Bruno. *La seconda parte del sefer ʾOklah weʾOklah: Edizione del ms. Halle, Universitätsbibliothek Y b 4° 10, ff. 68–124.* Textos y Estudios "Cardenal Cisneros" 57. Madrid: Instituto de Filología del CSIC; Fribourg: Éditions universitaires, 1995.

Paton, *Esther*

Paton, Lewis Bayles. *A Critical and Exegetical Commentary on the Book of*

Esther. International Critical Commentary. Edinburgh: T&T Clark, 1908. Repr., Edinburgh: T&T Clark, 1976.

Payne Smith, *Thesaurus*
Payne Smith, R., Etienne Marc Quatremère, Georg Heinrich Bernstein, D. S. Margoliouth, and Jessie Payne Smith Margoliouth. *Thesaurus syriacus.* 2 vols. Oxford: Clarendon, 1879–1901.

Perez Castro, Federico, et al., eds. *El Códice de Profetas de El Cairo.* 8 vols. Madrid: CSIC, 1979–1988; 4 vols. of indices, Madrid: CSIC, 1992–1997.

Peritz, "Zwei alte arabische Uebersetzungen"
Peritz, M. "Zwei alte arabische Uebersetzungen des Buches Rûth: Zum ersten Male herausgegeben und mit Anmerkungen versehen." *Monatsschrift für Geschichte und Wissenschaft des Judenthums* 43 (1899): 49–60, 113–16, 145–48, 210–17, 337–44, 401–8, 450–60.

Perles, "Threni 1,20"
Perles, Felix. "Was bedeutet כמות in Threni 1,20?" *Orientalistische Literaturzeitung* 23 (1920): 157–58.

Podechard, *L'Ecclésiaste*
Podechard, Emmanuel. *L'Ecclésiaste.* Etudes bibliques. Paris: J. Gabalda/V. Lecoffre, 1912.

Pschitta
Biblia Sacra juxta Versionem Simplicem quae dicitur Pschitta. 3 vols. Mosul: Typis Fratrum Praedicatorum, 1887.

Qafih, חמש מגילות
Qafih, Y. חמש מגילות. Jerusalem, 1962.

Qimhi, *Mikhlol*
Kimhi, David. *Mikhlol.* Edited by Yitshak ben Aharon Rittenberg. Lyck: Tsvi Hirsh Pettsal, 1842. Repr., Jerusalem, 1966.

Qimhi, *Sefer Ha-Shorashim*
Qimchi, David. *Sefer Ha-Shorashim.* Edited by Johann Heinrich Biesenthal and Fuerchtegott Lebrecht. Berlin: G. Bethge, 1847. Repr., Jerusalem, 1967.

Qimron, *Hebrew of the Dead Sea Scrolls*
Qimron, Elisha. *The Hebrew of the Dead Sea Scrolls.* Harvard Semitic Studies 29. Atlanta: Scholars Press, 1986.

Rahlfs, *Ruth griechisch*
Rahlfs, Alfred. *Das Buch Ruth griechisch als Probe einer kritischen Handausgabe der Septuaginta.* Stuttgart: Württembergische Bibelanstalt, 1922.

Rahlfs, *Septuaginta*
Rahlfs, Alfred, ed. *Septuaginta.* 2 vols. 9th ed. Stuttgart: Deutsche Bibelstiftung, 1979. (First edition: Stuttgart: Württembergische Bibelanstalt, 1935.)

Rahlfs, *Studie*
Rahlfs, Alfred. *Studie über den griechischen Text des Buches Ruth.* Mitteilungen des Septuaginta-Unternehmens 3/2. Berlin: Weidmann, 1922.

Reif, *Hebrew Manuscripts*
Reif, S. C. *Hebrew Manuscripts at Cambridge University Library: A Description and Introduction.* Cambridge: Cambridge University Press, 1997.

Revell, E. J. "The Leningrad Codex as a Representative of the Masoretic Text." Pages xxix–xlvi in *The Leningrad Codex.* Edited by D. N. Freedman, et al. Grand Rapids: Eerdmans; Leiden: Brill, 1998.

Rudolph, "Text der Klagelieder"
    Rudolph, Wilhelm. "Der Text der Klagelieder." *Zeitschrift für die alttesta-
    mentliche Wissenschaft* 56 (1938): 101–22.
Rudolph, "Textkritisches zum Estherbuch"
    Rudolph, Wilhelm. "Textkritisches zum Estherbuch." *Vetus Testamentum* 4
    (1954): 89–90.
Rudolph, *Ruth/Hohes Lied/Klagelieder*
    Rudolph, Wilhelm. *Das Buch Ruth, Das Hohe Lied, Die Klagelieder.* Kom-
    mentar zum Alten Testament 17/1–3. Gütersloh: Gerd Mohn, 1962.
Sabatier, *Bibliorum sacrorum*
    Sabatier, Pierre, and Vincent de La Rue, eds. *Bibliorum sacrorum latinæ ver-
    siones antiquæ, seu vetus italica.* 3 vols. in 6. 2d ed. Paris: Franciscus Didot, 1751.
Salkind, *Die Peschitta*
    Salkind, Jakob Meir. *Die Peschitta zu Schir-Haschirim textkritisch und in
    ihrem Verhältnisse zu MT und LXX untersucht.* Leiden: Brill, 1905.
Sasson, *Ruth*
    Sasson, Jack M. *Ruth: A New Translation with a Philological Commentary
    and a Formalist-Folklorist Interpretation.* Baltimore: Johns Hopkins Univer-
    sity Press, 1979.
Sassoon, *Ohel David*
    Sassoon, D. S. *Ohel David: Descriptive Catalogue of the Hebrew and Sa-
    maritan Manuscripts in the Sassoon Library, London.* 2 vols. Oxford: Oxford
    University Press; London: Humphrey Milford, 1932.
Scharfenberg, *Animadversiones*
    Scharfenberg, Johann Gottfried. *Animadversiones quibus fragmenta versio-
    num Graecarum V.T. a Bern. Montefalconio collecta illustrantur emendan-
    tur.* 2 vols. Leipzig: Guil. Gottlob Sommer, 1776–1781.
Schleusner, "Curae criticae"
    Schleusner, Johann Friedrich. "Curae criticae et exegeticae in Threnos Iere-
    miae," *Repertorium für Biblische und Morgenländische Litteratur* 12 (1783):
    1–57.
Schleusner, *Thesaurus*
    Schleusner, Johann Friedrich. *Novus thesaurus philologico-criticus sive lexi-
    con in LXX et reliquos interpretes graecos ac scriptores apocryphos Veteris
    Testamenti.* 5 vols. Leipzig: Weidmann, 1820–1821.
Schoors, *The Preacher Sought*
    Schoors, Antoon. *The Preacher Sought to Find Pleasing Words: A Study of
    the Language of Qoheleth.* Orientalia Lovanensia Analecta 41. Leuven:
    Peeters, 1992.
Schulz-Flügel, *Gregorius Eliberritanus*
    Schulz-Flügel, Eva, ed. *Gregorius Eliberritanus. Epithalamium sive explana-
    tio in Canticis Canticorum.* Aus der Geschichte der lateinischen Bibel 26.
    Freiburg: Herder, 1994.
Segal, *Mishnaic Hebrew*
    Segal, Moses Hirsch. *A Grammar of Mishnaic Hebrew.* Oxford: Clarendon,
    1927.
Serrano, "(Eccl 8, 10)"
    Serrano, J. J. "I saw the wicked buried (Eccl 8, 10)." *Catholic Biblical Quar-
    terly* 16 (1954): 168–70.

Siegfried, *Prediger und Hoheslied*
　　Siegfried, Carl J. *Prediger und Hoheslied.* Handkommentar zum Alten Testament II/3/2. Göttingen: Vandenhoeck & Ruprecht, 1898.
Sperber, *Bible in Aramaic*
　　Sperber, Alexander. *The Bible in Aramaic.* 5 vols. Leiden: Brill, 1959–1973.
Spicq, *Theological Lexicon*
　　Spicq, Ceslas. *Theological Lexicon of the New Testament.* 3 vols. Translated and edited by James D. Ernest. Peabody, Mass.: Hendrickson, 1994.
Striedl, "Untersuchung"
　　Striedl, Hans. "Untersuchung zur Syntax und Stilistik des hebräischen Buches Esther." *Zeitschrift für die alttestamentliche Wissenschaft* 55 (1937): 73–108.
Swete, *Introduction*
　　Swete, Henry Barclay. *An Introduction to the Old Testament in Greek.* 2d ed. Revised by R.R. Ottley. Cambridge: Cambridge University Press, 1914.
Swete, *Old Testament*
　　Swete, Henry Barclay. *The Old Testament in Greek.* 3 vols. 4th ed. Cambridge: Cambridge University Press, 1909–1922. Repr., Cambridge: Cambridge University Press, 1930.
Taradach, Madeleine, and Joan Ferrer. *Un Targum de Qohéleth: ms M-2 de Salamanca: editio princeps: texte araméen, traduction et commentaire critique.* Monde de la Bible 38. Geneva: Labor et Fides, 1998.
THAT
　　Jenni, Ernst, and Claus Westermann, editors. *Theologisches Handwörterbuch zum Alten Testament.* 2 vols. Munich: Chr. Kaiser, 1971, 1976.
Thornhill, "Greek Text"
　　Thornhill, Raymond. "The Greek Text of the Book of Ruth: A Grouping of Manuscripts according to Origen's Hexapla." *Vetus Testamentum* 3 (1953): 236–49.
ThWAT
　　Botterweck, G. Johannes, and Helmer Ringgren, editors. *Theologisches Handwörterbuch zum Alten Testament.* Stuttgart: W. Kohlhammer, 1970–.
Torczyner, "Anmerkungen"
　　Torczyner, Harry. "Anmerkungen zum Hebräischen und zur Bibel." *Zeitschrift der deutschen morgenländischen Gesellschaft* 66 (1912): 401–9.
Torrey, "Older Book"
　　Torrey, Charles Cutler. "The Older Book of Esther." *Harvard Theological Review* 37 (1944): 1–40.
Tournay, "Les chariots"
　　Tournay, Raymond Jacques. "Les chariots d'Aminadab (Cant. vi 12): Israël, peuple théophore." *Vetus Testamentum* 9 (1959): 288–309.
Tov, "The 'Lucianic' Text"
　　Tov, Emanuel. "The 'Lucianic' Text of the Canonical and the Apocryphal Sections of Esther: a Rewritten Biblical Book." *Textus* 10 (1982): 1–25.
Tov, "Three Manuscripts"
　　Tov, Emanuel. "Three Manuscripts (Abbreviated Texts?) of Canticum from Qumran Cave 4." *Journal of Semitic Studies* 46 (1995): 88–111.

Tov, *Textual Criticism*
> Tov, Emanuel. *Textual Criticism of the Hebrew Bible*. Minneapolis: Fortress; Assen and Maastricht: Van Gorcum, 1992.

Tov/Pfann, *Microfiche*
> Tov, Emanuel, with the collaboration of Stephen J. Pfann. *The Dead Sea Scrolls on Microfiche: A Comprehensive Facsimile Edition of the Texts from the Judaean Desert*. Leiden and New York: Brill; Leiden: IDC, 1993.

Ulrich, "Ezra and Qohelet"
> Ulrich, Eugene. "Ezra and Qohelet Manuscripts from Qumran (4QEzra, 4QQoh[a,b])." Pages 139–57 in *Priests, Prophets, and Scribes: Essays on the Formation and Heritage of Second Temple Judaism in Honour of Joseph Blenkinsopp*. Edited by Eugene Ulrich, John W. Wright, and Robert P. Carroll. Journal for the Study of the Old Testament: Supplement Series 149. Sheffield: JSOT Press, 1992.

Vaccari, *Cantici Canticorum*
> Vaccari, A. *Cantici Canticorum vetus latina translatio a S. Hieronymo ad graecum textum hexaplarem emendata*. Rome: Edizioni di Storia e Letteratura, 1959.

Vajda, *Deux commentaires karaïtes*
> Vajda, Georges. *Deux commentaires karaïtes sur l'Ecclésiaste*. Études sur le Judaïsme médiéval 4. Leiden: Brill, 1971.

van der Heide, *Yemenite Tradition*
> van der Heide, Albert. *The Yemenite Tradition of the Targum of Lamentations: Critical Text and Analysis of the Variant Readings*. Studia Postbiblica 32. Leiden: Brill, 1981.

Van Wyk, "The Peshitta"
> Van Wyk, W.C. "The Peshitta of the Song of Songs." *Die Oud-Testamentiese Werkgemeenskap in Suid-Afrika* 20/21 (1977–1978): 181–89.

Vilchez Lindez, *Eclesiastés*
> Vilchez Lindez, José. *Eclesiastés o Qohélet*. Nueva Biblia Española, Sapienciales 3. Estella: Verbo Divino, 1994.

Waltke/O'Connor, *Hebrew Syntax*
> Waltke, Bruce K. and Michael P. O'Connor. *An Introduction to Biblical Hebrew Syntax*. Winona Lake, Ind.: Eisenbrauns, 1990.

Walton, *Biblia Sacra Polyglotta*
> Walton, Brian, ed. *Biblia Sacra Polyglotta*. 6 vols. London: Thomas Roycroft, 1653–1657.

Weber, *Biblia sacra*[1]
> Weber, Robert, ed. *Biblia Sacra iuxta vulgatam versionem*. 2 vols. Stuttgart: Württembergische Bibelanstalt, 1969.

Weber, *Biblia Sacra*[2]
> Weber, Robert, ed. *Biblia Sacra iuxta vulgatam versionem*. 2 vols. 2d rev. ed. Stuttgart: Württembergische Bibelanstalt, 1975.

Weber, *Biblia Sacra*[4]
> Weber, Robert, ed. *Biblia Sacra iuxta vulgatam versionem*. 4th rev. ed. Prepared by Roger Gryson. Stuttgart: Deutsche Bibelgesellschaft, 1994.

Weil
> Weil, Gérard E. *Massorah gedolah iuxta codicem Leningradensem B 19a*. Vol. I: Catalogi. Rome: Pontifical Biblical Institute, 1971.

Weippert, "Kommentar zu Ruth"
  Weippert, M. "Ein neuer Kommentar zu Ruth." *Biblica* 59 (1978): 268–73.
White Crawford, "Has Esther been Found"
  White Crawford, Sidnie. "Has Esther been Found at Qumran? 4QProto-
  Esther and the Esther Corpus." *Revue de Qumrân* 17 (1996): 307–25.
Wickes, *Accentuation*
  Wickes, William. *Two Treatises on the Accentuation of the Old Testament.* 2
  vols. Oxford: Clarendon, 1881, 1887. Repr., 1 vol. New York: KTAV, 1970.
Wiesmann, *Klagelieder*
  Wiesmann, Hermann. *Die Klagelieder übersetzt und erklärt.* Edited by Wil-
  helm Koester. Frankfurt am Main: Philosophisch-theologische Hochschule
  Sankt Georgen, 1954.
Wildeboer, *Prediger*
  Wildeboer, Gerrit. *Der Prediger.* In *Die fünf Megillot: das Hohelied, das
  Buch Ruth, die Klagelieder, der Prediger, das Buch Esther,* by Karl Budde,
  Alfred Bertholet, and Gerrit Wildeboer. Kurzer Hand-Commentar zum Alten
  Testament 17. Freiburg im Breisgau: J.C.B. Mohr (Paul Siebeck), 1898.
Wright, *Ruth in Hebrew*
  Wright, Charles H. H. *The Book of Ruth in Hebrew, with a Critically-Revised
  Text. Various Readings, Including a New Collation of twenty-eight Hebrew
  MSS and a Grammatical and Critical Commentary.* London: Williams &
  Norgate, 1864.
Würthwein, "Das Hohelied"
  Würthwein, Ernst. "Das Hohelied." Pages 25–71 in *Die fünf Megilloth,* by
  Ernst Würthwein, Kurt Galling and Otto Plöger. 2d rev. ed. Handbuch zum
  Alten Testament, erste Reihe 18. Tübingen: J.C.B. Mohr (Paul Siebeck),
  1969.
Yadin, "DSD 4:20"
  Yadin, Yigael. "Note on DSD 4:20." *Journal of Biblical Literature* 74
  (1955): 40–43.
Yeivin, "Division into Sections"
  Yeivin, Israel. "The Division into Sections in the Book of Psalms." *Textus* 7
  (1969): 76–102.
Yeivin, *Tiberian Masorah*
  Yeivin, Israel. *Introduction to the Tiberian Masorah.* Translated and edited
  by E. J. Revell. Masoretic Studies 5. Missoula, Mont.: Scholars Press, 1980.
Ziegler, "Gebrauch des Artikels"
  Ziegler, Joseph. "Der Gebrauch des Artikels in der Septuaginta des Eccle-
  siastes." Edited by Detlef Fraenkel. Pages 83–120 in *Studien zur Septuagin-
  ta Robert Hanhart zu Ehren.* Edited by Detlef Fraenkel, Udo Quast and John
  William Wevers. Mitteilungen des Septuaginta-Unternehmens 20. Göttingen:
  Vandenhoeck & Ruprecht, 1990.
Ziegler, *Jeremias, Baruch, Threni*
  Ziegler, Joseph, ed. *Jeremias, Baruch, Threni, Epistula Jeremiae.* Vol. XV of
  *Septuaginta: Vetus Testamentum Graecum auctoritate Academiae Scientia-
  rum Gottingensis editum.* Göttingen: Vandenhoeck & Ruprecht, 1957.
Zimolong, "Ruth 2.7"
  Zimolong, Bertrand. "Zu Ruth 2.7." *Zeitschrift für die alttestamentliche Wis-
  senschaft* 58 (1940–1941): 156–58.

BIBLIA HEBRAICA QUINTA

18

MEGILLOTH

תורה נביאים וכתובים
BIBLIA HEBRAICA
quinta editione
cum apparatu critico novis curis elaborato

participantibus
R. Althann, P.B. Dirksen, N. Fernández Marcos, A. Gelston, A. Gianto,
L. Greenspoon, I. Himbaza, J. Lust, D. Marcus, C. McCarthy, M. Rösel,
M. Sæbø, R. Schäfer, S. Sipilä, P. Schwagmeier, A. Tal, Z. Talshir

consultis A. Dotan pro masora,
A. Groves et Soetjianto pro impressione electronica, R. Omanson pro redactione et stylo

communiter ediderunt
A. SCHENKER (praeses), Y.A.P. GOLDMAN, A. VAN DER KOOIJ,
G.J. NORTON, S. PISANO, J. DE WAARD, R.D. WEIS

General Introduction
and
MEGILLOTH מגלות

RUTH רות
J. de Waard

CANTICLES שיר השירים
P.B. Dirksen

QOHELETH קהלת
Y.A.P. Goldman

LAMENTATIONS איכה
R. Schäfer

ESTHER אסתר
M. Sæbø

DEUTSCHE BIBELGESELLSCHAFT

ISBN 3-438-05278-4

Biblia Hebraica Quinta, Fascicle 18: General Introduction and Megilloth
© 2004 Deutsche Bibelgesellschaft, Stuttgart

www.scholarly-bibles.com

CONTENTS

GENERAL INTRODUCTION

The first edition in the modern series of *Biblia Hebraica* (*BHK¹*) appeared at Leipzig in 1906 as the new century was getting under way. Throughout the century new editions of *Biblia Hebraica* have appeared, each retaining the basic structure of the original edition, but introducing changes as warranted by developments in text critical study. A second edition (*BHK²*), differing from the first only in minor corrections, was published in 1913, also at Leipzig. The third edition (*BHK³*) appeared in 1929–1937 at Stuttgart, and introduced major changes: a new base text, reproducing the text of the Leningrad Codex rather than the 1524–1525 Bomberg edition of Jacob ben Ḥayyim; and an entirely new apparatus. *Biblia Hebraica Stuttgartensia* (*BHS*, 1967–1977), the fourth edition in the series, followed *BHK³* in using the Leningrad codex as the base text, but introduced a new presentation of the manuscript's Masorah, as well as a new apparatus.

As the old century gives way to a new one, the increased availability of recent manuscript discoveries (especially the Dead Sea Scrolls), the developments of several decades' intensive research in the transmission of the text of the Hebrew Bible, and the concomitant shifts in our appreciation of the aims and limits of textual criticism occasion a new edition (the fifth) in the line of *Biblia Hebraica*, which thus may be known as *Biblia Hebraica Quinta* (*BHQ*). Since this is the first fascicle of the new edition, it is appropriate that we offer some explanation of the edition so as to situate it in relation to its predecessors.

This new edition comes about at the initiative of the United Bible Societies, and with the sponsorship of the German Bible Society, which has special responsibility for the publication of scientific editions, specifically including *Biblia Hebraica*. The character of *Biblia Hebraica Quinta* is shaped by two histories, that of the editions of *Biblia Hebraica*, and that of the Hebrew Old Testament Text Project of the United Bible Societies.

Several crucial decisions at stages in the development of the *Biblia Hebraica* have given the series a well-known character that continues in this edition. From the beginning, the editions in this series have been intended as *Handausgaben*. Also from the beginning, as a result of an explicit choice by Rudolf Kittel, the edition has not presented an eclectic text of the Hebrew Bible, but rather has printed the text of single edition or manuscript, and provided a critical apparatus that presents a selection of variants and conjectures for emending the text, emphasizing those most significant for exegesis and translation. In the first two editions, the text of the Bomberg edition of Jacob ben Ḥayyim was used as the base text. Starting with the third edition (1937), on the initiative of Paul Kahle, the text of codex EBP. I B 19a of the Russian National Library in St. Petersburg (i.e., M^L) has been printed as the base text. Kahle also emphasized the importance of printing the Masorah parva and magna of M^L as part of the edition. In the third edition, this aim was realized only for the Masorah parva. It was only with the fourth in the *Biblia Hebraica* series, *Biblia Hebraica Stuttgartensia*, that Kahle's aim was attempted so far as the Masorah magna is concerned. As the Dead Sea Scrolls began to appear in the late 1940's, the seventh impression of *BHK³*, on the initiative of

Otto Eissfeldt, added apparatuses giving a full report of the variants contained in 1QIsaᵃ and 1QpHab. *Biblia Hebraica Quinta* stands firmly within this tradition at many points, even as it refines and renews it at others.

As was true for its predecessors, this edition of *Biblia Hebraica* is intended as a *Handausgabe* for use by scholars, clergy, translators, and students who are not necessarily specialists in textual criticism. Because our field still lacks an *editio critica maior*, specialists in textual criticism should also find the edition of use, even though it is not principally intended for them. At the beginning of its work, the Editorial Committee considered the possibility of producing such an edition, but concluded that it was not practical at that time, and in any case would not meet the need to which the *Biblia Hebraica* responds. The committee hopes that this new edition of *Biblia Hebraica* may serve as a contribution toward the eventual publication of an *editio critica maior*.

Following the pattern of its predecessors, this edition will appear initially in fascicles, of which this fascicle containing the Megilloth is the first. Each fascicle will present the following items for the biblical books published therein:

– an introduction;
– lists of sigla, symbols and abbreviations;
– a glossary of common abbreviations used in the Masorah parva;
– the text and full Masorah of M^L;
– the critical apparatus reporting the readings of the witnesses to the text's transmission;
– a commentary on selected cases from the critical apparatus, the translation of the Masorah magna, and comments on difficult cases in the Masorah magna and parva.

This sequence implies a preferred order for reading the edition. By reading the introduction to a book before proceeding to the text and apparatus, a reader gains important perspective on the witnesses for that book. As the reader then proceeds to text and apparatus, the editors assume that the commentary will be consulted as points of interest arise in the reading of the text and apparatus.

At the end of the publication process, the edition will be published in two volumes, one containing text, Masorah, and critical apparatus along with the general introduction, sigla, symbols, and abbreviations (i.e., a single volume on the usual *BHK* pattern). The second volume will contain the introductions to the individual books, the textual and Masorah commentaries, and the translation of the notes of the Masorah magna.

This new edition of *Biblia Hebraica* follows the pattern set in 1937, presenting the text of a single good Masoretic manuscript as a base text and adding a critical apparatus offering the evidence of the text's transmission in relation to the point of reference provided by the base text. This is founded, of course, in Kittel's choice of such a structure for the 1906 edition, albeit then using the Bomberg text instead of a single manuscript. The Editorial Committee is well aware of the current discussion of the relative merits of an edition of this type as opposed to an edition presenting what is properly called an eclectic text. The committee chose to maintain the historic structure of the editions of *Biblia Hebraica* for three reasons. First, it was judged that, as yet, not enough is known about the history of the development of the text of the Hebrew Bible and its various textual traditions to give a sound basis for constructing an eclectic text. Second, an edition presenting an

eclectic text of the Hebrew Bible must choose to reconstruct that text at a particular point in its development. In the midst of the current lack of consensus about the appropriate stage of the text to aim at in such a reconstruction, it seems to the committee that an edition, which will be widely used by students and non-specialists, should not present as its running text a reconstruction based on one of the positions in the debate. Third, the committee takes the view that an eclectic text ought to be based on the presentation of all variants found in the surviving witnesses. Such a presentation is beyond the limits inherent in a one-volume edition.

THE TEXT

Continuing the practice established with the third edition of 1937, and refined in the *Stuttgartensia* edition, this edition offers as its base text a basically diplomatic presentation of M^L. In recent years, studies of M^L and its Masorah have indicated that in some respects it may be less than ideal as the base text of an edition (see the specific discussion below). Indeed, the committee gave due consideration to other options for providing a base text for the edition. It was decided not to use the Aleppo Codex (i.e., M^A) chiefly because the manuscript is incomplete. Moreover, since the Hebrew University Bible Project employs this manuscript as the base text for its splendid editions, and since it is also the text for the Bar-Ilan University edition of the Bible edited by M. Cohen, M^A is appearing before the scholarly public in edited form. The Editorial Committee also considered employing the earliest available ben Asher manuscript for each of the three divisions of the canon as the base text for *BHQ*. This option was abandoned in favor of the continued use of M^L for several reasons. First, M^L remains the earliest known manuscript of the entire Hebrew Bible. Second, the state of the manuscripts that met the indicated criterion would have led to a patchwork when their gaps had to be supplemented with another manuscript (e.g., in addition to its well-known lacuna in the Torah, the Aleppo Codex lacks several of the Writings entirely). Third, when it was assumed that the new edition would be typeset by traditional methods, the fact that the German Bible Society had in its possession a typeset text of M^L, which already had undergone several rounds of careful correction, was a significant pragmatic factor. Then, at the point where it was decided to move the project to fully computerized processes, it was equally significant that the text of M^L was already available in electronic form – the only one of the great Tiberian manuscripts then so available. While the processes of converting the text to the specific electronic form used in making this edition had introduced new errors into the electronic text, it had already undergone some degree of correction before its use in this project. In the course of making this edition, the electronic version of the text is undergoing thorough correction against color transparencies obtained from the Ancient Biblical Manuscript Center in Claremont, California, USA. The transparencies were produced from the new photographs of M^L taken in St. Petersburg by the Center's team formed by West Semitic Research of Los Angeles. The clarity and quality of the photographs are well beyond that which has been readily obtainable otherwise, and will undoubtedly lead to a number of corrections that were not possible for the text of *BHS* until the fifth impression exclusively (1997). The electronic text of M^L will be checked against these photos independently by the editors of the individual books and by academic collaborators to whom the task has been specifically assigned.

As with *BHS*, the text printed in *BHQ* will be the text of M^L, even when this shows obvious errors. The corrections will be noted in the apparatus on the basis of the other Tiberian manuscripts collated. On the other hand, the new photographs of M^L have revealed a small number of instances where damage to the manuscript has rendered some element of a word illegible (usually a vowel sign or accent). In such instances the edition will show a reconstructed reading in the base text, and will use an apparatus entry to report what can actually be discerned in M^L, as well as the readings of the other Tiberian witnesses that form the basis of the reconstruction. In still other cases, M^L displays a variation between the reading of the first hand, and a reading provided by a second hand (e.g., through errors in the course of re-inking accidentally damaged portions of the manuscript [see the discussion below]). In these cases the editor will include in the base text the reading judged to represent the valid reading of the manuscript, and will report the relevant data in an apparatus entry.

As far as the layout of the base text is concerned, *BHQ* follows its predecessors by departing from a fully diplomatic representation of M^L's page layout in that texts judged by the editor to be prose are set in a single column, and texts judged to be poetry are set stichographically. However, the criteria for determining the stichography have been altered from those used in previous editions. For poetic passages in prose texts that M^L presents stichographically in a traditional page layout, the text of this edition will follow the stichography of M^L. Otherwise, the stichography in this edition is based on the Masoretic accents. Stichoi are always defined by the primary disjunctive accents, except in cases where a different syntactic division from the one expressed in those accents is judged to be the preferred reading of the text. In such cases the preferred reading will determine the division of the stichoi. The grouping of stichoi into bi- and tri-cola is determined so far as possible by the hierarchy of precedence among those accents. Only where the result produces a line that would run over the edge of the page, or that would disrupt an obvious *parallelismus membrorum* is the grouping of the stichoi into bi- and tri-cola altered.

There are also a number of lists among the prose texts of M^L (e.g., Ezra 2:43-57) that, although there is no fixed tradition concerning their presentation, are arranged on the pages of M^L in a way that distinguishes them from the surrounding prose. In this edition they will be presented in a way that, so far as possible, replicates their presentation in the manuscript.

The various other phenomena associated with Masoretic manuscripts (e.g., enlarged letters, suspended letters, signals for reading sections, inverted *nûnîm*) are printed as they appear in M^L, as has been the practice since the 1937 edition. In particular, the *nûn-* or *zayin*-like sign found in the Masorah parva of M^L (ׯ) will be shown in a form that follows the manuscript as closely as possible. However, *sətumôt* and *pətuhôt* are not indicated by the manner of spacing lines, but by the interposition of ס and פ, as has been the practice from the beginning of the *Biblia Hebraica* series.

THE MASORAH

In his contribution to the foreword of the third edition, Kahle, pointing out that the text of M^L "vollständig wird . . . erst durch die ihm beigegebene Masora" (*BHK³*, VIII), expressed the aim of publishing the full Masorah of M^L in *Biblia Hebraica*.

In the event, that aim was realized only for the Masorah parva in the 1937 edition. *BHS* was intended to realize Kahle's aim of publishing both the Masorah parva and magna. The edition of M^L's Masorah produced for *BHS* by Gérard E. Weil was intended as a fully corrected and normalized realization of the Masorah of M^L, rather than a diplomatic representation of what was actually written in the manuscript. For this new edition, the Editorial Committee determined to reproduce both the Masorah parva and magna of M^L in an essentially diplomatic representation. Since the Masorah is part of the text of M^L that constitutes the base text of the edition, and the basic principle of its representation is diplomatic, it seemed to the committee inconsistent to present the Masorah in any other fashion. It is true that the Masorah magna and parva of M^L have their deficiencies, and they most certainly do not represent the totality of the data contained in the tradition of the Masorah. However, an edition that would address these matters would require the collation of the Masorah in other manuscripts, and would need more space than can reasonably be granted such matters in a one-volume edition.

This means that where the Masorah of M^L is not consistent with the text in the manuscript, it will not be corrected, as was the practice in *BHK³* and especially *BHS*. Such cases instead will be explained in a note in the commentary section of the edition. A glossary of common abbreviations used in the Masorah parva is included in this edition to aid readers in understanding those notes. Notes from the Masorah parva that cannot be translated reliably using the glossary will be translated in the commentary section, as will every note in the Masorah magna. Masorah notes that involve too much implicit information to be reasonably understood even from a translation will be discussed in the commentary section.

The edition will depart in two formal aspects from a diplomatic presentation of the Masorah magna in order to make it easier for readers to follow the text of the Masorah. At the beginning of each note, the numbers of the chapter and verse to which the note is judged to refer will be inserted. Masorah magna notes containing *sîmanîm* will appear with a point inserted between each *sîman*.

On more than one occasion M^L inserts a circellus in its text without a corresponding note in the Masorah parva. Likewise, notes occur in the Masorah parva without circelli indicating the words or phrases to which they refer, and notes occur in the Masorah magna that have no connection with the matter displayed on the pages of M^L on which they occur. So far as possible, *BHQ* attempts to represent this situation reliably. Circelli will be inserted in the text even when they do not have a corresponding note. Notes in the Masorah parva without a corresponding circellus will be associated with the word or phrase to which the editor judges they relate, but without the insertion of a circellus. Thus the note will occur in proximity to its probable referent, but a false certainty about that referent will not be conveyed. Notes in the Masorah magna that cannot be related to textual matter on the same or neighboring pages, will be associated with the first word on the manuscript page on which they occur, ensuring a location in the edition that approximates the note's location in the manuscript. In both Masorah magna and parva, numerals that lack the usual supralinear dot in M^L will have that dot supplied for the sake of clarity.

THE CRITICAL APPARATUS

As was the case for all the earlier editions in the series, the critical apparatus for this edition will present only a selection of textual cases, emphasizing those that are of substance for translation and exegesis. It is, however, at the point of the contents and presentation of the critical apparatus that *Biblia Hebraica Quinta* is most particularly shaped by the second history to which it is heir, that of the Hebrew Old Testament Text Project (HOTTP) of the United Bible Societies. The HOTTP was constituted in 1969 of a committee of six scholars of the Hebrew Bible (Dominique Barthélemy, Alexander R. Hulst, Norbert Lohfink, W.D. McHardy, Hans Peter Rüger, James A. Sanders). In addition, Eugene A. Nida of the United Bible Societies held the chair. At annual meetings over a period of eleven years, the committee reviewed over five thousand text critical cases forwarded to it from John A. Thompson on the basis of a comparison of the Revised Standard Version, the New English Bible, the Bible de Jérusalem, and the Revidierte Lutherbibel. The five-volume *Preliminary and Interim Report* of this committee, edited by Adrian Schenker, then secretary of the committee, was published between 1973 and 1980. To date, three volumes of the final report have been published under the title *Critique textuelle de l'Ancien Testament*, with the late Dominique Barthélemy of Fribourg as principal editor. The publication of two more volumes is anticipated.

The Hebrew Old Testament Text Project committee elaborated and implemented a particular approach to the task of textual criticism which clearly distinguishes between specific text critical matters and the history of the literary development of the text, and thus differentiates between cases proper to textual criticism as being founded in external evidence, and those proper to other scholarly methods that operate purely on the basis of internal evidence. This approach was adopted by the United Bible Societies as the basis for this new edition of *Biblia Hebraica*. An editorial committee of seven was named by the members of the HOTTP, and invited to a constituting meeting in August, 1990, at the University of Fribourg in Switzerland. Of the seven members of the Editorial Committee, Adrian Schenker of Fribourg was named the president. Following United Bible Societies practice, the Editorial Committee is international and interconfessional, as is the entire project team of twenty-nine. The Editorial Committee elaborated its conception of this edition of *Biblia Hebraica* and especially of the critical apparatus on the basis of its own work, the work of the editors of the individual books, responses and reactions to a sample chapter distributed to many colleagues around the world in 1992, and comments on an *extra seriem* fascicle distributed at scholarly meetings in 1998. This conception was expressed as a set of principles for the guidance of the editors of the individual books. These principles were given written formulation in the *Guidelines for Contributors* and subsequent supplements thereto.

The Selection of Cases and Inclusion of Witnesses

The function of the critical apparatus in *Biblia Hebraica Quinta* is to present and evaluate the evidence for the text's transmission. Accordingly, cases presented in the apparatus are selected for inclusion primarily on the basis of a thorough collation of the ancient witnesses, i.e., three major Tiberian manuscripts for the Torah, and

two for the Prophets and Writings (in addition to M^L); all available pre-Tiberian Hebrew textual witnesses; and all ancient versions that give evidence of independent knowledge of a Hebrew text. The editors intend that, so far as possible, the apparatus will include all cases of variation in these witnesses that meet two general criteria for inclusion. First, such a variation is judged to be text-critically significant. In other words, the reading arguably, but not necessarily, represents a Hebrew text differing from the edition's base text. Second, it is judged to be potentially significant for translation or exegesis. Entries for such cases will ordinarily indicate the force of the relevant evidence of all the collated witnesses on the point at issue.

Whenever the actual readings are presented, they ordinarily will be given in full and in their own language and script. In a minority of cases where a variant reading can be described clearly and economically, a description is given in preference to the reading. Readings consisting entirely of numbers may be translated as numerals in order to save space. Readings that consist entirely of a minus in relation to the base text will be indicated with the symbol >. Versional pluses that are longer than one verse and come from what amounts to a separate edition of the book in question (e.g., Esther) will be indicated (usually with the abbreviation "+ txt"), but not given in full, by reason of limitations of space. Similarly, lengthy readings that are judged to stand in a literary relation to the text represented in the base text (e.g., a parallel text) will be signaled (usually with the abbreviation "differ-txt"), but not given in full. Retroversion will be used only for a reading proposed as preferable to that found in the base text. Since the apparatus is devoted to the presentation and evaluation of the concrete evidence for the text's transmission, a hypothetical reading (i.e., a conjecture) will have place in the apparatus of *BHQ* only when it is the only explanation of the extant readings in a case.

The editors recognize that the two general criteria for inclusion of cases in the apparatus of *BHQ* represent a departure from the previous practice in *Biblia Hebraica*, as well as from the practice of textual criticism for many years. In order to enter into conversation with the pre-existing discussion, some additional cases that have long been treated as text critical cases on the basis of other criteria (e.g., exegetical difficulty), but that are not true text critical cases, have been included in the apparatus of *BHQ*. The presentation of these cases may take a more abbreviated form, however (e.g., when the matter at issue is purely linguistic rather than text critical).

In addition to the general principles for including cases in the critical apparatus, there are a number of additional principles that require the presentation of certain types of significant cases without at the same time overloading the apparatus with matter that does not affect translation or exegesis. Thus all cases arising from variants occurring in a Hebrew (or Aramaic for Daniel and Ezra) witness from Qumran, Maṣada or Murabbaᶜât, as well as all cases of kǝṯîḇ/qǝrê – where these variants are not purely orthographic – are included in the apparatus. Moreover, all cases arising from variants found in the Samaritan Pentateuch, where the variant is not purely orthographic or linguistic in character, are also included in the apparatus.

Correspondingly, certain supplementary principles were adopted to limit explicitly the contents of the apparatus in order to keep it substantive and verifiable. Thus the inclusion of materials from the Cairo Geniza is limited to materials that can be dated to the period before 1000 C.E. and that have been published, in the interests of relevance on the one hand, and of verifiability by the reader of the apparatus on the other. Biblical quotations in the Deuterocanon/Apocrypha, the

Pseudepigrapha, the Qumran literature, phylacteries, the works of Philo and Josephus, the New Testament, Tannaitic and Amoraic sources, and Patristic sources are included in the apparatus for specific textual cases only when they are judged possibly to have a variant Hebrew text behind them, and when they represent our only access to a particular reading or they are of particular weight. Individual textual cases in which the extant variants are all from the versions and are self-evidently translational (i.e., adjusting to the constraints and style of the receptor language of the version), paraphrastic or haggadic have been excluded from the apparatus unless they have received considerable attention in previous discussion. Analogously, when the Targum for a book, taken as a whole, is made unreliable as a witness to the Hebrew text due to extensive paraphrasis or haggadic expansion (e.g., the Targum to Canticles), it will not be cited constantly as a witness since to do so would overload the apparatus with matter that is not useful for the textual cases presented there.

A number of witnesses are not cited constantly because they cannot be regarded as regularly demonstrating independent access to a Hebrew *Vorlage*. On the other hand, they occasionally seem to report readings deriving from a Hebrew *Vorlage*, or are otherwise relevant for understanding cases entered in the apparatus. The Syro-Hexapla and kindred witnesses to the Origenian recension of the Old Greek are reported among the witnesses for a case only when their readings differ from both the Old Greek and the MT. The Old Latin will be reported only when it agrees with a Hebrew witness or arguably witnesses an independent reading, *and* does not agree with any Greek manuscript. The Samaritan Targum to the Pentateuch, the Gallican Psalter, and the Coptic versions will not be collated or recorded systematically, but their witness will be reported in those cases where an editor regards them as offering useful evidence.

BHQ makes a complete collation of *sətumôt* and *pətuḥôt* in the Tiberian manuscripts treated as constantly cited witnesses. However, only cases regarded as having significance for translation and exegesis are entered in the apparatus. In practice this means that only cases where there is a disagreement as to the presence or absence of a *sətumâ* or *pətuḥâ* will be included in the apparatus. A complete table of the occurrences of *sətumôt* and *pətuḥôt* in M^L and the collated Tiberian manuscripts will be included in the introduction to each book.

In distinction to earlier editions in the *Biblia Hebraica* series, *BHQ* will not cite the medieval manuscripts in the collations of Kennicott and de Rossi, or the editions of Ginsburg, as witnesses for cases in the apparatus. This is a consequence of following the carefully argued views of Moshe H. Goshen-Gottstein that these manuscripts are essentially derivative of the text and Masorah established by the great Tiberian Masoretes. Thus their evidence seems to add little that is independent of the great Tiberian manuscripts. References to the manuscripts collated by Kennicott, de Rossi, or Ginsburg will be found in characterizations of other readings or in comments on cases when the reading(s) found in Kennicott, de Rossi, or Ginsburg document an attitude or a stance toward the transmitted text that the editor also wishes to posit for another part of the textual tradition.

In quite another fashion, *BHQ* is in a different position from its predecessors in regard to the Dead Sea Scrolls and the Peshitta, and to a lesser extent in regard to the Septuagint and Vulgate. In the case of the Dead Sea Scrolls, the critical apparatus in this edition has been able to make full use of all extant biblical manuscripts among them, due to the rapid pace of publication during the last decade and thanks

to the gracious access to unpublished materials afforded by those responsible for them. In the case of the Peshitta, the work of the Leiden Peshitta Project has produced a series of excellent editions, and where these were not yet finished, project leaders graciously made available collations. Thus the evidence of the Peshitta cited in the apparatus of *BHQ* is derived from good and early manuscripts rather than from the older editions of varying quality upon which *BHK³* and *BHS* often relied. In the case of the Septuagint, some of the editions of the Göttingen Septuaginta-Unternehmen were of course available for *BHS*, but in the intervening years a goodly number of important volumes have been added to that series. Moreover, where volumes are still in process, the institute has graciously afforded *BHQ* book editors access to collations and other resources. For the Vulgate, *BHK³* and *BHS* were able to rely on some of the volumes of the San Girolamo edition, but not for all of the books. *BHQ* has the advantage that in the meantime that edition has been completed.

The Evaluation of the Evidence

The apparatus in *BHQ* aims not only to present the evidence of the text's transmission, but also to evaluate that evidence to discern when a reading not contained in the base text is to be preferred to the reading found there. Thus the apparatus will from time to time propose that a witnessed reading other than the one found in the base text is to be preferred. That the apparatus will make such judgments implies a necessarily subjective component in the presentation of cases. As often has been pointed out, such a subjective component is unavoidable if one engages in textual criticism. Since this subjective component cannot be removed from an apparatus that proposes preferred readings from the range of extant variants, the editors have determined, in keeping with an aim to make the apparatus as nearly transparent as possible, to make explicit their judgments concerning the character of the various readings in a case where this can be done with reasonable confidence and clarity. These judgments are expressed in their fullest form in the discussions of selected cases in the commentary on the apparatus, including all cases where a reading other than that in the edition's base text is preferred. In other cases they are expressed through the use of abbreviated characterizations inserted in the apparatus itself (see below for the list of abbreviations and definitions). The aim of this edition in rendering judgments in its apparatus is to indicate the earliest attainable form(s) of the text based on the available evidence. This objective is determined by the focus of the apparatus on the presentation and evaluation of the evidence of the ancient witnesses. This twofold role of the apparatus (presentation and evaluation) also underlies the structure for cases presented in the apparatus.

In weighing the evidence of each witness, the editors have taken account of the preceding decades of research into the process of textual transmission. Thus they recognize that the process of the transmission of the text was not only a mechanical matter, but that the text was in some degree transmitted in terms of its meaning for the copyists' and translators' communities. Consequently, the textual critic must be alert not only to the sorts of changes that may arise from the mechanics of manuscript production, but also to changes made in consequence of meanings assigned to the text. In the case of the versional witnesses, the editors are conscious that these must be considered, within the framework of each distinct translation

unit, with reference to the technique of translation and the characteristics of the translational language when compared with Hebrew.

The Structure and Presentation of Cases

The editors conceived their task as the presentation of the evidence in a way that allows readers of other viewpoints, or readers studying other aspects of the transmission of the text, to draw their own conclusions. Therefore, the primary part of each case entry, following the lemma drawn from the base text, is the presentation of the readings in the collated witnesses and the groupings among the witnesses. (See Fig. 1 for a sample case entry illustrating this discussion.) Entries in this apparatus are so structured that the lemma (base text) is followed by the variants from it and each reading – whether lemma or variant – is followed by the sigla for the witnesses supporting it. Ordinarily, the text of the principal witness for a variant reading is given. The first variant reading in the sequence is the reading that generates the text critical case. The sequence of the remaining variants (as well as of the listing of witnesses following a reading) is based on a sequence of language (i.e., Hebrew, Greek, Latin, others) and within a language by an approximate ascending chronology. If two variant readings generate a single case, they precede the other variants, and the sequence between the two is determined by the linguistic-chronological sequence just described.

Consistent with the emphasis of the apparatus on cases in which one or more of the witnesses arguably point to a Hebrew text differing from the base text, groupings among the witnesses are determined at the level of the possible Hebrew text. Thus, for example, two Greek witnesses that offer synonymous renderings of the same word or phrase may be grouped together when the editor judges that they witness the same *Vorlage* even though they do not use the same Greek word(s). Groupings among witnesses are determined with reference to the particular issue that is the focus of the case. Where a subsequent witness for a reading agrees on this focal matter with the initial witness for that reading, even though it differs in details outside the focus of the case, it is grouped with the initial witness, but enclosed in parentheses. To merit signaling in this way, variations of detail must arguably exist at the level of the possible Hebrew text.

Where a reading given in a case (including the lemma from the base text) is judged to be secondary and the editor has judged that an abbreviated characterization of the reading would be helpful and can be expressed with reasonable certainty, this characterization will appear following the sigla of the witnesses supporting that reading. These characterizations ordinarily describe the reading to which they are attached with reference to the preferred reading in the case. In those cases where one reading is characterized with reference to another reading, but not the preferred one, the siglum of the reading providing the point of reference for the characterization will be attached to the characterization. In identifying a versional reading as a variant in this apparatus, the question ordinarily is left open whether the variation exists at the level of the Hebrew text or at the level of the translation. In some cases the characterizations of versional readings will be marked to indicate the level to which the characterization applies (using "hebr" = level of the *Vorlage*; "vrs"/"vrss" = level of the version[s]).

In cases where the editor proposes that a reading other than that of the base text is to be preferred, this is presented in the concluding portion of the entry following

a double vertical stroke and the abbreviation "pref" (for "preferred reading"). The evidence supporting the preferred reading is recapitulated. If the preferred reading is not directly attested by any of the extant witnesses, but is only implied by their evidence, it is marked by the signal "(origin)", i.e., that it is the indirectly attested origin of the extant readings. If the grammatical form of the preferred reading is not found otherwise in Hebrew of the biblical period, it is marked either as "unat-test" (= "unattested") or as "conjec-phil" (= "philological conjecture"), depending on the kind of external support for the reading. Where the proposed reading is a conjecture, it is not introduced by the abbreviation "pref" (= "preferred reading"), but by the abbreviation "conjec" (= "conjecture"). In line with the focus of the apparatus on the evidence of the text's *transmission*, proposals for preferred read-ings will not seek to reconstruct the literary history of a text. Readings that are judged to derive from another literary tradition for a book will be characterized as "lit" (see the definitions of characterizations below).

Whenever a case receives further discussion in the edition's textual commen-tary, its entry in the apparatus will contain the symbol ❖. Whenever it is discussed in the commentary for another case, the entry in the apparatus will include the symbols →❖ and the reference for the verse at which the commentary is found. Each case entry in the apparatus concludes with the symbol •. When the same lemma in the base text requires more than one case entry in the apparatus, the conclusion to each case entry before the last is marked with the symbol ○. The end of the last one, of course, is marked with the symbol •.

THE LAYOUT OF A PAGE

The elements of the edition – base text, Masorah, apparatus, textual commentary, translations of Masoretic notes – are laid out in the following way. (See Fig. 2 for a sample page illustrating the features discussed here.) Beginning at the top of the page will be the text of M^L. Chapter and verse numbers will be inserted along the inner margin of the text. The indications of lectionary sections and similar Masoretic marginalia (e.g., inverted *nûnîm*), as they appear in M^L, will be given in the outside lateral margin. In addition, the names of the lectionary sections accord-ing to the annual cycle in current use will be presented in the Torah, with the book name in the running head at the top of the right-hand page.

The notes of the Masorah parva of M^L will be laid out in the outside lateral margin of the page. A reader is alerted to the connection of a note to a word or words in the text by the presence of circelli over or between the relevant word(s) in the text except in those few instances noted earlier where the manuscript pro-vides a note, but no circellus, or where it has a circellus in the text, but no note in the Masorah parva. As indicated above, the reader is expected to be able to trans-late the notes of the Masorah parva with the help of the glossary of abbreviations and terms provided with the edition. Notes which do not correspond to the text of M^L, and notes of particular difficulty will receive attention in the commentary sec-tion, so that the reader is advised to check there on such occasions.

The notes of the Masorah magna of M^L will be laid out in a separate register below the base text. As is the case in the manuscript, there is no particular signal in the text of the edition to indicate that a word has a note in the Masorah magna

although these notes typically occur for words already noted in the Masorah parva. In order to aid the reader in connecting notes in the Masorah magna with the relevant words or phrases in the text, this edition gives the notes in the order of the words in the biblical text even when this requires departing from the order of the notes on a given page of the manuscript. It also, as noted above, inserts the chapter and verse to which the note refers ahead of the note. Translations of notes in the Masorah magna will be available in the commentary section, as well as comments on difficult notes or notes that do not correspond to the text of M^L.

The text critical apparatus will be found at the bottom of the page, below the base text and Masorah magna. The editors determined not to introduce letters, numbers, or symbols into the base text of the edition to signal the connection of entries in the apparatus with the text. Instead the reader can rely on the full reproduction of the relevant word(s) from the base text as the lemma at the beginning of each case in the apparatus to make this connection. The apparatus is designed as an essentially self-contained entity, but whenever further discussion of a case is provided in the commentary section of the edition, this will be signaled as described above.

In the margin to the left of the first line of the critical apparatus, the edition will list the reference(s) for any text(s) parallel to the portion of the base text printed on that page. If this parallel text is cited as a witness in any case in the apparatus on that page it will be referred to by means of a symbol (//), or a general siglum (e.g., Neh), rather than a precise chapter and verse reference.

M^L, ITS TEXT AND MASORAH

The introductions to the individual biblical books will offer descriptions of the non-Tiberian witnesses used in the edition. However, since M^L is the same witness for all the books, we offer here an overall description of it rather than repeat this material unnecessarily by including it in the book introductions. In the section following this, we provide briefer overall descriptions of the other Tiberian Masoretic witnesses used in this edition.

The manuscript known by the shelf mark EBP. I B 19a, housed in the Russian National Library in St. Petersburg, Russia (previously known as the Saltykov-Shchedrin State Public Library [Leningrad], and before that as the Imperial Public Library [St. Petersburg]), known as Codex Leningradensis or the Leningrad Codex, received substantive codicological description in the 1875 catalogue of A. Harkavy and H. L. Strack (*Catalog der hebräischen Bibelhandschriften der kaiserlichen öffentlichen Bibliothek* [St. Petersburg: C. Ricker, 1875; Leipzig: J. C. Hinrichs, 1875]). Recently, this long-standard description has been surpassed by the much more thorough and up-to-date description in M. Beit-Arié, C. Sirat, and M. Glatzer (*Codices Hebraicis Litteris Exarati Quo Tempore Scripti Fuerint Exhibentes*, Tome 1, Jusqu'à 1020 [Monumenta Palaeographica Medii Aevi, Series Hebraica; Turnhout: Brepols, 1997], 114–31). The text and Masorah of the manuscript have received much scholarly attention, beginning with the work of Kahle. Notable recent descriptions of the text and Masorah of M^L include those of M. Breuer (כתר ארם צובה והנוסח המקובל של המקרא [Jerusalem: Mosad HaRav Kook, 1976]),

I. Yeivin (*Introduction to the Tiberian Masorah* [Missoula: Scholars Press, 1980]), E. J. Revell ("The Leningrad Codex as a Representative of the Masoretic Text," in *The Leningrad Codex* [ed. D. N. Freedman, et al.; Grand Rapids: William B. Eerdmans; Leiden: Brill, 1998], xxix–xlvi), and the numerous works of A. Dotan. The following discussion is based in part on these descriptions, and in part on the editors' own experience with M^L, although at the moment their experience is necessarily less a foundation for what follows than will be the case at the end of the project.

The codex was produced in Cairo by Shemu$^{\circ}$el ben Ya^{c}aqob for Rabbi Mevorak ben Joseph ha-Kohen. The year of its production is given according to five different calendars. These, however, yield four different year dates according to Common Era reckoning: 1008, 1009, 1010, and 1013. Following Beit-Arié, Sirat, and Glatzer, we accept 1008 as the year of the manuscript's production. Shemu$^{\circ}$el ben Ya^{c}aqob copied and corrected all aspects of the manuscript: consonantal text, pointing, and Masorah.

The codex consists of 491 parchment folios inscribed in black to dark brown ink. The first 463 folios contain the twenty-four books of the Hebrew Bible with vowels and accents, plus Masorah parva and magna. The biblical text is written three columns to a page (except for Psalms, Job, and Proverbs, which are written two columns to the page) with twenty-seven lines per column. The Masorah parva is written in the lateral and inter-columnar margins, and the Masorah magna is written in the top and bottom margins of each page. The codex exhibits the typical codicological characteristics for a medieval Middle Eastern manuscript. For a full codicological discussion with complete texts and translations of all the colophons, see the work by Beit-Arié, Sirat, and Glatzer cited above.

On the whole, the manuscript is well preserved. Page-by-page details of deterioration and damage may be found in the conservation notes that are part of the Eerdmans/Brill facsimile edition cited above. This damage does not often impinge on our ability to read the manuscript, but there are instances where it has an impact. For example, as is also true in neighboring columns, much of the original text in the bottom half of the right-hand column on folio 250r, containing Jer 7:28-31, has flaked off and then been re-inked by a later, cruder hand. However, in this column errors have crept into the text through the re-inking process. In v. 30 the first hand has clearly written נְאֻם־יְהֹוָה. Whoever re-inked the text misconstrued some of the remains of the original letters and mistakenly wrote נְאֻם־יְהוָה. That the text has been effaced and re-inked is clear enough from the black-and-white plate in the Eerdmans/Brill facsimile, but the details of what has happened become clear only from the color transparencies used by the project.

In the sixth of the manuscript's eight colophons (on f. 479r), Shemu$^{\circ}$el ben Ya^{c}aqob indicated that he corrected this manuscript from others produced and corrected by Aharon ben Mosheh ben Asher. The close conformity of the corrected text and Masorah of M^L to the ben Asher tradition, implied by this note, has been confirmed by numerous recent studies. In cases from *Kitāb al-khilāf* where ben Asher differs from ben Naphtali, M^A follows ben Asher in 94% and M^L follows in 92%. Both follow ben Asher in 90% of the cases where ben Asher and ben Naphtali agree against other authorities (Yeivin, *Tiberian Masorah*, 16 and 19; for an excellent edition of *Kitāb al-khilāf* see L. Lipschütz, *Kitāb al-khilāf: Mishael ben Uzziel's Treatise on the Differences between Ben Asher and Ben Naphtali* [Hebrew University Bible Project Monograph Series 2; Jerusalem: Magnes Press, 1965]).

This correspondence between M^A and M^L is closer than for any other extant representative of the ben Asher tradition. Thus M^L appears to be an excellent representative of the ben Asher tradition of the Tiberian Masoretic Text, second only to M^A in its adherence to that tradition, and the best surviving complete representative. As is now widely recognized, this Tiberian Masoretic Text is a carefully preserved descendant of a textual stream whose ancient antecedents are found among the Dead Sea Scrolls.

As is often remarked, M^L, although an excellent manuscript, is not as carefully prepared as M^A. The level of care, and of variation from M^A, varies from one aspect of the text to another. Variations in the consonantal text apart from medial vowel letters are few. In the use of medial vowel letters, M^L exhibits a mild preference for more common spellings. The variations in the reading tradition are similarly small. Variations in the use of *sᵊtumôt* and *pᵊtuḥôt* are somewhat greater.

The most notable variations between M^L and M^A, and the most notable instances of carelessness in the preparation of M^L, are in the Masorah. The substance of notes differs little between M^L and M^A, but which phenomena receive comment and the style of presentation of the information in the notes differ between the two manuscripts. As is well known from a number of studies and from the work of G. Weil in *BHS*, a number of notes in the Masorah of M^L do not correspond to the text of the manuscript, exhibit miscopied or confused references, or seem to be misplaced in the manuscript. On the other hand, in spite of its defects, the Masorah of M^L is of real value in view of the completeness of the manuscript, as well as some specific data unique to M^L.

THE OTHER TIBERIAN MASORETIC WITNESSES

Seven other Tiberian Masoretic manuscripts are collated for various portions of the Bible in this edition. The Aleppo Codex (M^A) has been collated for all the portions where it survives. For the Torah, Oriental Ms. 4445 of the British Library (M^B), manuscript EBP. II B 17 of the Russian National Library in St. Petersburg (M^{L17}), and manuscript Sassoon 507 (M^{S5}), now Heb. 24° 5702 of the National and University Library in Jerusalem, also have been collated. For the Prophets, the Cairo Codex (M^C) also has been collated. For the Writings, Additional Ms. 1753 of the Cambridge University Library (M^Y) also has been collated, and for books not surviving in the Aleppo Codex, either manuscript Sassoon 1053 (M^{S1}) or manuscript EBP. II B 34 of the Russian National Library in St. Petersburg (M^{L34}) has been collated. Here we offer brief descriptions of these witnesses and identify the editions and/or films used as their standards for collation and citation. In this first fascicle these descriptions are necessarily based more on existing discussions than on the direct experience of the editors. In addition to the specific works identified in the description of each witness, the relevant portions of Yeivin, *Tiberian Masorah*, have been relied on for this discussion.

– *The Aleppo Codex* (M^A) has received a great deal of attention among scholars, as is only appropriate to its value. The recent work of M. Beit-Arié, C. Sirat, and M. Glatzer (*Codices Hebraicis Litteris Exarati*, 1:65–72) provides a comprehensive codicological description. Unless otherwise cited, the following description is drawn from that of Beit-Arié, Sirat, and Glatzer. In *BHQ* this witness is cited

according to the facsimile edition by M. Goshen-Gottstein (*The Aleppo Codex.* Volume 1, The Plates [Jerusalem: Magnes Press, 1976]).

Although there is no colophon in the extant portions of the manuscript, the copying of the consonantal text in M^A is attributed to Solomon ben Buya^{c}a, and the addition and verification of the vowels, accents and Masorah is attributed to Aaron ben Asher himself. These attributions are based on information contained in four marginal dedicatory notes within the manuscript itself. It has also been argued that this is the manuscript that Maimonides reported using and stated had been corrected and verified by ben Asher. Based on these attributions, the manuscript is assumed to have been produced in Tiberias. Beit-Arié, Sirat, and Glatzer propose its date as ca. 930 C.E.

Of the original manuscript, 295 folios survive, containing the following portions of text: Deut 28:17 to the end of the book; Joshua; Judges; Samuel; Kings except for 2 Kgs 14:21–18:13; Isaiah; Jeremiah except 29:9–31:34 and parts of 32:1-25; Ezekiel; the Twelve Prophets except Amos 8:13 to the end, Obadiah, Jonah, Mic 1:1–5:1, Zeph 3:20 to the end, Haggai, Zech 1:1–9:17; Chronicles; Psalms except 15:1–25:1; Job; Proverbs; Ruth; Cant 1:1–3:11. For the folios that survive, the various forms of minor damage that the pages of the codex have suffered have not resulted in any loss of text except for folio 148, where parts of verses in Jer 32:1-25 have been lost. The manuscript is written on parchment in square script in dark brown ink with text mostly arranged in three columns per page, and in two columns per page in Job, Proverbs and Psalms. The Masorah parva is written in the lateral and intercolumnar margins, and the Masorah magna is written in the top and bottom margins.

The manuscript has been prepared with great care, and gives evidence of careful correction. It is the purest representative of the ben Asher tradition among the extant manuscripts of the Hebrew Bible. As stated above, M^A follows ben Asher in 94% in cases from *Kitāb al-khilāf* where ben Asher differs from ben Naphtali, and it follows ben Asher and ben Naphtali in 90% of the cases where these two agree against other authorities (Yeivin, *Tiberian Masorah*, 16).

– *Oriental Ms. 4445 of the British Library* (M^B) has received significant discussion in a variety of contexts. The works of G. Margoliouth (*Catalogue of the Hebrew and Samaritan Manuscripts in the British Museum* [London: British Museum, 1899], Part I, 36–39) and A. Dotan ("Reflections Towards a Critical Edition of Pentateuch Codex Or. 4445," in *Estudios Masoréticos (X Congreso de la IOMS): En memoria de Harry M. Orlinsky* [ed. E. Fernández Tejero and M. T. Ortega Monasterio; Madrid: Instituto de Filología del CSIC, 1993], 39–51) form the primary basis of the following description. In *BHQ*, M^B has been collated and cited according to a microfilm of the manuscript.

The manuscript lacks a colophon, but of the Tiberian witnesses used in this edition, it is held to be among the earliest. Margoliouth dated it to the middle of the ninth century (*Hebrew and Samaritan Manuscripts*, 36). Similarly, Dotan ("Codex Or. 4445," 50), although leaving the question finally open, inclines toward a date in the second half of the ninth century. Yeivin (*Tiberian Masorah*, 19) suggests a date ca. 925. It is generally held that the scribe and place of writing are unknown. However, Dotan proposes that the name of the scribe, Nissi ben Daniel ha-Kohen, is found as an acrostic in certain Masoretic notes, and that this scribe is responsible for the entirety of the manuscript, text, vowels and accents, and Masorah ("Codex Or. 4445," 50). Margoliouth and Dotan suggest the possibility of a Persian provenance.

M^B contains text and Masorah (Masorah parva and Masorah magna) for Gen 39:20–Deut 1:33 except for Num 7:46-73; 9:12–10:18. This ninth- or tenth-century text is found on 186 parchment folios laid out in three columns per page. The remaining portions of the Pentateuch were added on paper folios, which, according to a colophon, were produced in 1540.

According to Yeivin, M^B follows ben Asher in 80% of cases from *Kitāb al-khilāf* where ben Asher differs from ben Naphtali, and it follows ben Asher and ben Naphtali in 73% of the cases where these two agree against other authorities (Yeivin, *Tiberian Masorah*, 19). P. Kahle reports 83% correspondence to the ben Asher readings where these differ from ben Naphtali (P. Kahle, "The Hebrew Ben Asher Bible Manuscripts," *VT* 1 [1951]: 167). Margoliouth points to a number of divergences from established Tiberian tradition (e.g., in the placement of *sətumôt* and *pətuḥôt*). Both Margoliouth and Dotan regard some of these traits in text and accentuation (and Masorah in Dotan's case) as signs of the antiquity of the manuscript's tradition.

– The comprehensive codicological description of *manuscript EBP. II B 17 of the Russian National Library* in St. Petersburg (M^{L17}) by M. Beit-Arié, C. Sirat, and M. Glatzer (*Codices Hebraicis Litteris Exarati*, 1:53–64) provides a readily accessible account of this manuscript, and forms the basis of the following summary description unless otherwise noted. In *BHQ* this witness has been collated and cited according to a microfilm of the manuscript.

According to two colophons in the manuscript, its consonantal text was copied by Solomon ha-Levi ben Buya^{c}a, who was also the scribe of M^A. The vowels, accents, Masorah, and decoration were added by Ephraim ben Buya^{c}a, who also verified its text. The second colophon gives a date for the manuscript that translates to 929 C.E. This is a beautiful and carefully prepared manuscript. Yeivin maintains that in cases from *Kitāb al-khilāf* M^{L17} shows no definite tendency to agree with either ben Asher or ben Naphtali (*Tiberian Masorah*, 23).

This Pentateuchal manuscript, now of 242 folios, has suffered a good deal of damage, and contains numerous lacunae due to missing folios. The following portions of the Pentateuch survive: Gen 2:5–6:3; 8:9–20:9; 21:17–25:22; 27:6–41:43; Gen 42:35–Exod 23:7; Exod 25:2–Lev 19:20; Lev 20:8–25:17; Lev 25:44–Num 10:35; Num 17:6 to the end of Deuteronomy. The manuscript is written on parchment in square script in dark brown ink which often has flaked, especially on the flesh side of the folios. Except for the Song of the Sea and the Song of Moses, the text is arranged in three columns per page. The Masorah parva is written in the lateral and intercolumnar margins, and the Masorah magna is written in the top and bottom columns. Some first lines of text and some Masorah magna notes have been lost due to damage of the top edges of the pages.

– *The Damascus Pentateuch*, formerly known as *manuscript Sassoon 507*, now known as Heb. 24° 5702 of the National and University Library in Jerusalem (M^{S5}) is described in D. S. Sassoon's catalogue (*Ohel David: Descriptive Catalogue of the Hebrew and Samaritan Manuscripts in the Sassoon Library, London* [Oxford: Oxford University Press; London: Humphrey Milford, 1932], 1:22–23). This is the primary basis for the following description. In *BHQ* M^{S5} has been collated and cited according to a microfilm of the manuscript, or according to the facsimile edition of M. Beit-Arié (*The Damascus Pentateuch* [vol. 2 in *Early Hebrew Manuscripts in Facsimile*; ed. M. Beit-Arié; Copenhagen: Rosenkilden and Bagger; Baltimore: Johns Hopkins University Press, 1982]).

M^{S5} doubtless falls within the range set by the dates for M^B and M^L. However, within that range there is considerable variety in the date ascribed to M^{S5}. Yeivin (*Tiberian Masorah*, 21) dates the ms. to the tenth century, whereas Sassoon dates it to the ninth (*Ohel David*, 23). Loewinger also thinks in terms of a ninth century date, whereas Beit-Arié thinks of a date around 1000 C.E. (*CTAT*, 3:ix). There is a similar disagreement over its place of origin, Tiberias (Sassoon and Loewinger), or more generally Palestine or Egypt (Beit-Arié).

M^{S5} contains the vocalized text and Masorah (Masorah parva and Masorah magna) from Gen 9:26 to the end of Deuteronomy except for Exod 18:1-23. The text appears on 229 folios arranged in three columns per page.

The manuscript appears to have been carefully prepared, but has a less clear-cut alignment within the Masoretic tradition than some of the others used in *BHQ*. Yeivin reports that it uses a "mixed system" of marking accents. The ms. follows ben Asher in 52% in cases from *Kitāb al-khilāf* where ben Asher differs from ben Naphtali, and it follows ben Asher and ben Naphtali in 76% of the cases where these two agree against other authorities (Yeivin, *Tiberian Masorah*, 21). Sassoon suggests that although the Masorah follows the tradition of ben Asher, the text follows that of ben Naphtali (*Ohel David*, 22).

– *The Cairo Codex* (M^C) justly has received a considerable amount of attention among text critical scholars. In their recent work, M. Beit-Arié, C. Sirat, and M. Glatzer (*Codices Hebraicis Litteris Exarati*, 1:25–39) provide a comprehensive codicological description of the manuscript. Unless otherwise noted, this is the basis of the following description. In *BHQ* this witness is cited according to the edition of F. Perez Castro, et al. (*El Codice de Profetas de El Cairo* [7 vols. of text; Madrid: CSIC, 1979–1988; 4 vols. of indices; Madrid: CSIC, 1992–1997]).

One of the two colophons in the manuscript attributes the copying of the consonantal text and the vowels, accents and Masorah to Moses ben Asher, and dates and locates the production of the codex to 894/5 C.E. in Tiberias. A variety of factors, including the results of radiocarbon dating, lead Beit-Arié, Sirat, and Glatzer to doubt the authenticity of this attribution, and to date the codex to the end of the tenth century or the beginning of the eleventh.

M^C comprises 296 parchment folios containing the Former and Latter Prophets written in brown ink. There is no significant gap in the text of the Prophets due to damage or missing folios. Except for the various Canticles, which are arranged in one or two columns, the text is arranged in three columns per page. The Masorah parva is written in the lateral and intercolumnar margins, and the Masorah magna is written in the top and bottom margins.

Considering its attribution to Moses ben Asher, it is interesting that M^C follows ben Asher in only 33% of the cases from *Kitāb al-khilāf* where ben Asher differs from ben Naphtali, but it follows ben Naphtali in 64% of the cases. M^C follows ben Asher and ben Naphtali in 75% of the cases where these two agree against other authorities (Yeivin, *Tiberian Masorah*, 20). Sirat (*Codices Hebraicis Litteris Exarati*, 1:28) reviews various discussions that point out a number of ways in which M^C does not conform to the ben Asher tradition.

– *Additional Ms. 1753 of the Cambridge University Library* (M^Y) has received important descriptions in works by S. C. Reif (*Hebrew Manuscripts at Cambridge University Library: A Description and Introduction* [Cambridge: Cambridge University Press, 1997], 70–71) and I. Yeivin ("The Division into Sections in the Book of Psalms" *Textus* 7 [1969]: 76–102). These two descriptions form the basis

of what follows. This witness has been collated and cited according to a microfilm of the manuscript.

M^Y is a Yemenite manuscript whose scribe and date of production are unknown because the ms. lacks a colophon. Reif (*Hebrew Manuscripts*, 70) proposes a date in the fifteenth–sixteenth centuries, but Yeivin's proposal of a fourteenth–fifteenth century date seems more plausible since the sixth owner of the ms. purchased it in 1570.

In 145 parchment folios, the ms. contains for the Writings the text with vowels and accents, as well as Masorah parva and Masorah magna, in the following order (which matches that of M^L): Chronicles, Psalms, Job, Proverbs, Ruth, Canticles, Qoheleth, Lamentations, Esther, Daniel, Ezra-Nehemiah. The ms. also contains some Masoretic lists pertaining to the Torah and Writings.

Yeivin judges that M^Y is not itself a work of the ben Asher school, but regards it as "a second or third-hand copy" of a ben Asher ms., which in turn he considers "no less accurate and reliable than [M^A]." In spite of some carelessness in marking the accents and some obvious copyists' errors, "the details of the ancient tradition have been preserved with meticulous care" (Yeivin, "Division into Sections," 80). This care shows itself in several measures of the manuscript's faithfulness to the ben Asher tradition and its greatest exemplar, M^A. In those cases from *Kitāb al-khilāf* where ben Asher differs from ben Naphtali, M^Y follows ben Asher over 80% of the time. Its "spelling, especially of the words written plene and defective... is almost identical with [M^A]." In comparison to an anonymous ms. containing a list of open and closed sections in Psalms, M^A follows that list 90% of the time, and M^Y "surpasses, or is at least by no means inferior to," M^A in its conformity to the list. (Yeivin, "Division into Sections," 80.) Indeed, of all the mss. Yeivin compared to the list, he concluded that only four mss. can really be said to follow its various stipulations concerning the book of Psalms. These are M^A, M^Y, M^L, and Firkovich II.94. The first two mss., M^A, and M^Y, constitute a group that follows these stipulations nearly identically (Yeivin, "Division into Sections," 97).

– Manuscript *Sassoon 1053* (M^{S1}) is described on pages 1111–12 in volume 2 of D. S. Sassoon's *Ohel David: Descriptive Catalogue of the Hebrew and Samaritan Manuscripts in the Sassoon Library, London* (Oxford: Oxford University Press; London: Humphrey Milford, 1932). That description and Yeivin's in *Tiberian Masorah* (21–22) are the basis of this one. In *BHQ* M^{S1} has been collated and cited according to a microfilm of the manuscript.

Both Sassoon and Yeivin date the manuscript to the tenth century. However, there is no colophon that gives an exact date for the manuscript's production. Although the names of several owners are known from notes in the ms., neither the name of the person(s) who produced the ms., nor the site of its production are known.

In 396 folios M^{S1} contains the whole Bible, but with gaps (e.g., the first ten chapters of Genesis are lost). The vocalized and accented text is accompanied by Masorah parva and Masorah magna, but the Masorah magna is found only on some pages. The Latter Prophets occur in the order Jeremiah, Ezekiel, Isaiah, then the XII. The Writings occur in the same sequence as in M^L, that is, beginning rather than ending with Chronicles.

Yeivin judges M^{S1} to be carelessly prepared by comparison with other great Tiberian MT mss. It follows ben Asher in 40% of cases from *Kitāb al-khilāf* where ben Asher differs from ben Naphtali, and it follows ben Asher and ben Naphtali in

60% of the cases where these two agree against other authorities (Yeivin, *Tiberian Masorah*, 21–22).

– The following description of *manuscript EBP. II B 34 of the Russian National Library* in St. Petersburg (M^{L34}) is derived mostly from that found in P. Kahle, *Masoreten des Westens* (Stuttgart: W. Kohlhammer, 1927), 1:74–77. In *BHQ* this witness has been collated and cited according to a microfilm of the manuscript.

M^{L34} does not contain a reference to the date of its production. A colophon referring to its rebinding in 1130, and dedication notice dated to 1100 set the upper limit for its age. If another, undated note refers to an earlier rebinding, then the ms. probably predates the eleventh century. Yeivin suggests it was produced ca. 975 (Yeivin, *Tiberian Masorah*, 26). An undated dedicatory notice, which is apparently earlier than the dated one, associates the ms. with the Karaite community in Cairo.

In 201 folios M^{L34} contains substantial text from most of the Writings, but there are many gaps. The specific contents are as follows: 1 Chr 1:1-17, 5:24–6:4, 11:10-24, 17:26–18:14, 24:24–26:4; 2 Chr 1:9–2:5, 8:8–15:16, 24:6–28:27, 34:11–36:23; Pss 1:1–7:4, 9:19–30:4, 45:11–78:61, 80:3–94:3, 96:1–145:15, 147:15–150:6; Job 1:1–8:16, 9:27–22:6, 23:10–34:3, 34:36–42:17; Prov 1:1–3:23, 6:26–10:32, 14:12–15:8; Cant 7:3–8:14; Qoheleth; Lam 1:1–5:6; Esth 1:22–8:7, 9:15–10:3; Dan 1:1–3:29, 4:13–12:13; Ezra 1:1-3, 2:8-42, 4:9–6:21, 8:2-22, 9:1-12; Neh 7:8-41, 8:9–9:4. This text is accompanied by what Yeivin calls "short" Masorah parva and Masorah magna (*Tiberian Masorah*, 26).

The manuscript has been carefully prepared. M^{L34} follows ben Naphtali in somewhat more than half of the cases from *Kitāb al-khilāf* where it differs from ben Asher (Yeivin, *Tiberian Masorah*, 26).

ACKNOWLEDGMENTS

It is our pleasure and our duty to acknowledge a number of persons and institutions who have been instrumental in supporting this project and helping it achieve its aims. We are deeply grateful to the late Dominique Barthélemy, the late Hans Peter Rüger, and James A. Sanders of the United Bible Societies' Hebrew Old Testament Text Project for having seen the need for a new edition and convening the exploratory meeting of the Editorial Committee. We wish to express particular thanks to the United Bible Societies and Jan de Waard, then chair of the UBS Sub-Committee on Scholarly Editions, for the necessary support in the inaugural stages of the project. We are profoundly grateful to the late Siegfried Meurer, his successor Jan A. Bühner, and the German Bible Society for having seen, also from the side of the publisher, the need for a new *Biblia Hebraica*, and for providing the indispensable practical support needed to make the edition a reality. This edition has benefited from the flexibility and control of a new computerized production method in which all data to be included in the edition are entered into a database, which can then be converted into a variety of electronic and printed forms. This approach would not have been possible without the guidance and assistance of the project's Consultant in Information Systems, Alan Groves of Westminster Theological Seminary, his programming assistant Soetjianto, Winfried Bader and Rolf

Schäfer of the German Bible Society, and Edgar Szilagyi and Karl-Heinz Strößner of Universitätsdruckerei Stürtz, AG. We are most appreciative of all their efforts on behalf of *BHQ*. We are very grateful to the Ancient Biblical Manuscript Center of Claremont, California, and its then-president, James Sanders, and director, Michael Phelps, for making available the splendid color transparencies of M^L. We wish also to offer great thanks to Aron Dotan of the Tel Aviv University, who agreed to serve as the project's Consultant for Masorah, and has helped resolve a number of difficult problems in that area.

Several persons have made indispensable contributions to the everyday practical functioning of the project, and we here acknowledge with deep appreciation their important contributions. Rolf Schäfer of the German Bible Society has overseen the production of the edition from the side of the publisher, no small task, especially considering the difficulties associated with the new production process. Roger Omanson of the United Bible Societies willingly took on the task of copy-editing at a crucial moment in the life of the project. Harold P. Scanlin of the United Bible Societies facilitated the work of the project in many practical ways, especially in regard to access to manuscript and other resources. Sarah Lind, also of the United Bible Societies, helped polish the English style of the introduction and commentaries for Qoheleth. Norbert Rabe in Tübingen and Jonathan Kearney in Dublin checked the electronic version of the text of M^L for the Megilloth against the transparencies with great care. Last, but by no means least, Bernadette Schacher of the Institut Biblique in Fribourg kept information and materials flowing quickly and dependably to the members of the project team.

We particularly wish to remember here two members of the project who are no longer among our number. Martin Jan Mulder of Leiden University and Raymond Dillard of Westminster Theological Seminary were the initial book editors of Canticles and Esther respectively. Their untimely deaths soon after they had taken up their tasks prevented them from continuing with the project.

The editors are most grateful to their home institutions for their support of this work, as well as to the numerous colleagues who have both encouraged, and thoughtfully and helpfully criticized, the work of edition along its way. Notwithstanding all this help, and all the efforts the members of the *BHQ* project team have expended to make this edition as serviceable as possible for its readers, we follow our predecessors in finding in the sentences of Rudolf Kittel an appropriate conclusion (*BHK³*, XXVIII). "Even so the *Biblia Hebraica* will remain subject to the saying 'One day instructs another'. May it find everywhere fair critics, but especially readers worthy of the greatness of the subject!"

Stuttgart
February, 2004   THE EDITORIAL COMMITTEE

ALLGEMEINE EINLEITUNG

Die erste Auflage der von Rudolf Kittel herausgegebenen *Biblia Hebraica (BHK^1)* wurde am Anfang des 20. Jahrhunderts 1906 in Leipzig gedruckt. Im Laufe des ganzen Jahrhunderts erschienen weitere Auflagen der *Biblia Hebraica*, die sich einerseits in Form und Anlage an der Erstausgabe orientierten, andererseits aber auch mancherlei Änderungen erfuhren, die sich aus der Entwicklung der Textkritik ergaben. Zunächst kam 1913 in Leipzig eine zweite Ausgabe heraus (*BHK^2*), die sich von der ersten nur durch kleine Verbesserungen unterschied. Die dritte Ausgabe (*BHK^3*) jedoch, die von 1929 bis 1937 in Stuttgart erschien, wies gegenüber ihren beiden Vorgängerinnen einschneidendere Veränderungen auf: Während diesen noch der Text zugrunde lag, den Jakob ben Chajjim für die Druckausgabe von Daniel Bomberg 1524–1525 erstellt hatte, reproduzierte die neue dritte Ausgabe der *Biblia Hebraica* den Text des Codex Leningradensis. Sie bot desgleichen einen vollständig neu erarbeiteten textkritischen Apparat. Auch die *Biblia Hebraica Stuttgartensia (BHS)*, die 1967–1977 in Stuttgart als vierte Ausgabe der Biblia-Hebraica-Reihe erschien, übernahm wie *BHK^3* als Bibeltext den Text des Codex Leningradensis, bot aber dessen *Masora* in einer neuen, bearbeiteten und ergänzten Fassung und war mit einem völlig neu konstituierten textkritischen Apparat versehen.

Am Ausgang des 20. Jahrhunderts hat die Arbeit an einer weiteren Neuausgabe der *Biblia Hebraica* begonnen, die nun als fünfte in der Reihe ihrer Vorgängerinnen erscheint; sie mag deshalb als *Biblia Hebraica Quinta (BHQ)* bezeichnet werden. Verschiedene Umstände haben diese Neuausgabe erforderlich gemacht: Der Forschung stehen heute wesentlich mehr biblische Handschriften zur Verfügung, namentlich die Schriftrollen vom Toten Meer. Vor allem aber haben mehrere Jahrzehnte intensiver wissenschaftlicher Beschäftigung mit der Überlieferungsgeschichte des Textes der Hebräischen Bibel zu einer veränderten Sicht im Blick auf die Ziele und Grenzen der Textkritik geführt. Da der vorliegende Faszikel als erster Teil der neuen Ausgabe veröffentlicht wird, erscheint es angebracht, im Folgenden die Besonderheiten der *BHQ* im Vergleich mit den früheren Ausgaben der *Biblia Hebraica* etwas eingehender zu erläutern.

Die neue Ausgabe verdankt sich einer Initiative des Weltbundes der Bibelgesellschaften, und sie genießt die besondere Unterstützung der Deutschen Bibelgesellschaft, die als Verlag wissenschaftlicher Bibelausgaben, zu denen namentlich auch die *Biblia Hebraica* zu rechnen ist, eine lange Tradition hat. Die Eigenart der *Biblia Hebraica Quinta* ist das Resultat ihrer doppelten Vorgeschichte, einerseits in den früheren Ausgaben der *Biblia Hebraica* und andererseits im *Hebrew Old Testament Text Project* des Weltbundes der Bibelgesellschaften.

Mehrere wichtige Entscheidungen im Lauf der Geschichte der *Biblia Hebraica* haben der Reihe dieser Ausgaben charakteristische Merkmale verliehen, die auch für diese vorliegende Ausgabe kennzeichnend bleiben. Von Anfang an waren diese Ausgaben als *Handausgaben* gedacht. Gleichfalls von Anfang an wurde aufgrund einer ausdrücklichen Entscheidung Rudolf Kittels von einem eklektischen Text der Hebräischen Bibel Abstand genommen und stattdessen der Text einer einzigen

Ausgabe oder einer einzigen Handschrift wiedergegeben, dem ein kritischer Apparat mit ausgewählten Lesarten und Konjekturen zur Herstellung eines kritischen Textes beigefügt war. Ausschlaggebend bei der Auswahl der Varianten war deren Bedeutung für Exegese und Übersetzung. Die beiden ersten Ausgaben boten den Text der Bomberg'schen Druckausgabe von Jakob Ben Chajjim. In der dritten Ausgabe wurde auf Initiative von Paul Kahle 1937 der Text des Kodex EBP. I B 19a der Russischen Nationalbibliothek in St. Petersburg (Siglum M^L) als Bibeltext abgedruckt. Kahle legte ebenso Wert darauf, die *Masora magna* (Mm) und *parva* (Mp) von M^L als einen integralen Teil in die Ausgabe aufzunehmen. In der dritten Ausgabe (*BHK³*) wurde dies jedoch nur für die Mp verwirklicht. Erst die vierte Ausgabe der *Biblia Hebraica* Reihe, die *Biblia Hebraica Stuttgartensia* entsprach Kahles Konzeption auch hinsichtlich der Mm. Als gegen Ende der 40er-Jahre die ersten Handschriftenfunde aus Qumran veröffentlicht wurden, wurde die 7. Auflage der *BHK³* auf Veranlassung von Otto Eißfeldt um einen Apparat erweitert, der die Lesarten der Handschriften 1QIsaᵃ und 1QpHab bot. *Biblia Hebraica Quinta* steht in mancher Hinsicht bewusst in dieser Tradition, obgleich sie diese unter anderen Aspekten verfeinert und verändert.

Was für die vorhergehenden Ausgaben galt, das trifft auch auf diese neue Ausgabe zu: Sie ist eine *Handausgabe* für Exegeten, Geistliche, Theologen, Übersetzer und Studierende, die nicht unbedingt alle auch spezialisierte Textkritiker sind. Da eine vollständige *editio critica maior* der Hebräischen Bibel noch aussteht, soll diese Ausgabe jedoch auch für spezialisierte Textkritiker von Nutzen sein, obwohl sie nicht in erster Linie für diesen Personenkreis gedacht ist. Die Herausgeberkommission hat anfangs durchaus eine *editio critica maior* in Erwägung gezogen, doch sie musste sich bald eingestehen, dass ein solches Vorhaben für sie in absehbarer Zeit nicht realisierbar war, und dass eine solche Ausgabe auch nicht dem Zweck entsprechen würde, den die *Biblia Hebraica* erfüllen soll. Die Herausgeberkommission hofft indessen, dass diese Neuausgabe der *Biblia Hebraica* ihren Beitrag zur künftigen Erstellung einer *editio critica maior* leisten wird.

Wie ihre Vorgängerausgaben wird die BHQ zuerst in Faszikeln erscheinen, von denen der vorliegende mit den *Megilloth* der erste ist.

Jeder Faszikel enthält ein biblisches Buch samt den dazugehörigen Materialien und ist folgendermaßen aufgebaut:

– Einführung;
– Verzeichnis der Siglen, Zeichen und Abkürzungen;
– Glossar der in der *Masora parva* allgemein gebräuchlichen Abkürzungen;
– Text und vollständige *Masora* von M^L;
– kritischer Apparat mit den Lesarten der Textzeugen, die die Textgeschichte dokumentieren;
– Kommentar zu ausgewählten Fällen des kritischen Apparates, ferner die Übersetzung der *Masora magna* und Kommentare zu schwierigen Fällen in *Masora magna* und *Masora parva*.

Dieser in allen Faszikeln gleiche Aufbau der Ausgabe legt zugleich auch die sinnvollste Reihenfolge der Benutzung nahe. Die Einführung vermittelt die für Text und Apparat notwendige Einsicht in die Beschaffenheit der Textzeugen. Der Text und sein kritischer Apparat bedürfen ferner an bestimmten Punkten des Textkommentars, um vollständig einsichtig zu sein.

Sobald sämtliche Faszikel vorliegen, wird eine Gesamtausgabe in zwei Bänden

erscheinen; im ersten stehen Bibeltext, *Masora* und kritischer Apparat sowie die
Einleitung in die Gesamtausgabe, ferner die Sigeln, Zeichen und Abkürzungen
(d.h., er wird ein Band in der Art von *BHK* und *BHS* sein), während der zweite
Band Einleitungen in die einzelnen biblischen Bücher, den Text- und *Masora*-
Kommentar sowie die Übersetzung der *Masora magna* enthält.

Diese neue Ausgabe der *Biblia Hebraica* entspricht dem seit 1937 gebräuchlichen Modell einer Ausgabe, die den Text einer einzigen guten masoretischen
Handschrift wiedergibt, versehen mit einem kritischen Apparat, welcher die Textüberlieferung im Vergleich mit dem gewählten Text dokumentiert. Diese Option
geht auf Kittels Entscheidung von 1906 zurück, obgleich damals als Basistext
die Bomberg-Ausgabe an Stelle einer Handschrift herangezogen worden war. Die
Herausgeberkommission ist sich der Problematik einer solchen Ausgabe im
Gegensatz zu einer Ausgabe mit einem eklektischen Text bewusst. Die Herausgeberkommission hatte drei Gründe für die Beibehaltung der historisch ge-
wordenen Struktur der *Biblia Hebraica* seit deren Beginn. Erstens ist sie der Ansicht, dass die Geschichte der Textentwicklung der hebräischen Bibel mit ihren
verschiedenen Textüberlieferungen noch immer zu wenig gut bekannt ist, um eine
solide Grundlage für die Herstellung eines eklektischen Textes abzugeben. Zweitens muss eine Ausgabe mit einem eklektischen Text der hebräischen Bibel für die
Herstellung dieses Textes einen bestimmten zeitlichen Einschnitt in der Entwicklung des Textes wählen. Zur Zeit gibt es jedoch keine Einigkeit über die Phase der
Textgeschichte, welche ein solcher eklektischer Text repräsentieren müsste. Daher
verzichtete die Herausgeberkommission darauf, für ihre von Studierenden und
Nicht-Spezialisten benutzte Ausgabe einen Bibeltext zu erstellen, der einem
bestimmten Moment der Textgeschichte entsprechen würde, dem aber in mancher
Augen andere Phasen vorzuziehen gewesen wären. Drittens ist die Herausgeberkommission der Überzeugung, dass ein eklektischer Text sämtliche Lesarten der
vorhandenen Textzeugen einbeziehen und entsprechend verzeichnen muss. Eine
solche umfassende Ausgabe würde jedoch den Umfang einer einbändigen Ausgabe
sprengen.

DER TEXT

In der Linie der dritten Ausgabe der *Biblia Hebraica* von 1937 und der *Stuttgartensia* mit ihren Verfeinerungen legt auch diese vorliegende Ausgabe eine prinzipi-
ell diplomatische Wiedergabe von M^L als Bibeltext zugrunde. Neuere Untersuchungen von M^L und seiner *Masora* zeigen, dass sie keinen unter jeder Hinsicht
befriedigenden Text bieten und daher als Basistext einer kritischen Ausgabe zu
wünschen übrig lassen (siehe die ausführlichere Erörterung weiter unten). Die Herausgeberkommission hat tatsächlich auch andere mögliche Optionen sorgfältig ge-
prüft. Der Aleppo Kodex (M^A) wurde hauptsächlich deshalb nicht gewählt, weil
die Handschrift unvollständig ist. Überdies legt das *Hebrew University Bible Project* dieses Manuskript seiner bewundernswerten Ausgabe zugrunde, und es ist
ebenso der Bibeltext für die Ausgabe der Bar Ilan Universität, die M. Cohen
herausgibt. So liegt M^A in zwei wissenschaftlichen Ausgaben vor. Die Herausgeberkommission erwog ebenfalls die Möglichkeit, für jeden der drei Kanonteile
die jeweils älteste vorhandene *Ben Ascher*-Handschrift als Basistext für *BHQ* zu
benutzen. Mehrere Gründe sprachen jedoch dafür, auf diese Möglichkeit zugunsten

der durchgehenden Verwendung von M^L zu verzichten. Erstens ist M^L die älteste bekannte vollständige Handschrift der Hebräischen Bibel. Zweitens würde die Wahl der verschiedenen ältesten *Ben Ascher*-Handschriften zu einem Flickwerk geführt haben, da ihre Lücken mit Hilfe anderer Handschriften geschlossen werden müssten (z.B. fehlen im Aleppo Kodex nicht nur der Hauptteil der *Tora*, wie bekannt ist, sondern ebenso ganze Bücher aus den Hagiographen oder *Schriften*). Drittens wurde ursprünglich angenommen, dass die Deutsche Bibelgesellschaft die neue Ausgabe im traditionellen Druckverfahren herstellen und dafür ihren Text der Handschrift M^L benützen würde, der schon mehrmals sorgfältig revidiert wurde. Dieser Umstand fiel in pragmatischer Hinsicht ebenfalls ins Gewicht. Als dann die vollständig elektronische Herstellung der Ausgabe beschlossen wurde, war die schon vorhandene elektronische Fassung des Textes der Handschrift M^L ein nicht zu unterschätzender Vorteil, da damals keine andere der bedeutenden tiberiensischen Handschriften in elektronischer Form zur Verfügung stand. Obschon beim elektronischen Erfassen des Textes von M^L neue Fehler in diese Textform eingeführt worden waren, gab es bereits vor dem Beginn des *BHQ*-Projekts Revisionen, um den elektronischen Text zuverlässiger zu machen. Die Vorbereitung dieser neuen Ausgabe selbst schließt erneut eine sorgfältige Revision des elektronischen Textes von M^L ein, der mit Farbaufnahmen der Handschrift verglichen wird, die das *Ancient Biblical Manuscript Center* in Claremont, Kalifornien, lieferte. Diese Fotos entsprechen den neuen Aufnahmen der Handschrift M^L, welche die durch *West Semitic Research,* Los Angeles, ausgebildeten Spezialisten des *Centers* von Claremont in St. Petersburg gemacht haben. Genauigkeit und Qualität dieser Fotografien übertreffen alles, was bisher an Reproduktionen erhältlich war, und werden zu einer Reihe von Verbesserungen führen, die erst beginnend mit der fünften Auflage der *BHS* (1997) realisierbar sind. Sowohl die Bearbeiter der einzelnen biblischen Bücher selbst als auch unabhängig von ihnen eigens bestellte spezialisierte Mitarbeiter, denen diese besondere Aufgabe übertragen wurde, vergleichen den elektronischen Text mit den neuen Fotografien von M^L.

Wie schon *BHS* folgt auch *BHQ* dem M^L-Text selbst dort, wo dieser offenkundige Fehler enthält. Die Korrektur solcher Fehler wird im Apparat mit Hinweis auf die andern kollationierten tiberiensischen Handschriften verzeichnet. Anderseits zeigen die neuen Fotografien von M^L wenige Stellen, an denen kleine Elemente, gewöhnlich ein Vokalzeichen oder ein Akzent, wegen einer Beschädigung der Handschrift unleserlich geworden sind. In diesen Fällen bietet die Ausgabe eine rekonstruierte Lesart in ihrem Text, während der Apparat über das informiert, was in M^L gelesen werden kann, und die Lesarten der andern tiberiensischen Handschriften notiert, die der Rekonstruktion des Textes als Grundlage dienen. In anderen Fällen weist M^L eine erste und eine zweite Hand auf, z.B. wenn verblasste oder beschädigte Stellen von einer späteren Hand mit Tinte nachgezogen wurden (siehe dazu die Erörterung unten). Dabei kommen gelegentliche Divergenzen zwischen der ursprünglichen ersten und der zweiten Hand vor. In solchen Fällen nimmt der Herausgeber jene Graphie der Handschrift in den Text seiner Ausgabe auf, die er als authentisch betrachtet, und notiert die relevanten Elemente der Textsituation im Apparat.

Was die Wiedergabe des Textes von M^L anlangt, verzichtet *BHQ* wie schon ihre Vorgängerinnen auf eine vollständig diplomatische Reproduktion, insofern Prosatexte nicht in drei Kolumnen pro Seite, sondern einspaltig, und poetische Texte in stichographischer Anordnung gedruckt werden. Das Urteil, was als Prosa und was

als poetischer Text zu gelten habe, liegt jeweils beim Herausgeber des betreffenden biblischen Buches. Die Prinzipien der stichographischen Darstellung sind indessen nicht dieselben wie in den vorhergehenden Ausgaben. Alle Prosa- und Poesie-passagen, die M^L nach traditioneller Disposition in einer speziellen Stichographie darbietet, werden auch in dieser Ausgabe genau so wiedergegeben. Die Sticho-graphie der anderen poetischen Texte in dieser Ausgabe orientiert sich an den ma-soretischen Akzenten. Die Stichen werden stets durch die trennenden Hauptakzente definiert, außer in den Fällen, wo sich die durch die masoretischen Akzente ge-schaffene Gliederung im Vergleich mit einer andern bezeugten syntaktischen Struktur als sekundäre Lesart erweist. In solchen Beispielen bestimmt die vorgezo-gene Lesart die Versteilung. Die Gruppierung von Stichen in Bi- und Trikola folgt so weit als möglich der Hierarchie der Akzente. Nur dort, wo als Ergebnis dieses Prinzips eine Verszeile den Rand einer Seite überschreiten oder einen klaren *Par-allelismus membrorum* zerstören würde, erfolgt die Gruppierung in Bi- und Trikola gegen die Akzente. Es gibt auch eine Anzahl von Listen in den Prosasektionen von M^L (z.B. Esr 2:43-57), für die es zwar keine von der Tradition festgelegten Regeln der Darstellung gibt, die sich aber in M^L trotzdem von der sie umgebenden Prosa abheben. In der vorliegenden Ausgabe werden sie so getreu wie möglich der Form der Handschrift entsprechend wiedergegeben.

Die verschiedenen andern Eigentümlichkeiten der masoretischen Textgestaltung, z.B. größer geschriebene sowie hochgestellte Buchstaben, Zeichen für die gottes-dienstlichen Lesungen, umgekehrte *Nûnîm*, werden in dieser Ausgabe so wieder-geben, wie sie in M^L vorliegen, wie das ja auch in den Ausgaben der *Biblia He-braica* seit 1937 der Fall war. Namentlich das *Nûn-* oder *Zajin*-ähnliche Zeichen in der kleinen *Masora* auf den Rändern von M^L ( ) wird in einer der Handschrift möglichst ähnlichen Form wiedergegeben. Indessen erscheinen die *sətumôt* und *pətuhôt* nicht wie in M^L als spezifische Zeilenunterbrechungen, sondern sie wer-den, wie in der *Biblia Hebraica* von Anfang an üblich, durch die Buchstaben ס und פ angezeigt.

DIE MASORA

In den Prolegomena zur dritten Ausgabe war Paul Kahle ein eigener Abschnitt ein-geräumt worden. Darin hatte er die Wiedergabe der ganzen *Masora* von M^L in der *Biblia Hebraica* damit begründet, dass der Text von M^L "vollständig wird ... erst durch die ihm beigegebene *Masora*" (*BHK^3*, VIII). Faktisch wurde dieses Ziel in der Ausgabe von 1937 nur für die *Masora parva* verwirklicht. Erst die *BHS* wurde Kahles Absicht gerecht, indem sie sowohl die *Masora parva* als auch die *Masora magna* darbot. Die von Gérard E. Weil für die BHS erarbeitete Ausgabe der *Maso-ra* von M^L war freilich weniger als diplomatische Wiedergabe der Handschrift M^L denn als vervollständigte und von Irrtümern befreite *Masora* von M^L gedacht. Für die vorliegende neue Ausgabe beschloss die Herausgeberkommission demgegen-über, beide Masoren der Handschrift M^L im Wesentlichen diplomatisch zu repro-duzieren. Da die *Masora* einen Bestandteil des Textes von M^L darstellt, der die textliche Grundlage für diese Ausgabe abgibt und grundsätzlich in diplomatischer Form wiedergegeben wird, hätte es die Herausgeberkommission nicht für folge-richtig gehalten, die *Masora* in irgendeiner andern Form als in der von M^L gebo-tenen zu präsentieren. Es ist unbestritten, dass *Masora magna* und *Masora parva*

in M^L nicht fehlerfrei sind und selbstverständlich auch nicht die Gesamtheit der von den Masoreten gesammelten und tradierten Daten enthalten. Eine Ausgabe, die der masoretischen Tradition voll Rechnung tragen wollte, müsste die Masoren anderer Handschriften kollationieren und würde sehr viel mehr Raum in Anspruch nehmen, als bei einer einbändigen Handausgabe vernünftigerweise zur Verfügung steht.

Das hat zur Folge, dass Unstimmigkeiten zwischen *Masora* und Text der Handschrift M^L nicht korrigiert werden, anders als es gelegentlich in *BHK^3* und vor allem in *BHS* gehandhabt wurde. Solche Fälle werden stattdessen im Kommentarteil der Ausgabe erklärt. Ein Glossar der in der *Masora parva* gebräuchlichen Abkürzungen ist der Ausgabe beigefügt, um es der Leserschaft zu erleichtern, die masoretische Notation zu entschlüsseln. Formulierungen der *Masora parva*, die auch mit Hilfe des Glossars nicht zuverlässig interpretiert werden können, sind im Kommentarteil übersetzt, wie dies ebenfalls für sämtliche Notate der *Masora magna* gilt. Überall dort, wo die *Masora* stillschweigend zu viel an Information voraussetzt, sodass sie selbst in Übersetzung unverständlich bleibt, bietet der Kommentarteil eine Erläuterung.

In zweierlei Hinsicht weicht diese Ausgabe im Interesse größerer Übersichtlichkeit und bessern Verständnisses von einer diplomatischen Wiedergabe der *Masora magna* ab: Am Anfang jeder masoretischen Notiz bezeichnen Kapitel- und Versangaben die Stelle, zu der die Notiz nach dem Urteil des Herausgebers gehört. Ferner sind die *Sîmanîm* in den Notizen durch einen eingefügten Punkt voneinander getrennt.

Gelegentlich findet sich ein *Circellus* im Text von M^L, dem keine *Masora* am Rande entspricht. Ebenso gibt es am Rand masoretische Notizen ohne entsprechende *Circelli* über den Wörtern oder Phrasen im Text, auf die sie sich beziehen. Auch gibt es Notate der *Masora magna,* die keinen Bezug zum Text derjenigen Seite aufweisen, auf der diese *Masora magna* steht. Die *BHQ* versucht, diese Situationen in einer dem Manuskript möglichst ähnlichen Weise wiederzugeben. *Circelli* werden deshalb beibehalten, auch wenn in M^L eine entsprechende masoretische Randnotiz fehlt. Notizen der *Masora parva* ohne einen *circellus* im Text werden zwar mit dem Wort oder Ausdruck verbunden, auf die sie sich nach Meinung des Herausgebers beziehen, aber der *Circellus* wird nicht ergänzt; so erscheint ein solches masoretische Notat in der Nähe seines wahrscheinlichen Bezugspunktes im Text, aber es wird keine falsche Gewissheit über diesen Bezugspunkt erzeugt. *Masora magna* Notizen ohne Bezug zum Text der Manuskriptseite, auf der sie stehen, werden mit dem ersten Wort dieser Manuskriptseite verbunden; auf diese Weise erscheinen sie in der Druckausgabe an einer Stelle, die ungefähr ihrer Position im Manuskript entspricht. Sowohl in der *Masora magna* als auch in der *Masora parva* werden um der größeren Klarheit willen die supralinearen Punkte der Zahlbuchstaben überall stillschweigend ergänzt, wo sie in der Handschrift irrtümlicherweise fehlen.

DER KRITISCHE APPARAT

Wie es schon in allen früheren Ausgaben von *BHK* und *BHS* der Fall war, behandelt auch die *BHQ* in ihrem kritischen Apparat nur eine Auswahl der textkritischen Fragen, und zwar bevorzugt jene, die für Exegese und Übersetzung von Belang

sind. Inhalt und Form des kritischen Apparates sind indessen jener Teil der Ausgabe, in dem die *Biblia Hebraica Quinta* maßgeblich vom zweiten Strang ihrer oben erwähnten doppelten Vorgeschichte geprägt ist: dem *Hebrew Old Testament Text Project (HOTTP)* des Weltbundes der Bibelgesellschaften. Dieses Projekt wurde 1969 gegründet und einer Gruppe von sechs Gelehrten der Hebräischen Bibel übertragen: Dominique Barthélemy, Alexander R. Hulst, Norbert Lohfink, William D. McHardy, Hans Peter Rüger, James A. Sanders. Unter Vorsitz von Eugene A. Nida vom Weltbund der Bibelgesellschaften untersuchte dieses Komitee bei seinen jährlichen Zusammenkünften in einem Zeitraum von elf Jahren rund 5000 textkritische Probleme, die John A. Thompson aufgrund eines Vergleichs von Revised Standard Version, New English Bible, Bible de Jérusalem und Revidierter Lutherbibel ausgewählt und der Arbeitsgruppe unterbreitet hatte. Der fünfbändige *Preliminary and Interim Report* mit den Arbeitsergebnissen des *HOTTP*, herausgegeben von dessen Sekretär Adrian Schenker, erschien von 1973 bis 1980. Bis heute sind außerdem unter dem Titel *Critique textuelle de l'Ancien Testament* drei Bände eines ausführlichen Abschlussberichts erschienen. Dominique Barthélemy, Freiburg (Schweiz) ist dabei der Hauptverfasser. Er starb am 10. Februar 2002. Zwei weitere postum herausgegebene Bände sollen das ganze Werk vervollständigen.

Das Komitee des *Hebrew Old Testament Text Project* schuf und entwickelte eine besondere Konzeption der Aufgabe der Textkritik, bei der klar zwischen dem eigentlichen Gebiet der Textkritik und dem der Geschichte der literarischen Entwicklung der Texte unterschieden wird: Es gibt Fälle verschiedener Textformen, die eindeutig zum Gebiet der Textkritik gehören, weil sie durch externe Textzeugen belegt sind; davon verschieden sind literarkritische Fälle, die andere wissenschaftliche Methoden erfordern, weil sie nicht durch Textzeugen belegbar sind und daher nur nach internen Kriterien beurteilt werden können. Diese Art der Textkritik legte der Weltbund der Bibelgesellschaften der neuen Ausgabe der *Biblia Hebraica* zu Grunde. Eine Herausgeberkommission aus sieben Mitgliedern wurde vom *HOTTP* bestimmt und im August 1990 zu einer konstituierenden Sitzung an der Universität Freiburg in der Schweiz eingeladen. Von den sieben Mitgliedern der Herausgeberkommission wurde Adrian Schenker, Freiburg, zum Präsidenten bestimmt. In Übereinstimmung mit den Gepflogenheiten des Weltbundes der Bibelgesellschaften sind sowohl die Herausgeberkommission, als auch der weitere Kreis der Herausgeber, bestehend aus insgesamt 29 Personen, international und interkonfessionell zusammengesetzt. Die Herausgeberkommission konzipierte die neue Ausgabe der *Biblia Hebraica* und namentlich deren kritischen Apparat aufgrund ihrer eigenen Arbeit, aber auch aufgrund der Arbeit der Herausgeber der einzelnen biblischen Bücher und unter Berücksichtigung von Antworten und Reaktionen, die auf eine im Jahr 1992 weit gestreute Probeausgabe eines biblischen Kapitels von manchen Kollegen und Kolleginnen rund um die Welt eingingen. Hinzu kamen Hinweise und Meinungsäußerungen bei bibelwissenschaftlichen Kongressen nach der 1998 erfolgten Verteilung eines *extra seriem* Faszikels.

Die Konzeption der Ausgabe wurde in einer Anzahl von Editionsprinzipien konkretisiert, die für alle Herausgeber der einzelnen biblischen Bücher verbindlich sind. Diese Prinzipien liegen in schriftlicher Form unter dem Titel *Guidelines for Contributors* und in Ergänzungsheften zu diesen *Guidelines* vor.

Die Auswahl der Apparateinträge und
der jeweils genannten Textzeugen

Der kritische Apparat der *Biblia Hebraica Quinta* hat die Aufgabe, das für die Textüberlieferung relevante Material auszubreiten und zu beurteilen. Dementsprechend erfolgte die Auswahl der in den Apparat aufgenommenen Fälle vor allem aufgrund gründlicher Kollationierung der alten Textzeugen, d.h. von drei erstrangigen tiberiensischen Handschriften neben M^L für die Tora, bzw. von zwei solchen neben M^L für die Propheten und die Hagiographen (Schriften), ferner aller vorhandenen vortiberiensischen hebräischen Textzeugen sowie aller alten Übersetzungen, die einen unmittelbaren und unabhängigen Zugang zu einem hebräischen Text hatten.

Der Apparat ist in der Absicht der Herausgeber so gedacht, dass er nach Möglichkeit alle Varianten in diesen Textzeugen verzeichnet, soweit sie zwei allgemeine Aufnahmekriterien erfüllen: Erstens muss einer Variante textkritische Bedeutung zuerkannt werden können, d.h., eine gegebene Lesart muss zwar nicht notwendigerweise faktisch einer hebräischen Vorlage entsprechen, aber es muss zumindest denkbar sein, dass sie auf eine solche hebräische Vorlage zurückgeht, die sich vom Basistext der vorliegenden Ausgabe unterscheidet; und zweitens muss eine Variante potentiell für die Übersetzung oder die Exegese von Bedeutung sein. Die Notierung solcher Fälle verzeichnet normalerweise das Gewicht aller relevanten kollationierten Textzeugen für den zur Diskussion stehenden Punkt.

Lesarten werden in der Regel vollständig und in ihrer Originalsprache und -schrift zitiert. In einigen Fällen empfiehlt es sich jedoch, eine Lesart zu beschreiben statt sie zu zitieren, weil eine Beschreibung manchmal klarer und sparsamer ist als ein ganzes Zitat. Lesarten, die nur aus Zahlen bestehen, werden aus Platzgründen mit Zahlzeichen notiert, und für solche, die das ganze Lemma vermissen lassen, erscheint das Zeichen ">". Textüberschüsse von mehr als einem Vers in alten Übersetzungen, die eine andere Edition des in Frage stehenden Buches (z.B. Esther) darstellen, werden angezeigt (gewöhnlich durch die Abkürzung "+ txt"), aber nicht zitiert, um den Apparat nicht zu überlasten. Desgleichen wird auf lange Lesarten, die literarisch mit dem Basistext zusammenhängen, z.B. ein Paralleltext, hingewiesen (in der Regel durch die Abkürzung "differ-txt"), ohne dass sie im Wortlaut angeführt werden. Rückübersetzungen ins Hebräische beschränken sich auf Fälle, in denen einer nicht auf hebräisch überlieferten Lesart der Vorzug gegenüber dem hebräischen Basistext der Ausgabe gegeben wird. Da der Apparat dazu bestimmt ist, die konkreten Zeugen der Überlieferungsgeschichte des Textes anzuführen und zu gewichten, erscheinen hypothetische Lesarten, d.h. Konjekturen, nur dann im Apparat der *BHQ*, wenn allein sie die vorhandenen Lesarten eines Falles zu erklären vermögen.

Die Herausgeber sind sich bewusst, dass die beiden allgemeinen Kriterien für die Aufnahme von Fällen in den Apparat der *BHQ* eine Neuerung darstellen, und zwar sowohl gegenüber dem bisher in der *Biblia Hebraica* üblichen Auswahlverfahren als auch im Verhältnis zu einer langen Praxis der Textkritik. Daher erscheinen im Apparat der *BHQ* gelegentlich auch Fälle, die unter anderen Kriterien, z.B. jenem besonderer exegetischer Schwierigkeit, lange als textkritische Probleme betrachtet wurden, obwohl sie keine textkritische Frage im eigentlichen Sinn aufwerfen. Die Berücksichtigung solcher Fälle dokumentiert frühere textkritische Fragestellungen. Es liegt auf der Hand, dass die Darstellung dann in gerafterer Form

erfolgen kann, wenn z.B. das eigentliche Problem, um das es geht, rein lingui-
stisch-philologischer Natur ist und die Textkritik höchstens indirekt betrifft.

Zu den allgemeinen Kriterien für die Aufnahme von Fällen in den Apparat
kommen weitere ergänzend hinzu, um bestimmte textkritische Probleme von besonderer Bedeutung im Apparat zu registrieren, die sonst ausgeschlossen worden
wären. Der Apparat soll andererseits aber nicht unnötig mit Fällen befrachtet werden, die weder für die Exegese noch für die Übersetzung von Belang sind. So
werden alle Varianten, die in hebräischen Textzeugen aus Qumran, Masada oder
Murabbaᶜât auftreten, bzw. in aramäischen für Daniel und Esra, im Apparat verzeichnet. Gleichfalls finden sich alle kᵊṯîḇ-qᵊrê Lesarten im Apparat, sofern es sich
nicht um rein orthographische Varianten handelt. Überdies enthält der Apparat
ebenfalls alle divergierenden Lesarten des samaritanischen Pentateuch, die nicht
rein orthographischer oder linguistischer Natur sind.

In analoger Weise kommen bestimmte zusätzliche Kriterien in Anwendung, um
den Umfang des Apparates in Grenzen zu halten, denn er soll nicht mit Ballast befrachtet werden, und er soll auch verifizierbar bleiben. So wird aus der Geniza von
Kairo nur publiziertes und kein nach dem Jahr 1000 niedergeschriebenes Material
berücksichtigt, weil solches für textkritische Zwecke kaum relevant sein dürfte, und
weil die Leserschaft des Apparates unveröffentlichte Handschriften nicht nachprü-
fen kann. Biblische Zitate in der deuterokanonischen, bzw. apokryphen Literatur, in
den Pseudepigraphen, den Schriften von Qumran, in Phylakterien, in den Werken
des Philo von Alexandrien und des Flavius Josephus, im Neuen Testament, in der
tannaitischen und amoräischen Literatur und bei den Kirchenvätern erscheinen im
Apparat nur bei besonderen textkritischen Problemen, sofern diese Schriften als
Zeugen einer möglichen hebräischen Textform angesehen werden können und unser
einziger Zugang zu einer spezifischen Textform über sie führt, oder sofern ihr Gewicht besonders schwer wiegt. Individuelle Lesarten, deren Zeugen allesamt alte
Übersetzungen sind und die offenkundig aus der Wiedergabe in eine andere Sprache
resultieren, da sie deren linguistischer Struktur und Stil folgen, sowie paraphrasie-
rende oder haggadische Wiedergaben sind aus dem Apparat ausgeschlossen, es sei
denn, sie hätten in der früheren Textkritik eine bedeutende Rolle gespielt. In analoger Weise wird der Targum eines biblischen Buches dann nicht regelmäßig angeführt, wenn er nach seiner gesamten Ausrichtung kaum als eigentlicher Zeuge für
den hebräischen Text herangezogen werden kann, weil er durchwegs zu Paraphrasen
und haggadischer Ausgestaltung neigt, wie beispielsweise der Targum des Hoheelie-
des. Der Apparat soll ja nicht mit Material befrachtet werden, das für die dargebote-
nen Textprobleme irrelevant ist.

Es gibt eine Anzahl Textzeugen, die nicht regelmäßig angeführt werden, weil
sie nicht beanspruchen können, durchgehend und eigenständig auf hebräischen
Vorlagen zu basieren. Dennoch scheinen sie gelegentlich Lesarten zu überliefern,
die auf eine solche hebräische Vorlage zurückgehen mögen. Es kommt ebenfalls
vor, dass sie bei bestimmten Textproblemen Licht in das Verständnis der im Apparat ausgebreiteten Textsituation bringen. Die Syro-Hexapla und verwandte Zeugen
der origenianischen Rezension der Septuaginta figurieren nur dann unter den Zeugen eines Falles, wenn ihre Lesarten sowohl von der ursprünglichen Septuaginta
als auch vom MT abweichen. Die Vetus Latina erscheint nur dann im Apparat,
wenn sie einerseits mit einem hebräischen Zeugen übereinstimmt oder wenn dafür
argumentiert werden könnte, sie biete eine eigenständige Textvariante, und wenn
sie andererseits mit keinem griechischen Textzeugen zusammengeht. Der samaritani-

sche Targum, der gallikanische Psalter und die koptischen Übersetzungen werden nicht durchgehend verzeichnet, aber ihr Zeugnis tritt überall dort in Erscheinung, wo ein Herausgeber der Meinung ist, es könne aus ihnen eine nützliche Einsicht gewonnen werden.

BHQ kollationiert vollständig die *sətumôt* und *pətuḥôt* der tiberiensischen Handschriften, die jeweils als regelmäßig angeführte Textzeugen herangezogen werden. Im Apparat selbst erscheinen jedoch nur jene Variationen, die eine Bedeutung für Übersetzung und Exegese beanspruchen können. Praktisch heißt das, dass nur Fälle im Apparat zu finden sind, in denen die Zeugen hinsichtlich des Vorhandenseins oder Fehlens von *sətumôt* und *pətuḥôt* auseinandergehen. Eine vollständige Übersicht der in M^L und den kollationierten tiberiensischen Handschriften vorkommenden *sətumôt* und *pətuḥôt* findet sich in der Einführung zu jedem biblischen Buch.

Im Unterschied zu den früheren Ausgaben der *Biblia Hebraica* führt *BHQ* die mittelalterlichen Handschriften der Kollationen von Kennicott und de Rossi oder in den Bibelausgaben Ginsburgs im Apparat nicht als Textzeugen an. Dieser Verzicht ergibt sich aus der sorgfältig begründeten Ansicht von Moshe H. Goshen-Gottstein, derzufolge diese Handschriften im Wesentlichen auf den von den großen tiberiensischen Masoreten geschaffenen Text und *Masora* beruhen. Daraus folgt, dass sie zur Textkritik kaum etwas beitragen, das von den maßgeblichen tiberiensischen Handschriften unabhängig wäre. Es wird jedoch auf die von Kennicott, de Rossi oder Ginsburg kollationierten Handschriften und Druckausgaben Bezug genommen, wenn andere Lesarten charakterisiert werden, oder auch in Kommentaren zu Fällen, in denen die bei Kennicott und de Rossi oder Ginsburg verzeichneten Lesarten einen Hang oder Trend im Verhältnis zum überlieferten Text belegen, den ein Herausgeber auch bei andern Textzeugen feststellt und den er illustrieren möchte.

In ganz anderer Weise unterscheidet sich *BHQ* von ihren Vorgänger-Ausgaben hinsichtlich der Handschriften vom Toten Meer und der Peschitta sowie – in freilich geringerem Maß – ebenfalls hinsichtlich Septuaginta und Vulgata. Was die Schriften vom Toten Meer anlangt, so konnte der kritische Apparat vollen Gebrauch aller unter ihnen vorhandener Bibeltexte machen, weil die Veröffentlichung dieser Schriften in den letzten zehn Jahren rasch fortschritt, und weil die mit der Herausgabe beauftragten Gelehrten freundlicherweise Zugang zu unpubliziertem, in Bearbeitung befindlichem Material gewährten. Die Peschitta liegt nunmehr in einer Reihe ausgezeichneter, vom Peschitta Projekt in Leiden erstellter Ausgaben vor, und wo solche noch ausstehen, konnten mit freundlicher Erlaubnis die Kollationen eingesehen werden. So stammen die im Apparat der *BHQ* verzeichneten Lesarten der Peschitta aus guten und frühen handschriftlichen Textzeugen anstatt aus den überholten gedruckten Ausgaben von mehr oder weniger guter Qualität, aus denen *BHK*^{3} und *BHS* geschöpft haben. Für die Septuaginta konnte auch *BHS* bereits auf mehrere Bände des Göttinger Septuaginta-Unternehmens zurückgreifen, aber seither hat dieses eine stattliche Anzahl weiterer und wichtiger Ausgaben herausgebracht. Überdies hat auch dieses Institut den Herausgebern biblischer Bücher, deren Septuaginta-Ausgabe in Göttingen erst in Bearbeitung begriffen ist, großzügig Zugang zu Kollationen und anderem Material gewährt. *BHK*^{3} und *BHS* konnten schon mehrere Bände der Vulgata in der San-Girolamo-Ausgabe benutzen, aber noch nicht für alle biblischen Bücher. *BHQ* kann diese große kritische Vulgata Ausgabe nun vollständig nutzen.

Die Beurteilung der Daten

Der Apparat der *BHQ* stellt sich nicht bloß die Aufgabe, die Daten der Textüberlieferung zu verzeichnen, sondern diese Daten auch zu gewichten, um festzustellen, wann einer Lesart im Basistext eine andere vorzuziehen ist, die von diesem abweicht. Demgemäß schlägt der Apparat gelegentlich vor, einer bezeugten, aber vom Basistext verschiedenen Lesart den Vorzug zu geben. Die Tatsache solcher Vorschläge impliziert notgedrungen eine subjektive Komponente in der Beurteilung einer Textsituation. Wie schon oft festgestellt wurde, ist ein solches subjektives Moment in der textkritischen Arbeit nicht zu umgehen. Da also ein subjektives Moment in einem Apparat, der unter mehreren vorhandenen Lesarten eine bestimmte bevorzugt, nicht zu vermeiden ist, haben sich die Herausgeber entschieden, dass der jeweilige Herausgeber seine Beurteilung der verschiedenen Varianten eines gegebenen Textproblems expliziert, sofern dies mit vernünftiger Sicherheit und Klarheit möglich ist. Dadurch soll der Apparat so transparent wie möglich gemacht werden. Am ausführlichsten finden sich solche Gewichtungen im Kommentarteil, wo bestimmte ausgewählte Fälle des Apparates breiter erörtert werden. Alle Fälle, in denen eine Lesart gegenüber dem Basistext der Ausgabe bevorzugt wird, erfahren generell eine derartige Erörterung im Kommentarteil. In vielen andern Fällen ist die Beurteilung mit Hilfe von kurzen Charakteristiken im Apparat selbst zum Ausdruck gebracht (vgl. unten die Liste der Abkürzungen und Definitionen). Der Zweck, den diese Ausgabe mit der Beurteilung von Lesarten im Apparat verfolgt, ist es, die früheste(n) erreichbare(n) Form(en) des Texts aufgrund vorhandener Textzeugen zu bestimmen. Diese Zielsetzung ergibt sich aus der doppelten Perspektive des Apparates, der die Daten der alten Textzeugen sowohl ausbreitet als auch gewichtet. Der Doppelrolle des Apparates (Ausbreitung und Gewichtung der Daten) entspricht die Art und Weise, in der die textkritischen Fälle im Apparat dargestellt werden.

In der Gewichtung der Textzeugen und ihrer Lesarten gehen die Herausgeber von der neueren Forschung auf dem Gebiet der Überlieferungsgeschichte der biblischen Texte aus. So sehen sie im Prozess der Textüberlieferung keinen bloß mechanischen Gesetzen folgenden Ablauf. Der Text wurde vielmehr zugleich mit einer bestimmten Bedeutung weitergegeben, die man in ihm las, und welche für die Gemeinschaften der Schreiber und Übersetzer wichtig war. Daraus folgt, dass Textkritiker nicht nur materielle Verderbnisse gewärtigen dürfen, die bei der konkreten Handschriftenherstellung auftreten, sondern ebenso auf Änderungen des Textes achten müssen, die aufgrund bestimmter Deutungen erfolgt sind. Im Falle der alten Übersetzungen ist es in den Augen der Herausgeber auch notwendig, innerhalb der Gesamtübersetzung eventuell vorkommende Teilübersetzungen mit ihren jeweiligen Besonderheiten zu unterscheiden sowie das Übersetzungswerk auf seine Übersetzungstechnik und die linguistischen Eigengesetzlichkeiten der Zielsprache – im Vergleich mit dem Hebräischen als Ausgangssprache – zu prüfen.

Aufbau und Darstellung der Fälle

Die Herausgeber sehen ihre Aufgabe darin, das Material so anzuordnen, dass Leserschaften, die andere Auffassungen haben oder sich für andere Aspekte der Textüberlieferung interessieren, in die Lage versetzt werden, ihre eigenen Schlussfolgerungen aus dem vorgelegten Material ziehen zu können. Daher besteht der

Hauptteil des Apparates, unmittelbar auf das jeweilige Lemma aus dem Basistext der Ausgabe folgend, aus den Lesarten der kollationierten Textzeugen und aus der Anordnung dieser Zeugen. (Siehe Fig. 1, in der die folgenden Erläuterungen an einem Beispiel veranschaulicht werden.)

Die Notierung der Lesarten erfolgt im Apparat so, dass nach dem Lemma des Basistexts die abweichenden Lesarten zu stehen kommen. Nach jeder Lesart, ob Lemma oder Variante, folgen die Sigla der Zeugen, die sie stützen. In der Regel ist der Hauptzeuge für eine Variante im Wortlaut angeführt. Die in der Reihe der Varianten zuerst gebotene ist jene Lesart, die das Textproblem erzeugt. Die Reihenfolge der danach notierten Varianten sowie der aufgelisteten Zeugen nach jeder Variante entspricht einer Reihenfolge der Sprachen – nämlich: Hebräisch, Griechisch, Lateinisch, andere – und innerhalb einer jeden Sprache wird eine ungefähre aufsteigende chronologische Abfolge eingehalten. Wenn zwei Varianten ein Textproblem hervorbringen, stehen sie vor den andern Varianten, und die Abfolge unter ihnen gehorcht den soeben beschriebenen sprachlichen und chronologischen Kriterien.

Der Apparat von *BHQ* misst insbesondere solchen Fällen Bedeutung bei, in denen einer oder mehrere Textzeugen eine Lesart bieten, die begründeterweise als Wiedergabe einer vom Basistext abweichenden hebräischen Vorlage interpretiert werden kann. Daher entspricht die Zuordnung der Zeugen untereinander einem möglichen hebräischen Text, der ihnen zu Grunde liegen mag. So werden z.B. zwei griechische Zeugen mit verschiedenem Wortlaut, aber gleichwertiger Bedeutung einander zugeordnet, wenn der Herausgeber der Ansicht ist, dass sie beide trotz ihres verschiedenen Wortlauts der gleichen hebräischen Vorlage entsprechen. Zuordnungen hängen jeweils von dem besonderen Aspekt ab, unter dem das betreffende Textproblem betrachtet wird. Ein Textzeuge, der unter dem Aspekt des gestellten Textproblems mit dessen Hauptzeugen übereinstimmt, obschon er sich in anderer Hinsicht von ihm unterscheidet, erscheint hinter dem Hauptzeugen, aber in Klammern, zur Bezeichnung der zwischen beiden außerhalb des formellen Textproblems existierenden Unterschiede. Dabei ist immer vorausgesetzt, dass solche durch Klammern signalisierte Unterschiede einer möglichen hebräischen Vorlage entsprechen müssen, von der sie begründeterweise abgeleitet werden könnten.

Eine als sekundär beurteilte Lesart (wobei es sich durchaus auch um das Lemma des Basistextes handeln kann) kann der Herausgeber charakterisieren, sofern ihm dies sinnvoll und hinreichend wahrscheinlich erscheint. Er wählt dazu die entsprechende Abkürzung aus; sie erscheint in Klammern hinter den Siglen, welche die betreffende Lesart bezeugen. In der Regel charakterisiert diese Beschreibung eine für sekundär gehaltene Lesart im Vergleich mit der für originaler gehaltenen, bevorzugten Lesart. Wo eine Beschreibung jedoch eine sekundäre Lesart im Vergleich mit einer andern sekundären Lesart charakterisiert, steht hinter ihrer Charakterisierung die Sigel jener anderen verglichenen sekundären Lesart, auf die sich die Charakterisierung bezieht. Lesarten aus den alten Übersetzungen im Apparat lassen nicht erkennen, ob ihre Textunterschiede nur auf der Ebene der Übersetzer oder auch auf der ihrer hebräischen Vorlage liegen. Daher werden Lesarten der Übersetzungen gelegentlich ausdrücklich so beschrieben, dass die Stufe des Textunterschieds deutlich wird. Dabei bezeichnet "hebr" die Stufe der Vorlage, "vrs"/"vrss" die Ebene der Übersetzung(en).

In solchen Fällen, in denen nach Meinung des Herausgebers eine andere Lesart

als die des Basistextes vorzuziehen ist, steht diese bevorzugte Lesart am Ende des Eintrags, mit einem senkrechten Doppelstrich vom Vorhergehenden getrennt und mit der Abkürzung "pref" (*preferred*, bevorzugte Lesart) versehen. Die Textzeugen für die bevorzugte Lesart werden wiederholt. Wenn keiner der vorhandenen Textzeugen die bevorzugte Lesart direkt bietet, sodass diese aus den Textzeugen nur erschlossen ist, erhält sie die Bezeichnung "origin", d.h., sie wird als der indirekt bezeugte Ausgangspunkt der vorhandenen Lesarten betrachtet. Falls die sprachliche Form von so erschlossenen bevorzugten Lesarten in der Sprache der biblischen Periode nicht belegt ist, erhält sie die Qualifikation "unattest" (unbelegt) oder "conjec-phil" (philologische Konjektur), je nach der Art der externen Bezeugung solcher Lesarten. Wo die bevorzugte Lesart eine Konjektur ist, steht nicht die Abkürzung "pref" (*preferred*, bevorzugte Lesart), sondern die Qualifikation "conjec" (Konjektur). In Übereinstimmung mit Ausrichtung und Zielsetzung des Apparats, der die *Überlieferungsgeschichte* des Textes belegen will, ist mit den vorgeschlagenen bevorzugten Lesarten nicht beabsichtigt, die literarische Entstehungsgeschichte der Texte zu rekonstruieren. Lesarten, die im Urteil der Herausgeber in einem gegebenen Buch eine andere literarische Tradition als die des Basistextes der Ausgabe widerspiegeln, werden mit der Bezeichnung "lit" versehen (vgl. Definitionen und Charakterisierungen weiter unten).

Überall wo eine textkritische Frage im Kommentarteil der Ausgabe ausführlicher erörtert wird, steht im entsprechenden Eintrag im Apparat das Symbol ⁙. Wird das Textproblem jedoch im Zusammenhang mit einem andern Fall im Textkommentar behandelt, stehen im Apparateintrag die kombinierten Symbole →⁙ zusammen mit dem Verweis auf die Stelle, an der die Diskussion stattfindet. Jeder Eintrag im Apparat wird mit dem Symbol • geschlossen. Wenn dasselbe Lemma mehrere Einträge im Apparat erfordert, so sind diese Einträge durch das Zeichen ○ voneinander getrennt; erst der letzte dieser Einträge wird wieder mit dem Zeichen • abgeschlossen.

DIE ANORDNUNG DER SEITE

Die einzelnen Bestandteile dieser Ausgabe – Basistext, *Masora*, Apparat, Textkommentar, Übersetzung der masoretischen Einträge – werden wie folgt dargeboten (siehe dazu Fig. 2, in der an einem Beispiel der Aufbau einer Seite erläutert wird):

Den obern Teil der Seite nimmt der Text der Handschrift M^L ein. Die Zählung der Kapitel und Verse wird auf dem inneren Rand der Seite abgedruckt. Die Abschnitte der synagogalen Lesungen, wie sie M^L verzeichnet, und ähnliche masoretische Marginalien, z.B. umgekehrte *Nûnîm*, ebenso wie M^L sie bietet, stehen am äußeren Seitenrand. Zusätzlich stehen die allgemein gebräuchlichen Namen der Lesungen des Jahreszyklus im Pentateuch zusammen mit dem Namen des Buches fortlaufend in der Kopfleiste zuoberst auf der rechten Seite des aufgeschlagenen Buches.

Die Einträge der *Masora parva* von M^L kommen auf den äußeren Seitenrand zu stehen. Den Bezug einer solchen *Masora parva* zu einem Wort oder einer Wortgruppe im Text stellen *circelli* her, die im Text auf dem betreffendem Wort oder zwischen Wörtern eines ganzen Ausdrucks stehen. Ausnahmen bilden dabei jene wenigen Fälle, wo die Handschrift zwar eine *Masora parva,* aber keinen *circellus* im

Text bietet, oder wo sie umgekehrt einen *circellus* im Text aufweist, dem keine *Masora parva* am Rand entspricht. Wie schon gesagt soll das Glossar der masoretischen Termini und Abkürzungen, das der Ausgabe beigegeben ist, die Interpretation der *Masora parva* erschließen. Sofern Einträge der Mp dem Text nicht entsprechen oder schwer aufzuschlüsseln sind, werden sie im Kommentarteil ausführlich behandelt, so dass in allen diesen Fällen der Kommentar die nötigen Aufschlüsse gibt.

Die *Masora magna* von M^L wird unmittelbar unter dem Basistext in einem eigenen Register wiedergegeben. Wie auch in der Handschrift selber gibt es kein Verweiszeichen, das diese *Masora* mit den entsprechenden Wörtern oder Wortgruppen verknüpft. Doch die Einträge der *Masora magna* beziehen sich in der Regel auf Wörter und Ausdrücke, die auch durch eine entsprechende Notiz der *Masora parva* am Rand der betreffenden Zeile signalisiert werden. Um den Bezug der *Masora magna* zu den entsprechenden Wörtern und Wendungen im Text leicht auffindbar zu machen, führt die *BHQ* die Notate der *Masora magna* nach der Reihenfolge der Wörter und Ausdrücke im biblischen Text an, unerachtet der sich daraus ergebenden Abweichungen von der Anordnung der *Masora magna* auf einer gegebenen Seite in der Handschrift M^L. Es wurde schon erwähnt, dass außerdem am Anfang jedes Notats eine Kapitel- und Versangabe hinzugefügt wurde. Eine Übersetzung aller *Masora-magna*-Notate findet sich im Kommentarteil, wobei schwer verständliche oder mit dem Text von M^L auseinanderklaffende Einträge der *Masora magna* auch eingehender erörtert werden.

Der textkritische Apparat nimmt den unteren Seitenrand unterhalb des Basistextes und der *Masora magna* ein. Die Herausgeber verzichteten auf Buchstaben, Zahlen oder Symbole im Basistext der Ausgabe, um den Bezug zwischen Text und Apparateinträgen herzustellen. Stattdessen zeigt die vollständige Wiedergabe des betreffenden Wortes oder Wortgefüges aus dem Basistext am Anfang jedes Eintrags im Apparat als Lemma des behandelten Textproblems eindeutig, worauf sich der Apparateintrag bezieht. Der Apparat ist im wesentlichen ein in sich abgeschlossenes Ganzes. Sofern jedoch ein Fall im Kommentarteil der Ausgabe noch ausführlicher erörtert wird, weist ein Zeichen im Apparateintrag ausdrücklich darauf hin.

Am linken Rand der ersten Zeile des kritischen Apparates steht gegebenenfalls der Verweis auf parallele Texte, die dem auf derselben Seite abgedruckten Basistext entsprechen. Wenn dieser Paralleltext überdies als Textzeuge im Apparat angeführt wird, so wird auf ihn durch daneben das Zeichen für Textparallelen (//) oder durch das Kürzel des betreffenden Buches (z.B. Neh) verwiesen, in der Regel ohne weitere Kapitel- und Versangaben.

DIE HANDSCHRIFT M^L, IHR TEXT UND IHRE MASORA

In den Einleitungen zu den einzelnen biblischen Büchern sind die nicht-tiberiensischen Textzeugen beschrieben und die jeweiligen Ausgaben genannt, in denen sie bei der Bearbeitung herangezogen wurden. Da jedoch die Handschrift M^L der grundlegende Textzeuge für alle Bücher ist, beschreiben wir sie zusammenfassend hier in der allgemeinen Einleitung, damit die Charakteristika von M^L nicht bei jedem biblischen Buch wiederholt werden müssen. In einem weiteren Abschnitt folgt eine kurze Beschreibung der andern tiberiensischen masoretischen Textzeugen, die für diese Ausgabe benutzt werden.

Das Manuskript, das unter der Signatur EBP. I B 19a in der russischen Nationalbibliothek in St. Petersburg (früher: Öffentliche Staatsbibliothek Saltikow-
Schtschedrin, Leningrad; vor 1917: Kaiserliche öffentliche Bibliothek, St. Petersburg) aufbewahrt wird, ist unter der Bezeichnung *Codex Leningradensis, Kodex
Leningrad* bekannt. 1875 wurde sie von Harkavy und Strack kodikologisch beschrieben: A. Harkavy und H. L. Strack, *Catalog der hebräischen Bibelhandschriften der kaiserlichen öffentlichen Bibliothek* (St. Petersburg: C. Ricker, 1875; Leipzig: J. C. Hinrichs, 1875). Diese für lange Zeit autoritative Beschreibung ist vor
kurzem durch eine sehr viel gründlichere und dem heutigen Wissensstand
entsprechende neue Beschreibung ersetzt worden: M. Beit-Arié, C. Sirat, M. Glatzer, *Codices Hebraicis Litteris Exarati Quo Tempore Scripti Fuerint Exhibentes,*
Vol. 1, Jusqu'à 1020 (Monumenta Palaeographica Medii Aevi, Series Hebraica;
Turnhout: Brepols, 1997), 114–31. In der Forschung fanden Text und *Masora* der
Leningrader Handschrift viel Beachtung, angefangen mit Kahles Arbeiten. Bedeutende neuere Abhandlungen zu M^L finden sich in den Werken von M. Breuer
(כתר ארם צובה והנוסח המקובל של המקרא [Jerusalem: Mosad HaRav Kook,
1976]), I. Yeivin (*Introduction to the Tiberian Masorah* [Missoula: Scholars Press,
1980]), E. J. Revell ("The Leningrad Codex as a Representative of the Masoretic
Text", in *The Leningrad Codex* [ed. D. N. Freedman et al., Grand Rapids: William
B. Eerdmans; Leiden: Brill, 1998], xxix–xlvi) und in zahlreichen Werken A. Dotans. Die folgenden Ausführungen beruhen auf diesen Studien, aber auch auf der
eigenen Erfahrung der Herausgeber mit M^L, wobei diese Erfahrung sich bis zum
Abschluss des *BHQ*-Projektes ohne Zweifel vertiefen wird.

Der Kodex Leningradensis ist in Kairo entstanden. Shemuʾel ben Jaʿaqov
schrieb ihn für Rabbi Mevorak Ben Josef ha-Kohen. Das Entstehungsjahr wird
nach verschiedenen Kalendern angegeben. Diese ergeben jedoch bei ihrer Übertragung in die Chronologie der heute üblichen Zeitrechnung vier verschiedene
Jahre: 1008, 1009, 1010 und 1013. Im Anschluss an Beit-Arié, Sirat und Glatzer
halten wir 1008 als Entstehungsjahr fest. Shemuʾel ben Jaʿaqov schrieb und
korrigierte alle Teile der Handschrift: Konsonantentext, Punktierung und *Masora*.
Der Kodex umfasst 491 Pergamenblätter, beidseitig beschrieben mit schwarzer
oder dunkelbrauner Tinte. Die ersten 463 Blätter enthalten die 24 Bücher der hebräischen Bibel mit Vokalen und Akzenten sowie *Masora parva* und *magna*. Der
Bibeltext erscheint in drei Spalten zu je 27 Zeilen pro Seite, ausgenommen Psalmen, Ijjob und Sprüche, die in zwei Kolumnen pro Seite geschrieben sind, ebenfalls zu je 27 Zeilen. Die *Masora parva* steht an den seitlichen Rändern und zwischen den Spalten, die *Masora magna* am oberen und unteren Seitenrand. Die
Handschrift weist die typischen kodikologischen Eigentümlichkeiten der
mittelalterlichen Handschriften aus dem Nahen Osten auf. Eine ausführliche kodikologische Erörterung mit dem vollständigen Wortlaut und der Übersetzung aller
Kolophone findet sich in dem oben angeführten Werk von Beit-Arié, Sirat und
Glatzer.

Im großen Ganzen ist die Handschrift gut erhalten. Im Einzelnen gibt es jedoch
mancherlei Verderbnisse und Schäden, die in den Anmerkungen zum Erhaltungszustand der oben zitierten Facsimile-Ausgabe Eerdmans-Brill verzeichnet sind.
Diese Schäden führen nur selten zur Unleserlichkeit, aber es gibt Stellen, an denen
sie sich negativ auswirken. So ist beispielsweise ein guter Teil der Schrift in der
rechten Spalte auf fol 250r mit Jer 7:28-31 abgeblättert und von einer späteren,
weniger sorgfältigen Hand neu mit Tinte nachgezogen worden. Ähnliches lässt sich

auch in benachbarten Spalten feststellen. Dabei schlichen sich Fehler ein: in V. 30 hatte die erste Hand klar נְאָם־יְהֹוָה geschrieben. Wer immer es war, der die verblasste Schrift nachzog, missverstand die in Resten übriggebliebenen ursprünglichen Schriftzeichen und schrieb fälschlicherweise נְאֻם־יְהֹוה. Dass die Schrift gelöscht und neu geschrieben worden ist, ergibt sich mit hinreichender Deutlichkeit aus der Schwarzweiß-Aufnahme der Eerdmans-Brill Facsimile-Ausgabe, aber die Einzelheiten des Vorgefallenen lassen sich erst mit Hilfe der Farbaufnahmen klar interpretieren, die dem Projekt zur Verfügung stehen.

Im sechsten der insgesamt acht Kolophone (fol 479r) teilt Shemuʾel ben Jaᶜaqov mit, dass er seine Abschrift aufgrund anderer Handschriften korrigiert habe, die Aharon Ben Mosche Ben Ascher selbst geschrieben und korrigiert hatte. Diese Angabe impliziert eine weitgehende Übereinstimmung des korrigierten Textes und der *Masora* von M^L mit der Ben Ascher Tradition. Zahlreiche neuere Untersuchungen bestätigen Schemuʾels Angabe. In den im *Kitāb al-khilāf* verzeichneten Divergenzen zwischen Ben Ascher und Ben Naftali entspricht M^A in 94% der Fälle Ben Ascher, gefolgt von M^L mit 92% Übereinstimmungen mit Ben Ascher. Beide Handschriften folgen Ben Ascher in 90% derjenigen Fälle, in denen Ben Ascher und Ben Naftali sich gemeinsam von anderen masoretischen Traditionen unterscheiden (Yeivin, *Tiberian Masorah*, 16 und 19). Der *Kitāb al-khilāf* ist herausgegeben worden von L. Lipschütz, *Kitāb al-khilāf: Mishael ben Uzziel's Treatise on the Differences Between Ben Asher and Ben Naphtali* (The Hebrew University Bible Project Monograph Series, 2; Jerusalem: Magnes Press, 1965). Diese Entsprechung zwischen M^A und M^L ist weit enger als die mit irgendeinem andern Zeugen der Ben Ascher Tradition. So erscheint M^L als ein hervorragender Zeuge der Ben Ascher Tradition des tiberiensischen masoretischen Texts, ein Zeuge, der in seiner Konformität mit dieser Tradition nur noch von M^A um ein Weniges übertroffen wird und unter allen vollständig erhaltenen Zeugen diese Tradition am besten repräsentiert. Es ist heute eine weithin anerkannte Tatsache, dass es sich beim tiberiensischen masoretischen Text um den sorgfältig bewahrten Nachfahren einer Textüberlieferung handelt, deren Vorfahren unter den Schriftrollen vom Toten Meer zu finden sind.

Es wurde schon oft darauf hingewiesen, dass M^L bei aller Qualität doch nicht mit der gleichen Sorgfalt wie M^A geschrieben ist. Der Grad an Sorgfalt und die Zahl der Unterschiede gegenüber M^A sind aber für jeden Teil des Textes verschieden. Was den Konsonantentext betrifft, gibt es, abgesehen von den Vokalbuchstaben, nur wenig Varianten. Beim Gebrauch der Vokalbuchstaben zeigt M^L eine leichte Vorliebe für geläufigere Schreibweisen. Varianten in Bezug auf Punktuation und Akzente kommen ebenfalls nur selten vor. Etwas zahlreicher sind Unterschiede in der Plazierung der *sətumôt* und *pətuḥôt*.

Die wichtigsten Unterschiede zwischen M^L und M^A und die deutlichsten Beispiele für mangelnde Sorgfalt in M^L finden sich in der *Masora*. Der materielle Inhalt der masoretischen Einträge deckt sich in M^L ziemlich mit dem von M^A, aber welche Phänomene kommentiert werden, und in welcher Art und Weise die Information in den Einträgen dargeboten wird, ist in den beiden Handschriften verschieden. Wie aus mehreren Untersuchungen und aus dem Werk von G. Weil in *BHS* hervorgeht, gibt es in M^L eine Reihe von Beispielen dafür, dass die *Masora* nicht dem Text der Handschrift entspricht, dass Verweise auf Bibelstellen falsch abgeschrieben oder verwechselt worden sind, und dass masoretische Einträge am falschen Platz zu stehen scheinen. Dennoch behält die *Masora* von M^L trotz ihrer

Mängel einen echten Wert, weil M^L eine vollständige Handschrift ist und ihre *Masora* einige spezifische, nur in M^L vorkommende Elemente bietet.

DIE ANDEREN TIBERIENSISCHEN TEXTZEUGEN

Sieben andere tiberiensische masoretische Handschriften werden in dieser Ausgabe für verschiedene Teile der Bibel kollationiert. Der Aleppo Kodex (M^A) wird für alle Teile der Bibel kollationiert, in denen er erhalten ist. Für die Tora werden folgende Handschriften verglichen: Oriental Ms. 4445 der British Library (M^B), Handschrift EBP. II B 17 der russischen Nationalbibliothek in St. Petersburg (M^{L17}), Handschrift Sassoon 507 (M^{S5}), jetzt Heb 24° 5702 der National- und Universitätsbibliothek in Jerusalem. Für die Propheten wird der Kairoer Prophetenkodex (M^C) kollationiert. Für die Hagiographen (Schriften) wird Additional Ms. 1753 der Universitätsbibliothek Cambridge (M^Y) verglichen. Für die im Aleppo Kodex fehlenden Bücher werden entweder Handschrift Sassoon 1053 (M^{S1}) oder EBP. II B 34 der russischen Nationalbibliothek St. Petersburg (M^{L34}) herangezogen. Hier folgen kurze Beschreibungen dieser Handschriften und die Bezeichnung der Ausgaben oder/und Mikrofilme, die in dieser Ausgabe für die Kollation und die Zitate benützt werden. In diesem ersten Faszikel basieren die Beschreibungen mehr auf den einschlägigen Forschungen zu diesen Zeugen als auf ihrer direkten Benützung durch die Herausgeber der einzelnen biblischen Bücher. Zusätzlich zu der zitierten Bibliographie zu diesen handschriftlichen Zeugen ist in dieser Beschreibung auch Yeivin, *Tiberian Masorah*, benützt worden.

   – Der *Aleppo Kodex* (M^A) ist oft Gegenstand von Untersuchungen geworden, wie das ja auch bei seiner Bedeutung nicht anders zu erwarten ist. Das Werk von M. Beit-Arié, C. Sirat und M. Glatzer, *Codices Hebraicis Litteris Exarati*, 1:65–72, bietet eine detaillierte kodikologische Beschreibung. Die folgende Beschreibung beruht, wo nichts anderes vermerkt ist, auf dieser Untersuchung von Beit-Arié, Sirat und Glatzer. In der *BHQ* wird dieser Textzeuge nach der Faksimile-Ausgabe von M. Goshen-Gottstein, *The Aleppo Codex* (vol. 1, The Plates, Jerusalem: Magnes Press, 1976) zitiert.

   Obschon in den erhaltenen Teilen der Handschrift kein Kolophon vorhanden ist, wird der Konsonantentext von M^A Salomon Ben Buya^{c}a zugeschrieben. Die Vokalisierung, Akzentuierung und *Masora* sowie die Verifizierung des Textes werden als das Werk von Aaron Ben Ascher betrachtet. Diese Zuschreibungen ergeben sich aus Informationen, die in vier Widmungsangaben auf dem Rand der Handschrift selbst enthalten sind. Man hat die Meinung vertreten, es handle sich um jene Handschrift, die Maimonides benützt hat und von der er sagte, sie sei durch Ben Ascher korrigiert und verifiziert worden. Aufgrund dieser Zuschreibungen vermutete man, dass die Handschrift in Tiberias entstanden ist. Beit-Arié, Sirat und Glatzer nehmen für die Entstehung der Handschrift ein Datum um 930 an.

   Von der ursprünglichen Handschrift sind 295 Blätter erhalten, die folgenden Inhalt haben: Dt 28:17 bis zum Ende des Deuteronomiums, Josua, Richter, 1 und 2 Samuel, 1 und 2 Könige (ausgenommen 2 Kön 14:21–18:13), Jesaja, Jeremia (ausgenommen Jer 29:9–31:34 und Teile von Jer 32:1-25), Ezechiel, die Zwölf (ausgenommen Amos 8:13 bis Ende von Amos, Obadja, Jona, Micha 1:1–5:1, Zefanja 3:20 bis Ende von Zefanja, Haggai, Sach 1:1–9:17), 1 und 2 Chronik, Psalmen

(ausgenommen 15:1–25:1), Ijjob, Proverbien, Ruth, Hohelied 1:1–3:11. In den erhaltenen Blättern sind geringere Beschädigungen zu beklagen, die aber nirgends zu Textverlusten geführt haben. Die einzige Ausnahme ist Fol 148, wo Teile von Jer 32:1-25 verloren gingen. Die Handschrift ist auf Pergament in Quadratschrift geschrieben. Die Tinte ist dunkelbraun. Der Text ist meistens auf drei Kolumnen auf einer Seite verteilt. In Ijjob, Proverbien und Psalmen sind es zwei Kolumnen. Die *Masora parva* steht auf den Seitenrändern oder zwischen den Kolumnen, während die *Masora magna* den obern und untern Rand der Seite einnimmt.

Die Handschrift wurde mit großer Sorgfalt hergestellt. Sie weist Anzeichen einer sorgfältigen Korrektur auf und ist unter allen bekannten Handschriften der hebräischen Bibel die reinste Repräsentantin der Ben Ascher Tradition. Wie oben bereits erwähnt, entspricht M^A in 94% der Fälle, die im *Kitāb al-khilāf* als Divergenzen zwischen Ben Ascher und Ben Naftali aufgezählt werden, der Form von Ben Ascher. Überdies deckt sich M^A in 90% der Fälle mit Ben Ascher und Ben Naftali, wo diese beiden Masoreten sich von andern masoretischen Autoritäten gemeinsam unterscheiden (Yeivin, *Tiberian Masorah,* 16).

– Die Handschrift *Oriental Ms. 4445 der British Library* (M^B) wurde in verschiedenen Zusammenhängen Gegenstand der Forschung. Folgende zwei Studien liegen der hier vorgelegten Beschreibung zugrunde: G. Margoliouth, *Catalogue of the Hebrew and Samaritan Manuscripts in the British Museum* (London: British Museum, 1899), Part I, 36–39; A. Dotan, "Reflections Towards a Critical Edition of Pentateuch Codex Or. 4445", in *Estudios Masoréticos (X Congreso de la IOMS): En memoria de Harry M. Orlinsky* (ed. E. Fernández Tejero und M.T. Ortega Monasterio; Madrid: Instituto de Filología del CSIC, 1993), 39–51. In der *BHQ* wird M^B in einem Mikrofilm der Handschrift kollationiert und zitiert.

In der Handschrift fehlt ein Kolophon. Sie gilt als einer der frühesten tiberiensischen Zeugen, der in dieser Ausgabe benutzt wird. Margoliouth setzt ihre Entstehung in der Mitte des 9. Jh. an (*Hebrew and Samaritan Manuscripts,* 36), Dotan neigt der zweiten Hälfte des 9. Jh. zu, obgleich er die Frage der Entstehungszeit zuletzt unentschieden lässt ("Codex Or. 4445", 50). Yeivin denkt an ein Datum um 925 (*Tiberian Masorah*, 19). Schreiber und Herkunft der Handschrift sind nach allgemeiner Ansicht nicht bestimmbar. Immerhin hat Dotan den Schreiber als Nissi Ben Daniel ha-Kohen identifizieren wollen, weil dieser Name als Akrostichon in bestimmten masoretischen Notizen erscheint. Nach Dotan hat dieser Schreiber das ganze Manuskript: Konsonantentext, Vokalisierung, Akzentuierung, *Masora*, geschrieben ("Codex Or. 4445", 50). Margoliouth und Dotan halten eine persische Herkunft für möglich.

M^B enthält den Text und die *Masora* (*Masora magna* und *Masora parva*) von Gen 39:20 bis Dt 1:33, ausgenommen Num 7:46-73; 9:12–10:18. Die Handschrift umfasst 186 Pergamentblätter. Die Seiten sind in drei Kolumnen unterteilt. Die fehlenden Teile des Pentateuchs wurden später durch Papierblätter ergänzt, die nach einem Kolophon im Jahr 1540 entstanden sind.

Nach Yeivin folgt M^B in 80% der Fälle, in denen nach dem *Kitāb al-khilāf* Ben Ascher und Ben Naftali getrennte Wege gehen, dem Muster von Ben Ascher, und in 73% der Fälle geht die Handschrift dort mit Ben Ascher und Ben Naftali zusammen, wo diese beiden Masoreten sich von andern masoretischen Autoritäten gemeinsam unterscheiden (*Tiberian Masorah,* 19). Paul Kahle zählte 83% Übereinstimmungen zwischen M^B und Ben Ascher im Gegensatz zu Ben Naftali: P. Kahle, "The Hebrew Ben Asher Bible Manuscripts," *VT* 1 (1951): 167. Margoliouth weist

eine bestimmte Anzahl von Beispielen nach, wo M^B von der spezifischen tiberiensischen Tradition abweicht (z.B. in der Platzierung der *sətumôt* und *pətuḥôt*). Margoliouth und Dotan halten manche dieser Besonderheiten in Text und Akzentuierung (und in der *Masora* nach Dotans Untersuchung) für Zeichen des hohen Alters der in dieser Handschrift bezeugten Tradition.

– Die *Handschrift EBP. II B 17 (M^{L17})* in der russischen Nationalbibliothek in St. Petersburg haben M. Beit-Arié, C. Sirat und M. Glatzer kodikologisch beschrieben (*Codices Hebraicis Litteris Exarati*, 1:53–64). Diese leicht zugängliche Beschreibung der Handschrift bildet die Grundlage der folgenden summarischen Angaben, soweit keine andere bibliographische Quelle genannt ist. In der *BHQ* wird dieser Textzeuge in einem Mikrofilm gelesen und kollationiert.

Nach den beiden Kolophonen der Handschrift wurde der Konsonantentext von Salomon ha-Levi Ben Buyaᶜa niedergeschrieben, dem gleichen Schreiber, der M^A geschrieben hat. Vokale, Akzente, *Masora* und Buchschmuck sind das Werk von Efraim Ben Buyaᶜa, der den Text auch verifiziert hat. Im zweiten Kolophon findet sich eine Datumsangabe, die unserem Jahr 929 entspricht. Es ist eine sehr schöne und sorgfältige Handschrift. Yeivin ist der Ansicht, dass die Handschrift in den vom *Kitāb al-khilāf* verzeichneten Divergenzen Ben Ascher – Ben Naftali keine klare Übereinstimmung weder mit Ben Ascher noch mit Ben Naftali erkennen lässt (*Tiberian Masorah*, 23).

Diese Pentateuch-Handschrift umfasst heute 242 Blätter, die ziemlich viele Schäden und Lücken aufweisen. Erhalten sind folgende Teile der Tora: Gen 2:5–6:3; 8:9–20:9; 21:17–25:22; 27:6–41:43; Gen 42:35–Ex 23:7; Ex 25:2–Lev 19:20; Lev 20:8–25:17; Lev 25:44–Num 10:35; Num 17:6 bis Deuteronomium Ende. Es ist eine Pergament-Handschrift in Quadratschrift. Die Tinte ist dunkelbraun; oft ist sie flockig geworden, besonders auf der Fleischseite des Pergaments. Der Text erscheint, vom Schilfmeerlied, Ex 15, und dem Lied Moses, Dt 32, abgesehen, in drei Kolumnen. Die *Masora parva* steht am Seitenrand und zwischen den Kolumnen, die *Masora magna* auf dem obern und untern Rand der Seite. Manchmal sind die obersten Zeilen des Bibeltextes und *Masora magna* Notizen verschwunden, weil der obere Teil mancher Blätter Schaden gelitten hat.

– Der *Damaskus Pentateuch,* auch in einer älteren Bezeichnung als Handschrift *Sassoon 507* bekannt, jetzt unter der Signatur Heb. 24° 5702 in der National- und Universitätsbibliothek Jerusalem (M^{S5}), wird beschrieben von D.S. Sassoon, *Ohel David: Descriptive Catalogue of the Hebrew and Samaritan Manuscripts in the Sassoon Library, London* (Oxford: Oxford University Press; London: Humphrey Milford, 1932), 1:22–23. Dies ist die hauptsächliche Quelle für die folgenden Angaben. In *BHQ* wurde M^{S5} in einem Mikrofilm oder in der Faksimile-Ausgabe gelesen: M. Beit-Arié, *The Damascus Pentateuch* (vol. 2 in *Early Hebrew Manuscripts in Facsimile*; ed. M. Beit-Arié; Copenhagen: Rosenkilde and Bagger; Baltimore: The Johns Hopkins University Press, 1982).

Zeitlich steht M^{S5} zwischen den Daten von M^B und M^L. Das genauere Datum wird kontrovers diskutiert. Yeivin datiert die Handschrift ins 10. Jh. (*Tiberian Masorah*, 21), während Sassoon das 9. Jh. annimmt (*Ohel David*, 23). Das ist auch das von Loewinger vorgeschlagene Datum, während Beit-Arié an eine Zeit um das Jahr 1000 denkt (*CTAT*, 3:ix). Eine ähnliche Meinungsverschiedenheit herrscht in der Frage der Herkunft: Tiberias (Sassoon, Loewinger), allgemeiner Palästina oder Ägypten (Beit-Arié).

M^{S5} umfasst den vokalisierten Pentateuch von Gen 9:26 bis Deuteronomium

Ende, mit der Lücke Ex 18:1-23. Die Handschrift besitzt *Masora magna* und *parva*. Sie besteht aus 229 Blättern. Die Seite ist in drei Kolumnen aufgeteilt.

Das Manuskript ist sorgfältig, aber es lässt sich weniger klar in die masoretische Tradition einordnen als andere in *BHQ* verwendete Handschriften. Nach Yeivin benützt es für die Akzente ein "gemischtes System". In 52% der Fälle, wo nach dem *Kitāb al-khilāf* Ben Ascher und Ben Naftali auseinandergehen, folgt M^{S5} dem Modell Ben Aschers, und in 76% deckt es sich mit Ben Ascher-Ben Naftali, wo diese beiden gemeinsam gegen die andern masoretischen Autoritäten stehen (Yeivin, *Tiberian Masorah,* 21). Sassoon meint feststellen zu können, dass die *Masora* zwar Ben Ascher folge, aber der Text Ben Naftali entspreche (*Ohel David,* 22).

– Der *Kairo Kodex* (M^C) ist mit Recht sehr oft untersucht worden. M. Beit-Arié, C. Sirat und M. Glatzer haben die Handschrift kodikologisch beschrieben (*Codices Hebraicis Litteris Exarati,* 1:25–39). Ihre Beschreibung dient den folgenden Angaben als Quelle, es sei denn etwas anderes vermerkt. In *BHQ* wird die Handschrift nach der Ausgabe von F. Perez Castro et al. benützt: *El Codice de Profetas de El Cairo* (7 Bde. Text; Madrid: CSIC, 1979–1988; 4 Bde. Indices; Madrid: CSIC, 1992–1997).

Eines der beiden Kolophone der Handschrift schreibt Konsonantentext, Vokale, Akzente und *Masora* Moshe Ben Asher zu und nennt als Entstehungsdatum das Jahr 894/895 und als Entstehungsort Tiberias. Mehrere Argumente, u.a. auch der Radiokarbon-Test, lassen Beit-Arié, Sirat und Glatzer an der Authentizität dieses Kolophons zweifeln. Sie möchten die Handschrift an das Ende des 10. oder an den Anfang des 11. Jh. setzen.

M^C besteht aus 296 Pergamentsblättern, die die *Vorderen und Hinteren Propheten* enthalten. Die Tinte ist braun. Es gibt keine Lücken im Prophetentext. Es sind weder Beschädigungen noch fehlende Blätter zu beklagen. Der Text ist in drei Kolumnen pro Seite aufgeteilt, ausgenommen hymnische Stellen, die in einer oder in zwei Kolumnen geschrieben wurden. Die *Masora parva* steht auf den Seitenrändern und zwischen den Kolumnen, die *Masora magna* auf dem oberen und untern Seitenrand.

Was ihre Zuschreibung an Moshe Ben Ascher betrifft, so fällt auf, dass M^C nach Yeivin nur in 33% der vom *Kitāb al-khilāf* aufgelisteten Fällen mit den Divergenzen zwischen Ben Ascher und Ben Naftali dem Modell Ben Ascher folgt, während die Handschrift sich hingegen in 64% dieser Fälle mit Ben Naftali deckt. Wo Ben Ascher und Ben Naftali gemeinsam den andern masoretischen Autoritäten gegenüberstehen, entspricht M^C in 75% der Fälle Ben Ascher-Ben Naftali (Yeivin, *Tiberian Masorah,* 20). Sirat bespricht verschiedene Untersuchungen, die Beispiele nachweisen, in denen M^C nicht der Ben Ascher-Tradition entspricht (*Codices Hebraicis litteris exarati,* 1:28).

– Die Handschrift *Additional Ms. 1753* der Universitätsbibliothek Cambridge (M^Y) wird beschrieben von S.C. Reif, *Hebrew Manuscripts at Cambridge University Library: A Description and Introduction* (Cambridge: University Press, 1997), 70–71; I. Yeivin, "The Division into Sections in the Book of Psalms," *Textus* 7 (1969): 76–102. Auf diesen beiden Untersuchungen beruhen die folgenden Angaben zur Handschrift. Für die *BHQ* wird ein Mikrofilm der Handschrift benützt. M^Y ist eine jemenitische Handschrift. Ihr Schreiber und ihr genaues Alter sind unbekannt, weil kein Kolophon erhalten ist. Reif schlägt ein Datum im 15. oder 16. Jh. vor (*Hebrew Manuscripts,* 70), wohingegen Yeivins Annahme einer Datierung in

das 14.–15. Jh. überzeugender ist, weil der sechste Eigentümer die Handschrift im Jahr 1570 erwarb.

Sie besteht aus 145 Pergamentblättern und enthält den Konsonantentext, Vokale, Akzente, *Masora magna* und *parva* für die Hagiographen (Schriften). Diese erscheinen in der Reihenfolge: 1 und 2 Chronik, Psalmen, Ijob, Proverbien, Ruth, Hohelied, Kohelet, Klagelieder, Esther, Daniel, Esra-Nehemia. Die Handschrift bietet masoretische Listen, die sich auf Tora und Hagiographen beziehen.

Nach Yeivin kann die Handschrift nicht als Werk der Ben Ascher-Schule bezeichnet werden. Es stellt vielmehr die Abschrift zweiter oder dritter Hand eines Ben Ascher-Manuskripts dar, welches er hingegen als "nicht weniger genau und zuverlässig als (M^A)" beurteilt. Trotz mangelnder Sorgfalt in der Setzung der Akzente und manchen Schreibfehlern "wurden die Einzelheiten der alten Tradition mit peinlicher Sorgfalt bewahrt" (Yeivin, "Division into Sections," 80). Diese Sorgfalt ergibt sich aus der Nachprüfung der Übereinstimmung der Handschrift mit der Ben Ascher Tradition und mit deren Hauptvertreter, der Hs. M^A. In den Fällen, wo Ben Ascher und Ben Naftali nach dem Zeugnis des *Kitāb al-khilāf* differieren, stimmt M^Y in 80% der Fälle mit Ben Ascher überein. "Die Orthographie (von M^Y), namentlich was die *Plene-* und *Defective-Schreibung* betrifft, … ist mit (M^A) nahezu identisch." Im Vergleich mit einem anonymen Manuskript, das eine Liste von offenen und geschlossenen Abschnitten in den Psalmen enthält, entspricht M^A in 90% der Fälle dieser Liste, während M^Y darin "(M^A) noch überbietet, oder ihm jedenfalls nicht nachsteht" (Yeivin, "Division into Sections," 80). In der Tat können von allen Handschriften, die Yeivin mit dieser Liste verglichen hat, nur vier den Anspruch erheben, den Bedingungen der Liste im Buch der Psalmen zu entsprechen, nämlich M^A, M^Y, M^L, Firkowitsch II. 94 (EBP. II B 94 der russischen Nationalbibliothek, St. Petersburg). Die beiden erstgenannten, M^A und M^Y, bilden dabei eine Gruppe, die diesen Bedingungen nahezu vollständig entspricht (Yeivin, "Division into Sections," 97).

– Handschrift *Sassoon 1053* (M^{S1}) wird von D.S. Sassoon, *Ohel David: Descriptive Catalogue of the Hebrew and Samaritan Manuscripts in the Sassoon Library, London* (Oxford: University Press; London: Humphrey Milford, 1932) 2:1111–12 beschrieben. Zusammen mit den Angaben von Yeivin, *Tiberian Masorah*, 21–22, bildet Sassoons Beschreibung die Quelle für die hier angeführten Charakteristika der Handschrift. Für die *BHQ* wird ein Mikrofilm der Handschrift benützt.

Sassoon und Yeivin datieren die Handschrift ins 10. Jh. Es ist jedoch kein Kolophon vorhanden, das die genaue Entstehungszeit angäbe. Während die Namen mehrerer Eigentümer aus Notizen in der Handschrift hervorgehen, bleiben Schreiber, Punktatoren und Korrektoren unbekannt, wie auch die Herkunft in Dunkel gehüllt ist.

Die Handschrift M^{S1} enthält die ganze Bibel auf 396 Pergamentblättern. Aber es gibt Lücken, z.B. fehlen die ersten zehn Kapitel der Genesis. Der Konsonantentext ist vokalisiert und mit Akzenten versehen. Die *Masora parva* ist vorhanden, wohingegen die *Masora magna* nur auf einigen Blättern vorkommt. Die *Hinteren Propheten* stehen in der Reihenfolge: Jeremia, Ezechiel, Jesaja, die Zwölf. Die Hagiographen sind in der gleichen Reihenfolge wie in M^L angeordnet, d.h. 1–2 Chronik steht am Anfang statt am Ende.

Yeivin beurteilt M^{S1} als unsorgfältig im Vergleich mit andern großen tiberiensischen masoretischen Handschriften. Nach dem Maßstab des *Kitāb al-khilāf* folgt

M^{S1} in 40% der Fälle, in denen sich Ben Ascher und Ben Naftali unterscheiden, der Ben Ascher Tradition und geht mit Ben Ascher und Ben Naftali zusammen in 60% der Fälle, in denen die beiden den anderen masoretischen Autoritäten gegenüberstehen (Yeivin, *Tiberian Masorah*, 21–22).

– Die Beschreibung der *Handschrift EBP. II B 34* der russischen Nationalbibliothek in St. Petersburg (M^{L34}) beruht auf P. Kahle, *Masoreten des Westens* (Stuttgart: W. Kohlhammer, 1927), 1:74–77. In *BHQ* wird diese Handschrift in einem Mikrofilm benützt.

M^{L34} enthält keine Datumsangabe. Ein Kolophon erwähnt einen neuen Einband für die Handschrift im Jahre 1130, und eine Weihenotiz aus dem Jahr 1100 setzt den *terminus ante quem*. Es ist möglich, dass eine weitere, undatierte Notiz einen früheren Bucheinband erwähnt. In diesem Fall könnte die Handschrift vor dem 11. Jh. geschrieben worden sein. Yeivin nimmt eine Entstehungszeit um 975 an (*Tiberian Masorah*, 26). Eine undatierte Weihenotiz, welche anscheinend älter als die datierte ist, bringt die Handschrift in Verbindung mit der karäischen Gemeinde von Kairo.

Auf 201 Blättern aus Pergament bietet M^{L34} Textpartien aus fast allen Hagiographen (Schriften), aber die Lücken sind zahlreich. Hier die erhaltenen Partien: 1 Chr 1:1-17; 5:24–6:4; 11:10-24; 17:26–18:14; 24:24–26:4; 2 Chr 1:9–2:5; 8:8–15:16; 24:6–28:27; 34:11–36:23; Ps 1:1–7:4; 9:19–30:4; 45:11–78:61; 80:3–94:3; 96:1–145:15; 147:15–150:6; Ijob 1:1–8:16; 9:27–22:6; 23:10–34:3; 34:36–42:17; Prov 1:1–3:23; 6:26–10:32; 14:12–15:8; Hohel 7:3–8:14; Kohelet; Klagel 1:1–5:6; Est 1:22–8:7; 9:15–10:3; Dan 1:1–3:29; 4:13–12:13; Esr 1:1-3; 2:8-42; 4:9–6:21; 8:2-22; 9:1-12; Neh 7:8-41; 8:9–9:4. Dieser Text besitzt eine nach Yeivins Terminologie "kurze" *Masora parva und Masora magna* (*Tiberian Masorah*, 26).

M^{L34} ist eine sorgfältige Handschrift. Sie folgt Ben Naftali in etwas mehr als der Hälfte der Fälle, die der *Kitāb al-khilāf* als Differenzen zwischen Ben Ascher und Ben Naftali aufzählt (Yeivin, *Tiberian Masorah*, 26).

DANK

Es ist uns nicht nur eine angenehme Pflicht, sondern auch eine besondere Freude, an dieser Stelle einigen Personen und Institutionen ausdrücklich zu danken, die das *BHQ*-Projekt gefördert und an seiner Realisierung tatkräftig mitgewirkt haben. Allen voran nennen wir mit großer Dankbarkeit Dominique Barthélemy und Hans Peter Rüger, die verstorben sind, und James A. Sanders. Als Mitglieder des schon erwähnten *Hebrew Old Testament Text Project* haben sie seinerzeit erkannt, dass eine neue Ausgabe der *Biblia Hebraica* nötig war und daraufhin die Initiative ergriffen. Sie sorgten dafür, dass ein erstes Treffen der späteren Herausgeberkommission zustande kam, bei dem über die sich stellenden Probleme und die Konzeption der neuen Ausgabe beraten wurde. Dem Weltbund der Bibelgesellschaften haben wir in vielerlei Hinsicht zu danken und schließen in diesen Dank insbesondere Jan de Waard mit ein: Zu Beginn des *BHQ*-Projekts war er beim Weltbund der Bibelgesellschaften Vorsitzender des Subkomitees für wissenschaftliche Ausgaben und

ließ in dieser Eigenschaft dem Vorhaben einer Neubearbeitung der *Biblia Hebraica* alle Unterstützung zuteil werden, die besonders am Anfang nötig war.

Unsere tief empfundene Dankbarkeit gilt des weiteren der Deutschen Bibelgesellschaft, insbesondere ihrem inzwischen verstorbenen früheren Generalsekretär Siegfried Meurer und seinem Nachfolger Jan-A. Bühner. Sie waren sich auch von der verlegerischen Seite her bewusst, dass eine Neubearbeitung der *Biblia Hebraica* notwendig war, und stellten die dafür nötigen konkreten Mittel großzügig bereit, um diese Ausgabe Wirklichkeit werden zu lassen.

Bei der Ausarbeitung und Herstellung der *BHQ* werden die vielfältigen Anpassungs- und Kontrollmöglichkeiten einer neuen computergestützten Satztechnik genutzt. Alle von den einzelnen Bearbeitern und Herausgebern gesammelten Daten werden in einer elektronischen Datenbank gespeichert, aus der sie sich in eine Vielzahl verschiedener elektronischer und gedruckter Formen konvertieren lassen. Diese Möglichkeiten wären den Herausgebern ohne die Kompetenz und Mitwirkung des Beraters der Herausgeberkommission in Informatikfragen, Alan Groves, Westminster Theological Seminary, Philadelphia, seines Programmierungsassistenten Soetjianto und vonseiten Winfried Baders von der Deutschen Bibelgesellschaft, verschlossen geblieben. Unser Dank gilt in diesem Bereich besonders auch Rolf Schäfer, sowie Edgar Szilagyi und Karl-Heinz Strößner von der Universitätsdruckerei Stürtz AG in Würzburg. Wir schätzen ihren Einsatz für die *BHQ* außerordentlich hoch.

Dem *Ancient Biblical Manuscript Center* in Claremont, Kalifornien, seinem Präsidenten James A. Sanders und seinem Direktor Michael Phelps sind wir zu großem Dank verpflichtet, weil sie die vorzüglichen Farbaufnahmen der Handschrift M^L für die Ausarbeitung der *BHQ* zur Verfügung stellten. Professor Aron Dotan von der Universität Tel Aviv sprechen wir unseren herzlichen Dank dafür aus, dass er bereit war, dem Projekt als Experte in allen Fragen, die die *Masora* betreffen, zur Verfügung zu stehen. Er hat eine ganze Reihe von Schwierigkeiten auf diesem Gebiet gelöst.

Mehrere Personen leisteten unentbehrliche Dienste und Beiträge für den täglichen Fortschritt des Vorhabens, und es ist uns eine angenehme und vordringliche Pflicht, ihnen hier unsern Dank für ihre wichtige und wertvolle Hilfe auszusprechen. Rolf Schäfer von der Deutschen Bibelgesellschaft war die Verantwortung für die druck- und buchtechnische Realisierung anvertraut, eine sehr anspruchsvolle Aufgabe, wenn man die Probleme bedenkt, die die neuen Drucktechniken mit sich brachten. Roger Omanson vom Weltbund der Bibelgesellschaften übernahm zu einem für das Projekt entscheidenden Zeitpunkt die Aufgabe, Einheitlichkeit, Stil und Bibliographie der Ausgabe zu verbessern und zu vervollständigen. Harold P. Scanlin vom Weltbund der Bibelgesellschaften hat dem Projekt in vielen praktischen Belangen den Weg geebnet, insbesondere bei der Beschaffung von Handschriften-Mikrofilmen und anderem Material. Sarah Lind, ebenfalls vom Weltbund der Bibelgesellschaften, hat dem englischen Stil in Kohelet den letzten Schliff gegeben. Norbert Rabe, Tübingen, und Jonathan Kearney, Dublin, kollationierten zur Kontrolle mit großer Sorgfalt den elektronischen Text der *Megilloth* mit den Farbaufnahmen der Handschrift M^L. *Last, but not least*, ist Bernadette Schacher, Biblisches Institut der Universität Freiburg, Schweiz zu erwähnen, die die Informationen und Material rasch und zuverlässig unter der Herausgeberschaft zirkulieren ließ.

Es ist unsere Pflicht und unser Wunsch, zweier Herausgeber im Projekt der *BHQ* zu gedenken, die nicht mehr unter uns sind: Martin Mulder, Universität Lei-

den, und Raymond Dillard, Westminster Theological Seminary, Philadelphia. Der
erste war ursprünglicher Herausgeber des Hoheliedes, der zweite jener von Esther.
Ihr früher Tod kurz nach Übernahme ihrer herausgeberischen Aufgabe hat ihnen
die Vollendung aus der Hand genommen.

Die Herausgeber sind sich mit Dankbarkeit bewusst, dass ihre Institutionen, an
denen sie wirken, die Herausgabe der *BHQ* mittragen. Auch den zahlreichen
Kolleginnen und Kollegen fühlen sie sich zu Dank verpflichtet, die den Fortgang
des Projekts mit Interesse begleitet und die Herausgeber sowohl ermutigt als auch
mit Sachkenntnis und Hilfsbereitschaft kritisiert haben. Trotz all dieser Hilfe und
trotz aller von den Herausgebern unternommenen Anstrengungen, diese neue Ausgabe ihrer Leserschaft so nützlich wie nur irgend möglich zu gestalten, können wir
nur in den Fußstapfen unserer Vorgänger weitergehen und zum Abschluss mit Rudolf Kittels Vorwort zur dritten Ausgabe (1929) sagen (*BHK³*, V): "Auch so wird
es der BH. nicht erspart bleiben, dem *dies diem docet* ihren Tribut zu entrichten.
Möge sie überall billige Beurteiler, vor allem aber der Größe des Stoffes würdige
Leser finden."

Stuttgart im Februar 2004   DIE HERAUSGEBERKOMMISSION

INTRODUCCIÓN GENERAL

La primera edición en la serie moderna de la *Biblia Hebraica* (*BHK¹*) apareció en
Leipzig en 1906, cuando se abría paso el nuevo siglo. A lo largo del siglo han
aparecido nuevas ediciones de la *Biblia Hebraica*, manteniendo todas ellas la
estructura básica de la edición original, pero introduciendo cambios justificados
por el desarrollo de los estudios de crítica textual. En 1913 se publicó, también en
Leipzig, una segunda edición (*BHK²*), que sólo se diferenciaba de la primera en
pequeñas correcciones. La tercera edición (*BHK³*), apareció en Stuttgart en 1929–
1937, e introdujo cambios de mayor envergadura: un nuevo texto base que repro-
ducía el texto del códice de Leningrado en vez de la edición de Jacob ben Ḥayyim
de Bomberg (1524–1525), y un aparato crítico completamente nuevo. La *Biblia
Hebraica Stuttgartensia* (*BHS*, 1967–1977), la cuarta edición de la serie, siguió a
BHK³ en el uso del códice de Leningrado como texto base, pero introdujo una
nueva presentación de la masora del manuscrito y un nuevo aparato.

En el momento en que el viejo siglo cede el paso a uno nuevo, el creciente
aumento de descubrimientos de manuscritos (en especial los Rollos del Mar Muerto), los avances de la intensa investigación de muchas décadas en la transmisión
del texto de la Biblia hebrea, y las consiguientes transformaciones en nuestra apre-
ciación de los objetivos y límites de la crítica textual, justifican una nueva edición
(la quinta) en la línea de la *Biblia Hebraica*, que por ello puede denominarse *Biblia Hebraica Quinta* (*BHQ*). Puesto que éste es el primer fascículo de la nueva

Esta nueva edición surge por iniciativa de las Sociedades Bíblicas Unidas y con el mecenazgo de la Sociedad Bíblica de Alemania, que es especialmente responsable de la publicación de las ediciones científicas entre las que se incluye específicamente la *Biblia Hebraica*. El carácter de la *Biblia Hebraica Quinta* se configura a través de dos historias, la de las ediciones de la *Biblia Hebraica*, y la del Hebrew Old Testament Text Project de las Sociedades Bíblicas Unidas.

Muchas decisiones cruciales en los diversos estadios del desarrollo de la *Biblia Hebraica* dieron a la serie un carácter muy conocido que continúa en esta edición. Desde el comienzo las ediciones de la serie se proyectaron como *ediciones manuales*. También desde el comienzo, como resultado de una elección explícita de Rudolf Kittel, la edición no ofreció un texto ecléctico de la Biblia hebrea, sino que imprimió el texto de una sóla edición o manuscrito, provisto de un aparato crítico que presenta una selección de variantes y conjeturas para enmendar el texto, insistiendo en las que eran más significativas para la exégesis y la traducción. En las dos primeras ediciones se usó como texto base el de la edición de Bomberg de Jacob ben Ḥayyim. A partir de la tercera edición (1937) se imprimió como texto base, por iniciativa de Paul Kahle, el texto del códice EBP. I B 19a de la Biblioteca Nacional Rusa de San Petersburgo (en adelante M^L). Kahle insistió también en la importancia de imprimir las masoras parva y magna de M^L como parte de la edición. En la tercera edición este objetivo sólo se llevó a cabo con la masora parva. Por lo que a la masora magna se refiere, el objetivo de Kahle se intentó llevar a cabo por primera vez en la edición cuarta de la serie *Biblia Hebraica*, la *Biblia Hebraica Stuttgartensia*. Cuando comenzaron a aparecer los Rollos del Mar Muerto a finales de los años cuarenta, la séptima impresión de la *BHK³*, por iniciativa de Otto Eissfeldt, añadió aparatos que ofrecían información completa de las variantes contenidas en 1QIsaᵃ y 1QpHab. La *Biblia Hebraica Quinta* conserva esta tradición en muchos puntos, aunque la depura y renueva en otros.

Como ocurrió con sus predecesoras, esta edición de la *Biblia Hebraica* pretende ser una *edición manual*, para uso de profesores, teólogos, traductores y estudiantes que no están necesariamente especializados en crítica textual. Puesto que nuestro campo todavía carece de una *editio critica maior*, la edición debería ser útil también para los especialistas en crítica textual, aunque no vaya dirigida principalmente a ellos. El Comité Editorial al comienzo de su trabajo consideró la posibilidad de llevar a cabo una edición de ese tipo, pero llegó a la conclusión de que no era práctica en este momento, y en todo caso no satisfaría las necesidades a las que responde la *Biblia Hebraica*. El comité alberga la esperanza de que esta nueva edición de la *Biblia Hebraica* pueda contribuir a la publicación final de una *editio critica maior*.

Siguiendo el modelo de sus predecesoras esta edición aparecerá inicialmente en fascículos. Este fascículo, que contiene las Megilloth, es el primero de ellos. Cada fascículo ofrecerá los siguientes apartados de los libros bíblicos que se publiquen:
- una introducción;
- listas de siglas, símbolos y abreviaturas;
- un glosario de abreviaturas comunes usadas en la masora parva;
- el texto y la masora completa de M^L;
- el aparato crítico que registre las lecturas de los testimonios de la transmisión textual;
- un comentario sobre una selección de casos del aparato crítico, la traducción de la masora magna, y comentarios de casos difíciles de las masoras magna y parva.

Esta secuencia implica un orden de preferencia para la lectura de la edición. Al leer la introducción de un libro antes de pasar al texto y aparato, el lector adquiere una perspectiva importante sobre los testimonios de ese libro. Cuando el lector pasa al texto y aparato, los editores suponen que se consultará el comentario en el momento en que surjan puntos de interés en la lectura del texto y aparato.

Al final del proceso de publicación la edición se publicará en dos volúmenes: el primero contendrá el texto, la masora y el aparato crítico junto con la introducción, siglas, símbolos y abreviaturas (es decir, un único volumen según el modelo habitual de *BHK*). El segundo volumen contendrá el comentario textual y la traducción de las notas de la masora magna.

Esta nueva edición de la *Biblia Hebraica* sigue el modelo adoptado en 1937 al presentar el texto de un único manuscrito masorético de buena calidad como texto base y añadir un aparato crítico que ofrece los testimonios de la transmisión textual en relación con el punto de referencia del texto base. Se sigue, naturalmente, la estructura elegida por Kittel para la edición de 1906, aunque entonces se sirvió del texto de Bomberg en lugar de un único manuscrito. El Comité Editorial es muy consciente del debate actual sobre los méritos relativos de una edición de este tipo frente a una edición que presente lo que se llama, con razón, un texto ecléctico. El Comité prefirió mantener la estructura histórica de las ediciones de la *Biblia Hebraica* por tres motivos. Primero: se pensó que todavía no se conocía suficientemente la historia y evolución del texto de la Biblia hebrea y sus diversas tradiciones textuales como para ofrecer una base sólida para la reconstrucción de un texto ecléctico. Segundo: una edición que presente un texto ecléctico de la Biblia hebrea tiene que optar por la reconstrucción del texto en un momento particular de su evolución. Ante la carencia actual de un consenso sobre el estadio mas adecuado del texto que ha de ser la meta de tal reconstrucción, le pareció al Comité que una edición que va a ser ampliamente utilizada por estudiantes y no especialistas, no debería presentar como texto seguido una reconstrucción basada en una de las opciones del debate. Tercero: el Comité considera que un texto ecléctico debería basarse en la presentación de todas las variantes que se encuentran en los testimonios que han sobrevivido. Semejante presentación supera los límites propios de una edición en un volumen.

EL TEXTO

Siguiendo la práctica establecida en la tercera edición de 1937, mejorada en la edición *Stuttgartensia*, esta edición ofrece como texto base una reproducción fundamentalmente diplomática de M^L. En los últimos años los estudios de M^L y su masora han puesto de relieve que en algunos aspectos puede estar lejos de ser el ideal de texto base de una edición (ver más adelante el debate específico). En realidad el Comité reflexionó seriamente sobre otros posibles textos base para la edición. Se decidió no utilizar el códice de Alepo (en adelante M^A) sobre todo porque el manuscrito está incompleto. Es más, puesto que el Hebrew University Bible Project utiliza este manuscrito como texto base de sus espléndidas ediciones, y es también el texto de la edición de la Biblia de la universidad de Bar-Ilan editada por M. Cohen, M^A está apareciendo como edición ante el público especializado. El Comité Editorial consideró también la posibilidad de usar como texto base de la

BHQ el manuscrito ben Ašer más antiguo que se conservara para cada una de las tres divisiones del canon. Esta opción se abandonó en favor del uso seguido de M^L por varias razones. Primero: M^L sigue siendo el manuscrito más antiguo conocido de toda la Biblia hebrea. Segundo: el estado de los manuscritos que reunían el criterio indicado habría conducido a una amalgama porque sus lagunas tendrían que ser completadas con otro manuscrito (por ejemplo, además de la conocida laguna en la Torá, al códice de Alepo le faltan por completo varios de los Escritos). Tercero: cuando se suponía que la nueva edición sería realizada por los métodos tradicionales, el hecho de que la German Bible Society contara con un texto compuesto de M^L, texto que ya había experimentado varias revisiones de cuidadosa corrección, constituyó un factor pragmático de primer orden. En el momento en que se decidió pasar el proyecto a procesos totalmente informatizados, fue igualmente significativo que el texto de M^L estuviera ya disponible en forma electrónica, el único de los grandes manuscritos tiberienses disponible en esa forma. Aunque los procesos de conversión del texto a la forma electrónica específica para su uso en la preparación de esta edición introdujeron nuevos errores en el texto electrónico, dicho texto ya había sufrido algún grado de corrección antes de ser utilizado en el proyecto. Durante la preparación de esta edición la versión electrónica del texto está siendo sometida a una corrección minuciosa basada en las transparencias en color procedentes del Ancient Biblical Manuscript Center en Claremont, California, USA. Las transparencias se realizaron a partir de las nuevas fotografías de M^L tomadas en San Petersburgo por el equipo del Centro formado por la West Semitic Research de Los Angeles. La claridad y calidad de las fotografías supera con creces a las que se han obtenido por otras vías y sin duda generarán un número de correciones que no fueron posibles para el texto de *BHS* hasta su quinta impresión (1997) exclusive. Los editores de los libros individuales y los colaboradores científicos a los que se les ha asignado la tarea específica colacionarán a su vez el texto electrónico de M^L con estas fotografías.

Lo mismo que sucedió con *BHS*, el texto impreso en *BHQ* será el texto de M^L, incluso cuando éste presenta errores obvios. Las correcciones se anotarán en el aparato sobre la base de los otros manuscritos tiberienses colacionados. Por otra parte las nuevas fotografías de M^L han revelado un pequeño número de casos en los que el deterioro del manuscrito ha vuelto ilegible algún elemento de una palabra (de ordinario un signo vocálico o acento). En esos casos la edición ofrecerá una lectura reconstruida en el texto base y utilizará una entrada del aparato para informar de lo que en realidad se puede ver con claridad en M^L, así como las lecturas de los otros testimonios tiberienses que constituyen la base de la reconstrucción. Hay también casos en los que M^L presenta una discrepancia entre la lectura de la primera mano y una lectura de una segunda mano (por ejemplo, a través de errores cometidos accidentalmente al entintar de nuevo las partes dañadas del manuscrito [véase más adelante la explicación]). En estos casos el editor incluirá en el texto base la lectura que, a su juicio, es la genuina del manuscrito, e informará sobre los datos pertinentes en una entrada del aparato.

Por lo que toca a la disposición del texto base, *BHQ* sigue a sus predecesoras al apartarse de una reproducción totalmente diplomática de la disposición de la página de M^L en los siguientes puntos: los textos que el editor considera que son prosa van en forma seguida y los textos que considera poesía se disponen de forma esticográfica. Sin embargo, se han cambiado los criterios para determinar la esticografía frente a los usados en las ediciones previas. Para los pasajes poéticos de textos

en prosa que M^L presenta de forma esticográfica en una disposición tradicional de la página, el texto de esta edición seguirá la esticografía del manuscrito. De no ser así, la esticografía de esta edición se basa en los acentos masoréticos. Los esticos se definen siempre por medio de los acentos disyuntivos mayores, excepto en aquellos casos en los que se piensa que hay que preferir como lectura del texto una división sintáctica diferente de la expresada por esos acentos. En tales casos la lectura preferida condicionará la división de los esticos. La agrupación de los esticos en bi- y tricola se decidirá cuando sea posible por la jerarquía de prioridad entre esos acentos. Sólo cuando el resultado genere una línea que sobrepasaría el límite de la página, o cuando quiebre un obvio *parallelismus membrorum* se alterará la agrupación de los esticos en bi- y tricola.

Entre los textos en prosa de M^L también se dan una serie de listas (p. e. Esdras 2:43-57) que, aunque no haya una tradición fija respecto a su presentación, están dispuestas en las páginas de M^L de una forma que las distingue de la prosa que las circunda. En esta edición se presentarán de tal manera que reproduzcan, en cuanto sea posible, su presentación en el manuscrito.

Otros fenómenos asociados con los manuscritos masoréticos (por ejemplo, letras dilatadas, letras suspendidas, signos para las secciones de lectura, *nûnîm* invertidos) se imprimen tal cual aparecen en M^L, como ha sido usual desde la edición de 1937. En concreto el signo parecido a la *nûn* ó *zayin* que se encuentra en la masora parva de M^L (ן֗) aparecerá de tal forma que siga lo más estrechamente posible al manuscrito. Sin embargo las *sətumôt* y *pətuḥôt* no se indican mediante el espaciado de líneas, sino mediante la inserción de ס y פ, como se ha venido haciendo desde los comienzos de la serie *Biblia Hebraica*.

LA MASORA

En su contribución al prólogo de la tercera edición, Kahle, al señalar que el texto de M^L "vollständig wird ... erst durch die ihm beigegebene Masora" (*BHK³*, VIII), expresó el propósito de publicar la masora completa de M^L en la *Biblia Hebraica*. En realidad ese objetivo se cumplió sólo con la masora parva en la edición de 1937. *BHS* intentó llevar a cabo el objetivo de Kahle de publicar a la vez las masoras parva y magna. La edición de la masora de M^L preparada por Gérard Weil para *BHS* se concibió como una elaboración completa, corregida y normalizada, de la masora de M^L más que como una reproducción diplomática de lo que en realidad estaba escrito en el manuscrito. Para esta nueva edición el Comité Editorial decidió reproducir las dos masoras, parva y magna, de M^L en una presentación esencialmente diplomática. Puesto que la masora es parte del texto de M^L que constituye el texto base de la edición, y el principio básico de su presentación es diplomático, le pareció al Comité que no sería coherente presentar la masora de cualquier otra forma. Es verdad que las masoras parva y magna de M^L tienen sus deficiencias y que seguramente no reflejan la totalidad de los datos contenidos en la tradición masorética. Sin embargo, una edición que se ocupara de estos asuntos requeriría la colación de la masora de otros manuscritos y precisaría de mayor espacio del que se puede dedicar razonablemente a estos temas en una edición de un volumen.

Esto quiere decir que cuando la masora de M^L no concuerda con el texto del manuscrito, no se corregirá como era práctica habitual en BHK^3 y sobre todo en *BHS*. En su lugar se explicarán dichos casos en una nota en la sección del comentario de la edición. En esta edición se incluye un glosario de las abreviaturas comunes utilizadas en la masora parva para ayudar a los lectores a comprender esas notas. Las notas de la masora parva que no se puedan traducir con seguridad con la ayuda del glosario, se traducirán en la sección del comentario, lo mismo que todas las notas de la masora magna. Las notas de la masora que incluyen demasiada información implícita como para que puedan razonablemente ser comprendidas, incluso con la traducción, se discutirán en la sección del comentario.

La edición se aparta en dos aspectos formales de una presentación diplomática de la masora magna con el fin de que los lectores puedan seguir con más facilidad el texto de la masora. Al comienzo de cada nota se insertarán los números del capítulo y versículo a los que se piensa que hace referencia la nota. Las notas de masora magna que contienen *sîmanîm* aparecerán con un punto insertado entre cada *sîman*.

En más de una ocasión M^L inserta un circellus en su texto sin una nota correspondiente en la masora parva. Asimismo aparecen notas en la masora parva sin circelli que indiquen las palabras o frases a las que se refieren, y notas en la masora magna que no tienen conexión con el asunto presentado en las páginas de M^L en las que aparecen. En la medida de lo posible, *BHQ* intenta reflejar esta situación de forma fidedigna. Los circelli se insertarán en el texto incluso cuando no lleven su correspondiente nota. Las notas de la masora parva sin su correspondiente circellus se asociarán con la palabra o frase con la que el editor piense que están relacionadas, pero sin insertar un circellus. De esta forma la nota aparecerá próxima a su referente probable, pero no se transmitirá una falsa seguridad sobre dicho referente. Las notas de la masora magna que no puedan ponerse en relación con el tema textual de la misma página o de las páginas vecinas, se vincularán a la primera palabra de la página del manuscrito en la que aparecen, asegurando una localización en la edición que se aproxime a la localización de la nota en el manuscrito. Tanto en la masora magna como en la masora parva, a los numerales que carecen en M^L del punto supralinear usual, se les añadirá en consideración a la claridad.

EL APARATO CRÍTICO

Como en todas las ediciones anteriores de la serie, el aparato crítico de esta edición ofrecerá sólo una selección de casos textuales, poniendo el énfasis en aquellos que son importantes para la traducción y la exégesis. Sin embargo, precisamente en los contenidos y presentación del aparato crítico es donde la *Biblia Hebraica Quinta* ha sido más influida concretamente por la segunda historia de la que es heredera, la del Hebrew Old Testament Text Project (HOTTP) de las United Bible Societies. El HOTTP quedó constituido en 1969 por un Comité de seis profesores de la Biblia hebrea (Dominique Barthélemy, Alexander R. Hulst, Norbert Lohfink, W. D. McHardy, Hans Peter Rüger, James A. Sanders). Y además Eugene A. Nida de las United Bible Societies actuaba como presidente. En los encuentros anuales a lo largo de un período de once años el Comité revisó más de cinco mil casos de crítica textual que le proporcionaba John A. Thompson, basados en la comparación

de la Revised Standard Version, la New English Bible, la Biblia de Jerusalén y la Revidierte Lutherbibel. Los cinco volúmenes del *Preliminary and Interim Report* de este Comité, editados por Adrian Schenker, entonces secretario del Comité, se publicaron entre 1973 y 1980. Hasta la fecha se han publicado tres volúmenes del informe final bajo el título *Critique textuelle de l'Ancien Testament*, con Dominique Barthélemy de Friburgo como editor principal. Se espera la publicación de dos volumens más.

Este Comité del Hebrew Old Testament Text Project elaboró y puso en práctica un método particular para el trabajo de la crítica textual que distingue claramente entre temas específicos de la crítica textual, y la historia del desarrollo literario del texto y, en consecuencia, diferencia los casos propios de la crítica textual, en cuanto se basan en los datos externos, de aquellos que son propios de otros métodos científicos que operan únicamente sobre la base de los datos internos. Las United Bible Societies adoptaron este método como base para esta nueva edición de la *Biblia Hebraica*. Los miembros del HOTTP designaron un Comité Editorial de siete personas y los invitaron en agosto de 1990 a un encuentro constituyente en la universidad de Friburgo, Suiza. Adrian Schenker, de Friburgo, fue nombrado presidente de los siete miembros del Comité Editorial. Siguiendo la práctica de las United Bible Societies, el Comité Editorial es internacional e interconfesional como lo es todo el equipo de veintinueve profesores que integran el proyecto. El Comité Editorial elaboró su concepción de esta edición de la *Biblia Hebraica* y en especial de su aparato crítico sobre la base de su propio trabajo, el trabajo de los editores de los libros concretos, las respuestas y reacciones a un capítulo de muestra distribuido en 1992 entre muchos colegas de todo el mundo, y los comentarios a un fascículo fuera de serie, distribuido en los encuentros académicos en 1998. Esta concepción se expresó en una serie de principios que sirvieran de guía a los editores de los libros individuales. Estos principios recibieron una formulación escrita en las *Guidelines for Contributors* con sus sucesivos suplementos.

La selección de los casos y la inclusión de los testimonios

La función del aparato crítico en la *Biblia Hebraica Quinta* es presentar y evaluar los datos de la transmisión del texto. Por esta razón los casos presentados se seleccionan para ser incluidos en el aparato principalmente sobre la base de una colación completa de los testimonios antiguos, es decir, los tres principales manuscritos tiberienses para la Torá, y dos para los Profetas y Escritos (además de M^L); todos los testimonios textuales hebreos pretiberienses disponibles; y todas las versiones antiguas que atestigüan un conocimiento independiente del texto hebreo. Los editores pretenden que, en la medida de lo posible, el aparato incluya todos los casos de variantes de estos testimonios que reúnan dos criterios generales para su inclusión. Primero, si se juzga que la variante es significativa en crítica textual. En otras palabras, la lectura razonablemente, pero no necesariamente, refleja un texto hebreo diferente del texto base de la edición. Segundo, si se juzga que es potencialmente significativa para la traducción o la exégesis. Las entradas de tales casos indicarán de ordinario el peso de los datos pertinentes de todos los testimonios colacionados para el punto en cuestión.

Cuando se incluyan esas lecturas existentes, normalmente se darán al completo y en su propia lengua y escritura. En los pocos casos en los que la lectura variante se pueda describir de forma clara y breve, se optará preferentemente por una des-

cripción en vez de la lectura. Las lecturas que consisten en sólo números pueden darse como numerales para ahorrar espacio. Las lecturas que son sólo omisiones en relación con el texto base se indicarán con el símbolo >. Los añadidos de las versiones que superen la extensión de un verso y que procedan de textos equiparables a los de una edición distinta del libro en cuestión (por ejemplo, Ester), se indicarán (de ordinario con la abreviatura "+ txt"), pero no se darán al completo por limitaciones de espacio. Así mismo, las lecturas largas que, a juicio del editor, tienen una relación literaria con el texto representado en el texto base (p. e., un texto paralelo) se señalarán (de ordinario con la abreviatura "differ-txt"), pero no se darán al completo. La retroversión se usará sólo para la lectura que se propone como preferible a la que se encuentra en el texto base. Puesto que el aparato se dedica a la presentación y valoración de los datos concretos de la transmisión del texto, una lectura hipotética (es decir, una conjetura) sólo tendrá un lugar en el aparato de *BHQ* cuando sea la única explicación de la lecturas existentes en ese caso.

Los editores reconocen que los dos criterios generales para la inclusión de casos en el aparato de *BHQ* suponen un distanciamiento de los usos anteriores en la *Biblia Hebraica* y de la práctica de la crítica textual en las décadas recientes. Con el fin de entrar en diálogo con el debate ya existente se han incluido en el aparato de *BHQ* algunos casos adicionales que durante mucho tiempo se han tratado como casos de crítica textual sobre la base de otros criterios (por ejemplo, la dificultad exegética), pero que no son verdaderos casos de crítica textual. No obstante, la presentación de estos casos puede adoptar una forma más abreviada (por ejemplo, cuando el tema en cuestión es puramente lingüístico más que de crítica textual).

Además de los principios generales para incluir casos en el aparato crítico hay otros principios adicionales que requieren la presentación de ciertos tipos de casos significativos sin necesidad de sobrecargar el aparato con asuntos que no afectan a la traducción o a la exégesis. Así, todos los casos motivados por variantes que aparecen en un testimonio hebreo (o arameo en Daniel y Esdras) de Qumrán, Masada o Murabbaᶜât, así como todos los casos de *kətîb/qərê*, – cuando estas variantes no son puramente ortográficas – se incluyen en el aparato. Mas aún, también se incluyen en el aparato todos los casos motivados por variantes que se hallan en el Pentateuco Samaritano, cuando la variante no es puramente ortográfica o de carácter lingüístico.

También se adoptaron ciertos principios suplementarios para limitar expresamente los contenidos del aparato con el fin de mantener su identidad y hacerlo verificable. Así, la inclusión de materiales de la Genizá de El Cairo se limita a materiales que se puedan fechar en el período anterior al año 1000 E. C. y que estén publicados, atendiendo por un lado a su importancia y por otro a su posible verificación por parte del lector del aparato. Las citas bíblicas de los Deuterocanónicos/Apócrifos, Escritos pseudoepigráficos, literatura de Qumrán, filacterias, obras de Filón y Josefo, Nuevo Testamento, fuentes tannaítas o amoraítas, y fuentes patrísticas, se incluyen en el aparato en casos textuales específicos sólo cuando, a juicio del editor, existe la posibilidad de una variante textual hebrea detrás de ellas, y cuando constituyen nuestro único acceso a una lectura particular o tienen un peso especial. Los casos textuales individuales en los que todas las variantes existentes proceden de las versiones y son claramente de traducción (p. e. un ajuste a los límites y estilo de la lengua término de la versión), parafrásticas o hagádicas, se han excluido del aparato, a menos que hayan recibido una atención considerable

en el debate previo. Análogamente, cuando el Targum de un libro, tomado en su conjunto, no es una traducción fiable en cuanto testimonio del texto hebreo, debido a las extensas paráfrasis o a las expansiones hagádicas (por ejemplo, el Targum al Cantar de los cantares), no se citará de forma continua como testimonio, puesto que si se hiciera así recargaría el aparato con material que no es útil para los casos textuales que allí se presentan.

Hay una serie de testimonios que no se citan de forma constante porque no se puede considerar que demuestren regularmente una vía de acceso independiente a una *Vorlage* hebrea. Por otro lado, es probable que, ocasionalmente, recojan lecturas derivadas de una *Vorlage* hebrea o sean pertinentes para comprender casos registrados en el aparato. La Sirohexapla y los testimonios emparentados con la recensión origeniana de la Septuaginta Antigua sólo se incluirán entre los testimonios de un caso cuando sus lecturas discrepen a la vez de la Septuaginta Antigua y del TM. La *Vetus Latina* se recogerá sólo cuando concuerde con un testimonio hebreo o atestigüe razonablemente una lectura independiente *y* no concuerde con ningún manuscrito griego. El Targum Samaritano al Pentateuco, el Salterio Galicano y las versiones coptas no se colacionarán o registrarán sistemáticamente, pero su testimonio se recogerá en aquellos casos en los que un editor considere que ofrecen información útil.

BHQ realiza una colación completa de las *səṭumôṯ* y *pəṯuḥôṯ* en los manuscritos tiberienses que son tratados como testimonios citados de continuo. No obstante, sólo se recogen en el aparato los casos considerados significativos para la traducción y la exégesis. En la práctica esto quiere decir que sólo se incluirán en el aparato aquellos casos en los que existe un desacuerdo con relación a la presencia o ausencia de una *səṭumâ* y *pəṯuḥâ*. En la introducción de cada libro se incluirá una lista de las *səṭumôṯ* y *pəṯuḥôṯ* en M^L y en los manuscritos tiberienses colacionados.

A diferencia de las ediciones anteriores de la serie *Biblia Hebraica*, *BHQ* no citará los manuscritos medievales de las colaciones de Kennicott y de Rossi, o las ediciones de Ginsburg, como testimonios de los casos del aparato. Es la consecuencia de seguir los puntos de vista, cuidadosamente razonados, de Moshe H. Goshen-Gottstein según los cuales estos manuscritos derivan esencialmente del texto y masora fijados por los grandes masoretas tiberienses. Por eso parece que sus datos añaden poco que no dependa de los grandes manuscritos tiberienses. Las referencias a los manuscritos colacionados por Kennicott, de Rossi o Ginsburg se encontrarán en la caracterización de otras lecturas o en los comentarios a los casos cuando la(s) lectura(s) encontrada(s) en Kennicott, de Rossi o Ginsburg documenten una actitud o inclinación hacia el texto transmitido que el editor desee también postular para otra parte de la tradición textual.

En otro aspecto muy distinto, *BHQ* adopta una postura diferente de sus predecesoras con relación a los Rollos del Mar Muerto y la Peshitta, y en menor medida con relación a la Septuaginta y la Vulgata. En el caso de los Rollos del Mar Muerto, el aparato crítico de esta edición ha podido hacer uso completo de todos los manuscritos bíblicos existentes al respecto, debido al rápido ritmo de publicación en la última década y gracias al generoso acceso a los materiales inéditos que los responsables de los mismos han otorgado. En el caso de la Peshitta, el trabajo del Leiden Peshitta Project ha fructificado en una serie de ediciones excelentes y, cuando éstas aún no estaban terminadas, los directores del proyecto pusieron amablemente a nuestra disposición las colaciones. De esta forma la información sobre la Peshitta citada en el aparato de *BHQ* procede de manuscritos buenos y antiguos,

y no de viejas ediciones de calidad variable en las que con frecuencia se apoyaron *BHK³* y *BHS*. En el caso de la Septuaginta, *BHS* pudo disponer de algunas de las ediciones del Septuaginta-Unternehmen de Gotinga, pero en los años que han transcurrido se han sumado a la colección un buen número de volúmenes importantes. Más aún, cuando los volúmenes están todavía en proceso de edición, dicho Instituto ha permitido amablemente a los editores de los libros de *BHQ* acceder a las colaciones y a otros fondos. Para la Vulgata, *BHK³* y *BHS* pudieron apoyarse en algunos volúmenes de la edición de San Jerónimo, pero no en todos los libros. *BHQ* tiene la ventaja de que entre tanto esa edición se ha concluido.

La valoración de los datos

El aparato de *BHQ* se propone no sólo presentar los datos de la transmisión textual, sino también valorar esos datos con el fin de distinguir cuándo una lectura que no está en el texto base debe preferirse a la lectura que se encuentra en él. Por eso el aparato propondrá de vez en cuando la preferencia de una lectura atestigüada distinta de la que se encuentra en el texto base. El hecho de que el aparato emita tales juicios implica un componente necesariamente subjetivo en la presentación de los casos. Como se ha señalado con frecuencia, dicho componente subjetivo es inevitable en crítica textual. Puesto que no se puede evitar este componente subjetivo en un aparato que propone lecturas elegidas entre una gama de variantes reales, los editores han decidido, de acuerdo con el propósito de hacer el aparato lo más transparente posible, explicitar sus juicios sobre el carácter de las distintas lecturas, siempre que pueda hacerse con una confianza y claridad razonables. Estos juicios se expresarán de forma más completa en la discusión de los casos seleccionados en el comentario al aparato, incluyendo todos aquellos en los que se ha preferido una lectura distinta a la del texto base de la edición. En otros casos esos juicios se expresarán mediante el uso de calificaciones abreviadas insertas en el mismo aparato (ver mas adelante la lista de abreviaturas y definiciones). El propósito de esta edición al emitir juicios en su aparato es indicar la(s) forma(s) más antigua(s) del texto que se pueden alcanzar a partir de los datos disponibles. Este objetivo se consigue al centrarse el aparato en la presentación y valoración de los datos de los testimonios antiguos. Este doble papel del aparato (presentación y valoración) está subyaciendo también a la estructura de los casos presentados en el aparato.

Al sopesar los datos de cada testimonio los editores han tenido en cuenta las décadas precedentes de investigación en el proceso de la transmisión textual. De esta forma reconocen que el proceso de la transmisión textual no fue sólo un asunto mecánico sino que, en cierta medida, el texto se transmitió en función de su significado para las comunidades de copistas y traductores. En consecuencia, el crítico textual tiene que estar atento no sólo al tipo de cambios que pudieron surgir de la mecánica de la produción manuscrita, sino también a los cambios realizados a consecuencia de los sentidos que atribuyeron al texto. En el caso de los testimonios de las versiones, los editores son conscientes de que éstos deben considerarse, dentro del marco de cada unidad específica de traducción, en relación con la técnica de traducción y las características del lenguaje de traducción por comparación con el hebreo.

La estructura y presentación de los casos

Puesto que los editores concibieron su tarea como presentación de los datos en una forma que permita sacar sus propias conclusiones a lectores con puntos de vista diferentes o a lectores que estudian otros aspectos de la transmisión textual, la parte primordial de cada entrada, siguiendo el lema sacado del texto base, consiste en la presentación de las lecturas de los testimonios colacionados y la agrupación de los testimonios (ver Fig. 1 para la entrada de un caso como ejemplo que ilustra esta exposición). Las entradas en este aparato están estructuradas de tal manera que el lema (texto base) va seguido de sus variantes y cada lectura – ya sea lema o variante – va seguida de las siglas de los testimonios que la apoyan. De ordinario, se da el texto del testimonio principal para una lectura variante. La primera variante en la secuencia es la lectura que genera el caso de crítica textual. La secuencia de las restantes variantes (así como la lista de los testimonios que siguen una lectura) se basa en una secuencia lingüística (es decir, hebreo, griego, latín, otros) y dentro de una misma lengua se organiza mediante una cronología ascendente aproximada. Si dos variantes generan un único caso, preceden a las otras variantes, y la secuencia entre las dos se fija mediante la secuencia cronológico-lingüística antes descrita.

Las agrupaciones de entre los testimonios se determinan en el nivel del posible texto hebreo en consonancia con la insistencia del aparato en casos en los que uno o más testigos apuntan razonablemente a un texto hebreo distinto del texto base. Así, por ejemplo, dos testimonios griegos que ofrecen lecturas sinónimas de la misma palabra o frase pueden ser agrupados cuando el editor juzga que atestiguan la misma *Vorlage*, aunque no usen la(s) misma(s) palabra(s) griega(s). Las agrupaciones de los testimonios se determinan por referencia al tema particular que constituye el núcleo del caso. Cuando un testimonio ulterior de una lectura coincide en este tema nuclear con los testimonios iniciales de esa lectura, aunque difiera en detalles periféricos del caso, se agrupa con los testimonios iniciales pero encerrado entre paréntesis. Para merecer ser señalado de esta manera las variaciones de detalle deben darse razonablemente en el nivel del posible texto hebreo.

Cuando se piensa que una lectura dada en un caso (incluido el lema del texto base) es secundaria, y el editor cree que sería útil una caracterización abreviada de la lectura y que puede formularse con certeza razonable, dicha caracterización figurará a continuación de las siglas de los testimonios que apoyan esa lectura. Estas caracterizaciones de ordinario describen la lectura a la que se adjuntan en relación con la lectura preferida en el caso. En aquellos casos en los que una lectura se caracteriza con relación a otra lectura, pero no la preferida, se adjuntará a la caracterización la sigla de la lectura que suministra el punto de referencia de dicha caracterización. Al identificar una lectura de las versiones como variante en este aparato se deja abierta la cuestión de si la variante se da al nivel del texto hebreo o al nivel de la traducción. En algunos casos las caracterizaciones de las lecturas de las versiones irán señaladas para indicar el nivel al que se aplica la caracterización (usando "hebr" = nivel de la *Vorlage*; "vrs"/"vrss" = nivel de la[s] versión[es]).

En aquellos casos en los que el editor propone que se debe preferir una lectura distinta de la del texto base, ésta se presenta en la parte final de la entrada, después de una doble raya vertical y de la abreviatura "pref" (= "lectura preferida"). Se recapitulan los datos que apoyan la lectura preferida. Si la lectura preferida no está

directamente atestigüada en ninguno de los testimonios existentes sino que solamente está implicada en sus datos, se marca con el signo "(origin)", es decir, que es el origen indirectamente atestigüado de las lecturas existentes. Si la forma gramatical de la lectura preferida además no se encuentra en el hebreo del período bíblico, se la señala bien sea como "unattest" (= "no atestigüada"), o bien como "conjec-phil" (= "conjetura filológica"), dependiendo de la clase de apoyo externo de la lectura. Cuando la lectura propuesta es una conjetura, no se introduce mediante la abreviatura "pref" (= "lectura preferida") sino mediante la abreviatura "conjec" (= "conjetura"). En consonancia con la finalidad del aparato, que se centra en los datos de la *transmisión* textual, las propuestas de lecturas preferidas no han de buscar reconstruir la historia literaria del texto. Las lecturas que se consideran derivadas de una tradición literaria distinta para el libro se calificarán de "lit" (ver más adelante las definiciones de las caracterizaciones).

Cuando un caso sea objeto de una discusión más extensa en el comentario textual de la edición, su entrada en el aparato llevará el símbolo ⁜. Cuando se discuta en el comentario de otro caso, la entrada en el aparato incluirá el símbolo →⁜ y la remisión al versículo en el que se encuentra el comentario. Cada entrada de un caso en el aparato concluye con el símbolo ●. Cuando el mismo lema en el texto base requiere más de una entrada de caso en el aparato, la conclusión a cada entrada de caso anterior a la última se marca con el signo ○. El final de la última se marca, obviamente, con el signo ●.

LA DISPOSICIÓN DE LA PÁGINA

Los elementos de la edición – texto base, masora, aparato, comentario textual, traducciones de las notas masoréticas – están distribuidos de la siguiente forma (ver Fig. 2 para una página de muestra que ilustra los rasgos aquí expuestos). Al comienzo, en la parte superior de la página se encuentra el texto de M^L. Los números de los capítulos y versículos se insertan en el margen interior del texto. Las indicaciones de las secciones para la lectura tal como se encuentran en M^L y las notas masoréticas similares del margen (por ejemplo, *nûnîm* invertidos), tal como aparecen en M^L, se dan en el margen lateral exterior. Además, los nombres de las secciones para la lectura según el ciclo anual en el uso corriente se presentarán en la Torá en la cabecera correspondiente en la parte superior de la página derecha junto con el nombre del libro.

Las notas de la masora parva de M^L se presentarán en el margen lateral externo de la página. El lector es advertido de la relación de una nota con una palabra o palabras del texto por medio de circelli sobre o entre la(s) palabra(s) pertinente(s) del texto, excepto en los pocos ejemplos antes mencionados en los que el manuscrito tiene una nota pero no circellus, o cuando tiene un circellus en el texto pero carece de nota en la masora parva. Como antes se indicó, se espera que el lector sea capaz de traducir las notas de la masora parva con la ayuda del glosario de abreviaturas y términos incluidos en la edición. Las notas que no corresponden al texto de M^L, y las notas particularmente difíciles se explicarán en la sección del comentario, de modo que se aconseja al lector que lo consulte en tales ocasiones.

Las notas de la masora magna de M^L se dispondrán en un registro separado debajo del texto base. Como ocurre en el manuscrito, no hay un signo especial en

el texto de la edición para indicar que una palabra tiene una nota en la masora magna, aunque esas notas aparecen típicamente en palabras que ya han sido anotadas en la masora parva. Con el fin de ayudar al lector a conectar las notas de la masora magna con las palabras o frases pertinentes del texto, esta edición ofrece las notas en el orden de palabras del texto bíblico, incluso cuando esto exige apartarse del orden de las notas tal como se ofrece en una página dada del manuscrito. También se inserta al comienzo de la nota, como antes se dijo, el capítulo y versículo al que se refiere la nota. Las traducciones de las notas de la masora magna estarán a disposición del lector en la sección del comentario, lo mismo que los comentarios sobre notas difíciles o notas que no corresponden al texto de M^L.

El aparato crítico del texto se encontrará en la parte inferior de la página, debajo del texto base y de la masora magna. Los editores decidieron no introducir letras, números o símbolos en el texto base de la edición para señalar la conexión de las entradas del aparato con el texto. En su lugar el lector, al comienzo de cada caso en el aparato, puede apoyarse en la reproducción completa como lema de la(s) palabra(s) pertinente(s) del texto base para hacer esta conexión. El aparato está diseñado como una entidad básicamente completa en sí misma, pero cuando vaya acompañado de la discusión ulterior de un caso en la sección del comentario de la edición, se indicará en la forma antes descrita.

En el margen, a la izquierda de la primera línea del aparato crítico, la edición dará una lista con la(s) referencia(s) del(os) texto(s) paralelo(s) de la parte del texto base impreso en esa página. Si este texto paralelo es citado como testimonio de algún caso en el aparato de esa página, se hará referencia a él por medio del símbolo (//), o una sigla general (p. e. Neh), y no con la referencia precisa de capítulo y versículo.

M^L, SU TEXTO Y SU MASORA

Las introducciones a los libros bíblicos concretos ofrecerán descripciones de los testimonios utilizados en la edición. No obstante, puesto que M^L es el mismo testimonio para todos los libros, ofrecemos aquí una descripción general del manuscrito en vez de repetirla innecesariamente al incluirla en las introducciones de cada libro. En el apartado que viene a continuación de éste ofrecemos descripciones, en general más breves, de los otros testimonios masoréticos tiberienses utilizados en esta edición.

El manuscrito conocido por la signatura EBP. I B 19a, depositado en la Biblioteca Nacional Rusa de San Petersburgo, Rusia (previamente conocida como Biblioteca Pública del Estado Saltykov-Shchedrin [Leningrado], y con anterioridad como Biblioteca Pública Imperial [San Petersburgo]), conocido como Codex Leningradensis o Códice de Leningrado, fue objeto de una descripción codicológica substancial en el catálogo de A. Harkavy y H. L. Strack de 1875 (*Catalog der hebräischen Bibelhandschriften der kaiserlichen öffentlichen Bibliothek* [San Petersburgo: C. Ricker, 1875; Leipzig: J. C. Hinrichs, 1875]). Recientemente esta descripción, estándar durante mucho tiempo, ha sido superada por una descripción mucho más completa y actualizada en M. Beit-Arié, C. Sirat y M. Glatzer (*Codices Hebraicis Litteris Exarati Quo Tempore Scripti Fuerint Exhibentes*, Tome 1, Jusqu'à 1020 [Monumenta Palaeographica Medii Aevi, Series Hebraica: Turnhout:

Brepols, 1997], 114–31). Los especialistas, comenzando por la obra de Kahle, han prestado mucha atención al texto y a la masora del manuscrito. Entre las recientes descripciones importantes del texto y masora de M^L se cuentan las de M. Breuer (כתר ארם צובה והנוסח המקובל של המקרא) [Jerusalem: Mosad HaRav Kook, 1976]), I. Yeivin (*Introduction to the Tiberian Masorah* [Missoula: Scholars Press, 1980], E. J. Revell ("The Leningrad Codex as a Representative of the Masoretic Text", en *The Leningrad Codex* [ed. D. N. Freedman, et al.; Grand Rapids: William B. Eerdmans; Leiden: Brill, 1998], xxix–xlvi), y los numerosos trabajos de A. Dotan. La siguiente exposición en parte se basa en estas descripciones, y en parte en la propia experiencia de los editores con M^L, aunque en este momento su experiencia constituye necesariamente un fundamento menor para lo que sigue de lo que constituirá al final del proyecto.

El códice fue compuesto en El Cairo por Shemuʾel ben Yaʿaqob para Rabbi Mevorak ben Yosef ha-Kohen. El año de su composición se da según cinco calendarios diferentes. Sin embargo, éstos dan como fecha cuatro años distintos según el cómputo de la Era Común: 1008, 1009, 1010 y 1013. Siguiendo a Beit-Arié, Sirat y Glatzer, aceptamos el 1008 como año de la composición del manuscrito. Shemuʾel ben Yaʿaqob copió y corrigió todos los componentes del manuscrito: texto consonántico, puntuación, y masora.

El códice consta de 491 folios en pergamino escritos con tinta entre negra y marrón oscura. Los primeros 463 folios contienen los veinticuatro libros de la Biblia hebrea con vocales y acentos, además de las masoras parva y magna. El texto bíblico está escrito a tres columnas por página (excepto en los Salmos, Job y Proverbios que están escritos a dos columnas por página) con veintisiete líneas por columna. La masora parva está escrita en los márgenes lateral e interior de las columnas, y la masora magna está escrita en los márgenes superior e inferior de cada página. El códice presenta las características codicológicas típicas de un manuscrito medieval del Oriente Medio. Para una descripción codicológica completa, con los textos y traducciones íntegros de todos los colofones, ver la obra de Beit-Arié, Sirat y Glatzer antes citada.

En conjunto el manuscrito está bien conservado. Los detalles página por página del deterioro y las partes dañadas se pueden encontrar en las notas sobre la conservación que forman parte de la edición facsimilar de Eerdmans/Brill antes citada. Estos daños con frecuencia no constituyen un desafío a nuestra capacidad para leer el manuscrito, pero hay casos en los que la ponen a prueba. Por ejemplo (y lo mismo se puede decir de las columnas próximas), gran parte del texto original de la mitad inferior de la columna derecha del folio 250r, que contiene Jer 7,28-31 está desvaída y ha sido entintada de nuevo por una mano posterior más ruda. Amén de que en esta columna se han deslizado errores en el texto durante el proceso del nuevo entintado. En el v. 30 la primera mano había escrito claramente נְאָם־יְהוָֹה. El que entintó de nuevo el texto deformó algunos de los restos de las letras originales y escribió erróneamente נְאֻם־יְהֹוָה. Queda claro, a partir de la plancha en blanco y negro del facsímil de Eerdmans/Brill, que el texto se borró y fue entintato de nuevo, pero los detalles de lo que ocurrió sólo se aclaran a partir de las trasparencias en color utilizadas por el proyecto.

En el sexto de los ocho colofones del manuscrito (en el f. 479r) Shemuʾel ben Yaʿaqob indicó que corrigió este manuscrito a partir de otros compuestos y corregidos por Aharon ben Moseh ben Asher. La estrecha conformidad del texto corregido y de la masora de M^L con la tradición de ben Asher, que está implícita en la

nota, se ha visto confirmada por numerosos estudios recientes. En los casos del *Kitāb al-khilāf* en los que ben Asher discrepa de ben Naftalí, M^A sigue a ben Asher en un 94% y M^L lo sigue en un 92%. Ambos siguen a ben Asher en un 90% de los casos en los que ben Asher y ben Naftalí coinciden frente a otras autoridades (Yeivin, *Tiberian Masorah*, 16 y 19; para una edición excelente del *Kitāb al-khilāf* ver L. Lipschütz, *Kitāb al-khilāf: Mishael ben Uzziel's Treatise on the Differences between Ben Asher and Ben Naphtali:* [Hebrew University Bible Project Monograph Series 2; Jerusalem: Magnes Press, 1965]). Esta correspondencia entre M^A y M^L es más estrecha que la de cualquier otro representante conservado de la tradición de ben Asher. En consecuencia M^L es, al parecer, un excelente representante del texto masorético tiberiense de la tradición de ben Asher, el segundo después de M^A respecto a su fidelidad a esa tradición, y el mejor representante completo que se conserva de dicha tradición. Como se reconoce ahora sobradamente, el texto masorético tiberiense es un descendiente, cuidadosamente conservado, de una corriente textual cuyos antecedentes antiguos se encuentran entre los Rollos del Mar Muerto.

Como se ha observado con frecuencia, M^L, aunque es un excelente manuscrito, no está compuesto con tanto cuidado como M^A. El grado de rigor y de discrepancia con relación a M^A varía de un aspecto del texto a otro. Si exceptuamos las letras vocales intermedias, las variantes en el texto consonántico son pocas. En el uso de las letras vocales intermedias M^L presenta una ligera preferencia por las grafías más comunes. Las variantes en la tradición de lectura son igualmente pequeñas. Las variantes en el uso de las *sǝtumôt* y de las *pǝtuhôt* son un poco mayores.

Las diferencias más importantes entre M^L y M^A, y los ejemplos más llamativos de descuido en la composición de M^L, están en la masora. En lo substancial las diferencias entre las notas de M^L y M^A son pocas, pero los dos manuscritos difieren en los fenómenos que comentan y en la forma de presentar la información de las notas. Como se sabe por varios estudios y por la obra de G. Weil en *BHS*, varias notas de la masora de M^L no corresponden al texto del manuscrito, presentan referencias mal copiadas o confusas, o parecen estar mal colocadas en el manuscrito. Por otro lado, a pesar de sus defectos, la masora de M^L tiene un valor real, tanto por tratarse del manuscrito más completo como por algunos datos específicos que M^L tiene en exclusiva.

LOS OTROS TESTIMONIOS MASORÉTICOS TIBERIENSES

En esta edición se colacionan otros siete manuscritos masoréticos tiberienses para varias partes de la Biblia. El Códice de Alepo (M^A) se ha colacionado en todas las partes de la Biblia en las que se conserva. Para la Torá se han colacionado también el Oriental Ms. 4445 de la Biblioteca Británica (M^B), el manuscrito EBP. II B 17 de la Biblioteca Nacional Rusa de San Petersburgo (M^{L17}), y el manuscrito Sassoon 507 (M^{S5}), ahora Heb. 24° 5702 de la Biblioteca Nacional y Universitaria de Jerusalén. Para los Profetas también se ha colacionado el Códice de El Cairo (M^C). Para los Escritos también se ha colacionado el Additional Ms. 1753 de la Biblioteca Universitaria de Cambridge (M^Y), y para libros que no se conservan en el Códice de Alepo se han colacionado o bien el manuscrito Sassoon 1053 (M^{S1}) o bien el

manuscrito EBP. II B 34 de la Biblioteca Nacional Rusa de San Petersburgo (M^{L34}). A continuación ofrecemos breves descripciones de estos testimonios e identificamos las ediciones y/o microfilmes usados como modelos para la colación y las citas. En este primer fascículo estas descripciones se basan más en los estudios existentes que en la experiencia directa de los editores. Además de las obras específicas identificadas en la descripción de cada uno de los testimonios, nos hemos apoyado para este estudio en las partes pertinentes de Yeivin, *Tiberian Masorah.*

– El *Códice de Alepo* (M^A) ha recibido mucha atención por parte de los expertos, como corresponde a su valor. La reciente obra de M. Beit-Arié, C. Sirat y M. Glatzer (*Codices Hebraicis Litteris Exaratis*, 1:65–72) proporciona una amplia description codicológica. A menos que se diga otra cosa, la siguiente descripción está tomada de la de Beit-Arié, Sirat y Glatzer. En la *BHQ* este testimonio se cita según la edición facsimilar de M. Goshen-Gottstein (*The Aleppo Codex.* Volume 1, The Plates [Jerusalem: Magnes Press, 1976]).

Aunque las partes conservadas del manuscrito no tienen colofón, la copia del texto consonántico de M^A se atribuye a Salomón ben Buya^{c}a, y la adición y comprobación de las vocales, acentos y masora se atribuye al mismo Aarón ben Asher. Estas atribuciones están basadas en la información contenida en cuatro notas marginales de dedicatoria del manuscrito mismo. También se ha argumentado que éste es el manuscrito que Maimónides dijo haber usado, del que afirmó que había sido corregido y comprobado por Ben Asher. Sobre la base de estas atribuciones se supone que el manuscrito fue compuesto en Tiberias. Beit-Arié, Sirat y Glatzer proponen como fecha de su composición en torno al 930 E.C.

Se conservan 295 folios del manuscrito original que contienen las partes siguientes del texto: Deut 28,17 hasta el final del libro; Josué; Jueces; Samuel; Reyes con la excepción de 2 Reyes 14,21–18,13; Isaías; Jeremías excepto 29,9–31,34 y partes de 32,1-25; Ezequiel; los Doce Profetas excepto Amos 8,13 hasta el final, Abdías, Jonás, Miq 1,1–5,1, Sof 3,20 hasta el final, Ageo, Zac 1,1–9,17; Crónicas; Salmos excepto 15,1–25,1; Job; Proverbios; Rut; Cant 1,1–3,11. En los folios que se conservan las varias formas de deterioro menor que han sufrido las páginas del códice no han dado como resultado una pérdida de texto, salvo en el folio 148 en el que se han perdido partes de los versos de Jer 32,1-25. El manuscrito está escrito sobre pergamino en escritura cuadrada con tinta marrón oscura, con el texto distribuido en su mayoría en tres columnas por página, y en dos columnas por página en Job, Proverbios y Salmos. La masora parva está escrita en los márgenes laterales e intercolumnares, y la masora magna en los márgenes superior e inferior.

El manuscrito se preparó son sumo cuidado y da pruebas de una corrección cuidada. Es el representante más puro de la tradición de ben Asher de todos los manuscritos existentes de la Biblia hebrea. Como dijimos antes, M^A sigue a ben Asher en 94% de los casos del *Kitāb al-khilāf* en los que ben Asher se distingue de ben Naftalí; y sigue a ben Asher y ben Naftalí en 90% de los casos en los que estos dos coinciden frente a otras autoridades (Yeivin, *Tiberian Masorah*, 16).

– El *Oriental Ms. 4445 of the British Library* (M^B) ha sido objeto de importantes estudios en contextos variados. Las obras de G. Margoliouth (*Catalogue of the Hebrew and Samaritan Manuscripts in the British Museum* [Londres: Museo Británico, 1899], Part I, 36–39) y A. Dotan ("Reflections Towards a Critical Edition of Pentateuch Codex Or. 4445," en *Estudios Masoréticos (X Congreso de la IOMS):*

En memoria de Harry M. Orlinsky [ed. E. Fernández Tejero y M. T. Ortega Monasterio; Madrid: Instituto de Filología del CSIC, 1993], 39–51) constituyen la base principal de la siguiente descripción. En la *BHQ* M^B ha sido colacionado y citado según un microfilme del manuscrito.

El manuscrito carece de colofón pero puede mantenerse que es uno de los más antiguos de todos los testimonios tiberienses utilizados en esta edición. Margoliouth lo fechó a mediados del siglo IX (*Hebrew and Samaritan Manuscripts*, 36). Y lo mismo Dotan ("Codex Or. 4445", 50), quien aun dejando al final abierta la cuestión, se inclina hacia una fecha de la segunda mitad del siglo IX. Yeivin (*Tiberian Masorah*, 19) sugiere una fecha en torno al 925. En general se mantiene que tanto el escriba como el lugar en que fue escrito son desconocidos. Sin embargo, Dotan propone que el nombre del escriba, Nissi ben Daniel ha-Kohen, se halla como acróstico en ciertas notas masoréticas, y que este escriba es responsable del conjunto del manuscrito, texto, vocales y acentos, y masora ("Codex Or. 4445", 50). Margoliouth y Dotan sugieren la posibilidad de una procedencia persa.

M^B contiene texto y masora (masora parva y masora magna) de Gén 39,20–Deut 1,33 excepto Núm 7,46-73; 9,12–10,18. Este texto del siglo IX ó X se encuentra en 186 folios de pergamino, distribuido en tres columnas por página. Las restantes partes del Pentateuco fueron añadidas en folios de papel que, según un colofón, fueron compuestos en 1540.

Según Yeivin, M^B sigue a ben Asher en un 80% de los casos del *Kitāb al-khilāf* en los que ben Asher se distingue de ben Naftalí, y sigue a ben Asher y a ben Naftalí en el 73% de los casos en los que ambos coinciden frente a otras autoridades (Yeivin, *Tiberian Masorah*, 19). P. Kahle registra un 83% de correspondencia con las lecturas de ben Asher cuando éstas difieren de ben Naftalí (P. Kahle, "The Hebrew Ben Asher Bible Manuscripts," *VT* 1 [1951]: 167). Margoliouth señala un número de divergencias respecto a la tradición tiberiense establecida (p. e. en la colocación de las *sətumôt* y de las *pətuḥôt*). Tanto Margoliouth como Dotan consideran algunos de estos rasgos en el texto y en la acentuación (y en la masora en el caso de Dotan) como signos de la antigüedad de la tradición del manuscrito.

– La extensa descripción codicológica del *manuscrito EBP. II B 17 de la Biblioteca Nacional Rusa* en San Petersburgo (M^{L17}) a cargo de M. Beit-Arié, C. Sirat y M. Glatzer (*Codices Hebraicis Litteris Exaratis*, 1:53–64) ofrece una exposición fácil y accesible de este manuscrito, y constituye la base de la descripción abreviada que sigue, a menos que se indique otra cosa. En la *BHQ* este testimonio ha sido colacionado y citado según un microfilme del manuscrito.

Como indican dos colofones del manuscrito su texto consonántico fue copiado por Salomón ha-Levi ben Buyaᶜa, que fue también el escriba de M^A. Las vocales, acentos, masora y decoración fueron añadidos por Efraím ben Buyaᶜa, quien también comprobó su texto. El segundo colofón da una fecha para el manuscrito que lo lleva al 929 E.C. Es un manuscrito bello y cuidadosamente preparado. Yeivin mantiene que en los casos del *Kitāb al-khilāf* M^{L17} no muestra una tendencia definida a coincidir con ben Asher o con ben Naftalí (*Tiberian Masorah*, 23). Este manuscrito del Pentateuco, ahora de 242 folios, está bastante deteriorado y contiene numerosas lagunas debidas a los folios que faltan. Se conservan las siguientes partes del Pentateuco: Gén 2,5–6,3; 8,9–20,9; 21,17–25,22; 27,6–41,43; Gén 42,35–Éxod 23,7; Éxod 25,2–Lev 19,20; Lev 20,8–25,17; Lev 25,44–Núm 10,35; Núm 17,6 hasta el final del Deuteronomio. El manuscrito está escrito sobre pergamino en escritura cuadrada, con tinta marrón oscura, que con frecuencia ha

palidecido, en especial por el lado de los folios que iba pegado a la carne. Salvo en el Canto del Mar y el Canto de Moisés, el texto está distribuido en tres columnas por página. La masora parva está escrita en los márgenes laterales e intercolumnares, y la masora magna en los márgenes superior e inferior. Se han perdido algunas de las primeras líneas del texto y algunas notas de la masora magna debido al deterioro de los márgenes superiores de las páginas.

– El *Pentateuco de Damasco*, antes conocido como *manuscrito Sassoon 507*, ahora conocido como Heb. 24° 5702 de la Biblioteca Nacional y Universitaria de Jerusalén (M^{S5}), está descrito en el catálogo de D. S. Sassoon (*Ohel David: Descriptive Catalogue of the Hebrew and Samaritan Manuscripts in the Sassoon Library, London* [Oxford: Oxford University Press; Londres: Humphrey Milford, 1932], 1:22–23). Es la base principal para la descripción que sigue. En la *BHQ* M^{S5} ha sido colacionado y citado según un microfilme del manuscrito, o según la edición facsimilar de M. Beit-Arié (*The Damascus Pentateuch* [vol. 2 in *Early Hebrew Manuscripts in Facsimile*; ed. M. Beit-Arié; Copenhagen: Rosenkilde and Bagger; Baltimore: Johns Hopkins University Press, 1982]).

Sin duda M^{S5} cae dentro del marco establecido por las fechas de M^B y M^L. Sin embargo, dentro de ese marco hay una considerable variedad en la fecha que se le asigna al M^{S5}. Yeivin (*Tiberian Masorah*, 21) fecha el manuscrito en el s. X, mientras que Sassoon lo fecha en el IX (*Ohel David*, 23). Loewinger también piensa en términos que apuntan al s. IX como fecha, mientras que Bet-Arié piensa en una fecha que ronda el año 1000 E.C. (*CTAT*, 3:ix). Hay un desacuerdo semejante sobre su lugar de origen, Tiberias (Sassoon y Loewinger), o, más en general Palestina o Egipto (Beit-Arié).

M^{S5} contiene el texto vocalizado y la masora (masora parva y masora magna) desde Gén 9,26 hasta el final del Deuteronomio, con la excepción de Éxod 18,1-23. El texto aparece en 229 folios distribuidos en tres columnas por página.

El manuscrito, al parecer, fue cuidadosamente preparado, pero su alineación en la tradición masorética no es tan clara como la de algunos otros usados en la *BHQ*. Yeivin informa de que utiliza un "sistema mixto" al consignar los acentos. El ms. sigue a ben Asher en el 52% de los casos del *Kitāb al-khilāf* en los que ben Asher difiere de ben Naftalí, y que sigue a ben Asher y ben Naftalí en el 76% de los casos en los que ambos coinciden frente a otras autoridades (Yeivin, *Tiberian Masorah*, 21). Sassoon sugiere que, aunque la masora sigue la tradición de ben Asher, el texto sigue la de ben Naftalí (*Ohel David*, 22).

– El *Códice de El Cairo* (M^C) ha recibido con razón una atención considerable por parte de los expertos en crítica textual. En su obra reciente, M. Beit-Arié, C. Sirat y M. Glatzer (*Codices Hebraicis Litteris Exarati*, 1:25–39) ofrecen una extensa descripción codicológica del manuscrito. A menos que se diga otra cosa, ésta es la base de la descripción que sigue. En la *BHQ* este testimonio se cita según la edición de F. Pérez Castro (*El Codice de Profetas de El Cairo* [7 vols. of text; Madrid: CSIC, 1979–1988; 4 vols. of indices; Madrid: CSIC 1992–1997]).

Uno de los dos colofones del manuscrito atribuye la copia del texto consonántico y de las vocales, acentos y masora a Moses ben Asher, y fecha y sitúa la producción del códice en el 894/5 E.C. en Tiberias. Diversos factores, incluidos los resultados de la datación por radiocarbono, llevan a Beit-Arié, Sirat y Glatzer a dudar de la autenticidad de esta atribución, y a fechar el códice al final del s. X o comienzos del XI.

M^C consta de 296 folios de pergamino que contienen los Profetas Anteriores y

Posteriores escritos con tinta marrón. No hay ninguna laguna importante en el texto de los Profetas por deterioro o por folios que falten. Excepto en los diversos
Cantos, que están dispuestos en una o dos columnas, el texto está distribuido en
tres columnas por página. La masora parva está escrita en los márgenes laterales e
intercolumnares, y la masora magna está escrita en los márgenes superior e inferior.

Si se tiene en cuenta su atribución a Moses ben Asher, resulta interesante que
M^C sigue a ben Asher sólo en el 33% de los casos del *Kitāb al-khilāf* en los que
ben Asher difiere de ben Naftalí, pero sigue a ben Naftalí en el 64% de los casos.
M^C sigue a ben Asher y ben Naftalí en el 75% de los casos en los que ambos
coinciden contra otras autoridades (Yeivin, *Tiberian Masorah*, 20). Sirat (*Codices
Hebraicis Litteris Exarati*, 1:28) reseña varios argumentos que indican una serie de
formas en las que M^C no concuerda con la tradición de ben Asher.

– El *Additional Ms. 1753 de la Biblioteca Universitaria de Cambridge* (M^Y) ha
sido objeto de importantes descripciones en obras de S. C. Reif (*Hebrew Manuscripts at Cambridge University Library: A Description and Introduction* [Cam-
bridge: Cambridge University Press, 1997], 70–71) y I. Yeivin ("The Division into
Sections in the Book of Psalms," *Textus* 7 [1969]: 76–102). En estas dos descripciones se basa el texto que sigue. Este testimonio ha sido colacionado y citado
según un microfilme del manuscrito.

M^Y es un manuscrito yemení. Se desconoce el escriba y la fecha de composición, porque el ms. carece de colofón. Reif (*Hebrew Manuscripts*, 70) propone una
fecha entre los siglos XV–XVI, pero la propuesta de Yeivin de una fecha entre los
siglos XIV–XV parece más aceptable, puesto que el sexto proprietario del ms. lo
adquirió en 1570.

El ms. consta de 145 folios de pergamino que contienen el texto con vocales y
acentos, así como la masora parva y la masora magna de los Escritos en el siguiente orden (que se ajusta al de M^L): Crónicas, Salmos, Job, Proverbios, Rut, Cantar,
Qohelet, Lamentaciones, Ester, Daniel, Esdras-Nehemías. El ms. contiene también
algunas listas masoréticas que se refieren a la Torá y a los Escritos.

Yeivin cree que M^Y no es en sí mismo una obra de la escuela de ben Asher,
pero lo considera "a second or third-hand copy" de un ms. ben Asher, que, a su
vez, considera "no less accurate and reliable than [M^A]". A pesar de algunos des-
cuidos al marcar los acentos y algunos errores obvios de copista "the details of the
ancient tradition have been preserved with meticulous care" (Yeivin, "Division
into Sections," 80). Este cuidado se manifiesta en numerosas muestras de la fidelidad del manuscrito a la tradición de ben Asher y a su ejemplar más extenso, M^A.
En aquellos casos del *Kitāb al-khilāf* en los que ben Asher difiere de ben Naftalí,
M^Y sigue a ben Asher en más de un 80%. Su "spelling, especially of the words
written plene and defective ... is almost identical with [M^A]". Comparado con un
ms. anónimo que contiene una lista de secciones abiertas y cerradas en Salmos,
M^A sigue dicha lista en un 90% de veces, y M^Y "surpasses, or is at least by no
means inferior to", M^A en su concordancia con la lista (Yeivin, "Division into Sections," 80). En realidad, de todos los mss. que comparó con la lista Yeivin llegó a
la conclusión de que sólo de cuatro mss. puede afirmarse que sigan sus diversas
características por lo que al libro de los Salmos se refiere. Éstos son M^A, M^Y, M^L,
y Firkovich II.94. Los dos primeros mss., M^A, y M^Y, forman un grupo que sigue
estas características casi idénticamente (Yeivin, "Division into Sections," 97).

– El Manuscrito *Sassoon 1053* (M^{S1}) está descrito en las páginas 1111–12 del

volumen 2 de D. S. Sassoon *Ohel David: Descriptive Catalogue of the Hebrew and Samaritan Manuscripts in the Sassoon Library, London* (Oxford: Oxford University Press; Londres: Humphrey Milford, 1932). En esa descripción y la de Yeivin en *Tiberian Masorah* (21–22) se basa ésta. En la *BHQ* M^{S1} ha sido colacionado y citado según un microfilme del manuscrito.

Tanto Sassoon como Yeivin fechan el manuscrito en el s. X. Sin embargo, no hay colofón que ofrezca una fecha exacta de la composición del manuscrito. Aunque por las notas del ms. se conocen los nombres de numerosos propietarios, no se conocen ni el nombre de la(s) persona(s) que compusieron el ms., ni el lugar de su composición.

M^{S1} contiene toda la Biblia en 396 folios, pero con lagunas (p. e. los diez primeros capítulos del Génesis se han perdido). El texto vocalizado y acentuado va acompañado de la masora parva y de la masora magna, pero la masora magna se halla sólo en algunas páginas. Los Profetas Posteriores figuran en el orden Jeremías, Ezequiel, Isaías y los Doce. Los Escritos figuran en la misma secuencia que en M^L, es decir, comienzan en vez de terminar con Crónicas.

Yeivin cree que, comparado con otros grandes manuscritos masoréticos tiberienses, M^{S1}, está compuesto con descuido. Sigue a ben Asher en un 40% de los casos del *Kitāb al-khilāf* en los que ben Asher difiere de ben Naftalí, y sigue a ben Asher y a ben Naftalí en un 60% de los casos en los que ambos coinciden frente a otras autoridades (Yeivin, *Tiberian Masorah*, 21–22).

– La descripción que sigue del *manuscrito EBP. II B 34 de la Biblioteca Nacional Rusa* de San Petersburgo (M^{L34}) está tomada en su mayor parte de la que se encuentra en P. Kahle, *Masoreten des Westens* (Stuttgart: W. Kohlhammer, 1927), 1:74–77. En la *BHQ* este testimonio ha sido colacionado y citado según un microfilme del manuscrito.

M^{L34} no contiene referencia alguna sobre la fecha de su composición. Un colofón que hace referencia a su reencuadernación en 1130, y una noticia dedicatoria fechada en 1100 ponen el límite más alto a su edad. Si otra nota, que no lleva fecha, se refiere a una reencuadernación más temprana, en ese caso el ms. probablemente es de una fecha anterior al s. XI. Yeivin sugiere que fue compuesto en torno al 975 (Yeivin, *Tiberian Masorah*, 26). Una nota dedicatoria sin fecha, que, al parecer, es anterior a la que está fechada, asocia el ms. con la comunidad caraíta de El Cairo.

M^{L34} contiene en 201 folios texto importante de la mayor parte de los Escritos, pero tiene muchas lagunas. Los contenidos específicos son los siguientes: 1 Cr 1,1-17, 5,24–6,4, 11,10-24, 17,26–18,14, 24,24–26,4; 2 Cr 1,9–2,5, 8,8–15,16, 24,6–28,27, 34,11–36,23; Salmos 1,1–7,4, 9,19–30,4, 45,11–78,61, 80,3–94,3, 96,1–145,15, 147,15–150,6; Job 1,1–8,16, 9,27–22,6, 23,10–34,3, 34,36–42,17; Prov 1,1–3,23, 6,26–10,32, 14,12–15,8; Cant 7,3–8,14; Qohelet; Lam 1,1–5,6; Est 1,22–8,7, 9,15–10,3; Dan 1,1–3,29, 4,13–12,13; Esdras 1,1-3, 2,8-42, 4,9–6,21, 8,2-22, 9,1-12; Neh 7,8-41, 8,9–9,4. Este texto va acompañado por lo que Yeivin llama "short" masora parva y masora magna (*Tiberian Masorah*, 26).

El manuscrito ha sido compuesto con cuidado. M^{L34} sigue a ben Naftalí en algo más de la mitad de los casos del *Kitāb al-khilāf* en los que difiere de ben Asher (Yeivin, *Tiberian Masorah*, 26).

AGRADECIMIENTOS

Es un grato deber dar las gracias a un número de personas e instituciones que han contribuido a apoyar este proyecto y han ayudado a conseguir sus objetivos. Estamos profundamente agradecidos a Dominique Barthélemy y Hans Peter Rüger, ya fallecidos; y a James A. Sanders, los tres del Hebrew Old Testament Text Project de las Sociedades Bíblicas Unidas por haber comprendido la necesidad de una nueva edición y haber propiciado el encuentro inicial del Comité Editorial. Deseamos expresar un agradecimiento particular a las Sociedades Bíblicas Unidas y a Jan de Waard, entonces presidente del Subcomité de la UBS para las ediciones científicas, por el apoyo necesario en las etapas iniciales del proyecto. Estamos profundamente agradecidos a Siegfried Meurer ya fallecido, a su sucesor Jan A. Bühner y a la Sociedad Bíblica de Alemania por haber comprendido, también desde la perspectiva editorial, la necesidad de una nueva *Biblia Hebraica*, y por haber proporcionado el apoyo práctico indispensable que se necesitaba para convertir la edición en una realidad. Esta edición se ha beneficiado de la flexibilidad y control de un nuevo método de produción informatizada en el que se introducen en una base de datos todos los que han de incluirse en la edición, que pueden a partir de ahí transformarse en una variedad de formas electrónicas e impresas. Este procedimiento no habría sido posible sin la guía y asistencia del asesor del proyecto en sistemas de información, Alan Groves, del Westminster Theological Seminary, su ayudante de programación Soetjianto, Winfried Bader y Rolf Schäfer de la Sociedad Bíblica de Alemania, y Edgar Szilagyi y Karl-Heinz Strößner de la imprenta universitaria Stürtz, AG. Apreciamos enormemente todos sus esfuerzos en favor de la *BHQ*. Estamos muy agradecidos al Ancient Biblical Manuscript Center de Claremont, California, y a su entonces presidente, James Sanders, y al director, Michael Phelps, por poner a nuestra disposición las espléndidas transparencias en color del M^L. También deseamos expresar nuestro agradecimiento a Aron Dotan, de la Universidad de Tel Aviv, por haber accedido a participar como asesor del proyecto para la masora y por haber ayudado a solucionar un número de problemas difíciles en esta área.

Muchas personas han contribuido de forma imprescindible al funcionamiento práctico del día a día del proyecto y desde aquí agradecemos con profundo aprecio sus importantes contribuciones. Rolf Schäfer de la Sociedad Bíblica de Alemania ha supervisado la producción de la edición desde el punto de vista editorial, tarea no pequeña, sobre todo si se tienen en cuenta las dificultades inherentes al nuevo proceso de producción. Roger Omanson, de las Sociedades Bíblicas Unidas, asumió de buen grado la tarea de preparación del manuscrito para la edición en un momento crucial para la vida del proyecto. Harold P. Scanlin, de las Sociedades Bíblicas Unidas, facilitó el trabajo del proyecto de forma práctica en muchos aspectos, especialmente en el acceso al manuscrito y a otros fondos. Sarah Lind, también de las Sociedades Bíblicas Unidas, ayudó a pulir el estilo del inglés de la introducción y de los comentarios al Qoheleth. Norbert Rabe en Tübingen y Jonathan Kearney en Dublin compulsaron con gran cuidado la versión electrónica del texto de M^L para las Megilloth con las transparencias. Por fin, última en orden pero no en importancia, Bernadette Schacher del Institut Biblique de Friburgo distribuyó de forma fluida, rápida y segura la información y los materiales entre los miembros del equipo del proyecto.

Particularmente deseamos recordar aquí a dos miembros del proyecto que ya no están entre nosotros: Martin Jan Mulder, de la Universidad de Leiden, y Raymond Dillard, del Westminster Theological Seminary, quienes fueron los editores iniciales del Cantar y Ester respectivamente. Sus muertes prematuras al poco tiempo de haber emprendido sus tareas les impidieron continuar con el proyecto.

Los editores están muy agradecidos a las instituciones que los acogen por su apoyo a esta obra, así como a numerosos colegas que han animado, y también criticado con solicitud y provecho, la labor de edición a lo largo de su andadura. A pesar de toda esta ayuda y de todos los esfuerzos que los miembros del equipo de la *BHQ* han invertido para hacer esta edición lo más útil posible para sus lectores, seguimos a nuestros predecesores al descubrir en las frases de Rudolf Kittel una conclusión oportuna (*BHK³*, V): "Incluso así a la *Biblia Hebraica* se le aplicará el dicho, 'Dies diem docet'. ¡Ojalá encuentre en todas partes críticos honestos, pero sobre todo lectores dignos de la grandeza del tema!".

Stuttgart
Febrero, 2004   EL COMITÉ EDITORIAL

FIGURE 1
Sample of an Apparatus Entry (Jer 23:17)
Illustrating the Presentation of the Text Critical Cases

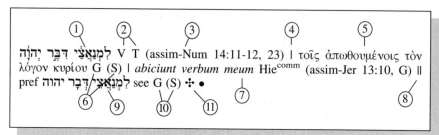

(1) **Lemma from M^L, the reference text**
(2) **Sigla for witnesses agreeing with the reference text**
(3) **Characterization of the reading from the reference text**
(4) **Separator line**
(5) **First reading differing from the reference text**
(6) **Sigla of witnesses attesting the reading**
(7) **Second reading differing from the reference text**
(8) **Separator line for the case conclusion**
(9) **Reading to be preferred over the reading in the reference text (the lemma)**
(10) **Sigla for witnesses supporting the preferred reading**
(11) **Symbol indicating that the commentary section has a discussion of this case**

(1) *Lemma aus M^L, dem Referenztext*
(2) *Sigla der Textzeugen, die mit dem Referenztext übereinstimmen*
(3) *Charakterisierung für die Lesart des Referenztextes*
(4) *Trennlinie*
(5) *Erste vom Referenztext abweichende Lesart*
(6) *Sigla der Textzeugen, in denen diese Lesart überliefert ist*
(7) *Zweite vom Referenztext abweichende Lesart*
(8) *Trennlinie vor der Schlussfolgerung zu diesem Fall*
(9) *Lesart, die gegenüber der Lesart des Referenztextes (Lemma) den Vorzug verdient*
(10) *Sigla der Textzeugen für die bevorzugte Lesart*
(11) *Hinweis darauf, dass der Kommentarteil weitere Erläuterungen zu diesem Fall enthält*

(1) Lema de M^L, texto de referencia
(2) Siglas de los testimonios que coinciden con el texto de referencia
(3) Caracterización de la lectura con relación al texto de referencia
(4) Línea de separación
(5) Primera lectura que difiere del texto de referencia
(6) Siglas de los testimonios que atestiguan la lectura
(7) Segunda lectura que difiere del texto de referencia
(8) Línea de separación para la conclusión de un caso
(9) Lectura preferida frente a la lectura del texto de referencia (lema)
(10) Siglas de los testimonios que apoyan la lectura preferida
(11) Símbolo indicativo de que la sección del comentario tiene una discusión sobre el caso

FIGURE 2

Sample Page Illustrating the Features of the Layout

(1) **Diplomatic presentation of the text of M^L (except for the insertion of verse numbers, the marking of poetic lines according to the Masoretic accents, and the omission of** *rapê***).**

(2) **Diplomatic presentation of the Masorah parva of M^L.**

(3) **Diplomatic presentation of the Masorah magna of M^L (except for verse numbers and reference separators); a translation is provided in the commentary section of the edition.**

(4) **Text critical apparatus with the evidence of witnesses to the Hebrew text for cases material to exegesis and/or translation; occasional expanded discussions in the commentary section of the edition.**

(1) *Diplomatische Wiedergabe des Bibeltextes aus M^L (abweichend von der Handschrift wurden Kapitel- und Versziffern hinzugefügt und poetische Passagen den masoretischen Akzenten folgend stichographisch angeordnet; außerdem wird rapê im Druck nicht wiedergegeben).*

(2) *Diplomatische Wiedergabe der Masora parva von M^L.*

(3) *Diplomatische Wiedergabe der Masora magna von M^L (abweichend von der Handschrift wurden Versziffern sowie Trennzeichen zwischen den einzelnen Verweisen hinzugefügt); im Kommentarteil findet sich dazu jeweils eine Übersetzung.*

(4) *Textkritischer Apparat mit dem Befund der antiken Textzeugen des Hebräischen Textes in denjenigen Fällen, die für Exegese und/oder Übersetzung möglicherweise bedeutsam sind; gelegentlich finden sich dazu weitere Erläuterungen im Kommentarteil.*

(1) Presentación diplomática del texto de M^L (excepto en la inserción de los números de versículo, la indicación de las líneas poéticas según los acentos masoréticos y la omisión del *rapê*).

(2) Presentación diplomática de la masora parva de M^L.

(3) Presentación diplomática de la masora magna de M^L (excepto en los números de versículo y los separadores de referencia); la traducción en la sección del comentario.

(4) Aparato crítico del texto con los datos de los testimonios del texto hebreo para el material de los casos que afectan a la exégesis y/o la traducción; ocasionalmente discusiones más extensas en la sección del comentario.

רות RUTH

1 וַיְהִ֗י בִּימֵי֙ שְׁפֹ֣ט הַשֹּׁפְטִ֔ים וַיְהִ֥י רָעָ֖ב בָּאָ֑רֶץ וַיֵּ֨לֶךְ אִ֜ישׁ מִבֵּ֧ית לֶ֣חֶם
ב̇ חד מל וחד חס ה̇

2 יְהוּדָ֗ה לָגוּר֙ בִּשְׂדֵ֣י מוֹאָ֔ב ה֥וּא וְאִשְׁתּ֖וֹ וּשְׁנֵ֥י בָנָֽיו׃ וְשֵׁ֣ם הָאִ֣ישׁ
ל
אֱ‍ֽלִימֶ֡לֶךְ וְשֵׁם֩ אִשְׁתּ֨וֹ נׇֽעֳמִ֜י וְשֵׁ֨ם שְׁנֵֽי־בָנָ֣יו ׀ מַחְל֤וֹן וְכִלְיוֹן֙ אֶפְרָתִ֔ים

3 מִבֵּ֥ית לֶ֖חֶם יְהוּדָ֑ה וַיָּבֹ֥אוּ שְׂדֵי־מוֹאָ֖ב וַיִּֽהְיוּ־שָֽׁם׃ וַיָּ֥מׇת אֱלִימֶ֖לֶךְ

4 אִ֣ישׁ נׇעֳמִ֑י וַתִּשָּׁאֵ֥ר הִ֖יא וּשְׁנֵ֥י בָנֶֽיהָ׃ וַיִּשְׂא֣וּ לָהֶ֗ם נָשִׁים֙ מֹֽאֲבִיּ֔וֹת שֵׁ֤ם
ב̇ מג̇
ל חס̇

5 הָֽאַחַת֙ עׇרְפָּ֔ה וְשֵׁ֥ם הַשֵּׁנִ֖ית ר֑וּת וַיֵּ֥שְׁבוּ שָׁ֖ם כְּעֶ֥שֶׂר שָׁנִֽים׃ וַיָּמ֤וּתוּ ל
גַם־שְׁנֵיהֶם֙ מַחְל֣וֹן וְכִלְי֔וֹן וַתִּשָּׁאֵר֙ הָֽאִשָּׁ֔ה מִשְּׁנֵ֥י יְלָדֶ֖יהָ וּמֵאִישָֽׁהּ׃ ל

6 וַתָּ֤קׇם הִיא֙ וְכַלֹּתֶ֔יהָ וַתָּ֖שׇב מִשְּׂדֵ֣י מוֹאָ֑ב כִּ֤י שָֽׁמְעָה֙ בִּשְׂדֵ֣ה מוֹאָ֔ב
ל חס̇
ב כתב ה

7 כִּֽי־פָקַ֤ד יְהוָה֙ אֶת־עַמּ֔וֹ לָתֵ֥ת לָהֶ֖ם לָ֑חֶם וַתֵּצֵ֗א מִן־הַמָּקוֹם֙ אֲשֶׁ֣ר
הָיְתָה־שָׁ֔מָּה וּשְׁתֵּ֥י כַלֹּתֶ֖יהָ עִמָּ֑הּ וַתֵּלַ֣כְנָה בַדֶּ֔רֶךְ לָשׁ֖וּב אֶל־אֶ֥רֶץ ב̇ חד מל

8 יְהוּדָֽה׃ וַתֹּ֤אמֶר נׇעֳמִי֙ לִשְׁתֵּ֣י כַלֹּתֶ֔יהָ לֵ֣כְנָה שֹּׁ֔בְנָה אִשָּׁ֖ה לְבֵ֣ית אִמָּ֑הּ
ב̇ ב̇
ב בנתי בנתי

9 יַ֣עַשׂ יְהוָ֤ה עִמָּכֶם֙ חֶ֔סֶד כַּאֲשֶׁ֧ר עֲשִׂיתֶ֛ם עִם־הַמֵּתִ֖ים וְעִמָּדִֽי׃ יִתֵּ֤ן
יעש ק̇
יְהוָה֙ לָכֶ֔ם וּמְצֶ֣אןָ מְנוּחָ֔ה אִשָּׁ֖ה בֵּ֣ית אִישָׁ֑הּ וַתִּשַּׁ֣ק לָהֶ֔ן וַתִּשֶּׂ֥אנָה ב

[1:1] תרין פסוק מיחדין ולית זוגה באורך רעב בארץ ב בטע וירד אברם . וילך איש :ס‎

1:1 בִּימֵי֙ שְׁפֹ֣ט הַשֹּׁפְטִ֔ים 4QRuthᵃ Gᴹˢˢ (V) (T) | ἐν τῷ κρίνειν τοὺς κριτάς G |
שְׁנֵ֥י בָנָֽיו ܚܡܫܐ ܕܢ‍ܐ S (facil-synt) ÷ • וְשֵׁם֩ 4QRuthᵃ 4QRuthᵇ Gᴹˢˢ V T | καὶ οἱ υἱοὶ
αὐτοῦ G S (implic) • **2** וְשֵׁם֩¹ 4QRuthᵃ G S T | שׁם 4QRuthᵇ | ipse vocabatur V
(transl) • אֱ‍ֽלִימֶ֡לֶךְ Gᴹˢˢ V S T | ̓Αβιμέλεχ G • וַיִּֽהְיוּ־ G T | וישבו 4QRuthᵃ
(assim-1:4?) | morabantur V (transl) | ܠܚܡܕ S (transl) ÷ • **3** אִ֣ישׁ נׇעֳמִ֑י G V S
T | vir eius La • **5** מִשְּׁנֵ֥י יְלָדֶ֖יהָ וּמֵאִישָֽׁהּ 4QRuthᵃ V T | ἀπὸ τοῦ ἀνδρὸς αὐτῆς
καὶ ἀπὸ τῶν δύο υἱῶν αὐτῆς G S (harm-chron) ÷ • **6** וְכַלֹּתֶ֔יהָ
T | prec δύο G (V)
S • **7** בַדֶּ֔רֶךְ G V (T) | > La S ÷ • **8** לִשְׁתֵּ֣י Gᴹˢˢ T | > G S | V (indet) • אִמָּ֑הּ G
T | τοῦ πατρὸς αὐτῆς Gᴹˢˢ (assim-cultur) | matris vestrae La V (assim-ctext) |
patris vestri Vᴹˢˢ (assim-cultur + assim-ctext) | ܕܐܒܘܟܝ S (assim-cultur + assim-
ctext) • יַ֣עַשׂ יעשה Mᵏᵉᵗ | יַ֣עַשׂ Mqᵉʳᵉ | G V S T (indet) • **9** לָכֶ֔ם G V | foll
ἔλεον Gᴸ S (ampl) | foll ... אגר טב שלים T (midr) ÷ •

SIGLA, SYMBOLS,
AND ABBREVIATIONS

The following list gives the sigla, symbols and abbreviations specific to this edition. Where no abbreviation has been specified otherwise, the edition follows the *The SBL Handbook of Style* (Peabody, Mass.: Hendrickson Publishers, 1999) in respect to abbreviations for the biblical books, extra-biblical sources, and conventional terms used in biblical studies. Standard English abbreviations not specified in this list, or in *The SBL Handbook of Style*, are derived from the lists and rules given in chapter 14 of *The Chicago Manual of Style: Fourteenth Edition, Revised and Expanded* (Chicago: University of Chicago, 1993). Abbreviations will appear without periods when used in the critical apparatus, regardless of the source.

In addition to the manuscript and witness sigla specific to this edition, which are listed below, the edition employs other manuscript sigla based on widely accepted standards. For the Old Greek, these are the sigla of the Göttingen Septuaginta Unternehmen, except in the case of the Alpha-Text of Esther for which the edition adopts the siglum G^{AT} (see below). For the materials from Qumran and other sites around the Dead Sea, the sigla follow the system of abbreviation described in J. A. Fitzmyer, S.J., *The Dead Sea Scrolls: Major Publications and Tools for Study* (SBLRBS, 20; rev. ed.; Atlanta: Scholars, 1990), 1–8. Where such an existing abbreviation is based on a document's name, this is used in preference to the abbreviation based on the document's number. For the Vulgate, the manuscript sigla are those of the San Girolamo edition of the Vulgate, i.e., *Biblia Sacra iuxta Latinam Vulgatam Versionem* (18 vols.; Rome: Typis Polyglottis Vaticanis, 1926–1995). For the Peshitta, the manuscript sigla of the Leiden Peshitta Project are used. Specific manuscripts of the versions will be indicated by placing the correct manuscript siglum in superscript to the witness siglum in question (e.g. S^{7a1}).

SIGLA FOR TEXTUAL WITNESSES

α'	Aquila
αλ'	ὁ ἄλλος, οἱ ἄλλοι
β'	Second column of the Hexapla
γ'	the "Three"
ε'	Quinta
εβρ'	ὁ ἑβραῖος
ετ'	οἱ ἕτεροι
ς'	Sexta
ζ'	Septima
θ'	Theodotion

ιω'	Ἰώσιππος, cf. J. Ziegler, *Jeremias, Baruch, Threni, Epistula Jeremiae*, p. 106
λ'	οἱ λοιποί
ο'	οἱ ἑβδομήκοντα
π'	πάντες
σ'	Symmachus
συρ'	ὁ Σύρος
⟨ ⟩	When placed around the siglum for a Hexaplaric witness (e. g., ⟨α'⟩), these brackets indicate that the Greek reading offered for the witness has been established by retroversion.

Note that hyphenated combinations of Hexaplaric readings (e.g., α'-σ'-θ') are used when a single reading is attributed by the same witness(es) to two or more of the Hexaplaric sources together.

Akh	Akhmimic
anon	anonymous (an otherwise unidentified Greek witness, usually reported by Jerome or Chrysostom – used in superscript with a source identification [e.g., Hie^{anon}])
ast	asterisk (※) Since the asterisk is used to witness to the proto-MT against the very source where the symbol is found, it is treated effectively as a witness in itself. The witness in which it is reported will be indicated in superscript (e.g., ast^{Syh}).
Barb	Barberini text of Habakkuk 3 (G mss. V 62 86 147 407)
Bo	Bohairic
G	Old Greek (as defined by the collation standard identified in the introduction to each book)
G*	the Old Greek reading in the judgment of the *BHQ* book editor, where this differs from the text established by the editor of the edition used as the standard of collation and citation
G^{Ms}	the reading for a single witness to the Old Greek as given in the apparatus of the relevant collation standard
G^{Mss}	the reading for more than one witness to the Old Greek as given in the apparatus of the relevant collation standard
Gα	where G offers "parallel" (i.e., literarily divergent) versions of the same text (e.g., Ezra, 1 Kgs 12:24), this signals the reading of the "first" version (e.g., Esdras α', 1 Kgs 12:24a–z)
Gβ	where G offers "parallel" (i.e., literarily divergent) versions of the same text (e.g., Ezra, 1 Kgs 12:24), this signals the reading of the "second" version (e.g., 1 Kgs 11:1–12:14, Esdras β')
G^{AT}	the Alpha-Text of Esther
G^{L}	the Lucianic Recension of the Old Greek
G^{O}	the Origenian Recension of the Old Greek
G^{P967}	papyrus 967 of the Old Greek (Ezekiel, Daniel, Esther)
Ga	Gallican Psalter
Gnz	fragments from the Cairo Geniza (always given in superscript with the siglum of the witness reported in the fragments, e.g., T^{Gnz}.)
Hbrs	*Psalterium iuxta Hebraeos*
Hev	the Greek Minor Prophets Scroll from Naḥal Ḥever

Hex		a Hexaplaric reading referred to without specification
Hie		Hieronymus (Jerome) (Note the variations Hie^{hebr}, used to designate an instance when Jerome reports the Hebrew text, and Hie^{comm}, where he comments on it.)
Hie^{SF}		Jerome's letter to Sunnia and Fretela
La		Old Latin (as defined by the appropriate collation standard)
	La^{Ambr}	quotations in the writings of Ambrosius
	La^{Ep}	the lemma text in the translation by Epiphanius Scholasticus of Philo of Carpasia's commentary on Canticles
	La^{169}	Salzburg, Abbey of St. Peter, Ms. IX 16
M		Masoretic Text (defined as the agreement of M^{L} and the other collated Tiberian MSS)
	M^{A}	Aleppo Codex
	M^{B}	British Library, Oriental Ms. 4445
	M^{C}	Cairo Codex of the Prophets
	M^{L}	the Leningrad Codex, manuscript EBP. I B 19a in the Russian National Library, St. Petersburg
	M^{L*}	a first hand reading in M^{L} (used only when a later hand reading is also recorded)
	M$^{L\,(qere)}$	the *qərê* for M^{L} alone
	M$^{L\,(ket)}$	the *kətîb* for M^{L} alone
	M^{L+}	a later hand in M^{L}
	M^{L17}	manuscript EBP. II B 17 in the Russian National Library, St. Petersburg
	M^{L34}	manuscript EBP. II B 34 in the Russian National Library, St. Petersburg
	M^{M1}	codex M1 in the Complutensian Library of Madrid
	M^{S1}	manuscript Sassoon 1053
	M^{S5}	manuscript Sassoon 507
	M^{Y}	Cambridge University, Add. Ms. 1753
Mur		Murabbaᶜât 88
obel		obelos [÷] Since the obelos is used to witness to the proto-MT against the very source where the symbol is found, it is treated effectively as a witness in itself. The witness in which it is reported will be indicated in superscript (e.g., obel^{Syh}).
S		Syriac (as defined by the collation standard identified in the introduction to each book)
	S*	the reading for the Syriac in the judgment of the *BHQ* book editor, where this differs from the text established in the collation standard being used for a given book
	S^{Ms}	the reading for a single witness to the Syriac as given in the apparatus of the relevant collation standard
	S^{Mss}	the reading for more than one witness to the Syriac as given in the apparatus of the relevant collation standard
Sa		Sahidic
Smr		Samaritan Pentateuch
Syh		Syro-Hexapla
T		Targum (In the Pentateuch this siglum signifies a reading attested by all extant Pentateuchal Targumim.)

T*	the reading for a Targum in the judgment of the *BHQ* book editor, where this differs from the text in the relevant collation standard. For the individual Pentateuchal Targumim this siglum takes the form of $T^{O}*$, $T^{J}*$, $T^{N}*$, $T^{F}*$
T^{Ms}	the reading for a single witness to a Targum as given in the apparatus of the relevant collation standard
T^{Mss}	the reading for more than one witness to a Targum as given in the apparatus of the relevant collation standard
T^{OJF}, T^{NJF}, T^{NJ}, etc.	multiple Pentateuchal Targumim witnessing the same reading
T^{Be}	the manuscript Berlin Orientalis 1213 of the Targum
T^{Br}	the Breslau manuscript of the Targum
T^{F}	the Fragment Targum to the Pentateuch
T^{J}	Targum Pseudo-Jonathan to the Pentateuch
T^{N}	Targum Neofiti to the Pentateuch
T^{O}	Targum Onqelos to the Pentateuch
T^{R}	Targum Rishon to Esther
T^{Sh}	Targum Sheni to Esther
T^{Smr}	Samaritan Pentateuch Targum
T^{U}	the manuscript Vaticanus Urbinas 1 of the Targum
T^{Z}	the Zamora edition of the Targum
V	Vulgate (as defined in the San Girolamo edition)
V*	the reading for the Vulgate in the judgment of the *BHQ* book editor, where this differs from the text established by the editor of the San Girolamo volume
V^{Ms}	the reading for a single witness to the Vulgate as given in the apparatus of the San Girolamo edition
V^{Mss}	the reading for more than one witness to the Vulgate as given in the apparatus of the San Girolamo edition
V^{We}	Weber, R., ed. *Biblia Sacra iuxta vulgatam versionem.* Two volumes. Stuttgart: Württembergische Bibelanstalt, 1975.

SYMBOLS USED IN THE APPARATUS

•	marks the end of a case in the apparatus
○	marks the end of a case in the apparatus when the next case also has the same lemma as the case ended by ○
‖	divides the presentation of variant readings and witnesses from final comments on a case
|	separates a reading and its witnesses from other readings and their witnesses within a case
( )	When parentheses are used around a portion of text within a variant reading, they signal that the words contained within them are not themselves part of the reading, but are the context of the words actually constituting the reading at issue in the case. When used around the siglum for a witness, they indicate that the reading in that witness agrees with the reading with which the witness is aligned on the mat-

ter at issue in the case, but varies in matters of detail that are not relevant to the case.

>   means "is lacking"

→   indicates a point to which the reader's attention is directed

√   means "lexical root"

⁜   denotes a case receiving further discussion in the commentary

1, 2, etc.   (given in superscript) first, second, etc.

+   indicates that the lemma (or its equivalent) plus the text after the sign constitutes the reading in question. It is used where "prec" or "foll" are too precise an indication.

?   When written as a superscript ($^?$), this is used to express doubt about one of two matters:

    – whether the reading represents the best form of that witness (e.g., $G^?$, $G^{*?}$);

    – the assignment of a reading to a Hexaplaric witness.

These usages are to be distinguished from cases where there is doubt about the alignment of the witnesses, in which case "indet" is used.

‖   used in an apparatus entry to indicate a reference to a "parallel passage," which will be indicated for the whole page in the margin to the left of the first line of the critical apparatus

*   This sign, when appended to the siglum for a manuscript (e.g., M^{A*}), indicates the uncorrected first hand of that manuscript. The same sign, when appended to the siglum for a witness (e.g., $G*$), rather than an individual manuscript, indicates the *BHQ* book editor's choice for the original reading of that witness. Such a decision will be explained in the commentary. In the case of a Hexaplaric witness (e.g., α'*), this sign may also indicate the *BHQ* book editor's choice about the assignment of the Hexaplaric reading to a witness. Such a decision also will be explained in the commentary.

ABBREVIATIONS

abbr	abbreviation
abs	absolute
act	active
adj	adjective
ampl	amplification
aram	Aramaic
art	article
assim	assimilation
caus	causative
cf	*confer*, see also
chron	chronology
cj	conjunction
cohort	cohortative
comm	commentary
confl	conflation

conjec	conjecture
conjec-phil	philological conjecture (This is used to signal that a preferred reading falls into one of three classes: its root is attested in Hebrew [or Aramaic for Daniel and Ezra] of the biblical period, but neither its *binyan* [conjugation] nor a corresponding *binyan* is attested; its root is attested in Hebrew of the biblical period, but not with the sense indicated in the case; its root is not attested in Hebrew of the biblical period.)
cons	of the consonantal text
conv	converted (imperfect/perfect)
copt	Coptic
cp	compare
crrp	corrupt
cstr	construct state
ctext	context
cultur	cultural
dbl	double reading/translation
differ	difference, different
differ-txt	different text – the standard notation used to *describe* a reading that will not otherwise be quoted (e.g., Syriac psalm superscriptions, parallel but different passages in Tanakh)
dissim	dissimilation
ditt	dittography
div	division of the consonantal text
elus	elusive motivation or cause
em scr	emendation of the scribes (i.e., any genuine case of scribal emendation whether or not it occurs in the list of tiqqune sopherim)
emph	giving emphasis
err	error
euphem	euphemism
exeg	exegesis
explic	making explicit
f	feminine
facil	facilitation
foll	followed by (Note also the use of "prec" and the sign +.)
frag	fragmentary
geogr	geography
gk	Greek
gram	grammar
graph	graphic/graphemic
hapl	haplography
harm	harmonization
hebr	Hebrew
hist	history, historical
homarc	homoioarcton
homtel	homoioteleuton
ideol	ideologically motivated
idiom	idiom/idiomatic
ign	ignorance (always with a specification [e.g., ign-lex])

illeg	illegible
impf	imperfect
implic	making implicit
impv	imperative
indet	indeterminate
indic	indicative
inf	infinitive
insuf	insufficient data for conclusion
interp	interpretation
interpol	interpolation
interr	interrogative
irrel	irrelevant to the case at hand
Jos, *Ap*	Josephus, *Contra Apionem*
Ant	Josephus, *Antiquitates Judaicae*
BJ	Josephus, *Bellum Judaicum*
Vit	Josephus, *Vita*
ket	*kǝṯîḇ* (always superscript with M [i.e., M^{ket}]; for a single ms. of M as follows: M$^{L(ket)}$)
KR	the manuscripts described in the editions of Kennicott and de Rossi
lacun	lacuna
lat	Latin
lem	lemma
lex	lexical
lib	liberty
lit	literary
loc	locative
m	masculine
metath	metathesis
Mf	Masorah finalis
mg	margin
midr	midrash
Mm	Masorah magna
modern	modernization
Mp	Masorah parva
ms	manuscript
mss	manuscripts
narr	narrative
neg	negative
obj	object
om	omission
order	word order
origin	origin (This term is used to designate a preferred reading when that reading explains the extant readings, but is not itself extant.)
orth	orthographic
par	parallel text
paraphr	paraphrase
part	particle
pass	passive
pf	perfect

Philo, *Abr*   *De Abrahamo*
   Aet   *De aeternitate mundi*
   Agr   *De agricultura*
   Cher *De cherubim*
   Conf *De confusione linguarum*
   Congr *De congressu quaerendae*
   Dec   *De decalogo*
   Det   *Quod deterius potiori*
   Ebr   *De ebrietate*
   Flacc *In Flaccum*
   Fug   *De fuga et inventione*
   Gaium *Legatio ad Gaium*
   Gig   *De gigantibus*
   Hyp   *Hypothetica [Apologia pro Iudaeis]*
   Jos   *De Iosepho*
   Leg Alleg *Legum allegoriae*
   Mig   *De migratione Abrahami*
   Mos   *De vita Mosis*
   Mut   *De mutatione nominum*
   Op   *De opificio mundi*
   Plant *De plantatione*
   Post *De posteritate Caini*
   Praem *De praemiis et poenis*
   Prov *De providentia*
   QE   *Quaestiones et solutiones in Exodum*
   QG   *Quaestiones et solutiones in Genesin*
   Quis Rerum *Quis rerum divinarum heres*
   Quod Deus *Quod Deus immutabilis sit*
   Quod Omn *Quod omnis probus liber sit*
   Sac   *De sacrificiis Abelis et Caini*
   Sob   *De sobrietate*
   Som   *De somniis*
   Spec Leg *De specialibus legibus*
   Virt   *De virtutibus*
   Vit Cont *De vita contemplativa*

phonol   phonological
pl   plural
prec   preceded by (Note also the use of "foll" and the sign +.)
pref   preferred reading (This indicates that this reading, from among those presented in the apparatus entry for a case, is to be preferred as the earliest attested text.)
prep   preposition
pron   pronoun
ptc   participle
qere   *qərê* (always superscript with M [i.e., M^{qere}]; for a single ms. of M as follows: $M^{L\,(qere)}$)
redund   redundancy
refl   reflexive
rest   restoration

seman	semantic
sfx	suffix
sg	singular
shift	shift of meaning
spont	spontaneous
styl	stylistic
subj	subject
subst	substantive
substit	substitution
synt	syntactic
syr	Syriac
syst	systematization
theol	theologically motivated
tiq soph	tiqqun sopherim (i.e., a case included in the traditional list of emendations of the scribes, whether or not the emendation is judged to be genuine)
transcr	transcription
transf	transfer
transl	translational
translit	transliteration
transp	transposition
txt	text
unattest	unattested (This is used to signal that a preferred reading established by retroversion belongs to a *binyan* [conjugation] for which no other form is attested in Hebrew [or Aramaic in Daniel and Ezra] of the biblical period, but for which a corresponding *binyan* is attested.)
unconv	unconverted (imperfect/perfect)
usu	usual expression
v	verse
vv	verses
vb	verb
via	identifies the Hebrew root or form judged to have served as the stimulus for a reading
vocal	vocalization
vocat	vocative
vrs	version
vrss	versions

DEFINITIONS AND ABBREVIATIONS
FOR THE TERMS
USED TO CHARACTERIZE READINGS

The following lists present the abbreviated characterizations used in the critical apparatus of this edition to signal the basic element(s) of the editor's judgment of the relation between the reading characterized and the preferred (or occasionally another) reading in the case. First the characterizations are listed according to their underlying typology. Then they are listed alphabetically with their definitions.

THE TYPOLOGY UNDERLYING THE CHARACTERIZATIONS

An editor employs characterizations in the presentation of a case when such judgments can be expressed with reasonable confidence, and with sufficient clarity to aid the reader. Such confidence and clarity is aided both by a diversity of expressions and by the organization of those expressions according to typological categories so that, taken together, they constitute a coherent language.

The following typology moves through increasing levels of specificity about the relationship between a particular variant reading and the preferred reading in a case. The first division is based on the criterion of relevance. The characterizations under heading I describe readings that do not bear on the case at hand. Those under headings II–VII describe readings that do bear on the case in some way. Then characterizations that merely identify that a certain type of difference exists between two readings (heading II) are distinguished from those that indicate that the characterized reading represents a change from the preferred reading (headings III–VII). The characterizations that describe one reading as a change from another are distinguished first of all on the basis of whether the characterization proposes a motivation for the change (headings IV–VII) or simply describes the movement of text involved in the change (heading III). The characterizations that propose a motivation for the change embodied in a particular reading are further subdivided into those that suggest that the change is an accident (heading IV), those that suggest that the change is intentional (heading VII), and those that suggest that the change is the result of an impulse that might represent either a conscious or unconscious process on the part of the tradent (e.g., copyist, translator), i.e., headings V–VI. Finally, the characterizations that describe a reading as the result of an intentional change (heading VII) are subdivided according to three degrees of specificity about that intention (none at all – VII A; in terms of its result – VII B; in terms of a specific purpose – VII C).

I.   Characterizations of a Reading as Not Bearing on the Issue in the Case

illeg   illegible
insuf   insufficient
indet   indeterminate
irrel   irrelevant
lit   literary

II.   Characterizations of One Reading as Differing from Another,
*   Identifying Only the Point of Difference*

differ   difference
                     differ-div
                     differ-gram
                     differ-graph
                     differ-orth
                     differ-phonol
                     differ-vocal

III. Characterizations of One Reading as Representing a Type of Change from
*   Another Reading, But Not Commenting on the Motivation of the Change*

confl   conflation
dbl   double reading/translation
gloss
metath   metathesis
om   omission
spont   spontaneous
transp   transposition

IV.   Characterizations of a Reading as Representing a Change Arising Through
*   Accident*

ditt   dittography
hapl   haplography
homarc   homoioarcton
homtel   homoioteleuton

V.   Characterizations of a Reading as Representing a Change Arising Through
*   Ignorance or Error*

ign   ignorance
                     ign-cultur
                     ign-geogr
                     ign-gram
                     ign-lex
err   error
                     err-chron
                     err-geogr
                     err-gram
                     err-graph

                    err-hist
                    err-lex
                    err-phonol
                    err-synt

VI.   *Characterizations of a Reading as Representing a Change That Arises in Reaction to Some Textual/Linguistic Element*

   A. *In Reaction to Some Difficulty in Source Texts: Hebrew and Versional Witnesses and Their* Vorlagen

   facil   facilitation
                    facil-gram
                    facil-lex
                    facil-seman
                    facil-styl
                    facil-synt

   B. *In Reaction to Some Aspect of the Receptor Language (Versions Only)*

   transl   translational adjustment

VII. *Characterizations of a Reading as Representing a Change Arising Through the Intention of a Tradent*

   A. *Through an Intention Which Is Not Further Specified, Instead the Type of Change Is Specified*

   lib   liberty
                    lib-seman
                    lib-synt
   abbr   abbreviation
   ampl   amplification
   emph   giving emphasis
   explic   making implicit information explicit
   implic   making explicit information implicit
   interpol   interpolation
   paraphr   paraphrase
   rest   restoration
   shift   shift of meaning
   substit   substitution
   transcr   transcription
   translit   transliteration

   B. *Through an Intention Which Is Further Specified In Terms of the Results of the Change*

   assim   assimilation
                    assim-[reference]
                    assim-ctext
                    assim-cultur

	assim-par
	assim-styl
	assim-usu
harm	harmonization
	harm-[reference]
	harm-chron
	harm-ctext
	harm-styl
	harm-synt
modern	modernization
syst	systematization

C. *Through an Intention Which Is Further Specified In Terms of the Purpose of the Change*

exeg	exegesis
euphem	euphemism
interp	interpretation
midr	midrash
narr	narrative
theol	theologically motivated
ideol	ideologically motivated

VIII. *Miscellaneous Terms*

base	
crrp	corrupt
elus	elusive
em scr	emendation of the scribes
tiq soph	tiqqun sopherim
via	
via √	

ALPHABETICAL LIST
OF THE CHARACTERIZATIONS AND THEIR DEFINITIONS

abbr = abbreviation   This term characterizes a reading as arising from the shortening of the text (i.e., the deletion of textual matter) through scribal activity (as opposed to a literary [i.e., redactional] abridgment). It signals an initiative on the part of the copyist or translator, but does not specify the nature of the motivation behind the initiative.

ampl = amplification   This term characterizes a reading as arising from the scribal activity of filling out a text (as opposed to a literary [i.e., redactional] expansion). It signals an initiative on the part of the copyist or translator, but does not specify the nature of the motivation behind the initiative. "Ampl" is to be distinguished from "lit" in that the former refers to developments within the textual transmission of a single edition of a book, whereas the latter presupposes the survival of more than one edition of a book.

assim = assimilation   This characterization suggests that a particular force in generating the reading of a witness in the case has been an impulse to create or increase a degree of similarity with a text or contextual element with which a certain degree of similarity may already exist. The nature of the assimilation will be further specified by indicating that to which the reading is made similar (e.g., another passage, words or phrases in the context of the current passage).

assim-[reference] = assimilation to the particular passage whose reference is given (e.g., assim-Hab 1:4)

assim-ctext = assimilation to specific words or phrases in the context of the current passage

assim-cultur = assimilation to the cultural pattern prevailing at the time of the translator or copyist

assim-par = assimilation to a parallel text

assim-styl = assimilation to the prevailing style of the current passage

assim-usu = assimilation to the typical form of the expression as found in Biblical Hebrew/Aramaic

base   This term designates a text that is regarded as the basis for another extant reading. The reading designated as "base" need not be extant itself. However, in labeling something as "base" the editor is either referring to an extant reading, or is positing that such a reading actually existed at one time as a *Vorlage*. When such a degree of certainty concerning the actual existence of a reading is impossible, the term "via" (for which see below) will be used.

confl = conflation   This term characterizes a reading as arising from the merging of two otherwise attested readings.

crrp = corrupt   This term signals a judgment that the text is disturbed in some way that cannot be adequately deciphered.

dbl = double reading/translation – This term characterizes a reading as containing two forms or renderings of the same text.

differ = difference   This characterization makes no attempt to suggest anything about the origin of a witness's reading. It simply calls attention to the existence of a difference between readings. "Differ" will appear with an additional term specifying the point at which the readings differ. The following combinations will be found:

differ-div = difference in the division of the text

differ-gram = difference in grammar

differ-graph = difference in the writing of the consonantal text (other than orthographic differences)

differ-orth = difference in orthography

differ-phonol = difference in phonology

differ-vocal = difference in vocalization

ditt = dittography   This term characterizes a reading as arising from the accidental repetition of a letter or letters, or word or words.

elus = elusive   This term signals that the motivation for a reading is difficult to ascertain.

em scr = emendation of the scribes   This term identifies a case as a genuine instance of scribal emendation, whether or not it occurs in the traditional lists of the tiqqune sopherim. Note also "theol" (for which see below).

emph = giving emphasis   This term describes the effect of a change, i.e., making

an expression more emphatic, judged to have been introduced by the copyist or translator.

err = error   This term communicates a judgment that the origin of a reading is to be found in a mistake on the part of the ancient copyist or translator. "Err" is further specified using one of the following combinations:

err-chron = error in chronology
err-geogr = error of geography
err-gram = error in grammar
err-graph = error in writing the consonantal text
err-hist = error in historical matters
err-lex = error in lexical matters
err-phonol = error in phonology
err-synt = error of syntax

euphem = euphemism   This term communicates a judgment that a reading arises from the desire to substitute an agreeable or inoffensive expression for one that may offend or may suggest something unpleasant.

exeg = exegesis   This characterization points to an initiative on the part of a witness to develop the meaning of the lemma. "Exeg" is thus a broad term for a class of changes, and the characterizations "euphem," "interp," "midr," "narr," "theol," and "ideol" highlight more specific phenomena within that category.

explic = making implicit information explicit   This term expresses the judgment that the witness is not really adding new information to the text, but rather is making explicit information already implicit in the text. "Explic" is to be distinguished from "interp" (for which see below).

facil = facilitation   This characterization suggests that a reading arises from an impulse to ease some difficulty or awkwardness in the way the passage containing the case reads.

This is to be distinguished from "harm" (= harmonization). Harmonization emphasizes the making consistent of something which the copyist or translator perceived (whether consciously or unconsciously) to be inconsistent. Facilitation emphasizes rather that the passage would have been perceived to be difficult, awkward, containing an unresolved tension – to be "rough" in some way, and that the reading arises as a "smoother" form of the text, relieving the reader's difficulty. "Facil" may be used alone, or the nature of the facilitation may be further specified by indicating the aspect of the text in which the ancient reader/copyist/translator is judged to have experienced difficulty.

facil-gram = facilitation of a grammatical difficulty
facil-lex = facilitation of a lexical difficulty
facil-seman = facilitation of a semantic difficulty
facil-styl = facilitation of a stylistic difficulty
facil-synt = facilitation of a syntactical difficulty

gloss   This term indicates a judgment that the reading in question may result from the interpolation into the text itself of a short comment on the text, which was originally located between the lines or in the margin of the text.

hapl = haplography   This term characterizes a reading as arising from the accidental omission of similar and contiguous letters or words.

harm = harmonization   This term suggests that a particular force in the generation of the reading of a witness appears to have been an impulse to make the

text read in a way that is consistent with some external frame of reference. This does not mean that the reading is made like these other materials. The emphasis rather is on the possibility that it could have been perceived to be inconsistent with them in some way. The reading then would have been generated as a way to achieve consistency, not necessarily similarity. "Harm" may be used alone, or the nature of the harmonization may be further specified by indicating either the frame of reference for the harmonization (e.g., another text, the context of the case), or the textual aspect that is harmonized (e.g., syntax, style, chron). (See also "facil.")

harm-[reference] = harmonization with the particular passage identified by the reference (e.g., harm-Hab 2:1)

harm-chron = harmonization of chronology

harm-ctext = harmonization with the context

harm-styl = harmonization of style

harm-synt = harmonization of syntax

homarc = homoioarcton   This term characterizes the absence in a witness of a reading or elements of a reading as an accidental omission attributable to the identity of beginning between two words at the boundaries of the omitted phrase, line, or clause.

homtel = homoioteleuton   This term characterizes the absence in a witness of a reading or elements of a reading as an accidental omission attributable to the identity of ending between two words at the boundaries of the omitted phrase, line, or clause.

ideol = ideologically motivated   This term proposes that the reading has been adjusted to conform to a particular ideological perspective which is not necessarily or overtly theological.

ign = ignorance   This term communicates a judgment that the origin of a reading is to be found in the copyist's or translator's lack of data or understanding concerning their *Vorlage*. In distinction to "err," the use of the characterization "ign" emphasizes the tradents' lack of knowledge, not their mistake. "Ign" will be further specified using one of the following combinations:

ign-cultur = ignorance of cultural information

ign-geogr = ignorance of geography

ign-gram = ignorance of grammar

ign-lex = ignorance of lexical information

illeg = illegible   This characterization is reserved in this edition for use in apparatus cases generated due to damage to the main text of M^L. It is applied to the reading reported for M^L to indicate that it cannot be read with sufficient clarity and completeness to provide a reading for the base text of the edition.

implic = making explicit information implicit   This term expresses the judgment that the witness is not removing existing information from the text, but is suppressing the explicit communication of that information, leaving it implicit.

indet = indeterminate   This characterization indicates that the cited witness is unusable for resolving the particular difficulty at issue in the case (e.g., the Latin versions in the case of the presence or absence of the definite article, or the Greek and Latin versions in the case of the masculine or feminine gender of a verbal form).

insuf = insufficient   This term indicates that a manuscript other than M^L has been

damaged in some way so that its reading, although present, cannot be determined with enough confidence to be cited.

This is to be distinguished from the use of "frag" (=fragmentary) as a superscript qualification of a manuscript witness, which signals that the reading in the indicated manuscript, while incomplete, is sufficiently complete to bear with some degree of confidence upon the case under discussion.

interp = interpretation   This characterization proposes that the Hebrew/Aramaic text of the lemma contained some ambiguity as to its meaning, and the ancient witness in question has made a decision concerning this ambiguity. This ambiguity is not necessarily a difficulty or awkwardness, and pertains more to obtaining a clear meaning from a text rather than to its basic intelligibility, thus distinguishing "interp" from "facil." "Interp" is also to be distinguished from "explic" (for which see above). Both terms refer to a process of making implicit information explicit. "Explic," however, presupposes that the implicit information made explicit is clear to the copyist or translator, requiring no decision. "Interp" presupposes an ambiguity concerning which the ancient copyist or translator, as reader, had to decide.

interpol = interpolation   This term characterizes the reading as having arisen from the insertion into the text of textual matter from another document, or another part of the same document.

irrel = irrelevant   This term marks the reading of a particular witness as irrelevant to the specific issue under consideration in a case.

lib = liberty   This characterization proposes that the primary force generating the reading in question is the initiative of the copyist or translator rather than phenomena in the source text, or some interaction of the source text and a broader context, or the demands of a version's receptor language. "Lib" suggests that the change may have some degree of intentionality, that this intentionality is not driven by some reference point outside of the copyist or translator, and that the intention behind the reading is not specified further. "Lib" may appear alone, or with a further specification to indicate the linguistic aspect in which liberty was exercised.

lib-seman = liberty in respect to semantic matters

lib-synt = liberty in respect to syntactic matters

lit = literary   This term indicates that a reading represents a discrete literary tradition (i.e., one of two or more surviving editions for a book) that should not itself be used to correct another text coming from a different literary tradition (i.e., another edition) represented in the reading of another witness. Samuel and Jeremiah, for example, each offer a number of such cases.

metath = metathesis   This term characterizes a reading as arising from the transposition of letters within a word. No statement is being made about the motivation for the change, but it is more likely to be regarded as accidental than intentional. "Metath," which pertains to letters within a word, is to be distinguished from "transp," which pertains to words (see "transp" below).

midr = midrash   This term proposes that the reading is inspired by an extant midrashic tradition.

modern = modernization   This term characterizes a reading as arising from assimilation to the lexical or grammatical usage prevailing at the time of the translator or copyist.

narr = narrative   This term proposes that the reading has arisen from an adjustment to conform to some narrative structure or technique.

om = omission   This term characterizes the absence in a witness of a reading, or elements of a reading, as the accidental or intentional omission of that reading or those elements by the copyist or translator.

paraphr = paraphrase   This term communicates a judgment that a reading is best characterized as a restatement in other form of the meaning of another (therefore prior) reading.

rest = restoration   This term signals the judgment that a witness attempted to restore a text (its *Vorlage*) that it thought had been corrupted in previous transmission.

shift = shift of meaning   This term signals the judgment that a version tried to give a new sense to the totality of a passage by rewriting part of the text's elements, and that the variation observed in the case in question arose from that rewriting process.

spont = spontaneous   This term proposes that a particular variant reading that seems to be supported by independent witnesses in fact arose spontaneously and independently in those witnesses in response to the same difficulty with the Hebrew text.

substit = substitution   This term signals the judgment that the word or words of the reading have been substituted for another word or words at the free initiative of the copyist or translator, but without further specification of the motivation for the substitution.

syst = systematization   This term communicates a judgment that the reading in question arises as part of a process by which the copyist or translator gives a passage (including the case in question) a more uniform literary structure.

theol = theologically motivated   This term proposes that the reading has been adjusted to conform to theological norms. Note also "tiq soph" (for which see below) and "em scr" (for which see above).

tiq soph = tiqqun sopherim   This term identifies a case as one included in the traditional lists of emendations of the scribes, whether or not the case is judged actually to be such an emendation. Note also "theol" (for which see above).

transcr = transcription   This term suggests that a versional reading arose, not from the translation of the version's *Vorlage*, but from the reproduction – according to the phonological system of the versional language – of the spoken form of the *Vorlage* (i.e., the way it sounded).

transl = translational adjustment   This characterization of a reading points to the role of the constraints and opportunities provided by the receptor language of a version, and the way those aspects necessarily shape the rendering of the particularities of the source text and language.

translit = transliteration   This term suggests that a versional reading arose, not from the translation of the version's *Vorlage*, but from the reproduction – based on some character-for-character equivalence – of the written form of the *Vorlage* (i.e., its spelling), regardless of whether the resulting versional form imitated the sound of the *Vorlage* or would have been regarded as orthographically "strange" in the versional language.

transp = transposition   This term characterizes a reading as arising from two words or groups of words having exchanged locations within the sequence of

the text. No statement is being made about the motivation for the change, but it is more likely to be regarded as accidental than intentional. "Transp," which pertains to words, is to be distinguished from "metath," which pertains to letters within a word (see "metath" above).

via   This term indicates the Hebrew form that is judged to have served as the stimulus for a particular extant reading. In so marking a form, no position is taken as to whether the reading was an actual *Vorlage* (written in a manuscript) or a virtual *Vorlage* (in the mind of the translator or copyist), or even whether one could properly label the form a *Vorlage*.

via √   This term indicates the Hebrew *root* that is judged to have served as the stimulus for a particular extant reading. The root is understood as a kind of hermeneutical key that appears to have shaped the way the copyist or translator understood their *Vorlage*.

GLOSSARY OF COMMON TERMS
IN THE MASORAH PARVA

Prepared by A. Schenker

word beginning with ʾalep̄,   א
the letter ʾalep̄, the accent ʾatnah

one, once   אَ

the alphabet,   א״ב, אלפא ביתא
alphabetical order, Ps 119

the first two letters of the   א׳ ב׳ ב׳ ג׳ ד׳
word follow the order of
the alphabet

the tetragrammaton   אדכר, אדכרה
(= הזכרה)

the Pentateuch   או, אור, אורי׳, אורייתא

letter, letters   אות, אותיות

suspended letters   אות תלויות

other   אחרי׳

they   אינון

there is/are   אית

there is/are in them   אית בהון

woman   אית = איתא

within, the middle,   אמ׳, אמצע, אמצעא
the interior (of a clause or word)

Job, Proverbs, Psalms   אמ״ת
(the three poetical books)

the whole Bible   אנ״ך

man's name   אנש, בר נש, שום בר נש,
שם גברא

woman's name   אנת, אנתתא, אתת, אתתא

ʾatnah and sôp̄ pasûq   א״סף, אתנ וסוף פסו

one verse is the sîman   אפ״ס

Aramaic   ארמֹ

letter, letters   את, אתא, אתין

ʾatnah   אתנ, אתנח, אתנחתא

woman's name   אתת, אתתא

except for one (two, . . .)   בֹ מֹ אֹ (בֹ . . .),
בר מן אֹ (בֹ . . .)

in them   בהון

in it   ביה

between them   ביניה, ביניהון

Genesis   ברא, בראשית

man   ברנש, בר נש

after   בתר, בתרא,

man's name   גבר, גברא

gaʿyâ   גע׳, געיא, גיעיה

gereš   גרש, גריש

Chronicles   דב הי, דב ימֹ, ד״ה

after   דבתר, (ד)בתריה

daḡeš   דגש, דיג, דיגשא

this one   דין

similar, like it, like them   דכ, דכו, דכות,
דכותיה, דכותהון

masculine   דכר

incomplete   דלוג

similar   דמיין

fifteen (15)   ה׳י

these   הלין

codex Hilleli   הללי׳

here   הכא

word with *waw* prefixed to it   וא

and another   וא׳

and one   וא

waw   ואו

Numbers   וידבר

pair, pairs   זוג, זוגין

masculine   זכר

small (letter[s])   זעיר, זעירא, זעירין

zâqep̄   זק, זקף, זקף, זקפא

zarqâ   זרק, זרקא

its companion   חב, חבי, וחב, חברו, וחברו

one, once   חד, חדה, חדא

English	Hebrew
one of, unique among	חד מן
ordinary (profane)	חול
the Pentateuch	חומש
without gaᶜyâ (i.e., short)	חטף
difference, variation	חלוף, חילופ, חילוף
defective, defectively written	חס, חסי, חסיר, ח, חסר
doubly defective	חס וחס
middle, half	חצי
accent, with accent	טע, טעם, בטע, בטעמא
once	יחד
unusual	יחיד, מיחד, מיוחד, יחידאין, מיחדין
the Tetragrammaton	יי, ייי, יה
Joshua, Judges, Psalms	י ש ת
superfluous	יתי, יתיר, יתירין
here	כה, כאן
like, similar	כות, כותהון
written thus, thus written	כ״כ, כתיב כן, כן כתיב
all	כל, כ״ל, כול
written, kəṯîḇ	כת, כתיב, כתוב, כתיבא, כתבן
the Writings	כתי, כתו, כתיב, כתיבין, כתוביא
unique	ל, לית, ליתא
ləḡarmeh	לג, לגר, לגרמ, לגרמיה
form, meaning, language, gender	ליש, לישנ, בליש, בלישנא, לשון
above	לעיל
below	לרע
changed, put behind	מאוחר
mêrəḵâ	מארכ, מארכא, מאריכין
the Esther scroll	מג, מגלה
Easterners	מדנ, מדנח, למד, למדנ, מדנחאי
correct text, corrected text	מוג, סיפ מוג, ספר מוגא
doubled, repeated	מוכפ, מוכפל
put in front	מוקדם
variant, variants	מחליפ, מחל, מחלפ, מחלפין
they are mistaken	מטע, מטעין, דמטע
unusual	מיחד, מיוחד, מיחדין
word, words	מילה, מלה, מלה, מילין, מלין
number	מינין
in their midst	מיסיהון
plene	מל, מ״ל, מלא
twice plene	מל דמל, מ״ל דמ״ל, מלא דמלא
milᶜêl, stress on the penultima	מלע, מלעיל
milraᶜ, stress on the ultima	מלר, מלרע
among them, from them	מנה, מנהון
musical meaning (of the טע׳)	מנוגן
vocalized	מנוקד, מנוקדין
Masorah finalis	מס׳ רבתא
Westerners	מע, מער, מערבאי
middle of the verse	מ״ק, מצע פסוק
mappîq, they pronounce the final hê	מפ, מפיק, מפיקין
within	מצ׳, מצעא, מיצעא, מציעא
Masorah parva	מ ק
Deuteronomy	מ״ת, משנה תורה
different	משני, משנין
Kings, Isaiah, Jeremiah, the Twelve	מ׳ש׳ר׳ת׳
similar, the same	מתא, מתאימין, מתאמין
variant, variants	מתח, מתחלפ, מתחלפין
in the midst of the word	מ״ת, מצע תיבותא
another text	נ״א, נוסחא אחרינא, נוסח אחר
the Prophets	נב, נביא, נביי, נבי, נביאי
musical meaning (of the טע׳)	נגן
capital nûn	נון רבתי
lower case nûn	נון זעיר
the Prophets and the Writings	נ״ך
with, including, added	נסיב, נסיב, נסיבין, נסבה, נסבא
points	נקוד, נקודות
feminine	נקיבה
seḏer, lectionary section	ס
another book, other books	ס״א, ספרין אחריין
presumed reading (not to be introduced into the text)	סביר, סביר, סבירין
mnemonic note, reference, their mnemonic note(s), their reference(s)	סי, סימ, סימן, סימנהון
book	סיפ, סיפרא
end	סיפא
sum, total	סכום

connected with,	סמיכ, סמיך, סמיכין
closely preceding,	
closely following, constructed with	
sôp pasûq,	ס פ, ס״פ, סוף פס, סוף פסוק
the end of a verse	
the end	ס״ת, סוף תיבותא, סופי תיבותא
of a word	
context, section	עינ, עינינ, עניָן, ענינא
at the end	עקב', עקבא
difference,	פלג, פולג, פלוג, פלוגתא, פלגתא
division, discordance (of opinion)	
someone	פלוני
verse	פסו, פס, פסוק
paseq	פס, פסק, פסיק, פסיקתא
parašâ, lectionary section	פרש, פרשה
paṭaḥ	פת, פתח, פתחין
səḡôl	פת קטן
qərê	ק, קר, קרי, קריין
first	קד, קדמ, קדמא, קדמיה
holy, Hebrew	קדש, לשון קדש
(i.e., the holy tongue)	
qameṣ	קמ, קמצ
ṣerê	קמצ קטן
bald (i.e., without prefixed *waw*)	קרחי
Holy Scripture	קריא, קרי
place name	קריה, קרתא
the beginning	ר, ראש
the beginning of the verse	ר״פ, רא פס
the beginning of a word	ראש תיבותא
great, large	רב, רבת, רבתי
plural	רבים, לשון רבים
rêš, beginning	ריש
rapê	רפ, רפי, רפה, רפין
(i.e., without *daḡeš*	
or quiescent laryngeal)	
the rest, the others	שא, שאר, שארא
(personal) name,	שום, שם, שמא, שמו', שמוא'
names	
list	שיטה, שטה
the following	שלא, שלאה, שלאחריו
(word, clause, etc.)	
Samuel	שמו, שמוא
the Torah	ת, תו, תור
word	תיב, תיבו, תיבות, תיבותא
Leviticus	ת״כ, תורת כוהנין
second	תינ'
suspended (letter)	תלוי
Psalms	תלים, תלין
three, *səḡôl*	תלת
second	תנינא
the Bible	תנ״ך
second	תל, תרי, תרתי, תרין, תרתין
the Twelve Prophets,	ת״ע, תל עש, תרי עשר
Dodekapropheton	
two meanings	תל לישׁנ
targum	תרג, תרגום

TABLE OF ACCENTS

ACCENTS FOR THE TWENTY-ONE PROSE BOOKS

(The horizontal lines divide the accents into grades of equivalent strength.)

Disjunctive accents

Sign	Name(s)	Example
	sillûq (*always at the verse end* [sôp̄ pasûq]); *or* sôp̄ pasûq	דָּבָר׃
	ᵓaṯnaḥ	דָּבָר
	səḡôltâ (*postpositive*)	דָּבָר֒
	šalšeleṯ	דָּבָר׀
	zaqep̄ qaṭan	דָּבָר
	mûnaḥ-zaqep̄	וְהָאָדָ֜ם
	zaqep̄ gaḏôl	דָּבָר
	məṯîḡâ-zaqep̄	וְכִסּוֹ
	ṭip̄ḥâ (*comes before* ᵓaṯnaḥ *or* sillûq)	דָּבָר
	rəḇîaᶜ	דָּבָר
	zarqâ (*postpositive; comes before* səḡôltâ)	דָּבָר֮
	paštâ (*postpositive*)	דָּבָר֙
	paštâ	מֶלֶךְ
	yəṯîḇ (*prepositive; a substitute for* paštâ)	מֶלֶךְ
	təḇîr	דָּבָר
	gereš *or* ṭeres	דָּבָר
	geršayim	דָּבָר
	pazer *or* pazer qaṭan	דָּבָר
	pazer gaḏôl *or* qarnê p̄arâ	דָּבָר
	təlîšâ gəḏôlâ (*prepositive*)	דָּבָר
	ləḡarmeh (*comes before* rəḇîaᶜ)	דָּבָר׀

Conjunctive accents

Sign	Name(s)	Example
	mûnaḥ *or* šôp̄ar mûnaḥ, šôp̄ar ᶜillûy, *or* šôp̄ar məḵarbel	דָּבָר
	mahpak *or* šôp̄ar hapûḵ *or* məhuppaḵ	דָּבָר
	mêrəḵâ	דָּבָר
	mêrəḵâ kəp̄ûlâ	דָּבָר
	dargâ	דָּבָר
	ᵓazlâ	דָּבָר
	təlîšâ qəṭannâ (*postpositive*)	דָּבָר֩
	galgal *or* yeraḥ	דָּבָר
	mâyəlâ (*rare; looks like* ṭip̄ḥâ, *but always used as a secondary accent on the same phonetic unit as* ᵓaṯnaḥ *or* sillûq)	וַיֵּצֵא־נֹחַ

Additional signs

Sign	Name(s)	Example
	gaᶜyâ *or* meteḡ (*always used ahead of another accent*)	וַיְלַמְּדָהּ
	maqqep̄	אִמְרִי־לִי
	paseq	הַבּוֹגֵד ׀ בּוֹגֵד

ACCENTS FOR THE THREE POETICAL BOOKS
(PSALMS, JOB AND PROVERBS)

(The horizontal lines divide the accents into grades of equivalent strength.)

Disjunctive accents

Sign	Name(s)	Example
	sillûq (*always at the verse end* [sôp̄ pasûq]); *or* sôp̄ pasûq	דָּבָר׃
	ᶜolê wəyôreḏ	דָּבָר
	ʾaṯnaḥ	דָּבָר
	rəḇîaᶜ gaḏôl	דָּבָר
	rəḇîaᶜ muḡraš	דָּבָר
	šalšeleṯ gəḏôlâ	דָּבָר |
	ṣinnôr *or* zarqâ (*postpositive*)	דָּבָר
	rəḇîaᶜ qaṭan	דָּבָר
	dəḥî (*prepositive*)	דָּבָר
	pazer *or* pazer qaṭan	דָּבָר
	məhuppaḵ ləḡarmeh	דָּבָר |
	ʾazlâ ləḡarmeh	דָּבָר |

Conjunctive accents

Sign	Name(s)	Example
	mûnaḥ *or* šôp̄ar mûnaḥ	דָּבָר
	mêrəḵâ	דָּבָר
	ᶜillûy *or* šôp̄ar ᶜillûy	דָּבָר
	ṭarḥâ	דָּבָר
	galgal *or* yeraḥ	דָּבָר
	šôp̄ar mahpaḵ *or* šôp̄ar məhuppaḵ	דָּבָר
	ʾazlâ	דָּבָר
	šalšeleṯ qəṭannâ	דָּבָר
	ṣinnôrîṯ (*comes before* mêrəḵâ *or* šôp̄ar mahpaḵ *on an open syllable*)	דָּבָר

Additional signs

Sign	Name(s)	Example
	gaᶜyâ *or* meteḡ (*always used ahead of another accent*)	וַיְלַמְּדָה
	maqqep̄	אִמְרֵי־לִי
	məṯîḡâ (*used as a secondary accent on the syllable before* mêrəḵâ)	חָכְמָה
	paseq	הַבּוֹגֵד | בּוֹגֵד

MEGILLOTH
מגלות

RUTH רות
prepared by J. de Waard

CANTICLES שיר השירים
prepared by P.B. Dirksen

QOHELETH קהלת
prepared by Y.A.P. Goldman

LAMENTATIONS איכה
prepared by R. Schäfer

ESTHER אסתר
prepared by M. Sæbø

RUTH רות

1 וַיְהִ֗י בִּימֵי֙ שְׁפֹ֣ט הַשֹּׁפְטִ֔ים וַיְהִ֥י רָעָ֖ב בָּאָ֑רֶץ וַיֵּ֨לֶךְ אִ֜ישׁ מִבֵּ֧ית לֶ֣חֶם   <small>ל֖</small>
<small>ב֞ חד מל וחד חס</small>

2 יְהוּדָ֗ה לָגוּר֙ בִּשְׂדֵ֣י מוֹאָ֔ב ה֥וּא וְאִשְׁתּ֖וֹ וּשְׁנֵ֣י בָנָֽיו׃ וְשֵׁ֣ם הָאִ֣ישׁ   <small>ל֖</small>

אֱלִימֶ֡לֶךְ וְשֵׁם֩ אִשְׁתּ֨וֹ נָעֳמִ֜י וְשֵׁ֣ם שְׁנֵֽי־בָנָ֣יו ׀ מַחְל֤וֹן וְכִלְיוֹן֙ אֶפְרָתִ֔ים

3 מִבֵּ֥ית לֶ֖חֶם יְהוּדָ֑ה וַיָּבֹ֥אוּ שְׂדֵי־מוֹאָ֖ב וַיִּֽהְיוּ־שָֽׁם׃ וַיָּ֥מָת אֱלִימֶ֖לֶךְ

4 אִ֣ישׁ נָעֳמִ֑י וַתִּשָּׁאֵ֥ר הִ֖יא וּשְׁנֵ֥י בָנֶֽיהָ׃ וַיִּשְׂא֣וּ לָהֶ֗ם נָשִׁים֙ מֹֽאֲבִיּ֔וֹת שֵׁ֤ם   <small>ב֞ מ֞ג</small>
<small>ל וחס</small>

5 הָֽאַחַת֙ עָרְפָּ֔ה וְשֵׁ֥ם הַשֵּׁנִ֖ית ר֑וּת וַיֵּ֥שְׁבוּ שָׁ֖ם כְּעֶ֥שֶׂר שָׁנִֽים׃ וַיָּמ֥וּתוּ   <small>ל֖</small>

גַם־שְׁנֵיהֶ֖ם מַחְל֣וֹן וְכִלְי֑וֹן וַתִּשָּׁאֵר֙ הָֽאִשָּׁ֔ה מִשְּׁנֵ֥י יְלָדֶ֖יהָ וּמֵאִישָֽׁהּ׃   <small>ל֖</small>

6 וַתָּ֤קָם הִיא֙ וְכַלֹּתֶ֔יהָ וַתָּ֖שָׁב מִשְּׂדֵ֣י מוֹאָ֑ב כִּ֤י שָֽׁמְעָה֙ בִּשְׂדֵ֣ה מוֹאָ֔ב   <small>ל וחס</small>
<small>ב֞ כתבה ה</small>

7 כִּֽי־פָקַ֤ד יְהוָה֙ אֶת־עַמּ֔וֹ לָתֵ֥ת לָהֶ֖ם לָ֑חֶם וַתֵּצֵ֗א מִן־הַמָּקוֹם֙ אֲשֶׁ֣ר   <small>ב֞ חד מל</small>

הָיְתָה־שָׁ֔מָּה וּשְׁתֵּ֥י כַלֹּתֶ֖יהָ עִמָּ֑הּ וַתֵּלַ֣כְנָה בַדֶּ֔רֶךְ לָשׁ֖וּב אֶל־אֶ֥רֶץ

8 יְהוּדָֽה׃ וַתֹּ֤אמֶר נָעֳמִי֙ לִשְׁתֵּ֣י כַלֹּתֶ֔יהָ לֵ֣כְנָה שֹּׁ֔בְנָה אִשָּׁ֖ה לְבֵ֣ית אִמָּ֑הּ   <small>ב֞ ב֞</small>
<small>ב֞ בנתי בנתי</small>

9 יַ֣עַשׂ יְהוָ֤ה עִמָּכֶם֙ חֶ֔סֶד כַּאֲשֶׁ֧ר עֲשִׂיתֶ֛ם עִם־הַמֵּתִ֖ים וְעִמָּדִֽי׃ יִתֵּ֨ן   <small>יעש֖</small>
<small>ק</small>

יְהוָ֜ה לָכֶ֗ם וּמְצֶ֤אןָ מְנוּחָ֔ה אִשָּׁ֖ה בֵּ֣ית אִישָׁ֑הּ וַתִּשַּׁ֣ק לָהֶ֔ן וַתִּשֶּׂ֥אנָה   <small>ב֞</small>

<small>[1:1] תרין פסוק מיחדין ולית זוגה ויהי רעב בארץ ב֞ בטע וירד אברם . וילך איש :o:</small>

1:1 בִּימֵ֣י שְׁפֹ֣ט הַשֹּׁפְטִ֔ים 4QRuth^a G^Mss (V) (T) | ἐν τῷ κρίνειν τοὺς κριτάς G | ܘܒܢ̈ܝ ܕܝܠܗ S (facil-synt) �︎ • וּשְׁנֵ֣י בָנָֽיו׃ 4QRuth^a 4QRuth^b G^Mss V T | καὶ οἱ υἱοὶ αὐτοῦ G S (implic) • **2** וְשֵׁ֣ם 4QRuth^a G S T | שם 4QRuth^b | ipse vocabatur V (transl) • אֱלִימֶ֖לֶךְ G^Mss V S T | ’Αβιμέλεχ G • וַיִּֽהְיוּ־ G T | וישבו 4QRuth^a (assim-1:4?) | morabantur V (transl) | ܠܚܕܬܐ S (transl) �︎ • **3** אִ֣ישׁ נָעֳמִ֑י G V S T | vir eius La • **5** מִשְּׁנֵ֥י יְלָדֶ֖יהָ וּמֵאִישָֽׁהּ׃ 4QRuth^a V T | ἀπὸ τοῦ ἀνδρὸς αὐτῆς καὶ ἀπὸ τῶν δύο υἱῶν αὐτῆς G S (harm-chron) �︎ • **6** וְכַלֹּתֶ֔יהָ T | prec δύο G (V) S • **7** בַדֶּ֔רֶךְ G V (T) | > La S �︎ • **8** לִשְׁתֵּ֣י G^Mss T | > G S | V (indet) • אִמָּ֑הּ G T | τοῦ πατρὸς αὐτῆς G^Mss (assim-cultur) | matris vestrae La V (assim-ctext) | patris vestri V^Mss (assim-cultur + assim-ctext) | ܠܒܝܬ S (assim-cultur + assim-ctext) • וַתִּשֶּׂ֥אנָה T (midr) ✿ • **9** לָכֶ֗ם G V | foll ἔλεον G^L S (ampl) | foll ... אגר טב שלים T (midr) ✿ •

קוֹלָ֖ן וַתִּבְכֶּ֑ינָה וַתֹּאמַ֣רְנָה־לָּ֔הּ כִּי־אִתָּ֥ךְ נָשׁ֖וּב לְעַמֵּֽךְ׃ וַתֹּ֣אמֶר 10

נָעֳמִ֗י שֹׁ֤בְנָה בְנֹתַי֙ לָ֣מָּה תֵלַ֣כְנָה עִמִּ֔י הַֽעֽוֹד־לִ֤י בָנִים֙ בְּֽמֵעַ֔י וְהָי֥וּ 11

לָכֶ֖ם לַאֲנָשִֽׁים׃ שֹׁ֤בְנָה בְנֹתַי֙ לֵ֔כְןָ כִּ֥י זָקַ֖נְתִּי מִהְי֣וֹת לְאִ֑ישׁ כִּ֤י אָמַ֙רְתִּי֙ 12

יֶשׁ־לִ֣י תִקְוָ֔ה גַּ֣ם הָיִ֤יתִי הַלַּ֙יְלָה֙ לְאִ֔ישׁ וְגַ֖ם יָלַ֥דְתִּי בָנִֽים׃ הֲלָהֵ֣ן ׀ 13

תְּשַׂבֵּ֗רְנָה עַ֚ד אֲשֶׁ֣ר יִגְדָּ֔לוּ הֲלָהֵן֙ תֵּֽעָגֵ֔נָה לְבִלְתִּ֖י הֱי֣וֹת לְאִ֑ישׁ אַ֣ל

בְּנֹתַ֗י כִּֽי־מַר־לִ֤י מְאֹד֙ מִכֶּ֔ם כִּֽי־יָצְאָ֥ה בִ֖י יַד־יְהוָֽה׃ וַתִּשֶּׂ֣נָה קוֹלָ֔ן 14

וַתִּבְכֶּ֖ינָה ע֑וֹד וַתִּשַּׁ֤ק עָרְפָּה֙ לַחֲמוֹתָ֔הּ וְר֖וּת דָּ֥בְקָה בָּֽהּ׃ וַתֹּ֗אמֶר 15

הִנֵּה֙ שָׁ֣בָה יְבִמְתֵּ֔ךְ אֶל־עַמָּ֖הּ וְאֶל־אֱלֹהֶ֑יהָ שׁ֖וּבִי אַחֲרֵ֥י יְבִמְתֵּֽךְ׃ 16

וַתֹּ֤אמֶר רוּת֙ אַל־תִּפְגְּעִי־בִ֔י לְעָזְבֵ֖ךְ לָשׁ֣וּב מֵאַחֲרָ֑יִךְ כִּ֠י אֶל־אֲשֶׁ֨ר 17

תֵּלְכִ֜י אֵלֵ֗ךְ וּבַאֲשֶׁ֤ר תָּלִ֙ינִי֙ אָלִ֔ין עַמֵּ֣ךְ עַמִּ֔י וֵאלֹהַ֖יִךְ אֱלֹהָֽי׃ בַּאֲשֶׁ֤ר

תָּמ֙וּתִי֙ אָמ֔וּת וְשָׁ֖ם אֶקָּבֵ֑ר כֹּה֩ יַעֲשֶׂ֨ה יְהוָ֥ה לִי֙ וְכֹ֣ה יֹסִ֔יף כִּ֣י הַמָּ֔וֶת 18

יַפְרִ֖יד בֵּינִ֥י וּבֵינֵֽךְ׃ וַתֵּ֕רֶא כִּֽי־מִתְאַמֶּ֥צֶת הִ֖יא לָלֶ֣כֶת אִתָּ֑הּ וַתֶּחְדַּ֖ל 19

לְדַבֵּ֥ר אֵלֶֽיהָ׃ וַתֵּלַ֣כְנָה שְׁתֵּיהֶ֔ם עַד־בֹּאָ֖נָה בֵּ֣ית לָ֑חֶם וַיְהִ֗י כְּבֹאָ֙נָה֙ 20

בֵּ֣ית לֶ֔חֶם וַתֵּהֹ֤ם כָּל־הָעִיר֙ עֲלֵיהֶ֔ן וַתֹּאמַ֖רְנָה הֲזֹ֣את נָעֳמִֽי׃ וַתֹּ֣אמֶר

---

[10] ח בטע וסימנה ויצא נח . בשבעתיכם . מאפליה . קפדה בא . ובאת שמה . ובאו
שמה . וישבו בה . ותאמרנה לה :o: ותרין ומזון לכלא בה . וחביר . [11] לאנשים ו
פתח וסימנ התחזקו ב בו . ולקחתי את לחמי . ויצקו לאנשים . קחו נשים והולידו .
והיו לכם לאנשים . וחד ויעש דוד לאבנר :o: [16] אל אשר ה וסימנהון ועתה לך נחה .
והתנחלתם . יהיה שמה הרוח . וקרבו . תלכי אלך :o: וחלופיהן אשר אל ו ועשית שתי
טבעת זהב . וחבירו . ויהי כקרא יהודי . ויבא אתי . והבנין אשר . ומחוצה לשער :o:
עמך ה וסימנהון והשביע הכהן . בפרסות . נשים . ושכחי . רות :o: [19] ותהם ג
הארץ . הקריה . כל העיר :o:

---

9 לֶ֣כְןָ • **12** קוֹלָ֖ן G S T | קולם 4QRuthª | prec ἑκάστη GᴸL | *quae elevata voce* V ✣ • V T | > G S | διὰ τοῦτο Gᴹˢˢ (differ-vocal: לְכֵן) ✣ • הַלַּ֙יְלָה֙ V T | > G S (euphem) | λελαϊκωμένην Gᴹˢˢ (via חָלִילָה?) | βεβηλωμένη α' (via חֲלִילָה?) | *odie* La (euphem) ✣ • בָנִֽים G V S T | prec שֵׁנִ֥ית 4QRuthᵇ • **14** לַחֲמוֹתָ֔הּ 4QRuthᵇ | foll καὶ ἐπέστρεψεν εἰς τὸν λαὸν αὐτῆς G (explic) | foll *et habiit* La (explic) | foll *ac reversa* V (explic) | foll ܘܗܦܟܬ ܠܘܬ ܥܡܗ S (explic) | foll ואזלת לאורח T (explic) ✣ • וְאֶל־אֱלֹהֶ֑יהָ 4QRuthᵇ | G V S T (indet) • אֶל־עַמָּ֖ה | ל[ע]מּ[ה] | (emph) ✣ • **15** אֶל־עַמָּ֖הּ | ל[ע]מּ[ה] | (emph) ✣ • ולאלהיה 4QRuthᵇ | > S | G V T (indet) • שׁ֖וּבִי (V) T | foll δὴ καὶ σύ G S (emph) ✣ • **19** וַיְהִ֗י כְּבֹאָ֙נָה֙ בֵּ֣ית לֶ֔חֶם Gᴹˢˢ (V) S T | > G (homtel) • וַתֵּהֹ֤ם T | καὶ ἤχησεν G (via וַתַּהֹם?) | *audibit* La (interp) | *velox ... fama percrebuit* V (interp) | ܘܙܥܬ S (interp) ✣ •

אֵלֵיהֶן אַל־תִּקְרֶאנָה לִי נָעֳמִי קְרֶאןָ לִי מָרָא כִּי־הֵמַר שַׁדַּי לִי   ה . ל חסֿ .

21 מְאֹד: אֲנִי מְלֵאָה הָלַכְתִּי וְרֵיקָם הֱשִׁיבַנִי יְהוָה לָמָּה תִקְרֶאנָה לִי   ל כת אׁ

22 נָעֳמִי וַיהוָה עָנָה בִי וְשַׁדַּי הֵרַע לִי: וַתָּשָׁב נָעֳמִי וְרוּת הַמּוֹאֲבִיָּה   דׁ וחד ושב והרע

כַלָּתָהּ עִמָּהּ הַשָּׁבָה מִשְּׂדֵי מוֹאָב וְהֵמָּה בָּאוּ בֵּית לֶחֶם בִּתְחִלַּת

2 קְצִיר שְׂעֹרִים: וּלְנָעֳמִי מוֹדָע לְאִישָׁהּ אִישׁ גִּבּוֹר חַיִל מִמִּשְׁפַּחַת   מודע קׁ

2 אֱלִימֶלֶךְ וּשְׁמוֹ בֹּעַז: וַתֹּאמֶר רוּת הַמּוֹאֲבִיָּה אֶל־נָעֳמִי אֵלְכָה־נָּא

הַשָּׂדֶה וַאֲלַקֳטָה בַשִּׁבֳּלִים אַחַר אֲשֶׁר אֶמְצָא־חֵן בְּעֵינָיו וַתֹּאמֶר   ל . ל . נׁא

3 לָהּ לְכִי בִתִּי: וַתֵּלֶךְ וַתָּבוֹא וַתְּלַקֵּט בַּשָּׂדֶה אַחֲרֵי הַקֹּצְרִים וַיִּקֶר   ל

4 מִקְרֶהָ חֶלְקַת הַשָּׂדֶה לְבֹעַז אֲשֶׁר מִמִּשְׁפַּחַת אֱלִימֶלֶךְ: וְהִנֵּה־בֹעַז   ל

בָּא מִבֵּית לֶחֶם וַיֹּאמֶר לַקּוֹצְרִים יְהוָה עִמָּכֶם וַיֹּאמְרוּ לוֹ יְבָרֶכְךָ   דׁ מלׄ

5 יְהוָה: וַיֹּאמֶר בֹּעַז לְנַעֲרוֹ הַנִּצָּב עַל־הַקּוֹצְרִים לְמִי הַנַּעֲרָה הַזֹּאת: דׁ מלׄ

6 וַיַּעַן הַנַּעַר הַנִּצָּב עַל־הַקּוֹצְרִים וַיֹּאמַר נַעֲרָה מוֹאֲבִיָּה הִיא

7 הַשָּׁבָה עִם־נָעֳמִי מִשְּׂדֵה מוֹאָב: וַתֹּאמֶר אֲלַקֳטָה־נָּא וְאָסַפְתִּי   ל

בָעֳמָרִים אַחֲרֵי הַקּוֹצְרִים וַתָּבוֹא וַתַּעֲמוֹד מֵאָז הַבֹּקֶר וְעַד־עַתָּה   דׁ מלׄ

8 זֶה שִׁבְתָּהּ הַבַּיִת מְעָט: וַיֹּאמֶר בֹּעַז אֶל־רוּת הֲלוֹא שָׁמַעַתְּ בִּתִּי   טׁ מלׄ בכתׄ

אַל־תֵּלְכִי לִלְקֹט בְּשָׂדֶה אַחֵר וְגַם לֹא תַעֲבוּרִי מִזֶּה וְכֹה תִדְבָּקִין   ה . בׁ

9 עִם־נַעֲרֹתָי: עֵינַיִךְ בַּשָּׂדֶה אֲשֶׁר־יִקְצֹרוּן וְהָלַכְתְּ אַחֲרֵיהֶן הֲלוֹא   ל . ל

צִוִּיתִי אֶת־הַנְּעָרִים לְבִלְתִּי נָגְעֵךְ וְצָמִת וְהָלַכְתְּ אֶל־הַכֵּלִים   ל . ל

[2:4] קוצרים דׁ מל והנה בעז . ושלאחׁ ושלאׁ ושלאחר :oׄ [8] הלוא טׁ מל בכתוב
וסימנהון שמעת . צויתי . משנאיך . יתעו . כתובים דמגלת אסתר . תאנף בנו .
ביראת . כה עשׂו . חטא שלמה מלך :oׄ בשדה ה רפיין וסימנה לא נעבר בשדה . לא
נטה . הוי מגיעי בית . אל תלכי ללקט . ולא־יפגעו בך בשדה אחר :oׄ

---

21 עָנָה T | ἐταπείνωσεν G V S (via עִנָּה) ⋄ • • **2:1** מוֹדָע M^ket | מידע M^qere | G V S T (indet) • **2** וַאֲלַקֳטָה M^A M^Y • בַשִּׁבֳּלִים M^L | וַאֲלַקֳטָה M^L (err) | בַשִּׁבֳּלִים M^A M^Y • **6** הַנִּצָּב עַל־הַקֹּצְרִים G T | > G^Mss V S (implic) • נַעֲרָה מוֹאֲבִיָּה T | ἡ παῖς ἡ Μωαβῖτις G (exeg) | La V S (indet) • **7** עַתָּה G^Mss V T | ἑσπέρας G (exeg) | > S ⋄ • זֶה שִׁבְתָּהּ הַבַּיִת T | οὐ κατέπαυσεν ἐν τῷ ἀγρῷ G (neg + via שָׁבְתָה + explic) | ut pausaret in domum La (via שָׁבְתָה) | ne … domum reversa est V (via שָׁבָה + neg) | ܠܒܝܬܐ S (abbr) ⋄ • **9** וְהָלַכְתְּ M^L | וְהָלַכְתְּ M^A M^Y •

ל   וַתִּשְׁתַּ֤חוּ אֶֽרְצָה   וַתִּפֹּל֙ עַל־פָּנֶ֔יהָ   וְשָׁתִ֥ית מֵאֲשֶׁ֖ר יִשְׁאֲב֣וּן הַנְּעָרִ֑ים׃   10

ל   וָאֹנֹכִ֖י נָכְרִיָּֽה׃   וַתֹּ֣אמֶר אֵלָ֗יו מַדּוּעַ֩ מָצָ֨אתִי חֵ֤ן בְּעֵינֶ֙יךָ֙ לְהַכִּירֵ֔נִי   11

ל   אֶת־חֲמוֹתֵ֔ךְ   וַיַּ֤עַן בֹּ֨עַז֙ וַיֹּ֣אמֶר לָ֔הּ הֻגֵּ֨ד הֻגַּ֜ד לִ֗י כֹּ֤ל אֲשֶׁר־עָשִׂ֙ית֙

ל   וַתֵּ֣לְכִ֔י   אַחֲרֵ֖י מ֣וֹת אִישֵׁ֑ךְ וַתַּֽעַזְבִ֞י אָבִ֣יךְ וְאִמֵּ֗ךְ וְאֶ֙רֶץ֙ מֽוֹלַדְתֵּ֔ךְ

ל   וּתְהִ֣י   אֶל־עַ֕ם אֲשֶׁ֥ר לֹא־יָדַ֖עַתְּ תְּמ֣וֹל שִׁלְשֽׁוֹם׃ יְשַׁלֵּ֥ם יְהוָ֖ה פָּעֳלֵ֑ךְ   12

ל ס   לַחֲס֖וֹת   מַשְׂכֻּרְתֵּ֗ךְ שְׁלֵמָ֗ה מֵעִ֤ם יְהוָה֙ אֱלֹהֵ֣י יִשְׂרָאֵ֔ל אֲשֶׁר־בָּ֖את

לוחד עזרתני   ל   וְכִ֤י   תַּֽחַת־כְּנָפָֽיו׃ וַ֠תֹּאמֶר אֶמְצָא־חֵ֨ן בְּעֵינֶ֤יךָ אֲדֹנִי֙ כִּ֣י נִֽחַמְתָּ֔נִי   13

ל חס ו   וַיֹּ֨אמֶר   דִבַּ֖רְתָּ עַל־לֵ֣ב שִׁפְחָתֶ֑ךָ וְאָנֹכִי֙ לֹ֣א אֶֽהְיֶ֔ה כְּאַחַ֖ת שִׁפְחֹתֶֽיךָ׃   14

ג רפ . ל . ל   פִּתֵּךְ֙   לָ֣הּ בֹ֠עַז לְעֵ֤ת הָאֹ֙כֶל֙ גֹּ֣שִֽׁי הֲלֹ֔ם וְאָכַ֣לְתְּ מִן־הַלֶּ֔חֶם וְטָבַ֥לְתְּ

יב . ל   וַתִּשְׂבַּ֖ע   בַּחֹ֔מֶץ וַתֵּ֙שֶׁב֙ מִצַּ֣ד הַקּֽוֹצְרִ֔ים וַיִּצְבָּט־לָ֣הּ קָלִ֔י וַתֹּ֥אכַל

לוחס   ל   הָעֳמָרִ֑ים   וַתֹּתַֽר׃ וַתָּ֣קָם לְלַקֵּ֑ט וַיְצַו֩ בֹּ֨עַז אֶת־נְעָרָ֤יו לֵאמֹר֙ גַּ֣ם בֵּ֤ין   15

לומל . ל   וַעֲזַבְתֶּ֖ם   תְּלַקֵּ֖ט וְלֹ֣א תַכְלִימֽוּהָ׃ וְגַ֛ם שֹׁל־תָּשֹׁ֥לּוּ לָ֖הּ מִן־הַצְּבָתִ֑ים   16

ל   אֶת־   וְלִקְּטָ֖ה וְלֹ֥א תִגְעֲרוּ־בָֽהּ׃ וַתְּלַקֵּ֥ט בַּשָּׂדֶ֖ה עַד־הָעָ֑רֶב וַתַּחְבֹּט֙   17

ב . ל   וַתֵּ֤רֶא   אֲשֶׁר־לִקֵּ֔טָה וַיְהִ֖י כְּאֵיפָ֥ה שְׂעֹרִֽים׃ וַתִּשָּׂא֙ וַתָּב֣וֹא הָעִ֔יר   18

ג . לוחס   הוֹתִ֖רָה   חֲמוֹתָ֖הּ אֵ֣ת אֲשֶׁר־לִקֵּ֑טָה וַתּוֹצֵא֙ וַתִּתֶּן־לָ֔הּ אֵ֥ת אֲשֶׁר־

ל   יְהִ֣י   מִשָּׂבְעָֽהּ׃ וַתֹּאמֶר֩ לָ֨הּ חֲמוֹתָ֜הּ אֵיפֹ֨ה לִקַּ֤טְתְּ הַיּוֹם֙ וְאָ֣נָה עָשִׂ֔ית   19

ל   שֵׁ֤ם   מַכִּירֵ֖ךְ בָּר֑וּךְ וַתַּגֵּ֣ד לַחֲמוֹתָ֗הּ אֵ֤ת אֲשֶׁר־עָשְׂתָה֙ עִמּ֔וֹ וַתֹּ֗אמֶר

ל   בָּר֣וּךְ   הָאִ֛ישׁ אֲשֶׁ֥ר עָשִׂ֛יתִי עִמּ֖וֹ הַיּ֣וֹם בֹּֽעַז׃ וַתֹּ֨אמֶר נָעֳמִ֜י לְכַלָּתָ֗הּ   20

ל   וְאֶת־הַמֵּתִ֑ים   ה֣וּא לַֽיהוָ֔ה אֲשֶׁר֙ לֹא־עָזַ֣ב חַסְדּ֔וֹ אֶת־הַחַיִּ֖ים

חצי הספ   וַתֹּ֤אמֶר לָהּ֙ נָעֳמִ֔י קָר֥וֹב לָ֙נוּ֙ הָאִ֔ישׁ מִֽגֹּאֲלֵ֖נוּ הֽוּא׃ וַתֹּ֙אמֶר֙ ר֣וּת   21

[12] וּתְהִי יד וסימנהון אחריתי . פלשתים . אתננה . שנים בו פלשתים . להשות . להשאות . סכנת . כתבה . שמעו . החרש . נחמתי . ותהי משכרתך :ס [20] קדמיה דאורית אשר לא עזב חסדו בתר דרות אשר לא עזב חסדו :ס

10 וָאֹנֹכִ֖י M[L] | וְאָנֹכִ֖י M[A] M[Y] • **11** אָבִ֣יךְ M[L] | אָבִ֣יךְ M[A] M[Y] • **13** לֹ֣א V T | ἰδού G (via הֲלֹא/לֹא?) | > La S (interp) • **14** לְעֵ֤ת S T | ἤδη ὥρα G (V) (differ-div) ✤ • וַיִּצְבָּט־ 2QRuth[a] La S T | καὶ ἐβούνισεν G (via צבר) | et congessit … sibi V (via צבר? → G?) ✤ • **18** וַתֵּ֤רֶא G T | et ostendit V S (differ-vocal: וַתַּרְא, cf KR) ✤ • אֵ֤ת אֲשֶׁר־עָשְׂתָה֙ עִמּ֔וֹ 2QRuth[a] | משבעה G (S) (T) | בשבעה 2QRuth[a] (V) • **19** מִשָּׂבְעָֽהּ V (T) | ποῦ ἐποίησεν G S (assim-ctext) ✤ • **20** לַֽיהוָ֔ה 2QRuth[a] G V T | dominus La S (via יהוה, harm-synt, cf KR) • **21** ר֣וּת V T | foll πρὸς τὴν πενθερὰν αὐτῆς G S •

הַמּוֹאֲבִיָּ֑ה גַּ֣ם ׀ כִּֽי־אָמַ֣ר אֵלַ֗י עִם־הַנְּעָרִ֤ים אֲשֶׁר־לִי֙ תִּדְבָּקִ֔ין עַ֣ד — ב
22 אִם־כִּלּ֔וּ אֵ֥ת כָּל־הַקָּצִ֖יר אֲשֶׁר־לִֽי׃ וַתֹּ֥אמֶר נָעֳמִ֖י אֶל־ר֣וּת — ב
כַּלָּתָ֑הּ ט֣וֹב בִּתִּ֗י כִּ֤י תֵֽצְאִי֙ עִם־נַ֣עֲרוֹתָ֔יו וְלֹ֥א יִפְגְּעוּ־בָ֖ךְ בְּשָׂדֶ֥ה — ג . ב מל . ה רפ
23 אַחֵֽר׃ וַתִּדְבַּ֞ק בְּנַעֲר֤וֹת בֹּ֙עַז֙ לְלַקֵּ֔ט עַד־כְּל֥וֹת קְצִֽיר־הַשְּׂעֹרִ֖ים — ל
3 וּקְצִ֣יר הַֽחִטִּ֑ים וַתֵּ֖שֶׁב אֶת־חֲמוֹתָֽהּ׃ וַתֹּ֥אמֶר לָ֖הּ נָעֳמִ֣י חֲמוֹתָ֑הּ בִּתִּ֗י — ל . יב
2 הֲלֹ֧א אֲבַקֶּשׁ־לָ֛ךְ מָנ֖וֹחַ אֲשֶׁ֥ר יִֽיטַב־לָֽךְ׃ וְעַתָּ֗ה הֲלֹ֥א בֹ֙עַז֙ מֹֽדַעְתָּ֔נוּ — ל וכת
אֲשֶׁ֥ר הָיִ֖ית אֶת־נַעֲרוֹתָ֑יו הִנֵּה־ה֗וּא זֹרֶ֛ה אֶת־גֹּ֥רֶן הַשְּׂעֹרִ֖ים — ב מל . ב
3 הַלָּֽיְלָה׃ וְרָחַ֣צְתְּ ׀ וָסַ֗כְתְּ וְשַׂ֧מְתְּ שִׂמְלֹתֵ֛ךְ עָלַ֖יִךְ וְיָרַ֣דְתִּי הַגֹּ֑רֶן — ל . תיך ק . וירדת ק
4 אַל־תִּוָּדְעִ֣י לָאִ֔ישׁ עַ֥ד כַּלֹּת֖וֹ לֶאֱכֹ֥ל וְלִשְׁתּֽוֹת׃ וִיהִ֣י בְשָׁכְב֗וֹ וְיָדַ֙עַתְּ֙ — לב . ז
אֶת־הַמָּקוֹם֙ אֲשֶׁ֣ר יִשְׁכַּב־שָׁ֔ם וּבָ֛את וְגִלִּ֥ית מַרְגְּלֹתָ֖יו וְשָׁכָ֑בְתְּי וְהוּא֙ — ה . ושכבת ק
5 יַגִּ֣יד לָ֔ךְ אֵ֖ת אֲשֶׁ֥ר תַּעֲשִֽׂין׃ וַתֹּ֖אמֶר אֵלֶ֑יהָ כֹּ֛ל אֲשֶׁר־תֹּאמְרִ֥י ‌ ‌ — ל . אלי ק ולא כת
6 7 אֶֽעֱשֶֽׂה׃ וַתֵּ֖רֶד הַגֹּ֑רֶן וַתַּ֕עַשׂ כְּכֹ֥ל אֲשֶׁר־צִוַּ֖תָּה חֲמוֹתָֽהּ׃ וַיֹּ֨אכַל בֹּ֤עַז — ל
וַיֵּשְׁתְּ֙ וַיִּיטַ֣ב לִבּ֔וֹ וַיָּבֹ֕א לִשְׁכַּ֖ב בִּקְצֵ֣ה הָעֲרֵמָ֑ה וַתָּבֹ֣א בַלָּ֔ט וַתְּגַ֥ל — ה . ב בכת
8 מַרְגְּלֹתָ֖יו וַתִּשְׁכָּֽב׃ וַיְהִי֙ בַּחֲצִ֣י הַלַּ֔יְלָה וַיֶּחֱרַ֥ד הָאִ֖ישׁ וַיִּלָּפֵ֑ת וְהִנֵּ֣ה — ב . ל
9 אִשָּׁ֔ה שֹׁכֶ֖בֶת מַרְגְּלֹתָֽיו׃ וַיֹּ֖אמֶר מִי־אָ֑תְּ וַתֹּ֗אמֶר אָנֹכִי֙ ר֣וּת אֲמָתֶ֔ךָ
10 וּפָרַשְׂתָּ֤ כְנָפֶ֙ךָ֙ עַל־אֲמָ֣תְךָ֔ כִּ֥י גֹאֵ֖ל אָֽתָּה׃ וַיֹּ֗אמֶר בְּרוּכָ֨ה אַ֤תְּ — ל חס למערב . ל וחד וברוכה

[3:4] וידעת ז̇ וסימנהון והיו מלכים אמניך . וינקת חלב גוים . והקימתי אני . ונחלת בך . וארשתיך לי . ונלוו גוים רבים :o: [5] אלין קרין ולא כתבין בני . פרת . איש . כן . בניו . צבאות . באים . לה . ככל . אלי . אלי :o: [7] בלט ד̇ חד יתיר א̇ וסימנהון ותבוא אליו בלאט . ויצו שאול את עבדיו . ויקם דוד ויכרת . ותבא בלט :o: [8] בחצי הלילה ג̇ וסימנה̇ ויהוה הכה כל בכור . וישכב שמשון עד חצי הלילה . ויהי בחצי הלילה ויחרד האיש :o:

21 הַמּוֹאֲבִיָּ֑ה 2QRuth^{a} T | > G V S ✣ • אֵלַ֗י | לי 2QRuth^{a} | G V S T (indet) • הַנְּעָרִ֤ים 2QRuth^{a} G S | τῶν κορασίων G^{Mss} T (assim-ctext) | V (indet) • **22** נַ֣עֲרוֹתָ֔יו G V S T | נערותו 2QRuth^{a} (err-graph) • **23** לְלַקֵּ֔ט G S T | ללוט 2QRuth^{a*} (err-graph) | *et tamdiu cum eis messuit* V (lib) ✣ • וַתֵּ֖שֶׁב אֶת־ G S T | *reversa est ad* V (shift, cf KR) | > La | 2QRuth^{a} (insuf) ✣ • **3:3** שִׂמְלֹתֵ֛ךְ | שמלתך M^{ket} G | שִׂמְלֹתַיִךְ M^{qere} 2QRuth^{a} V S T • וְיָרַ֣דְתִּי | וירדתי M^{ket} | וְיָרַדְתְּ M^{qere} | G V S T (indet) • **4** וְשָׁכָ֑בְתְּי | ושכבתי M^{ket} | וְשָׁכָבְתְּ M^{qere} | G V S T (indet) • **5** ‌ ‌ | > M^{ket} G V | אֵלַי M^{qere} S T (emph) • **7** וַיֵּשְׁתְּ֙ 2QRuth^{a} La V S T | > G • **9** אָ֑תְּ M^{L} (err) | אָ֑תְּ M^{A} M^{Y} •

לַֽיהוָ֗ה בִּתִּ֚י הֵיטַ֣בְתְּ חַסְדֵּ֛ךְ הָאַחֲר֖וֹן מִן־הָרִאשׁ֑וֹן לְבִלְתִּי־לֶ֙כֶת֙   סֵּ֖ד

אַחֲרֵי֙ הַבַּ֣חוּרִ֔ים אִם־דַּ֖ל וְאִם־עָשִֽׁיר׃ וְעַתָּ֣ה בִּתִּי֩ אַל־תִּ֨ירְאִ֜י כֹּ֤ל   ל . יב   **1**

אֲשֶׁר־תֹּאמְרִי֙ אֶֽעֱשֶׂה־לָּ֔ךְ כִּ֤י יוֹדֵ֙עַ֙ כָּל־שַׁ֣עַר עַמִּ֔י כִּ֛י אֵ֥שֶׁת חַ֖יִל

אָֽתְּ׃ וְעַתָּה֙ כִּ֣י אָמְנָ֔ם כִּ֥י *אם* גֹּאֵ֖ל אָנֹ֑כִי וְגַ֛ם יֵ֥שׁ גֹּאֵ֖ל קָר֥וֹב מִמֶּֽנִּי׃   **2**
   אם כת
   ולא ק

לִ֣ינִי ׀ הַלַּ֗יְלָה וְהָיָ֤ה בַבֹּ֙קֶר֙ אִם־יִגְאָלֵ֥ךְ טוֹב֙ יִגְאָ֔ל וְאִם־לֹ֨א יַחְפֹּ֜ץ   **3**
   ל וכול
   שם ברנש

לְגָֽאֳלֵ֤ךְ וּגְאַלְתִּ֙יךְ֙ אָנֹ֔כִי חַי־יְהוָ֖ה שִׁכְבִ֥י עַד־הַבֹּֽקֶר׃ וַתִּשְׁכַּ֤ב   **4**
   ח בטע בנוך

מַרְגְּלוֹתָו֙ עַד־הַבֹּ֔קֶר וַתָּ֕קָם *בְּטֶרֶם* יַכִּ֥יר אִ֖ישׁ אֶת־רֵעֵ֑הוּ וַיֹּ֙אמֶר֙   **5**
   מרגלותי . יתיר ו
   ק

אַל־יִוָּדַ֕ע כִּי־בָ֥אָה הָאִשָּׁ֖ה הַגֹּֽרֶן׃ וַיֹּ֕אמֶר הָ֤בִי הַמִּטְפַּ֙חַת֙   ל בטע

אֲשֶׁר־עָלַ֖יִךְ וְאֶֽחֳזִי־בָ֑הּ וַתֹּ֣אחֶז בָּ֔הּ וַיָּ֤מָד שֵׁשׁ־שְׂעֹרִים֙ וַיָּ֣שֶׁת עָלֶ֔יהָ   ל . ב . ו

וַיָּבֹ֖א הָעִֽיר׃ וַתָּבוֹא֙ אֶל־חֲמוֹתָ֔הּ וַתֹּ֖אמֶר מִי־אַ֣תְּ בִּתִּ֑י וַתַּ֙גֶּד־לָ֔הּ   **6**

אֵ֛ת כָּל־אֲשֶׁ֥ר עָֽשָׂה־לָ֖הּ הָאִֽישׁ׃ וַתֹּ֕אמֶר שֵׁ֧שׁ־הַשְּׂעֹרִ֛ים הָאֵ֖לֶּה נָ֣תַן   **7**

לִ֑י כִּ֚י אָמַ֣ר ׄ ׄ ׄ אַל־תָּב֥וֹאִי רֵיקָ֖ם אֶל־חֲמוֹתֵֽךְ׃ וַתֹּ֙אמֶר֙ שְׁבִ֣י בִתִּ֔י   **8**
   אלי ק ולא כת .
   ב ומל

עַ֚ד אֲשֶׁ֣ר תֵּֽדְעִ֔ין אֵ֖יךְ יִפֹּ֣ל דָּבָ֑ר כִּ֣י לֹ֤א יִשְׁקֹט֙ הָאִ֔ישׁ כִּֽי־אִם־כִּלָּ֥ה   ל

הַדָּבָ֖ר הַיּֽוֹם׃ וּבֹ֨עַז עָלָ֣ה הַשַּׁעַר֮ וַיֵּ֣שֶׁב שָׁם֒ וְהִנֵּ֨ה הַגֹּאֵ֤ל עֹבֵר֙ אֲשֶׁ֣ר   **4**

דִּבֶּר־בֹּ֔עַז וַיֹּ֛אמֶר ס֥וּרָה שְׁבָה־פֹּ֖ה פְּלֹנִ֣י אַלְמֹנִ֑י וַיָּ֖סַר וַיֵּשֵֽׁב׃ וַיִּקַּ֞ח   ל בטע . ג . ל   **2**

עֲשָׂרָ֧ה אֲנָשִׁ֛ים מִזִּקְנֵ֥י הָעִ֖יר וַיֹּ֣אמֶר שְׁבוּ־פֹ֑ה וַיֵּשֵֽׁבוּ׃ וַיֹּ֙אמֶר֙ לַגֹּאֵ֔ל   ל   **3**

חֶלְקַת֙ הַשָּׂדֶ֔ה אֲשֶׁ֥ר לְאָחִ֖ינוּ לֶאֱלִימֶ֑לֶךְ מָכְרָ֣ה נָעֳמִ֔י הַשָּׁ֖בָה מִשְּׂדֵ֥ה   ב כת כן בסיפ

[12] אלין כתב ולא קרי וסימנ׳ נא . את . ידרך . חמש דנגב . במקום . כאשר ‍:ס
[13] אנכי ח בטע בנון וסימנהון כי ערם . דברים . לוי . מצרי . ימיני . כי בוקר .
הראש כלב . ליני . וכל זקף ואתנ׳ וסוף פסוק כות׳ ב מ׳ ‍:ס [15] וישת ו וסימנהון לו
עדרים . על ראש אפר . אל המדבר פניו . וישת עליהם תבל . חשרת מים . שש
שערים ‍:ס

---

11 תֹּאמְרִ֖י G | foll πρός με G^Mss V S T (explic) • **12** אִם כִּ֥י אם | כי אם M^ket (ditt) |
מַרְגְּלוֹתָו֙ M^L | מַרְגְּלֹתָ֖יו M^A M^Y ∘ מרגלותו M^ket (err-graph) | מַרְגְּלֹתָ֖יו M^qere 2QRuth^b G V S T •
כִּ֥י M^qere T | > G V S ‖ pref *omit* כִּ֥י אם see G V S ∴ • **14** מַרְגְּלוֹתָו֙ M^L | מַרְגְּלֹתָ֖יו
M^A M^Y ∘ מרגלותו M^ket (err-graph) | מַרְגְּלֹתָ֖יו M^qere 2QRuth^b G V S T • וַיֹּ֙אמֶר֙ | foll
בְּטֶ֖רֶם M^ket (err-graph) | בְּטֶ֖רֶם M^qere | G V S T (indet) • בְּטֶ֖רֶם | foll
Βόος G V (explic) | foll Βόος αὐτῇ G^Mss (explic) | ܠܗ ܐܡܪܬ S (assim-ctext) |
foll לעולימוי T (explic) ∴ • הָאִשָּׁ֖ה T | > 2QRuth^b V S | γυνή G (hapl?) •
15 וַיָּ֣מָד G V T | foll שם 2QRuth^b | foll ܠܗ S | וַיָּבֹ֖א G T | καὶ εἰσῆλθεν Ῥούθ
G^Mss (V) (S) (harm-synt, cf KR) ∴ • **16** מִ֥י G S T | מֹ֖ה 2QRuth^b* G^Mss V • **17**
ׄ ׄ ׄ | > M^ket V (hapl?) | אֵלַ֖י M^qere G (S) T (explic?) •

4 מוֹאָב֒ וַאֲנִ֣י אָמַ֡רְתִּי אֶגְלֶ֣ה אָזְנְךָ֩ לֵאמֹ֨ר קְ֠נֵה נֶ֥גֶד הַיֹּשְׁבִים֮ וְנֶ֣גֶד זִקְנֵ֣י

עַמִּי֒ אִם־תִּגְאַל֙ גְּאָ֔ל וְאִם־לֹ֨א יִגְאַ֜ל הַגִּ֣ידָה לִּ֗י וְאֵֽדְעָה֙ כִּ֣י אֵ֤ין זוּלָֽתְךָ֙   ל ו ואדעה ק ב

5 לִגְא֔וֹל וְאָנֹכִ֖י אַחֲרֶ֑יךָ וַיֹּ֖אמֶר אָנֹכִ֥י אֶגְאָֽל׃ וַיֹּ֣אמֶר בֹּ֗עַז   ב

בְּיוֹם־קְנוֹתְךָ֥ הַשָּׂדֶ֖ה מִיַּ֣ד נָעֳמִ֑י וּ֠מֵאֵת ר֣וּת הַמּוֹאֲבִיָּ֤ה אֵֽשֶׁת־הַמֵּת֙   ל ומל

6 קָנִ֔יתִי לְהָקִ֥ים שֵׁם־הַמֵּ֖ת עַל־נַחֲלָתֽוֹ׃ וַיֹּ֣אמֶר הַגֹּאֵ֗ל לֹ֤א אוּכַל֙   קניתה ק

לִגְאָל־לִ֔י פֶּן־אַשְׁחִ֖ית אֶת־נַחֲלָתִ֑י גְּאַל־לְךָ֤ אַתָּה֙ אֶת־גְּאֻלָּתִ֔י כִּ֥י   יתיר ו

7 לֹא־אוּכַ֖ל לִגְאֹֽל׃ וְזֹאת֩ לְפָנִ֨ים בְּיִשְׂרָאֵ֜ל עַל־הַגְּאוּלָּ֤ה וְעַל־   יו ראש פסוק

הַתְּמוּרָה֙ לְקַיֵּ֣ם כָּל־דָּבָ֔ר שָׁלַ֥ף אִ֛ישׁ נַעֲל֖וֹ וְנָתַ֣ן לְרֵעֵ֑הוּ וְזֹ֥את

8 הַתְּעוּדָ֖ה בְּיִשְׂרָאֵֽל׃ וַיֹּ֧אמֶר הַגֹּאֵ֛ל לְבֹ֖עַז קְנֵה־לָ֑ךְ וַיִּשְׁלֹ֖ף נַעֲלֽוֹ׃

9 וַיֹּאמֶר֩ בֹּ֨עַז לַזְּקֵנִ֜ים וְכָל־הָעָ֗ם עֵדִ֤ים אַתֶּם֙ הַיּ֔וֹם כִּ֤י קָנִ֨יתִי֙   ג באמצ פסוק

אֶת־כָּל־אֲשֶׁ֣ר לֶֽאֱלִימֶ֔לֶךְ וְאֵ֛ת כָּל־אֲשֶׁ֥ר לְכִלְי֖וֹן וּמַחְל֑וֹן מִיַּ֖ד   ל וכול קרי חלוף

10 נָעֳמִֽי׃ וְגַ֣ם אֶת־ר֣וּת הַמֹּאֲבִיָּה֩ אֵ֨שֶׁת מַחְל֜וֹן קָנִ֧יתִי לִ֣י לְאִשָּׁ֗ה   ל ושאר אשת המת

לְהָקִ֤ים שֵׁם־הַמֵּת֙ עַל־נַחֲלָת֔וֹ וְלֹא־יִכָּרֵ֧ת שֵׁם־הַמֵּ֛ת מֵעִ֥ם אֶחָ֖יו   ד

11 וּמִשַּׁ֣עַר מְקוֹמ֑וֹ עֵדִ֥ים אַתֶּ֖ם הַיּֽוֹם׃ וַיֹּ֨אמְר֜וּ כָּל־הָעָ֧ם אֲשֶׁר־בַּשַּׁ֛עַר

וְהַזְּקֵנִ֖ים עֵדִ֑ים יִתֵּן֩ יְהוָ֨ה אֶֽת־הָאִשָּׁ֜ה הַבָּאָ֣ה אֶל־בֵּיתֶ֗ךָ כְּרָחֵ֤ל | ג בטע. ל

[4:4] זולתך ב וסימנהון אלהים זולתך יעשה למחכה לו . ואדעה כי אין זולתך
לגאול o: [7] וזאת יו ראש פס וסימנה התרומה . האשם . השלמים . המנחה .
התורה . המצוה . המצוה . עשו . משמרת . הנזיר . הברכה . ליהודה . וזאת לכם
האות . וזאת שנית תעשו . וזאת תהיגה המגפה . וזאת לפני בישראל o:

4:4 וְאֵֽדְעָה֙ יִגְאַ֜ל (err-graph?) | ἀγχιστεύεις G S (V) (T) (assim?, cf KR) ✧ • וְאֵֽדְעָה Mket G S | וְאֵֽדְעָה Mqere | La V T (indet) • **5** וּמֵאֵת G T | *et (Ruth)* La S (transl) | *(Ruth) quoque* V (transl) ✧ • קָנִ֨יתִי | קניתי Mket (err-graph?) | קָנִ֔יתִי קניתה Mqere G V S T • **7** וְזֹאת֩ | foll τὸ δικαίωμα G (S) (explic) | foll *mos* V (T) (explic) • **8** קְנֵה־לָ֑ךְ La S T | foll τὴν ἀγχιστείαν μου G (explic) | foll *(tolle) calciamentum* V (anticipation) • נַעֲלֽוֹ׃ V S | foll καὶ ἔδωκεν αὐτῷ G (explic) | foll וקנא מניה T (explic) • **10** וּמִשַּׁ֣עַר מְקוֹמ֑וֹ α' σ' T | καὶ ἐκ τῆς φυλῆς λαοῦ αὐτοῦ G (synecdoche) | καὶ ἐκ τῆς φυλῆς αὐτοῦ GMss S (synecdoche) | *de tribu loci ipsius* La (synecdoche) | *et populo* V (synecdoche) • **11** וְהַזְּקֵנִ֖ים עֵדִ֑ים La V T | μάρτυρες. καὶ οἱ πρεσβύτεροι (εἴποσαν) G (exeg) | (ܘܗܡܘ ܣܗ̈ܕܐ) ܘܣ̈ܒܐ ܘܟܠܗ ܥܡܐ ܕܒܬܪܥܐ S (ampl + inversion → 4:9) ✧ •

וּכְלֵאָה אֲשֶׁר בָּנוּ שְׁתֵּיהֶם אֶת־בֵּית יִשְׂרָאֵל וַעֲשֵׂה־חַיִל בְּאֶפְרָתָה

וּקְרָא־שֵׁם בְּבֵית לָחֶם: וִיהִי בֵיתְךָ כְּבֵית פֶּרֶץ אֲשֶׁר־יָלְדָה תָמָר

לִיהוּדָה מִן־הַזֶּרַע אֲשֶׁר יִתֵּן יְהוָה לְךָ מִן־הַנַּעֲרָה הַזֹּאת: וַיִּקַּח

בֹּעַז אֶת־רוּת וַתְּהִי־לוֹ לְאִשָּׁה וַיָּבֹא אֵלֶיהָ וַיִּתֵּן יְהוָה לָהּ הֵרָיוֹן

וַתֵּלֶד בֵּן: וַתֹּאמַרְנָה הַנָּשִׁים אֶל־נָעֳמִי בָּרוּךְ יְהוָה אֲשֶׁר לֹא

הִשְׁבִּית לָךְ גֹּאֵל הַיּוֹם וְיִקָּרֵא שְׁמוֹ בְּיִשְׂרָאֵל: וְהָיָה לָךְ לְמֵשִׁיב נֶפֶשׁ

וּלְכַלְכֵּל אֶת־שֵׂיבָתֵךְ כִּי כַלָּתֵךְ אֲשֶׁר־אֲהֵבַתֶךְ יְלָדַתּוּ אֲשֶׁר־הִיא

טוֹבָה לָךְ מִשִּׁבְעָה בָּנִים: וַתִּקַּח נָעֳמִי אֶת־הַיֶּלֶד וַתְּשִׁתֵהוּ בְחֵיקָהּ

וַתְּהִי־לוֹ לְאֹמֶנֶת: וַתִּקְרֶאנָה לוֹ הַשְּׁכֵנוֹת שֵׁם לֵאמֹר יֻלַּד־בֵּן

לְנָעֳמִי וַתִּקְרֶאנָה שְׁמוֹ עוֹבֵד הוּא אֲבִי־יִשַׁי אֲבִי דָוִד: פ

וְאֵלֶּה תּוֹלְדוֹת פָּרֶץ פֶּרֶץ הוֹלִיד אֶת־חֶצְרוֹן: וְחֶצְרוֹן הוֹלִיד

אֶת־רָם וְרָם הוֹלִיד אֶת־עַמִּינָדָב: וְעַמִּינָדָב הוֹלִיד אֶת־נַחְשׁוֹן

וְנַחְשׁוֹן הוֹלִיד אֶת־שַׂלְמָה: וְשַׂלְמוֹן הוֹלִיד אֶת־בֹּעַז וּבֹעַז הוֹלִיד

אֶת־עוֹבֵד: וְעֹבֵד הוֹלִיד אֶת־יִשָׁי וְיִשַׁי הוֹלִיד אֶת־דָוִד:

סכום הפסוקים שלספר פֿ הֿ

[11] שתיהם ב̇ ותלכנה שתיהם . אשר בנו שתיהם :o [14] ויקרא ב̇ ויקרא בהם שמי .
ויקרא שמו בישראל :o [17] עובד ב̇ מל ותקראנה לו . ושלמון . וכל דבר יֹמֿ כו ב̇ מֹ
עבד אדם :o

14 שְׁמוֹ V S T ǀ τὸ ὄνομά σου G (harm) • **16** וַתְּשִׁתֵהוּ בְחֵיקָהּ G^Mss S T ǀ καὶ
ἔθηκεν εἰς τὸν κόλπον αὐτῆς G V (implic) •

שיר השירים CANTICLES

ל	1 שִׁיר הַשִּׁירִים אֲשֶׁר לִשְׁלֹמֹה:
ל . ל וחד ונעתרות נשיקות	2 יִשָּׁקֵנִי מִנְּשִׁיקוֹת פִּיהוּ כִּי־טוֹבִים דֹּדֶיךָ מִיָּיִן:
יֹ . ל	3 לְרֵיחַ שְׁמָנֶיךָ טוֹבִים שֶׁמֶן תּוּרַק שְׁמֶךָ
ד	עַל־כֵּן עֲלָמוֹת אֲהֵבוּךָ:
ל	4 מָשְׁכֵנִי אַחֲרֶיךָ נָּרוּצָה
ד . ל וחד וחדריו	הֱבִיאַנִי הַמֶּלֶךְ חֲדָרָיו נָגִילָה וְנִשְׂמְחָה בָּךְ
גֹ	נַזְכִּירָה דֹדֶיךָ מִיַּיִן מֵישָׁרִים אֲהֵבוּךָ: ס
ל . ל	5 שְׁחוֹרָה אֲנִי וְנָאוָה בְּנוֹת יְרוּשָׁלָםִ
ל . הֹ מל	כְּאָהֳלֵי קֵדָר כִּירִיעוֹת שְׁלֹמֹה:
ל ומל . ל . ל	6 אַל־תִּרְאוּנִי שֶׁאֲנִי שְׁחַרְחֹרֶת שֶׁשֱּׁזָפַתְנִי הַשָּׁמֶשׁ

[1:3] לריח יֹו וסימנהון ולקחת . ואת הכבש דואלה שמות . ראשית . והקטירם . ואת כל חלבה . ואת הקרב . מעל כפיהם . וזרק . מעיני . אך בכור . עלת תמיד . בכורים . ראש שנה . ולחמי אשר נתתי . שמניך טובים ס: [4] הביאני דֹ וסימֹ בצדקתי הביאני יהוה . במראות אלהים . הביאני המלך . הביאני אל בית היין ודגלו ס:

1:2 דֹּדֶיךָ S T | μαστοί σου G V (differ-vocal) | 6QCant (indet) ‖ → v 4; 4:10; 7:13 • **3** לְרֵיחַ שְׁמָנֶיךָ טוֹבִים (6QCant) (V) S | καὶ ὀσμὴ μύρων σου ὑπὲρ πάντα τὰ ἀρώματα G (assim-4:10) • מֵרָן] שֶׁמֶן תּוּרַק G S | שמנים 6QCant V • שְׁמָנֶיךָ G S | שמנים 6QCant V • תּוּרַק] μύρον ἐκκενωθέν G | ἔλαιον ἐκχεόμενον ⟨α'⟩ ⟨ε'⟩ V T | ܡܫܚܐ ܕ S ÷ • **4** מָשְׁכֵנִי α' σ' V S | 3 pl pf G (differ-vocal) | 2 sg pf ⟨ε'⟩ | משכני 6QCant ° מָשְׁכֵנִי 6QCant α' σ' (⟨ε'⟩) V S | 2 sg sfx G (harm-ctext) • אַחֲרֶיךָ ⟨α'⟩ V S | foll εἰς ὀσμὴν μύρων σου G ⟨ε'⟩ (assim-v 3) ÷ • נָּרוּצָה G ⟨α'⟩ ⟨θ'⟩ V S T | 1 sg ⟨ε'⟩ (exeg) | 6QCant (insuf) • הֱבִיאַנִי G V | impv σ' S (differ-vocal) | 6QCant (indet) • נָגִילָה וְנִשְׂמְחָה (exeg) 6QCant ⟨α'⟩ ⟨σ'⟩ ⟨ε'⟩ V | sg G | ܠܡܫܒܚܗ S (exeg) • חֲדָרָיו 6QCant ⟨α'⟩ ⟨σ'⟩ ⟨ε'⟩ V | sg G | ⟨ε'⟩ S | • דֹדֶיךָ ⟨ε'⟩ V S T | 1 sg ⟨ε'⟩ • נַזְכִּירָה G V S | נשמחה 6QCant S [ונגילה G V | μαστούς σου G V | 6QCant (indet) ‖ → v 2 • מֵישָׁרִים אֲהֵבוּךָ G ⟨α'⟩ σ' ⟨ε'⟩ V | מישרים אהובים (S) • שְׁלֹמֹה: ÷ • **5** בְּנוֹת G V S | בנתי 6QCant ÷ • בָּנוֹת

בְּנֵ֧י אִמִּ֣י נִֽחֲרוּ־בִ֗י   שָׂמֻ֙נִי֙ נֹטֵרָ֣ה אֶת־הַכְּרָמִ֔ים | ל חס . ל

כַּרְמִ֥י שֶׁלִּ֖י לֹ֥א נָטָֽרְתִּי: | ל

7 הַגִּ֣ידָה לִּ֗י שֶׁ֤אָהֲבָה֙ נַפְשִׁ֔י   אֵיכָ֣ה תִרְעֶ֔ה | ב . ̇ה

אֵיכָ֖ה תַּרְבִּ֣יץ בַּֽצָּהֳרָ֑יִם

שַׁלָּמָ֤ה אֶֽהְיֶה֙ כְּעֹ֣טְיָ֔ה   עַ֖ל עֶדְרֵ֥י חֲבֵרֶֽיךָ: | ל . ל

8 אִם־לֹ֤א תֵדְעִי֙ לָ֔ךְ   הַיָּפָ֖ה בַּנָּשִׁ֑ים | ̇ה ראש פסוק

צְֽאִי־לָ֞ךְ בְּעִקְבֵ֣י הַצֹּ֗אן   וּרְעִי֙ אֶת־גְּדִיֹּתַ֔יִךְ | ל . ל וכת

עַ֖ל מִשְׁכְּנ֥וֹת הָרֹעִֽים: ס

9 לְסֻֽסָתִי֙ בְּרִכְבֵ֣י פַרְעֹ֔ה   דִּמִּיתִ֖יךְ רַעְיָתִֽי: | ל . ל

10 נָאו֤וּ לְחָיַ֙יִךְ֙ בַּתֹּרִ֔ים   צַוָּארֵ֖ךְ בַּחֲרוּזִֽים: | ב . ל וחס . ל ומל

11 תּוֹרֵ֤י זָהָב֙ נַעֲשֶׂה־לָּ֔ךְ   עִ֖ם נְקֻדּ֥וֹת הַכָּֽסֶף: | ב סב

12 עַד־שֶׁ֤הַמֶּ֙לֶךְ֙ בִּמְסִבּ֔וֹ   נִרְדִּ֖י נָתַ֥ן רֵיחֽוֹ: | ל . ל

13 צְר֤וֹר הַמֹּר֙ ׀ דּוֹדִ֣י לִ֔י   בֵּ֥ין שָׁדַ֖י יָלִֽין:

14 אֶשְׁכֹּ֨ל הַכֹּ֤פֶר ׀ דּוֹדִי֙ לִ֔י   בְּכַרְמֵ֖י עֵ֥ין גֶּֽדִי: ס | ̇ה חס

15 הִנָּ֤ךְ יָפָה֙ רַעְיָתִ֔י   הִנָּ֥ךְ יָפָ֖ה עֵינַ֥יִךְ יוֹנִֽים: | ל בסיפ

16 הִנְּךָ֨ יָפֶ֤ה דוֹדִי֙ אַ֣ף נָעִ֔ים   אַף־עַרְשֵׂ֖נוּ רַעֲנָֽנָה: | ̇ה . ל . ל בטע

17 קֹר֤וֹת בָּתֵּ֙ינוּ֙ אֲרָזִ֔ים   רַחִיטֵ֖נוּ בְּרוֹתִֽים: | רהיטנו ז̇
ק

2 אֲנִי֙ חֲבַצֶּ֣לֶת הַשָּׁר֔וֹן   שֽׁוֹשַׁנַּ֖ת הָעֲמָקִֽים: | ל

2 כְּשֽׁוֹשַׁנָּה֙ בֵּ֣ין הַחוֹחִ֔ים   כֵּ֥ן רַעְיָתִ֖י בֵּ֥ין הַבָּנֽוֹת: | ל

3 כְּתַפּ֙וּחַ֙ בַּעֲצֵ֣י הַיַּ֔עַר   כֵּ֥ן דּוֹדִ֖י בֵּ֣ין הַבָּנִ֑ים | ל

---

[10] נאוו ב̇ מה נאוו על ההרים . לחייך בתורים :o: [14] אשכל ̇ה חס וסימנהון ויבא
הפליט ויגד . בלעדי רק אשר אכלו הנערים . ויבאו עד נחל אשכל . ויפנו ויעלו
ההרה . אשכל הכפר :o:

---

6 בְּנֵ֧י G V S ∣ sg ⟨θ'⟩ • נִֽחֲרוּ G σ' V S ∣ 3 sg θ' ✤ • שָׂמֻ֙נִי֙ (6QCant) G (σ') V S ∣
3 sg θ' ✤ • **7** כְּעֹ֣טְיָ֔ה 6QCant G ∣ (ὡς) ἐκβεβλημένη or ἀπολελυμένη ⟨α'⟩ ∣ (ὡς)
ῥεμβομένη σ' S ∣ *ne vagari incipiam* V T ✤ • **8** צְֽאִי־לָ֞ךְ G α' ⟨θ'⟩ ε' (V) S ∣
ἐξελθοῦσα πορεύου σ' ✤ • **10** נָאוֽוּ V S ∣ prec τί G T (lib-styl) • בַּתֹּרִ֔ים σ' S ∣
ὡς τρυγόνες G (via כתרים, e.g. KR) ∣ *sicut turturis* La V • בַּחֲרוּזִֽים: S ∣ ὡς
ὁρμίσκοι G V (via כחרוזים) ∣ ܓܒܝ̈ܐ G α' σ' V ∣ **11** תּוֹרֵ֤י ✤ • **12** עַד־שֶׁ֤הַמֶּ֙לֶךְ֙ G α' σ' V ∣
S • **17** רַחִיטֵ֖נוּ M^ket רחיטנו M^qere ∣ G σ' ⟨ε'⟩ V S (indet) ✤ •
2:1 הָעֲמָקִֽים: G V ∣ sg ⟨ε'⟩ S T •

בְּצִלּוֹ חִמַּדְתִּי וְיָשַׁבְתִּי   וּפִרְיוֹ מָתוֹק לְחִכִּי׃   ל

4 הֱבִיאַנִי אֶל־בֵּית הַיַּיִן   וְדִגְלוֹ עָלַי אַהֲבָה׃   ה . ל זקף קמׄ

5 סַמְּכוּנִי בָּאֲשִׁישׁוֹת   רַפְּדוּנִי בַּתַּפּוּחִים   ל . ל
כִּי־חוֹלַת אַהֲבָה אָנִי׃   ל ומל

6 שְׂמֹאלוֹ תַּחַת לְרֹאשִׁי   וִימִינוֹ תְּחַבְּקֵנִי׃   ד . ב

7 הִשְׁבַּעְתִּי אֶתְכֶם בְּנוֹת יְרוּשָׁלַ͏ִם בִּצְבָאוֹת   ב
אוֹ בְּאַיְלוֹת הַשָּׂדֶה
אִם־תָּעִירוּ ׀ וְאִם־תְּעוֹרְרוּ אֶת־הָאַהֲבָה עַד שֶׁתֶּחְפָּץ׃ ס   יאׄ בטעׄ בסוף פסוק . גׄ

8 קוֹל דּוֹדִי   הִנֵּה־זֶה בָּא
מְדַלֵּג עַל־הֶהָרִים   מְקַפֵּץ עַל־הַגְּבָעוֹת׃

9 דּוֹמֶה דוֹדִי לִצְבִי   אוֹ לְעֹפֶר הָאַיָּלִים
הִנֵּה־זֶה עוֹמֵד אַחַר כָּתְלֵנוּ   מַשְׁגִּיחַ מִן־הַחַלֹּנוֹת   וׄ מלׄ . לׄ . לׄ . לׄ
מֵצִיץ מִן־הַחֲרַכִּים׃   גׄ חסׄ

10 עָנָה דוֹדִי וְאָמַר לִי   בׄ מה אדבר
קוּמִי לָךְ רַעְיָתִי יָפָתִי   וּלְכִי־לָךְ׃

11 כִּי־הִנֵּה הַסְּתָו עָבָר   הסתיו ק
הַגֶּשֶׁם חָלַף הָלַךְ לוֹ׃

12 הַנִּצָּנִים נִרְאוּ בָאָרֶץ   עֵת הַזָּמִיר הִגִּיעַ

[2:3] וּפִרְיוֹ בׄ וסימנהון מתוך לחכי . שרף מעופף ‏:o [6] לראשׄי דׄ שומר לראשׄי . סוף חבוש . סכותה . שמאלו קדמיה ‏:o [9] החלונות גׄ חסׄ וסימׄ כהחלונות האלה . והחלונות מכסות . משגיח ‏:o

---

4 הֱבִיאַנִי V T | pl impv + sfx G S (differ-vocal) • וְדִגְלוֹ T | τάξατε G S | ἔταξεν α' V | ἐπισωρεύσατε σ' ⋆ • **5** בָּאֲשִׁישׁוֹת G (V) (S) | sg σ' • **7** הָאַהֲבָה G S | *dilectam* V ⋆ • **9** הָאַיָּלִים V S | foll ἐπὶ τὰ ὄρη Βαιθήλ G (assim-v 17) • **10** עָנָה G σ'* S T | > V ⋆ • לָךְ 4QCantᵇ S T | ἐλθέ G | *propera* V ⋆ • רַעְיָתִי 4QCantᵇ G V S | foll *columba mea* V^Mss (assim-5:2, cp the following) • יָפָתִי 4QCantᵇ V S | foll περιστερά μου G (cp v 14; 5:2; 6:9) • וּלְכִי־לָךְ 4QCantᵇ V S T | > G • **11** הַסְּתָו M^A M^Y | הסתו M^L(ket) | הַסְּתָיו M^L(qere) | G V S (indet) ⋆ • **12** הַנִּצָּנִים G V S | prec הנה 4QCantᵇ •

וְקוֹל הַתּוֹר נִשְׁמַע בְּאַרְצֵנוּ:   ל מל

13 הַתְּאֵנָה חָנְטָה פַגֶּיהָ   וְהַגְּפָנִים | סְמָדַר נָתְנוּ רֵיחַ   ל

קוּמִי לָכְ֒י רַעְיָתִי יָפָתִי   וּלְכִי־לָךְ: ס   לך קר

14 יוֹנָתִי בְּחַגְוֵי הַסֶּלַע   בְּסֵתֶר הַמַּדְרֵגָה   ג . ל

הַרְאִינִי אֶת־מַרְאַיִךְ   הַשְׁמִיעִינִי אֶת־קוֹלֵךְ   ל . ב

כִּי־קוֹלֵךְ עָרֵב   וּמַרְאֵיךְ נָאוֶה: ס   ל ומל

15 אֶחֱזוּ־לָנוּ | שׁוּעָלִים   שׁוּעָלִים קְטַנִּים   מְחַבְּלִים כְּרָמִים   ל

וּכְרָמֵינוּ סְמָדַר:

16 דּוֹדִי לִי וַאֲנִי לוֹ   הָרֹעֶה בַּשּׁוֹשַׁנִּים:

17 עַד שֶׁיָּפוּחַ הַיּוֹם   וְנָסוּ הַצְּלָלִים   ב ומל . ד

סֹב דְּמֵה־לְךָ דוֹדִי לִצְבִי   אוֹ לְעֹפֶר הָאַיָּלִים

עַל־הָרֵי בָתֶר: ס   ל

3 עַל־מִשְׁכָּבִי בַּלֵּילוֹת   בִּקַּשְׁתִּי אֵת שֶׁאָהֲבָה נַפְשִׁי   ד

בִּקַּשְׁתִּיו וְלֹא מְצָאתִיו:

[14] בחגוי ג יונתי בחגוי . שכני בחגוי סלע . בחגוי הסלע o: [3:1] בלילות ד וסימנה
בלילות בקשתי . ואמונתך בליות . העמדים בבית יהוה . מפחד בלילות o:

13 הַתְּאֵנָה G V S | הנה התנאה 4QCant[b] ⁜ • לְכִֿי | לכי M[ket] G | לָךְ M[qere]
4QCant[b] V S T ‖ pref לָךְ M[qere] 4QCant[b] V S T ⁜ • רַעְיָתִי יָפָתִי 4QCant[b] G V T |
בְּחַגְוֵי S (transp) • יָפָתִי V S | foll περιστερά μου G ‖ → v 10 • **14** בְּחַגְוֵי
V T | sg G ⟨σ'⟩ S • הַמַּדְרֵגָה T | המדלגה 4QCant[b] | (ἐχόμενα) τοῦ
προτειχίσματος G | maceriae V S ⁜ • אֶת־ M[L] (err) | אֶת־ M[A] M[Y] • קוֹלֵךְ G
V S | שמעך 4QCant[b] • וּמַרְאַיִךְ M[A] M[L] | G V S (indet) | M[Y] (insuf) ‖ conjec
וּמַרְאֵיךְ • **15** שׁוּעָלִים[2] λ' V S | > 4QCant[b] G V[Mss] (hapl, e.g. KR) ⁜ • וּכְרָמֵינוּ
G S | sg V (err-graph, e.g. KR) • **17** v 17 ⁜ • וְנָסוּ 4QCant[b] | καὶ κινηθῶσιν G |
καὶ κλιθῶσιν σ' V S ⁜ • הַצְּלָלִים | הטללים 4QCant[b] | G σ' V S (indet) • סֹב
(4QCant[b]) | ἀπόστρεψον G V S (via √שוב) • הָרֵי בָתֶר: | הררי בתר 4QCant[b] | G
V S (indet) ⁜ • **3:1** בַּלֵּילוֹת G V S | בלילות 4QCant[b] | [בלי]לות בלילות 4QCant[b] (ditt) • בִּקַּשְׁתִּי |
בשקתי 4QCant[b] (metath) | G V S (indet) • בִּקַּשְׁתִּיו | [בקשתי]הו 4QCant[b] | G V S
(indet) • מְצָאתִיו | מצתיהו 4QCant[b] | G V S (indet) o מְצָאתִיו: (4QCant[b]) V S |
foll ἐκάλεσα αὐτόν καὶ οὐχ ὑπήκουσέν μου G (assim-5:6) •

2 אָק֣וּמָה נָּ֗א וַאֲסוֹבְבָ֣ה בָעִ֔יר   בַּשְּׁוָקִים֙ וּבָ֣רְחֹב֔וֹת   ג . בֿ חד מל . ל
אֲבַקְשָׁ֕ה אֵ֥ת שֶׁאָהֲבָ֖ה נַפְשִׁ֑י
בִּקַּשְׁתִּ֖יו וְלֹ֥א מְצָאתִֽיו׃

3 מְצָא֙וּנִי֙ הַשֹּׁ֣מְרִ֔ים   הַסֹּבְבִ֖ים בָּעִ֑יר
אֵ֧ת שֶׁאָהֲבָ֛ה נַפְשִׁ֖י רְאִיתֶֽם׃

4 כִּמְעַט֙ שֶׁעָבַ֣רְתִּי מֵהֶ֔ם   עַ֣ד שֶׁמָּצָ֔אתִי   אֵ֥ת שֶׁאָהֲבָ֖ה נַפְשִׁ֑י   ל . ל
אֲחַזְתִּיו֙ וְלֹ֣א אַרְפֶּ֔נּוּ   עַד־שֶׁהֲבֵיאתִיו֙ אֶל־בֵּ֣ית אִמִּ֔י   ל . ל
וְאֶל־חֶ֖דֶר הוֹרָתִֽי׃   ל ומל

5 הִשְׁבַּ֨עְתִּי אֶתְכֶ֜ם בְּנ֤וֹת יְרוּשָׁלִַ֙ם֙ בִּצְבָא֔וֹת
א֖וֹ בְּאַיְל֣וֹת הַשָּׂדֶ֑ה   ב֯ ומל

אִם־תָּעִ֧ירוּ ׀ וְֽאִם־תְּע֛וֹרְרוּ אֶת־הָאַהֲבָ֖ה עַ֥ד שֶׁתֶּחְפָּֽץ׃   ס   ב . י֯א בטע֯ . ג֯

6 מִ֣י זֹ֗את עֹלָה֙ מִן־הַמִּדְבָּ֔ר   כְּתִֽימֲר֖וֹת עָשָׁ֑ן   ל ומל
מְקֻטֶּ֤רֶת מוֹר֙ וּלְבוֹנָ֔ה   מִכֹּ֖ל אַבְקַ֥ת רוֹכֵֽל׃   ל . ל

7 הִנֵּ֗ה מִטָּתוֹ֙ שֶׁלִּשְׁלֹמֹ֔ה   שִׁשִּׁ֥ים גִּבֹּרִ֖ים סָבִ֣יב לָ֑הּ   ל . ז֯ חס֯
מִגִּבֹּרֵ֖י יִשְׂרָאֵֽל׃   ה֯ חס֯

8 כֻּלָּם֙ אֲחֻ֣זֵי חֶ֔רֶב   מְלֻמְּדֵ֖י מִלְחָמָ֑ה   ל . ל
אִ֤ישׁ חַרְבּוֹ֙ עַל־יְרֵכ֔וֹ   מִפַּ֖חַד בַּלֵּילֽוֹת׃   ס

9 אַפִּרְי֗וֹן עָ֤שָׂה לוֹ֙ הַמֶּ֣לֶךְ שְׁלֹמֹ֔ה   מֵעֲצֵ֖י הַלְּבָנֽוֹן׃

---

[2] אקומה ג֯ ויאמר אבנר אל דוד . גם עוילים . נא ואסבבה ס: [7] גברים ז֯ חס֯ וכל
אנשיה גברים . קשת גברים חתים . איך נפלו גברים דיהונתן . אתה ידעת את אביך
ואת אנשיו . והיו כגברים בוסים בטיט חוצת . עיר גברים עלה . הנה מטתו
שלשלמה ס: [8] מלמדי ב֯ שיר בית יהוה . כלם אחזי חרב ֯ ס:

---

2 אָק֣וּמָה G V S | אקום 4QCant[b] • בַּשְּׁוָקִים֙ G V S T | sg La • **5** אֶתְכֶ֜ם 4QCant[a] |
אתכ]מה 4QCant[b] | G V S (indet) • הָאַהֲבָ֖ה → ✥ 2:7 • **6** vv **6-8** 4QCant[a] G V S |
> 4QCant[b] ‖ see Introd. • כְּתִֽימֲר֖וֹת | sg G σ' V S | ὡς ὁμοίωσις α' La[Ep] (via
כתמונת) ‖ cf Schleusner, *Thesaurus*, 4:87 • מְקֻטֶּ֤רֶת G S | ἀπὸ θυμιάματος α' (V)
T (differ-vocal) • **8** בַּלֵּילֽוֹת׃ M[L] (err) | בַּלֵּילֽוֹת M[A] M[Y] •

<table>
<tr><td>ד מל . ל</td><td>10 עַמּוּדָיו עָשָׂה כֶסֶף   רְפִידָתוֹ זָהָב   מֶרְכָּבוֹ אַרְגָּמָן</td></tr>
<tr><td>ל ומל</td><td>תּוֹכוֹ רָצוּף אַהֲבָה   מִבְּנוֹת יְרוּשָׁלָ͏ִם:</td></tr>
<tr><td>ל . ל</td><td>11 צְאֶינָה | וּרְאֶינָה בְּנוֹת צִיּוֹן בַּמֶּלֶךְ שְׁלֹמֹה</td></tr>
<tr><td>ל . ל . ל</td><td>בָּעֲטָרָה שֶׁעִטְּרָה־לּוֹ אִמּוֹ בְּיוֹם חֲתֻנָּתוֹ</td></tr>
<tr><td></td><td>וּבְיוֹם שִׂמְחַת לִבּוֹ: ס</td></tr>
<tr><td>ב . ב</td><td>4 הִנָּךְ יָפָה רַעְיָתִי הִנָּךְ יָפָה   עֵינַיִךְ יוֹנִים   מִבַּעַד לְצַמָּתֵךְ</td></tr>
<tr><td>ב . ל</td><td>שַׂעְרֵךְ כְּעֵדֶר הָעִזִּים   שֶׁגָּלְשׁוּ מֵהַר גִּלְעָד:</td></tr>
<tr><td>ל . ל</td><td>2 שִׁנַּיִךְ כְּעֵדֶר הַקְּצוּבוֹת   שֶׁעָלוּ מִן־הָרַחְצָה</td></tr>
<tr><td>ב ומל . ב חס</td><td>שֶׁכֻּלָּם מַתְאִימוֹת   וְשַׁכֻּלָה אֵין בָּהֶם:</td></tr>
<tr><td>ל . ל</td><td>3 כְּחוּט הַשָּׁנִי שִׂפְתֹתַיִךְ   וּמִדְבָּרֵיךְ נָאוֶה</td></tr>
<tr><td>ג</td><td>כְּפֶלַח הָרִמּוֹן רַקָּתֵךְ   מִבַּעַד לְצַמָּתֵךְ:</td></tr>
<tr><td>ה מל</td><td>4 כְּמִגְדַּל דָּוִיד צַוָּארֵךְ   בָּנוּי לְתַלְפִּיּוֹת</td></tr>
<tr><td>ג</td><td>אֶלֶף הַמָּגֵן תָּלוּי עָלָיו   כֹּל שִׁלְטֵי הַגִּבּוֹרִים:</td></tr>
<tr><td>ל מל</td><td>5 שְׁנֵי שָׁדַיִךְ כִּשְׁנֵי עֳפָרִים   תְּאוֹמֵי צְבִיָּה</td></tr>
<tr><td></td><td>הָרוֹעִים בַּשּׁוֹשַׁנִּים:</td></tr>
</table>

[10] עמודיו ד מל ואת עמודיו חמשה ואת וויהם . ויקם משה את . וזאת משמרת . עמודיו עשה o: [4:4] תלוי ג וסימנה כי קללת אלהים תלוי . ראיתי את אבשלום . אלף המגן תלוי עליו o:

11 בְּנוֹת צִיּוֹן G^Ms V S T | > G • צִיּוֹן G^Ms V S T | ירושלם 4QCant^a (harm-1:5 etc) • וּבְיוֹם G V | > cj 4QCant^a S • **4:1** מִבַּעַד G S | prec cj V | 4QCant^a 4QCant^b (insuf) || → v 3 • לְצַמָּתֵךְ ✥ 4QCant^b G V S | שַׂעְרֵךְ כְּעֵדֶר הָעִזִּים 4QCant^b G V S | כְּעֵדֶר 4QCant^a 4QCant^b La^Ambr La^169 S | pl G | העזים שערך] 4QCant^a • שֶׁגָּלְשׁוּ שגלש]ות 4QCant^a | αἳ ἀπεκαλύφθησαν G | αἳ ἀνεφάνησαν σ' | quae ascenderunt (La^Ep) V S ✥ • גִּלְעָד: מֵהַר 4QCant^a σ' La^Ambr La^169 V S T | ἀπὸ τοῦ Γαλααδ G (assim-6:5, e.g. KR) • **2** שִׁנַּיִךְ כְּעֵדֶר הַקְּצוּבוֹת 4QCant^b G V | כעדר הקצובות שניך 4QCant^a • כְּעֵדֶר 4QCant^a 4QCant^b La S T | pl G V • שֶׁעָלוּ עלו 4QCant^a | G V S | • וּמִדְבָּרֵיךְ 3 • אֵין אינה 4QCant^a | G V S (indet) • רַקָּתֵךְ מזקנתך 4QCant^a | רַקָּתֵךְ 4QCant^b G σ' V S | ✥ • ומדברך 4QCant^b G V S ✥ • מִבַּעַד 4QCant^a G σ' S | prec cj 4QCant^b V || → v 1 • לְצַמָּתֵךְ: ✥ 4:1 • **4 vv 4-7** 4QCant^a G V S | > 4QCant^b || see Introd. • עָלָיו G S | בו 4QCant^a | ex ea V • **5** צְבִיָּה G V (S) | הֿ] 4QCant^a • הָרוֹעִים G σ' | רעים 4QCant^a | V S (indet) •

⁶ עַד שֶׁיָּפ֙וּחַ֙ הַיּ֔וֹם   וְנָ֖סוּ הַצְּלָלִ֑ים

אֵלֶךְ לִי אֶל־הַ֣ר הַמּ֔וֹר   וְאֶל־גִּבְעַ֖ת הַלְּבוֹנָֽה׃

⁷ כֻּלָּ֤ךְ יָפָה֙ רַעְיָתִ֔י   וּמ֖וּם אֵ֥ין בָּֽךְ׃ ס

⁸ אִתִּ֤י מִלְּבָנוֹן֙ כַּלָּ֔ה   אִתִּ֖י מִלְּבָנ֣וֹן תָּב֑וֹאִי

תָּשׁ֣וּרִי ׀ מֵרֹ֣אשׁ אֲמָנָ֗ה   מֵרֹ֤אשׁ שְׂנִיר֙ וְחֶרְמ֔וֹן

מִמְּעֹנ֣וֹת אֲרָי֔וֹת   מֵֽהַרְרֵ֖י נְמֵרִֽים׃

⁹ לִבַּבְתִּ֖נִי אֲחֹתִ֣י כַלָּ֑ה

לִבַּבְתִּ֙ינִי֙ בְּאַחַ֣ד מֵֽעֵינַ֔יִךְ   בְּאַחַ֥ד עֲנָ֖ק מִצַּוְּרֹנָֽיִךְ׃

¹⁰ מַה־יָּפ֥וּ דֹדַ֛יִךְ אֲחֹתִ֥י כַלָּ֑ה

מַה־טֹּ֤בוּ דֹדַ֙יִךְ֙ מִיַּ֔יִן   וְרֵ֥יחַ שְׁמָנַ֖יִךְ מִכָּל־בְּשָׂמִֽים׃

¹¹ נֹ֛פֶת תִּטֹּ֥פְנָה שִׂפְתוֹתַ֖יִךְ כַּלָּ֑ה

דְּבַ֤שׁ וְחָלָב֙ תַּ֣חַת לְשׁוֹנֵ֔ךְ   וְרֵ֥יחַ שַׂלְמֹתַ֖יִךְ כְּרֵ֥יחַ לְבָנֽוֹן׃ ס

Masorah parva

ב . ד

יֹו וכל כרמל
הכרמל כות

ג . ל

ב וׄמׄל

ל . ג . ב

ג

ב וחס
באחת
ק . ל .

ב חס א בליש

ב אהליך . הׄ

יׄא ראש פסו נון
וסוף נון

ג . הׄ

Masorah magna

[9] אלין קר תׄ ולא כתב וסימ ותקרא . הכרתי . בפעם . עשרת . אמות .
המתקדשים . תהלת . קומת . לא ירתק . בת . ירימות . באחת מעיניך קדמי
דפסוק :ס [11] יׄא פסוק בקרי ראש נון וסוף נון וסימנהון נגע . נחנו . נביא . נודו .
נשקי . נהר . נחית . נגד . נפת . נפתי . נר יהוה :ס

Apparatus

6 וְנָ֖סוּ → ✛ 2:17 • אֵלֶךְ G α' V | 2 m sg impv S • וְאֶל־ G α' V S | > cj 4QCant^a • הַלְּבוֹנָֽה׃ 4QCant^a V S | τοῦ Λιβάνου G α' ‖ → vv 11, 14 • **8 4:8 – 6:10** 4QCant^b G V S | > 4QCant^a ‖ see Introd. • אִתִּי¹ and אִתִּי² T | את^{1,2} 4QCant^b | δεῦρο^{1,2} G V S (via אתה√) ✛ • מִלְּבָנוֹן¹ and מִלְּבָנ֣וֹן² | מן לבנון^{1,2} 4QCant^b | G σ' V S (indet) ✛ • תָּב֑וֹאִי G S | אבאי 4QCant^b (err-graph) | veni V • תָּשׁ֣וּרִי 4QCant^b (G) (S) | coronaberis V • מֵרֹאשׁ¹ G V S | מן ראשי 4QCant^b • אֲמָנָ֗ה α' σ' V (S) T | אומנן 4QCant^b | πίστεως G (via √ אמן) • וְחֶרְמ֔וֹן שְׂנִיר֙ מֵרֹ֤אשׁ G V S | > 4QCant^b (homtel) ✛ • מֵֽהַרְרֵ֖י | מן הררי 4QCant^b | G V S (indet) • **9** לִבַּבְתִּ֖נִי 4QCant^b σ' V S | 1 pl sfx G • לִבַּבְתִּ֙ינִי֙ (4QCant^b) σ' V S | 1 pl sfx G • בְּאַחַד¹ | באחד 4QCant^b | בְּאַחַ֣ד M^{ket} בְּאַחַ֥ת M^{qere} | G V S (indet) • מִצַּוְּרֹנָֽיִךְ | (מצורֹנׄיך M^{ket} באחד 4QCant^b | τραχήλων σου G (α') (σ') (ε') V S (via מצוארי/ך) • **10** דֹדַ֛יִךְ¹ and דֹדַ֙יִךְ֙² T | μαστοί σου^{1,2} G V S | 4QCant^b (indet) ‖ → 1:2 • מִיַּ֔יִן | מן יין 4QCant^b | G V S (indet) • שְׁמָנַ֖יִךְ V S | שמנך 4QCant^b | ἱματίων σου G (via ;שלמתיך cp v 11) • מִכָּל־ | מן כל 4QCant^b | G V S (indet) • בְּשָׂמִֽים׃ | בשמין 4QCant^b | G V S (indet) • **11** דְּבַ֤שׁ כַּלָּ֑ה G V | ܓܠܐ ܕܒܫ S (via כל הדבש) | prec 4QCant^b | G V S (indet) • לְבָנֽוֹן׃ G S T | turis V (via לבונה) | אחותי 4QCant^b (assim-ctext) • ‖ → v 6 • לְבָנֽוֹן׃ M^L | | לְבָנֽוֹן: גֶּן M^Y • לְבָנֽוֹן: ס גַּן M^L |

גַּן | נָעוּל אֲחֹתִי כַלָּה   12

גַּל נָעוּל מַעְיָן חָתוּם:

שְׁלָחַ֫יִךְ פַּרְדֵּ֫ס רִמּוֹנִים   עִם פְּרִי מְגָדִים   13   ל̇ . ל̇ וחד שומר הפרדס

כְּפָרִים עִם־נְרָדִים: ל̇

נֵרְדְּ | וְכַרְכֹּם   קָנֶה וְקִנָּמ֫וֹן   עִם כָּל־עֲצֵי לְבוֹנָה   14   ל̇ . ל̇ . ב̇

מֹר וַאֲהָל֫וֹת   עִם כָּל־רָאשֵׁי בְשָׂמִים: ב̇ ומל̇ . עה̇

מַעְיַן גַּנִּ֫ים   בְּאֵר מַיִם חַיִּ֫ים   15   ד̇

וְנֹזְלִים מִן־לְבָנוֹן:

ע֫וּרִי צָפוֹן וּבוֹאִי תֵימָן   הָפִ֫יחִי גַנִּי יִזְּלוּ בְשָׂמָיו   16   ל̇ מל̇ . ל̇

יָבֹא דוֹדִי לְגַנּ֫וֹ   וְיֹאכַל פְּרִי מְגָדָיו: ה̇ חס̇ . ה̇

בָּ֫אתִי לְגַנִּי֫ אֲחֹתִי כַלָּה֫   אָרִ֫יתִי מוֹרִי עִם־בְּשָׂמִ֫י   5

אָכַ֫לְתִּי יַעְרִי֫ עִם־דִּבְשִׁי   שָׁתִ֫יתִי יֵינִי עִם־חֲלָבִ֫י   ל̇ . ל̇

אִכְלוּ רֵעִ֫ים   שְׁתוּ וְשִׁכְרוּ דּוֹדִ֫ים: ס   ל̇ מל̇

אֲנִי יְשֵׁנָה וְלִבִּי עֵר   2   **ס**

ק֫וֹל | דּוֹדִי דוֹפֵק   פִּתְחִי־לִי אֲחֹתִי רַעְיָתִי יוֹנָתִי תַמָּתִ֫י   ל̇ ומל̇ . ל̇ . ב̇

שֶׁרֹאשִׁי֫ נִמְלָא־טָ֫ל   קְוֻצּוֹתַי רְסִיסֵי לָיְלָה: ל̇ . ל̇ . ל̇

[5:1] דודים ד̇ ג̇ חס̇ מל̇ וסימנ̇ והנה עתך עת דדים . בני בבל למשכב . לכה נרוה דדים . באתי לגני בתרא מל̇ ס: [2] ישנה ב̇ חד מל̇ וחד חס̇ ואמתך מל̇ . אני . למדנח תרויהון חס̇ ס:

---

12 גַּל M^L (err) | גַּל M^Y ○ גַּל | κῆπος G V S || pref גַּן see G V S ✥ • **13** נְרָדִים: G | sg V S • **14** כָּל־עֲצֵי G V T | ‏ܡܫ‎ S | לְבוֹנָה S T | τοῦ Λιβάνου G V (via מן ג]דיו) G V | פְּרִי מְגָדָיו V | ἀρώματά μου G S • **16** בְשָׂמָיו V || → v 6 • (לבנון 4QCant^b (exeg) | ‏ܠܓܒܐ,‎ S • **5:1** כַלָּה G V | foll ‏ܡܥ ܦܐܠܐ ܘܐܚܒܬܘܗܝ,‎ S • בְשָׂמִי pl G V S (differ-vocal) | 4QCant^b (indet) • אָכַלְתִּי to חֲלָבִי G V S | שתיתי 4QCant^b (transp) ✥ • יַעְרִי 4QCant^b | ἄρτον]אכלתי יערי עם חלבי יינ֯י עם חלבי 4QCant^b (transp) ✥ • יַעְרִי μου G (ign-lex) | τὸν δρυμόν μου σ' (via יַעַר, "thicket") | favum V | ‏ܟܟܪܝܬܐ,‎ S • רֵעִים G α'-σ' V | οἱ πλησίον μου G^Mss S • דּוֹדִים: G V | fratres mei La | ‏ܪܚܡܝ,‎ S* ✥ • **2** דּוֹפֵק V S | foll ἐπὶ τὴν θύραν G (ampl; cp Judg 19:22) • תַמָּתִי G V | ‏ܬܡܝܡܬܝ (ܘܝܘܢܝ) S || → 6:9 •

ל . ב . ב בטע	3 פָּשַׁ֙טְתִּי֙ אֶת־כֻּתׇּנְתִּ֔י אֵיכָ֖כָה אֶלְבָּשֶׁ֑נָּה
ב בטע . ל	רָחַ֥צְתִּי אֶת־רַגְלַ֖י אֵיכָ֥כָה אֲטַנְּפֵֽם׃
ל . ל . ל	4 דּוֹדִ֗י שָׁלַ֤ח יָדוֹ֙ מִן־הַחֹ֔ר וּמֵעַ֖י הָמ֥וּ עָלָֽיו׃
	5 קַ֥מְתִּֽי אֲנִ֖י לִפְתֹּ֣חַ לְדוֹדִ֑י
ל . ג מל בסיפֿ . ל וחד אצבעתי	וְיָדַ֣י נָֽטְפוּ־מ֗וֹר וְאֶצְבְּעֹתַי֙ מ֣וֹר עֹבֵ֔ר
ל	עַ֖ל כַּפּ֥וֹת הַמַּנְעֽוּל׃
ל	6 פָּתַ֤חְתִּֽי אֲנִי֙ לְדוֹדִ֔י וְדוֹדִ֖י חָמַ֣ק עָבָ֑ר
ל . ל	נַפְשִׁי֙ יָֽצְאָ֣ה בְדַבְּר֔וֹ בִּקַּשְׁתִּ֙יהוּ֙ וְלֹ֣א מְצָאתִ֔יהוּ
	קְרָאתִ֖יו וְלֹ֥א עָנָֽנִי׃
ל חס . ג . ל ומל	7 מְצָאֻ֧נִי הַשֹּׁמְרִ֛ים הַסֹּבְבִ֥ים בָּעִ֖יר הִכּ֣וּנִי פְצָע֑וּנִי
ל . ז כתב	נָשְׂא֤וּ אֶת־רְדִידִי֙ מֵֽעָלַ֔י שֹׁמְרֵ֖י הַחֹמֽוֹת׃
	8 הִשְׁבַּ֥עְתִּי אֶתְכֶ֖ם בְּנ֣וֹת יְרוּשָׁלָ֑͏ִם
	אִֽם־תִּמְצְאוּ֙ אֶת־דּוֹדִ֔י מַה־תַּגִּ֣ידוּ ל֔וֹ
ל ומל	שֶׁחוֹלַ֥ת אַהֲבָ֖ה אָֽנִי׃
ב	9 מַה־דּוֹדֵ֣ךְ מִדּ֔וֹד הַיָּפָ֖ה בַּנָּשִׁ֑ים
ג מל בסיפֿ . ג	מַה־דּוֹדֵ֣ךְ מִדּ֔וֹד שֶׁכָּ֖כָה הִשְׁבַּעְתָּֽנוּ׃
ל מל	10 דּוֹדִ֥י צַח֙ וְאָד֔וֹם דָּג֖וּל מֵרְבָבָֽה׃
	11 רֹאשׁ֖וֹ כֶּ֣תֶם פָּ֑ז
ל . ל . ל . ל וחד כערב	קְוֻצּוֹתָיו֙ תַּלְתַּלִּ֔ים שְׁחֹר֖וֹת כָּעוֹרֵֽב׃
	12 עֵינָ֕יו כְּיוֹנִ֖ים עַל־אֲפִ֣יקֵי מָ֑יִם
ל . ד	רֹֽחֲצוֹת֙ בֶּֽחָלָ֔ב יֹשְׁב֖וֹת עַל־מִלֵּֽאת׃

[3] כתנתי ב בפי כתנתי . פשטתי את כתנתי :o| [5] מור ג מל בסיפֿ וסימ̇ קמתי אני ב
בפסוק . נטפות מור עבר :o

---

5 וְיָדַ֣י נָֽטְפוּ־ (G) (V) | sg S • **6** חָמַ֣ק α' σ' V S | > G • **8** יְרוּשָׁלָ͏ִם V S | foll ἐν
ταῖς δυνάμεσιν καὶ ἐν ταῖς ἰσχύσεσιν τοῦ ἀγροῦ G (assim-2:7; 3:5) • מַה־ G
V | > S • תַּגִּ֣ידוּ G V | impv S • **10** מֵרְבָבָֽה׃ α'-σ'-θ' La Syh | pl G ε' V S T ✣ •
11 כֶּ֣תֶם (α') ⟨⟨σ')Ms⟩ (θ') ε' V | prec ὡς σ'Ms S | foll καί G ⟨ζ'⟩ • תַּלְתַּלִּ֔ים G S |
prec ὡς αλ' V •

לְחָיָו כַּעֲרוּגַת הַבֹּשֶׂם מִגְדְּלוֹת מֶרְקָחִים 13 ל . ל
שִׂפְתוֹתָיו שׁוֹשַׁנִּים נֹטְפוֹת מוֹר עֹבֵר:

יָדָיו גְּלִילֵי זָהָב מְמֻלָּאִים בַּתַּרְשִׁישׁ 14 ל בטע
מֵעָיו עֶשֶׁת שֵׁן מְעֻלֶּפֶת סַפִּירִים: ל . ל . ל וחד בספירים

שׁוֹקָיו עַמּוּדֵי שֵׁשׁ מְיֻסָּדִים עַל־אַדְנֵי־פָז 15
מַרְאֵהוּ כַּלְּבָנוֹן בָּחוּר כָּאֲרָזִים: ל וחד כארזים

חִכּוֹ מַמְתַקִּים וְכֻלּוֹ מַחֲמַדִּים 16 ל
זֶה דוֹדִי וְזֶה רֵעִי בְּנוֹת יְרוּשָׁלָ͏ִם:

6 אָנָה הָלַךְ דּוֹדֵךְ הַיָּפָה בַּנָּשִׁים ד
אָנָה פָּנָה דוֹדֵךְ וּנְבַקְשֶׁנּוּ עִמָּךְ: ד

דּוֹדִי יָרַד לְגַנּוֹ לַעֲרוּגוֹת הַבֹּשֶׂם 2 ל
לִרְעוֹת בַּגַּנִּים וְלִלְקֹט שׁוֹשַׁנִּים: ל וב ללקט

אֲנִי לְדוֹדִי וְדוֹדִי לִי הָרֹעֶה בַּשׁוֹשַׁנִּים: ס 3

יָפָה אַתְּ רַעְיָתִי כְּתִרְצָה נָאוָה כִּירוּשָׁלָ͏ִם 4 ל . ה . ל
אֲיֻמָּה כַּנִּדְגָּלוֹת: ב . ב

הָסֵבִּי עֵינַיִךְ מִנֶּגְדִּי שֶׁהֵם הִרְהִיבֻנִי 5 ל . ב
שַׂעְרֵךְ כְּעֵדֶר הָעִזִּים שֶׁגָּלְשׁוּ מִן־הַגִּלְעָד: ב . ב

שִׁנַּיִךְ כְּעֵדֶר הָרְחֵלִים שֶׁעָלוּ מִן־הָרַחְצָה 6 ב
שֶׁכֻּלָּם מַתְאִימוֹת וְשַׁכֻּלָה אֵין בָּהֶם: ל ומל

[6:2] ללקט וללקט ג̇ יצאו מן העם . בשדה אחר . וללקט שושנים :ס

13 כַּעֲרוּגַת | pl G α'-σ' V S (differ-vocal, e.g. KR) ‖ → 6:2 • הַבֹּשֶׂם G | pl V S • מִגְדְּלוֹת מֶרְקָחִים | φύουσαι μυρεψικά G T | *consitae a pigmentariis* V | > S ✛ • **14** גְּלִילֵי G V | prec ܐܝܟ S • עֶשֶׁת G S | > V • **15** כָּאֲרָזִים: G V S | sg σ' • **16** מַחֲמַדִּים M^L (err) | (וְכֻלּוֹ) S (via ܘܟܠܗܘܢ) • וְכֻלּוֹ G V | • מַחֲמַדִּים M^Y • **6:2** לַעֲרוּגוֹת G α'-σ' (S) | sg V (differ-vocal, e.g. KR) • **3** בַּשׁוֹשַׁנִּים: M^L (err) | כְּעֵדֶר **5** בַּשׁוֹשַׁנִּים M^Y • **4** כְּתִרְצָה | ὡς εὐδοκία G α' σ' θ' ε' V S T (via √רצה) La V S | pl G V^Mss • שֶׁגָּלְשׁוּ → ✛ 4:1 • מִן־הַגִּלְעָד G V | *a monte Galaad* La S T (assim-4:1, e.g. KR) • **6** כְּעֵדֶר La V S | pl G α' σ' V^Mss • הָרְחֵלִים α' σ' V T | τῶν κεκαρμένων G S (assim-4:2) • בָּהֶם: V S | foll ὡς σπαρτίον τὸ κόκκινον χείλη σου καὶ ἡ λαλιά σου ὡραία G* (α') (σ') (αλ') (assim-4:3) ✛ •

כְּפֶ֤לַח הָרִמּוֹן֙ רַקָּתֵ֔ךְ   מִבַּ֖עַד לְצַמָּתֵֽךְ: ⁷

ב חס   שִׁשִּׁ֥ים הֵ֙מָּה֙ מְלָכ֔וֹת   וּשְׁמֹנִ֖ים פִּֽילַגְשִׁ֑ים ⁸

ל   וַעֲלָמ֖וֹת אֵ֥ין מִסְפָּֽר:

אַחַ֥ת הִיא֙ יוֹנָתִ֣י תַמָּתִ֔י   אַחַ֥ת הִיא֙ לְאִמָּ֔הּ ⁹
ה כת ה. ה. ל   בָּרָ֥ה הִ֖יא לְיֽוֹלַדְתָּ֑הּ

ב. ל   ס   רָא֤וּהָ בָנוֹת֙ וַֽיְאַשְּׁר֔וּהָ   מְלָכ֥וֹת וּפִֽילַגְשִׁ֖ים וַֽיְהַלְלֽוּהָ:

ל בטע ז.   מִי־זֹ֥את הַנִּשְׁקָפָ֖ה כְּמוֹ־שָׁ֑חַר ¹⁰

ל   ס   יָפָ֣ה כַלְּבָנָ֗ה   בָּרָה֙ כַּֽחַמָּ֔ה   אֲיֻמָּ֖ה כַּנִּדְגָּלֽוֹת:

אֶל־גִּנַּ֤ת אֱגוֹז֙ יָרַ֔דְתִּי   לִרְא֖וֹת בְּאִבֵּ֣י הַנָּ֑חַל ¹¹
ל. ל חס בכת   לִרְאוֹת֙ הֲפָֽרְחָ֣ה הַגֶּ֔פֶן   הֵנֵ֖צוּ הָרִמֹּנִֽים:

ל. ד   לֹ֣א יָדַ֔עְתִּי נַפְשִׁ֣י שָׂמַ֔תְנִי   מַרְכְּב֖וֹת עַמִּי־נָדִֽיב: ¹²

ל ומל   שׁ֤וּבִי שׁ֙וּבִי֙ הַשּׁ֣וּלַמִּ֔ית   שׁ֥וּבִי שׁ֖וּבִי וְנֶחֱזֶה־בָּ֑ךְ ⁷

ל. ל. ל וחס   מַֽה־תֶּחֱזוּ֙ בַּשּׁ֣וּלַמִּ֔ית   כִּמְחֹלַ֖ת הַֽמַּחֲנָֽיִם:

ב   מַה־יָּפ֧וּ פְעָמַ֛יִךְ בַּנְּעָלִ֖ים בַּת־נָדִ֑יב ²

ל. ל. ל   חַמּוּקֵ֣י יְרֵכַ֔יִךְ   כְּמ֣וֹ חֲלָאִ֔ים   מַעֲשֵׂ֖ה יְדֵ֥י אָמָּֽן:

ל. ל. ל. ל   שָׁרְרֵךְ֙ אַגַּ֣ן הַסַּ֔הַר   אַל־יֶחְסַ֖ר הַמָּ֑זֶג ³

[8] שמנים ב׳ חס ויעש מהם . ששים המה . וכל קריה דכותה ב׳ מ׳ ו׳ מל :o: [9] ברה ה׳
כת ה׳ וסימנה עד בית ברה שנים בו . מצות יהוה . הנשקפה . וכל לשון
אכיל דכות כגון . ואברה מידך . אם אברה חסידה :o: ויאשרוה ב׳ ראוה בנות
ויאשרוה . קמו בניה ויאשרוה :o: [12] מרכבות ד׳ מרכבות פרעה . מרכבות השמש .
מרכבות כבודך . עמינדיב . :o:

7 לְצַמָּתֵ֖ךְ → 4:1 ✣ • **9** תַמָּתִי G σ' V | ‫ܬܡܝܡܬܝ‬ (‫ܬܡ‬) S || → 5:2 • **10** כַּנִּדְגָּלוֹת G
σ' V T | ὡς μεγαλυνόμεναι ε' (ζ') (via √ גדל) | ὡς ἐπιφάνεια αλ' | ‫ܐܝܟ ܕܓܠܐ‬
S ✣ • **11** בְּאִבֵּי G σ' V | sg G^Mss αλ' S | הַנָּחַל G σ' V | pl αλ' S |
אם] הֲפָרְחָה G σ' V | ✣ • הָרִמֹּנִים V S | foll ἐκεῖ δώσω τοὺς μαστούς
μου σοί G (assim-7:13) • **12** שָׂמַתְנִי G ε' S | ἠπόρησέ με σ' V | posuisti me
La^Ambr La^169 (differ-vocal) ✣ • **7:1** הַשּׁוּלַמִּית G V S | עַמִּי־נָדִיב: ✣ •
εἰρηνεύουσα α' ε' | ἡ ἐσκυλευμένη σ' ✣ • שׁוּבִי² G V S | 4QCant^a (insuf)
✣ • בַּשּׁוּלַמִּית • ✣ • כִּמְחֹלַת הַמַּחֲנָיִם | ἡ ἐρχομένη ὡς χοροὶ τῶν παρεμβολῶν G |
διερχομένην ὡς χορὸν τῶν παρεμβολῶν ε' | ἐν τρώσεσι τῶν παρεμβολῶν σ' |
nisi choros castrorum V | ‫ܐܝܟ ܢܫܝܢ ܕܐܬܕܪܟ ܒܚܝܠܘܬܐ ܣܓܝܐܐ‬ S ✣ •

בִּטְנֵךְ עֲרֵמַת חִטִּים סוּגָה בַּשּׁוֹשַׁנִּים:	ל בסיפֿ . ל
4 שְׁנֵי שָׁדַיִךְ כִּשְׁנֵי עֳפָרִים תָּאֳמֵי צְבִיָּה:	ל
5 צַוָּארֵךְ כְּמִגְדַּל הַשֵּׁן	
עֵינַיִךְ בְּרֵכוֹת בְּחֶשְׁבּוֹן עַל־שַׁעַר בַּת־רַבִּים	בֿ . בֿ
אַפֵּךְ כְּמִגְדַּל הַלְּבָנוֹן צוֹפֶה פְּנֵי דַמָּשֶׂק:	בֿ מל
6 רֹאשֵׁךְ עָלַיִךְ כַּכַּרְמֶל וְדַלַּת רֹאשֵׁךְ כָּאַרְגָּמָן	ל . ל
מֶלֶךְ אָסוּר בָּרְהָטִים:	
7 מַה־יָּפִית וּמַה־נָּעַמְתְּ אַהֲבָה בַּתַּעֲנוּגִים:	ל . ל . ל
8 זֹאת קוֹמָתֵךְ דָּמְתָה לְתָמָר וְשָׁדַיִךְ לְאַשְׁכֹּלוֹת:	ל . ל
9 אָמַרְתִּי אֶעֱלֶה בְתָמָר אֹחֲזָה בְּסַנְסִנָּיו	ל
וְיִהְיוּ־נָא שָׁדַיִךְ כְּאֶשְׁכְּלוֹת הַגֶּפֶן וְרֵיחַ אַפֵּךְ כַּתַּפּוּחִים:	ל . הֿ . ל
10 וְחִכֵּךְ כְּיֵין הַטּוֹב הוֹלֵךְ לְדוֹדִי לְמֵישָׁרִים	ל
דּוֹבֵב שִׂפְתֵי יְשֵׁנִים:	ל ומל
11 אֲנִי לְדוֹדִי וְעָלַי תְּשׁוּקָתוֹ: ס	הֿ . בֿ
12 לְכָה דוֹדִי נֵצֵא הַשָּׂדֶה נָלִינָה בַּכְּפָרִים:	ל
13 נַשְׁכִּימָה לַכְּרָמִים נִרְאֶה אִם פָּרְחָה הַגֶּפֶן פִּתַּח הַסְּמָדַר	ל . בֿ . ל
הֵנֵצוּ הָרִמּוֹנִים	

[7:11] ועלי ה וסימנהון מי ישׂימני שפט בארץ . ועלי לתת לך עשׂרה כסף . שׂמו כל
ישׂראל פניהם למלך . ועלי תשׁוקתו . ועלי הטה חסד o: [13] נראה גֿ האמרים .
כחשׁו ביהוה . לאמר כי ארץ מצרים נבא . באורך נראה אור . נשׂכימה לכרמים
נראה o: וחד ונראה כי אין o:

3 עֲרֵמַת G S | prec ὡς σ' La V • 4 צְבִיָּה G V | pl and foll ܘܬܐܡܐ ܕܛܒܝܐ S
(assim-4:5) • 5 בְּרֵכוֹת 4QCantᵃ | prec ὡς G σ' V S T ✣ • שַׁעַר V S T | pl G •
6 עָלַיִךְ G S | > V • וְדַלַּת G α'-σ' | pl V S (differ-vocal) • כָּאַרְגָּמָן מֶלֶךְ G | ὡς
πορφύρα βασιλέως α' σ' V S (differ-div) | 4QCantᵃ (indet) • 7 וּמַה־ G V S | >
cj 4QCantᵃ • בַּתַּעֲנוּגִים: (G) אַהֲבָה 4QCantᵃ ✣ • אַהֲבָה G T | ἀγαπητή σ' V S | א]הבה
σ' V T | θυγάτηρ τρυφῶν α' S ‖ pref בַּת תַּעֲנוּגִים see α' S ✣ • 8 זֹאת G α' σ' (S) |
> La V • 9 בְתָמָר | ἐν τῷ φοίνικι G (differ-vocal) | V S (indet) • 10 הוֹלֵךְ G
S | ἁρμόζων σ' (V) (exeg) • יְשֵׁנִים: T | χείλεσίν μου καὶ ὀδοῦσιν G (α')
(V) | אֱזܬ‎, ܡܦܩ S ‖ pref שִׂפְתֵי וְשִׁנֵּי see G (α') (V) S ✣ • 11 תְּשׁוּקָתוֹ: S | ἡ
ἐπιστροφή αὐτοῦ G V (via תשובתו ?) • 13 אִם Mᴸ (err) | אִם־ Mʸ ✣ •

שָׁם אֶתֵּן אֶת־דֹּדַי לָֽךְ׃

ב

14 הַֽדוּדָאִים נָֽתְנוּ־רֵ֗יחַ   וְעַל־פְּתָחֵ֨ינוּ֙ כָּל־מְגָדִ֔ים

ב

חֲדָשִׁ֖ים גַּם־יְשָׁנִ֑ים

דּוֹדִ֖י צָפַ֥נְתִּי לָֽךְ׃

8 מִ֤י יִתֶּנְךָ֙ כְּאָ֣ח לִ֔י   יוֹנֵ֖ק שְׁדֵ֣י אִמִּ֑י

ב

אֶֽמְצָאֲךָ֤ בַחוּץ֙ אֶשָּׁ֣קְךָ֔   גַּ֖ם לֹא־יָב֥וּזוּ לִֽי׃

ל . ל

2 אֶנְהָֽגֲךָ֗ אֲבִֽיאֲךָ֛ אֶל־בֵּ֥ית אִמִּ֖י תְּלַמְּדֵ֑נִי

ל . ל

אַשְׁקְךָ֙ מִיַּ֣יִן הָרֶ֔קַח   מֵעֲסִ֖יס רִמֹּנִֽי׃

ל . ל

3 שְׂמֹאלוֹ֙ תַּ֣חַת רֹאשִׁ֔י   וִימִינ֖וֹ תְּחַבְּקֵֽנִי׃

ל . ב

4 הִשְׁבַּ֥עְתִּי אֶתְכֶ֖ם   בְּנ֣וֹת יְרוּשָׁלָ֑͏ִם

5 מַה־תָּעִ֧ירוּ ׀ וּֽמַה־תְּעֹֽרְר֛וּ אֶת־הָאַהֲבָ֖ה עַ֥ד שֶׁתֶּחְפָּֽץ׃ ס   ל . ל . יא בטע

5 מִ֣י זֹ֗את עֹלָה֙ מִן־הַמִּדְבָּ֔ר   מִתְרַפֶּ֖קֶת עַל־דּוֹדָ֑הּ   ל . ל

תַּ֤חַת הַתַּפּ֨וּחַ֙ עֽוֹרַרְתִּ֔יךָ   שָׁ֚מָּה חִבְּלַ֣תְךָ אִמֶּ֔ךָ   ל ומל

שָׁ֖מָּה חִבְּלָ֥ה יְלָדַֽתְךָ׃   ל

6 שִׂימֵ֨נִי כַֽחוֹתָ֜ם עַל־לִבֶּ֗ךָ   כַּֽחוֹתָם֙ עַל־זְרוֹעֶ֔ךָ   ג

כִּֽי־עַזָּ֤ה כַמָּ֨וֶת֙ אַהֲבָ֔ה   קָשָׁ֥ה כִשְׁא֖וֹל קִנְאָ֑ה   ג

רְשָׁפֶ֕יהָ רִשְׁפֵּ֕י אֵ֖שׁ שַׁלְהֶ֥בֶתְיָֽה׃   ל . ל דגש . ל

[8:1] יבוזו ג̇ חד חס̇ וב̇ מל̇ וסימנהון אמצאך בחוץ . ונהרות לא ישטפוה . לא יבוזו
לוֹ גנב כי יגנוב ׃o

13 דֹּדַי αλ' | τοὺς μαστούς μου G V S ‖ → 1:2 • **8:1** כְּאָ֣ח α' S T | > prep G V
(hapl) • אֶשָּׁ֣קְךָ֔ M[L] (err) | אשקך M[Y] • **2** תְּלַמְּדֵ֑נִי V T | καὶ εἰς ταμίειον τῆς
συλλαβούσης με G S | καὶ εἰς ταμ(ί)ειον τῆς συλλαβούσης με ⁑ διδάξεις με ⸔
⟨Syh⟩ La[Ambr] ⁑ • מִיַּ֣יִן הָרֶ֔קַח (S) | ἀπὸ οἴνου τοῦ μυρεψικοῦ G | σ' V (indet)
⁑ : רִמֹּנִֽי | ῥοῶν μου G V S (differ-vocal) • **4** יְרוּשָׁלָ֑͏ִם V S | foll ἐν ταῖς
δυνάμεσιν καὶ ἐν ταῖς ἰσχύσεσιν τοῦ ἀγροῦ G (α') (assim-2:7; 3:5; 5:8, e.g.
KR) • הָאַהֲבָ֖ה ⁑ ↔ 2:7 • **5** מִן־הַמִּדְבָּ֔ר λ' V S T | λελευκανθισμένη G (elus)
| עֽוֹרַרְתִּ֔יךָ הַתַּפּ֨וּחַ֙ M[L] (err) | התפוח M[Y] • הַמִּדְבָּ֔ר (G) S | foll *deliciis affluens* V •
2 f sg sfx S | G α' V (indet) • חִבְּלַ֣תְךָ אִמֶּ֔ךָ | 2 f sg sfx S | G V (indet) •
חִבְּלָ֥ה σ' (V) S | foll σε G (assim-v 5b) | יְלָדַֽתְךָ׃ : ἡ τεκοῦσά σου G σ' V |
ܫܠܗܒܝܬܐ S ⁑ • **6** שַׁלְהֶ֥בֶתְיָֽה׃ | φλόγες αὐτῆς G | *atque flammarum* V | ܫܠܗܒܝܬܗ
S ⁑ •

מַ֣יִם רַבִּ֗ים לֹ֤א יֽוּכְלוּ֙ לְכַבּ֣וֹת אֶת־הָֽאַהֲבָ֔ה   7   יֵא

וּנְהָר֖וֹת לֹ֣א יִשְׁטְפ֑וּהָ   ל

אִם־יִתֵּ֨ן אִ֜ישׁ אֶת־כָּל־ה֤וֹן בֵּיתוֹ֙ בָּאַהֲבָ֔ה   ג

בּ֖וֹז יָב֥וּזוּ לֽוֹ׃   ס

אָח֥וֹת לָ֙נוּ֙ קְטַנָּ֔ה   וְשָׁדַ֖יִם אֵ֣ין לָ֑הּ   8

מַֽה־נַּעֲשֶׂה֙ לַאֲחֹתֵ֔נוּ   בַּיּ֖וֹם שֶׁיְּדֻבַּר־בָּֽהּ׃   ב בסיפ

אִם־חוֹמָ֣ה הִ֔יא   נִבְנֶ֥ה עָלֶ֖יהָ טִ֣ירַת כָּ֑סֶף   9   ל

וְאִם־דֶּ֣לֶת הִ֔יא   נָצ֥וּר עָלֶ֖יהָ ל֥וּחַ אָֽרֶז׃   ל

אֲנִ֣י חוֹמָ֔ה   וְשָׁדַ֖י כַּמִּגְדָּל֑וֹת   10   ל ומל

אָ֛ז הָיִ֥יתִי בְעֵינָ֖יו   כְּמוֹצְאֵ֥ת שָׁלֽוֹם׃   ל ומל

כֶּ֣רֶם הָיָ֤ה לִשְׁלֹמֹה֙ בְּבַ֣עַל הָמ֔וֹן   נָתַ֥ן אֶת־הַכֶּ֖רֶם לַנֹּטְרִ֑ים   11   ל

אִ֛ישׁ יָבִ֥א בְּפִרְי֖וֹ   אֶ֥לֶף כָּֽסֶף׃   ה חס

כַּרְמִ֥י שֶׁלִּ֖י לְפָנָ֑י   12   ב

הָאֶ֤לֶף לְךָ֙ שְׁלֹמֹ֔ה   וּמָאתַ֖יִם לְנֹטְרִ֥ים אֶת־פִּרְיֽוֹ׃   ג . ל

הַיּוֹשֶׁ֣בֶת בַּגַּנִּ֗ים   חֲבֵרִ֛ים מַקְשִׁיבִ֥ים לְקוֹלֵ֖ךְ   הַשְׁמִיעִֽינִי׃   13   ל . ב

בְּרַ֣ח ׀ דּוֹדִ֗י   וּֽדְמֵה־לְךָ֤ לִצְבִי֙ א֚וֹ לְעֹ֣פֶר הָֽאַיָּלִ֔ים   14   ל

עַ֖ל הָרֵ֥י בְשָׂמִֽים׃   ל

קי״ז

[8] אחותינו ד׳ ג֗ חס֗ וא֗ מל֗ אחותנו את חיי . לתת אחתנו . הכזוונה יעשה את . מה נעשה לאחת ס׃ [12] האלף ד֗ וסימנהון ואת האלף ושבע המאות . וצלע האלף תיניֿ . האלף לך שלמה . תביא לשר האלף ס׃

8 אֵ֣ין לָ֑הּ GVS | οὐκ ἔχεις ε' (err-graph) • **9** טִ֣ירַת | pl GVST (differ-vocal) • ל֥וּחַ GT | pl σ' La VS • **10** כַּמִּגְדָּל֑וֹת G (V) T | > prep G^Ms S • אָ֛ז α' ST | ἐγώ G | ex quo V • כְּמוֹצְאֵ֥ת GVS | > prep G^Ms α' • **11** נָתַ֥ן GV | 1 sg pf S • **12** כַּרְמִ֥י M^L (err) | כַּרמִי M^Y • **13** הַיּוֹשֶׁ֣בֶת M^L? (err) | M^Y (insuf) ÷ ○ הַיּוֹשֶׁ֣בֶת α' σ' VT | m sg ptc G θ'-ε' | qui sedent La^169 | m pl ptc S • חֲבֵרִ֛ים GV T | > S • לְקוֹלֵ֖ךְ | 2 m sg sfx S | GV (indet) •

1 דִּבְרֵי֙ קֹהֶ֔לֶת בֶּן־דָּוִ֖ד מֶ֥לֶךְ בִּירוּשָׁלָֽ͏ִם׃   ל

2 הֲבֵ֤ל הֲבָלִים֙ אָמַ֣ר קֹהֶ֔לֶת   הֲבֵ֥ל הֲבָלִ֖ים הַכֹּ֥ל הָֽבֶל׃   ג̇

3 מַה־יִּתְר֖וֹן לָֽאָדָ֑ם בְּכָל־עֲמָל֔וֹ   שֶֽׁיַּעֲמֹ֖ל תַּ֥חַת הַשָּֽׁמֶשׁ׃

4 דּ֤וֹר הֹלֵךְ֙ וְד֣וֹר בָּ֔א   וְהָאָ֖רֶץ לְעוֹלָ֥ם עֹמָֽדֶת׃   ד חס בסיפ̇ . ל̇

5 וְזָרַ֤ח הַשֶּׁ֙מֶשׁ֙ וּבָ֣א הַשָּׁ֔מֶשׁ   ג̇

וְאֶ֨ל־מְקוֹמ֔וֹ שׁוֹאֵ֛ף   זוֹרֵ֥חַֽ ה֖וּא שָֽׁם׃   ל . ל מל

6 הוֹלֵךְ֙ אֶל־דָּר֔וֹם   וְסוֹבֵ֖ב אֶל־צָפ֑וֹן   ל

סוֹבֵ֤ב ׀ סֹבֵב֙   הוֹלֵ֣ךְ הָר֔וּחַ   ב

וְעַל־סְבִיבֹתָ֖יו   שָׁ֥ב הָרֽוּחַ׃   ל

7 כָּל־הַנְּחָלִים֙ הֹלְכִ֣ים אֶל־הַיָּ֔ם   וְהַיָּ֖ם אֵינֶ֣נּוּ מָלֵ֑א   ל בסיפ̇ . ז̇

אֶל־מְק֗וֹם שֶׁ֤הַנְּחָלִים֙ הֹֽלְכִ֔ים   שָׁ֛ם הֵ֥ם שָׁבִ֖ים לָלָֽכֶת׃   ל . ל̇

8 כָּל־הַדְּבָרִ֣ים יְגֵעִ֔ים   לֹא־יוּכַ֥ל אִ֖ישׁ לְדַבֵּ֑ר   ל

לֹא־תִשְׂבַּ֥ע עַ֙יִן֙ לִרְא֔וֹת   וְלֹא־תִמָּלֵ֥א אֹ֖זֶן מִשְּׁמֹֽעַ׃   כה̇ . ד חס

9 מַה־שֶּֽׁהָיָה֙ ה֣וּא שֶׁיִּהְיֶ֔ה   וּמַה־שֶּׁנַּֽעֲשָׂ֔ה ה֖וּא שֶׁיֵּעָשֶׂ֑ה   ג̇ . ב̇

וְאֵ֥ין כָּל־חָדָ֖שׁ תַּ֥חַת הַשָּֽׁמֶשׁ׃   ב

[1:5] וזרח ג וסימנה משעיר למו . וזרח בחשך אורך . השמש ובא השמש ‪:ס‬ [6] סבב חס האחד פישון סובב . סבב תי̇נ דפסוק ‪:ס‬ [8] משמע ד̇ חס וסימנה נעויתי שחותי . משמוע דמים . מסיר אזנו . ולא תמלא ‪:ס‬ [9] שיהיה ג מה שהיה הוא שיהיה ושנאתי . כי אינ̇נו יודע מה שיהיה ‪:ס‬

1:1 בִּירוּשָׁלָ͏ִם T | βασιλέως Ἰσραὴλ ἐν Ἰερουσαλήμ G (facil) | regis *Hierusalem* V Hie^lem S (facil) ✢ • **2** קֹהֶלֶת (assim-1:1) | ὁ ἐκκλησιαστής G | V S T (indet) ‖ pref הַקֹּהֶלֶת see G ✢ ✢ • **3** עֲמָלוֹ G V T (assim-usu) | > sfx α' S ‖ pref הֶעָמָל see α' S ✢ • :הַשָּׁמֶשׁ G V S^Mss T (assim-usu?) | ܫܡܫܐ S* ✢ ✢ • **5** וְזָרַח ⟨α'⟩ | καὶ ἀνατέλλει G ⟨σ'⟩ | > cj V Hie^lem S | וידנח T ‖ pref וְזָרַח see G ⟨σ'⟩ ✢ • שׁוֹאֵף ✢ ✢ | זוֹרֵחַ G | prec cj V Hie^lem T (facil) | ܢܓܕ S ‖ → ✢ ✢ • **8** ²לֹא־ V | וְזָרַח ✢ ✢ Hie^lem | prec cj G S T •

¹⁰ יֵ֣שׁ דָּבָ֥ר שֶׁיֹּאמַ֛ר   רְאֵה־זֶ֥ה חָדָ֖שׁ ה֑וּא

כְּבָר֙ הָיָ֣ה לְעֹֽלָמִ֔ים   אֲשֶׁ֥ר הָיָ֖ה מִלְּפָנֵֽנוּ:   ג חס . ג בסיפ

¹¹ אֵ֥ין זִכְר֖וֹן לָרִֽאשֹׁנִ֑ים   וְגַ֤ם לָאַֽחֲרֹנִים֙ שֶׁיִּֽהְי֔וּ   ג . ג

לֹֽא־יִהְיֶ֤ה לָהֶם֙ זִכָּר֔וֹן   עִ֥ם שֶׁיִּֽהְי֖וּ לָאַֽחֲרֹנָֽה: פ   ג . ב

¹²¹³ אֲנִ֣י קֹהֶ֗לֶת הָיִ֥יתִי מֶ֛לֶךְ עַל־יִשְׂרָאֵ֖ל בִּירֽוּשָׁלָ֑͏ִם: וְנָתַ֣תִּי אֶת־לִבִּ֗י   ה

לִדְר֤וֹשׁ וְלָתוּר֙ בַּֽחָכְמָ֔ה עַ֛ל כָּל־אֲשֶׁ֥ר נַֽעֲשָׂ֖ה תַּ֣חַת הַשָּׁמָ֑יִם ה֣וּא | ג בסיפ

עִנְיַ֣ן רָ֗ע נָתַ֧ן אֱלֹהִ֛ים לִבְנֵ֥י הָֽאָדָ֖ם לַֽעֲנ֥וֹת בּֽוֹ:

¹⁴ רָאִ֙יתִי֙ אֶת־כָּל־הַֽמַּעֲשִׂ֔ים   שֶֽׁנַּעֲשׂ֖וּ תַּ֣חַת הַשָּׁ֑מֶשׁ   ל

וְהִנֵּ֥ה הַכֹּ֛ל הֶ֖בֶל וּרְע֥וּת רֽוּחַ:

¹⁵ מְעֻוָּ֖ת לֹֽא־יוּכַ֣ל לִתְקֹ֑ן   וְחֶסְר֖וֹן לֹא־יוּכַ֥ל לְהִמָּנֽוֹת: ל . ל וחס . ל ומל . ל ומל

¹⁶ דִּבַּ֨רְתִּי אֲנִ֤י עִם־לִבִּי֙ לֵאמֹ֔ר אֲנִ֗י הִנֵּ֨ה הִגְדַּ֤לְתִּי וְהוֹסַ֙פְתִּי֙ חָכְמָ֔ה עַ֛ל   ב ראש פסוק . ד

כָּל־אֲשֶׁר־הָיָ֥ה לְפָנַ֖י עַל־יְרֽוּשָׁלָ֑͏ִם וְלִבִּ֛י רָאָ֥ה הַרְבֵּ֖ה חָכְמָ֥ה

וָדָֽעַת: ¹⁷ וָאֶתְּנָ֣ה לִבִּ֗י לָדַ֤עַת חָכְמָה֙ וְדַ֣עַת הֽוֹלֵל֖וֹת וְשִׂכְל֑וּת יָדַ֕עְתִּי   ד . ל . ל כת

שֶׁגַּם־זֶ֥ה ה֖וּא רַעְי֥וֹן רֽוּחַ:

[11] זכרון ג וסימנהון זכרון תרועה מקרא קדש . אין זכרון לראשנים . כי אין זכרון
לחכם :o

10 יֵ֣שׁ דָּבָ֥ר שֶׁיֹּאמַ֛ר (Hie^{lem}) T | ὃς λαλήσει καὶ ἐρεῖ G S (interp) | *putasne est qui possit dicere* σ' | *nec valet quisquam dicere* V (exeg) ✣ • הָיָ֖ה² σ' | pl G V Hie^{lem} T | S (indet) ✣ • **13** הַשָּׁמָ֑יִם G S* | *sole* V Hie^{lem} S^{Mss} T (assim-usu) ✣ • | ה֑וּא ⟨σ'⟩ V Hie^{lem} | ὅτι G (crrp via כי?) | > S | T (indet) ✣ • אֱלֹהִ֛ים (theol) | ὁ θεός G | V S T (indet) ‖ pref הָֽאֱלֹהִ֛ים see G ✣ • **14** שֶֽׁנַּעֲשׂ֖וּ | אשר נעשו 4QQoh^b | G V S T (indet) ✣ • **15** לְהִמָּנֽוֹת: G V Hie^{lem} S^{Mss} T | ܠܡܚܠܡܘܬܗ S | ἀναπληρῶσαι ἀριθμόν σ' (confl) | ܘܚܘܣܪܢܐ ܕ... θ' ✣ • **16** הִגְדַּ֤לְתִּי | ἐμεγαλύνθην G V Hie^{lem} S (assim-2:9) | T (indet) ✣ • הָיָ֥ה² Syh^{anon} | pl G V Hie^{lem} S T ‖ → ✣ 1:10 • עַל־יְרֽוּשָׁלָ֑͏ִם | ἐν Ἰερουσαλήμ G V Hie^{lem} S T ✣ • **17** וְדַ֣עַת | καὶ γνῶσιν G V Hie^{lem} S (T) ‖ pref וָדָֽעַת see G V Hie^{lem} S (T) ✣ • הֽוֹלֵל֖וֹת (interp) | παραβολάς G (S) (interp) | πλάνας α' V (interp) | παραφοράς θ' | וחולחולתא דמלכותא T* | והולהולתא דמלכותא T (err) ‖ pref הֽוֹלֵל֖וֹת (origin) ✣ • וְשִׂכְל֑וּת | καὶ ἐπιστήμην G S T (interp) | *et stultitiam* V Hie^{lem} ‖ pref וְסִכְל֑וּת see V Hie^{lem} ✣ • רַעְי֥וֹן יָדַ֕עְתִּי | G^{Mss} Hie^{lem} | ἔγνων ἐγώ G* | *et agnovi* V S | למידע T (interp) ✣ • רַעְי֥וֹן G α' Hie^{lem} S T | *labor et adflictio* V | ܥܡܠܐ ܘܛܘܪܦܐ S^{Ms} (assim-1:14) •

לֹג 18 כִּי בְּרֹב חָכְמָה רָב־כָּעַס וְיוֹסִיף דַּעַת יוֹסִיף מַכְאוֹב׃

2 אָמַרְתִּי אֲנִי בְּלִבִּי

ל. ד 　　לְכָה־נָּא אֲנַסְּכָה בְשִׂמְחָה וּרְאֵה בְטוֹב

וְהִנֵּה גַם־הוּא הָבֶל׃

ל ומל . ג . / י . 2 לִשְׂחוֹק אָמַרְתִּי מְהוֹלָל וּלְשִׂמְחָה מַה־זֹּה עֹשָׂה׃

ל ומל. ד . ל 3 תַּרְתִּי בְלִבִּי לִמְשׁוֹךְ בַּיַּיִן אֶת־בְּשָׂרִי וְלִבִּי נֹהֵג בַּחָכְמָה וְלֶאֱחֹז

בְּסִכְלוּת עַד אֲשֶׁר־אֶרְאֶה אֵי־זֶה טוֹב לִבְנֵי הָאָדָם אֲשֶׁר יַעֲשׂוּ

ג בסיפ 　　תַּחַת הַשָּׁמַיִם מִסְפַּר יְמֵי חַיֵּיהֶם׃

4 הִגְדַּלְתִּי מַעֲשָׂי

בָּנִיתִי לִי בָּתִּים נָטַעְתִּי לִי כְּרָמִים׃

ג ראׁ פסוק . ל 5 עָשִׂיתִי לִי גַּנּוֹת וּפַרְדֵּסִים

וְנָטַעְתִּי בָהֶם עֵץ כָּל־פֶּרִי׃

ג ראש פסוק 6 עָשִׂיתִי לִי בְּרֵכוֹת מָיִם

ל ומל 　　לְהַשְׁקוֹת מֵהֶם יַעַר צוֹמֵחַ עֵצִים׃

ה 7 קָנִיתִי עֲבָדִים וּשְׁפָחוֹת וּבְנֵי־בַיִת הָיָה לִי

ד 　　גַּם מִקְנֶה בָקָר וָצֹאן הַרְבֵּה הָיָה לִי

ל 　　מִכֹּל שֶׁהָיוּ לְפָנַי בִּירוּשָׁלָ͏ִם׃

[2:2] ולשמחה ג וסימנהון לדגון אלהיהם . צום הרביעי . לשחוק אמרתי ס: [6] ברכות
ב בחשבון . עשיתי לי ס: [7] יצאו ד וסימנהון וכל מעשר בקר . ויזבח בלק בקר
וצאן . דחזקיה . גם מקנה בקר וצאן הרבה היה לי ס:

---

18 כָּעַס ⟨α'-θ'⟩ ⟨σ'⟩ V Hie^lem S T | γνώσεως G (theol) • **2:2** מְהוֹלָל G α' σ' θ' V
Hie^lem | עֹשָׂה ⟨σ'-θ'⟩ (T) | ليצنות T ٭ • ﹕ • : ٭ • ليصنوت S | עֹשָׂה ⟨σ'-θ'⟩ (T) | ποιεῖς G V Hie^lem
S • **3** תַּרְתִּי בְלִבִּי לִמְשׁוֹךְ בַּיַּיִן Hie^lem S T | καὶ κατεσκεψάμην εἰ ἡ καρδία μου
ἑλκύσει ὡς οἶνον G* | καὶ διενοήθην ἐν τῇ καρδίᾳ μου ἑλκῦσαι ὡς οἶνον ⟨θ'⟩ |
cogitavi in corde meo abstrahere a vino V ٭ • נֹהֵג S^Ms | ὡδήγησεν G (interp) |
ὡδήγησέν με G^Mss Hie^lem (interp) | μεταγάγω σ' V (interp) | ܘ S T ٭ • בְּסִכְלוּת
G V Hie^lem T* | ἐπ' εὐφροσύνῃ G^Mss (crrp) | ܒܚܕܘܬܐ S ٭ • הַשָּׁמַיִם
| τὸν ἥλιον G V Hie^lem S T (assim-usu) ‖ → ٭ • 1:3 הַשֶּׁמֶשׁ **4** מַעֲשָׂי σ' V
Hie^lem S | ποίημά μου G | עובדין טבין T ٭ • **7** קָנִיתִי G Hie^lem T | *possedi* V
(interp) | ܩܢܝܬ S (assim-ctext) ٭ • וּבְנֵי־בַיִת הָיָה לִי G Hie^lem T | *multamque
familiam habui* V S ٭ • הָיָה | pl G Hie^lem S T (transl) | *habui* V ٭ •
• ٭ מִכֹּל שֶׁהָיוּ • וּבְנֵי־בַיִת הָיָה לִי ٭ → הַרְבֵּה

8 כָּנַ֨סְתִּי לִ֤י גַּם־כֶּ֨סֶף֙ וְזָהָ֔ב וּסְגֻלַּ֥ת מְלָכִ֖ים וְהַמְּדִינ֑וֹת	ל וחס̇ . ל ל ומל̇ וחד למדינות
עָשִׂ֨יתִי לִ֤י שָׁרִים֙ וְשָׁר֔וֹת וְתַעֲנוּגֹ֖ת בְּנֵ֣י הָאָדָ֑ם שִׁדָּ֖ה וְשִׁדּֽוֹת׃	ל . ל . ל
9 וְגָדַ֣לְתִּי וְהוֹסַ֔פְתִּי מִכֹּ֛ל שֶׁהָיָ֥ה לְפָנַ֖י בִּירוּשָׁלָ֑͏ִם	ל̇
אַ֥ף חָכְמָתִ֖י עָ֥מְדָה לִּֽי׃	
10 וְכֹל֙ אֲשֶׁ֣ר שָֽׁאֲל֣וּ עֵינַ֔י לֹ֥א אָצַ֖לְתִּי מֵהֶ֑ם	ל . ל
לֹֽא־מָנַ֨עְתִּי אֶת־לִבִּ֜י מִכָּל־שִׂמְחָ֗ה	
כִּֽי־לִבִּ֣י שָׂמֵ֗חַ מִכָּל־עֲמָלִ֑י	
וְזֶֽה־הָיָ֥ה חֶלְקִ֖י מִכָּל־עֲמָלִֽי׃	
11 וּפָנִ֣יתִֽי אֲנִ֗י בְּכָל־מַעֲשַׂי֙ שֶֽׁעָשׂ֣וּ יָדַ֔י	כֹ̇ב
וּבֶֽעָמָ֖ל שֶׁעָמַ֣לְתִּי לַעֲשׂ֑וֹת	ג̇
וְהִנֵּ֥ה הַכֹּ֛ל הֶ֥בֶל וּרְע֣וּת ר֔וּחַ	
וְאֵ֥ין יִתְר֖וֹן תַּ֥חַת הַשָּֽׁמֶשׁ׃	
12 וּפָנִ֤יתִֽי אֲנִי֙ לִרְא֣וֹת חָכְמָ֔ה וְהוֹלֵל֖וֹת וְסִכְל֑וּת	
כִּ֣י ׀ מֶ֣ה הָאָדָ֗ם שֶׁיָּבוֹא֙ אַחֲרֵ֣י הַמֶּ֔לֶךְ	כֹ̇ד . ל ומל̇

[8] שרים ה̇ וסימנהון קדמו שרים אחר נגנים . ושרים כחללים . בקול . וכנורת . עשיתי לי . בקינותיהם :ס̇ ב̇ מיללין דמין חס̇ בליש מבית תעגניה . ותענגות בני :ס̇ [9] עמדה ד̇ וסימ̇ כי עמדה מלדת . וגם האשרה . במישור . אף חכמתי עמדה לי :ס̇

8 וְזָהָ֔ב G^{Mss} S T (assim-ctext?) | καὶ γε χρυσίον G* | V (indet) ✣ ● וּסְגֻלַּ֥ת S (assim-usu?) | pl G α' σ' V Hie^{lem} T ✣ ● שָׁרִ֣ים וְשָׁר֔וֹת • שָׂדֶ֖ה → :✣ ● שִׁדָּ֖ה וְשִׁדּֽוֹת: | pl G α' σ' V Hie^{lem} T ✣ ● וְשִׁדּֽוֹת: | *sadda et saddoth* Hie^{comm} (differ-vocal) | οἰνοχόον καὶ οἰνοχόας G θ' | κυλίκιον καὶ κυλίκια α' | *mensurarum species et appositiones* σ' | *scyphos et urceos in ministerio ad vina fundenda* V | ܟ̈ܣܐ S | *ministros vini et ministras* Hie^{lem} | ܟ T ✣ ● מרזיבין דשדיין מיא פשורי ומרזבין דשדין מיא חמימי T ✣ ● **9** שֶׁהָיָ֥ה | pl G V Hie^{lem} S T ‖ → ✣ 1:10 ● **10** לֹ֥א2 G | prec cj V Hie^{lem} S T ● מִכָּל־2 σ' T (assim-ctext) | ἐν παντί G V Hie^{lem} S ‖ pref בְּכָל see G V Hie^{lem} S ✣ ● **11** וּבֶֽעָמָ֖ל G V Hie^{lem} T | καὶ τὸν πόνον σ' | ܘܒܥܡܠ S (assim-ctext) ✣ ● **12** וְהוֹלֵל֖וֹת ✣ α'-θ' V Hie^{lem} | καὶ παραφοράν G^{Ms} | καὶ περιφοράν G S | וחלחולתא דמלכותא T (interp) ‖ pref וְהוֹלֵל֖וֹת see G S ✣ ● מֶ֣ה הָאָדָ֗ם G^{Mss} σ' V Hie^{lem} S | τίς ἄνθρωπος G* (hapl) | מה הנאה אית לגבר T ✣ ● הַמֶּ֔לֶךְ ⟨α'⟩ ⟨θ'⟩ V Hie^{lem} S T | τῆς βουλῆς G σ' (exeg) ✣ ●

אֶת אֲשֶׁר־כְּבָר עָשֽׂוּהוּ:   ל

13   וְרָאִ֫יתִי אָ֗נִי שֶׁיֵּ֤שׁ יִתְרוֹן֙ לַֽחָכְמָ֔ה מִן־הַסִּכְל֑וּת כִּיתְר֥וֹן הָא֖וֹר מִן־   נֵ בסיפ . ל ומל
הַחֹֽשֶׁךְ:

14   הֶֽחָכָם֙ עֵינָ֣יו בְּרֹאשׁ֔וֹ   וְהַכְּסִ֖יל בַּחֹ֣שֶׁךְ הוֹלֵ֑ךְ   יד

וְיָדַ֣עְתִּי גַם־אָ֔נִי   שֶׁמִּקְרֶ֥ה אֶחָ֖ד יִקְרֶ֥ה אֶת־כֻּלָּֽם: ל

15   וְאָמַ֨רְתִּ֤י אֲנִי֙ בְּלִבִּ֔י   ל

כְּמִקְרֵ֤ה הַכְּסִיל֙   גַּם־אֲנִ֣י יִקְרֵ֔נִי

וְלָ֧מָּה חָכַ֛מְתִּי אֲנִ֖י אָ֣ז יוֹתֵ֑ר

וְדִבַּ֣רְתִּי בְלִבִּ֔י שֶׁגַּם־זֶ֥ה הָֽבֶל: ג

16   כִּי֩ אֵ֨ין זִכְר֧וֹן לֶחָכָ֛ם   עִֽם־הַכְּסִ֖יל לְעוֹלָ֑ם   ג

בְּשֶׁכְּבָ֞ר הַיָּמִ֤ים הַבָּאִים֙   הַכֹּ֣ל נִשְׁכָּ֔ח   ל . ל

וְאֵ֛יךְ יָמ֥וּת הֶחָכָ֖ם עִֽם־הַכְּסִֽיל:

17   וְשָׂנֵ֙אתִי֙ אֶת־הַֽחַיִּ֔ים

כִּ֣י רַ֤ע עָלַי֙ הַֽמַּעֲשֶׂ֔ה   שֶֽׁנַּעֲשָׂ֖ה תַּ֣חַת הַשָּׁ֑מֶשׁ

כִּֽי־הַכֹּ֥ל הֶ֖בֶל וּרְע֥וּת רֽוּחַ:

18   וְשָׂנֵ֤אתִֽי אֲנִי֙ אֶת־כָּל־עֲמָלִ֔י שֶֽׁאֲנִ֥י עָמֵ֖ל תַּ֣חַת הַשָּׁ֑מֶשׁ שֶׁ֣אַנִּיחֶ֔נּוּ   ב . ה בסיפ . ל

19   לָֽאָדָ֖ם שֶׁיִּהְיֶ֥ה אַחֲרָֽי: וּמִ֣י י֥וֹדֵ֗עַ הֶֽחָכָ֤ם יִהְיֶה֙ א֣וֹ סָכָ֔ל וְיִשְׁלַט֙ בְּכָל־   ג . ל

20   עֲמָלִ֔י שֶֽׁעָמַ֛לְתִּי וְשֶׁחָכַ֖מְתִּי תַּ֣חַת הַשָּׁ֑מֶשׁ גַּם־זֶ֥ה הָֽבֶל: וְסַבּ֥וֹתִֽי אֲנִ֖י   ג . ל

12 כְּבָ֫ר T | > G ⟨θ'⟩ V S | *ante* Hie^lem ‖ pref *omit* כְּבָ֫ר see G ⟨θ'⟩ V S ✣ •
עָשֽׂוּהוּ (theol) | ἐποίησεν αὐτήν G | *factorem suum* V Hie^lem | ܥܒܕܗ(ܘ) S |
13 כִּיתְר֥וֹן see G V Hie^lem S ✣ • **15** אָ֣ז G
Hie^comm T | > G^Mss Hie^lem | V S (indet) ✣ • וְדִבַּ֣רְתִּי V Hie^lem S T | > cj G ‖ → ✣ •
הָֽבֶל V T | + διότι ἄφρων ἐκ περισσεύματος λαλεῖ G S (gloss) ✣ •
17 וְשָׂנֵ֙אתִי֙ G Hie^lem | foll pron G^Mss (V) S T (assim-v 18) • **19** י֥וֹדֵ֗עַ G Hie^lem |
ܢܕܥ S | *ignoro* V (lib) | T (indet) •

ל. כִּי־יֵשׁ ²¹ לִֽי־אָ֗שׁ אֶת־לִבִּ֑י עַ֚ל כָּל־הֶ֣עָמָ֔ל שֶׁעָמַ֖לְתִּי תַּ֥חַת הַשָּׁ֑מֶשׁ׃ כִּי־יֵ֣שׁ

ל בסיפ. אָדָ֗ם שֶׁעֲמָל֤וֹ בְּחָכְמָ֥ה וּבְדַ֖עַת וּבְכִשְׁר֑וֹן וּלְאָדָ֞ם שֶׁלֹּ֤א עָֽמַל־בּוֹ

ב ביום אשמתו
ט. ב. ²² יִתְּנֶ֣נּוּ חֶלְק֔וֹ גַּם־זֶ֥ה הֶ֖בֶל וְרָעָ֣ה רַבָּ֑ה כִּ֣י מֶֽה־הֹוֶ֣ה לָֽאָדָ֔ם בְּכָל־

ל. ה בסיפ. ²³ עֲמָל֔וֹ וּבְרַעְי֖וֹן לִבּ֑וֹ שֶׁה֥וּא עָמֵ֖ל תַּ֣חַת הַשָּׁ֑מֶשׁ כִּ֥י כָל־יָמָ֣יו

ל חס ²³ מַכְאֹבִ֣ים וָכַ֗עַס עִנְיָנ֔וֹ גַּם־בַּלַּ֖יְלָה לֹא־שָׁכַ֣ב לִבּ֑וֹ גַּם־זֶ֖ה הֶ֥בֶל הֽוּא׃

ב ²⁴ אֵֽין־ט֤וֹב בָּֽאָדָם֙ שֶׁיֹּאכַ֣ל וְשָׁתָ֔ה וְהֶרְאָ֧ה אֶת־נַפְשׁ֛וֹ ט֖וֹב בַּעֲמָל֑וֹ גַּם־

י. נ. ד בליש ²⁵ זֹ֤ה רָאִ֨יתִי֙ אָ֔נִי כִּ֥י מִיַּ֖ד הָאֱלֹהִ֥ים הִֽיא׃ כִּ֣י מִ֤י יֹאכַל֙ וּמִ֣י יָח֔וּשׁ ח֖וּץ

ל בסיפ ²⁶ מִמֶּֽנִּי׃ כִּ֤י לְאָדָם֙ שֶׁטּ֣וֹב לְפָנָ֔יו נָתַ֛ן חָכְמָ֥ה וְדַ֖עַת וְשִׂמְחָ֑ה וְלַחוֹטֶא֩

ג בסוף פסוק נָתַ֨ן עִנְיָ֜ן לֶאֱסֹ֣וף וְלִכְנ֗וֹס לָתֵת֙ לְטוֹב֙ לִפְנֵ֣י הָֽאֱלֹהִ֔ים גַּם־זֶ֥ה הֶ֖בֶל

וּרְע֥וּת רֽוּחַ׃

ג בסיפ. ל	עֵת֙	ס וְעֵ֥ת לְכָל־חֵ֖פֶץ תַּ֣חַת הַשָּׁמָֽיִם׃ לַכֹּ֖ל זְמָ֑ן **3**
	וְעֵ֖ת	לָלֶ֖דֶת
	עֵ֥ת	לָמ֑וּת
ל	וְעֵ֖ת	לָטַ֖עַת
ל. ל ³	עֵ֥ת	לַעֲק֖וֹר נָטֽוּעַ׃
ב מל	וְעֵ֖ת	לַהֲר֑וֹג
	עֵ֥ת	לִרְפֹּֽוא

[26] כל סיפרא קמצ ב מ̇ ב̇ כי לאדם שטוב . ולאדם שלא עמל בו :o: זה הבל ורעות
רוח ג בסוף פס כי לאדם שטוב לפניו . כי היא קנאת . טוב מראה מהלך נפש :o:
[3:3] לרפא ב̇ חד חס מל̇ וסימנהון והוא לא יוכל לרפא לכם . עת להרוג ועת
לרפוא :o: לרפא ב̇ חד חס ומל̇ חד מל̇ והוא לא יוכל לרפא לכם . עת להרוג :o:

21 וּלְאָדָ֞ם (V) Hie^lem S T I καὶ ἄνθρωπος G • **22** כִּ֣י מֶֽה־הֹוֶ֣ה V T I ὅτι γίνεται
G* I ὅτι γὰρ περιγέγονεν σ' I *quid enim fit* Hie^lem I ܡܢ ܪܚܒܬ S ‖ pref
כִּיהֹוֶ֣ה see G* ✢ • לִבּ֑וֹ M^L (err) I לִבֹּ֑ו M^L34 M^Y • **23** עִנְיָנ֔וֹ G S T I *pleni sunt* V (exeg) I
curarumque Hie^lem ✢ • **24** בָּֽאָדָם֙ G^Mss T* I τῷ ἀνθρώπῳ G* Hie^lem S (facil) I >
V (facil) I בני אנשא T^Ms (crrp) I ‖ → ✢ ✢ • שֶׁיֹּאכַ֣ל G^Mss I εἰ μὴ ὃ φάγεται G*
Hie^lem S T I φαγεῖν ⟨σ'⟩ V I ὃ ἐσθίει ⟨θ'⟩ ‖ pref מְשֶׁיֹּאכַל see G* Hie^lem S
T ✢ • **25** יָח֔וּשׁ I πίεται G* ⟨θ'⟩ S (interp) I φείσεται α' ⟨σ'⟩ Hie^lem I *deliciis*
affluet V (interp) ✢ • מִמֶּֽנִּי׃ (V) T I 3 m sg sfx G Hie^lem S ‖ pref מִמֶּֽנּוּ see G
Hie^lem S ✢ • **3:3** לַהֲר֑וֹג ✢ •

	וְעֵת	לִפְרוֹץ
	עֵת	⁴ לִבְנוֹת:
	וְעֵת	לִבְכּוֹת
	עֵת	לִשְׂחוֹק
ג מל	וְעֵת	סְפוֹד
ל	עֵת	⁵ רְקוֹד:
	וְעֵת	לְהַשְׁלִיךְ אֲבָנִים
	עֵת	כְּנוֹס אֲבָנִים
ל	וְעֵת	לַחֲבוֹק
ד חס בכתיב . ל	עֵת	⁶ לִרְחֹק מֵחַבֵּק:
	וְעֵת	לְבַקֵּשׁ
	עֵת	לְאַבֵּד
ח מל	וְעֵת	לִשְׁמוֹר
	עֵת	⁷ לְהַשְׁלִיךְ:
ל ומל	וְעֵת	לִקְרוֹעַ
ל ומל	עֵת	לִתְפּוֹר
ל	וְעֵת	לַחֲשׁוֹת
	עֵת	⁸ לְדַבֵּר:
	וְעֵת	לֶאֱהֹב
	עֵת	לִשְׂנֹא
	וְעֵת	מִלְחָמָה
	מַה־	⁹ שָׁלוֹם: ס

הוֹ . ה בסיפ   יִתְרוֹן הָעוֹשֶׂה   בַּאֲשֶׁר הוּא עָמֵל:

ב בסיפ   ¹⁰ ¹¹ רָאִיתִי אֶת־הָעִנְיָן אֲשֶׁר נָתַן אֱלֹהִים לִבְנֵי הָאָדָם לַעֲנוֹת בּוֹ: אֶת־

[9] מה יתרון העשה למערב חס ולמדנ שלמ :o:

6 הָעוֹשֶׂה G Hie^lem | עֵת לְבַקֵּשׁ G V Hie^lem T | ܘܒܠܐ ܠܚܒܒܕܗ S (transp) ÷ • **9** הָעוֹשֶׂה G Hie^lem |
homo V (lib-seman) | ܠܒܕ ܐܢܫ ܚܒܒܐ S (transl) | לגברא פלח T (transl) •
| T (transl) | אֶת־הַכֹּל T | **10** אֱלֹהִים | ὁ θεός G | V S T (indet) ‖ pref הָאֱלֹהִים see G ÷ • **11**
σύμπαντα G* | τὰ σύμπαντα G^Mss | V S (indet) ÷ •

הַכֹּל עָשָׂה יָפֶה בְעִתּוֹ גַּם אֶת־הָעֹלָם נָתַן בְּלִבָּם מִבְּלִי אֲשֶׁר לֹא־   הֵ . בׄ חסׄ
למעׄר . טׄ

יִמְצָא הָאָדָם אֶת־הַמַּעֲשֶׂה אֲשֶׁר־עָשָׂה הָאֱלֹהִים מֵרֹאשׁ וְעַד־

12 סֽוֹף: יָדַעְתִּי כִּי אֵין טוֹב בָּם כִּי אִם־לִשְׂמוֹחַ וְלַעֲשׂוֹת טוֹב בְּחַיָּיו: בׄ מלׄ

13 𝕭   וְגַם כָּל־הָאָדָם שֶׁיֹּאכַל וְשָׁתָה וְרָאָה טוֹב בְּכָל־עֲמָלוֹ מַתַּת ׄ   בׄ . בׄ

14 אֱלֹהִים הִיא: יָדַעְתִּי כִּי כָּל־אֲשֶׁר יַעֲשֶׂה הָאֱלֹהִים הוּא יִהְיֶה   בׄ מכל התעבות

לְעוֹלָם עָלָיו אֵין לְהוֹסִיף וּמִמֶּנּוּ אֵין לִגְרֹעַ וְהָאֱלֹהִים עָשָׂה שֶׁיִּרְאוּ   בׄ . לׄ . לׄ חסׄ

מִלְּפָנָיו: חׄ

15 מַה־שֶּׁהָיָה כְּבָר הוּא   וַאֲשֶׁר לִהְיוֹת כְּבָר הָיָה

וְהָאֱלֹהִים יְבַקֵּשׁ אֶת־נִרְדָּף: זׄ . בׄ

16 וְעוֹד רָאִיתִי תַּחַת הַשָּׁמֶשׁ   חׄ רֹא פסוק

מְקוֹם הַמִּשְׁפָּט   שָׁמָּה הָרֶשַׁע

וּמְקוֹם הַצֶּדֶק   שָׁמָּה הָרָשַׁע: גׄ . לׄ

17 אָמַרְתִּי אֲנִי בְּלִבִּי

אֶת־הַצַּדִּיק וְאֶת־הָרָשָׁע יִשְׁפֹּט הָאֱלֹהִים   לׄ . לׄ

כִּי־עֵת לְכָל־חֵפֶץ וְעַל כָּל־הַמַּעֲשֶׂה שָׁם:

---

[11] יפה הֵ . וכאבשלום לא היה איש יפה . יפה בעתו יפה . ראיתי . יפה דודי ׃ס
[14] וממנו בׄ . וממנו אין לגרע . וממנו הורם התמיד ׃ס [15] והאלהים זׄ . נסה את
אברהם . יעננו בקול . אנה לידו . לא תבנה בית . נגף את ירבעם . עשה שיראו .
יבקש את נרדף ׃ס [16] ומקום גׄ . וסימנהון ומקום רגלי . ומקום משכן כבודך . ומקום
הצדק ׃ס . ומקום גׄ . ומקום רגלי . ומקום משכן כבודך . ומקום הצדק ׃ס

---

11 עָשָׂה Gᴹˢˢ V Hieˡᵉᵐ T (theol?) | ἃ ἐποίησεν G* S ⸆ • הָעֹלָם G V Hieˡᵉᵐ S* (T) |
prec πάντα Gᴹˢˢ | ܟܠܗ Sᴹˢˢ (crrp) • **12** בָּם G S T | > V Hieˡᵉᵐ ⸆ • **13** הָאָדָם
Gᴹˢˢ | > art G* | V S T (indet) ⸆ • מַתַּת G T | prec hoc V S (explic) | ex dono
Hieˡᵉᵐ • **14** יַעֲשֶׂה T | ἐποίησεν G V Hieˡᵉᵐ S (interp) • **16** הָרֶשַׁע V Hieˡᵉᵐ S | ὁ
ἀσεβής G (assim-ctext) | T (indet) ‖ ⸆ ⸆ הַצֶּדֶק • הַצֶּדֶק α' V Hieˡᵉᵐ S (harm-
ctext) | τοῦ δικαίου G T ‖ pref הַצַּדִּיק see G T ⸆ • הָרָשַׁע V Hieˡᵉᵐ S | ὁ
ἀσεβής G T | ὁ εὐσεβής Gᴹˢˢ (crrp) ‖ pref הָרָשָׁע see G T ⸆ • **17** שָׁם: G* Hieˡᵉᵐ
S T | tunc erit V (interp) ⸆ •

אָמַ֣רְתִּי אֲנִ֣י בְּלִבִּ֗י עַל־דִּבְרַת֙ בְּנֵ֣י הָֽאָדָ֔ם לְבָרָ֖ם הָאֱלֹהִ֑ים וְלִרְא֕וֹת   ל . ג 18

שְׁהֶם־בְּהֵמָ֥ה הֵ֖מָּה לָהֶֽם: כִּ֣י מִקְרֶ֣ה בְֽנֵי־הָ֠אָדָם וּמִקְרֶ֨ה הַבְּהֵמָ֜ה   ל . ב 19

וּמִקְרֶ֣ה אֶחָד֩ לָהֶ֨ם כְּמ֥וֹת זֶה֙ כֵּ֣ן מ֣וֹת זֶ֔ה וְר֥וּחַ אֶחָ֖ד לַכֹּ֑ל וּמוֹתַ֨ר   ל

הָאָדָ֤ם מִן־הַבְּהֵמָה֙ אָ֔יִן כִּ֥י הַכֹּ֖ל הָֽבֶל:

הַכֹּ֥ל הוֹלֵ֖ךְ אֶל־מָק֣וֹם אֶחָ֑ד   ג 20

הַכֹּל֙ הָיָ֣ה מִן־הֶֽעָפָ֔ר וְהַכֹּ֖ל שָׁ֥ב אֶל־הֶעָפָֽר: ל

מִ֣י יוֹדֵ֗עַ ר֚וּחַ בְּנֵ֣י הָֽאָדָ֔ם הָעֹלָ֥ה הִ֖יא לְמָ֑עְלָה   ל 21

וְר֙וּחַ֙ הַבְּהֵמָ֔ה הַיֹּרֶ֥דֶת הִ֖יא לְמַ֥טָּה לָאָֽרֶץ: ל וחס

וְרָאִ֗יתִי כִּ֣י אֵ֥ין טוֹב֙ מֵאֲשֶׁ֨ר יִשְׂמַ֤ח הָֽאָדָם֙ בְּֽמַעֲשָׂ֔יו כִּי־ה֖וּא חֶלְק֑וֹ   יב 22

כִּ֣י מִ֤י יְבִיאֶ֙נּוּ֙ לִרְא֔וֹת בְּמֶ֖ה שֶׁיִּהְיֶ֥ה אַחֲרָֽיו: וְשַׁ֣בְתִּֽי אֲנִ֗י וָֽאֶרְאֶה֙ אֶת־   ל 4

כָּל־הָ֣עֲשֻׁקִ֔ים אֲשֶׁ֥ר נַעֲשִׂ֖ים תַּ֣חַת הַשָּׁ֑מֶשׁ   ג

וְהִנֵּ֣ה |

דִּמְעַ֣ת הָעֲשֻׁקִ֗ים וְאֵ֤ין לָהֶם֙ מְנַחֵ֔ם   ג

וּמִיַּ֤ד עֹֽשְׁקֵיהֶם֙ כֹּ֔חַ וְאֵ֥ין לָהֶ֖ם מְנַחֵֽם: ל וחס . ג

וְשַׁבֵּ֧חַ אֲנִ֛י אֶת־הַמֵּתִ֖ים שֶׁכְּבָ֣ר מֵ֑תוּ   2

ל וחד את החיים
ואת המתים . ל

---

[18] ‏ ולראות ‏ ג ‏ שהם בבהמה ‏ . ‏ טובה ‏ . ‏ ולראות את העניין ‏ :o: ‏ המה להם ‏ ב ‏ וסימנה ‏ ב ‏ וביבנו גם המה ‏ . ‏ שהם בבהמה המה ‏ :o: ‏ [19] ‏ ומותר האדם מן הבהמה ‏ אָ֔יִן ‏ ל ‏ זק ‏ קמ ‏ וחד ‏ ואדם אָ֔יִן ‏ :o: ‏ [20] ‏ אל מקום אחד ‏ ג ‏ וסימנהון יקוו המים ‏ . ‏ הכל הולך ‏ . ‏ הלוא אל מקום אחד שהם בבהמה ‏ :o:

18 לְבָרָ֖ם (differ-orth) | ὅτι διακρινεῖ αὐτούς G Hie^lem | ut probaret eos V | וְלִרְא֕וֹת ❖ • see S | S ‏ דבא אוׄא‎ ‎‏ | pref לְבָרָם T ‖ לנסיאיהון ובגין למבחנהון T | καὶ τοῦ δεῖξαι G V Hie^lem S (interp) ❖ • לָהֶֽם: Hie^lem T | καὶ γε αὐτοῖς G | transf להם to v 19 S (differ-div) | V (indet) ‖ pref לָהֶם גַּם see G ❖ • **19** כִּ֣י Hie^lem S* T | ὡς G* (assim-ctext) | > G^Mss | S ‏ ܡܢ‎ ‎‏ (crrp) | V (indet) ❖ • מִקְרֶ֣ה (theol) | cstr G V Hie^lem S T ‖ pref ❖ • וּמִקְרֶ֨ה | (theol) | καὶ συνάντημα (τοῦ) G V Hie^lem S T* ‖ pref וּמִקְרֶ֣ה see G V Hie^lem S T* ❖ • מִקְרֶ֣ה V | > cj G Hie^lem S T ‖ pref מִקְרֶ֣ה^2 see G Hie^lem S T ❖ • וּמוֹתַ֨ר Hie^lem S T | καὶ τί ἐπερίσσευσεν G σ' θ' | et nihil habet (...) amplius V ❖ • **21** מִ֣י V T (theol) | καὶ τίς G Hie^lem S ‖ pref וּמִי see G Hie^lem S ❖ • הָעֹלָ֥ה (theol) | εἰ ἀναβαίνει G V Hie^lem S T ‖ pref הָעֹלָה see G V Hie^lem S T ❖ • הַיֹּרֶ֥דֶת (theol) | εἰ καταβαίνει G V Hie^lem S T ‖ pref הַיֹּרֶדֶת see G V Hie^lem S T ❖ • **22** בְּמֶ֖ה σ' V Hie^lem T | S ‏ ܡܕܡ ܓ‎ ‎‏ • **4:1** וּמִיַּ֤ד G (S) (T) | et in manibus Hie^lem | V (indet) ❖ • **2** וְשַׁבֵּ֧חַ | καὶ ἐπήνεσα G σ' V Hie^lem S T ❖ •

מִן־הַחַיִּ֔ים   אֲשֶׁ֥ר הֵ֖מָּה חַיִּ֥ים עֲדֶֽנָה׃   ל

וְט֣וֹב מִשְּׁנֵיהֶ֔ם   אֵ֥ת אֲשֶׁר־עֲדֶ֖ן לֹ֣א הָיָ֑ה   3   זֹ . ל

אֲשֶׁ֤ר לֹֽא־רָאָה֙ אֶת־הַמַּעֲשֶׂ֣ה הָרָ֔ע   בֹ קמצׁ דסמׁ

אֲשֶׁ֥ר נַעֲשָׂ֖ה תַּ֥חַת הַשָּֽׁמֶשׁ׃

וְרָאִ֨יתִֽי אֲנִ֜י אֶת־כָּל־עָמָ֗ל וְאֵת֙ כָּל־כִּשְׁר֣וֹן הַֽמַּעֲשֶׂ֔ה כִּ֛י הִ֥יא   4   יֹב . בׄ

קִנְאַת־אִ֖ישׁ מֵרֵעֵ֑הוּ גַּם־זֶ֥ה הֶ֖בֶל וּרְע֥וּת רֽוּחַ׃

הַכְּסִיל֙ חֹבֵ֣ק אֶת־יָדָ֔יו   וְאֹכֵ֖ל אֶת־בְּשָׂרֽוֹ׃   5   ל וחׂס

ט֕וֹב מְלֹ֥א כַ֖ף נָ֑חַת   מִמְּלֹ֥א חָפְנַ֛יִם עָמָ֖ל וּרְע֥וּת רֽוּחַ׃   6   ל וחׂס

וְשַׁ֧בְתִּי אֲנִ֛י וָאֶרְאֶ֥ה הֶ֖בֶל תַּ֥חַת הַשָּֽׁמֶשׁ׃   7

יֵ֣שׁ אֶחָד֩ וְאֵ֨ין שֵׁנִ֜י   גַּ֣ם בֵּ֧ן וָאָ֣ח אֵֽין־ל֗וֹ   8   ל

וְאֵ֥ין קֵץ֙ לְכָל־עֲמָל֔וֹ   גַּם־עֵינ֖וֹ לֹא־תִשְׂבַּ֣ע עֹ֑שֶׁר   עינו ק

וּלְמִ֣י ׀ אֲנִ֣י עָמֵ֗ל   וּמְחַסֵּ֤ר אֶת־נַפְשִׁי֙ מִטּוֹבָ֔ה   גׄ . הׄ בׄסיפׄ . ל

גַּם־זֶ֥ה הֶ֖בֶל   וְעִנְיַ֥ן רָ֖ע הֽוּא׃   ל

טוֹבִ֥ים הַשְּׁנַ֖יִם מִן־הָאֶחָ֑ד   9   בׄ יעמדו

אֲשֶׁ֧ר יֵשׁ־לָהֶ֛ם שָׂכָ֥ר ט֖וֹב בַּעֲמָלָֽם׃   ל

כִּ֣י אִם־יִפֹּ֔לוּ   הָאֶחָ֖ד יָקִ֣ים אֶת־חֲבֵר֑וֹ   10   ל

וְאִ֣יל֗וֹ הָֽאֶחָד֙ שֶׁיִּפּ֔וֹל   וְאֵ֥ין שֵׁנִ֖י לַהֲקִימֽוֹ׃   ל . בׄ . לׄ וחד ולהקימו

גַּ֛ם אִם־יִשְׁכְּב֥וּ שְׁנַ֖יִם וְחַ֣ם לָהֶ֑ם   וּלְאֶחָ֖ד אֵ֥יךְ יֵחָֽם׃   גׄ . לׄ . בׄ חד פתׁ

[4:8] ס: ולמי ג̇ אלה לפניך . כל חמדת ישראל . אני עמל ומחסר את נפשי :ס

4 עָמָ֖ל‬ | τὸν μόχθον G | *labores* V S | Hie^lem T (indet) ✤ • **5** חֹבֵק σ' V S T |
περιέλαβεν G Hie^lem ✤ • וְאֹכֵל V Hie^lem S | καὶ ἔφαγεν G | ייכול T (interp) ✤ •
בְּשָׂרֽוֹ: S T | τὰς σάρκας αὐτοῦ G V Hie^lem ✤ • **6** נָחַת G S | μετὰ ἀναπαύσεως
σ' V Hie^lem T (interp) ✤ • עָמֵל → ✤ • נָחַת **8** וְאָח G^Mss Hie^lem S | καί γε ἀδελφός
G* T | V (indet) ✤ • עֵינוֹ | עיניו M^ket V | עינו M^qere G Hie^lem S T • **10** יִפֹּלוּ G
⟨α'-σ'-θ'⟩ S* | sg G^Mss V Hie^lem S T (facil-synt) • וְאִיל֗וֹ | καὶ οὐαὶ αὐτῷ G
(V) Hie^lem S | ואלו T (ign-lex) ‖ pref וְאִ֣י ל֗וֹ see G (V) Hie^lem S ✤ • שֶׁיִּפּ֔וֹל |
ὅταν πέσῃ G V Hie^lem T | נפל דהא S • **11** וְחַם T | καὶ θέρμη G Hie^lem (via
וְחֹם) | V S (indet) • וּלְאֶחָד ⟨α'-θ'⟩ T (assim-ctext) | καὶ ὁ εἷς G (V) Hie^lem S ‖
pref וְהָאֶחָד see G (V) Hie^lem S ✤ •

וְאִם־יִתְקְפוֹ֙ הָֽאֶחָ֔ד   הַשְּׁנַ֖יִם יַעַמְד֣וּ נֶגְדּ֑וֹ   12

וְהַחוּט֙ הַֽמְשֻׁלָּ֔שׁ   לֹ֥א בִמְהֵרָ֖ה יִנָּתֵֽק׃

ט֛וֹב יֶ֥לֶד מִסְכֵּ֖ן וְחָכָ֑ם   מִמֶּ֤לֶךְ זָקֵן֙ וּכְסִ֔יל   13

אֲשֶׁ֛ר לֹא־יָדַ֥ע לְהִזָּהֵ֖ר עֽוֹד׃

כִּֽי־מִבֵּ֥ית הָסוּרִ֖ים   יָצָ֣א לִמְלֹ֑ךְ   14

כִּ֛י גַּ֥ם בְּמַלְכוּת֖וֹ   נוֹלַ֥ד רָֽשׁ׃

רָאִ֨יתִי֙ אֶת־כָּל־הַ֣חַיִּ֔ים   הַֽמְהַלְּכִ֖ים תַּ֣חַת הַשָּׁ֑מֶשׁ   15

עִ֚ם הַיֶּ֣לֶד הַשֵּׁנִ֔י   אֲשֶׁ֥ר יַעֲמֹ֖ד תַּחְתָּֽיו׃

אֵֽין־קֵ֣ץ לְכָל־הָעָ֗ם   לְכֹ֤ל אֲשֶׁר־הָיָה֙ לִפְנֵיהֶ֔ם   16

גַּ֥ם הָאַחֲרוֹנִ֖ים   לֹ֣א יִשְׂמְחוּ־ב֑וֹ

כִּֽי־גַם־זֶ֥ה הֶ֖בֶל וְרַעְי֥וֹן רֽוּחַ׃

שְׁמֹ֣ר רַגְלְךָ֗   כַּאֲשֶׁ֤ר תֵּלֵךְ֙ אֶל־בֵּ֣ית הָאֱלֹהִ֔ים   17

וְקָר֣וֹב לִשְׁמֹ֔עַ   מִתֵּ֥ת הַכְּסִילִ֖ים זָ֑בַח

כִּֽי־אֵינָ֥ם יוֹדְעִ֖ים לַעֲשׂ֥וֹת רָֽע׃

אַל־תְּבַהֵ֨ל עַל־פִּ֜יךָ   וְלִבְּךָ֧ אַל־יְמַהֵ֛ר   5

לְהוֹצִ֥יא דָבָ֖ר לִפְנֵ֣י הָאֱלֹהִ֑ים

כִּ֤י הָאֱלֹהִים֙ בַּשָּׁמַ֔יִם   וְאַתָּ֖ה עַל־הָאָ֑רֶץ

Masorah marginalia (right margin):
ב
ל . ג
ד
ל
ל . ג
ל
ו פסוק דמיין מטע . ל
רגלך ק
ד
ד מל
ה
ו

[14] למלך ג וסימנה ועלי שמו כל ישראל . ויהי בשמנים שנה . כי מבית הסורים ‪:ס‬

[17] יודעים ד מל וסימנה שמר רגלך . כי החיים שנים בו . ושלח אלי ‪:ס‬ [5:1] כי האלהים ו וסימנהון ועתה לא אתם . והיה כי תבאינה . כל אשר בלבבך דדברי הימי׳ . כי האלהים בשמים . כי האלהים מענה . כי האלהים שמחם ‪:ס‬

---

12 יִתְקְפוֹ V Hie^lem | יִתְקוֹף ἐπικραταιωθῇ G S | ὑπερισχύσῃ σ' | T (indet) ‖ pref see G S ⊹ • **14** מִבֵּית הָסוּרִים G σ' Hie^lem S (ign-lex) | *et de carcere catenisque* V (dbl) ⊹ • יָצָא σ' T | ἐξελεύσεται G | *egreditur* Hie^lem | *egrediatur* V | نفخ S (indet) ⊹ • **16** הָיָה ⟨σ'⟩ T | pl G V Hie^lem S ‖ → ⊹ 1:10 • לִפְנֵיהֶם G ⟨σ'⟩ Hie^lem T | *ante eum* V S (assim-ctext) • **17** רַגְלֶיךָ | רגלך M^ket M^qere G V Hie^lem S T ⊹ • כַּאֲשֶׁר T | ἐν ᾧ G ⟨θ'⟩ | V S (indet) ⊹ • מִתֵּת (T) | ὑπὲρ δόμα G (S) (facil-synt) | δόμα ⟨α'-θ'⟩ Hie^lem | V (indet) ⊹ • זָבַח ⟨α'-θ'⟩ Hie^lem T | θυσία σου G | *victimae* V S •

עַל־כֵּ֥ן יִהְי֖וּ דְבָרֶ֣יךָ מְעַטִּֽים: ג̇ יהיו ימיו

2   כִּ֛י בָּ֥א הַחֲל֖וֹם בְּרֹ֣ב עִנְיָ֑ן

וְק֥וֹל כְּסִ֖יל בְּרֹ֥ב דְּבָרִֽים:

3   כַּאֲשֶׁר֩ תִּדֹּ֨ר נֶ֜דֶר לֵֽאלֹהִ֗ים אַל־תְּאַחֵר֙ לְשַׁלְּמ֔וֹ   ל̇ . ד̇

כִּ֣י אֵ֥ין חֵ֖פֶץ בַּכְּסִילִ֑ים אֵ֥ת אֲשֶׁר־תִּדֹּ֖ר שַׁלֵּֽם:

4   ט֖וֹב אֲשֶׁ֣ר לֹֽא־תִדֹּ֑ר מִשֶּׁתִּדּ֖וֹר וְלֹ֥א תְשַׁלֵּֽם: ל̇ ומ̇ל

5   אַל־תִּתֵּ֤ן אֶת־פִּ֨יךָ֙ לַחֲטִ֣יא אֶת־בְּשָׂרֶ֔ךָ   ל̇

וְאַל־תֹּאמַר֙ לִפְנֵ֣י הַמַּלְאָ֔ךְ כִּ֥י שְׁגָגָ֖ה הִ֑יא   ל̇

לָ֣מָּה יִקְצֹ֤ף הָֽאֱלֹהִים֙ עַל־קוֹלֶ֔ךָ   ל̇

וְחִבֵּ֖ל אֶת־מַעֲשֵׂ֥ה יָדֶֽיךָ:   יא̇ מ̇ל

6   כִּ֣י בְרֹ֤ב חֲלֹמוֹת֙ וַהֲבָלִ֔ים וּדְבָרִ֖ים הַרְבֵּ֑ה   ב̇ אחדים

כִּ֥י אֶת־הָאֱלֹהִ֖ים יְרָֽא: ד̇

7   אִם־עֹ֣שֶׁק רָ֠שׁ וְגֵ֨זֶל מִשְׁפָּ֤ט וָצֶ֨דֶק֙ תִּרְאֶ֣ה בַמְּדִינָ֔ה אַל־תִּתְמַ֖הּ עַל־   ל̇ . ד̇ . ב̇ . ל̇

8   הַחֵ֑פֶץ כִּ֣י גָבֹ֜הַּ מֵעַ֤ל גָּבֹ֨הַּ֙ שֹׁמֵ֔ר וּגְבֹהִ֖ים עֲלֵיהֶֽם: וְיִתְר֥וֹן אֶ֛רֶץ בַּכֹּ֖ל   ג̇ . ל̇ וחס̇ . ז̇   דגש

הִ֥יא מֶ֖לֶךְ לְשָׂדֶ֥ה נֶעֱבָֽד: הוא . ל̇   ק

9   אֹהֵ֥ב כֶּ֨סֶף֙ לֹֽא־יִשְׂבַּ֣ע כֶּ֔סֶף

---

[3] תאחר ד̇ וסימנהון מלאתך ודמעך . כי תדר נדר ליהוה אלהיך . קרבתי צדקתי . כאשר תדר נדר וג̇ תאחר ‹o›: [8] ה̇ דכותה היא וקר הוא וסימנהון ואחשבה . ויתרון פלילים . וביתה . הכיננו ‹o›:

5:2 הַחֲל֖וֹם | > art G σ' | V Hie^{lem} S T (indet) ÷ • עִנְיָ֑ן G (V) Hie^{lem} S (T) | πειρασμοῦ G^{Mss} (crrp) | ἀνομίας σ' (err-graph) ÷ • **3** אֵ֥ת ⟨θ'⟩ V Hie^{lem} | σὺ οὖν G* | σύ ⟨α'⟩ S | ואנת ית ד̇־ T ‖ pref אַ֩תָּ see ⟨α'⟩ S T ÷ • **4** מִשֶּׁתִּדּ֖וֹר M^L (err) | מִשֶּׁתִּדֹּ֖ר M^{L34} M^Y • **5** הַמַּלְאָ֔ךְ ⟨α'-σ'-θ'⟩ V Hie^{lem} T (theol?) | τοῦ θεοῦ G S (theol?) ÷ • לָ֣מָּה T | ἵνα μή G V Hie^{lem} S ÷ • מַעֲשֵׂ֥ה S | pl G V Hie^{lem} T • **6** כִּ֥י אֶת־ G^{Mss} ⟨σ'⟩ Hie^{lem} | ὅτι σύ G* | tu vero V | ܐܢ S | T (indet) ÷ • **7** גָבֹ֜הַּ M^L M^Y | גָּבֹ֨הַּ M^{L34} • שֹׁמֵ֔ר Hie^{lem} S T | φυλάξαι G | V (indet) • **8** בַּכֹּ֖ל G^{Mss} ⟨θ'⟩ Hie^{lem} S (ideol) | ἐπὶ παντί G* σ' T | V (indet) ‖ pref עַל־כֹּל see G* σ' T ÷ • הִ֥יא היא M^{ket} T | הוא M^{qere} G σ' ⟨θ'⟩ Hie^{lem} S | V (indet) ÷ •

ד בסוף פסוק

וּמִי־אֹהֵב בֶּהָמוֹן לֹא תְבוּאָה גַּם־זֶה הָבֶל׃

ל ומל

10 בִּרְבוֹת הַטּוֹבָה רַבּוּ אוֹכְלֶיהָ

ראות
ק

וּמַה־כִּשְׁרוֹן לִבְעָלֶיהָ כִּי אִם־רְאִית עֵינָיו׃

יג

11 מְתוּקָה שְׁנַת הָעֹבֵד אִם־מְעַט וְאִם־הַרְבֵּה יֹאכֵל

ל ומל

וְהַשָּׂבָע לֶעָשִׁיר אֵינֶנּוּ מַנִּיחַ לוֹ לִישׁוֹן׃

12 יֵשׁ רָעָה חוֹלָה רָאִיתִי תַּחַת הַשָּׁמֶשׁ

ב כי למועד

עֹשֶׁר שָׁמוּר לִבְעָלָיו לְרָעָתוֹ׃

13 וְאָבַד הָעֹשֶׁר הַהוּא בְּעִנְיַן רָע

וְהוֹלִיד בֵּן וְאֵין בְּיָדוֹ מְאוּמָה׃

ל

14 כַּאֲשֶׁר יָצָא מִבֶּטֶן אִמּוֹ עָרוֹם יָשׁוּב לָלֶכֶת כְּשֶׁבָּא

ב . לז

וּמְאוּמָה לֹא־יִשָּׂא בַעֲמָלוֹ שֶׁיֹּלֵךְ בְּיָדוֹ׃

ל . י

15 וְגַם־זֹה רָעָה חוֹלָה

כָּל־עֻמַּת שֶׁבָּא כֵּן יֵלֵךְ

ג

וּמַה־יִּתְרוֹן לוֹ שֶׁיַּעֲמֹל לָרוּחַ׃

[9] גם זה הבל ג וסימ ומי יודע . אהב כסף . כי כקול הסירים . ובכן ראיתי ס׃

9 אָהֵב² V Hie^lem S | ἠγάπησεν G | impf T (assim-ctext) • בֶּהָמוֹן G | ܪܚܡ̈ܐ S T (interp) | δῶρα ἐν πλήθει αλ' (dbl) | divitias V Hie^lem ‖ → ✣ • לֹא • לֹא תְבוּאָה αλ' V Hie^lem S | αὐτῶν γένημα G | αὐτοῦ γένημα G^Mss | לית ליה שבח תְבוּאָה ... לעלמא דאתי ... דלית ליה אגר עלל למיכל T (dbl) ‖ pref מְתבוּאָה (origin) ✣ • כִּי אִם־ • T ✣ • **10** הַטּוֹבָה G^Mss α' | > art G* | opes V Hie^lem | ܛܒ̈ܬܐ S | טיבותא T ✣ • רְאִית | σ' ⟨θ'⟩ V Hie^lem S T | ὅτι ἀρχή G* | ὅτι ἀλλ' ἤ G^Mss (confl) ✣ • רְאִית M^ket רְאוּת M^qere | τοῦ ὁρᾶν G ⟨θ'⟩ V Hie^lem T | σ' S (indet) ‖ pref רְאוֹת see G ⟨θ'⟩ V Hie^lem T ✣ • **11** הָעֹבֵד V Hie^lem S T (ideol) | τοῦ δούλου G ⟨σ'-θ'⟩ ‖ pref הָעֹבֵד see G ⟨σ'-θ'⟩ ✣ • וְהַשָּׂבָע לֶעָשִׁיר σ' V Hie^lem S (T) | καὶ τῷ ἐμπλησθέντι τοῦ πλουτῆσαι G ✣ • **12** רָעָה חוֹלָה σ' V Hie^lem S T (ideol?) | ἀρρωστία G ‖ pref חָלִי see G ✣ • **14** כַּאֲשֶׁר G V Hie^lem S | prec כיא 4QQoh^a* | הי כמא ד ⁻ T • שֶׁיֹּלֵךְ (T) | ἵνα πορευθῇ G Hie^lem S | ὃ συναπελεύσεται σ' | > V (facil-styl) ✣ • **15** וְגַם־ G Hie^lem S T | גם 4QQoh^a | prorsus V ‖ → 7:6 • כָּל־עֻמַּת (err-graph?) | ὥσπερ γάρ G Hie^lem S | quomodo V | דכל קבל ד T (confl) ‖ pref כִּי לְעֻמַּת see G Hie^lem S ✣ •

גם כָּל־יָמָ֛יו   בַּחֹ֥שֶׁךְ יֹאכֵ֖ל   16

וְכָעַ֥ס הַרְבֵּ֖ה   וְחׇלְי֥וֹ וָקָֽצֶף׃

הִנֵּ֞ה אֲשֶׁר־רָאִ֣יתִי אָ֗נִי ט֣וֹב אֲשֶׁר־יָפֶ֣ה לֶאֱכוֹל־וְֽלִשְׁתּ֜וֹת וְלִרְא֣וֹת   17

טוֹבָ֗ה בְּכׇל־עֲמָל֣וֹ ׀ שֶׁיַּעֲמֹ֣ל תַּֽחַת־הַשֶּׁ֗מֶשׁ מִסְפַּ֧ר יְמֵֽי־חַיָּ֛ו אֲשֶׁר־

נָֽתַן־ל֥וֹ הָאֱלֹהִ֖ים כִּי־ה֥וּא חֶלְקֽוֹ׃ גַּ֣ם כָּֽל־הָאָדָ֡ם אֲשֶׁ֣ר נָֽתַן־   18

ל֣וֹ הָאֱלֹהִ֡ים עֹ֩שֶׁר֩ וּנְכָסִ֨ים וְהִשְׁלִיט֜וֹ לֶאֱכֹ֤ל מִמֶּ֙נּוּ֙ וְלָשֵׂ֣את אֶת־

חֶלְק֔וֹ וְלִשְׂמֹ֖חַ בַּעֲמָל֑וֹ זֹ֕ה מַתַּ֥ת אֱלֹהִ֖ים הִֽיא׃ כִּ֚י לֹ֣א הַרְבֵּ֣ה יִזְכֹּ֔ר   19

אֶת־יְמֵ֖י חַיָּ֑יו כִּ֧י הָאֱלֹהִ֛ים מַעֲנֶ֖ה בְּשִׂמְחַ֥ת לִבּֽוֹ׃   יֵ֣שׁ רָעָ֔ה אֲשֶׁ֥ר   **6**

רָאִ֖יתִי תַּ֣חַת הַשָּׁ֑מֶשׁ וְרַבָּ֥ה הִ֖יא עַל־הָאָדָֽם׃ אִ֣ישׁ אֲשֶׁ֣ר יִתֶּן־ל֣וֹ   2

הָאֱלֹהִ֡ים עֹ֩שֶׁר֩ וּנְכָסִ֨ים וְכָב֜וֹד וְֽאֵינֶ֨נּוּ חָסֵ֥ר לְנַפְשׁ֣וֹ ׀ מִכֹּ֣ל אֲשֶׁר־

יִתְאַוֶּ֗ה וְלֹֽא־יַשְׁלִיטֶ֤נּוּ הָֽאֱלֹהִים֙ לֶאֱכֹ֣ל מִמֶּ֔נּוּ כִּ֛י אִ֥ישׁ נׇכְרִ֖י יֹֽאכְלֶ֑נּוּ

זֶ֥ה הֶ֛בֶל וׇחֳלִ֥י רָ֖ע הֽוּא׃

אִם־יוֹלִ֨יד אִ֜ישׁ מֵאָ֗ה   וְשָׁנִים֮ רַבּ֣וֹת יִֽחְיֶה֒   3

וְרַ֣ב ׀ שֶׁיִּהְי֣וּ יְמֵֽי־שָׁנָ֗יו   וְנַפְשׁוֹ֙ לֹא־תִשְׂבַּ֣ע מִן־הַטּוֹבָ֔ה

וְגַם־קְבוּרָ֖ה לֹא־הָ֣יְתָה לּ֑וֹ

אָמַ֕רְתִּי ט֥וֹב מִמֶּ֖נּוּ הַנָּֽפֶל׃

כִּֽי־בַהֶ֥בֶל בָּ֖א   וּבַחֹ֣שֶׁךְ יֵלֵ֑ךְ   4

וּבַחֹ֖שֶׁךְ שְׁמ֥וֹ יְכֻסֶּֽה׃

---

[17] חיו ד׳ חס׳ וסימנה ואבשלום לקח . וארח דמלכים . ושנֹה דירמֹ . הנה אשר :o:

[6:1] קדמיה יש רעה חולה . תיניְנה יש רעה אשר ראיתי :o: ורבה ד׳ וסימנה עליך

חית . ורבה העזובה בק . ורבה משטמה . ורבה היא על האדם :o: על האדם ג׳ וסימנה

ויפל יהוה אלהים תרדמה . ויצו יהוה אלהים . ורבה היא . וכול על הארץ ועל

הבהמה דכותהון :o:

---

16 בַּחֹ֥שֶׁךְ יֹאכֵ֖ל V Hie^lem (S) T | ἐν σκότει καὶ ἐν πένθει G* | ἐν σκότει καὶ πένθει G^Mss ✣ • וְכָעַס (facil-synt) | καὶ θυμῷ G V Hie^lem S T* | [כעס] 4QQoh^a (indet) ‖ pref וְכָעַ֥ס see G V Hie^lem S T* ✣ • וְחׇלְי֥וֹ | καὶ ἀρρωστίᾳ G V Hie^lem S T ‖ pref וְחׇלִי see G V Hie^lem S T ✣ • **17** אָ֣נִי 4QQoh^a G V Hie^lem T | foll אלהא S • **18** הָאָדָ֡ם G^Mss | > art G* | V S T (indet) ✣ • **19** מַעֲנֶ֖ה V Hie^lem (spont) | περισπᾷ αὐτόν G S | T (indet) ‖ pref מַעֲנֵהוּ see G S ✣ • **6:3** מִמֶּ֖נּוּ G V Hie^lem S T | הנפל ממנו 4QQoh^a • **4** יֵלֵ֑ךְ S T (facil) | הלך 4QQoh^a | הַנָּֽפֶל׃ G V Hie^lem S T | הנפל ממנו 4QQoh^a • πορεύεται G V Hie^lem (facil) ‖ pref הָלַךְ 4QQoh^a ✣ •

5 גַּם־שֶׁ֥מֶשׁ לֹא־רָאָ֖ה   וְלֹ֣א יָ֑דַ֖ע

נַ֥חַת לָזֶ֖ה מִזֶּֽה׃

6 וְאִלּ֣וּ חָיָ֗ה אֶ֤לֶף שָׁנִים֙ פַּעֲמַ֔יִם   וְטוֹבָ֖ה לֹ֣א רָאָ֑ה

הֲלֹ֛א אֶל־מָק֥וֹם אֶחָ֖ד הַכֹּ֥ל הוֹלֵֽךְ׃

7 כָּל־עֲמַ֥ל הָאָדָ֖ם לְפִ֑יהוּ   וְגַם־הַנֶּ֖פֶשׁ לֹ֥א תִמָּלֵֽא׃

8 כִּ֛י מַה־יּוֹתֵ֥ר לֶחָכָ֖ם מִן־הַכְּסִ֑יל

מַה־לֶּעָנִ֣י יוֹדֵ֔עַ   לַהֲלֹ֖ךְ נֶ֥גֶד הַֽחַיִּֽים׃

9 ט֛וֹב מַרְאֵ֥ה עֵינַ֖יִם   מֵֽהֲלָךְ־נָ֑פֶשׁ

גַּם־זֶ֥ה הֶ֖בֶל וּרְע֥וּת רֽוּחַ׃

10 מַה־שֶּֽׁהָיָ֗ה כְּבָר֙ נִקְרָ֣א שְׁמ֔וֹ   וְנוֹדָ֖ע אֲשֶׁר־ה֣וּא אָדָ֑ם

וְלֹא־י֣וּכַל לָדִ֔ין   עִ֖ם שֶׁהַתַּקִּ֥יף מִמֶּֽנּוּ׃

11 כִּ֛י יֵשׁ־דְּבָרִ֥ים הַרְבֵּ֖ה   מַרְבִּ֣ים הָ֑בֶל

מַה־יֹּתֵ֖ר לָאָדָֽם׃

12 כִּ֣י מִֽי־יוֹדֵעַ֩ מַה־טּ֨וֹב לָֽאָדָ֜ם בַּֽחַיִּ֗ים

מִסְפַּ֛ר יְמֵי־חַיֵּ֥י הֶבְל֖וֹ   וְיַעֲשֵׂ֣ם כַּצֵּ֑ל

אֲשֶׁר֙ מִֽי־יַגִּ֣יד לָֽאָדָ֔ם   מַה־יִּהְיֶ֥ה אַחֲרָ֖יו תַּ֥חַת הַשָּֽׁמֶשׁ׃

[5] לזה ג וסימנהון נחת לזה מזה . הלוא לזה יענו במחלות . את כל אשר לזה ‎:ס
[6] ואלו ב יה . לעבדים ולשפחות ‎:ס [10] ולא יוכל ד פתח וחד קמצ וסימנ וכסה
את עין הארץ . יהוה עוד לשאת . לדין עם שתקיף . ובא אל מקדשו להתפלל ולא
יוכל . בתרי קמץ ‎:ס [12] כצל ה דגשין וסימנהון כצל ימינו . ויברח כצל ולא יעמד .
ויצורי כצל כלם . ולא יאריך ימים . כצל ‎:ס

5 נַ֥חַת יָ֑דַ֖ע ✠ • נַחַת 4QQohᵃ ✠ | ἐπειράθη διαφορᾶς σ' V T | ‏ידע נוחת‎ G Hieˡᵉᵐ S | ❘
Gᴹˢ ⟨α'-σ'-θ'⟩ Hieˡᵉᵐ S | נוחת 4QQohᵃ | ἀναπαύσεις G* | διαφορᾶς σ' V T (exeg)
✠ • 6 וְאִלּ֣וּ G V Hieˡᵉᵐ S T | ואם לוא 4QQohᵃ (err) • פַּעֲמַ֔יִם 4QQohᵃ V Hieˡᵉᵐ S
T | καθόδους G (interp) • 8 כִּ֤י מַה־יּוֹתֵ֥ר Gᴹˢˢ ⟨α'-θ'⟩ σ' (V) Hieˡᵉᵐ T | ‏כמה יותר‎
4QQohᵃ (ideol) | ὅτι περισσεία G* S (ideol) ✠ • מַה־לֶּעָנִ֣י ⟨σ'⟩ Hieˡᵉᵐ T* | διότι
ὁ πένης G | ‏ܡܢܐ ܠܡܣܟܢܐ‎ Syh | et quid pauper V | ‏ܡܗܠܟ ܡ ܠܡܣܟܢܐ‎ S ✠ • 9
‎‏מֵֽהֲלָךְ‎ | σ' V S | ὑπὲρ πορευόμενον G ⟨θ'⟩ Hieˡᵉᵐ | מן דיזיל T (indet) ✠ • 10
‎| שֶׁהַתַּקִּ֥יף שהתקיף Mᵏᵉᵗ | שֶׁתַּקִּיף Mqᵉʳᵉ G V Hieˡᵉᵐ S T ‖ pref שְׁתַקִּיף Mqᵉʳᵉ G V Hieˡᵉᵐ S T
✠ • 12 כַּצֵּ֑ל V Hieˡᵉᵐ S T* | ἐν σκιᾷ G ‖ pref בַּצֵּל see G ✠ •

ס

ל   7 טֹ֥וב שֵׁ֖ם מִשֶּׁ֣מֶן ט֑וֹב   וְי֣וֹם הַמָּ֔וֶת מִיּ֖וֹם הִוָּלְדֽוֹ׃

ל   2 ט֞וֹב לָלֶ֣כֶת אֶל־בֵּֽית־אֵ֗בֶל   מִלֶּ֙כֶת֙ אֶל־בֵּ֣ית מִשְׁתֶּ֔ה

הֹ֒יֹ֒.ֹגֹ֒.ֹלֹ֒.ֹל   בַּאֲשֶׁ֕ר ה֖וּא ס֣וֹף כָּל־הָאָדָ֑ם   וְהַחַ֖י יִתֵּ֥ן אֶל־לִבּֽוֹ׃

   3 ט֥וֹב כַּ֖עַס מִשְּׂחֹ֑ק   כִּֽי־בְרֹ֥עַ פָּנִ֖ים יִ֥יטַב לֵֽב׃

ל   4 לֵ֤ב חֲכָמִים֙ בְּבֵ֣ית אֵ֔בֶל   וְלֵ֥ב כְּסִילִ֖ים בְּבֵ֥ית שִׂמְחָֽה׃

   5 ט֕וֹב לִשְׁמֹ֖עַ גַּעֲרַ֣ת חָכָ֑ם   מֵאִ֕ישׁ שֹׁמֵ֖עַ שִׁ֥יר כְּסִילִֽים׃

יֹ֒.ֹל   6 כִּ֣י כְק֤וֹל הַסִּירִים֙ תַּ֣חַת הַסִּ֔יר   כֵּ֖ן שְׂחֹ֣ק הַכְּסִ֑יל

ל   וְגַם־זֶ֖ה הָֽבֶל׃

גֹ֒.ֹב   7 כִּ֥י הָעֹ֖שֶׁק יְהוֹלֵ֣ל חָכָ֑ם   וִֽיאַבֵּ֥ד אֶת־לֵ֖ב מַתָּנָֽה׃

ג בטע בסיפֹ.ֹב   8 ט֤וֹב אַחֲרִ֣ית דָּבָ֔ר מֵֽרֵאשִׁית֑וֹ   ט֥וֹב אֶֽרֶךְ־ר֖וּחַ מִגְּבַהּ־רֽוּחַ׃

ל מֹל   9 אַל־תְּבַהֵ֥ל בְּרֽוּחֲךָ֖ לִכְע֑וֹס   כִּ֣י כַ֔עַס בְּחֵ֥יק כְּסִילִ֖ים יָנֽוּחַ׃

ל   10 אַל־תֹּאמַר֙ מֶ֣ה הָיָ֔ה   שֶׁ֤הַיָּמִים֙ הָרִ֣אשֹׁנִ֔ים הָי֥וּ טוֹבִ֖ים מֵאֵ֑לֶּה

   כִּ֛י לֹ֥א מֵחָכְמָ֖ה שָׁאַ֥לְתָּ עַל־זֶֽה׃

ל וחֹס   11 טוֹבָ֥ה חָכְמָ֖ה עִֽם־נַחֲלָ֑ה   וְיֹתֵ֖ר לְרֹאֵ֥י הַשָּֽׁמֶשׁ׃

7:1 שֵׁם 4QQohᵃ G Hieˡᵉᵐ S | ὄνομα ἀγαθόν ⟨σ'⟩ V T (interp) • הִוָּלְדֽוֹ׃ Gᴹˢˢ α' Hieˡᵉᵐ | לֹדֹ[...] 4QQohᵃ | > sfx G* V S | דאתיליד רשיעא בעלמא T ‡ • **2** מִלֶּכֶת T | ἢ ὅτι πορευθῆναι G S | quam (ire) V Hieˡᵉᵐ ‡ • מִשְׁתֶּה G V Hieˡᵉᵐ S T | ס֣וֹף כָּל־ • בַּאֲשֶׁר → ‡ 4:17 • כַּאֲשֶׁר[ש] 4QQohᵃ (assim-v 4) • בַּאֲשֶׁר → ‡ 4:17 • ס֣וֹף כָּל־ | כול סוף 4QQohᵃ (err) ‡ • הָאָדָם Gᴹˢˢ T | > art G* | ἀνθρώπων ⟨α'⟩ V S | hominis Hieˡᵉᵐ ‖ → 5:18 • יִתֵּן σ' V Hieˡᵉᵐ T | δώσει ἀγαθόν G* S ‡ • **4** בְּבֵית G Hieᶜᵒᵐᵐ S | בית 4QQohᵃ | V T (indet) • **5** גַּעֲרַת G Hieˡᵉᵐ S | גערות 4QQohᵃ | V T (indet) • מֵאִישׁ שֹׁמֵעַ G Hieˡᵉᵐ S T | לשמוע[מ] 4QQohᵃ | V (indet) ‡ • **6** כִּי 4QQohᵃ Gᴹˢˢ V Hieˡᵉᵐ S T | > G* Sᴹˢˢ ‡ • הַכְּסִיל 4QQohᵃ V Hieˡᵉᵐ T | pl G S (assim-ctext) ‡ • וְגַם־ G V Hieˡᵉᵐ S T | גם 4QQohᵃ Tᴹˢˢ ‖ → 5:15 • **7** וְיאַבֵּד G* V Hieˡᵉᵐ S T | ויעוֹה 4QQohᵃ ‡ • מַתָּנָה׃ σ' S T (ign-lex) | εὐτονίας αὐτοῦ G α'-θ' V Hieˡᵉᵐ (differ-vocal) | εὐγενείας αὐτοῦ Gᴹˢˢ (crrp) | מתונה Midr Qoh (via √מתן) ‡ • **8** דָּבָר σ' V Hieˡᵉᵐ S T | pl G (ditt?) • **10** מֵחָכְמָה | ἐν σοφίᾳ G S (facil) | φρονίμως σ' Hieˡᵉᵐ | על חכמתא T (interp) | V (indet) ‡ •

12 כִּי בְּצֵל הַחָכְמָה   בְּצֵל הַכָּסֶף
וְיִתְרוֹן דַּעַת   הַחָכְמָה תְּחַיֶּה בְעָלֶיהָ:   ג

13 רְאֵה אֶת־מַעֲשֵׂה הָאֱלֹהִים
כִּי מִי יוּכַל לְתַקֵּן אֵת אֲשֶׁר עִוְּתוֹ:   ל . ל

14 בְּיוֹם טוֹבָה   הֱיֵה בְטוֹב   וּבְיוֹם רָעָה   רְאֵה   ד
גַּם אֶת־זֶה לְעֻמַּת־זֶה   עָשָׂה הָאֱלֹהִים
עַל־דִּבְרַת שֶׁלֹּא יִמְצָא הָאָדָם אַחֲרָיו מְאוּמָה: ד

15 אֶת־הַכֹּל רָאִיתִי   בִּימֵי הֶבְלִי
יֵשׁ צַדִּיק אֹבֵד בְּצִדְקוֹ   וְיֵשׁ רָשָׁע מַאֲרִיךְ בְּרָעָתוֹ:   ל . ל וחד ומאריך

16 אַל־תְּהִי צַדִּיק הַרְבֵּה   וְאַל־תִּתְחַכַּם יוֹתֵר
לָמָּה תִּשּׁוֹמֵם:

17 אַל־תִּרְשַׁע הַרְבֵּה   וְאַל־תְּהִי סָכָל
לָמָּה תָמוּת בְּלֹא עִתֶּךָ:   ב חד מל

18 טוֹב אֲשֶׁר תֶּאֱחֹז בָּזֶה   וְגַם־מִזֶּה אַל־תַּנַּח אֶת־יָדֶךָ   ג
כִּי־יְרֵא אֱלֹהִים יֵצֵא אֶת־כֻּלָּם: ד . ל בֿ

19 הַחָכְמָה תָּעֹז לֶחָכָם   מֵעֲשָׂרָה שַׁלִּיטִים אֲשֶׁר הָיוּ בָּעִיר: ל

20 כִּי אָדָם אֵין צַדִּיק בָּאָרֶץ   אֲשֶׁר יַעֲשֶׂה־טּוֹב וְלֹא יֶחֱטָא:

21 גַּם לְכָל־הַדְּבָרִים אֲשֶׁר יְדַבֵּרוּ   אַל־תִּתֵּן לִבֶּךָ   ל

12 בְּצֵל and בְּצֵל (T) | ἐν σκιᾷ αὐτῆς ... ὡς σκιά G | ὡς σκέπει ... ὁμοίως σκέπει ⟨σ'⟩ V Hie^lem | ܒܛܠܠ ... ܐܝܟ S ‖ pref בְּצֵל ... בְּצֵל see G ✣ • בְּצֵל ... ܒܛܠܠ S ‖ pref כְּצֵל see G ✣ • **13** מַעֲשֵׂה S T | pl G σ' V Hie^lem ✣ • **14** הֱיֵה σ' Hie^lem S T | ζῆθι G ⟨α'-θ'⟩ | fruere (bonis) V ✣ • וּבְיוֹם רָעָה רְאֵה σ' V Hie^lem S (interp) | καὶ ἴδε ἐν ἡμέρᾳ κακίας. ἴδε G* | וּרְאֵה T ‖ pref | בגין דלא תיתי עלך יום בישא חזי ואסתכל | בְּיוֹם רָעָה see G* ✣ • אֶת־ G^Mss T* (explic) | l > G* | V Hie^lem S (indet) ‖ pref omit אֶת see G* ✣ • **18** אַל־תַּנַּח ⟨θ'⟩ V Hie^lem S T | μὴ μιάνῃς G* | μὴ ἀφῇς ⟨α'-σ'⟩ ✣ • **19** תָּעֹז α' V Hie^lem S (ideol) | תעזֹר 4QQoh^a G T (ideol) ‖ pref תָּעֹז (origin) ✣ • שֶׁנַּעֲשׂוּ • אֲשֶׁר הָיוּ | ש[היו] 4QQoh^a | G V S T (indet) ‖ → ✣ 1:14 • שֶׁנַּעֲשׂוּ **20** אֲשֶׁר יַעֲשֶׂה־ | ש[יע/]שה 4QQoh^a | G V S T (indet) ‖ → ✣ 1:14 • **21** אֲשֶׁר יְדַבֵּרוּ G^Mss σ' V Hie^lem | οὓς λαλήσουσιν ἀσεβεῖς G* S T* (gloss) ✣ •

אֲשֶׁר לֹא־תִשְׁמַע אֶת־עַבְדְּךָ מְקַלְלֶךָ׃   ל

22 כִּי גַּם־פְּעָמִים רַבּוֹת יָדַע לִבֶּךָ

אֲשֶׁר גַּם־אַתְּ קִלַּלְתָּ אֲחֵרִים׃   ן אתה ק

23 כָּל־זֹה נִסִּיתִי בַחָכְמָה   י . ב

אָמַרְתִּי אֶחְכָּמָה וְהִיא רְחוֹקָה מִמֶּנִּי׃   ל בסיפ מוגה נז

24 רָחוֹק מַה־שֶּׁהָיָה וְעָמֹק ׀ עָמֹק מִי יִמְצָאֶנּוּ׃

25 סַבּוֹתִי אֲנִי וְלִבִּי לָדַעַת וְלָתוּר וּבַקֵּשׁ חָכְמָה וְחֶשְׁבּוֹן   ל

וְלָדַעַת רֶשַׁע כֶּסֶל וְהַסִּכְלוּת הוֹלֵלוֹת׃   ה . ח . ל

26 וּמוֹצֶא אֲנִי מַר מִמָּוֶת אֶת־הָאִשָּׁה   ל

אֲשֶׁר־הִיא מְצוֹדִים וַחֲרָמִים לִבָּהּ אֲסוּרִים יָדֶיהָ   ב ומל

טוֹב לִפְנֵי הָאֱלֹהִים יִמָּלֵט מִמֶּנָּה וְחוֹטֵא יִלָּכֶד בָּהּ׃   ג . ל

27 רְאֵה זֶה מָצָאתִי אָמְרָה קֹהֶלֶת

אַחַת לְאַחַת לִמְצֹא חֶשְׁבּוֹן׃   ל

28 אֲשֶׁר עוֹד־בִּקְשָׁה נַפְשִׁי וְלֹא מָצָאתִי   ה

[7:23] זה י וסימנהון העיר . והלשכה . לעגם . ועדותי . חולה . וגדולה . שיאכל . מתת . נסיתי . ולשמחה o: נסיתי ב כי לא נסיתי . כל זה נסיתי בחכמה [28] o: ולא מצאתי ה עלילות . פלשתים . חרפה שברה לבי . ואבקש . בקשה קדמיה דפסוק o:

22 יָדַע V Hie^lem S T* | κακώσει G (err-graph) | πονηρεύσεται σ' (err-graph) ⁙ • **23** רְחוֹקָה S | ἐμακρύνθη G V Hie^lem T ‖ pref רָחֲקָה see G V Hie^lem T ⁙ • **24** מַה־שֶּׁהָיָה T (facil) | ὑπὲρ ὃ ἦν G V Hie^lem | ‎ܡܕܡ ܕܗܘ ܗܠܟ S ‖ pref מְשֶׁהָיָה | וְעָמֹק ׀ עָמֹק | καὶ βαθὺ βάθος G V Hie^lem (facil) | ‎ܥܘܡܩܐ ‎ܥܘܡܩܐ S | T (indet) ⁙ • יִמְצָאֶנּוּ׃ G ⟨α'-θ'⟩ S T | εὑρήσει αὐτήν G^Mss V Hie^lem | ὃ (οὐδεὶς) εὑρήσει σ' ⁙ • **25** וְלִבִּי G Hie^lem S | sensu meo σ' V | לחשבא T (interp) ⁙ • וְהַסִּכְלוּת הוֹלֵלוֹת׃ • | וְהַסִּכְלוּת הוֹלֵלוֹת → רֶשַׁע כֶּסֶל ⁙ • בלבבי T (theol) | καὶ σκληρίαν καὶ περιφοράν G S | καὶ ὀχληρίαν καὶ περιφοράν G^Mss | et errorem inprudentium V Hie^lem | καὶ ἀφροσύνην πλάνας α'* ‖ pref וְסִכְלוּת וְהוֹלֵלוּת see G S ⁙ • **26** וּמוֹצֶא אֲנִי Hie^lem | καὶ εὑρίσκω ἐγὼ αὐτὴν καὶ ἐρῶ G* (ampl) | et inveni V S | ואשכחית אנא T ⁙ • אֲסוּרִים יָדֶיהָ ⟨α'⟩ σ' V Hie^lem T* | δεσμὸς εἰς χεῖρας αὐτῆς G* | ‎ܘܐܣܘܪܐ ܒܐܝܕܝܗ S ⁙ • **27** אָמְרָה קֹהֶלֶת | εἶπεν ὁ Ἐκκλησιαστής G | dicit Ecclesiastes V Hie^lem S T (indet) ‖ pref אָמַר הַקֹּהֶלֶת see G ⁙ •

אָדָ֤ם אֶחָד֙ מֵאֶ֣לֶף מָצָ֔אתִי

וְאִשָּׁ֥ה בְכָל־אֵ֖לֶּה לֹ֥א מָצָֽאתִי׃

29 לְבַד֙ רְאֵה־זֶ֣ה מָצָ֔אתִי

אֲשֶׁ֨ר עָשָׂ֧ה הָאֱלֹהִ֛ים אֶת־הָאָדָ֖ם יָשָׁ֑ר

וְהֵ֥מָּה בִקְשׁ֖וּ חִשְּׁבֹנ֥וֹת רַבִּֽים׃

           ב

8 מִ֚י כְּהֶ֣חָכָ֔ם וּמִ֥י יוֹדֵ֖עַ פֵּ֣שֶׁר דָּבָ֑ר

      ל . ‍ֹ . ל

חָכְמַ֤ת אָדָם֙ תָּאִ֣יר פָּנָ֔יו וְעֹ֥ז פָּנָ֖יו יְשֻׁנֶּֽא׃

           ל

2 אֲנִי֙ פִּי־מֶ֣לֶךְ שְׁמ֔וֹר וְעַ֕ל דִּבְרַ֖ת שְׁבוּעַ֥ת אֱלֹהִֽים׃

   ל . ל מל ‍ֹ‍ֹ חס .
   ‍ֵ וחד ושבועת

3 אַל־תִּבָּהֵ֤ל מִפָּנָיו֙ תֵּלֵ֔ךְ אַֽל־תַּעֲמֹ֖ד בְּדָבָ֣ר רָ֑ע

כִּ֛י כָּל־אֲשֶׁ֥ר יַחְפֹּ֖ץ יַעֲשֶֽׂה׃

       ב ראש פס

4 בַּאֲשֶׁ֥ר דְּבַר־מֶ֖לֶךְ שִׁלְט֑וֹן

           ב

וּמִ֥י יֹֽאמַר־ל֖וֹ מַֽה־תַּעֲשֶֽׂה׃

5 שׁוֹמֵ֣ר מִצְוָ֔ה לֹ֥א יֵדַ֖ע דָּבָ֣ר רָ֑ע

       ג מל

וְעֵ֣ת וּמִשְׁפָּ֔ט יֵדַ֖ע לֵ֥ב חָכָֽם׃

[8:1] ‏ וישנא את בגדי דמלכֿ . כן יתן לידידו שנא . ועז פניו ישנא . ישנא הכתם . כֿתֿ
אֿ ‏ :‎ ‏o [2] למערבֿ אני פי מלך שמור ולמדנחֿ חסֿ ‏:‎o שבועת הֿ וסימנה יהוה תהיה . כל
נדר וכל . ויחמל המלך . ומדוע לא שמרת . אני פי מלך שמֿר . וחד ושבועת שקר ‏:‎o
[5] שומֿר ‏ֹ‏ מל וסימנהון על יד . הנה . שוא שקד . אהביו . צנים . הברית .
מצוה . וחבר דו . חלדה הנביאה ‏:‎o

---

28 אָדָ֤ם V Hie^lem S T | prec cj G* ✥ • **8:1** מִ֚י כְּהֶ֣חָכָ֔ם Hie^lem S | τίς οἶδεν
σοφούς G (crrp) | τίς ὧδε σοφός α' V (err-gram) | τίς οὕτως σοφός σ' (crrp) | מִן
הוא חכימא דיכול למקם קבל חכמא דייי T ✥ • וְעֹ֥ז (ideol) | καὶ ἀναιδής G |
et potentissimus V Hie^lem | ܡܬܢܢܝܦ S T* ‖ pref וְעַ֕ל see G ✥ • יְשֻׁנֶּֽא׃ T |
μισηθήσεται G S (err-lex) | *commutavit* V | *commutabit* V^Mss Hie^lem ‖ pref יְשַׁנֶּא
see V^Mss Hie^lem ✥ • **2** אֲנִי֙ V Hie^lem (theol) | ἐγώ παραινῶ σ' (theol) | > G S T ‖
pref *omit* אֲנִי see G S T ✥ • שְׁמ֔וֹר G S T | *observo* V Hie^lem (exeg) ‖ → ✥ • אֲנִ֙י
3 אַל־תִּבָּהֵ֤ל V Hie^lem | transf to end of v 2 G σ' S (differ-div) | T (indet) ✥ •
אַֽל־תַּעֲמֹ֖ד G | prec cj V Hie^lem S (facil) | T (indet) | (μὴ) ἐπίμενε σ' (insuf) •
4 בַּאֲשֶׁ֥ר σ' T | καθώς G Hie^lem S | *et* V (lib) ‖ → ✥ 4:17 כַּאֲשֶׁר • דְּבַר־ σ' V T |
> G* | *dixerit* Hie^lem S | λαλεῖ transf to end of v 4a G^Mss | ἐλάλησε ⟨α'⟩ ✥ •
שִׁלְט֑וֹן σ' V Hie^lem | ἐξουσιάζων G S T ✥ • **5** וּמִשְׁפָּ֔ט V Hie^lem S T | > cj G •
יֵדַ֖ע² (harm-v 7a) | γινώσκει G V Hie^lem S T ‖ pref יָדַע see G V Hie^lem S T ✥ •

כִּי לְכָל־חֵפֶץ   יֵשׁ עֵת וּמִשְׁפָּט   6

כִּי־רָעַת הָאָדָם רַבָּה עָלָיו׃

כִּי־אֵינֶנּוּ יֹדֵעַ   מַה־שֶׁיִּהְיֶה   7

כִּי כַּאֲשֶׁר יִהְיֶה   מִי יַגִּיד לוֹ׃

אֵין אָדָם שַׁלִּיט בָּרוּחַ   לִכְלוֹא אֶת־הָרוּחַ   8   ג̇ . ל̇ וכת̇ כן

וְאֵין שִׁלְטוֹן בְּיוֹם הַמָּוֶת   וְאֵין מִשְׁלַחַת בַּמִּלְחָמָה   ב̇

וְלֹא־יְמַלֵּט רֶשַׁע אֶת־בְּעָלָיו׃   ח̇ וחד וימלט . יח̇

אֶת־כָּל־זֶה רָאִיתִי   וְנָתוֹן אֶת־לִבִּי   9   יו̇

לְכָל־מַעֲשֶׂה   אֲשֶׁר נַעֲשָׂה תַּחַת הַשָּׁמֶשׁ   ל̇

עֵת אֲשֶׁר שָׁלַט הָאָדָם בְּאָדָם לְרַע לוֹ׃   ד̇ . ב̇

וּבְכֵן רָאִיתִי רְשָׁעִים קְבֻרִים וָבָאוּ   10   ב̇ . ל̇

וּמִמְּקוֹם קָדוֹשׁ יְהַלֵּכוּ   וְיִשְׁתַּכְּחוּ בָעִיר אֲשֶׁר כֵּן־עָשׂוּ   ל̇ . ל̇

גַּם־זֶה הָבֶל׃

אֲשֶׁר אֵין־נַעֲשָׂה פִתְגָם   מַעֲשֵׂה הָרָעָה מְהֵרָה   11   ב̇ ונשמע

עַל־כֵּן מָלֵא לֵב בְּנֵי־הָאָדָם   בָּהֶם לַעֲשׂוֹת רָע׃   ט̇ בטע̇

[9] באדם ד̇ וסימנהון נגע צרעת . אשר יגע . אשר שלט . ובוגדים באדם . וחד
ובאדם ס׃

6 רָעַת σ′ V Hie^comm S T | γνῶσις G 〈θ′〉 (err-graph) • **7** כִּי כַּאֲשֶׁר יִהְיֶה G Hie^lem
T* | (τίς) γὰρ τὰ ἐσόμενα σ′ V (S) T^Mss (lib) ⊹ • **8** הַמָּוֶת G^Mss | > art G* |
V Hie^lem S T (indet) ⊹ • בַּמִּלְחָמָה σ′ V Hie^lem T | ἐν ἡμέρᾳ πολέμου G*
S ⊹ • **9** אֶת¹ Hie^lem T | prec cj G S • עֵת אֲשֶׁר α′ σ′ V (S) T | τὰ ὅσα G | et
Hie^lem • קְבֻרִים α′ σ′ V | τοῦ κακῶσαι αὐτόν G 〈θ′〉 Hie^lem S T ⊹ • **10**
וָבָאוּ (V) Hie^lem T (crrp) | εἰς τάφους εἰσαχθέντας G (crrp) | … καὶ ἦλθον α′ |
καὶ ὅποτε περιῆσαν σ′ | ܘܡܛܝ̈ S (lib) ‖ pref קְבֻרִים יָבֹאוּ (origin)
⊹ • וּמִמְּקוֹם קָדוֹשׁ 〈α′〉 Hie^lem S T | καὶ ἐκ τοῦ ἁγίου G* | ἐν τόπῳ ἁγίῳ σ′ V ‖
pref וּבְמִקְדָּשׁ (origin) ⊹ • יְהַלֵּכוּ σ′ Hie^lem S | καὶ ἐπορεύθησαν G* 〈α′-θ′〉 T |
erant V ⊹ • וְיִשְׁתַּכְּחוּ S T (crrp) | καὶ ἐπῃνέθησαν G 〈α′-θ′〉 〈σ′〉 V Hie^lem ‖
pref וְיִשְׁתַּבְּחוּ see G 〈α′-θ′〉 〈σ′〉 V Hie^lem ⊹ • **11** פִתְגָם → ⊹ • מַעֲשֵׂה הָרָעָה
• מַעֲשֵׂה הָרָעָה | ἀπὸ τῶν ποιούντων τὸ πονηρόν G S | contra malos V Hie^lem |
רשיעיא על עובדיהון בישיא T (paraphr) ⊹ • רָע׃ T (assim-v 12a?) | τὸ πονηρόν
G S | V Hie^lem (indet) •

אֲשֶׁ֣ר חֹטֶ֗א עֹשֶׂ֥ה רָ֛ע מְאַ֖ת וּמַאֲרִ֣יךְ ל֑וֹ ‏12

כִּ֚י גַּם־יוֹדֵ֣עַ אָ֔נִי אֲשֶׁ֤ר יִֽהְיֶה־טּוֹב֙ לְיִרְאֵ֣י הָֽאֱלֹהִ֔ים

אֲשֶׁ֥ר יִֽירְא֖וּ מִלְּפָנָֽיו׃

וְטוֹב֙ לֹא־יִֽהְיֶ֣ה לָֽרָשָׁ֔ע וְלֹֽא־יַאֲרִ֥יךְ יָמִ֖ים כַּצֵּ֑ל ‏13

אֲשֶׁ֛ר אֵינֶ֥נּוּ יָרֵ֖א מִלִּפְנֵ֥י אֱלֹהִֽים׃

יֶשׁ־הֶבֶל֮ אֲשֶׁ֣ר נַעֲשָׂ֣ה עַל־הָאָרֶץ֒ ‏14

אֲשֶׁ֣ר ׀ יֵ֣שׁ צַדִּיקִ֗ים אֲשֶׁ֨ר מַגִּ֤יעַ אֲלֵהֶם֙ כְּמַעֲשֵׂ֣ה הָרְשָׁעִ֔ים

וְיֵ֣שׁ רְשָׁעִ֔ים שֶׁמַּגִּ֥יעַ אֲלֵהֶ֖ם כְּמַעֲשֵׂ֣ה הַצַּדִּיקִ֑ים

אָמַ֕רְתִּי שֶׁגַּם־זֶ֖ה הָֽבֶל׃

וְשִׁבַּ֤חְתִּֽי אֲנִי֙ אֶת־הַשִּׂמְחָ֔ה אֲשֶׁ֨ר אֵֽין־ט֤וֹב לָֽאָדָם֙ תַּ֣חַת הַשֶּׁ֔מֶשׁ כִּ֖י ‏15

אִם־לֶאֱכ֣וֹל וְלִשְׁתּ֣וֹת וְלִשְׂמ֑וֹחַ וְה֞וּא יִלְוֶ֣נּוּ בַעֲמָל֗וֹ יְמֵ֧י חַיָּ֛יו אֲשֶׁר־

נָֽתַן־ל֥וֹ הָאֱלֹהִ֖ים תַּ֥חַת הַשָּֽׁמֶשׁ׃ כַּאֲשֶׁ֨ר נָתַ֤תִּי אֶת־לִבִּי֙ לָדַ֣עַת ‏16

חָכְמָ֔ה וְלִרְאוֹת֙ אֶת־הָ֣עִנְיָ֔ן אֲשֶׁ֥ר נַעֲשָׂ֖ה עַל־הָאָ֑רֶץ כִּ֣י גַ֤ם בַּיּוֹם֙

וּבַלַּ֔יְלָה שֵׁנָ֕ה בְּעֵינָ֖יו אֵינֶ֥נּוּ רֹאֶֽה׃ וְרָאִ֘יתִי֮ אֶת־כָּל־מַעֲשֵׂ֣ה הָאֱלֹהִים֒ ‏17

כִּי֩ לֹ֨א יוּכַ֜ל הָאָדָ֗ם לִמְצוֹא֙ אֶת־הַֽמַּעֲשֶׂה֙ אֲשֶׁ֣ר נַעֲשָׂ֣ה תַֽחַת־

הַשֶּׁ֔מֶשׁ בְּ֠שֶׁל אֲשֶׁ֨ר יַעֲמֹ֤ל הָֽאָדָם֙ לְבַקֵּ֔שׁ וְלֹ֣א יִמְצָ֑א וְגַ֨ם אִם־יֹאמַ֤ר

הֶֽחָכָם֙ לָדַ֔עַת לֹ֥א יוּכַ֖ל לִמְצֹֽא׃

---

[12] חטא ג̇ חס̇ וסימ̇ הוי גוי חטא . אשר חטא עשה . כטוב כחטא ס̇: [13] מלפני
אלהים ב̇ יען רך ב̇דדבר יֹמֹ . ולא יאריך יֹמֹ . [17] וראיתי יֹב̇ וסימנהון ופסחתי עליכם .
וראיתי מה והגדתי לך . עליהם גידים . שיש יתרון . מאשר ישמח האדם . את כל
עמל . את כל מעשה האלהים . כי איככה אוכל ב̇ בו . לבית . אני דניאל . אני
דניאל ס̇:

---

12 חֹטֶא σ' V Hie^{lem} T | ἥμαρτεν G | S (indet) • עֹשֶׂה σ' V Hie^{lem} T | ἐποίησεν
G | S (indet) ✠ • מְאַת V Hie^{lem} S | ἀπὸ τότε G (via מאז) | ἀπέθανεν σ' α'-σ'-θ'
(ign-lex) | מאה שנין T (interp) ✠ • וּמַאֲרִיךְ σ' V Hie^{lem} S T | καὶ ἀπὸ
μακρότητος G ✠ • לוֹ σ' V Hie^{lem} S T | αὐτῶν G* (assim-v 12b) ✠ • **13** כַּצֵּל V
Hie^{lem} S T | ἐν σκιᾷ G | > σ' ✠ • **16** כַּאֲשֶׁר T | ἐν οἷς G | διό σ' Hie^{lem} S
(interp) | et V (indet) ‖ → ✠ 4:17 • **17** מַעֲשֵׂה S T | pl G σ' V Hie^{lem} → ✠ 7:13 •
הָאָדָם^1 σ' | > art G | V S T (indet) ✠ •

ב̇ חס̇ בסיפ̇ .
כַּבֶּ . ל̇

ל̇

יֹ̇ . ה̇ דגש

ל̇ בסיפ̇

ב̇ חס̇ בסיפ̇

ל̇ . ב̇ חס̇
בסיפ̇ ו̇ .

ל̇

ג̇

ה̇ . יֹב̇
יֹ̇ פסוק לא ולא
לא . ב̇ מל̇
ל̇ . ב̇ בסיפ̇

ל	9 כִּ֣י אֶת־כָּל־זֶ֞ה נָתַ֤תִּי אֶל־לִבִּי֙ וְלָב֣וּר אֶת־כָּל־זֶ֗ה
ו . ל . ל	אֲשֶׁ֨ר הַצַּדִּיקִ֧ים וְהַחֲכָמִ֛ים וַעֲבָדֵיהֶ֖ם בְּיַ֣ד הָאֱלֹהִ֑ים
	גַּֽם־אַהֲבָ֣ה גַם־שִׂנְאָ֗ה אֵ֤ין יוֹדֵ֙עַ֙ הָֽאָדָ֔ם
י	2 הַכֹּ֖ל לִפְנֵיהֶֽם׃ הַכֹּ֞ל כַּאֲשֶׁ֤ר לַכֹּל֙ מִקְרֶ֣ה אֶחָ֔ד
ב . ב . ל	לַצַּדִּ֤יק וְלָרָשָׁע֙ לַטּוֹב֙ וְלַטָּה֣וֹר וְלַטָּמֵ֔א
	וְלַ֨זֹּבֵ֔חַ וְלַ֣אֲשֶׁ֔ר אֵינֶ֖נּוּ זֹבֵ֑חַ
ג חס	כַּטּוֹב֙ כַּֽחֹטֶ֔א הַנִּשְׁבָּ֕ע כַּאֲשֶׁ֖ר שְׁבוּעָ֥ה יָרֵֽא׃
ג בטע ברא פסוק	3 זֶ֣ה ׀ רָ֗ע בְּכֹ֤ל אֲשֶֽׁר־נַעֲשָׂה֙ תַּ֣חַת הַשֶּׁ֔מֶשׁ כִּֽי־מִקְרֶ֥ה אֶחָ֖ד לַכֹּ֑ל וְגַ֣ם לֵ֣ב בְּֽנֵי־הָ֠אָדָם מָֽלֵא־רָ֨ע וְהוֹלֵל֤וֹת בִּלְבָבָם֙ בְּחַיֵּיהֶ֔ם וְאַחֲרָ֖יו אֶל־הַמֵּתִֽים׃
ן יחבר . ל ק'	4 כִּי־מִי֙ אֲשֶׁ֣ר יְבֻחַ֔ר אֶ֥ל כָּל־הַחַיִּ֖ים יֵ֣שׁ בִּטָּח֑וֹן
ל	כִּֽי־לְכֶ֤לֶב חַי֙ ה֣וּא ט֔וֹב מִן־הָאַרְיֵ֖ה הַמֵּֽת׃
ד מל	5 כִּ֧י הַֽחַיִּ֛ים יוֹדְעִ֖ים שֶׁיָּמֻ֑תוּ וְהַמֵּתִ֞ים אֵינָ֤ם יוֹדְעִים֙ מְא֔וּמָה
	וְאֵֽין־ע֤וֹד לָהֶם֙ שָׂכָ֔ר כִּ֥י נִשְׁכַּ֖ח זִכְרָֽם׃
יב יחיד דרא פסו אית בהון מן ג̇ ג̇ מלין קרחי	6 גַּ֣ם אַהֲבָתָ֧ם גַּם־שִׂנְאָתָ֛ם גַּם־קִנְאָתָ֖ם כְּבָ֣ר אָבָ֑דָה
	וְחֵ֨לֶק אֵין־לָהֶ֥ם עוֹד֙ לְעוֹלָ֔ם

[9:2] ולרשע ב̇ אמר אלהים מה לך . לצדיק ולרשע ב̇ :ס [3] זה ג̇ בטע ברא פסוק יתנו
כל העבר . לחמנו חם . רע בכל אשר נעשה . וחד וזה פרשגן הנשתון :ס

9:1 וְלָב֣וּר V Hie^lem T (hapl?) | καὶ καρδία μου (...) εἶδεν G | ut ventilarem ⟨σ'⟩ |
ܡܠܒ ܘܝ S ‖ pref וְלִבִּ֥י רָאָ֖ה see S ✥ • הַכֹּ֖ל לִפְנֵיהֶֽם׃ (err-graph) | τὰ
πάντα πρὸ προσώπου αὐτῶν ματαιότης G | τὰ πάντα ἔμπροσθεν αὐτοῦ ἄδηλα
σ' (V) | omnia in facie eorum Hie^lem | ܚܠ ܕܡܩܕܡܝܗܘܢ، ܚܒܠܐ، ܚܠ S (confl) | T
(indet) ‖ pref: הַכֹּ֖ל לִפְנֵיהֶ֥ם הָבֶל see G ✥ • **2** כַּאֲשֶׁ֤ר לַכֹּל֙ ⟨σ'⟩ V S | ἐν τοῖς
πᾶσιν G Hie^lem | T (indet) ‖ pref בַּאֲשֶׁ֥ר לַכֹּל see G Hie^lem ✥ • לַטּוֹב֙ T | τῷ
ἀγαθῷ καὶ τῷ κακῷ G V Hie^lem (S) (ampl) ✥ • הַנִּשְׁבָּ֕ע | ὡς ὁ ὀμνύων G V
Hie^lem S T (assim-ctext) • **3** וְהוֹלֵל֤וֹת α' Hie^lem | καὶ περιφέρεια G | καὶ
αὐθαδείας σ' V | ܘܚܣܡܐ S | וחולחולתא T ‖ pref וְהוֹלֵל֤וֹת see G σ' V S T ✥ •
וְאַחֲרָ֖יו V Hie^lem T | καὶ ὀπίσω αὐτῶν G (assim-ctext) | τὰ δὲ τελευταῖα αὐτῶν
σ' S (harm-ctext) ✥ • **4** יְבֻחַ֔ר | יבחר M^ket יְחֻבַּ֔ר M^qere σ' V S T* | κοινωνεῖ G
Hie^lem ‖ pref יְחֻבַּ֔ר M^qere σ' V S T* ✥ • **5** יוֹדְעִ֖ים V Hie^lem S T | γνώσονται G •

בְּכֹל אֲשֶׁר־נַעֲשָׂה תַּחַת הַשָּׁמֶשׁ׃

‏ל   ס᷑ 7 לֵךְ אֱכֹל בְּשִׂמְחָה לַחְמֶךָ   וּשֲׁתֵה בְלֶב־טוֹב יֵינֶךָ

‏ב. ל   כִּי כְבָר רָצָה הָאֱלֹהִים אֶת־מַעֲשֶׂיךָ׃

8 בְּכָל־עֵת יִהְיוּ בְגָדֶיךָ לְבָנִים
וְשֶׁמֶן עַל־רֹאשְׁךָ אַל־יֶחְסָר׃

‏ב וחס   9 רְאֵה חַיִּים עִם־אִשָּׁה אֲשֶׁר־אָהַבְתָּ   כָּל־יְמֵי חַיֵּי הֶבְלֶךָ
אֲשֶׁר נָתַן־לְךָ תַּחַת הַשֶּׁמֶשׁ   כֹּל יְמֵי הֶבְלֶךָ
כִּי הוּא חֶלְקְךָ בַּחַיִּים
‏ה בסיפ   וּבַעֲמָלְךָ   אֲשֶׁר־אַתָּה עָמֵל תַּחַת הַשָּׁמֶשׁ׃

10 כֹּל אֲשֶׁר תִּמְצָא יָדְךָ לַעֲשׂוֹת   בְּכֹחֲךָ עֲשֵׂה
‏י   כִּי אֵין מַעֲשֶׂה וְחֶשְׁבּוֹן   וְדַעַת וְחָכְמָה
‏ד חס בסיפ   בִּשְׁאוֹל   אֲשֶׁר אַתָּה הֹלֵךְ שָׁמָּה׃ ס

11 שַׁבְתִּי וְרָאֹה תַחַת־הַשֶּׁמֶשׁ
‏ל. ל   כִּי לֹא לַקַּלִּים הַמֵּרוֹץ   וְלֹא לַגִּבּוֹרִים הַמִּלְחָמָה
וְגַם לֹא לַחֲכָמִים לֶחֶם   וְגַם לֹא לַנְּבֹנִים עֹשֶׁר
וְגַם לֹא לַיֹּדְעִים חֵן
‏ב   כִּי־עֵת וָפֶגַע יִקְרֶה אֶת־כֻּלָּם׃

‏יֹ   12 כִּי גַּם לֹא־יֵדַע הָאָדָם אֶת־עִתּוֹ
‏ל   כַּדָּגִים   שֶׁנֶּאֱחָזִים בִּמְצוֹדָה רָעָה
‏ל. ל   וְכַצִּפֳּרִים   הָאֲחֻזוֹת בַּפָּח
‏ל   כָּהֵם יוּקָשִׁים בְּנֵי הָאָדָם   לְעֵת רָעָה
‏ל ומל   כְּשֶׁתִּפּוֹל עֲלֵיהֶם פִּתְאֹם׃

[7] רצה האלהים ב וסימנ כי כבד פה . בי רצה להמליך :ס [10] מעשה י וסימנהון
כל כלי מעשה . בשם . למצרים . כי יאמר . מרקחים . החל . להסיר . את כל זה .
תמצא ידך . כי את כל מעשה :ס

9 רְאֵה σ' V Hie^lem T | prec cj G* S • אֲשֶׁר² to הֶבְלֶךָ² G^Mss V Hie^lem I > G* S I
נָתַן T | τὰς δοθείσας G^Mss V Hie^lem (facil-synt) I > G*
S • כָּל יְמֵי הֶבְלֶךָ G^Mss α' V Hie^lem I > G* S T ⊹ • **10** בְּכֹחֲךָ Hie^lem S (T) I ὡς ἡ
δύναμίς σου G I *instanter* V || pref כְּכֹחֲךָ see G ⊹ • **12** יֵדַע I pf G T I *nescit* V
Hie^lem I ـبـ S (indet) • ⊹ • הָאֲחֻזוֹת

י . ב . 13 גַּם־זֹ֤ה רָאִ֙יתִי֙ חָכְמָ֔ה תַּ֖חַת הַשָּׁ֑מֶשׁ   וּגְדוֹלָ֥ה הִ֖יא אֵלָֽי׃

ג 14 עִ֣יר קְטַנָּ֔ה וַאֲנָשִׁ֥ים בָּ֖הּ מְעָ֑ט וּבָֽא־אֵלֶ֜יהָ מֶ֤לֶךְ גָּדוֹל֙ וְסָבַ֣ב אֹתָ֔הּ

ל בסיפׄ מוגהׄ . ל 15 וּבָנָ֥ה עָלֶ֖יהָ מְצוֹדִ֣ים גְּדֹלִ֑ים וּמָ֣צָא בָ֗הּ אִ֤ישׁ מִסְכֵּן֙ חָכָ֔ם וּמִלַּט־

ט . ל הֽוּא אֶת־הָעִ֖יר בְּחָכְמָת֑וֹ וְאָדָם֙ לֹ֣א זָכַ֔ר אֶת־הָאִ֥ישׁ הַמִּסְכֵּ֖ן
הַהֽוּא׃

16 וְאָמַ֣רְתִּי אָ֔נִי   טוֹבָ֥ה חָכְמָ֖ה מִגְּבוּרָ֑ה

ל . ה וְחָכְמַ֤ת הַמִּסְכֵּן֙ בְּזוּיָ֔ה   וּדְבָרָ֖יו אֵינָ֥ם נִשְׁמָעִֽים׃

ז 17 דִּבְרֵ֣י חֲכָמִ֔ים   בְּנַ֖חַת נִשְׁמָעִ֑ים

מִֽזַּעֲקַ֥ת מוֹשֵׁ֖ל בַּכְּסִילִֽים׃

18 טוֹבָ֥ה חָכְמָ֖ה   מִכְּלֵ֣י קְרָ֑ב

וְחוֹטֶ֣א אֶחָ֔ד יְאַבֵּ֖ד טוֹבָ֥ה הַרְבֵּֽה׃

ל . ל . ב מלׄ 10 זְבוּבֵ֣י מָ֔וֶת   יַבְאִ֥ישׁ יַבִּ֖יעַ שֶׁ֣מֶן רוֹקֵ֑חַ

ל יָקָ֛ר מֵחָכְמָ֥ה מִכָּב֖וֹד סִכְל֥וּת מְעָֽט׃

2 לֵ֤ב חָכָם֙ לִֽימִינ֔וֹ   וְלֵ֥ב כְּסִ֖יל לִשְׂמֹאלֽוֹ׃

יתיר ה . ל . ל 3 וְגַם־בַּדֶּ֙רֶךְ֙ כְּשֶׁהַסָּכָ֣ל הֹלֵ֔ךְ   לִבּ֥וֹ חָסֵ֑ר
ד חסׄ בסׄ . ד

---

[14] ובא אליה ב וסימנהון כי יקח איש איש אשה . מלך גדול וסבב אתה :o. וסבב ג
וסימנהון ביתאל והגלגל . לעפל ויגביהה . עיר קטנה ואנשים בה מעט :o. מצודים ב
ומל וסימנהון ובנה עליה מצודים . אשר היא מצודים וחרמים :o. [10:3] הלך ד חסׄ
דור הלך ודור בא . בשאול אשר אתה . וגם בדרך כשהסכל הלך . כי הלך האדם על
בית עלמו :o.

---

14 מְצוֹדִים T | ἀποτείχισμα σ' | χάρακας G S | *machinam* Hie^lem | *munitiones* V
(indet) ‖ pref מְצוּרִים see G S ✣ • **17** מוֹשֵׁל σ' V Hie^lem S T | pl G (assim-
ctext) • **10:1** זְבוּבֵי מָוֶת Hie^lem | μυῖαι θανατοῦσαι G | μυιῶν θάνατος σ'
(interp) | *muscae morientes* V S (interp) ✣ • יַבְאִישׁ σ' T |
pl G V Hie^lem S ‖ pref יַבְאִישׁוּ see G V Hie^lem S ✣ • יַבִּיעַ (crrp) | > G σ' V
Hie^lem S T ‖ pref *omit* יַבִּיעַ see G σ' V Hie^lem S T ✣ • יָקָר to
מְעָט (Hie^lem) (T) | τίμιον ὀλίγον σοφίας ὑπὲρ δόξαν ἀφροσύνης μεγάλης G |
pretiosior est sapientia et gloria parva ad tempus stultitia V | ܚܟܡܬܐ ܚ ܝܩܝܪܐ
ܩܠܝܠ S ✣ • מִכָּבוֹד G | prec cj V Hie^lem (S) T •
3 כְּשֶׁסָּכָל | M^ket | כְּשֶׁהַסָּכָל M^qere G | V S T (indet) •

וְאָמַ֥ר לַכֹּ֖ל סָכָ֥ל הֽוּא׃

4 אִם־ר֤וּחַ הַמּוֹשֵׁל֙ תַּעֲלֶ֣ה עָלֶ֔יךָ מְקֽוֹמְךָ֖ אַל־תַּנַּ֑ח ג
כִּ֣י מַרְפֵּ֔א יַנִּ֖יחַ חֲטָאִ֥ים גְּדוֹלִֽים׃ ו מל

5 יֵ֥שׁ רָעָ֛ה רָאִ֖יתִי תַּ֣חַת הַשָּׁ֑מֶשׁ
כִּשְׁגָגָ֕ה שֶׁיֹּצָ֖א מִלִּפְנֵ֥י הַשַּׁלִּֽיט׃ ל . ל

6 נִתַּ֣ן הַסֶּ֔כֶל בַּמְּרוֹמִ֖ים רַבִּ֑ים
וַעֲשִׁירִ֖ים בַּשֵּׁ֥פֶל יֵשֵֽׁבוּ׃ ל . ל . ד

7 רָאִ֥יתִי עֲבָדִ֖ים עַל־סוּסִ֑ים
וְשָׂרִ֛ים הֹלְכִ֥ים כַּעֲבָדִ֖ים עַל־הָאָֽרֶץ׃

8 חֹפֵ֥ר גּוּמָּ֖ץ בּ֣וֹ יִפּ֑וֹל וּפֹרֵ֥ץ גָּדֵ֖ר יִשְּׁכֶ֥נּוּ נָחָֽשׁ׃ ל . ל . ל

9 מַסִּ֣יעַ אֲבָנִ֔ים יֵעָצֵ֖ב בָּהֶ֑ם בּוֹקֵ֥עַ עֵצִ֖ים יִסָּ֥כֶן בָּֽם׃ ל . ב . ג

10 אִם־קֵהָ֣ה הַבַּרְזֶ֗ל וְהוּא֙ לֹא־פָנִ֣ים קִלְקַ֔ל ב
וַחֲיָלִ֖ים יְגַבֵּ֑ר וְיִתְר֥וֹן הכשיר הַכְשֵׁ֥יר חָכְמָֽה׃ ל . ל . יתיר י

11 אִם־יִשֹּׁ֥ךְ הַנָּחָ֖שׁ בְּלוֹא־לָ֑חַשׁ וְאֵ֣ין יִתְר֔וֹן לְבַ֖עַל הַלָּשֽׁוֹן׃ ל . ו מל

12 דִּבְרֵ֥י פִי־חָכָ֖ם חֵ֑ן וְשִׂפְת֥וֹת כְּסִ֖יל תְּבַלְּעֶֽנּוּ׃

13 תְּחִלַּ֥ת דִּבְרֵי־פִ֖יהוּ סִכְל֑וּת וְאַחֲרִ֣ית פִּ֔יהוּ הוֹלֵל֖וּת רָעָֽה׃ ג ראש פסוק

14 וְהַסָּכָ֖ל יַרְבֶּ֣ה דְבָרִ֑ים
לֹא־יֵדַ֤ע הָאָדָם֙ מַה־שֶּׁיִּֽהְיֶ֔ה
וַאֲשֶׁ֤ר יִֽהְיֶה֙ מֵֽאַחֲרָ֔יו מִ֖י יַגִּ֥יד לֽוֹ׃ יט

---

[4] תנח ג טוב אשר תאחז בזה . אם רוח המושל . בבקר זרע את זרעך . וחד ותנח
בגדו אצלה :o [11] בלוא ו מל וסימנהון הוי כל צמא לכו ב בו . למה תשקלו כסף ב
בו . בלוא יועיל . בלוא לחש :o

---

3 וְאָמַ֥ר לַכֹּ֖ל (σ') (V) (Hie^lem) | καὶ ἃ λογιεῖται πάντα G | ܘܟܠܐ S | ‹ואז› ‹ ⫶ • **5** שֶׁיֹּצָ֖א V Hie^lem S T | ἐξῆλθεν G* | ἐξελθόν σ' | ὁ ἐξῆλθεν
G^Mss ‖ pref שֶׁיֹּצָ֖א (origin) ⫶ • **6** הַסֶּ֔כֶל | ὁ ἄφρων G α' σ' V Hie^lem S T •
9 בּוֹקֵ֥עַ G | prec cj V Hie^lem S T • **10** לֹא V Hie^lem T | > G S ⫶ •
הַכְשֵׁ֥יר | הכשיר M^ket | הַכְשֵׁ֥ר M^qere | τοῦ ἀνδρείου G (S) | ὁ γοργευσάμενος σ' |
industriam V | *fortitudinis* Hie^lem | אכשרות T ⫶ • **11** הַנָּחָ֖שׁ G^Mss (spont) | > art
G* | pl T | V S (indet) ‖ pref נָחָשׁ see G* ⫶ • **14** לֹא ⫶ • יֵדַ֤ע T | ἔγνω G |
ignorat V Hie^lem | ܢܕܥ S ⫶ • שֶּׁיִּֽהְיֶ֔ה T | τὸ γενόμενον G σ' V Hie^lem S ⫶ •

עֲמַ֥ל הַכְּסִילִ֖ים תְּיַגְּעֶ֑נּוּ   אֲשֶׁ֥ר לֹֽא־יָדַ֖ע לָלֶ֥כֶת אֶל־עִֽיר׃   15   ל

אִֽי־לָ֣ךְ אֶ֔רֶץ שֶׁמַּלְכֵּ֖ךְ נָ֑עַר   וְשָׂרַ֖יִךְ בַּבֹּ֥קֶר יֹאכֵֽלוּ׃   16   ב

אַשְׁרֵ֣יךְ אֶ֔רֶץ שֶׁמַּלְכֵּ֖ךְ בֶּן־חוֹרִ֑ים   וְשָׂרַ֙יִךְ֙ בָּעֵ֣ת יֹאכֵ֔לוּ   17

בִּגְבוּרָ֖ה וְלֹ֥א בַשְּׁתִֽי׃

ל וכול ערב כות
ב מ א
ל . ל . ל . ל וחד
ואת ידלף

בַּעֲצַלְתַּ֖יִם יִמַּ֣ךְ הַמְּקָרֶ֑ה   וּבְשִׁפְל֥וּת יָדַ֖יִם יִדְלֹ֥ף הַבָּֽיִת׃   18

לִשְׂחוֹק֙ עֹשִׂ֣ים לֶ֔חֶם   וְיַ֖יִן יְשַׂמַּ֣ח חַיִּ֑ים   19   ז

וְהַכֶּ֖סֶף יַעֲנֶ֥ה אֶת־הַכֹּֽל׃

גַּ֣ם בְּמַדָּֽעֲךָ֙ מֶ֣לֶךְ אַל־תְּקַלֵּ֔ל   20   ל

וּבְחַדְרֵי֙ מִשְׁכָּ֣בְךָ֔ אַל־תְּקַלֵּ֖ל עָשִׁ֑יר

כִּ֣י ע֤וֹף הַשָּׁמַ֙יִם֙ יוֹלִ֣יךְ אֶת־הַקּ֔וֹל   ב חד חס

וּבַ֥עַל הַכְּנָפַ֖יִם יַגֵּ֥יד דָּבָֽר׃   כנפים ן   ק

שַׁלַּ֥ח לַחְמְךָ֖ עַל־פְּנֵ֣י הַמָּ֑יִם   11

כִּֽי־בְרֹ֥ב הַיָּמִ֖ים תִּמְצָאֶֽנּוּ׃

תֶּן־חֵ֥לֶק לְשִׁבְעָ֖ה וְגַ֣ם לִשְׁמוֹנָ֑ה   2   ל מל וכול דברי ימים דכות

כִּ֚י לֹ֣א תֵדַ֔ע מַה־יִּהְיֶ֥ה רָעָ֖ה עַל־הָאָֽרֶץ׃

אִם־יִמָּלְא֨וּ הֶעָבִ֥ים גֶּ֙שֶׁם֙ עַל־הָאָ֣רֶץ יָרִ֔יקוּ   3

וְאִם־יִפּ֥וֹל עֵ֛ץ בַּדָּר֖וֹם וְאִ֣ם בַּצָּפ֑וֹן   ב . ל

מְק֛וֹם שֶׁיִּפּ֥וֹל הָעֵ֖ץ שָׁ֥ם יְהֽוּא׃   ב חד מל וחד חס

שֹׁמֵ֥ר ר֖וּחַ לֹ֣א יִזְרָ֑ע   וְרֹאֶ֥ה בֶעָבִ֖ים לֹ֥א יִקְצֽוֹר׃   4

כַּאֲשֶׁ֨ר אֵֽינְךָ֤ יוֹדֵ֙עַ֙   מַה־דֶּ֣רֶךְ הָר֔וּחַ   5

15 עֲמַ֥ל הַכְּסִילִ֖ים תְּיַגְּעֶ֑נּוּ (crrp) | μόχθος τῶν ἀφρόνων κοπώσει αὐτούς G V Hie[lem] S | עֲמַל הַכְּסִיל מָתַי יְיַגְּעֶנּוּ conjec ‖ ... טרחות שטיא ... משלהי ליה T ✣ ● **17** בַשְּׁתִֽי׃ S | αἰσχυνθήσονται G | in confusione Hie[lem] | ad luxuriam V | T (indet) ✣ ● **19** וְיַ֖יִן יְשַׂמַּ֣ח G T | καὶ οἶνον τοῦ εὐφρανθῆναι ⟨θ'⟩* V Hie[lem] | καὶ οἶνον καὶ ἔλαιον τοῦ εὐφρανθῆναι G[Mss] S ✣ ● **20** וּבְחַדְרֵי G | sg V Hie[lem] S T (interp) ● הַכְּנָפַ֖יִם M[ket] G ⟨α'⟩ | כְּנָפַים M[qere] ⟨θ'⟩ | ⟨σ'⟩ V Hie[lem] S T (indet) ✣ ● **11:3** יְהֽוּא׃ ✣ ● **5** כַּאֲשֶׁ֨ר V Hie[lem] T | ἐν οἷς G | ἐν ᾧ a' | ἐπεί σ' | ר ܪ S ‖ → ✣ 4:17 ● אֵֽינְךָ֤ יוֹדֵ֙עַ֙ a' σ' V Hie[lem] S T | οὐκ ἔστιν γινώσκων G ‖ pref אֵין יוֹדֵעַ see G ✣ ●

כַּעֲצָמִים֙   בְּבֶ֣טֶן הַמְּלֵאָ֔ה

כָּ֣כָה לֹ֤א תֵדַע֙   אֶת־מַעֲשֵׂ֣ה הָֽאֱלֹהִ֔ים

אֲשֶׁ֥ר יַעֲשֶׂ֖ה אֶת־הַכֹּֽל׃

6 בַּבֹּ֙קֶר֙ זְרַ֣ע אֶת־זַרְעֶ֔ךָ   וְלָעֶ֖רֶב אַל־תַּנַּ֣ח יָדֶ֑ךָ

כִּי֩ אֵֽינְךָ֨ יוֹדֵ֜עַ   אֵ֣י זֶ֤ה יִכְשָׁר֙   הֲזֶ֣ה אוֹ־זֶ֔ה

וְאִם־שְׁנֵיהֶ֥ם כְּאֶחָ֖ד טוֹבִֽים׃

7 וּמָת֖וֹק הָא֑וֹר   וְט֥וֹב לַֽעֵינַ֖יִם לִרְא֥וֹת אֶת־הַשָּֽׁמֶשׁ׃

8 כִּ֣י אִם־שָׁנִ֥ים הַרְבֵּ֛ה יִחְיֶ֥ה הָאָדָ֖ם   בְּכֻלָּ֣ם יִשְׂמָ֑ח

וְיִזְכֹּר֙ אֶת־יְמֵ֣י הַחֹ֔שֶׁךְ   כִּֽי־הַרְבֵּ֥ה יִהְי֖וּ כָּל־שֶׁבָּ֥א הָֽבֶל׃

9 שְׂמַ֧ח בָּח֣וּר בְּיַלְדוּתֶ֗יךָ   וִֽיטִֽיבְךָ֤ לִבְּךָ֙ בִּימֵ֣י בְחוּרוֹתֶ֔ךָ

וְהַלֵּךְ֙ בְּדַרְכֵ֣י לִבְּךָ֔   וּבְמַרְאֵ֖י עֵינֶ֑יךָ

וְדָ֕ע כִּ֧י עַל־כָּל־אֵ֛לֶּה   יְבִֽיאֲךָ֥ הָאֱלֹהִ֖ים בַּמִּשְׁפָּֽט׃

10 וְהָסֵ֥ר כַּ֙עַס֙ מִלִּבֶּ֔ךָ   וְהַעֲבֵ֥ר רָעָ֖ה מִבְּשָׂרֶ֑ךָ

כִּֽי־הַיַּלְד֥וּת וְהַֽשַּׁחֲר֖וּת הָֽבֶל׃

12 וּזְכֹר֙ אֶת־בּ֣וֹרְאֶ֔יךָ   בִּימֵ֖י בְּחוּרֹתֶ֑יךָ

עַ֣ד אֲשֶׁ֤ר לֹא־יָבֹ֙אוּ֙   יְמֵ֣י הָֽרָעָ֔ה

וְהִגִּ֣יעוּ שָׁנִ֔ים אֲשֶׁ֣ר תֹּאמַ֔ר   אֵֽין־לִ֥י בָהֶ֖ם חֵֽפֶץ׃

2 עַ֣ד אֲשֶׁ֤ר לֹֽא־תֶחְשַׁךְ֙ הַשֶּׁ֣מֶשׁ וְהָא֔וֹר   וְהַיָּרֵ֖חַ וְהַכּוֹכָבִ֑ים

וְשָׁ֥בוּ הֶעָבִ֖ים   אַחַ֥ר הַגָּֽשֶׁם׃

3 בַּיּ֗וֹם שֶׁיָּזֻ֙עוּ֙ שֹׁמְרֵ֣י הַבַּ֔יִת   וְהִֽתְעַוְּת֖וּ אַנְשֵׁ֣י הֶחָ֑יִל

[11:9] במשפט חׄ דגשין לא תעשו עול . ויגבה יהוה צבאות . על כן לא יקמו רשעים במשפט . ידרך ענוים במשפט . שאת פני רשע . שמח בחור בילדותיך . וכל איוב דכותהון בׄ מׄ אׄ ואתי תביא במשפט עמך ס׃

5 כַּעֲצָמִים֙ see T ✣ • בַּעֲצָמִ֣ים G (V) (Hie^lem) (S) | בגוף עולימא שלילא T ‖ pref
בְּדַרְכֵ֣י לִבְּךָ֔ → ✣ 7:13 • 6 יוֹדֵ֜עַ M^L (err) | יֹדֵ֜עַ M^{L34} M^Y • 9
וּבְמַרְאֵ֖י V Hie^lem S | ἐν ὁδοῖς καρδίας σου ἄμωμος καὶ μὴ ἐν ὁράσει G*
(gloss) | וּבְמַרְאֵ֖י sg G V Hie^lem | T בענוותנותא עם ארחי לבך ותחי זהיר בחיזו |
S T ✣ • 12:1 בּ֣וֹרְאֶ֔יךָ ✣ •

וּבֻטְּלוּ הַטֹּחֲנוֹת כִּי מִעֵטוּ   וְחָשְׁכוּ הָרֹאוֹת בָּאֲרֻבּוֹת: ל . ל . ד . ב

4 וְסֻגְּרוּ דְלָתַיִם בַּשּׁוּק   בִּשְׁפַל קוֹל הַטַּחֲנָה   ב

וְיָקוּם לְקוֹל הַצִּפּוֹר   וְיִשַּׁחוּ כָּל־בְּנוֹת הַשִּׁיר: ל . ל

5 גַּם מִגָּבֹהַּ יִרָאוּ   וְחַתְחַתִּים בַּדֶּרֶךְ   ל

וְיָנֵאץ הַשָּׁקֵד   וְיִסְתַּבֵּל הֶחָגָב   וְתָפֵר הָאֲבִיּוֹנָה   ל וְיתִּיר א̇ .
ל . ל

כִּי־הֹלֵךְ הָאָדָם אֶל־בֵּית עוֹלָמוֹ   וְסָבְבוּ בַשּׁוּק הַסֹּפְדִים: ד חס̇ בסיפ̇ . ב

6 עַד אֲשֶׁר לֹא־יֵרָחֵק חֶבֶל הַכֶּסֶף   וְתָרֻץ גֻּלַּת הַזָּהָב   ירתק ק̇ . ל בס̇ . ל

וְתִשָּׁבֶר כַּד עַל־הַמַּבּוּעַ   וְנָרֹץ הַגַּלְגַּל אֶל־הַבּוֹר: ל . ל

7 וְיָשֹׁב הֶעָפָר עַל־הָאָרֶץ כְּשֶׁהָיָה   הֹ

וְהָרוּחַ תָּשׁוּב אֶל־הָאֱלֹהִים אֲשֶׁר נְתָנָהּ:

8 הֲבֵל הֲבָלִים אָמַר הַקּוֹהֶלֶת   הַכֹּל הָבֶל: ל ומל̇

9 וְיֹתֵר שֶׁהָיָה קֹהֶלֶת חָכָם

עוֹד לִמַּד־דַּעַת אֶת־הָעָם   ל

וְאִזֵּן וְחִקֵּר   תִּקֵּן מְשָׁלִים הַרְבֵּה: ל . ל

10 בִּקֵּשׁ קֹהֶלֶת   לִמְצֹא דִּבְרֵי־חֵפֶץ   הֹ

[12:3] הראות ד̇ וסימנהון עיניכם הראות אשר עשה יהוה . את כל מעשה יהוה . את
כל אשר עשה . וחשכו הראות בא o: הראות ד̇ עיניכם הראת . את כל מעשה . את
כל אשר עשה . וחשכו הראות o: בארבות ב̇ בן חסד . וחשכו o: [4] וסגרו ב̇ דלתים
בשוק . על מסגר . וחד ערי הנגב סגרו o:

4 וְסֻגְּרוּ α' S ǀ καὶ κλείσουσιν G V Hie^lem ǀ T (indet) ✛ • וְיָקוּם G (σ') Hie^lem S
(T) ǀ pl G^Mss V ✛ • **5** יִרָאוּ V Hie^lem ǀ ὄψονται G ⟨σ'⟩ (err-voc) ܢܣܒ S ǀ T
(indet) ✛ • וְיָנֵאץ ✛ • וְיִסְתַּבֵּל ǀ παχυνθῇ G V Hie^lem (interp) ǀ ܗܣܒܐ S
(interp) ǀ ויתנפחון T (interp) ✛ • וְתָפֵר (interp) ǀ καὶ διασκεδασθῇ G V Hie^lem ǀ
καὶ διαλυθῇ σ' ǀ καὶ καρπεύσει α' ǀ ܪܕܒܠ ܪܒܕܐ (ܪܒܕ) ܗܕܒܠ ܪܒܕܝ (ܚܒܢܘܐܟܐ) S (confl) ǀ
T (indet) ‖ pref וְתָפֵר see G σ' V Hie^lem ✛ • בַּשּׁוּק M^L (err) בַשּׁוּק M^L34 M^Y •
6 יֵרָחֵק (ign-gram) ǀ ירחק M^ket יֵרָתֵק M^qere T ǀ ἀνατραπῇ G ǀ κοπῆναι σ' V
Hie^lem S ‖ pref יָנֵתֵק see σ' V Hie^lem S ✛ • וְתָרֻץ α' ⟨θ'⟩ V Hie^lem (err-voc) ǀ καὶ
συνθλιβῇ G σ' S T* ‖ pref וְתֵרֹץ see G σ' S T* ✛ • וְנָרֹץ V Hie^lem ǀ καὶ
συντροχάσῃ G S T ‖ pref וְיָרֹץ see G S T ✛ • **7** וְיָשֹׁב ✛ • **9** הָעָם G^Mss α'-σ' V
Hie^lem S T (theol?) ǀ τὸν ἄνθρωπον G* ✛ • וְאִזֵּן וְחִקֵּר ǀ καὶ οὖς ἐξιχνιάσεται G
(ign-gram) ǀ et enarravit quae fecerit et investigans V Hie^lem (ign-lex) ǀ καὶ
ἠνωτίσατο καὶ ἠρεύνησε α' S T (ign-lex) ✛ •

וְכָתוּב יֹ֖שֶׁר דִּבְרֵי אֱמֶֽת׃

ל

11 דִּבְרֵי חֲכָמִים֙ כַּדָּ֣רְבֹנ֔וֹת

ל . ל . ל

וּֽכְמַשְׂמְר֥וֹת נְטוּעִ֖ים בַּעֲלֵ֣י אֲסֻפּ֑וֹת

ו . ב

נִתְּנ֖וּ מֵרֹעֶ֥ה אֶחָֽד׃

ב . ל

12 וְיֹתֵ֥ר מֵהֵ֖מָּה בְּנִ֣י הִזָּהֵ֑ר

עֲשׂ֨וֹת סְפָרִ֤ים הַרְבֵּה֙ אֵ֣ין קֵ֔ץ

ל . ל

וְלַ֥הַג הַרְבֵּ֖ה יְגִעַ֥ת בָּשָֽׂר׃

ג

13 ס֥וֹף דָּבָ֖ר הַכֹּ֣ל נִשְׁמָ֑ע

ג

אֶת־הָאֱלֹהִ֤ים יְרָא֙ וְאֶת־מִצְוֺתָ֣יו שְׁמ֔וֹר

כִּי־זֶ֖ה כָּל־הָאָדָֽם׃

י . ה חס

14 כִּ֤י אֶת־כָּל־מַֽעֲשֶׂ֔ה הָאֱלֹהִ֖ים יָבִ֣א בְמִשְׁפָּ֑ט

ב . ב בקול יי
אלהינו

עַ֚ל כָּל־נֶעְלָ֔ם אִם־ט֖וֹב וְאִם־רָֽע׃

רלב

[11] נתנו ו וסימנה חקך וחק בניך . למות . אדום . שממו . נתנו קברותיה . מרעה ׃ס

[13] ואת מצותיו ג וסימ׳ ושמרת את חקיו . אחרי יהוה אלהיכם . סוף ׃ס

10 וְכָתוּב יֹ֖שֶׁר T | καὶ γεγραμμένον εὐθύτητος G | καὶ συνέγραψεν ὀρθῶς α' Hie^lem | *et conscripsit (sermones) rectissimos* V (lib) | ◌◌◌◌ ◌◌◌◌ S ✣ • | σ' **13** נִשְׁמָ֑ע G^Mss ⟨α'-θ'⟩ V Hie^lem T | ἄκουε G* S | ◌◌◌◌ Syh ✣ • **14** מַעֲשֶׂ֔ה Hie^lem T | τὸ ποίημα G | τὰ ἔργα τοῦ ἀνθρώπου ⟨θ'⟩ | pl (V) S ✣ •

LAMENTATIONS איכה

1 אֵיכָ֣ה | יָשְׁבָ֣ה בָדָ֗ד הָעִיר֙ רַבָּ֣תִי עָ֔ם
הָיְתָ֖ה כְּאַלְמָנָ֑ה רַבָּ֣תִי בַגּוֹיִ֗ם
שָׂרָ֙תִי֙ בַּמְּדִינ֔וֹת הָיְתָ֖ה לָמַֽס׃ ס

2 בָּכ֨וֹ תִבְכֶּ֜ה בַּלַּ֗יְלָה וְדִמְעָתָהּ֙ עַ֣ל לֶֽחֱיָ֔הּ
אֵֽין־לָ֥הּ מְנַחֵ֖ם מִכָּל־אֹהֲבֶ֑יהָ
כָּל־רֵעֶ֙יהָ֙ בָּ֣גְדוּ בָ֔הּ הָ֥יוּ לָ֖הּ לְאֹיְבִֽים׃ ס

3 גָּֽלְתָ֨ה יְהוּדָ֤ה מֵעֹ֙נִי֙ וּמֵרֹ֣ב עֲבֹדָ֔ה
הִ֚יא יָשְׁבָ֣ה בַגּוֹיִ֔ם לֹ֥א מָצְאָ֖ה מָנ֑וֹחַ
כָּל־רֹדְפֶ֥יהָ הִשִּׂיג֖וּהָ בֵּ֥ין הַמְּצָרִֽים׃ ס

4 דַּרְכֵ֨י צִיּ֜וֹן אֲבֵל֗וֹת מִבְּלִי֙ בָּאֵ֣י מוֹעֵ֔ד
כָּל־שְׁעָרֶ֙יהָ֙ שֽׁוֹמֵמִ֔ין כֹּהֲנֶ֖יהָ נֶאֱנָחִ֑ים
בְּתוּלֹתֶ֥יהָ נּוּג֖וֹת וְהִ֥יא מַר־לָֽהּ׃ ס

5 הָי֨וּ צָרֶ֤יהָ לְרֹאשׁ֙ אֹיְבֶ֣יהָ שָׁל֔וּ
כִּֽי־יְהוָ֥ה הוֹגָ֖הּ עַ֣ל רֹב־פְּשָׁעֶ֑יהָ
עוֹלָלֶ֛יהָ הָלְכ֥וּ שְׁבִ֖י לִפְנֵי־צָֽר׃ ס

[1:1] בדד ח וסימנהון כל ימי אשר . ינחנו ואין עמו . וישכן ישראל . כי עיר בצורה .
קומו . ישבתי . ישבה :o

1:1 | אֵיכָ֣ה V S | prec preface G V^Mss T (exeg) • רַבָּ֣תִי M^L (err) | רַבָּתִי M^L34
M^Y • **2** וְדִמְעָתָהּ֙ G V | + vb S (T) (explic) | ודן[מעתה 4QLam • לֶֽחֱיָ֔הּ T | pl
noun G V S T^Mss (assim-usu) • **3** מֵעֹ֙נִי֙ V S T | + 3 f sg sfx G (assim-ctext) •
עֲבֹדָ֔ה V S T | + 3 f sg sfx G (assim-ctext) • הִ֚יא S T | > G V (transl) ✣ •
הַמְּצָרִֽים׃ V (S) T | τῶν θλιβόντων G (differ-gram) | τῶν θλιβόντων αὐτήν G^Mss
(differ-gram + explic) ✣ • **4** נּוּג֖וֹת V S T | ἀγόμεναι G (via √נהג) | διωκόμεναι
⟨σ'⟩ (via √נהג) | αἰχμάλωτοι ⟨σ'⟩* (via √נהג) ✣ • **5** הוֹגָ֖הּ G S T | locutus est super
eam V (via √הגה^I) | ἐφθέγξατο ⟨α'⟩ (via √הגה^I) | ἐπήγαγεν σ' (via √נהג) • שְׁבִ֖י
V | prec prep G S T (assim-usu) •

<table>
<tr><td>מבת . ל
קׄ</td><td style="text-align:right">6 וַיֵּצֵא מִן־בַּת־צִיּוֹן   כָּל־הֲדָרָהּ</td></tr>
<tr><td>דׄ</td><td style="text-align:right">הָיוּ שָׂרֶיהָ כְּאַיָּלִים   לֹא־מָצְאוּ מִרְעֶה</td></tr>
<tr><td>ל מלׄ</td><td style="text-align:right">וַיֵּלְכוּ בְלֹא־כֹחַ   לִפְנֵי רוֹדֵף׃ ס</td></tr>
<tr><td></td><td style="text-align:right">7 זָכְרָה יְרוּשָׁלַ͏ִם   יְמֵי עָנְיָהּ וּמְרוּדֶיהָ</td></tr>
<tr><td>ל וכתׄ</td><td style="text-align:right">כֹּל מַחֲמֻדֶיהָ   אֲשֶׁר הָיוּ מִימֵי קֶדֶם</td></tr>
<tr><td>וׄ</td><td style="text-align:right">בִּנְפֹל עַמָּהּ בְּיַד־צָר   וְאֵין עוֹזֵר לָהּ</td></tr>
<tr><td>ל וחסׄ</td><td style="text-align:right">רָאוּהָ צָרִים   שָׂחֲקוּ עַל מִשְׁבַּתֶּהָ׃ ס</td></tr>
<tr><td>ל . דׄ</td><td style="text-align:right">8 חֵטְא חָטְאָה יְרוּשָׁלַ͏ִם   עַל־כֵּן לְנִידָה הָיָתָה</td></tr>
<tr><td>ל ומלׄ</td><td style="text-align:right">כָּל־מְכַבְּדֶיהָ הִזִּילוּהָ   כִּי־רָאוּ עֶרְוָתָהּ</td></tr>
<tr><td>בׄ</td><td style="text-align:right">גַּם־הִיא נֶאֶנְחָה   וַתָּשָׁב אָחוֹר׃ ס</td></tr>
<tr><td>ל ומלׄ</td><td style="text-align:right">9 טֻמְאָתָהּ בְּשׁוּלֶיהָ   לֹא זָכְרָה אַחֲרִיתָהּ</td></tr>
</table>

[6] ח מילין כת תרתין וקר חדה חדה וסימנהון כטוב . מבנימין . למרבה . מהמערה . מאתו . בהרבותיהם . מבת . כיעינים :ס [8] היתה דׄ וסימנהֹ אם לא כאשר דמיתי . ומלחמה לא היתה . ציון . על כן לנידה :ס

6 וַיֵּצֵא GMss V S T | καὶ ἐξήρθη G (theol) ✛ • | מן בת Mket | מבת
Mqere 4QLam (differ-orth) | G V S T (indet) ‖ pref בַּת מִן Mket ✛ • | לֹא־ G V (S)
(T) | לוֹא לֹא 4QLam (ditt) • מָצְאוּ מִרְעֶה G V S T | מצא ומרעה 4QLam (differ-
div) | בְלֹא־ G S | בלי 4QLam (differ) | V T (indet) • **7** זָכְרָה יְרוּשָׁלַ͏ִם G V S T
(assim-ctext) | זכרה יהוה 4QLam ‖ pref זָכְרָה יְהוָה (origin) ✛ • | יְמֵי עָנְיָהּ
וּמְרוּדֶיהָ G V S (T) (ampl) | > 4QLam ‖ pref omit 4QLam ✛ • | יְמֵי עָנְיָהּ וּמְרוּדֶיהָ
וּמְרוּדֶיהָ | καὶ ἀπωσμῶν αὐτῆς G (lib) | καὶ ἀποστάσεως [αὐτῆς] ⟨α'⟩ V (T)
(via √מרד) | ܡܣܪܕܘܬܗ S (transcr) • כֹּל to קֶדֶם ✛ • מַחֲמֻדֶיהָ G V S T (crrp) |
מכאובנו 4QLam (facil) ‖ pref מְרוּדֶיהָ (origin) ✛ • לָהּ G S T | > 4QLam V •
רָאוּהָ V S T | > 4QLam | ἰδόντες G • צָרִים V T | צריה 4QLam G S (assim-
ctext) ✛ • עַל G V S T | ל[...] עַל 4QLam (ampl) ✛ • מִשְׁבַּתֶּהָ: σ' (T) |
κατοικεσίᾳ αὐτῆς G (err-lex via ישׁב) | καθέδρᾳ [αὐτῆς] ⟨α'⟩ (err-lex via √ישׁב)
sabbata eius V (elus) | משבריה 4QLam (S) (err-graph) ✛ • **8** חֵטְא G V S T |
חטוא 4QLam (assim-usu) • לְנִידָה לנוד 4QLam G V T | ܢܕܐ S (via
לְנִדָה(?) | εἰς κεχωρισμένην ⟨α'⟩ | σίκχος ἀνάστατον σ' (dbl) ✛ • הִזִּילוּהָ G V
S T | > sfx 4QLam •

וַתֵּרֶד פְּלָאִים   אֵין מְנַחֵם לָהּ   ל

רְאֵה יְהוָה אֶת־עָנְיִי   כִּי הִגְדִּיל אוֹיֵב׃   ס

10 יָדוֹ פָּרַשׂ צָר   עַל כָּל־מַחֲמַדֶּיהָ   ב

כִּי־רָאֲתָה גוֹיִם   בָּאוּ מִקְדָּשָׁהּ   ל

אֲשֶׁר צִוִּיתָה   לֹא־יָבֹאוּ בַקָּהָל לָךְ׃   ד דגש   ס

11 כָּל־עַמָּהּ נֶאֱנָחִים   מְבַקְשִׁים לֶחֶם

נָתְנוּ מַחֲמוֹדֵּיהֶם בְּאֹכֶל   לְהָשִׁיב נָפֶשׁ   יתיר ו

רְאֵה יְהוָה וְהַבִּיטָה   כִּי הָיִיתִי זוֹלֵלָה׃   ל   ס

12 לוֹא אֲלֵיכֶם כָּל־עֹבְרֵי דֶרֶךְ   הַבִּיטוּ וּרְאוּ   לה מל

אִם־יֵשׁ מַכְאוֹב כְּמַכְאֹבִי   אֲשֶׁר עוֹלַל לִי   ג חס . ל

אֲשֶׁר הוֹגָה יְהוָה   בְּיוֹם חֲרוֹן אַפּוֹ׃   ג   ס

13 מִמָּרוֹם שָׁלַח־אֵשׁ בְּעַצְמֹתַי   וַיִּרְדֶּנָּה   ה חס . ל

[10] בקהל ד דגשין וסימנ אשר לא עלה עליה . כי רבת בקהל . קמתי . לא יבאו בקהל :ס [13] עצמתי ה חס בליש וסימנהון והעליתם . וחבירו . הניחו את עצמתיכם . עצר בעצמׂ . ממרום :ס

9 וַתֵּרֶד ⟨α'⟩ S ǀ καὶ κατεβίβασεν G (via וַתּוֹרֶד) ǀ καὶ κατήχθη ⟨σ'⟩ V (via וַתֵּרֶד ǀ ܐܬܒܚܬ S) ǀ ונחתת ונפלת T (ampl) ✣ • פְּלָאִים [פ]לאות 4QLam (assim-usu) ǀ פְּלָאִים G V ǀ ܐܬܕ... ǀ אֵין G V ǀ ואין 4QLam S T (facil-styl) • עָנְיִי G V S T ǀ 3 f sg sfx La Bo (assim-ctext) • **10** יָדוֹ G V T ǀ pl G^Mss S (assim-usu) • v 10 בַקָּהָל to v 11 נָתְנוּ G V S (T) ǀ > 4QLam (homtel?) ǀ בקהל] 3QLam • v 10 וְהוּת פרישן T (lib) • אֵין G V ǀ ואין 4QLam S T (facil-styl) • עָנְיִי G V S T • **11** מַחֲמוֹדֵּיהֶם σ' La T^Mss ǀ מחמדיה 4QLam G (assim-v 10) ǀ מְבַקְשִׁים ✣ • נָפֶשׁ G V S ǀ + 3 f sg sfx 4QLam (explic) ǀ + 3 m pl sfx T (explic) ✣ • זוֹלֵלָה׃ G S T ǀ זולל 4QLam (exeg) ǀ V (indet) ✣ • **12** לוֹא אֲלֵיכֶם G σ' S ǀ לוא אליכי 4QLam (interp?) ǀ ὦ ὑμᾶς ⟨σ'⟩ V (differ-vocal) ǀ > G^L ǀ אשבעית לכון T (explic via לוא) ǀ οἳ πρὸς ὑμᾶς G^Mss (elus) ✣ • אֲשֶׁר עוֹלַל לִי σ' T Bo ǀ אשר עוללו לי 4QLam (facil-gram) ǀ > לִי G (implic) ǀ ὃ ἐπεφύλλισέ(ν) μοι G^O G^L V (differ-vocal: עוֹלֵל) (interp) ǀ + 1 sg sfx G S T (explic) ǀ אשר הוגירני י[הוה ǀ אֲשֶׁר הוֹגָה יְהוָה 4QLam ǀ ܢܓܕ ... ܥܠ S (explic) ✣ • ἀνεκάλεσε κύριος σ' V (via √הגה) ǀ φθεγξάμενος ἐν ἐμοὶ ἐταπείνωσέ με κύριος G^Mss (dbl) ǀ אשר הוֹגָה] 3QLam (insuf) ✣ • חֲרוֹן אַפּוֹ ǀ חרו[נו 4QLam G^Ms ✣ • **13** וַיִּרְדֶּנָּה ⟨σ'⟩ ⟨⟨α'⟩⟩ (V) (T) ǀ κατήγαγεν αὐτὸ G ǀ ויורידני 4QLam S (facil) ‖ pref יוֹרְדֶנָּה see G, cf 4QLam S ✣ •

פָּרַשׂ רֶשֶׁת לְרַגְלַי֙   הֱשִׁיבַ֣נִי אָח֔וֹר

ג . ב   נְתָנַ֨נִי֙ שֹֽׁמֵמָ֔ה   כָּל־הַיּ֖וֹם דָּוָֽה׃ ס

ל . ל   14   נִשְׂקַד֩ עֹ֨ל פְּשָׁעַ֜י   בְּיָד֗וֹ יִשְׂתָּֽרְג֛וּ

עָל֥וּ עַל־צַוָּארִ֖י   הִכְשִׁ֣יל כֹּחִ֑י

יד כת כן בסיפֿ   נְתָנַ֣נִי אֲדֹנָ֔י   בִּידֵ֖י לֹא־אוּכַ֥ל קֽוּם׃ ס

ב . יד כת בסיפֿ   15   סִלָּ֣ה כָל־אַבִּירַ֣י ׀   אֲדֹנָי֮ בְּקִרְבִּי֒

קָרָ֥א עָלַ֛י מוֹעֵ֖ד   לִשְׁבֹּ֣ר בַּחוּרָ֑י

גַּ֚ת דָּרַ֣ךְ אֲדֹנָ֔י   לִבְתוּלַ֖ת בַּת־יְהוּדָֽה׃ ס

ל ומל . ל   16   עַל־אֵ֣לֶּה ׀ אֲנִ֣י בוֹכִיָּ֗ה   עֵינִ֣י ׀ עֵינִי֮ יֹ֣רְדָה מַּ֒יִם֒

כִּֽי־רָחַ֥ק מִמֶּ֛נִּי מְנַחֵ֖ם   מֵשִׁ֣יב נַפְשִׁ֑י

ל   הָי֤וּ בָנַי֙ שֽׁוֹמֵמִ֔ים   כִּ֥י גָבַ֖ר אוֹיֵֽב׃ ס

שוממה ג ב חס וחד מל וסימנה ותשב תמר ושממה . כי רבים בני שוממה . נתני
שוממה ס: דוה ג וסימנה ואשה אשר ישכב את אשה . תזרם כמו . כל היום דוה ס:

13 הֱשִׁיבַ֣נִי G V S T | חשיבני 4QLam (err-graph) ● שֹֽׁמֵמָ֔ה G V (S) T | שומם 4QLam
(exeg) ‖ → ✤ v 11 • דָּוָֽה׃ G V (S) T | דוןי 4QLam (exeg) ‖ → ✤ v 11 • זֹלְלָה:
KR) | ἐγρηγόρησεν GᴸV (via √שקד) | ܘܒܚܰܟ̈ S (via √שקד) | נקשרה 4QLam (metath, crrp) | ἐγρηγορήθη G (via שקד, see
KR) | ἐγρηγόρησεν GᴸV (via √שקד) | ܘܒܚܰܟ̈ S (via √שקד) | אתיקר T* • ✤ • עֹ֨ל V T* | על 4QLam G (differ-vocal: עַל) | ܚܠ S (lib via עַל) • בְּיָד֗וֹ 4QLam
V T | ἐν χερσί μου G (exeg) | ܒ̈ܐܝܕܰܘܗܝ S (assim-usu) • יִשְׂתָּֽרְג֛וּ G V S (T) | sg
4QLam (err-synt) | συνέπλεξέ(ν) με Gᴸ (err-graph?) ○ יִשְׂתָּֽרְג֛וּ G V S | prec cj
4QLam T (err-synt) • עָל֥וּ G V T | עולו 4QLam σ' (differ-vocal) | ܘܣܠܩܘ S
(differ-vocal) | ἐβάρυνε(ν) τὸν ζυγὸν αὐτοῦ Gᴸ (dbl) ✤ • אֲדֹנָ֔י | יהוה 4QLam |
G V S T (indet) • בִּידֵ֖י Sᴹˢˢ | ביד 4QLam V S T (assim-usu) | ἐν χερσί μου G
(differ-vocal) • קֽוּם׃ | לקום 4QLam T (assim-usu) | G V S (indet) • 15 | אַבִּירַ֣י
G V S T | אבידי 4QLam (err-graph) • אֲדֹנָ֔י² | יהוה 4QLam | G V S T (indet) •
16 vv 16-17 G V S T | v 16 (ע) follows v 17 (פ) 4QLam ✤ • אֲנִ֣י בוֹכִיָּ֗ה G V S
T | בכו 4QLam (facil-styl) • עֵינִ֣י | עֵינִי֮ | ὁ ὀφθαλμός μου G V (om, e.g. KR) |
עיני, i.e., pl 4QLam Gᴹˢˢ (S) (facil) | ותרתית עיני T (paraphr) | ὁ ὀφθαλμός μου
ἀδιαλείπτως ⟨σ'⟩ (interp) ✤ • מַּ֒יִם G V S T | דמעתי 4QLam (Gᴹˢ) (⟨σ'⟩)
(explic) | a fletu La (exeg) • נַפְשִׁ֑י G V S T | > sfx 4QLam (om) •

פֵּרְשָׂ֨ה צִיּ֜וֹן בְּיָדֶ֗יהָ   אֵ֤ין מְנַחֵם֙ לָ֔הּ   17   ז

צִוָּ֧ה יְהוָ֛ה לְיַעֲקֹ֖ב   סְבִיבָ֣יו צָרָ֑יו

הָיְתָ֧ה יְרוּשָׁלִַ֛ם   לְנִדָּ֖ה בֵּינֵיהֶֽם׃   ס

צַדִּ֥יק ה֛וּא יְהוָ֖ה   כִּ֣י פִ֣יהוּ מָרִ֑יתִי   18   כב . ב מנהון בס

שִׁמְעוּ־נָ֣א כָל־הָֽעַמִּים֮   וּרְאוּ֮ מַכְאֹבִי֒   נ העמים   ק

בְּתוּלֹתַ֥י וּבַחוּרַ֖י   הָלְכ֥וּ בַשֶּֽׁבִי׃   ס

קָרָ֤אתִי לַֽמְאַהֲבַי֙   הֵ֣מָּה רִמּ֔וּנִי   19   ל . ל

כֹּהֲנַ֥י וּזְקֵנַ֖י   בָּעִ֣יר גָּוָ֑עוּ   ל . ל

כִּֽי־בִקְשׁ֥וּ אֹ֙כֶל֙ לָ֔מוֹ   וְיָשִׁ֖יבוּ אֶת־נַפְשָֽׁם׃   ס   ז

רְאֵ֨ה יְהוָ֤ה כִּֽי־צַר־לִי֙   מֵעַ֣י חֳמַרְמָ֔רוּ   20   ל

נֶהְפַּ֤ךְ לִבִּי֙ בְּקִרְבִּ֔י   כִּ֥י מָר֖וֹ מָרִ֑יתִי   ל . ב ואנכי

מִח֥וּץ שִׁכְּלָה־חֶ֖רֶב   בַּבַּ֥יִת כַּמָּֽוֶת׃   ס

שָׁמְע֞וּ כִּ֧י נֶאֱנָחָ֣ה אָ֗נִי   אֵ֤ין מְנַחֵם֙ לִ֔י   21   ג ראש פסוק

כָּל־אֹ֨יְבַ֜י שָׁמְע֤וּ רָֽעָתִי֙ שָׂ֔שׂוּ   כִּ֥י אַתָּ֖ה עָשִׂ֑יתָ   ל

הֵבֵ֛אתָ יוֹם־קָרָ֖אתָ   וְיִֽהְי֥וּ כָמֽוֹנִי׃   ס   יא . ל חס

---

[17] בידיה ג וסימנה֜ וכל אשה חכמת לב . ואולת בידיה תהרסנו . פרשה ציון
בידיה ‖ ס: [21] שמעו ג ראש פסוק גוים ירגזון . גוים קלונך . כי נאנחה אני ‖ ס:

17 לָ֔הּ G V S T | foll + 4QLam (ampl) ✧ • צִוָּ֧ה G V
S T (theol) | צפה 4QLam ‖ pref צִוָּ֧ה 4QLam ✧ • יְהוָ֛ה T | אדוני 4QLam | G V
S (indet) • לְנִדָּ֖ה בֵּינֵיהֶֽם: G V S | ציון 4QLam (assim-v17a) • יְרוּשָׁלִַ֛ם G V S
(T) | לנדוח בניהמה 4QLam (err-graph) • **18** יְהוָ֖ה | אֲדוני 4QLam | G V S T
(indet) • מָרִ֑יתִי T | παρεπίκρανα G S (via √מרר) | ad iracundiam provocavi V
(lib) • עַמִּים֮ | עמים M^{ket} G^{Ms} G^O G^L ‖ הָֽעַמִּים֮ M^{qere} G S T | V (indet) •
19 נַפְשָֽׁם: V T | + καὶ οὐχ εὗρον G S (gloss) • **20** חֳמַרְמָ֔רוּ G V S T | + a fletu
meo La (assim-2:11) • מָרִ֑יתִי T | παραπικραίνουσα παραπίκρανα G (V) S
(via √מרר) • בַּבַּ֥יִת כַּמָּֽוֶת: ✧ • **21** שָׁמְע֞וּ V | ἀκούσατε δή G (differ-vocal) | ܐܫܬܡܥ
S (assim-v 20) | + עממיא T (explic) • הֵבֵ֛אתָ G V | + עלי T (explic) | ܐܬܐ S
(assim-ctext) • יוֹם־קָרָ֖אתָ S | ἡμέραν, ἐκάλεσας καιρόν G (err-synt + assim-v
15b) | diem consolationis V (exeg) | יום פורענות ערעת עלי מערע לצדותני T
(ampl) •

תָּבֹא כָל־רָעָתָם לְפָנֶיךָ   וְעוֹלֵל לָמוֹ 22

כַּאֲשֶׁר עוֹלַלְתָּ לִי   עַל   כָּל־פְּשָׁעָי

כִּי־רַבּוֹת אַנְחֹתַי   וְלִבִּי דַוָּי: פ

אֵיכָה יָעִיב בְּאַפּוֹ | אֲדֹנָי אֶת־בַּת־צִיּוֹן 2

הִשְׁלִיךְ מִשָּׁמַיִם אֶרֶץ   תִּפְאֶרֶת יִשְׂרָאֵל

וְלֹא־זָכַר הֲדֹם־רַגְלָיו   בְּיוֹם אַפּוֹ: ס

בִּלַּע אֲדֹנָי לֹא חָמַל   אֵת כָּל־נְאוֹת יַעֲקֹב 2

הָרַס בְּעֶבְרָתוֹ   מִבְצְרֵי בַת־יְהוּדָה

הִגִּיעַ לָאָרֶץ   חִלֵּל מַמְלָכָה וְשָׂרֶיהָ: ס

גָּדַע בָּחֳרִי אַף   כֹּל קֶרֶן יִשְׂרָאֵל 3

הֵשִׁיב אָחוֹר יְמִינוֹ   מִפְּנֵי אוֹיֵב

וַיִּבְעַר בְּיַעֲקֹב כְּאֵשׁ לֶהָבָה   אָכְלָה סָבִיב: ס

דָּרַךְ קַשְׁתּוֹ כְּאוֹיֵב   נִצָּב יְמִינוֹ כְּצָר 4

וַיַּהֲרֹג כֹּל   מַחֲמַדֵּי־עָיִן

בְּאֹהֶל בַּת־צִיּוֹן   שָׁפַךְ כָּאֵשׁ חֲמָתוֹ: ס

הָיָה אֲדֹנָי | כְּאוֹיֵב   בִּלַּע יִשְׂרָאֵל 5

בִּלַּע כָּל־אַרְמְנוֹתֶיהָ   שִׁחֵת מִבְצָרָיו

וַיֶּרֶב בְּבַת־יְהוּדָה   תַּאֲנִיָּה וַאֲנִיָּה: ס

Masora (left margin, top to bottom):

ל

ל וחס . ג

זז פסוק . יד
כת כן בסיפֿ

ג

ב ראֹ פסוק
המות . ולֹא
קֿ

ל

ל

ל

ב מטעֹ . ל

ב והמתי

ב . ב

Masora (bottom):

[2:1] ולֹא זכר ג וסימנה שר המשקים . יואש המלך . הדם רגליו ביום אפו :o

[5] תאניה ואניה ב והיתה תאניה ואניה . וירב בבת יהודה :o

Apparatus:

22 לְ G^Mss V S T | > G (implic?) • **2:1** אַפּוֹ G V | ὀργῆς θυμοῦ αὐτοῦ G^Mss S T (assim-1:12) • **2** לֹא | לֹא, M^ket G | וְלֹא M^qere V S T (spont, e.g. KR) ‖ pref חִלֵּל מַמְלָכָה לֹא M^ket G ÷ • בַת־ G S | *virginis* V (cf 1:15) | בֵית T (assim-usu) • ÷ • V T | ἐβεβήλωσε βασιλέα αὐτῆς G (explic) | ܡܠܟܬܗ ܚܠܠܬ S (differ-div) ÷ • מַמְלָכָה V T | βασιλέα αὐτῆς G (exeg) | pl G^Ms G^L S (exeg, assim-ctxt) ÷ • **3** בָּחֳרִי אַף M^L (err) | בָּחֳרִי־אַף M^L34 M^Y • אַף V T^Mss | + 3 m sg sfx G V^Mss S T (assim-ctext) • אָכְלָה סָבִיב: V T | καὶ κατέφαγε πάντα τὰ κύκλῳ G (ditt) | ܟܠܗܘܢ ܕܚܕܪܝܗ̇ S (err-graph, syr) ÷ • **4** נִצָּב יְמִינוֹ ÷ • עָיִן V T | ὀφθαλμῶν μου G • ÷ • **5** אַרְמְנוֹתֶיהָ S ܣܚܢ̈ | G

6 וַיַּחְמֹס כַּגַּן שֻׂכּוֹ   שִׁחֵת מוֹעֲדוֹ   ל . ל כת שׂ

שִׁכַּח יְהוָה | בְּצִיּוֹן   מוֹעֵד וְשַׁבָּת   ב חס

וַיִּנְאַץ בְּזַעַם־אַפּוֹ   מֶלֶךְ וְכֹהֵן: ס   ב חד ראש פסו וחד סוף פסוק

7 זָנַח אֲדֹנָי | מִזְבְּחוֹ   נִאֵר מִקְדָּשׁוֹ

הִסְגִּיר בְּיַד־אוֹיֵב   חוֹמֹת אַרְמְנוֹתֶיהָ   ח

קוֹל נָתְנוּ בְּבֵית־יְהוָה   כְּיוֹם מוֹעֵד: ס   לט . יא

8 חָשַׁב יְהוָה | לְהַשְׁחִית   חוֹמַת בַּת־צִיּוֹן

נָטָה קָו   לֹא־הֵשִׁיב יָדוֹ מִבַּלֵּעַ   ל

וַיַּאֲבֶל־חֵל וְחוֹמָה   יַחְדָּו אֻמְלָלוּ: ס   ל

9 טָבְעוּ בָאָרֶץ שְׁעָרֶיהָ   אִבַּד וְשִׁבַּר בְּרִיחֶיהָ   ב ורא פסוק . ב מל

מַלְכָּהּ וְשָׂרֶיהָ בַגּוֹיִם   אֵין תּוֹרָה

גַּם־נְבִיאֶיהָ   לֹא־מָצְאוּ חָזוֹן מֵיְהוָה: ס   ד

10 יֵשְׁבוּ לָאָרֶץ יִדְּמוּ   זִקְנֵי בַת־צִיּוֹן   כ

הֶעֱלוּ עָפָר עַל־רֹאשָׁם   חָגְרוּ שַׂקִּים

[6] מעדו ג חס בליש וסימנהון וידבר משה את מעדי יהוה . במעד שנת השמטה . ויחמס כגן שכו: וכול במעדו דכותה ב מ ב מל ויעשו בני ישראל . את קרבני לחמי o:
[7] מזבחו ג וסימנהון ויקרא לו ביום ההוא ירבעל . אם אלהים הוא . זנח אדני מזבחו o:

6 וַיַּחְמֹס כַּגַּן | καὶ διεπέτασεν ὡς ἄμπελον G* (exeg) ✣ • מֶלֶךְ וְכֹהֵן: V S T* | + καὶ ἄρχοντα G (ampl) | **7** נִאֵר • מלכא וכהנא רבא T (interp) | ἀπετίναξεν G (via √נער?ᴵᴵ) | κατηράσατο ⟨α'⟩ ⟨⟨σ'⟩⟩ V (via √ארר?) | ܐܣ S (via √נאץ?) | בעט T (lib-seman) • הִסְגִּיר σ' V (S) T | συνέτριψεν G (interp) | συνέκλεισεν ⟨α'⟩ (interp) ✣ • חוֹמֹת V S T | sg G (differ-vocal, assim-2:8) • **8** חָשַׁב Gᴹˢˢ V S T | καὶ ἐπέστρεψε G (err-graph) ✣ • קָו G S | + 3 m sg sfx V (err-phonol) | משקוליתהא T (lib) • וַיַּאֲבֶל־ S | καὶ ἐπένθησε G V T (differ-vocal) | ἐπένθησαν Gᴸ (transl) ✣ • חֵל G V T | ἐπὶ τῷ περιβόλῳ ⟨σ'⟩ (explic) | δυνάμεις Gᴸ (S) (err-lex) ✣ • אֻמְלָלוּ: **9** אִבַּד וְשִׁבַּר G V T | pl S (exeg) ✣ • לֹא־מָצְאוּ V S T | οὐκ εἶδον G (lib) • **10** יֵשְׁבוּ | ἐκάθισαν G V S (assim-ctext) | יִדְּמוּ | ἐσιώπησαν G V (S) (assim-ctext) | ישבו → ✣ T || ותשתקין T ✣ • יִדְּמוּ יתבין T ✣ • עַל־רֹאשָׁם G | capita sua V S T (facil-styl) •

הוֹרִ֧ידוּ לָאָ֣רֶץ רֹאשָׁ֗ן   ס   בְּתוּלֹ֖ת יְרוּשָׁלִָֽם׃   *ל . ב בסיפֿ*

11 כָּל֨וּ בַדְּמָע֤וֹת עֵינַי֙   חֳמַרְמְר֣וּ מֵעַ֔י   *ל דגש*

נִשְׁפַּ֤ךְ לָאָ֙רֶץ֙ כְּבֵדִ֔י   עַל־שֶׁ֖בֶר בַּת־עַמִּ֑י   *ל*

בֵּֽעָטֵ֤ף עוֹלֵל֙ וְיוֹנֵ֔ק   בִּרְחֹב֖וֹת קִרְיָֽה׃   ס   *ל*

12 לְאִמֹּתָם֙ יֹֽאמְר֔וּ   אַיֵּ֖ה דָּגָ֣ן וָיָ֑יִן   *ל וחד לְאָמֹתם . ז̇*

בְּהִֽתְעַטְּפָ֤ם כֶּֽחָלָל֙   בִּרְחֹב֣וֹת עִ֔יר   *ל*

בְּהִשְׁתַּפֵּ֣ךְ נַפְשָׁ֔ם   אֶל־חֵ֖יק אִמֹּתָֽם׃   ס   *ל*

13 מָֽה־אֲעִידֵ֞ךְ מָ֣ה אֲדַמֶּה־לָּ֗ךְ   הַבַּת֙ יְר֣וּשָׁלִַ֔ם

מָ֤ה אַשְׁוֶה־לָּךְ֙ וַאֲנַֽחֲמֵ֔ךְ   בְּתוּלַ֖ת בַּת־צִיּ֑וֹן

כִּֽי־גָד֥וֹל כַּיָּ֛ם שִׁבְרֵ֖ךְ   מִ֥י יִרְפָּא־לָֽךְ׃   ס   *ד̇*

14 נְבִיאַ֗יִךְ חָ֤זוּ לָךְ֙   שָׁ֣וְא וְתָפֵ֔ל   *כול מל*

וְלֹֽא־גִלּ֥וּ עַל־עֲוֺנֵ֖ךְ   לְהָשִׁ֣יב שביתך   *שבותך ק*

וַיֶּֽחֱזוּ לָ֔ךְ   מַשְׂא֥וֹת שָׁ֖וְא וּמַדּוּחִֽים׃   ס   *ב̇ . ב . ל ומל*

15 סָפְק֨וּ עָלַ֤יִךְ כַּפַּ֙יִם֙   כָּל־עֹ֣בְרֵי דֶ֔רֶךְ

שָֽׁרְקוּ֙ וַיָּנִ֣עוּ רֹאשָׁ֔ם   עַל־בַּ֖ת יְרוּשָׁלִָ֑ם   *ל חס*

הֲזֹ֣את הָעִ֗יר שֶׁיֹּֽאמְרוּ֙ כְּלִ֣ילַת יֹ֔פִי   מָשׂ֖וֹשׂ לְכָל־הָאָֽרֶץ׃   ס   *ה̇ . כול מל . ד̇*

---

[14] ויחזו ב̇ וסימ̇ את האלהים . לך משאות :ס [15] ג̇ חס בליש וינעם במדבר . והנעותי בכל . וינעו :ס משוש ד̇ וסימנהון כי על בתי משוש . שישו אתה . גילה ועמה . לכל הארץ :ס

---

10 הוֹרִידוּ to יְרוּשָׁלִָם׃ V (S) T^{Mss} | κατήγαγον εἰς γῆν ἀρχηγοὺς παρθένους Ἰερουσαλήμ G (err-synt) | κατήγαγον εἰς γῆν ἀρχηγοὺς παρθένου θυγατρὸς Ἰερουσαλήμ G^L (err-synt + assim-ctxt) | בתולתא דבירשלם T (homtel, aram) ✥ • **11** כְּבֵדִי V T | ἡ δόξα μου G S (differ-vocal: כְּבֹדִי) • **12** דָּגָן וָיָיִן G V T | + נַפְשָׁם T^{Mss} | ψυχὰς αὐτῶν G V S T (facil-styl) • **13** וַאֲנַחֲמֵךְ to מָה^3 G ⟨σ'⟩ V S T | τίς σώσει σε καὶ παρακαλέσει σε G^{Mss} (crrp, gk) ✥ • כַּיָּם V S (T) | ποτήριον G (err-graph: כוס, e.g. KR) • **14** שְׁבוּתֵךְ M^{ket} G | שְׁבִיתֵךְ M^{qere} (V) (T) | S (indet) ✥ • **15** כַּפַּיִם G V | + 3 m pl sfx S T (lib) • רֹאשָׁם G V | pl G^{Ms} S T (facil-styl) • הֲזֹאת G V | prec ܡ S (T) • שֶׁיֹּאמְרוּ to הָאָרֶץ׃ ✥ • כְּלִילַת יֹפִי ⟨α'⟩ V S T | στέφανος δόξης G (err-lex) ✥ •

16 פָּצוּ עָלַיִךְ פִּיהֶם֙ כָּל־אֹ֣יְבַ֔יִךְ

ל . ל   שָֽׁרְקוּ֙ וַיַּֽחַרְקוּ־שֵׁ֔ן אָֽמְר֖וּ בִּלָּ֑עְנוּ

ל . ל   אַ֣ךְ זֶ֧ה הַיּ֛וֹם שֶׁקִּוִּינֻ֖הוּ מָצָ֥אנוּ רָאִֽינוּ׃   ס

ב ראש פסוק .
ל . ל   17 עָשָׂ֨ה יְהוָ֜ה אֲשֶׁ֣ר זָמָ֗ם בִּצַּ֤ע אֶמְרָתוֹ֙

אֲשֶׁ֣ר צִוָּ֣ה מִֽימֵי־קֶ֔דֶם הָרַ֖ס וְלֹ֣א חָמָ֑ל

ל וחד ושמח   וַיְשַׂמַּ֤ח עָלַ֙יִךְ֙ אוֹיֵ֔ב הֵרִ֖ים קֶ֥רֶן צָרָֽיִךְ׃   ס

ב אל המלך   18 צָעַ֥ק לִבָּ֖ם אֶל־אֲדֹנָ֑י חוֹמַ֣ת בַּת־צִיּ֗וֹן

ל בטע   הוֹרִ֤ידִי כַנַּ֙חַל֙ דִּמְעָ֔ה יוֹמָ֖ם וָלַ֑יְלָה

ל בסיפֿ מוג
ד ראש פסוֿ .
ל . בלילה
ק ן   אַל־תִּתְּנִ֤י פוּגַת֙ לָ֔ךְ אַל־תִּדֹּ֖ם בַּת־עֵינֵֽךְ׃   ס

ל . ל . יד כת כן   19 ק֣וּמִי ׀ רֹ֤נִּי בַלַּ֙יְלָ֙ה֙ לְרֹאשׁ֙ אַשְׁמֻר֔וֹת

שִׁפְכִ֤י כַמַּ֙יִם֙ לִבֵּ֔ךְ נֹ֖כַח פְּנֵ֣י אֲדֹנָ֑י

ח . ב   שְׂאִ֧י אֵלָ֣יו כַּפַּ֗יִךְ עַל־נֶ֙פֶשׁ֙ עֽוֹלָלַ֔יִךְ

הָעֲטוּפִ֥ים בְּרָעָ֖ב בְּרֹ֥אשׁ כָּל־חוּצֽוֹת׃   ס

כול חס   20 רְאֵ֤ה יְהוָה֙ וְֽהַבִּ֔יטָה לְמִ֖י עוֹלַ֣לְתָּ כֹּ֑ה

---

[17] עשה ב ראש פסוק עשה ירח . עשה יהוה :o [19] קומי ד ראש פסוק אורי .
ובאי . ודושי . רני :o

---

16 vv 16-17 G V T | v 16 (פ) follows v 17 (ע) G^L S (spont, e.g. KR) ⟐ • בִּלָּֽעְנוּ
V T | + 3 f sg sfx G S (explic) • רָאִֽינוּ׃ G
V T | prec cj ⟨σ'⟩ S | + 3 f sg sfx La (explic) | prec cj + foll 3 f sg sfx G^L •
17 אֶמְרָתוֹ֙ La V S T | ῥήματα αὐτοῦ G (differ-vocal) • אוֹיֵ֔ב G V T^U | pl S
(harm-styl) | pl + 2 f sg sfx T (harm-styl) • צָרָֽיִךְ׃ V S T | sg G (harm-styl) •
18 צָעַ֥ק לִבָּ֖ם ⟐ • אֲדֹנָ֑י M^L | יְהוָ֑ה M^{L34} M^Y | G V S T (indet) • חוֹמַ֣ת T | pl G
(V) (S) (differ-vocal) ⟐ • בַּת־צִיּ֗וֹן V S T (assim-ctext) | > בַּת G ‖ pref *omit* בַּת
see G ⟐ • הוֹרִ֤ידִי V S T | καταγάγετε G (via הוֹרִידוּ) ⟐ • אַל־2 G | prec cj V S
T (spont, e.g. KR) • **19** בַלַּ֙יְלָ֙ה֙ | בליל M^{ket} | בַלַּיְלָה M^{qere} | G V S T (indet) •
לְרֹאשׁ֙ La V S T | pl G (lib?) ⟐ • אַשְׁמֻר֔וֹת V | φυλακῆς σου G (lib?) | sg S T
(lib) ⟐ • אֲדֹנָ֑י M^L | יְהוָ֑ה M^{L34} M^Y | G V S T (indet) • אֵלָ֣יו G V S T | *ad
Dominum* La (explic) • חוּצֽוֹת׃ to הָעֲטוּפִ֥ים ⟐ •

אִם־תֹּאכַ֨לְנָה נָשִׁ֤ים פִּרְיָם֙   עֹלֲלֵ֣י טִפֻּחִ֔ים   כול חס

אִם־יֵהָרֵ֛ג בְּמִקְדַּ֥שׁ אֲדֹנָ֖י   כֹּהֵ֥ן וְנָבִֽיא׃ ס   ז בלשן נביאיה

21 שָׁכְב֨וּ לָאָ֤רֶץ חוּצוֹת֙   נַ֣עַר וְזָקֵ֔ן

בְּתוּלֹתַ֥י וּבַחוּרַ֖י   נָפְל֣וּ בֶחָ֑רֶב

הָרַ֙גְתָּ֙ בְּי֣וֹם אַפֶּ֔ךָ   טָבַ֖חְתָּ לֹ֥א חָמָֽלְתָּ׃ ס

22 תִּקְרָא֩ כְי֨וֹם מוֹעֵ֤ד   מְגוּרַי֙ מִסָּבִ֔יב   יֹ֟א

וְלֹ֥א הָיָ֛ה בְּי֥וֹם אַף־יְהוָ֖ה   פָּלִ֣יט וְשָׂרִ֑יד   כֹה. ב.

אֲשֶׁר־טִפַּ֥חְתִּי וְרִבִּ֖יתִי   אֹיְבִ֥י כִלָּֽם׃ פ   ל.ב.י.

3 אֲנִ֤י הַגֶּ֙בֶר֙ רָאָ֣ה עֳנִ֔י   בְּשֵׁ֖בֶט עֶבְרָתֽוֹ׃   ל.ו.

2 אוֹתִ֥י נָהַ֛ג וַיֹּלַ֖ךְ   חֹ֥שֶׁךְ וְלֹא־אֽוֹר׃   ל מל בס. ל.

3 אַ֣ךְ בִּ֥י יָשֻׁ֛ב יַהֲפֹ֥ךְ יָד֖וֹ   כָּל־הַיּֽוֹם׃ ס   ב חס

4 בִּלָּ֤ה בְשָׂרִי֙ וְעוֹרִ֔י   שִׁבַּ֖ר עַצְמוֹתָֽי׃

5 בָּנָ֥ה עָלַ֛י וַיַּקַּ֖ף   רֹ֥אשׁ וּתְלָאָֽה׃   ל.ל.

6 בְּמַחֲשַׁכִּ֥ים הוֹשִׁיבַ֖נִי   כְּמֵתֵ֥י עוֹלָֽם׃ ס   ב

7 גָּדַ֧ר בַּעֲדִ֛י וְלֹ֥א אֵצֵ֖א   הִכְבִּ֥יד נְחָשְׁתִּֽי׃   ג.ב.ל.

[3:6] במחשכים ג̇ הושיבני כמתי ע̇ . במחשכים במצלות . במחשכים הושיבני ס:

[7] גדר ג̇ וסימנה ארחי גדר . גדר דרכי . גדר בעדי ס:

20 פִּרְיָם֙ V | καρπὸν κοιλίας αὐτῶν G (T) (explic) | pl S • עֹלֲלֵ֣י טִפֻּחִ֔ים T | ἐπιφυλλίδα ἐποίησε μάγειρος φονευθήσονται νήπια θηλάζοντα μαστούς G* (dbl) | βρέφη παλαιστῆς ⟨α′⟩ V (err-lex) | ܠܛܠܝܐ ܘܠܥܘܠܐ S (err-lex?) ✠ • **21** נָפְל֣וּ V S T | ἐπορεύθησαν ἐν αἰχμαλωσίᾳ G* (assim-1:18c) ✠ • בֶחָ֑רֶב G V S T | > G^O G^L (assim-1:18c) | + καὶ ἐν λιμῷ G^{Mss} (assim-usu) • לֹ֥א G | prec cj G^{Mss} V S T (spont, e.g. KR) ‖ cf 3:43 • **22** תִּקְרָא֩ G^{Mss} V S T | 3 sg G (hapl) • אֹיְבִ֥י כִלָּֽם׃ V | ἐχθρούς μου πάντας G (differ-vocal) | ܡܠܒܫܬܢܝ ܟܠܗܘܢ ܐܢܘܢ S T (lib) • **3:1** עֳנִ֔י G T | + 1 sg sfx ⟨σ′⟩ V S (spont, e.g. KR) • **2** אוֹתִ֥י נָהַ֛ג G V S T | ἐπ᾽ ἐμέ· παρέλαβέ(ν) με G^{Mss} (err-synt + explic) • וַיֹּלַ֖ךְ G V T | + 1 sg sfx G^{Mss} S (explic) • **3** יָשֻׁ֛ב יַהֲפֹ֥ךְ ⟨⟨σ′⟩⟩ (V) (S) (T) | ἐπέστρεψε G (hapl, gk) • **5** וַיַּקַּ֖ף G | + 1 sg sfx G^L V S (explic) | + קרתא T (interp) • רֹ֥אשׁ V S* | κεφαλήν μου G (err-lex) | עמא וא T (err-lex, paraphr) ✠ • וּתְלָאָֽה V | καὶ ἐμόχθησεν G (differ-vocal) | ܡܘܬܒܐ S (lib-seman) | ושלהי אינון T* (paraphr) ✠ • וּתְלָאָֽה: M^Y | וּתְלָאָֽה: ס בְּמַחֲשַׁכִּ֥ים M^L M^{L34} | בְּמַחֲשַׁכִּ֥ים ✠ •

8	גַּם כִּי אֶזְעַק וַאֲשַׁוֵּעַ	שָׂתַם תְּפִלָּתִי:	בֹּ חד כת שֹ וחד כת סֹ
9	גָּדַר דְּרָכַי בְּגָזִית	נְתִיבֹתַי עִוָּה ס	גֹ . בֹ
10	דֹּב אֹרֵב הוּא לִי	אֲרִיה בְּמִסְתָּרִים:	נ אֲרִי . גֹ ק
11	דְּרָכַי סוֹרֵר וַיְפַשְּׁחֵנִי	שָׂמַנִי שֹׁמֵם:	לֹ כול חסֹ
12	דָּרַךְ קַשְׁתּוֹ וַיַּצִּיבֵנִי	כַּמַּטָּרָא לַחֵץ: ס	לֹ ומל . לֹ וכת אֹ
13	הֵבִיא בְּכִלְיוֹתָי	בְּנֵי אַשְׁפָּתוֹ:	לֹ ראשֹ פסֹ . גֹ ד חסֹ בכתיֹ . גֹ סבר עמים וקרֹ עמי
14	הָיִיתִי שְּׂחֹק לְכָל־עַמִּי	נְגִינָתָם כָּל־הַיּוֹם:	
15	הִשְׂבִּיעַנִי בַמְּרוֹרִים	הִרְוַנִי לַעֲנָה: ס	לֹ . לֹ
16	וַיַּגְרֵס בֶּחָצָץ שִׁנָּי	הִכְפִּישַׁנִי בָּאֵפֶר:	לֹ וכתֹ . לֹ
17	וַתִּזְנַח מִשָּׁלוֹם נַפְשִׁי	נָשִׁיתִי טוֹבָה:	בֹ לא נשיתי
18	וָאֹמַר אָבַד נִצְחִי	וְתוֹחַלְתִּי מֵיהוָה: ס	
19	זְכָר־עָנְיִי וּמְרוּדִי	לַעֲנָה וָרֹאשׁ:	בֹּ . בֹּ
20	זָכוֹר תִּזְכּוֹר	וְתָשִׁיחַ עָלַי נַפְשִׁי:	נ ותשוח ק

[8] שתם בֹ חד כת סֹ וחד כת שֹ והוא יחזקיהו סתם . שתם תפלתי :סֹ [9] נתיבותי בֹ חד מלֹ
ארחי גדר . נתיבתי עוה :סֹ [10] במסתרים גֹ רפֹ וסימֹ דמינו כאריה . דב אורב הוא .
תבכה נפשי מפני גוה :סֹ

9 בְּגָזִית V T | ἐνέφραξε G (paraphr?) | ܟܪܒܐ S (err-graph) ✛ • **10** אֲרִיה |
אריה Mket TU | אֲרִי Mqere | G V S T (indet) • **11** דְּרָכַי V S | κατεδίωξεν G
(via aram √דרך) | sg T (differ-vocal) ✛ • וַיְפַשְּׁחֵנִי | καὶ διεσπάραξέ(ν) με GL V
(S) T (via aram √פשח) | καὶ ἐχώλανέ με ⟨α'⟩ (via √פסח) | καὶ κατέπαυσέ(ν) με
G* ✛ • **12** קַשְׁתּוֹ ML (err) קַשְׁתּוֹ ML34 MY • **14** עַמִּי G V (T) | ܥܡܡܐ S (exeg,
e.g. KR) ✛ • **16** וַיַּגְרֵס V S T | καὶ ἐξέβαλεν G ⟨⟨α'⟩⟩ (via וַיַּגְרֵשׁ) | [καὶ] ἐξέβαλε
. . . καὶ ἐξετίναξεν ⟨σ'⟩ (dbl) ✛ • הִכְפִּישַׁנִי ⟨σ'⟩ T | ἐψώμισέ με G V (exeg) |
ܗܦܟ S (ign-lex) ✛ • **17** וַתִּזְנַח T | 3 m sg G (assim-ctext) | et repulsa est V S
(differ-vocal) • **18** מֵיהוָה ML ML34 | זְכָר־: ס זְכָר־ MY ✛ • **19** זְכָר־ ⟨α'⟩
V S T | ἐμνήσθην G (lib?) ✛ • וּמְרוּדִי | καὶ ἐκ διωγμοῦ μου G (via prep מן +
√רדד/רדה) | καὶ ἀποστασίας μου ⟨α'⟩ V (via √רוד or √מרד) | ܡܪܘܕܘܬܝ S
(transcr) | ומא דמרידו בי סנאי T (exeg via √מרד) | ומה דאמרירו בי סנאי TMss
(via √מרר = err-graph) ✛ • וָרֹאשׁ: זָכוֹר ML MY | וְרֹאשׁ ML34 || → ✛ v 18 •
20 תִּזְכּוֹר ✛ • וְתָשִׁיחַ | ותשיח Mket | וְתָשׁוֹחַ Mqere ⟨σ'⟩ T (via √שׁחח) | καὶ
καταδολεσχήσει G σ' (via √שׁיחII) | καὶ τακήσεται GL V (via √שׁיח) | ܡܦܢܐ S
(via √שׁוב hifil, assim-1:11, 16, 19) || pref וְתָשִׁיחַ see G σ' (cf Mket) ✛ • נַפְשִׁי: ✛ •

<table>
<tr><td>יֹ</td><td>ס</td><td>זֹאת אָשִׁיב אֶל־לִבִּי　　עַל־כֵּן אוֹחִיל:</td><td>21</td></tr>
<tr><td>לׁ</td><td></td><td>חַסְדֵי יְהוָה כִּי לֹא־תָמְנוּ　　כִּי לֹא־כָלוּ רַחֲמָיו:</td><td>22</td></tr>
<tr><td>דׁ</td><td></td><td>חֲדָשִׁים לַבְּקָרִים　　רַבָּה אֱמוּנָתֶךָ:</td><td>23</td></tr>
<tr><td>יֹ</td><td>ס</td><td>חֶלְקִי יְהוָה אָמְרָה נַפְשִׁי　　עַל־כֵּן אוֹחִיל לוֹ:</td><td>24</td></tr>
<tr><td></td><td></td><td>טוֹב יְהוָה לְקֹוָו　　לְנֶפֶשׁ תִּדְרְשֶׁנּוּ:</td><td>25</td></tr>
<tr><td>לׁ לׁ</td><td></td><td>טוֹב וְיָחִיל וְדוּמָם　　לִתְשׁוּעַת יְהוָה:</td><td>26</td></tr>
<tr><td>לׁזֹ . ל מל</td><td>ס</td><td>טוֹב לַגֶּבֶר　　כִּי־יִשָּׂא עֹל בִּנְעוּרָיו:</td><td>27</td></tr>
<tr><td></td><td></td><td>יֵשֵׁב בָּדָד וְיִדֹּם　　כִּי נָטַל עָלָיו:</td><td>28</td></tr>
<tr><td>כֹּבֹ</td><td></td><td>יִתֵּן בֶּעָפָר פִּיהוּ　　אוּלַי יֵשׁ תִּקְוָה:</td><td>29</td></tr>
<tr><td></td><td>ס</td><td>יִתֵּן לְמַכֵּהוּ לֶחִי　　יִשְׂבַּע בְּחֶרְפָּה:</td><td>30</td></tr>
<tr><td>יד כת בסיפ</td><td></td><td>כִּי לֹא יִזְנַח לְעוֹלָם　　אֲדֹנָי:</td><td>31</td></tr>
<tr><td>גׁ . חסדיו ק</td><td></td><td>כִּי אִם־הוֹגָה וְרִחַם　　כְּרֹב חֲסָדָו:</td><td>32</td></tr>
<tr><td>יׁ</td><td>ס</td><td>כִּי לֹא עִנָּה מִלִּבּוֹ　　וַיַּגֶּה בְּנֵי־אִישׁ:</td><td>33</td></tr>
<tr><td>חצי הספ לׁ</td><td></td><td>לְדַכֵּא תַּחַת רַגְלָיו　　כֹּל אֲסִירֵי אָרֶץ:</td><td>34</td></tr>
<tr><td>לׁ זק . ל</td><td></td><td>לְהַטּוֹת מִשְׁפַּט־גָּבֶר　　נֶגֶד פְּנֵי עֶלְיוֹן:</td><td>35</td></tr>
<tr><td>דׁ</td><td>ס</td><td>לְעַוֵּת אָדָם בְּרִיבוֹ　　אֲדֹנָי לֹא רָאָה:</td><td>36</td></tr>
<tr><td>לׁ</td><td></td><td>מִי זֶה אָמַר וַתֶּהִי　　אֲדֹנָי לֹא צִוָּה:</td><td>37</td></tr>
</table>

21 אָשִׁיב V S T | τάξω G (via אָשִׂים) | μνησθήσομαι ⟨σ'⟩ (explic) • אוֹחִיל: G V
T | + 3 m sg sfx G^L S (assim-3:24b) • **22 vv 22-24** V S T | > G (homtel) • תָמְנוּ
⟨α'⟩ ⟨σ'⟩ V | > G | ἐξέλιπέν με G^{Mss} (crrp, gk) | 3 pl S T (assim-3:22b)
✧ • **25** לְקֹוָו | לקוו M^{ket} S | לְקוָֹיו M^{qere} G V (T) (assim-usu) ‖ pref לְקֹוָו M^{ket} S
✧ • **26** וְיָחִיל וְדוּמָם (V) | καὶ ὑπομενεῖ καὶ ἡσυχάσει G (differ-vocal) |
ὑπομένειν καὶ ἡσυχάζειν ⟨α'⟩ T (facil-synt) | ܠܒ ܢܣܒܪ ܘܢܫܬܘܩ S* (lib) ✧ •
27 עֹל G V T | ζυγὸν βαρύν G^L (ampl) | ܢܝܪ S (theol) • בִּנְעוּרָיו: G S | ἐκ
νεότητος αὐτοῦ G^L V T (assim-usu; e.g. KR) ✧ • **28** עָלָיו: G V | + ζυγὸν βαρύν
G^L (explic, cf 27b) | + ܢܝܪ S (explic, cf 27b) | differ-txt T (exeg) • **29 v 29** G^{Mss}
V S T | > G (homarc) • **32** הוֹגָה (G) V S | ἐπήγαγε ⟨σ'⟩ (via √נהג?) | ܒܪܝܫܐ
T (explic) ✧ • חֲסָדָו: | חסדו M$^{L(ket)}$ G T | חֲסָדָיו M$^{L(qere)}$ M$^{L34(frag)}$ M^Y ⟨σ'⟩
V (assim-3:22) | ܘܥܒܕܗ, S ‖ pref חַסְדּוֹ M$^{L(ket)}$ G T ✧ • **33** וַיַּגֶּה ✧ • בְּנֵי־
M^L (err) | בְּנֵי M^{L34} M^Y • **34** רַגְלָיו M^L | רַגְלֵיו M^{L34} M^Y • **36** רָאָה:
✧ • **37** צִוָּה: M^{L+} M^{L34} M^Y | עוה M^{L*} (err) •

מִפִּי עֶלְיוֹן לֹא תֵצֵא   הָרָעוֹת וְהַטּוֹב: 38 ד

מַה־יִּתְאוֹנֵן אָדָם חָי   גֶּבֶר עַל־חֲטָאָו: 39 ל . ל זק חטאיו ק

נַחְפְּשָׂה דְרָכֵינוּ וְנַחְקֹרָה   וְנָשׁוּבָה עַד־יְהוָה: 40 ז . ה

נִשָּׂא לְבָבֵנוּ אֶל־כַּפָּיִם   אֶל־אֵל בַּשָּׁמָיִם: 41 ו . ד וחס . ל

נַחְנוּ פָשַׁעְנוּ וּמָרִינוּ   אַתָּה לֹא סָלָחְתָּ: ס 42 ג

סַכֹּתָה בָאַף וַתִּרְדְּפֵנוּ   הָרַגְתָּ לֹא חָמָלְתָּ: 43 ג

סַכּוֹתָה בֶעָנָן לָךְ   מֵעֲבוֹר תְּפִלָּה: 44 ג . ל מל

סְחִי וּמָאוֹס תְּשִׂימֵנוּ   בְּקֶרֶב הָעַמִּים: ס 45 ל וחד שחי . ב מל

פָּצוּ עָלֵינוּ פִּיהֶם   כָּל־אֹיְבֵינוּ: 46

פַּחַד וָפַחַת הָיָה לָנוּ   הַשֵּׁאת וְהַשָּׁבֶר: 47 ל

---

[38] והטוב ד וסימנ̇ ועשית הישר והטוב . אנה יהוה . וחביר̇ . מפי עליון לא תצא :o [40] עד יהוה ד וסימ̇ ושבת עד יהוה . ושבת עד יהוה . ונגף יהוה את מצרים . שובה ישראל . נחפשה לבבנו :o [41] לבבנו ד וחס אנחנו עלים . ונשמע וימס . להטות לבבנו אל . נשא לבבנו אל כפים :o [42] נחנו ג פתח נחנו נעבר חלוצים . פשענו ומרינו . בני איש אחד :o [44] סכותה ג חד חס וב̇ מל̇ וסימנה סכתה לראשי . סכותה באף . בענן לך :o

---

38 וְהַטּוֹב G (T) | pl G^L V S (facil-styl) • **39** יִתְאוֹנֵן G V | ܐܠ̇ܬܘܢܢ S (via יתבוֹנן) | אוֹן T (via ממון ישכח) • חָ֣י גֶּבֶר ✤ • חֲטָאָו M^ket G | חֲטָאָיו M^qere V S T (theol) ‖ pref חֲטָאוֹ M^ket G ✤ • **40** נַחְפְּשָׂה and וְנַחְקֹרָה (G^Mss) V S T | ἐξηρευνήθη . . . καὶ ἠτάσθη G (differ-vocal) ✤ • דְרָכֵינוּ V S T | ἡ ὁδὸς ἡμῶν G (differ-vocal) ✤ • **41** לְבָבֵנוּ G^Ms T | καρδίας ἡμῶν G V S (spont, e.g. KR) • אֶל־¹ ⟨σ'⟩ V | ἐπί G S (via עַל) | ונדכי . . . מגזילין T (midr) ✤ • כַּפָּיִם G V | + 1 pl sfx G^Mss S T (assim-ctext) • **42** וּמָרִינוּ V T | > cj G* (hapl) | ἠσεβήσαμεν καὶ παρεπικράναμεν G^Mss (dbl) | + 2 m sg sfx S (explic) ✤ • **43** לֹא G | prec cj G^Mss V S T (spont, e.g. KR) ‖ cf 2:21 • **44** מֵעֲבוֹר ⟨σ'⟩ La V | + πρός σε G^L T (explic) | ܡܢ ܥܒܪܐ S (lib) | εἵνεκεν G (via בַּעֲבוּר) ✤ • תְּפִלָּה G V T | + 1 sg sfx G^L (explic) | + 1 pl sfx La S (explic) • **45** סְחִי ⟨σ'⟩ | καμ(μ)ύσαι με G* (elus) | λαλιάν ⟨α'⟩ G^L (via √שׂיח) | eradicationem V (S) (via √נסח) | כניעותא T (lib) | טלטילין T* (midr) ✤ • **46 vv 46-51** G V T | vv 46-48 (פ) follow vv 49-51 (ע) G^L S (spont, e.g. KR) ✤ • **47** וָפַחַת | καὶ θυμός G* (transl?) | καὶ θάμβος G^Mss (transl) | καὶ τρόμος G^L S T (transl) | et laqueus V (via פַּח) ✤ • הַשֵּׁאת | ἔπαρσις G ⟨α'⟩ (via נשׂא) | ἔκστασις G^L (V) (via נשׂא) | ܬܡܗܐ S (err-graph?) | רתיתא T (lib-seman) ✤ •

ס	48 פַּלְגֵי־מַיִם תֵּרַד עֵינִי עַל־שֶׁבֶר בַּת־עַמִּי:
כֹּט . בׄ . לׄ	49 עֵינִי נִגְּרָה וְלֹא תִדְמֶה מֵאֵין הֲפֻגוֹת:
גׄ	50 עַד־יַשְׁקִיף וְיֵרֶא יְהוָה מִשָּׁמָיִם:
ל ומל	51 עֵינִי עוֹלְלָה לְנַפְשִׁי מִכֹּל בְּנוֹת עִירִי: ס
ל . לׄ . גׄ	52 צוֹד צָדוּנִי כַּצִּפּוֹר אֹיְבַי חִנָּם:
ל . ל זק קמׄ . ל	53 צָמְתוּ בַבּוֹר חַיָּי וַיַּדּוּ־אֶבֶן בִּי:
ל . ל	54 צָפוּ־מַיִם עַל־רֹאשִׁי אָמַרְתִּי נִגְזָרְתִּי: ס
זׄ	55 קָרָאתִי שִׁמְךָ יְהוָה מִבּוֹר תַּחְתִּיּוֹת:
ל . ל	56 קוֹלִי שָׁמָעְתָּ אַל־תַּעְלֵם אָזְנְךָ לְרַוְחָתִי לְשַׁוְעָתִי:
בׄ דגשׄ	57 קָרַבְתָּ בְּיוֹם אֶקְרָאֶךָ אָמַרְתָּ אַל־תִּירָא: ס
יׄד כׄת כן	58 רַבְתָּ אֲדֹנָי רִיבֵי נַפְשִׁי גָּאַלְתָּ חַיָּי:
ל . בׄ . יׄוׄ	59 רָאִיתָה יְהוָה עַוָּתָתִי שָׁפְטָה מִשְׁפָּטִי:
ל	60 רָאִיתָה כָּל־נִקְמָתָם כָּל־מַחְשְׁבֹתָם לִי: ס
ל	61 שָׁמַעְתָּ חֶרְפָּתָם יְהוָה כָּל־מַחְשְׁבֹתָם עָלָי:
ל ומל	62 שִׂפְתֵי קָמַי וְהֶגְיוֹנָם עָלַי כָּל־הַיּוֹם:
ל . ל	63 שִׁבְתָּם וְקִימָתָם הַבִּיטָה אֲנִי מַנְגִּינָתָם: ס
	64 תָּשִׁיב לָהֶם גְּמוּל יְהוָה כְּמַעֲשֵׂה יְדֵיהֶם:

[50] וירא גׄ וסימנה וירא וירב את ריבי . כי מי עמד בסׄ . עד ישקיף וירא o:
[64] תשיב יׄ וסימנה השמר לך פן . השב תשיב לו את העבוט . ואיך תשיב . ואיך
תשיב . אם תשיב משבת רגלך . אף תשיב צור חרבו . למה תשיב ידך וימינך . כי
תשיב אל אל רוחך . תשיב להם גמול o:

49 תִדְמֶה σ′ V S T | 1 sg G (facil-styl) ✣ • **51** בְּנוֹת עִירִי V (S) (T) | > 1 sg sfx G (err-graph) ✣ • צוֹד: ס צוֹד M^L M^Y • עִירִי: צָדוּ M^{L34} ✣ • **56** אָזְנְךָ V S T | pl noun G (facil-styl) • לְשַׁוְעָתִי (V) | εἰς τὴν βοήθειάν μου G (S) (via √ישע) | καὶ εἰς τὸ σῶσαι ⟨σ′⟩ (via √ישע) | לבעותי T (interp) • **57** אָמַרְתָּ G^{Ms} V T | + μοι G (S) (explic) • **58** רִיבֵי G | sg V S (assim-usu) | לעבדין מצותא T (interp) ✣ • גָּאַלְתָּ G (S) T | redemptor V (via √גאל) ✣ • **59** עַוָּתָתִי V S T | pl G ⟨σ′⟩ (differ-vocal: עִוְּתַי) • שָׁפְטָה ⟨α′⟩ V T | ἔκρινας G S (assim-ctext) ✣ • **60** כָּל־2 G V T | prec καί G^{Mss} S (facil-styl) | prec εἰς G^{Mss} (elus) • לִי: G | ἐπ' ἐμοί G^{Mss} V S T (assim-v 61b) • **61** יְהוָה V S T | > G (elus) • **64** גְּמוּל G V T | + 3 m pl sfx S (explic) • כְּמַעֲשֵׂה S | pl cstr G V T (err-phonol) •

ל . ל	65	תִּתֵּן לָהֶם מְגִנַּת־לֵב תַּאֲלָתְךָ לָהֶם׃
ל . ל וחד שמי יהוה	66	תִּרְדֹּף בְּאַף וְתַשְׁמִידֵם מִתַּחַת שְׁמֵי יְהוָה׃ פ
ל . ז	4	אֵיכָה יוּעַם זָהָב יִשְׁנֶא הַכֶּתֶם הַטּוֹב
ל		תִּשְׁתַּפֵּכְנָה אַבְנֵי־קֹדֶשׁ בְּרֹאשׁ כָּל־חוּצוֹת׃ ס
ל . ל	2	בְּנֵי צִיּוֹן הַיְקָרִים הַמְסֻלָּאִים בַּפָּז
ל . ז		אֵיכָה נֶחְשְׁבוּ לְנִבְלֵי־חֶרֶשׂ מַעֲשֵׂה יְדֵי יוֹצֵר׃ ס
תנים ק . ל . ל כיענים ק	3	גַּם־תַּנִּין חָלְצוּ שַׁד הֵינִיקוּ גּוּרֵיהֶן
		בַּת־עַמִּי לְאַכְזָר כַּי עֵנִים בַּמִּדְבָּר׃ ס
	4	דָּבַק לְשׁוֹן יוֹנֵק אֶל־חִכּוֹ בַּצָּמָא
		עוֹלָלִים שָׁאֲלוּ לֶחֶם פֹּרֵשׂ אֵין לָהֶם׃ ס
ל וחד ויתן מעדנים	5	הָאֹכְלִים לְמַעֲדַנִּים נָשַׁמּוּ בַּחוּצוֹת
ל וחס . ב		הָאֱמֻנִים עֲלֵי תוֹלָע חִבְּקוּ אַשְׁפַּתּוֹת׃ ס
ל ומל . ל	6	וַיִּגְדַּל עֲוֺן בַּת־עַמִּי מֵחַטַּאת סְדֹם
		הַהֲפוּכָה כְמוֹ־רָגַע וְלֹא־חָלוּ בָהּ יָדָיִם׃ ס
ג . ב	7	זַכּוּ נְזִירֶיהָ מִשֶּׁלֶג צַחוּ מֵחָלָב
ל		אָדְמוּ עֶצֶם מִפְּנִינִים סַפִּיר גִּזְרָתָם׃ ס

---

65 תַּאֲלָתְךָ | θρῆνον τὸν ἀπό σου ⟨σ'⟩ (via √אלה[II]) | μόχθον σου G V (T) (via תלאתך) | ܡ̈ܫܐܠܬܟ S (via תלאתך?) ⁜ • **66** תִּרְדֹּף • ⁜ • בְּאַף G V T | + 2 m sg sfx G[O] G[L] (S) (explic) • מִתַּחַת שְׁמֵי יְהוָה T | ὑποκάτω τοῦ οὐρανοῦ, κύριε G V | דבית ܕ S ⁜ • **4:1** זָהָב G V | + ܐܒܠ S (harm-styl) | + ܡܢ ܥܠܝ ܒܝܬ ܨܗܝܘܢ S ⁜ • הַכֶּתֶם | color V S (lib) | τὸ ἀργύριον G (lib) | זיו יקר מקדשא T (exeg) • **2** מַעֲשֵׂה V S T | pl cstr G T[U] (err-phonol) ⁜ • **3** תַּנִּין | תנין M[ket] εβρ' (T) | תַּנִּים M[qere] | G σ' V S (indet) ‖ pref תַּנִּין M[ket] εβρ' (T) ⁜ • בַּת־ G[Ms] V S | pl G T • כַּי עֵנִים | כי ענים M[ket] (differ-div) | כַּיְעֵנִים M[qere] (G) σ' (V) (S) T ‖ pref כַּיְעֵנִים M[qere] (G) σ' (V) (S) T ⁜ • **4** חִכּוֹ M[L] (err) | חִכּוֹ M[L34] M[Y] • **6** חָלוּ ⁜ • **7** נְזִירֶיהָ ⁜ • אָדְמוּ עֶצֶם מִפְּנִינִים 5QLam[a] σ' (S) T | ἐπυρρώθησαν ὑπὲρ λίθους G (om עֶצֶם) | rubicundiores ebore antiquo V (lib) ⁜ • גִּזְרָתָם׃ • ⁜

8 חָשַׁךְ מִשְּׁחוֹר תָּאֳרָם   לֹא נִכְּרוּ בַּחוּצוֹת
צָפַד עוֹרָם עַל־עַצְמָם   יָבֵשׁ הָיָה כָעֵץ׃ ס

9 טוֹבִים הָיוּ חַלְלֵי־חֶרֶב   מֵחַלְלֵי רָעָב
שֶׁהֵם יָזוּבוּ מְדֻקָּרִים   מִתְּנוּבֹת שָׂדָי׃ ס

10 יְדֵי נָשִׁים רַחֲמָנִיּוֹת   בִּשְּׁלוּ יַלְדֵיהֶן
הָיוּ לְבָרוֹת לָמוֹ   בְּשֶׁבֶר בַּת־עַמִּי׃ ס

11 כִּלָּה יְהוָה אֶת־חֲמָתוֹ   שָׁפַךְ חֲרוֹן אַפּוֹ
וַיַּצֶּת־אֵשׁ בְּצִיּוֹן   וַתֹּאכַל יְסוֹדֹתֶיהָ׃ ס

12 לֹא הֶאֱמִינוּ מַלְכֵי־אֶרֶץ   וְכֹל יֹשְׁבֵי תֵבֵל
כִּי יָבֹא צַר וְאוֹיֵב   בְּשַׁעֲרֵי יְרוּשָׁלָ͏ִם׃ ס

13 מֵחַטֹּאת נְבִיאֶיהָ   עֲוֺנֹת כֹּהֲנֶיהָ
הַשֹּׁפְכִים בְּקִרְבָּהּ   דַּם צַדִּיקִים׃ ס

14 נָעוּ עִוְרִים בַּחוּצוֹת   נְגֹאֲלוּ בַּדָּם
בְּלֹא יוּכְלוּ   יִגְּעוּ בִּלְבֻשֵׁיהֶם׃ ס

15 סוּרוּ טָמֵא קָרְאוּ לָמוֹ   סוּרוּ סוּרוּ אַל־תִּגָּעוּ

Masora parva (left margin):
ד . ל מל . ל
ל
ב הרהיבוני . ב
ל
ל
ל . ב
נ (ק / כל)
ב חס בט . ב
ב
יא . ל וחס

Masora magna:

[4:8] חשך ד וסימנהון אעיק שמשא משכנא דשחורא ‎:ס חשך ד וסימנה חשך
בעריפיה . חשך השמש בצאתו . אור חשך באהלו . חשך משחור תארם ‎:ס [14] יוכלו
יא וסימנהון לקום לפני אויביהם . אמחצם ולא יוכלו קום . כי לא יוכלו להראות .
צפיו עורים כלם . ונלחמו אליך . ונלחמו . על מי אדברה ואעידה . זנח עגלך
שמרון . נעו עורים בחוצות . מביא . מים רבים ‎:ס

Apparatus:

8 עַצְמָם | pl G (V) S T (explic) • **9** שֶׁהֵם to
יָבֵשׁ הָיָה (V) (S) T | pl G ✣ • שָׂדָי: ✣ • יָזוּבוּ S (T) | ἐπορεύθησαν G (via ?יזלו) | *extabuerunt* V (lib-seman)
• ✣ • **10** לְבָרוֹת) (לְבָרוֹת) למסעד T^U (via לְבָרוּת) | εἰς βρῶσιν G V S T (via לְבָרוֹת ✣ • ✣
12 וְכֹל | וכל M^{ket} V S T (facil-styl) | כֹּל M^{qere} G ‖ pref כֹּל M^{qere} G ✣ •
צַר וְאוֹיֵב] 5QLam^a | ἐχθρὸς καὶ ἐκθλίβων G S (transp) | צר וא]ויב V T | וְאוֹיֵב
13 דַּם צַדִּיקִים: V S T | דם צד]יקים[5QLam^a | αἷμα δίκαιον G* ✣ • **14** עִוְרִים •
σ' V T | ἐγρήγοροι αὐτῆς G (via √עורII) | νεανίσκοι αὐτῆς G^L (via (וְעָרִים |
ܚ S (via שָׂרִים) | ם[5QLam^a (insuf) ✣ • בְּלֹא | בל G (V) | בל 5QLam^a (facil-
synt) | ܠܐ S (interp) | ועל דלא T (interp) ✣ • יִגְּעוּ G V (S) T | ו]בגן[...] 5QLam^a
(?differ) ✣ • **15** טָמֵא (T) | טמאו 5QLam^a | ἀκαθάρτων G V (S) (via ?טמאים) ✣ •
קָרְאוּ לָמוֹ V | καλέσατε αὐτούς G S (differ-vocal) | קראו למו 5QLam^a (indet) | T
(indet) ✣ • סוּרוּ סוּרוּ ✣ •

כִּֽי־נָצ֤וּ גַם־נָ֙עוּ֙   אָמְרוּ֙ בַּגּוֹיִ֔ם לֹ֥א יוֹסִ֖פוּ לָגֽוּר׃   ל . ל   ס

16   פְּנֵ֤י יְהוָה֙ חִלְּקָ֔ם   לֹ֥א יוֹסִ֖יף לְהַבִּיטָ֑ם   ל

פְּנֵ֤י כֹֽהֲנִים֙ לֹ֣א נָשָׂ֔אוּ   זְקֵנִ֖ים לֹ֥א חָנָֽנוּ׃   ס   זקנים ק   נ

17   עוֹדֵ֙ינוּ֙ תִּכְלֶ֣ינָה עֵינֵ֔ינוּ   אֶל־עֶזְרָתֵ֖נוּ הָ֑בֶל   עודינו ק   נ

בְּצִפִּיָּתֵ֣נוּ צִפִּ֔ינוּ   אֶל־גּ֖וֹי לֹ֥א יוֹשִֽׁעַ׃   ס   ל . ל . ב חס

18   צָד֣וּ צְעָדֵ֔ינוּ   מִלֶּ֖כֶת בִּרְחֹבֹתֵ֑ינוּ

קָרֵ֥ב קִצֵּ֙ינוּ֙ מָלְא֣וּ יָמֵ֔ינוּ   כִּי־בָ֖א קִצֵּֽינוּ׃   ס   ב

19   קַלִּ֤ים הָיוּ֙ רֹדְפֵ֔ינוּ   מִנִּשְׁרֵ֖י שָׁמָ֑יִם

עַל־הֶהָרִ֣ים דְּלָקֻ֔נוּ   בַּמִּדְבָּ֖ר אָ֥רְבוּ לָֽנוּ׃   ס   ל וחס

20   ר֤וּחַ אַפֵּ֙ינוּ֙ מְשִׁ֣יחַ יְהוָ֔ה   נִלְכַּ֖ד בִּשְׁחִיתוֹתָ֑ם   ל וכול שמואל כות ב מ א

אֲשֶׁ֣ר אָמַ֔רְנוּ   בְּצִלּ֖וֹ נִֽחְיֶ֥ה בַגּוֹיִֽם׃   ס

21   שִׂ֤ישִׂי וְשִׂמְחִי֙ בַּת־אֱד֔וֹם   יוֹשַׁבְתִּ֖י בְּאֶ֣רֶץ ע֑וּץ   יושבת ק

[17] אלין כת ה וקר ו וסימנה יקרחה . שפכה . נסברה . נצתה . עלה . והיה . היה .
יזנה . נושבה . שממה . שפכה . חמרמרה . עודינה :o: יושע ב חס וסימ ושח עינים
יושיע . אל גוי לא :o:

ܐܡܪܘ ܒܝܬ ܥܡܡܐ 15 אָמְרוּ בַגּוֹיִ֖ם V (T) | εἴπατε ἐν τοῖς ἔθνεσιν G (differ-vocal) |
S ✦ • 16 vv 16-17 5QLamᵃ G V Tᴹˢˢ | v 16 (פ) follows v 17 (ע) (Gᴸ) S (spont,
e.g. KR) | > v 17 T ✦ • חִלְּקָ֔ם V S (T) | μερὶς αὐτῶν G (via חֶלְקָם) |
διαμέρισον αὐτούς ⟨α'⟩ (differ-vocal) • לֹ֣א נָשָׂ֔אוּ G S T | οὐ κατῃσχύνθησαν ⟨σ'⟩
V (lib) • זְקֵנִ֖ים | וּזְקֵנִים Mᵏᵉᵗ G | זקנים Mᴸ⁽�qᵉʳᵉ⁾ Mʸ⁽qᵉʳᵉ⁾ V S T ✦ •
17 עוֹדֵ֙ינוּ | עודינה | [עוֹד]ֵינה 5QLamᵇ (Tᵁ) | עודינה Mᵏᵉᵗ | עוֹדֵ֙ינוּ Mᴸ⁽qᵉʳᵉ⁾ Mʸ⁽qᵉʳᵉ⁾ G
V S | עודנו Mᴸ³⁴⁽qᵉʳᵉ⁾ | > v 17 T • בְּצִפִּיָּתֵ֣נוּ צִפִּ֔ינוּ Tᴹˢˢ | ἀποσκοπευόντων
ἡμῶν ἀπεσκοπεύσαμεν G (via בְּצִפּוֹתֵנוּ צָפִינוּ) | cum respiceremus adtenti V
(lib) | ܕܡܐ ܕܨܡܚ S (lib) | > T • 18 צָד֣וּ 5QLamᵇ ⟨α'⟩ Tᴹˢˢ | ἐθήρευσαν ⟨σ'⟩ Gᴸ S T
(via √צוד) | ἐθηρεύσαμεν G (via √צוד + assim-ctext) | lubricaverunt V (lib) ✦ •
כִּֽי־ צְעָדֵ֔ינוּ ⟨α'⟩ ⟨σ'⟩ V T | μικρούς ἡμῶν G (S) (via צְעִירֵינוּ) | 5QLamᵇ (insuf) •
V S T | > G • 20 מְשִׁ֣יחַ יְהוָ֔ה ✦ • בִּשְׁחִיתוֹתָ֑ם G (S) T | 1 pl sfx Gᴹˢˢ V (theol) |
5QLamᵃ (insuf) ✦ • 21 יוֹשַׁבְתִּ֖י | יושבתי Mᵏᵉᵗ | יוֹשֶׁבֶת Mqᵉʳᵉ (assim-usu) | G V S
T (indet) ‖ pref יוֹשַׁבְתִּי Mᵏᵉᵗ ✦ • בְּאֶ֣רֶץ ע֑וּץ V S | ἐπὶ τῆς γῆς G (homtel) |
בארע ארמוניה T (exeg) ✦ •

ל	גַּם־עָלַ֣יִךְ תַּעֲבָר־כּ֔וֹס תִּשְׁכְּרִ֖י וְתִתְעָרִֽי׃ ס
ל מל בכת	22 תַּם־עֲוֺנֵךְ֙ בַּת־צִיּ֔וֹן לֹ֥א יוֹסִ֖יף לְהַגְלוֹתֵ֑ךְ
ה חס	פָּקַ֤ד עֲוֺנֵךְ֙ בַּת־אֱד֔וֹם גִּלָּ֖ה עַל־חַטֹּאתָֽיִךְ׃ פ
הביטה ק נ	5 זְכֹ֤ר יְהוָה֙ מֶֽה־הָ֣יָה לָ֔נוּ הַבֵּ֖יט וּרְאֵ֥ה אֶת־חֶרְפָּתֵֽנוּ׃
ל	2 נַחֲלָתֵ֙נוּ֙ נֶֽהֶפְכָ֣ה לְזָרִ֔ים בָּתֵּ֖ינוּ לְנָכְרִֽים׃
ואין ק נ	3 יְתוֹמִ֤ים הָיִ֙ינוּ֙ אֵ֣ין אָ֔ב אִמֹּתֵ֖ינוּ כְּאַלְמָנֽוֹת׃
הׄ.חׄ.	4 מֵימֵ֙ינוּ֙ בְּכֶ֣סֶף שָׁתִ֔ינוּ עֵצֵ֖ינוּ בִּמְחִ֥יר יָבֹֽאוּ׃
ולא ק נ	5 עַ֤ל צַוָּארֵ֙נוּ֙ נִרְדָּ֔פְנוּ יָגַ֖עְנוּ לֹ֥א הֽוּנַֽח לָֽנוּ׃
ג דגש. בׄ.	6 מִצְרַ֙יִם֙ נָתַ֣נּוּ יָ֔ד אַשּׁ֖וּר לִשְׂבֹּ֥עַ לָֽחֶם׃
ואינם ק ואנחנו ק נׄ.	7 אֲבֹתֵ֤ינוּ חָֽטְאוּ֙ אֵינָ֔ם אֲנַ֖חְנוּ עֲוֺנֹתֵיהֶ֥ם סָבָֽלְנוּ׃

[5:6] נתנו ג דגש בׄ פתח וחד קמצׄ וסימנׄ בעזבוניך . ומידך נתנו . מצרים נתנו . וחד
ונתנו את בנתינו ‪:ס‬

21 כּ֔וֹס 5QLamᵃ V S | ποτήριον κυρίου G (exeg) | כס פורענותא T (explic) ⸖ •
תִּשְׁכְּרִ֖י 5QLamᵃ G V S* T | prec πίεσαι καὶ Gᴸ (explic) ⸖ • וְתִתְעָרִֽי׃ V |
καὶ ἀποχεεῖς G T (via √ערה piel?) | ἀσχημονήσεις ⟨σ′⟩ (lib-seman) | ܘܬܬܠܚܡܝܢ
S (lib?) | adhuc La (elus) ⸖ • **22** עֲוֺנֵךְ֙ (5QLamᵃ) Gᴹˢˢ V T | pl G S • :חַטֹּאתָֽיִךְ
G V S T | + θρῆνοι στίχων ϙʹ Gᴹˢˢ (exeg) | + θρῆνοι Ἰερεμίου προφήτου Gᴹˢ
(exeg) | + explicit lamentatio (h)ieremi(a)e (one ms + prophete) Vᴹˢˢ (exeg) |
[vacat חטׄ]אותיך 5QLamᵃ • **5:1** זְכֹ֤ר 5QLamᵃ G V S T | prec προσευχή (few mss
+ Ἰερεμίου) Gᴹˢˢ (exeg) | prec προσευχὴ καὶ θρῆνος Ἰερεμίου Gᴹˢ (exeg) |
prec incipit oratio (h)ieremi(a)e (few mss + prophetae) Vᴹˢˢ (exeg) • הַבֵּ֖יט | הביט
Mᵏᵉᵗ הביטה 5QLamᵃ Mᑫᵉʳᵉ | G V S T (indet) ‖ pref הַבֵּ֖יט Mᵏᵉᵗ ⸖ • חֶרְפָּתֵֽנוּ G
V S T | pl 5QLamᵃ Gᴹˢˢ • **2** לְנָכְרִֽים: | לנוכריאם 5QLamᵃ (differ-orth) | G V S
T (indet) ⸖ • **3** אֵ֣ין ‫ ‬ | אין Mᵏᵉᵗ G ⟨σ′⟩ V (S) (T) | וְאֵ֣ין Mᑫᵉʳᵉ (facil-styl) ‖ pref אֵ֣ין
Mᵏᵉᵗ G ⟨σ′⟩ V (S) (T) ⸖ • :כְּאַלְמָנֽוֹת G V S T | בנות ואלמנות 5QLamᵃ
(ampl) • **4** מֵימֵ֙ינוּ֙ Gᴹˢˢ V S T | ἐξ ἡμερῶν ἡμῶν G (via מִימֵינוּ) | ὕδωρ ἡμῶν
. . . ἐξ ἡμερῶν ἡμῶν Gᴸ (dbl) ⸖ • בְּכֶ֣סֶף שָׁתִ֔ינוּ Gᴹˢˢ V S T | > G • יָבֹֽאוּ G S T |
ἐτρυγῶμεν ⟨σ′⟩ (interp) | ἐλάβομεν Gᴸ (facil) | conparavimus V (facil) ⸖ • **5** עַ֤ל
צַוָּארֵ֙נוּ֙ G S T | pl La (V) (spont, e.g. KR) | prec ζυγός (= עֹל) σ′ ⸖ • נִרְדָּ֔פְנוּ G
S | minabamur V (lib) | curvati sumus La (lib) | אטעננא T (lib) ⸖ • לֹ֥א ‫ ‬ | לא
Mᵏᵉᵗ G V | וְלֹ֥א Mᑫᵉʳᵉ S T (facil-styl) ‖ pref לֹ֥א Mᵏᵉᵗ G V ⸖ • הֽוּנַֽח לָֽנוּ Mᴸ
(differ-orth) | הֽוּנַֽח־לָֽנוּ Mᴸ³⁴ Mʸ • **6** נָתַ֣נּוּ σ′ V T | ἔδωκε G (S) (err-synt) ⸖ •
7 אֵינָ֔ם ‫ ‬ | אינם Mᵏᵉᵗ G | וְאֵינָ֔ם Mᑫᵉʳᵉ Gᴹˢˢ V S T ‖ pref אֵינָ֔ם Mᵏᵉᵗ G ⸖ • אֲנַ֖חְנוּ |
אנחנו Mᵏᵉᵗ G Tᴹˢ | וַאֲנַ֖חְנוּ Mᑫᵉʳᵉ V S T (facil-styl) | אנ[חנ]וׄ 5QLamᵃ (insuf) ‖ pref

8 עֲבָדִים֙ מָ֣שְׁלוּ בָ֔נוּ   פֹּרֵ֖ק אֵ֥ין מִיָּדָֽם׃   ב̇ וחס̇ ואין מציל

9 בְּנַפְשֵׁ֙נוּ֙ נָבִ֣יא לַחְמֵ֔נוּ   מִפְּנֵ֖י חֶ֥רֶב הַמִּדְבָּֽר׃

10 עוֹרֵ֙נוּ֙ כְּתַנּ֣וּר נִכְמָ֔רוּ   מִפְּנֵ֖י זַלְעֲפ֥וֹת רָעָֽב׃   ל̇ . ל̇ . ל̇ וחד זלעפות

11 נָשִׁים֙ בְּצִיּ֣וֹן עִנּ֔וּ   בְּתֻלֹ֖ת בְּעָרֵ֥י יְהוּדָֽה׃

12 שָׂרִים֙ בְּיָדָ֣ם נִתְל֔וּ   פְּנֵ֥י זְקֵנִ֖ים לֹ֥א נֶהְדָּֽרוּ׃

13 בַּחוּרִים֙ טְח֣וֹן נָשָׂ֔אוּ   וּנְעָרִ֖ים בָּעֵ֥ץ כָּשָֽׁלוּ׃   ל̇ וחד טחון . ב̇

14 זְקֵנִים֙ מִשַּׁ֣עַר שָׁבָ֔תוּ   בַּחוּרִ֖ים מִנְּגִינָתָֽם׃   ל̇ . ל̇

15 שָׁבַת֙ מְשׂ֣וֹשׂ לִבֵּ֔נוּ   נֶהְפַּ֥ךְ לְאֵ֖בֶל מְחֹלֵֽנוּ׃   ל̇ וכת̇ כן

16 נָֽפְלָה֙ עֲטֶ֣רֶת רֹאשֵׁ֔נוּ   אֽוֹי־נָ֥א לָ֖נוּ כִּ֥י חָטָֽאנוּ׃   ל̇

17 עַל־זֶ֗ה הָיָ֤ה דָוֶה֙ לִבֵּ֔נוּ   עַל־אֵ֖לֶּה חָשְׁכ֥וּ עֵינֵֽינוּ׃

18 עַ֤ל הַר־צִיּוֹן֙ שֶׁשָּׁמֵ֔ם   שׁוּעָלִ֖ים הִלְּכוּ־בֽוֹ׃ פ   ל̇ . ב̇ מל̇ . ב̇ דגש וחד רפ̇

19 אַתָּ֤ה יְהוָה֙ לְעוֹלָ֣ם תֵּשֵׁ֔ב   כִּסְאֲךָ֖ לְדֹ֥ר וָדֽוֹר׃

20 לָ֤מָּה לָנֶ֙צַח֙ תִּשְׁכָּחֵ֔נוּ   תַּֽעַזְבֵ֖נוּ לְאֹ֥רֶךְ יָמִֽים׃   ג̇

21 הֲשִׁיבֵ֙נוּ יְהוָ֤ה ׀ אֵלֶ֙יךָ֙ וְֽנָשׁ֔וּבָה   חַדֵּ֥שׁ יָמֵ֖ינוּ כְּקֶֽדֶם׃   ונשובה ז̇ ק̇

22 כִּ֚י אִם־מָאֹ֣ס מְאַסְתָּ֔נוּ   קָצַ֥פְתָּ עָלֵ֖ינוּ עַד־מְאֹֽד׃   ג̇

קֻנֹּד

[21] למערב̇ השיבנו יהוה כת̇ ולמדנח̇ אדני כת̇ ׃ס׃ וחילוף ליה תריין ׃ס׃ ונשובה ז̇
וסימ̇ אליכם . נתנה ראש . לנערו . הרבה . לכו . נחפשה . השיבנו . דהרבה ונשבה
כת̇ ׃ס׃ [22] מאוס ג̇ וסימנהון לדעתו . כי בטרם . כי בטרם . וחד סחי־ומאוס קדמ̇
ובתר מל̇ ב̇ מציע̇ ׃ס׃

אֲנַ֫חְנוּ Mket G TMs ✠ • 10 עוֹרֵ֙נוּ֙ G V T | עורי־.] 5QLama S (facil-synt; e.g.
KR) ✠ • נִכְמָ֔רוּ 5QLama T | sg G (⟨α´⟩) (V) (transl) | ἐπελιώθη, συνεσπάσθησαν
GMss (S) (dbl) ✠ • זַלְעֲפ֥וֹת G V | זלפות 5QLama (differ-orth) | sg ⟨σ´⟩ GL
S T ✠ • 12 פְּנֵ֥י V (S) T | > G (hapl, gk) • 14 זְקֵנִ֖ים V S T | prec cj G (ditt?) •
15 מְחֹלֵֽנוּ׃ ML+ ML34 MY | מחולנו ML* • 18 בֽוֹ׃ V S T | ἐν αὐτῇ G •
19 אַתָּ֤ה T | prec cj G V S • 21 וְֽנָשׁ֔וּבָה | ונשוב Mket וְנָשׁ֔וּבָה Mqere | G V S T
(indet) • 22 כִּ֚י אִם־ V T | > אם G S (facil) | εἰ δέ ⟨σ´⟩ (lib) ✠ •

ESTHER אסתר

1 וַיְהִ֖י בִּימֵ֣י אֲחַשְׁוֵר֑וֹשׁ ה֣וּא אֲחַשְׁוֵר֗וֹשׁ הַמֹּלֵךְ֙ מֵהֹ֣דּוּ וְעַד־כּ֔וּשׁ שֶׁ֥בַע

2 וְעֶשְׂרִ֖ים וּמֵאָ֣ה מְדִינָֽה׃ בַּיָּמִ֣ים הָהֵ֔ם כְּשֶׁ֣בֶת ׀ הַמֶּ֣לֶךְ אֲחַשְׁוֵר֗וֹשׁ עַ֚ל

3 כִּסֵּ֣א מַלְכוּת֔וֹ אֲשֶׁ֖ר בְּשׁוּשַׁ֥ן הַבִּירָֽה׃ בִּשְׁנַ֤ת שָׁלוֹשׁ֙ לְמָלְכ֔וֹ עָשָׂ֣ה

מִשְׁתֶּ֗ה לְכָל־שָׂרָ֖יו וַעֲבָדָ֑יו חֵ֣יל ׀ פָּרַ֣ס וּמָדַ֗י הַֽפַּרְתְּמִ֛ים וְשָׂרֵ֥י

[1:1] ויהי בימי ה׳ וסימנה יהויקים . אחז . אמרפל . שפט . אחשורוש . וחד ויהי רעב
בימי ׃ ס

1:1 o וַיְהִ֣י בִּימֵ֣י V S T^R | prec A 1-17 G (lit) | prec A 1-18 G^AT (lit) o וַיְהִ֣י בִּימֵ֣י S V S T^R | καὶ ἐγένετο μετὰ τοὺς λόγους τούτους ἐν ταῖς ἡμέραις G (G^AT) (assim-ctext) | In diebus V (facil-styl) ❖ • אֲחַשְׁוֵר֑וֹשׁ¹ S T^R | Ἀρταξέρξου G (substit) | Ἀσσυήρου G^AT (assim) | Asueri V (assim) ❖ • ה֣וּא אֲחַשְׁוֵר֗וֹשׁ S T^R | οὗτος ὁ Ἀρταξέρξης G (substit) | > G^AT V (facil-styl) ❖ • וְעַד־כּ֔וּשׁ S | > G (abbr) | ἕως τῆς Αἰθιοπίας G^AT V (substit) | ועד מערבא דכוש T^R (lib) • שֶׁ֥בַע וְעֶשְׂרִ֖ים וּמֵאָ֣ה G G^AT V T^R | ܡܐܐ ܘܥܣܪܝܢ ܘܫܒܥ S (assim) ❖ • 2 בַּיָּמִ֣ים הָהֵ֔ם G S (T^R) (ampl) | > G^AT V (facil-styl) • כְּשֶׁ֣בֶת (G^AT) | ὅτε ἐθρονίσθη G (interp) | quando sedit La V S T^Sh (interp) | כד בעא ... למיתב T^R (lib) ❖ • עַ֚ל כִּסֵּ֣א מַלְכוּת֔וֹ G^AT (V) S | > G (facil-styl) | in tribunali regni sui La (assim-cultur) | על כורסיה דשלמה T^R (ampl) • בְּשׁוּשַׁ֥ן הַבִּירָֽה׃ T^R T^Sh | ἐν Σούσοις τῇ πόλει G (facil-lex) | > G^AT (facil-styl) | Susa civitas regni eius (exordium fuit) V (lib-seman) | ܫܘܫܢ ܒܝܪܬܐ S (differ-gram) ❖ • 3 בִּשְׁנַ֤ת שָׁלוֹשׁ֙ לְמָלְכ֔וֹ G V S T^R T^Sh | > G^AT (facil-styl) • מִשְׁתֶּ֗ה (G) G^AT T^Sh | δοχὴν μεγάλην G^Mss V S T^R (ampl) • לְכָל־שָׂרָ֖יו וַעֲבָדָ֑יו V S T^R | τοῖς φίλοις καὶ τοῖς λοιποῖς ἔθνεσιν G (lib) | τοῖς ἄρχουσι G^AT (abbr) • חֵ֣יל S T^R | > G G^AT (facil-styl) | fortissimis V (assim-styl) ❖ • הַֽפַּרְתְּמִ֛ים וְשָׂרֵ֥י הַמְּדִינֹ֖ות (T^Sh) | τοῖς (Περσῶν καὶ Μήδων) ἐνδόξοις καὶ τοῖς ἄρχουσιν τῶν σατραπῶν G (lib-synt) | καὶ οἱ ἄρχοντες τῶν χωρῶν G^AT V (facil-styl) | ܐܣܛܪܛܝܓܝܢ ܕܦܪܣ ܘܡܐܕܝ, ܘܪܘܪܒܢܐ ܕܫܠܝܛܝܢ ܥܠ ܐܬܘܬܐ S (ampl) | ורבנין דממנן על פילכיא T^R (lib) ❖ •

ל וחד בְּהֵרָאֹתוּ

⁴ הַמְּדִינוֹת לְפָנָיו: בְּהַרְאֹתוֹ אֶת־עֹשֶׁר כְּבוֹד מַלְכוּתוֹ וְאֶת־יְקָר

ל ומל . ל . ב . ורא פסוק

⁵ תִּפְאֶרֶת גְּדוּלָּתוֹ יָמִים רַבִּים שְׁמוֹנִים וּמְאַת יוֹם: וּבִמְלוֹאת |

ה קמ . ל

הַיָּמִים הָאֵלֶּה עָשָׂה הַמֶּלֶךְ לְכָל־הָעָם הַנִּמְצְאִים בְּשׁוּשַׁן הַבִּירָה

לְמִגָּדוֹל וְעַד־קָטָן מִשְׁתֶּה שִׁבְעַת יָמִים בַּחֲצַר גִּנַּת בִּיתַן הַמֶּלֶךְ:

ל . ד . ב . ל בטע

⁶ חוּר | כַּרְפַּס וּתְכֵלֶת אָחוּז בְּחַבְלֵי־בוּץ וְאַרְגָּמָן עַל־גְּלִילֵי כֶסֶף

ב . ל . ל

וְעַמּוּדֵי שֵׁשׁ מִטּוֹת | זָהָב וָכֶסֶף עַל רִצְפַת בַּהַט־וָשֵׁשׁ וְדַר

ל . ב

⁷ וְסֹחָרֶת: וְהַשְׁקוֹת בִּכְלֵי זָהָב וְכֵלִים מִכֵּלִים שׁוֹנִים וְיֵין מַלְכוּת רָב

---

[5] קטן הקטן ה קמצין וסימנהון ויגד לרבקה . עוד שאר . ולמפיבשת . אחד למאה .
ובמלואת . וכול אתנה וסוף פסוק דכותהון :o [6] אחוז ד וחד ואחוז וסימ וממחצית
בני־ישראל . כרפס ותכלת . ויכתבם שמעיה . שלשה בו :o

---

4 בְּהַרְאֹתוֹ (S) | καὶ μετὰ ταῦτα, μετὰ τὸ δεῖξαι αὐτοῖς G (ampl) | εἰς τὸ ἐπιδειχθῆναι G^AT (V) (interp) | אחוי להון T^R (lib) ✣ • אֶת־עֹשֶׁר כְּבוֹד־מַלְכוּתוֹ G^AT V | τὸν πλοῦτον τῆς βασιλείας αὐτοῦ G (facil-styl) | ܥܘܬܪܐ ܕܡܠܟܘܬܗ S (facil-styl) | עותריה T^R (facil-styl) ✣ • וְאֶת־יְקָר תִּפְאֶרֶת גְּדוּלָּתוֹ S | καὶ τὴν δόξαν τῆς εὐφροσύνης τοῦ πλούτου αὐτοῦ G (assim-styl) | καὶ τὴν τιμὴν τῆς καυχήσεως αὐτοῦ G^AT (lib-seman) | *ac magnitudinem atque iactantiam potentiae suae* V (lib-seman) | ובההוא עותרא תקף יקריה וסגא תקוף מלכותיה T^R (paraphr) • יָמִים רַבִּים (V) S T^R | > G G^AT (facil-styl) ✣ •
5 וּבִמְלוֹאת T^R | ὅτε δὲ ἀνεπληρώθησαν G (G^AT) V S (transl) | ובאשלמות T^R (transl) ✣ • הַיָּמִים הָאֵלֶּה (G^AT) S | + τοῦ γάμου G (interp) | + *convivii* V T^R (interp) • הַנִּמְצָאִים בְּשׁוּשַׁן הַבִּירָה (G^AT) S | τοῖς εὑρεθεῖσιν εἰς τὴν πόλιν G (facil-styl) | *qui erant inventi in Susis Thebari* La (ign-lex) | *qui inventus est Susis* V (facil-styl) | דאישתכחו חייביא בשושן בירנותא T^R (paraphr) • שְׁבְעַת יָמִים G^AT V S T^R | ἡμέρας ἓξ G (theol) | > La (abbr) ✣ • בַּחֲצַר גִּנַּת בִּיתַן הַמֶּלֶךְ: S (T^R) | ἐν αὐλῇ οἴκου τοῦ βασιλέως G (facil-styl) | ἔνδον ἐν τῇ αὐλῇ τοῦ βασιλέως G^AT (lib-seman) | > La (abbr) | *in vestibulo horti et nemoris* V (lib-seman) • **6** חוּר | βυσσίνοις καὶ καρπασίνοις G (G^AT) (lib-seman) | > La (abbr) | *coloris et carpasini* V (lib-seman) | ܟܪܦܣ ܕܒܘܨ ... S (lib-seman) | ירִיען דבוץ גון חיוור כספירין וכרתנין T^R (lib-seman) | > T^Sh (abbr) ✣ • מִטּוֹת G (V) | καὶ κλῖναι G^AT S (facil-synt) | דרגשין T^R (interp) • רִצְפַת בַּהַט־וָשֵׁשׁ וְדַר | λιθοστρώτου σμαραγδίτου λίθου καὶ πινίνου καὶ παρίνου λίθου G (paraphr) | λιθόστρωτον σμαράγδου G^AT (facil-styl) | *lapides marmoratos et pictura varia* La (facil-styl) | *pavimentum zmaragdino et pario stratum lapide* V (lib-seman) | ... S (lib-seman) | סטיו כביש קרוסטלינין ומרמרין ודורא דבכרכי ימא רבא T^R (paraphr) ✣ •

ל . ב . ל . ל‎   8 כִּי־כֵן ׀ יִסַּד הַמֶּלֶךְ עַל כָּל־ כַיַד הַמֶּלֶךְ: וְהַשְּׁתִיָּה כַדָּת אֵין אֹנֵס כִּי־כֵן ׀

ל . ל . ד‎   9 עָשְׂתָה הַמַּלְכָּה וַשְׁתִּי גַּם אִישׁ־וָאִישׁ כִּרְצוֹן לַעֲשׂוֹת בֵּיתוֹ רַב

ג ראש פסוק‎   10 בַּיּוֹם‎ ס אֲחַשְׁוֵרוֹשׁ לַמֶּלֶךְ אֲשֶׁר הַמַּלְכוּת בֵּית נָשִׁים מִשְׁתֵּה

ד . ל . ב‎   חַרְבוֹנָא בַּזְּתָא לִמְהוּמָן אָמַר בַּיַּיִן הַמֶּלֶךְ לֵב כְּטוֹב הַשְּׁבִיעִי

ל‎   אֶת־פְּנֵי הַמְשָׁרְתִים הַסָּרִיסִים שִׁבְעַת וְכַרְכַּס זֵתַר וַאֲבַגְתָא בִגְתָא

ד‎   11 בְּכֶתֶר הַמֶּלֶךְ לִפְנֵי הַמַּלְכָּה אֶת־וַשְׁתִּי לְהָבִיא אֲחַשְׁוֵרוֹשׁ הַמֶּלֶךְ

ג . ב‎   מַרְאֶה כִּי־טוֹבַת אֶת־יָפְיָהּ וְהַשָּׂרִים הָעַמִּים לְהַרְאוֹת מַלְכוּת

ג‎   12 בְּיַד אֲשֶׁר הַמֶּלֶךְ בִּדְבַר לָבוֹא וַשְׁתִּי הַמַּלְכָּה וַתְּמָאֵן הִיא:

ל‎   13 הַמֶּלֶךְ‎ וַיֹּאמֶר בוֹ: בָעֲרָה וַחֲמָתוֹ מְאֹד הַמֶּלֶךְ וַיִּקְצֹף הַסָּרִיסִים

דָת כָּל־יֹדְעֵי לִפְנֵי הַמֶּלֶךְ דְּבַר כִּי־כֵן הָעִתִּים יֹדְעֵי לַחֲכָמִים

ל . ל חס . ל‎
ב חד כת י וחד‎
כת ה . י חס‎
בכתי‎   14 מַרְסְנָא מֶרֶס תַּרְשִׁישׁ אַדְמָתָא שֵׁתָר כַּרְשְׁנָא אֵלָיו וְהַקָּרֹב וָדִין:

ל‎   רִאשֹׁנָה הַיֹּשְׁבִים הַמֶּלֶךְ פְּנֵי רֹאֵי וּמָדַי פָּרַס ׀ שָׂרֵי שִׁבְעַת מְמוּכָן

15 עָשְׂתָה לֹא־ אֲשֶׁר ׀ עַל וַשְׁתִּי בַּמַּלְכָּה לַעֲשׂוֹת מַה־ כְּדָת בַּמַּלְכוּת:

ל וחד ואת מאמר‎   16 וַיֹּאמֶר‎ ס הַסָּרִיסִים בְּיַד אֲחַשְׁוֵרוֹשׁ הַמֶּלֶךְ אֶת־מַאֲמַר

מומכן‎
ק‎ ן‎ . ל . ד‎
ד וחד מעל כל‎
השרים‎   וַשְׁתִּי עָוְתָה לְבַדּוֹ הַמֶּלֶךְ עַל לֹא הַשָּׂרִים וְהַשָּׂרִים לִפְנֵי מוֹמְכָן

בְּכָל־ אֲשֶׁר הָעַמִּים וְעַל־כָּל־ הַשָּׂרִים כִּי־עַל־כָּל־ הַמַּלְכָּה

[9] ושתי המלכה ד וסימנה גם ושתי המלכה . לה להביא את ושתי . עותה ושתי
המלכה . אמר להביא את־ושתי‎ :o

9 גַּם וַשְׁתִּי הַמַּלְכָּה V (T^R) ׀ καὶ Ἀστὶν ἡ βασίλισσα G (G^AT) S (facil-styl) •
10 לִמְהוּמָן T^R ׀ Ἀμάν G (err-hist) ׀ > G^AT T^Sh (abbr) ׀ Maosma La (lib) ׀
Mauman V (lib) ׀ ܡܗܘܡܢ S (err-lex) ⁝ • וַאֲבַגְתָא (T^R) ׀ καὶ Ζαθολθά G (err-
hist) ׀ > G^AT ׀ et Achedes La (lib) ׀ et Abgatha V (differ-orth) ׀ ܘܐܒܓܬܐ
S (lib-seman) ⁝ • **11** בְּכֶתֶר מַלְכוּת G^AT S (T^R) ׀ τὸ διάδημα G V T^Sh
(lib-seman) • **13** יֹדְעֵי הָעִתִּים S (T^R) T^Sh ׀ > G G^AT V (abbr) ⁝ • **14** וְהַקָּרֹב ׀
καὶ προσῆλθεν G (G^AT) (lib-synt) ׀ erant . . . proximi V S T^R (assim-ctext) ⁝ •
שִׁבְעַת V T^R ׀ > G G^AT S (abbr) • **15** כְּדָת (G) (V) T^R ׀ > G^AT ׀ ܘܐ S (facil-
synt) ⁝ • **16** מוֹמְכָן ׀ מומכן M^ket (err-graph) ׀ סבן עצתא T^Sh (interp) ⁝ • **16**
M^qere V T^R ׀ Μουχαῖος G (lib) ׀ Βουγαῖος G^AT (lib) ׀ Mardochaeus La (lib) ׀
ܡܘܡܟܢ S (differ-graph) ‖ pref מְמוּכָן M^qere V (S) T^R ⁝ •

מְדִינוֹת הַמֶּלֶךְ אֲחַשְׁוֵרוֹשׁ: כִּי־יֵצֵא דְבַר־הַמַּלְכָּה עַל־כָּל־הַנָּשִׁים 17 ל

לְהַבְזוֹת בַּעְלֵיהֶן בְּעֵינֵיהֶן בְּאָמְרָם הַמֶּלֶךְ אֲחַשְׁוֵרוֹשׁ אָמַר לְהָבִיא ל.ל.ל

אֶת־וַשְׁתִּי הַמַּלְכָּה לְפָנָיו וְלֹא־בָאָה: וְהַיּוֹם הַזֶּה תֹּאמַרְנָה ׀ שָׂרוֹת 18 ד.ב.ב

פָּרַס־וּמָדַי אֲשֶׁר שָׁמְעוּ אֶת־דְּבַר הַמַּלְכָּה לְכֹל שָׂרֵי הַמֶּלֶךְ וּכְדַי ל

בִּזָּיוֹן וָקָצֶף: אִם־עַל־הַמֶּלֶךְ טוֹב יֵצֵא דְבַר־מַלְכוּת מִלְּפָנָיו 19 ל.ב

וְיִכָּתֵב בְּדָתֵי פָרַס־וּמָדַי וְלֹא יַעֲבוֹר אֲשֶׁר לֹא־תָבוֹא וַשְׁתִּי לִפְנֵי ג מל בכת

הַמֶּלֶךְ אֲחַשְׁוֵרוֹשׁ וּמַלְכוּתָהּ יִתֵּן הַמֶּלֶךְ לִרְעוּתָהּ הַטּוֹבָה מִמֶּנָּה: ל

וְנִשְׁמַע פִּתְגָם הַמֶּלֶךְ אֲשֶׁר־יַעֲשֶׂה בְּכָל־מַלְכוּתוֹ כִּי רַבָּה הִיא 20 ב

וְכָל־הַנָּשִׁים יִתְּנוּ יְקָר לְבַעְלֵיהֶן לְמִגָּדוֹל וְעַד־קָטָן: וַיִּיטַב הַדָּבָר 21 ל.ל.ג

בְּעֵינֵי הַמֶּלֶךְ וְהַשָּׂרִים וַיַּעַשׂ הַמֶּלֶךְ כִּדְבַר מְמוּכָן: וַיִּשְׁלַח סְפָרִים 22 ב

אֶל־כָּל־מְדִינוֹת הַמֶּלֶךְ אֶל־מְדִינָה וּמְדִינָה כִּכְתָבָהּ וְאֶל־עַם־עָם ג.ו

וָעָם כִּלְשׁוֹנוֹ לִהְיוֹת כָּל־אִישׁ שֹׂרֵר בְּבֵיתוֹ וּמְדַבֵּר כִּלְשׁוֹן ל

עַמּוֹ:   פ   אַחַר הַדְּבָרִים הָאֵלֶּה כְּשֹׁךְ חֲמַת הַמֶּלֶךְ אֲחַשְׁוֵרוֹשׁ 2 ג ראש פסוק.
ל וחס

זָכַר אֶת־וַשְׁתִּי וְאֵת אֲשֶׁר־עָשָׂתָה וְאֵת אֲשֶׁר־נִגְזַר עָלֶיהָ: וַיֹּאמְרוּ 2 ג

---

[16] מדינות המלך אחשורוש ד וסימנה עותה ושתי . ביום אחד . נקהלו היהודים .
ויכתב מרדכי ‎:ס: [18] והיום הזה ב וסימ' לא תבשר . תאמרנה שרות ‎:ס: וקצף ב וסימ'
וכדי בזיון וקצף . וכעס הרבה ‎:ס: [20] וכל הנשים ג וסימנה אשר נשא לבן . העמדות
קהל גדול . יתנו יקר לבעליהן א בתור א בנביא א בכתוב ‎:ס: [2:1] נגזר ג וסימנה כי
נגזר מארץ חיים . מבית יהוה . ואת אשר נגזר עליה ‎:ס:

---

17 עַל־כָּל־הַנָּשִׁים V S Tᴿ | αὐτοῖς G (lib-seman) | > Gᴬᵀ (abbr) | *etiam ab
omnibus mulieribus* La (lib-seman) ⁖ • **18** תֹּאמַרְנָה S (Tᴿ) | > G Gᴬᵀ (elus) |
negligent La (lib) | *parvipendent* V (lib) ⁖ • **19** בְּדָתֵי פָרַס־וּמָדַי (G) | > Gᴬᵀ |
secundum legem Persarum et Medorum La (V) Tᴿ (lib) | ܒܢܡܘܣܐ ܡܕܝ ܘܦܪܣ S
(lib) • **20** כִּי רַבָּה הִיא S | > G Gᴬᵀ (abbr) | *quod latissimum est* V (lib) • **אֲרוּם
גְּזֵירְתָא רַבָּא הִיא Tᴿ (interp) ⁖ • **22** וּמְדַבֵּר כִּלְשׁוֹן עַמּוֹ S (Tᴿ) | ὥστε εἶναι φόβον
αὐτοῖς ἐν ταῖς οἰκίαις αὐτῶν G (substit) | > Gᴬᵀ (abbr) | *et fuit timor magnus
in omni muliere* La (substit) | *et hoc per cunctos populos divulgari* V (substit)
⁖ • **2:1** אַחַר הַדְּבָרִים הָאֵלֶּה G (V) S Tᴿ | > Gᴬᵀ (abbr) • **זָכַר** V S | καὶ οὐκέτι
ἐμνήσθη G (lib-seman) | καὶ οὕτως ἔστη τοῦ μνημονεύειν Gᴬᵀ (lib-seman) |
שָׂרֵי לַמֶּדְכֵּר Tᴿ (interp) | > Tˢʰ (abbr) •

נַעֲרֵי־הַמֶּ֫לֶךְ מְשָׁרְתָ֖יו יְבַקְשׁ֥וּ לַמֶּ֛לֶךְ נְעָר֥וֹת בְּתוּל֖וֹת טוֹב֥וֹת

ב . ד . ז ³ מַרְאֶ֑ה וְיַפְקֵ֨ד הַמֶּ֜לֶךְ פְּקִידִ֗ים בְּכָל־מְדִינ֣וֹת מַלְכוּת֒וֹ וְיִקְבְּצ֣וּ

אֶֽת־כָּל־נַעֲרָֽה־בְ֠תוּלָה טוֹבַ֨ת מַרְאֶ֜ה אֶל־שׁוּשַׁ֤ן הַבִּירָה֙ אֶל־בֵּ֣ית

ז . ל חס̇ הַנָּשִׁ֔ים אֶל־יַ֥ד הֵגֶ֛א סְרִ֥יס הַמֶּ֖לֶךְ שֹׁמֵ֣ר הַנָּשִׁ֑ים וְנָת֖וֹן תַּמְרוּקֵיהֶֽן׃

ל וחד ותיטב ⁴ וְהַֽנַּעֲרָ֗ה אֲשֶׁ֤ר תִּיטַב֙ בְּעֵינֵ֣י הַמֶּ֔לֶךְ תִּמְלֹ֖ךְ תַּ֣חַת וַשְׁתִּ֑י וַיִּיטַ֧ב הַדָּבָ֛ר

ל ראש פסוק ⁵ בְּעֵינֵ֥י הַמֶּ֖לֶךְ וַיַּ֥עַשׂ כֵּֽן׃ ס   אִ֣ישׁ יְהוּדִ֔י הָיָ֖ה בְּשׁוּשַׁ֣ן הַבִּירָ֑ה

ל . ז̇ ⁶ וּשְׁמ֣וֹ מָרְדֳּכַ֗י בֶּ֣ן יָאִ֧יר בֶּן־שִׁמְעִ֛י בֶּן־קִ֖ישׁ אִ֥ישׁ יְמִינִֽי׃ אֲשֶׁ֤ר הָגְלָה֙

ד מל̇ . ב̇ חס̇ מִיר֣וּשָׁלַ֔יִם עִם־הַגֹּלָה֙ אֲשֶׁ֣ר הָגְלְתָ֔ה עִ֖ם יְכָנְיָ֣ה מֶֽלֶךְ־יְהוּדָ֑ה אֲשֶׁ֣ר

ל וחס̇ . ל ⁷ הֶגְלָ֔ה נְבוּכַדְנֶאצַּ֖ר מֶ֥לֶךְ בָּבֶֽל׃ וַיְהִ֨י אֹמֵ֜ן אֶת־הֲדַסָּ֗ה הִ֤יא אֶסְתֵּר֙

ב בַּת־דֹּד֔וֹ כִּ֛י אֵ֥ין לָ֖הּ אָ֣ב וָאֵ֑ם וְהַנַּעֲרָ֤ה יְפַת־תֹּ֨אַר֙ וְטוֹבַ֣ת מַרְאֶ֔ה

ל ⁸ וּבְמ֤וֹת אָבִ֨יהָ֙ וְאִמָּ֔הּ לְקָחָ֧הּ מָרְדֳּכַ֛י ל֖וֹ לְבַ֑ת וַיְהִ֗י בְּהִשָּׁמַ֤ע דְּבַר־

ב הַמֶּ֨לֶךְ֙ וְדָת֔וֹ וּֽבְהִקָּבֵ֞ץ נְעָר֥וֹת רַבּ֛וֹת אֶל־שׁוּשַׁ֥ן הַבִּירָ֖ה אֶל־יַ֣ד הֵגָ֑י

[5] אֶת בֶּן הַבֹּקֶר . בֶּן הַיִשְׂרְאֵלִית . בֶּן יְבֶרֶכְיָהוּ . בֶּן יָאִיר . בֶּן יְבֶרֶכְיָהוּ o:

[6] יְרוּשָׁלַיִם ד מל̇ וסימנהון עיין תהיה . יְהוֹעָדָן . אֲשֶׁר הָגְלָה . וְאֵלֶּה נוֹלְדוּ לוֹ
בִירוּשָׁלָ͏ם . וְחַד אַחַר זֶה שָׁלַח סַנְחֵרִיב מֶלֶךְ אַשּׁוּר עֲבָדָיו o: הָגְלָה ב̇ חס̇ וסימ̇ וַיֵּשְׁבוּ
תַּחְתֵּיהֶם . אֲשֶׁר הָגְלָה מִירוּשָׁלַ͏ם o:

2 נַעֲרֵי־הַמֶּ֫לֶךְ מְשָׁרְתָ֖יו T^R | οἱ διάκονοι τοῦ βασιλέως G (G^{AT}) (facil-styl) |
amici ejus La (facil-styl) | *pueri regis ac ministri eius* V S (facil-styl) ❖ •
3 פְּקִידִ֗ים T^R | κωμάρχας G (lib-seman) | > G^{AT} V (abbr) | ܩܘܡܛܐ S (differ-
graph) • כָּל־נַעֲרָֽה־בְתוּלָה (S) T^R | κοράσια παρθενικά G V (explic) | > G^{AT} •
אֶל־שׁוּשַׁ֤ן הַבִּירָה֙ T^R | εἰς Σουσὰν τὴν πόλιν G V (facil-lex) | > G^{AT} S (abbr) •
דתמן מתמני (הגי) T^R אֶל־יַ֥ד V | τῷ εὐνούχῳ G (differ-gram) | ܐܝܕܐ S (facil-styl) |
על ידוי T^{Sh} (differ-gram) ❖ • הֵגֶ֛א M^{L34} V | הגיא M^Y (differ-
graph) | > G (abbr) | Γωγαίου G^{AT} (substit) | *Oggeo* La (substit) | ܓܝ S T^R
(differ-graph) | שעשגז T^{Sh} (substit) ❖ • תַּמְרוּקֵיהֶֽן׃ T^{Sh} | σμῆγμα καὶ ἡ λοιπὴ
ἐπιμέλεια G (V) (paraphr) | > G^{AT} (abbr) | *et nitores* La (S) (lib) | סמתר משחהון
T^R (ampl) • **6** מֶֽלֶךְ־יְהוּדָ֑ה to עִם־הַגֹּלָה (S) T^R | > G G^{AT} (abbr) | *eo tempore quo
Iechoniam regem Iuda ... transtulerat* V (assim-ctext) ❖ • **7** הֲדַסָּ֗ה S T^R | > G
G^{AT} (abbr) | *Edessae* V (transcr) | דֹּד֔וֹ G^{AT} S T^R T^{Sh} | Ἀμιναδὰβ ἀδελφοῦ
πατρὸς αὐτοῦ G (explic) | *fratris ejus* La (V) (lib) ❖ • לְקָחָ֧הּ מָרְדֳּכַ֛י ל֖וֹ לְבַ֑ת׃ V
S T^{Sh} | ἐπαίδευσεν αὐτὴν ἑαυτῷ εἰς γυναῖκα G (explic) | > G^{AT} (abbr) |
nutrivit eam ut filiam propriam La (lib) | ונסבה מרדכי ליה בביתיה והוה קרי לה
ברתי T^R (paraphr) ❖ • **8** הֵגָ֑י (V) S T^R | Γαί G (substit) | Βουγαῖος G^{AT}
(substit) | *Oggei* La (substit) ❖ •

9 וַתִּיטַ֨ב הַנַּעֲרָ֣ה בְעֵינָיו֮ וַתִּשָּׂ֣א חֶ֣סֶד לְפָנָיו֒ וַ֠יְבַהֵל אֶת־תַּמְרוּקֶ֤יהָ וְאֶת־

וַתִּלָּקַ֨ח אֶסְתֵּ֜ר אֶל־בֵּ֤ית הַמֶּ֙לֶךְ֙ אֶל־יַ֣ד הֵגַ֔י שֹׁמֵ֖ר הַנָּשִׁ֑ים וַתִּיטַ֨ב

מָנוֹתֶ֙הָ֙ לָתֵ֣ת לָ֔הּ וְאֵת֙ שֶׁ֣בַע הַנְּעָר֔וֹת הָרְאֻי֥וֹת לָֽתֶת־לָ֖הּ מִבֵּ֣ית

10 הַמֶּ֑לֶךְ וַיְשַׁנֶּ֧הָ וְאֶת־נַעֲרוֹתֶ֛יהָ לְט֖וֹב בֵּ֥ית הַנָּשִֽׁים׃ לֹא־הִגִּ֣ידָה אֶסְתֵּ֔ר

אֶת־עַמָּ֖הּ וְאֶת־מֽוֹלַדְתָּ֑הּ כִּ֧י מָרְדֳּכַ֛י צִוָּ֥ה עָלֶ֖יהָ אֲשֶׁ֥ר לֹא־תַגִּֽיד׃

11 וּבְכָל־י֣וֹם וָי֔וֹם מָרְדֳּכַי֙ מִתְהַלֵּ֔ךְ לִפְנֵ֖י חֲצַ֣ר בֵּית־הַנָּשִׁ֑ים לָדַ֙עַת֙

12 אֶת־שְׁל֣וֹם אֶסְתֵּ֔ר וּמַה־יֵּעָשֶׂ֖ה בָּֽהּ׃ וּבְהַגִּ֡יעַ תֹּר֩ נַעֲרָ֨ה וְנַעֲרָ֜ה לָב֣וֹא ׀

אֶל־הַמֶּ֣לֶךְ אֲחַשְׁוֵר֗וֹשׁ מִקֵּץ֩ הֱי֨וֹת לָ֜הּ כְּדָ֤ת הַנָּשִׁים֙ שְׁנֵ֣ים עָשָׂ֣ר

חֹ֔דֶשׁ כִּ֛י כֵּ֥ן יִמְלְא֖וּ יְמֵ֣י מְרוּקֵיהֶ֑ן שִׁשָּׁ֤ה חֳדָשִׁים֙ בְּשֶׁ֣מֶן הַמֹּ֔ר וְשִׁשָּׁ֤ה

13 חֳדָשִׁים֙ בַּבְּשָׂמִ֔ים וּבְתַמְרוּקֵ֖י הַנָּשִֽׁים׃ וּבָזֶ֕ה הַנַּעֲרָ֖ה בָּאָ֣ה אֶל־

הַמֶּ֑לֶךְ אֵת֩ כָּל־אֲשֶׁ֨ר תֹּאמַ֜ר יִנָּ֤תֵֽן לָהּ֙ לָב֣וֹא עִמָּ֔הּ מִבֵּ֖ית הַנָּשִׁ֑ים

14 עַד־בֵּ֣ית הַמֶּֽלֶךְ׃ בָּעֶ֣רֶב ׀ הִ֣יא בָאָ֗ה וּ֠בַבֹּקֶר הִ֣יא שָׁבָ֞ה אֶל־בֵּ֤ית

הַנָּשִׁים֙ שֵׁנִ֔י אֶל־יַ֧ד שַֽׁעַשְׁגַ֛ז סְרִ֥יס הַמֶּ֖לֶךְ שֹׁמֵ֣ר הַפִּֽילַגְשִׁ֑ים לֹא־

תָב֥וֹא עוֹד֙ אֶל־הַמֶּ֔לֶךְ כִּ֣י אִם־חָפֵ֥ץ בָּ֛הּ הַמֶּ֖לֶךְ וְנִקְרְאָ֥ה בְשֵֽׁם׃

---

[11] יום ויום ב̇ ובכל יום ויום . ויהי באמרם אליו ‹o›: [12] בשמן ו̇ רפ̇ ועשירית .
ועשרון . והצילו . מצאתי . מצאתיו . קרני . המור ‹o›: [13] באה יא̇ בטע̇ באלף וסימנהון
השלום לו . והנה ארחת ישמעאלים . ותאמר לנעריה עברו לפני . ואנכי מע מעשיהם
ומחשבתיהם . קול שמועה הנה באה . ויקם יונה לברח תרשישה . ואם משפחת
מצרים . תוחלת ממשכה מחלה לב . ובזה הנערה . בערב היא באה ‹o›: וכל מלכ
ויחזקאל כות ב̇ מ̇ ב̇ ‹o›:

---

9 לְט֖וֹב בֵּ֥ית הַנָּשִֽׁים (T^{Sh}) | ἐχρήσατο αὐτῇ καλῶς καὶ ταῖς ἅβραις αὐτῆς ἐν τῷ
γυναικῶνι G (lib-seman) | > G^{AT} (abbr) | *in conventu mulierum* La (abbr) |
ornaret atque excoleret V (lib-seman) | ܠܒܫ ܡܢ ܚܠܡܝ ܢܟܐ S (lib-seman) |
לאוטבא להון ולפנוקותהון בבית נשיא T^R (lib-seman) ✛ • **11** שְׁל֣וֹם (La) (V) T^R | >
G G^{AT} (abbr) | ܐܒܠ S (lib-seman) • **12** הֱי֨וֹת לָ֜הּ כְּדָ֤ת הַנָּשִׁים֙ (S) T^R | > G G^{AT}
(abbr) | *quae ad cultum muliebrem pertinebant* V (facil-styl) ✛ • חֹ֔דֶשׁ G V (T^R)
T^{Sh} | > G^{AT} (abbr) | ܚܒ̈ S (substit) ✛ • **13** וּבָזֶ֕ה (S) (T^{Sh}) | καὶ τότε G T^R
(interp) | > G^{AT} V (facil-styl) ✛ • **14** שֵׁנִ֔י G V T^R | > G^{AT} S (abbr) ✛ •
אֶל־יַ֧ד | οὗ G (differ-gram) | > G^{AT} (abbr) | *sub manu* V (transl) ܒܠ ܒܝ S (differ-gram) |
לידא T^R T^{Sh} (differ-gram) ✛ • שַֽׁעַשְׁגַ֛ז (V) T^{Sh} | Γαί G (substit) | > G^{AT} (abbr) |
ܫܥܫܓܙ S (lib) | (ד)שעגז T^R (lib) ✛ • חָפֵ֥ץ בָּ֛הּ S T^R | > G G^{AT} (abbr) |
voluisset V (facil-styl) •

גֹ 15 וּבְהַגִּיעַ תֹּר־אֶסְתֵּר בַּת־אֲבִיחַיִל דֹּד מָרְדֳּכַי אֲשֶׁר לָקַח־לוֹ לְבַת

לֹ לָבוֹא אֶל־הַמֶּלֶךְ לֹא בִקְשָׁה דָּבָר כִּי אִם אֶת־אֲשֶׁר יֹאמַר הֵגַי

סְרִיס־הַמֶּלֶךְ שֹׁמֵר הַנָּשִׁים וַתְּהִי אֶסְתֵּר נֹשֵׂאת חֵן בְּעֵינֵי כָּל־

לֹ 16 רֹאֶיהָ׃ וַתִּלָּקַח אֶסְתֵּר אֶל־הַמֶּלֶךְ אֲחַשְׁוֵרוֹשׁ אֶל־בֵּית מַלְכוּתוֹ

לֹ 17 בַּחֹדֶשׁ הָעֲשִׂירִי הוּא־חֹדֶשׁ טֵבֵת בִּשְׁנַת־שֶׁבַע לְמַלְכוּתוֹ׃ וַיֶּאֱהַב

ה 18 הַמֶּלֶךְ אֶת־אֶסְתֵּר מִכָּל־הַנָּשִׁים וַתִּשָּׂא־חֵן וָחֶסֶד לְפָנָיו מִכָּל־

גֹ בסיפֹ . לֹ הַבְּתוּלֹת וַיָּשֶׂם כֶּתֶר־מַלְכוּת בְּרֹאשָׁהּ וַיַּמְלִיכֶהָ תַּחַת וַשְׁתִּי׃ וַיַּעַשׂ

הַמֶּלֶךְ מִשְׁתֶּה גָדוֹל לְכָל־שָׂרָיו וַעֲבָדָיו אֵת מִשְׁתֵּה אֶסְתֵּר וַהֲנָחָה

לֹ וחד 19 לַמְּדִינוֹת עָשָׂה וַיִּתֵּן מַשְׂאֵת כְּיַד הַמֶּלֶךְ׃ וּבְהִקָּבֵץ בְּתוּלוֹת שֵׁנִית

במדינות . חֹ

לֹ חֹס בסיפֹ 20 וּמָרְדֳּכַי יֹשֵׁב בְּשַׁעַר־הַמֶּלֶךְ׃ אֵין אֶסְתֵּר מַגֶּדֶת מוֹלַדְתָּהּ וְאֶת־

לֹ וחד את עַמָּהּ כַּאֲשֶׁר צִוָּה עָלֶיהָ מָרְדֳּכָי וְאֶת־מַאֲמַר מָרְדֳּכַי אֶסְתֵּר עֹשָׂה

מאמר . זָֹ

לֹ . בֹ בסיפֹ 21 כַּאֲשֶׁר הָיְתָה בְאָמְנָה אִתּוֹ׃   ס   בַּיָּמִים הָהֵם וּמָרְדֳּכַי יֹשֵׁב

---

[18] משאת ומשאת והמשאת הֹ בליש ועל בית הכרם שאו משאת . נוגי ממועד אספתי .
והנחה למדינות עשה . ויתן לו רב טבחים ארוחה . והמשאת החלה :o: וחד בשאת :o:
[20] עשֹה וָֹ אשר הוא עשה . רוח סערה . ימין יהוה רומֹ רוממה . רנה . ולשמחה .
מרדכי :o:

---

15 אֲבִיחַיִל (V) S Tᴿ I ᾿Αμιναδάβ G (substit) I > Gᴬᵀ (abbr) I *Chihel* La (substit) I
אֶל־בֵּית מַלְכוּתוֹ (Gᴬᵀ) V Tᴿ I καὶ εἰσῆλθεν G S (lib-seman) • **16** • ✠
(S) Tˢʰ I > G Gᴬᵀ (abbr) I *ad cubiculum regis* V (interp) I
לוֹת אידרון בֵית מלכותיה Tᴿ (paraphr) • הָעֲשִׂירִי V S Tᴿ I τῷ δωδεκάτῳ G (substit) I > Gᴬᵀ
(abbr) • טֵבֵת V (S) Tᴿ I ᾿Αδάρ G (substit) I > Gᴬᵀ (abbr) • שֶׁבַע G V Tᴿ I >
Gᴬᵀ I ܐܬܒܕ S (interp) • **17** מִכָּל־הַנָּשִׁים (Gᴬᵀ) V S Tᴿ I > G (facil-styl) •
חֵן Gᴬᵀ V (Tᴿ) I χάριν G S (facil-styl) • וַיָּשֶׂם G Gᴬᵀ V Tᴿ I ܘܣܒܠܗ S (lib-
seman) • **18** שָׂרָיו וַעֲבָדָיו V Tᴿ I τοῖς φίλοις αὐτοῦ καὶ ταῖς δυνάμεσιν G (lib-
seman) I > Gᴬᵀ (abbr) I ܠܥܒܕܘܗܝ, ܠܪܘܪܒܢܘܗܝ S (facil-styl) •
(V) וַיִּתֵּן מַשְׂאֵת כְּיַד הַמֶּלֶךְ׃ S I > G Gᴬᵀ (abbr) I
ומתנן Tᴿ (paraphr) I ויהב לה מתנן וחולק כמיסת ידא דמלכא Tˢʰ (lib-seman) ✠ • **vv 19-23** G V S Tᴿ Tˢʰ I > Gᴬᵀ (abbr) •
19 וּבְהִקָּבֵץ בְּתוּלוֹת שֵׁנִית S Tᴿ Tˢʰ I > G (abbr) I *cumque et secundo quaererentur*
virgines et congregarentur V (ampl) ✠ • **20** מוֹלַדְתָּהּ וְאֶת־עַמָּהּ (La) V S Tᴿ I τὴν
πατρίδα αὐτῆς G (facil-styl) I עמה ותלדות' Tˢʰ (transp) • צִוָּה עָלֶיהָ מָרְדֳּכָי (G)
S Tᴿ I *mandatum eius* V (lib-synt) • בְאָמְנָה I > G (facil-styl) I *eam parvulam*
nutriebat V (lib-seman) I מתרביא Tᴿ (Tˢʰ) (explic) I ܡܬܪܒܝܐ S (theol?) ✠ •

בְּשַׁעַר־הַמֶּ֫לֶךְ קָצַף בִּגְתָ֣ן וָתֶ֔רֶשׁ שְׁנֵֽי־סָרִיסֵ֥י הַמֶּ֛לֶךְ מִשֹּׁמְרֵ֥י הַסַּ֖ף

ל . 22 וַיְבַקְשׁוּ֙ לִשְׁלֹ֣חַ יָ֔ד בַּמֶּ֖לֶךְ אֲחַשְׁוֵרֹֽשׁ: וַיִּוָּדַ֣ע הַדָּבָר֮ לְמָרְדֳּכַי֒ וַיַּגֵּ֣ד

יד . ל . 23 לְאֶסְתֵּ֣ר הַמַּלְכָּ֑ה וַתֹּ֧אמֶר אֶסְתֵּ֛ר לַמֶּ֖לֶךְ בְּשֵׁ֥ם מָרְדֳּכָֽי: וַיְבֻקַּ֣שׁ

ז . ג . בסיפ הַדָּבָר֙ וַיִּמָּצֵ֔א וַיִּתָּל֥וּ שְׁנֵיהֶ֖ם עַל־עֵ֑ץ וַיִּכָּתֵ֗ב בְּסֵ֛פֶר דִּבְרֵ֥י הַיָּמִ֖ים

ג . בסיפ לִפְנֵ֥י הַמֶּֽלֶךְ:   פ   אַחַ֣ר ׀ הַדְּבָרִ֣ים הָאֵ֗לֶּה גִּדַּל֩ הַמֶּ֨לֶךְ **3**

ל . ג . בסיפ אֲחַשְׁוֵרֹ֜ושׁ אֶת־הָמָ֧ן בֶּֽן־הַמְּדָ֛תָא הָאֲגָגִ֖י וַֽיְנַשְּׂאֵ֑הוּ וַיָּ֨שֶׂם֙ אֶת־כִּסְא֔וֹ

ל . 2 מֵעַ֕ל כָּל־הַשָּׂרִ֖ים אֲשֶׁ֣ר אִתּֽוֹ: וְכָל־עַבְדֵ֨י הַמֶּ֜לֶךְ אֲשֶׁר־בְּשַׁ֣עַר

ל . הַמֶּ֗לֶךְ כֹּרְעִ֤ים וּמִֽשְׁתַּחֲוִים֙ לְהָמָ֔ן כִּי־כֵ֖ן צִוָּה־ל֣וֹ הַמֶּ֑לֶךְ וּמָ֨רְדֳּכַ֔י

ג . וחד ואשתחוה 3 לֹ֥א יִכְרַ֖ע וְלֹ֥א יִֽשְׁתַּחֲוֶֽה: וַיֹּ֨אמְר֜וּ עַבְדֵ֥י הַמֶּ֛לֶךְ אֲשֶׁר־בְּשַׁ֥עַר הַמֶּ֖לֶךְ
ב מל בכת
כאמרם
ק

ל . לְמָרְדֳּכָ֑י מַדּ֙וּעַ֙ אַתָּ֣ה עוֹבֵ֔ר אֵ֖ת מִצְוַ֣ת הַמֶּ֑לֶךְ: וַיְהִ֗י בְּאָמְרָ֤ם אֵלָיו֙ 4

ג . ומל בסיפ י֣וֹם וָי֔וֹם וְלֹ֥א שָׁמַ֖ע אֲלֵיהֶ֑ם וַיַּגִּ֣ידוּ לְהָמָ֗ן לִרְאוֹת֙ הֲיַעַמְדוּ֙ דִּבְרֵ֣י

ז . מָרְדֳּכַ֔י כִּֽי־הִגִּ֥יד לָהֶ֖ם אֲשֶׁר־ה֣וּא יְהוּדִ֑י: וַיַּ֣רְא הָמָ֔ן כִּי־אֵ֥ין 5

ז . ב הבכרה מָרְדֳּכַ֔י כֹּרֵ֥עַ וּמִֽשְׁתַּחֲוֶ֖ה ל֑וֹ וַיִּמָּלֵ֥א הָמָ֖ן חֵמָֽה: וַיִּ֣בֶז בְּעֵינָ֗יו לִשְׁלֹ֤חַ 6
נא

---

[23] ויכתב ג בסיפ וסימנהון בספר . ככל אשר צוה המן . מרדכי o: [3:1] כל תהלים
ואיוב ומשלי וחומשה ודניאל . יש הבל שנים בפסוק o: [2] ישתחוה ג ויהי דוד בא .
ומרדכי לא יכרע . ולפניהם o: [5] וימלא ו וסימנהון שבעת ימים . החכמה . הבית .
בית הבעל . וימלא המן . וימלא המן o:

---

21 בִּגְתָ֣ן וָתֶ֔רֶשׁ (V) S T^R | > G (abbr) ✶ •
22 הַמַּלְכָּ֑ה V S T^R | > G (abbr) • | בְּשֵׁ֥ם מָרְדֳּכָֽי: (V) S (T^R) | > G (abbr) | *et nomen Mardochaei* La (lib) • **3:1** הָמָ֧ן בֶּֽן־הַמְּדָ֛תָא הָאֲגָגִ֖י S | Ἀμὰν Ἀμαδάθου Βουγαῖον G G^{AT} (substit) | *Aman* La (abbr) | *Aman filium Amadathi qui erat de stirpe Agag* V (explic) | המן בר המדתא דמזרעית אגג בר עמלק רשיעא T^R (midr) • **2** כֹּרְעִ֤ים וּמִֽשְׁתַּחֲוִים֙ לְהָמָ֔ן V S T^{Sh} | עַבְדֵ֨י הַמֶּ֜לֶךְ V S T^R | > G (G^{AT}) (abbr) • (πάντες...) προσεκύνουν αὐτῷ G (facil-styl) | (πάντων οὖν) προσκυνούντων αὐτῷ G^{AT} (facil-styl) | חמטין וגחנין לאנדרטא די הקים המן בחדייה וסגדין להמן T^R (midr) • **4** בְּאָמְרָ֤ם | באמרם M$^{L(ket)}$ M^{L34} M^Y (G) (V) (S) T^R ‖ pref בְּאָמְרָ֤ם M$^{L(ket)}$ M^{L34} M^Y (G) (V) (S) T^R ✶ • **5:** וַיִּמָּלֵ֥א הָמָ֖ן חֵמָֽה: | ἐθυμώθη σφόδρα G V (facil-styl) | ἐθυμώθη τῷ Μαρδοχαίῳ, καὶ ὀργὴ ἐξεκαύθη ἐν αὐτῷ G^{AT} (ampl) | foll ܚܡܬܐ S (explic) | ואיתמלי המן עילוי מרדכי ריתחא T^R (explic) • **6** וַיִּ֣בֶז בְּעֵינָ֗יו T^{Sh} | > G G^{AT} (abbr) | *et pro nihilo duxit* V (S) (lib) | והוה חוך קומוי T^R (paraphr) ✶ • לִשְׁלֹ֤חַ M^L (err) | לִשְׁלֹ֤חַ M^{L34} M^Y •

יָד֙ בְּמָרְדֳּכַ֣י לְבַדּ֔וֹ כִּֽי־הִגִּ֥ידוּ ל֖וֹ אֶת־עַ֣ם מָרְדֳּכָ֑י וַיְבַקֵּ֣שׁ הָמָ֗ן ג

לְהַשְׁמִ֧יד אֶת־כָּל־הַיְּהוּדִ֛ים אֲשֶׁ֛ר בְּכָל־מַלְכ֥וּת אֲחַשְׁוֵר֖וֹשׁ עַ֥ם ל . ב

מָרְדֳּכָֽי׃ 7 בַּחֹ֤דֶשׁ הָרִאשׁוֹן֙ הוּא־חֹ֣דֶשׁ נִיסָ֔ן בִּשְׁנַת֙ שְׁתֵּ֣ים עֶשְׂרֵ֔ה ז ראׁ פסׁ . סׁד . ב

לַמֶּ֖לֶךְ אֲחַשְׁוֵר֑וֹשׁ הִפִּ֣יל פּוּר֩ ה֨וּא הַגּוֹרָ֜ל לִפְנֵ֣י הָמָ֗ן מִיּ֧וֹם ׀

לְי֛וֹם וּמֵחֹ֛דֶשׁ לְחֹ֥דֶשׁ שְׁנֵים־עָשָׂ֖ר הוּא־חֹ֥דֶשׁ אֲדָֽר׃ ס ל

8 וַיֹּ֤אמֶר הָמָן֙ לַמֶּ֣לֶךְ אֲחַשְׁוֵר֔וֹשׁ יֶשְׁנ֣וֹ עַם־אֶחָ֗ד מְפֻזָּ֤ר וּמְפֹרָד֙ ד . ל

בֵּ֣ין הָֽעַמִּ֔ים בְּכֹ֖ל מְדִינ֣וֹת מַלְכוּתֶ֑ךָ וְדָתֵיהֶ֞ם שֹׁנ֣וֹת מִכָּל־עָ֗ם ל . ל . ל . יׁד

וְאֶת־דָּתֵ֤י הַמֶּ֙לֶךְ֙ אֵינָ֣ם עֹשִׂ֔ים וְלַמֶּ֥לֶךְ אֵין־שֹׁוֶ֖ה לְהַנִּיחָֽם׃ בׁ־ליהוה . גׁ

9 אִם־עַל־הַמֶּ֣לֶךְ ט֔וֹב יִכָּתֵ֖ב לְאַבְּדָ֑ם וַעֲשֶׂ֨רֶת אֲלָפִ֜ים כִּכַּר־

כֶּ֗סֶף אֶשְׁקוֹל֙ עַל־יְדֵי֙ עֹשֵׂ֣י הַמְּלָאכָ֔ה לְהָבִ֖יא אֶל־גִּנְזֵ֥י ל מלׁ . ב כתׁ ו

הַמֶּֽלֶךְ׃ 10 וַיָּ֧סַר הַמֶּ֛לֶךְ אֶת־טַבַּעְתּ֖וֹ מֵעַ֣ל יָד֑וֹ וַֽיִּתְּנָ֔הּ לְהָמָ֞ן

11 בֶּֽן־הַמְּדָ֧תָא הָאֲגָגִ֛י צֹרֵ֥ר הַיְּהוּדִֽים׃ וַיֹּ֤אמֶר הַמֶּ֙לֶךְ֙ לְהָמָ֔ן כולׁ חסׁ . ב

[8] ישנו ד׳ וסימנהון כי את אשר ישנו פה . ביהונתן בני . וחפשתי אתו . ישנו עם אחד
מפזר ס: [11] ויאמר המלך להמן ב׳ הכסף נתון לך . מהר קח את הלבוש ס: ויאמר
המלך להמן ב׳ וסימנה הכסף נתון לך . מהר קח את הלבוש ואת הסוס ס:

6 עַם² מָרְדֳּכָי S Tᴿ | > G Gᴬᵀ (abbr) | *et Mardochaeum et genus ejus* La (lib-synt) | *nationem* V (facil-styl) ⊹ • **7** בַּחֹדֶשׁ הָרִאשׁוֹן הוּא־חֹדֶשׁ נִיסָן La (V) S Tᴿ | > G Gᴬᵀ (abbr) • פּוּר הוּא הַגּוֹרָל (V) | κλήρους G (assim-cultur) | > Gᴬᵀ (abbr) | ܡܠܬܐ ܗܘ ܥܒܕܐ S (lib-synt) | פייסא Tᴿ (transl) | ܡܠܬܐ ܗܘ ܥܒܕܐ Tˢʰ (exeg) • וּמֵחֹדֶשׁ לְחֹדֶשׁ שְׁנֵים־עָשָׂר (hapl) | ὥστε ἀπολέσαι ἐν μιᾷ ἡμέρᾳ τὸ γένος Μαρδοχαίου, καὶ ἔπεσεν ὁ κλῆρος εἰς τὴν τεσσαρεσκαιδεκάτην τοῦ μηνός G (interp) | καὶ βάλλει κλήρους εἰς τὴν τρισκαιδεκάτην τοῦ μηνός Gᴬᵀ (interp) | (*quo die et*) *quo mense gens Iudaeorum deberet interfici et exivit mensis duodecimus* V (interp) | ומן ירחא לירחא S | ܘܡܢ ܝܪܚܐ ܠܝܪܚܐ Tˢʰ (facil) | Tᴿ (indet) || pref וּמֵחֹדֶשׁ לְחֹדֶשׁ שְׁנֵים־עָשָׂר see S ⊹ • **8** מְפֻזָּר וּמְפֹרָד S Tᴿ | διεσπαρμένον G (Gᴬᵀ) (facil-styl) | *dispersus et a se mutuo separatus* V (lib-synt) | מתבדר ומטלטל Tˢʰ (lib-seman) • בֵּין הָעַמִּים G Tᴿ | > Gᴬᵀ V S (facil-styl) • **9** יִכָּתֵב לְאַבְּדָם Tᴿ | δογματισάτω ἀπολέσαι αὐτούς G (S) (lib-synt) | δοθήτω μοι τὸ ἔθνος εἰς ἀπώλειαν Gᴬᵀ (lib-seman) | *decerne ut pereat* V (lib-synt) | יכתב כתבא למובדא יתהון Tˢʰ (ampl) • עַל־יְדֵי S Tᴿ | > G Gᴬᵀ V (facil-styl) ⊹ • **10** בֶּן־הַמְּדָתָא הָאֲגָגִי צֹרֵר הַיְּהוּדִים S (Tᴿ) | > G Gᴬᵀ (abbr) ⊹ •

הַכֶּ֣סֶף נָת֣וּן לָ֔ךְ וְהָעָ֕ם לַעֲשׂ֥וֹת בּ֖וֹ כַּטּ֥וֹב בְּעֵינֶֽיךָ׃ וַיִּקָּרְאוּ֩ 12

סֹפְרֵ֨י הַמֶּ֜לֶךְ בַּחֹ֣דֶשׁ הָרִאשׁ֗וֹן בִּשְׁלוֹשָׁ֨ה עָשָׂ֣ר יוֹם֮ בּוֹ֒ וַיִּכָּתֵ֣ב כְּֽכָל־

אֲשֶׁר־צִוָּ֣ה הָמָ֡ן אֶ֣ל אֲחַשְׁדַּרְפְּנֵֽי־הַ֠מֶּלֶךְ וְֽאֶל־הַפַּחוֹת֩ אֲשֶׁ֨ר ׀ עַל־

מְדִינָ֜ה וּמְדִינָ֗ה וְאֶל־שָׂ֤רֵי עַם֙ וָעָ֔ם מְדִינָ֤ה וּמְדִינָה֙ כִּכְתָבָ֔הּ וְעַ֥ם

וָעָ֖ם כִּלְשׁוֹנ֑וֹ בְּשֵׁ֨ם הַמֶּ֤לֶךְ אֲחַשְׁוֵרֹשׁ֙ נִכְתָּ֔ב וְנֶחְתָּ֖ם בְּטַבַּ֥עַת הַמֶּֽלֶךְ׃

וְנִשְׁל֨וֹחַ סְפָרִ֜ים בְּיַ֣ד הָרָצִים֮ אֶל־כָּל־מְדִינ֣וֹת הַמֶּלֶךְ֒ לְהַשְׁמִ֡יד 13

לַהֲרֹ֣ג וּלְאַבֵּ֣ד אֶת־כָּל־הַ֠יְּהוּדִים מִנַּ֨עַר וְעַד־זָקֵ֜ן טַ֤ף וְנָשִׁים֙ בְּי֣וֹם

אֶחָ֔ד בִּשְׁלוֹשָׁ֥ה עָשָׂ֛ר לְחֹ֥דֶשׁ שְׁנֵים־עָשָׂ֖ר הוּא־חֹ֣דֶשׁ אֲדָ֑ר וּשְׁלָלָ֖ם

לָבֽוֹז׃ פַּתְשֶׁ֣גֶן הַכְּתָ֗ב לְהִנָּ֤תֵֽן דָּת֙ בְּכָל־מְדִינָ֣ה וּמְדִינָ֔ה גָּל֖וּי לְכָל־ 14

הָֽעַמִּ֑ים לִהְי֥וֹת עֲתִדִ֖ים לַיּ֥וֹם הַזֶּֽה׃ הָרָצִ֞ים יָצְא֤וּ דְחוּפִים֙ בִּדְבַ֣ר 15

הַמֶּ֔לֶךְ וְהַדָּ֥ת נִתְּנָ֖ה בְּשׁוּשַׁ֣ן הַבִּירָ֑ה וְהַמֶּ֤לֶךְ וְהָמָן֙ יָשְׁב֣וּ לִשְׁתּ֔וֹת

וְהָעִ֥יר שׁוּשָׁ֖ן נָבֽוֹכָה׃   פ   וּמָרְדֳּכַ֗י יָדַע֙ אֶת־כָּל־אֲשֶׁ֣ר נַעֲשָׂ֔ה 4

וַיִּקְרַ֤ע מָרְדֳּכַי֙ אֶת־בְּגָדָ֔יו וַיִּלְבַּ֥שׁ שַׂ֖ק וָאֵ֑פֶר וַיֵּצֵא֙ בְּת֣וֹךְ הָעִ֔יר

וַיִּזְעַ֛ק זְעָקָ֥ה גְדֹלָ֖ה וּמָרָֽה׃ וַיָּב֕וֹא עַ֖ד לִפְנֵ֣י שַֽׁעַר־הַמֶּ֑לֶךְ כִּ֣י אֵ֥ין 2

לָב֛וֹא אֶל־שַׁ֥עַר הַמֶּ֖לֶךְ בִּלְב֥וּשׁ שָֽׂק׃ וּבְכָל־מְדִינָ֣ה וּמְדִינָ֗ה מְקוֹם֙ 3

אֲשֶׁ֨ר דְּבַר־הַמֶּ֤לֶךְ וְדָתוֹ֙ מַגִּ֔יעַ אֵ֤בֶל גָּדוֹל֙ לַיְּהוּדִ֔ים וְצ֥וֹם וּבְכִ֖י

Masorah parva (right margin, top to bottom):

ג . ב̇
סד̇ . ב̇ . ג̇ בסיפ̇ . ג̇ בכת̇
ל̇
ל̇
ד̇ חס̇
ל̇ ומל̇ . כ̇ו פסוק אית בהון אלף בית

ל̇ . ג̇ ב בסיפ̇
ב̇ חד חס̇ . ל̇ ומל̇
ל̇ ומל̇ . ב̇ רא̇ פס̇
ל̇ . כול סיפ̇ מל̇ ב̇ מ̇ חס̇
ל̇

Masorah magna (below text):

נתון ג̇ ומל̇ וסימנה החכמה והמדע נתון לך . בלשכת בית . הכסף נתון לך ‹:o› נתון ג̇
ומל̇ וסימנה החכמה והמדע . נתון בלשכת בית . הכסף נתון לך ‹:o› [12] בשלשה עשר
יום בו ב̇ ויקראו ספרי המלך . ובשנים עשר חדש ‹:o› [13] לבוז ב̇ וסימנה ויבא יהושפט
ועמו לבוז את שלל . ושללם לבוז . ושללם לבוז ‹:o› [4:1] ומרדכי ב̇ רא̇ פסוק ידע
את כל אשר נעשה ‹:o›

11 הַכֶּ֣סֶף (G) (G^AT) T^R | *argentum quod polliceris* V (explic) | ܚܣܦܐ S
(explic) • **12** וַיִּכָּתֵ֣ב (La) V T^R | καὶ ἔγραψαν G (lib-synt) | > G^AT (abbr) •
אֲחַשְׁדַּרְפְּנֵֽי־הַ֠מֶּלֶךְ T^R | τοῖς στρατηγοῖς G (lib-seman) | > G^AT (abbr) | *et ducibus
regis* La (lib-seman) | *omnes satrapas regis* V (lib-seman) | ܘܠܪܘ̈ܪܒܢܐ S
(lib-seman) | יקירוי דמלכא T^Sh (lib-seman) ⁜ • **13** וְנָשִׁים֙ to לְהַשְׁמִ֡יד S T^R |
ἀφανίσαι τὸ γένος τῶν Ἰουδαίων G (abbr) | > G^AT (abbr) | *ut occiderent atque
delerent omnes Iudaeos a puero usque ad senem parvulos et mulieres* V (facil-styl)
⁜ • בִּשְׁלוֹשָׁ֥ה עָשָׂ֛ר V S T^R | > G G^AT (abbr) • לָבֽוֹז׃ V S T^R | foll B 1-7 G (lit) |
foll 3:14-18 G^AT (lit) • **14** גָּל֖וּי (T^R) T^Sh | καὶ προσετάγη G S (explic) | > G^AT
(abbr) | *scirent* V (explic) • **4:3 v 3** (G) (V) S T^R | > G^AT (abbr) ⁜ •

4 וּמִסְפֵּד שַׂק וָאֵפֶר יֻצַּע לָֽרַבִּֽים׃ וַתָּבוֹאנָה נַעֲרוֹת אֶסְתֵּר וְסָרִיסֶיהָ   ב. ד. ל מל

וַיַּגִּידוּ לָהּ וַתִּתְחַלְחַל הַמַּלְכָּה מְאֹד וַתִּשְׁלַח בְּגָדִים לְהַלְבִּישׁ אֶת־   ל

5 מׇרְדֳּכַי וּלְהָסִיר שַׂקּוֹ מֵעָלָיו וְלֹא קִבֵּֽל׃ וַתִּקְרָא אֶסְתֵּר לַהֲתָךְ   ל

מִסָּרִיסֵי הַמֶּלֶךְ אֲשֶׁר הֶעֱמִיד לְפָנֶיהָ וַתְּצַוֵּהוּ עַֽל־מׇרְדֳּכָי לָדַעַת   ב

6 מַה־זֶּה וְעַל־מַה־זֶּֽה׃ וַיֵּצֵא הֲתָךְ אֶֽל־מׇרְדֳּכָי אֶל־רְחוֹב הָעִיר   ל וחד על מה זה אתה מבקש

7 אֲשֶׁר לִפְנֵי שַֽׁעַר־הַמֶּֽלֶךְ׃ וַיַּגֶּד־לוֹ מׇרְדֳּכַי אֵת כׇּל־אֲשֶׁר קָרָהוּ   ג

וְאֵת ׀ פָּרָשַׁת הַכֶּסֶף אֲשֶׁר אָמַר הָמָן לִשְׁקוֹל עַל־גִּנְזֵי הַמֶּלֶךְ   ל מל. ל

8 *בַּיְּהוּדִֽיִּים* לְאַבְּדָֽם׃ וְאֶת־פַּתְשֶׁגֶן כְּתָֽב־הַדָּת אֲשֶׁר־נִתַּן בְּשׁוּשָׁן   יתיר י. כא

לְהַשְׁמִידָם נָתַן לוֹ לְהַרְאוֹת אֶת־אֶסְתֵּר וּלְהַגִּיד לָהּ וּלְצַוּוֹת עָלֶיהָ   ג. ל ומל

9 לָבוֹא אֶל־הַמֶּלֶךְ לְהִֽתְחַנֶּן־לוֹ וּלְבַקֵּשׁ מִלְּפָנָיו עַל־עַמָּֽהּ׃ וַיָּבוֹא   ד

10 הֲתָךְ וַיַּגֵּד לְאֶסְתֵּר אֵת דִּבְרֵי מׇרְדֳּכָֽי׃ וַתֹּאמֶר אֶסְתֵּר לַהֲתָךְ

11 וַתְּצַוֵּהוּ אֶֽל־מׇרְדֳּכָֽי׃ כׇּל־עַבְדֵי הַמֶּלֶךְ וְעַם־מְדִינוֹת הַמֶּלֶךְ

יֽוֹדְעִים אֲשֶׁר כׇּל־אִישׁ וְאִשָּׁה אֲשֶׁר יָבֽוֹא־אֶל־הַמֶּלֶךְ אֶל־הֶחָצֵר   ד בטע

הַפְּנִימִית אֲשֶׁר לֹֽא־יִקָּרֵא אַחַת דָּתוֹ לְהָמִית לְבַד מֵאֲשֶׁר יֽוֹשִׁיט־

לוֹ הַמֶּלֶךְ אֶת־שַׁרְבִיט הַזָּהָב וְחָיָה וַאֲנִי לֹא נִקְרֵאתִי לָבוֹא אֶל־   ו. ב

---

[3] יצע ב̇ שק ואפר יצע . תחתיך יצע רמה ׃o [5] על מרדכי ב̇ ותקרא אסתר
להתך . ויצא המן ביום ההוא ׃o [11] יקרא כא̇ וסימנהון לזאת יקרא אשה . את שמך
אברם . כי ביצחק . שמך עוד יעקב . כי ביצחק . וילך שפי . ההוא יקרא ארץ
רפאים . כי יקרא קן צפור לפניך . יקרא לפנים . שפטיך . והחזיקו . לעולם .
ולכילי . יהגה . מסלול ודרך . והביאותים . וגאלך . חפצי בה . ולך יקרא דרושה .
התפת . נבון . כל עבדי המלך ׃o נקראתי ב̇ נקרא נקראתי ׃o ואני לא נקראתי ׃o

---

4 נַעֲרוֹת אֶסְתֵּר וְסָרִיסֶיהָ V T^R T^{Sh} | αἱ ἅβραι καὶ οἱ εὐνοῦχοι τῆς βασιλίσσης G
(transp) | > G^{AT} (abbr) | ܐܢܫ̈ܐ ܕܡܗܝܡܢܝܢ ܥܠܝܗ̇ S (transp) • **5** לַהֲתָךְ (V)
T^R | ʾΑχραθαῖον G (lib) | > G^{AT} (abbr) | ܠܗܡܢ S (lib) | לדניאל דמתקרי התך T^R
(paraphr) • אֲשֶׁר הֶעֱמִיד | ὃς παρειστήκει G S T^{Sh} (differ-gram) | > G^{AT} (abbr) |
quem (rex ministrum) ei dederat V (lib-seman) | > T^R (abbr) ÷ • עַֽל־מׇרְדֳּכָי (V)
T^R | > G G^{AT} (abbr) | ܥܠ ܡܪܕܟܝ S (differ-gram) • **10** אֶֽל־מׇרְדֳּכָי G S | αὐτῷ
G^{AT} (facil-styl) | Mardocheo V (differ-gram) | על עיסק מרדכי T^R (differ-gram) |
מטול מרדכי T^{Sh} (lib-seman) ÷ • **11** נִקְרֵאתִי M^L (err) | נִקְרֵאתִי M^{L34} M^Y •

<table>
<tr><td>ב מל בכתיב</td><td>12</td><td>הַמֶּלֶךְ זֶה שְׁלוֹשִׁים יוֹם: וַיַּגִּידוּ לְמָרְדֳּכַי אֵת דִּבְרֵי אֶסְתֵּר: פ</td></tr>
</table>

ל זק קמׂ . ל . ל   **13**   וַיֹּאמֶר מָרְדֳּכַי לְהָשִׁיב אֶל אֶסְתֵּר אַל תְּדַמִּי בְנַפְשֵׁךְ לְהִמָּלֵט

ל   **14**   בֵּית הַמֶּלֶךְ מִכָּל הַיְּהוּדִים: כִּי אִם הַחֲרֵשׁ תַּחֲרִישִׁי בָּעֵת הַזֹּאת

ל וחד ורוח   רֶוַח וְהַצָּלָה יַעֲמוֹד לַיְּהוּדִים מִמָּקוֹם אַחֵר וְאַתְּ וּבֵית אָבִיךְ

ל וטעין . ג . ל . ל   **15**   תֹּאבֵדוּ וּמִי יוֹדֵעַ אִם לְעֵת כָּזֹאת הִגַּעַתְּ לַמַּלְכוּת: וַתֹּאמֶר אֶסְתֵּר

ל ומל . ל . ג   **16**   לְהָשִׁיב אֶל מָרְדֳּכָי: לֵךְ כְּנוֹס אֶת כָּל הַיְּהוּדִים הַנִּמְצְאִים

בְּשׁוּשָׁן וְצוּמוּ עָלַי וְאַל תֹּאכְלוּ וְאַל תִּשְׁתּוּ שְׁלֹשֶׁת יָמִים לַיְלָה

וָיוֹם גַּם אֲנִי וְנַעֲרֹתַי אָצוּם כֵּן וּבְכֵן אָבוֹא אֶל הַמֶּלֶךְ אֲשֶׁר לֹא

ל   **17**   כַדָּת וְכַאֲשֶׁר אָבַדְתִּי אָבָדְתִּי: וַיַּעֲבֹר מָרְדֳּכָי וַיַּעַשׂ כְּכֹל אֲשֶׁר

צִוְּתָה עָלָיו אֶסְתֵּר: ס   וַיְהִי | בַּיּוֹם הַשְּׁלִישִׁי וַתִּלְבַּשׁ אֶסְתֵּר   **5**

ל   מַלְכוּת וַתַּעֲמֹד בַּחֲצַר בֵּית הַמֶּלֶךְ הַפְּנִימִית נֹכַח בֵּית הַמֶּלֶךְ

ה זוגין מׂ ב ב / מיחד בבית וחד / בית . ל   וְהַמֶּלֶךְ יוֹשֵׁב עַל כִּסֵּא מַלְכוּתוֹ בְּבֵית הַמַּלְכוּת נֹכַח פֶּתַח הַבָּיִת:

ל   **2**   וַיְהִי כִרְאוֹת הַמֶּלֶךְ אֶת אֶסְתֵּר הַמַּלְכָּה עֹמֶדֶת בֶּחָצֵר נָשְׂאָה חֵן

שלושים ב מל בכתוב וסימנה ויחלא אסא . ואני לא נקראתי :ס [16] ובכן ב אבוא אל
המלך . ראיתי רשעים קבורים :ס ובכן ב אבוא אל המלך . ראיתי רשעים :ס ה [5:1]
זוגין מן ב ב מיחדין חד בבית וחד בית וסימנהון בבית הבור . בית הבור . בבית
החפשית . בית החפשית . בבית רשע . בית רשע . בבית אבל . בית אבל . בבית
המלכות . בית המלכות :ס

---

11 שְׁלוֹשִׁים G G^(AT) V T^(R) | ܐܠܐ S (lib-seman) • **12** וַיַּגִּידוּ T^(Sh) | καὶ ἀπήγγειλεν
Ἀχραθαῖος G S (harm-ctext) | > G^(AT) V T^(R) (abbr) • **13** לְהִמָּלֵט בֵּית הַמֶּלֶךְ
(T^(Sh)) | ὅτι σωθήσῃ μόνη ἐν τῇ βασιλείᾳ G (lib-seman) | > G^(AT) (abbr) | + *uxor*
regis La (lib-seman) | *animam tuam tantum liberes quia in domo regis es* V (lib-
seman) | הִגַּעַתְּ • **14** ܕܗܪ ܒܝܬ ܚܠܦܐ ܐܝܬ, ܡܬܦܠܟܠ ܐܝܬ, S (T^(R)) (explic) ✥ • **14** לַמַּלְכוּת
V T^(Sh) | ἐβασίλευσας G G^(AT) (explic) | ܐܝܬܬ ܕܬܡܠܟ ܠܬܚܠܕܬܐ S
(ampl) | את מטיא למיחסן מלכותא T^(R) (explic) ✥ • **16** וְאַל תֹּאכְלוּ G S | > G^(AT)
(abbr) | *non comedatis* V T^(R) (lib-synt) ✥ • גַּם | κἀγὼ δέ G G^(AT) V S T^(R) (lib-
synt) | > La (abbr) • וּבְכֵן T^(Sh) | καὶ τότε G V (lib-seman) | *post haec* La S T^(R)
(lib-seman) | > G^(AT) (abbr) ✥ • **17** אֶסְתֵּר: V S T^(R) | foll C 1-30 G (lit) | foll 4:12-
29 G^(AT) (lit) • **5:1** וַיְהִי V S T^(R) | prec D 1-16 G (lit) | prec 5 (D) 1-24 G^(AT) (lit)
✥ • מַלְכוּת | τὴν δόξαν αὐτῆς G (explic) | τὰ ἱμάτια τῆς δόξης G^(AT) (explic) |
regalibus vestimentis V (explic) | ܠܒܘܫ ܕܡܠܟܘܬܐ S T^(R) (explic) ✥ • בְּבֵית
הַמַּלְכוּת T^(R) | > G G^(AT) S (abbr) | *in consistorio palatii* V (assim-cultur) •

בְּעֵינָיו וַיּוֹשֶׁט הַמֶּלֶךְ לְאֶסְתֵּר אֶת־שַׁרְבִיט הַזָּהָב אֲשֶׁר בְּיָדֹו

3 וַתִּקְרַב אֶסְתֵּר וַתִּגַּע בְּרֹאשׁ הַשַּׁרְבִיט: ס וַיֹּאמֶר לָהּ הַמֶּלֶךְ

מַה־לָּךְ אֶסְתֵּר הַמַּלְכָּה וּמַה־בַּקָּשָׁתֵךְ עַד־חֲצִי הַמַּלְכוּת וְיִנָּתֵן

4 לָךְ: וַתֹּאמֶר אֶסְתֵּר אִם־עַל־הַמֶּלֶךְ טוֹב יָבוֹא הַמֶּלֶךְ וְהָמָן הַיּוֹם

5 אֶל־הַמִּשְׁתֶּה אֲשֶׁר־עָשִׂיתִי לֹו: וַיֹּאמֶר הַמֶּלֶךְ מַהֲרוּ אֶת־הָמָן

לַעֲשׂוֹת אֶת־דְּבַר אֶסְתֵּר וַיָּבֹא הַמֶּלֶךְ וְהָמָן אֶל־הַמִּשְׁתֶּה אֲשֶׁר־

6 עָשְׂתָה אֶסְתֵּר: וַיֹּאמֶר הַמֶּלֶךְ לְאֶסְתֵּר בְּמִשְׁתֵּה הַיַּיִן מַה־שְּׁאֵלָתֵךְ

7 וְיִנָּתֵן לָךְ וּמַה־בַּקָּשָׁתֵךְ עַד־חֲצִי הַמַּלְכוּת וְתֵעָשׂ: וַתַּעַן אֶסְתֵּר

8 וַתֹּאמַר שְׁאֵלָתִי וּבַקָּשָׁתִי: אִם־מָצָאתִי חֵן בְּעֵינֵי הַמֶּלֶךְ וְאִם־עַל־

הַמֶּלֶךְ טוֹב לָתֵת אֶת־שְׁאֵלָתִי וְלַעֲשׂוֹת אֶת־בַּקָּשָׁתִי יָבוֹא הַמֶּלֶךְ

וְהָמָן אֶל־הַמִּשְׁתֶּה אֲשֶׁר אֶעֱשֶׂה לָהֶם וּמָחָר אֶעֱשֶׂה כִּדְבַר הַמֶּלֶךְ:

9 וַיֵּצֵא הָמָן בַּיּוֹם הַהוּא שָׂמֵחַ וְטֹוב לֵב וְכִרְאֹות הָמָן אֶת־מָרְדֳּכַי

בְּשַׁעַר הַמֶּלֶךְ וְלֹא־קָם וְלֹא־זָע מִמֶּנּוּ וַיִּמָּלֵא הָמָן עַל־מָרְדֳּכַי

10 חֵמָה: וַיִּתְאַפַּק הָמָן וַיָּבוֹא אֶל־בֵּיתֹו וַיִּשְׁלַח וַיָּבֵא אֶת־אֹהֲבָיו

11 וְאֶת־זֶרֶשׁ אִשְׁתֹּו: וַיְסַפֵּר לָהֶם הָמָן אֶת־כְּבֹוד עָשְׁרֹו וְרֹב בָּנָיו וְאֵת

Marginal Masorah (right to left, outer column):
נא . ל בסיפ
ב
ל סוף פסוק
ד
ב חס בסיפ
ה . ל וחד ולעשות את בקשתי
הי . ל
ו
יו . ב
ב נביא עוד . ל . ו . ב
נא

---

[5] מהרו ד ועלו . עשו . ללכת . את המן . וג מהרו בניך . הלוים . שכחו :o: כול
ויבוא דבסיפ מל ב מן ב וסימנה אל המשתה . לשתות :o: [8] ומחר ו וסימנהון וקדשתם
היום . ומחר אשלחך . אתה ובניך . תמרדו . אעשה כדבר . ומחר אתן :o:
[9] וכראות ב שאול את דוד . המן את מרדכי . וחד ובראות יהוה כי נכנעו :o:
וכראות ב וסימנהון שאול את דוד . המן את מרדכֵי . וחד ובראות יהוה כי נכנעו :o:
[10] ויתאפק ב ויאמר שימו לחם . המן :o:

---

4 וְהָמָן G (V) S T^R | foll ὁ φίλος σου G^AT (lib-seman) | et amicus tuus La (substit) • **5** מַהֲרוּ אֶת־הָמָן | הַיּוֹם G V T^R | αὔριον G^AT (substit) | > S (abbr) ✥ • **5** אֲשֶׁר־עָשְׂתָה אֶסְתֵּר G^AT G G^AT (V) T^R | > La (abbr) | حصل ... S (lib) • אֲשֶׁר־עָשְׂתָה אֶסְתֵּר G^AT T^R | ἣν εἶπεν Ἐσθήρ G (assim-ctext) | > La S (abbr) | quod eis regina paraverat V (lib-synt) • **8** אֲשֶׁר to הַמֶּלֶךְ: (V) (T^Sh) | (ἔτι τὴν αὔριον εἰς τὴν δοχήν,) ἣν ποιήσω αὐτοῖς· καὶ αὔριον ποιήσω τὰ αὐτά G (lib-seman) | (εἰς τὴν δοχήν,) ἣν ποιήσω αὐτοῖς καὶ τῇ αὔριον· καὶ αὔριον γὰρ ποιήσω κατὰ τὰ αὐτά G^AT (lib-seman) | > La (abbr) | ... S (lib-seman) | > La (abbr) | ... S (lib-seman) ✥ • T^R (lib-seman) ✥ • ... T^R (lib-seman) ✥ • **10** וַיִּתְאַפַּק (V) T^R | > G G^AT (abbr) | ... S (substit) • וְאֶת־זֶרֶשׁ V S T^R | καὶ Ζωσάραν G G^AT (metath?) •

ל.ב | כָּל־אֲשֶׁ֨ר גִּדְּל֤וֹ הַמֶּ֙לֶךְ֙ וְאֵ֣ת אֲשֶׁ֣ר נִשְּׂא֔וֹ עַל־הַשָּׂרִ֖ים וְעַבְדֵ֥י הַמֶּֽלֶךְ׃

יֹב בטעֹ ברא פֿסוק | 2 וַיֹּ֣אמֶר֮ הָמָן֒ אַ֣ף לֹא־הֵבִ֩יאָה֩ אֶסְתֵּ֨ר הַמַּלְכָּ֧ה עִם־הַמֶּ֛לֶךְ אֶל־

ה בסיפֿ . ה . ל | הַמִּשְׁתֶּ֥ה אֲשֶׁר־עָשָׂ֖תָה כִּ֣י אִם־אוֹתִ֑י וְגַם־לְמָחָ֛ר אֲנִ֥י קָרֽוּא־לָ֖הּ

3 | עִם־הַמֶּֽלֶךְ׃ וְכָל־זֶ֗ה אֵינֶ֤נּוּ שֹׁוֶה֙ לִ֔י בְּכָל־עֵ֗ת אֲשֶׁ֤ר אֲנִי֙ רֹאֶ֔ה אֶת־

ל | 4 מָרְדֳּכַ֣י הַיְּהוּדִ֔י יוֹשֵׁ֖ב בְּשַׁ֣עַר הַמֶּֽלֶךְ׃ וַתֹּ֣אמֶר ל֣וֹ זֶ֣רֶשׁ אִשְׁתּ֗וֹ וְכָל־

ו.ב | אֹֽהֲבָ֞יו יַֽעֲשׂוּ־עֵ֣ץ גָּבֹ֣הַּ חֲמִשִּׁ֣ים אַמָּ֗ה וּבַבֹּ֣קֶר ׀ אֱמֹ֤ר לַמֶּ֙לֶךְ֙ וְיִתְל֣וּ

ב בליש | אֶֽת־מָרְדֳּכַי֙ עָלָ֔יו וּבֹֽא־עִם־הַמֶּ֥לֶךְ אֶל־הַמִּשְׁתֶּ֖ה שָׂמֵ֑חַ וַיִּיטַ֧ב

ב בליש | הַדָּבָ֛ר לִפְנֵ֥י הָמָ֖ן וַיַּ֥עַשׂ הָעֵֽץ׃ פ **6** בַּלַּ֣יְלָה הַה֔וּא נָדְדָ֖ה שְׁנַ֣ת

ל | הַמֶּ֑לֶךְ וַיֹּ֗אמֶר לְהָבִ֞יא אֶת־סֵ֤פֶר הַזִּכְרֹנוֹת֙ דִּבְרֵ֣י הַיָּמִ֔ים וַיִּֽהְי֥וּ

ל.ל | 2 נִקְרָאִ֖ים לִפְנֵ֥י הַמֶּֽלֶךְ׃ וַיִּמָּצֵ֣א כָת֗וּב אֲשֶׁר֩ הִגִּ֨יד מָרְדֳּכַ֜י עַל־בִּגְתָ֣נָא

יא | וָתֶ֗רֶשׁ שְׁנֵי֙ סָרִיסֵ֣י הַמֶּ֔לֶךְ מִשֹּׁמְרֵ֖י הַסַּ֑ף אֲשֶׁ֤ר בִּקְשׁוּ֙ לִשְׁלֹ֣חַ יָ֔ד

3 | בַּמֶּ֖לֶךְ אֲחַשְׁוֵרֽוֹשׁ׃ וַיֹּ֣אמֶר הַמֶּ֗לֶךְ מַֽה־נַּעֲשָׂ֞ה יְקָ֧ר וּגְדוּלָּ֛ה לְמָרְדֳּכַ֖י

4 | עַל־זֶ֑ה וַיֹּ֨אמְר֜וּ נַעֲרֵ֤י הַמֶּ֙לֶךְ֙ מְשָׁ֣רְתָ֔יו לֹֽא־נַעֲשָׂ֥ה עִמּ֖וֹ דָּבָֽר׃ וַיֹּ֥אמֶר

ל | הַמֶּ֙לֶךְ֙ מִ֣י בֶֽחָצֵ֔ר וְהָמָ֣ן בָּ֗א לַֽחֲצַ֤ר בֵּית־הַמֶּ֙לֶךְ֙ הַחִֽיצוֹנָ֔ה לֵאמֹ֣ר

ב | 5 לַמֶּ֔לֶךְ לִתְלוֹת֙ אֶֽת־מָרְדֳּכַ֔י עַל־הָעֵ֖ץ אֲשֶׁר־הֵכִ֣ין ל֑וֹ וַיֹּ֤אמְר֣וּ

---

[14] אמר למלך ב' ולגבירה . ובבקר ב' ובא ב' בלשון ביאה ובא עם המלך . ובא
בשערי ירושֹ o: [6:2] וימצא ז' וסימנה הגביע . כתוב . מבני הכהנים . ביעזיר גלעד .
ויבקש . בקשוהו . ויבקשוהו o: [4] לתלות ב' וסימֹ את מרדכי . עליו o:

---

11 כָּל־ T^Sh | > G G^AT V S T^R (lib-seman) ÷ • גִּדְּלוֹ (S) T^Sh | καὶ τὴν δόξαν, ἣν (ὁ βασιλεὺς) αὐτῷ περιέθηκεν G (facil-styl) | > G^AT (abbr) | *epulentiam gloriae suae* La (facil-styl) | *(quanta) eum gloria* V (facil-styl) | > T^R (abbr) ÷ • עַל־הַשָּׂרִים וְעַבְדֵי הַמֶּלֶךְ: | αὐτὸν πρωτεύειν G (lib-seman) | > G^AT (abbr) | *super omnes principes et servos suos* V T^R (lib) ܠܟ ܕܐܬܒܪܟ ܡܢ ܚܒܪ, ܚܠܟ S (lib) ÷ • **13** יוֹשֵׁב בְּשַׁעַר הַמֶּלֶךְ (V) S (T^Sh) | ἐν τῇ αὐλῇ G (abbr) | + καὶ μὴ προσκυνεῖ με G^AT (ampl) | *non adorantem me* La (substit) יתיב בסנהדרין עם T^R (paraphr) ÷ • **14** הַמִּשְׁתֶּה M^L (err) | עוּלְמִיא בתרע פלטירין דמלכא M^L34 M^Y M^S1 • לִפְנֵי הָמָן T^R | τῷ Ἀμάν G G^AT (assim-styl) | > אֶל־הַמִּשְׁתֶּה La (abbr) | *(placuit) ei (consilium)* V (facil-styl) | ܚܒܝܬܗ، ܕܗܡܢ S (substit) ÷ • **6:1** נָדְדָה שְׁנַת S T^R | ὁ δὲ κύριος ἀπέστησεν τὸν ὕπνον G (G^AT) (theol) | > La (abbr) | *(noctem illam rex) duxit insomnem* V (lib-synt) ÷ • **2** בִּגְתָנָא וָתֶרֶשׁ → ÷ • 2:21 • **3** נַעֲרֵי הַמֶּלֶךְ מְשָׁרְתָיו T^R | οἱ διάκονοι τοῦ βασιλέως G (facil-styl) | > G^AT (abbr) | *servi illius ac ministri* V S (lib-synt) • **4** לַחָצֵר (V) S T^R | > G G^AT (abbr) ÷ •

נַעֲרֵי הַמֶּ֫לֶךְ אֵלָ֫יו הִנֵּ֥ה הָמָ֖ן עֹמֵ֣ד בֶּחָצֵ֑ר וַיֹּ֥אמֶר הַמֶּ֖לֶךְ יָבֽוֹא׃

כול סיפ מל ב מ
ב חס

6 וַיָּבוֹא֮ הָמָן֒ וַיֹּ֤אמֶר לוֹ֙ הַמֶּ֔לֶךְ מַֽה־לַעֲשׂ֔וֹת בָּאִ֕ישׁ אֲשֶׁ֥ר הַמֶּ֖לֶךְ חָפֵ֣ץ

ל . ז מל
בִּֽיקָר֑וֹ וַיֹּ֤אמֶר הָמָן֙ בְּלִבּ֔וֹ לְמִ֞י יַחְפֹּ֥ץ הַמֶּ֛לֶךְ לַעֲשׂ֥וֹת יְקָ֖ר יוֹתֵ֥ר

7 מִמֶּֽנִּי׃ וַיֹּ֥אמֶר הָמָ֖ן אֶל־הַמֶּ֑לֶךְ אִ֕ישׁ אֲשֶׁ֥ר הַמֶּ֖לֶךְ חָפֵ֥ץ בִּיקָרֽוֹ׃

8 יָבִ֙יאוּ֙ לְב֣וּשׁ מַלְכ֔וּת אֲשֶׁ֥ר לָֽבַשׁ־בּ֖וֹ הַמֶּ֑לֶךְ וְס֗וּס אֲשֶׁ֙ר רָכַ֤ב עָלָיו֙ ט

כא . יד . ז .
ל בסיפ
9 הַמֶּ֔לֶךְ וַאֲשֶׁ֥ר נִתַּ֛ן כֶּ֥תֶר מַלְכ֖וּת בְּרֹאשֽׁוֹ׃ וְנָת֨וֹן הַלְּב֜וּשׁ וְהַסּ֗וּס עַל־

ג
יַד־אִ֞ישׁ מִשָּׂרֵ֤י הַמֶּ֙לֶךְ֙ הַֽפַּרְתְּמִ֔ים וְהִלְבִּ֙ישׁוּ֙ אֶת־הָאִ֔ישׁ אֲשֶׁ֥ר הַמֶּ֖לֶךְ

ל וכא . ו
חָפֵ֣ץ בִּֽיקָר֑וֹ וְהִרְכִּיבֻ֤הוּ עַל־הַסּוּס֙ בִּרְח֣וֹב הָעִ֔יר וְקָרְא֣וּ לְפָנָ֔יו

10 כָּ֚כָה יֵעָשֶׂ֣ה לָאִ֔ישׁ אֲשֶׁ֥ר הַמֶּ֖לֶךְ חָפֵ֥ץ בִּֽיקָרֽוֹ׃ וַיֹּ֨אמֶר הַמֶּ֜לֶךְ לְהָמָ֗ן

ד . לו . לב
מַ֠הֵר קַ֣ח אֶת־הַלְּב֤וּשׁ וְאֶת־הַסּוּס֙ כַּאֲשֶׁ֣ר דִּבַּ֔רְתָּ וַֽעֲשֵׂה־כֵן֙

ל וחד וַתַּפֵּל
לְמָרְדֳּכַ֣י הַיְּהוּדִ֔י הַיּוֹשֵׁ֖ב בְּשַׁ֣עַר הַמֶּ֑לֶךְ אַל־תַּפֵּ֣ל דָּבָ֔ר מִכֹּ֖ל אֲשֶׁ֥ר

ס
11 דִּבַּֽרְתָּ׃ וַיִּקַּ֤ח הָמָן֙ אֶת־הַלְּב֣וּשׁ וְאֶת־הַסּ֔וּס וַיַּלְבֵּ֖שׁ אֶֽת־מָרְדֳּכָ֑י

ד . לו . לב
וַיַּ֨רְכִּיבֵ֙הוּ֙ בִּרְח֣וֹב הָעִ֔יר וַיִּקְרָ֣א לְפָנָ֔יו כָּ֚כָה יֵעָשֶׂ֣ה לָאִ֔ישׁ אֲשֶׁ֥ר

ב
12 הַמֶּ֖לֶךְ חָפֵ֣ץ בִּֽיקָרֽוֹ׃ וַיָּ֥שָׁב מָרְדֳּכַ֖י אֶל־שַׁ֣עַר הַמֶּ֑לֶךְ וְהָמָן֙ נִדְחַ֣ף

ל
13 אֶל־בֵּית֔וֹ אָבֵ֖ל וַחֲפ֥וּי רֹֽאשׁ׃ וַיְסַפֵּ֙ר הָמָ֜ן לְזֶ֤רֶשׁ אִשְׁתּוֹ֙ וּלְכָל־

אֹֽהֲבָ֔יו אֵ֖ת כָּל־אֲשֶׁ֣ר קָרָ֑הוּ וַיֹּ֩אמְרוּ֩ ל֨וֹ חֲכָמָ֜יו וְזֶ֣רֶשׁ אִשְׁתּ֗וֹ אִם

ב
מִזֶּ֣רַע הַיְּהוּדִ֡ים מָרְדֳּכַ֞י אֲשֶׁר֩ הַחִלּ֨וֹתָ לִנְפֹּ֤ל לְפָנָיו֙ לֹא־תוּכַ֣ל ל֔וֹ

---

[6] יוֹתֵר ז מל בליש וסימנה איש אל יותר . ואת היותר . ואל תתחכם . ויותר ממנו .
וחב . מה לעני יודע . למי יחפץ . ונתון ז ויקראו לפניו אברך . העלה עליהם
קהל . ונתון את אלהיהם באש . ונתון לו ככר לחם ליום . את כל זה ראיתי ונתון אל
לבי דקהלת . תמרוקיהן . הלבוש והסוס על יד איש ס: כל מגלת אסתר אל יד ב מ
חד על יד ונתון הלבוש והסוס וכול קריה דכות בר מן ה אל יד ס: יעשה לאיש ככה
יעשה אשר לא יבנה את בית אביו . אשר המלך חפץ . וחביר ס:

---

6 בָּאִ֕ישׁ | τῷ ἀνθρώπῳ G V S TR (transl) | τῷ ἀνδρί GAT (facil-styl) ⸤ •
8 וַאֲשֶׁ֥ר to בְּרֹאשֽׁוֹ: (TSh) | > G GAT (abbr) | et accipere regium diadema super
caput suum V (lib-synt) | ܡܠܟܘܬܐ ܟܠܝܠܐ ܢܣܒ ܘܐܦ S (lib-synt) |
דִי־ S (lib-synt) | וְהִלְבִּ֙ישׁוּ֙ (G) (GAT) TR (interp) ⸤ • 9 אִתיהיב כלילא דמלכותא ברישיה TR (interp) ⸤ • 9 וְהִלְבִּ֙ישׁוּ֙
> V (abbr) | ܘܢܠܒܫܘܢܝܗ S (lib-synt) ⸤ • וְהִרְכִּיבֻ֤הוּ (G) (GAT) TR TSh | > V
(abbr) | ܘܢܪܟܒܘܢܝܗ S (ampl) ⸤ • וְקָרְא֣וּ (G) (GAT) S TR | clamet ac dicat V (TSh)
(ampl) ⸤ • 10 קַ֣ח (GAT) (V) S TR (TSh) | > G (abbr) • 13 חֲכָמָ֜יו GAT (V) TR |
οἱ φίλοι G S (assim-ctext) ⸤ •

כִּי־נָפֹ֣ול תִּפֹּ֣ול לְפָנָ֑יו: עֹודָ֣ם מְדַבְּרִ֣ים עִמֹּ֔ו וְסָרִיסֵ֥י הַמֶּ֖לֶךְ הִגִּ֑יעוּ גמל בכתֿ ג

7 וַֽיַּבְהִ֙לוּ֙ לְהָבִ֣יא אֶת־הָמָ֔ן אֶל־הַמִּשְׁתֶּ֖ה אֲשֶׁר־עָשְׂתָ֥ה אֶסְתֵּֽר: וַיָּבֹ֨א ל וחסֿ . ב חֿ
בסיֿפ

הַמֶּ֤לֶךְ וְהָמָן֙ לִשְׁתֹּ֔ות עִם־אֶסְתֵּ֖ר הַמַּלְכָּֽה: וַיֹּאמֶר֩ הַמֶּ֨לֶךְ לְאֶסְתֵּ֜ר יד

גַּ֣ם בַּיֹּ֤ום הַשֵּׁנִי֙ בְּמִשְׁתֵּ֣ה הַיַּ֔יִן מַה־שְּׁאֵלָתֵ֛ךְ אֶסְתֵּ֥ר הַמַּלְכָּ֖ה וְתִנָּ֣תֵֽן

לָ֑ךְ וּמַה־בַּקָּשָׁתֵ֛ךְ עַד־חֲצִ֥י הַמַּלְכ֖וּת וְתֵעָֽשׂ: וַתַּ֨עַן אֶסְתֵּ֤ר הַמַּלְכָּה֙ יד

וַתֹּאמַ֔ר אִם־מָצָ֨אתִי חֵ֤ן בְּעֵינֶ֙יךָ֙ הַמֶּ֔לֶךְ וְאִם־עַל־הַמֶּ֖לֶךְ טֹ֑וב ה

תִּנָּֽתֶן־לִ֤י נַפְשִׁי֙ בִּשְׁאֵ֣לָתִ֔י וְעַמִּ֖י בְּבַקָּשָׁתִֽי: כִּ֤י נִמְכַּ֙רְנוּ֙ אֲנִ֣י וְעַמִּ֔י יא . יֿ

לְהַשְׁמִ֖יד לַהֲרֹ֣וג וּלְאַבֵּ֑ד וְ֠אִלּוּ לַעֲבָדִ֨ים וְלִשְׁפָחֹ֤ות נִמְכַּ֙רְנוּ֙

הֶחֱרַ֔שְׁתִּי כִּ֣י אֵ֥ין הַצָּ֛ר שֹׁוֶ֖ה בְּנֵ֥זֶק הַמֶּֽלֶךְ: ס וַיֹּ֙אמֶר֙ הַמֶּ֣לֶךְ גֿבֿ . ג

אֲחַשְׁוֵרֹ֔ושׁ וַיֹּ֖אמֶר לְאֶסְתֵּ֣ר הַמַּלְכָּ֑ה מִ֣י ה֥וּא זֶה֙ וְאֵֽי־זֶ֣ה ה֔וּא אֲשֶׁר־ יד . ג

מְלָאֹ֥ו לִבֹּ֖ו לַעֲשֹׂ֥ות כֵּֽן: וַתֹּ֣אמֶר־אֶסְתֵּ֔ר אִ֚ישׁ צַ֣ר וְאֹויֵ֔ב הָמָ֥ן הָרָ֖ע ל

הַזֶּ֑ה וְהָמָ֣ן נִבְעַ֔ת מִלִּפְנֵ֥י הַמֶּ֖לֶךְ וְהַמַּלְכָּֽה: וְהַמֶּ֜לֶךְ קָ֤ם בַּחֲמָתֹו֙ ב

מִמִּשְׁתֵּ֣ה הַיַּ֔יִן אֶל־גִּנַּ֖ת הַבִּיתָ֑ן וְהָמָ֣ן עָמַ֗ד לְבַקֵּ֤שׁ עַל־נַפְשֹׁו֙ מֵֽאֶסְתֵּ֣ר

[7:4] הצר ג חד פתֿ וב̇ קמ̇ וסימנֿ על הצר הצרר אתכם . וליוצא ולבא אין שלום מן
הצר . כי אין הצר שוה :ȯ [5] מי הוא זה ג וסימנהון כי מי הוא זה ערב . מלך
הכבוד . ואי זה הוא אשר :ȯ

---

13 לְפָנָ֑יו²: V S T^R | foll ὅτι θεὸς ζῶν μετ' αὐτοῦ G (theol) | foll ὅτι ὁ θεὸς ἐν
αὐτοῖς G^AT (theol) | foll *non poteris repugnare ei, quia jam propheta est* La
(theol) • **14** וְתִנָּ֣תֵֽן G V (S) T^R | > G^AT (abbr) | וְסָרִיסֵ֥י G V (S) T^R | > וٖשלטונוי T^Sh (lib) • **7:2**
לָ֑ךְ V T^R T^Sh | > G G^AT S (abbr) ÷ • **4** וְ֠אִלּוּ S T^R T^Sh | > G G^AT V (ign-lex?)
÷ • כִּ֣י אֵ֥ין to הַמֶּֽלֶךְ: | οὐ γὰρ ἄξιος ὁ διάβολος τῆς αὐλῆς τοῦ βασιλέως G
(lib-seman) | ἵνα μὴ λυπήσω τὸν κύριόν μου G^AT (substit) | *nunc autem hostis
noster est cuius crudelitas redundat in regem* V (lib-seman) | ܐܠܐ ܕܒܥܠ
ܕܒܒܐ ܕܢܗܘܐ ܠܚܠܒܐ S (lib-seman) | ארום לית למעיקא טמין ורווחא באוזינקא
דמלכא T^R (lib-seman) | ארום לית בעיל־דבבא שתיק בטננא דמלכא T^Sh (lib-
seman) ÷ • **5** וַיֹּ֙אמֶר֙ to הַמַּלְכָּ֑ה (S) T^R | εἶπεν δὲ ὁ βασιλεύς G (abbr) | καὶ
ἐθυμώθη ὁ βασιλεὺς καὶ εἶπεν G^AT (abbr+substit) | *dixit autem rex reginae
Hester* La (abbr) | *respondensque rex Asuerus ait* V (abbr) | ואמ' מלכֿ אחשוֿ
T^Sh (paraphr) ÷ • אֲשֶׁר־מְלָאֹ֥ו לִבֹּ֖ו | למתרגמניה ואמר מתתרגמניה לאסתֿ מלכֿ
G G^AT V (lib-seman) | ܐܬܚܫܒ ܒܠܒܗ S (lib-seman) | די אמלכיה
T^R (lib-seman) | דחשיב לביה T^Sh (lib-seman) ÷ • **6** וַתֹּ֣אמֶר־אֶסְתֵּ֔ר M^L |
> *maqqēp* M^L34 M^Y M^S1 (differ-graph) •

הַמַּלְכָּ֔ה כִּ֣י רָאָ֔ה כִּֽי־כָלְתָ֥ה אֵלָ֛יו הָרָעָ֖ה מֵאֵ֣ת הַמֶּ֑לֶךְ ׃ וְהַמֶּ֡לֶךְ שָׁב֩ ⁸

מִגִּנַּ֨ת הַבִּיתָ֜ן אֶל־בֵּ֣ית ׀ מִשְׁתֵּ֣ה הַיַּ֗יִן וְהָמָן֙ נֹפֵ֔ל עַל־הַמִּטָּה֙ אֲשֶׁ֣ר   ג

אֶסְתֵּ֣ר עָלֶ֔יהָ וַיֹּ֣אמֶר הַמֶּ֔לֶךְ הֲ֠גַם לִכְבּ֧וֹשׁ אֶת־הַמַּלְכָּ֛ה עִמִּ֖י בַּבָּ֑יִת   ב חד חס

הַדָּבָ֗ר יָצָא֙ מִפִּ֣י הַמֶּ֔לֶךְ וּפְנֵ֥י הָמָ֖ן חָפֽוּ ׃ ס וַיֹּ֣אמֶר חַרְבוֹנָ֣ה ⁹   יו.ב.ב חד / כת א

אֶחָ֨ד מִן־הַסָּרִיסִ֜ים לִפְנֵ֣י הַמֶּ֗לֶךְ גַּ֣ם הִנֵּֽה־הָעֵ֞ץ אֲשֶׁר־עָשָׂ֣ה הָמָ֣ן   יו בטע

לְמָרְדֳּכַ֞י אֲשֶׁ֧ר דִּבֶּר־ט֣וֹב עַל־הַמֶּ֗לֶךְ עֹמֵד֙ בְּבֵ֣ית הָמָ֔ן גָּבֹ֖הַּ   ב

חֲמִשִּׁ֣ים אַמָּ֑ה וַיֹּ֥אמֶר הַמֶּ֖לֶךְ תְּלֻ֣הוּ עָלָֽיו ׃ וַיִּתְלוּ֙ אֶת־הָמָ֔ן עַל־הָעֵ֖ץ ¹⁰   ל וחס. ב

אֲשֶׁר־הֵכִ֣ין לְמָרְדֳּכָ֑י וַחֲמַ֥ת הַמֶּ֖לֶךְ שָׁכָֽכָה ׃ ס בַּיּ֣וֹם הַה֗וּא **8**   ל

נָתַ֞ן הַמֶּ֤לֶךְ אֲחַשְׁוֵרוֹשׁ֙ לְאֶסְתֵּ֣ר הַמַּלְכָּ֔ה אֶת־בֵּ֥ית הָמָ֖ן צֹרֵ֣ר

הַיְּהוּדִ֑ים וּמָרְדֳּכַ֗י בָּ֚א לִפְנֵ֣י הַמֶּ֔לֶךְ כִּֽי־הִגִּ֥ידָה אֶסְתֵּ֖ר מַ֥ה הֽוּא־   היהודיים / ק

לָֽהּ ׃ וַיָּ֨סַר הַמֶּ֜לֶךְ אֶת־טַבַּעְתּ֗וֹ אֲשֶׁ֤ר הֶעֱבִיר֙ מֵֽהָמָ֔ן וַֽיִּתְּנָ֖הּ לְמָרְדֳּכָ֑י ²   ל

וַתָּ֧שֶׂם אֶסְתֵּ֛ר אֶֽת־מָרְדֳּכַ֖י עַל־בֵּ֥ית הָמָֽן ׃ פ וַתּ֣וֹסֶף אֶסְתֵּ֗ר ³   יו.ג מל

וַתְּדַבֵּר֙ לִפְנֵ֣י הַמֶּ֔לֶךְ וַתִּפֹּ֖ל לִפְנֵ֣י רַגְלָ֑יו וַתֵּ֣בְךְּ וַתִּתְחַנֶּן־ל֗וֹ לְהַעֲבִיר֙

אֶת־רָעַת֙ הָמָ֣ן הָֽאֲגָגִ֔י וְאֵת֙ מַֽחֲשַׁבְתּ֔וֹ אֲשֶׁ֥ר חָשַׁ֖ב עַל־הַיְּהוּדִֽים ׃   ל חס בן המדתא

וַיּ֤וֹשֶׁט הַמֶּ֨לֶךְ֙ לְאֶסְתֵּ֔ר אֵ֖ת שַׁרְבִ֣ט הַזָּהָ֑ב וַתָּ֣קָם אֶסְתֵּ֔ר וַֽתַּעֲמֹ֖ד לִפְנֵ֥י ⁴   ל חס למע

הַמֶּֽלֶךְ ׃ וַ֠תֹּאמֶר אִם־עַל־הַמֶּ֨לֶךְ ט֜וֹב וְאִם־מָצָ֧אתִי חֵ֣ן לְפָנָ֗יו וְכָשֵׁ֤ר ⁵   ל.ל

---

[9] חרבונא ב̇ חד כת א וחד כת ה̇ וסימנהון בזתא חרבונא כת . ויאמר חרבונה כת :ס
[10] ויתלו ב̇ על הברכה . את המן על . וחד ויתלו את מרדכי :ס [8:1] ו̇ כת יהודיים
תריין יוד וקרין יהודים וסימנה . נתתי . פתשגן . נתן . פתשגן ויגד . והיהודים ראש פסוק .
ויקהלו . ואינון בחד סיפ :ס [3] ותוסף ג̇ מל וסימנה ותוסף המלחמה . אל תזונתיה .
ותוסף אסתר :ס

7 אֵלָ֛יו | > G G^AT (abbr) | *se in malis esse* La (transl) | *sibi* V (transl) | حلهم S T^R T^Sh (assim-ctext) ÷ • **8** עַל־ ÷ • חָפֽוּ | διετράπη G (substit) | > G^AT V (abbr) | حسف S (T^R) T^Sh (lib-synt) ÷ • **9** חַרְבוֹנָ֣ה V T^R | Βουγαθάν G (substit) | Ἀγαθᾶς G^AT (substit) | ايحבون S (differ) ÷ • דִּבֶּר־ט֣וֹב עַל־ (G^AT) S (T^R) (T^Sh) | τῷ λαλήσαντι περί G (abbr) | > La (abbr) | *qui locutus est pro* V (facil-styl) ÷ • **8:1** מַה הֽוּא־לָֽהּ (T^Sh) | ὅτι ἐνοικείωται αὐτῇ G (interp) | > G^AT (abbr) | *quod Mardochaeus erat de genere reginae* La (interp) | *quod esset patruus suus* V (interp) | حام لام S (differ-gram) | מאן הוא לה T^R (interp) ÷ • **4** וַתָּ֣קָם G (V) (T^R) T^Sh | > G^AT (abbr) | ممكله S (explic) • **5** אִם־עַל־הַמֶּלֶךְ ט֣וֹב V S T^R | εἰ δοκεῖ σοι G (facil-styl) | > G^AT (abbr) | *si placet domino meo* La (facil-styl) •

הַדָּבָר לִפְנֵי הַמֶּלֶךְ וְטוֹבָ֖ה אֲנִ֣י בְּעֵינָ֑יו יִכָּתֵ֞ב לְהָשִׁ֣יב אֶת־הַסְּפָרִ֗ים
מַחֲשֶׁ֜בֶת הָמָ֣ן בֶּֽן־הַמְּדָ֗תָא הָאֲגָגִי֙ אֲשֶׁ֣ר כָּתַ֔ב לְאַבֵּד֙ אֶת־הַיְּהוּדִ֔ים

6 אֲשֶׁ֖ר בְּכָל־מְדִינ֣וֹת הַמֶּ֑לֶךְ כִּ֣י אֵֽיכָכָ֣ה אוּכַל֮ וְֽרָאִ֙יתִי֙ בָּֽרָעָ֔ה

אֲשֶׁר־יִמְצָ֖א אֶת־עַמִּ֑י וְאֵֽיכָכָ֤ה אוּכַל֙ וְֽרָאִ֔יתִי בְּאָבְדַ֖ן

7 מוֹלַדְתִּֽי׃ ס   וַיֹּ֨אמֶר הַמֶּ֤לֶךְ אֲחַשְׁוֵרֹושׁ֙ לְאֶסְתֵּ֣ר הַמַּלְכָּ֔ה

וּֽלְמָרְדֳּכַ֖י הַיְּהוּדִ֑י הִנֵּ֨ה בֵית־הָמָ֜ן נָתַ֣תִּי לְאֶסְתֵּ֗ר וְאֹתוֹ֙ תָּל֣וּ עַל־

8 הָעֵ֔ץ עַ֛ל אֲשֶׁר־שָׁלַ֥ח יָד֖וֹ בַּיְּהוּדִֽיים׃ וְ֠אַתֶּם כִּתְב֨וּ עַל־הַיְּהוּדִ֜ים

כַּטּ֤וֹב בְּעֵֽינֵיכֶם֙ בְּשֵׁ֣ם הַמֶּ֔לֶךְ וְחִתְמ֖וּ בְּטַבַּ֣עַת הַמֶּ֑לֶךְ כִּֽי־כְתָ֞ב

אֲשֶׁר־נִכְתָּ֣ב בְּשֵׁם־הַמֶּ֗לֶךְ וְנַחְתּ֛וֹם בְּטַבַּ֥עַת הַמֶּ֖לֶךְ אֵ֥ין לְהָשִֽׁיב׃

9 וַיִּקָּרְא֣וּ סֹפְרֵֽי־הַמֶּ֣לֶךְ בָּֽעֵת־הַ֠הִיא בַּחֹ֨דֶשׁ הַשְּׁלִישִׁ֜י הוּא־חֹ֣דֶשׁ

סִיוָ֗ן בִּשְׁלוֹשָׁ֤ה וְעֶשְׂרִים֙ בּ֔וֹ וַיִּכָּתֵ֞ב כְּֽכָל־אֲשֶׁר־צִוָּ֣ה מָרְדֳּכַ֣י אֶל־

הַיְּהוּדִ֡ים וְאֶ֣ל הָאֲחַשְׁדַּרְפְּנִֽים־וְהַפַּחוֹת֩ וְשָׂרֵ֨י הַמְּדִינ֜וֹת אֲשֶׁ֣ר ׀

מֵהֹ֣דּוּ וְעַד־כּ֗וּשׁ שֶׁ֣בַע וְעֶשְׂרִ֤ים וּמֵאָה֙ מְדִינָ֔ה מְדִינָ֥ה וּמְדִינָ֖ה

10 כִּכְתָבָ֑הּ וְעַ֣ם וָעָ֖ם כִּלְשֹׁנ֑וֹ וְאֶ֨ל־הַיְּהוּדִ֔ים כִּכְתָבָ֖ם וְכִלְשׁוֹנָֽם׃ וַיִּכְתֹּ֗ב

בְּשֵׁם֙ הַמֶּ֣לֶךְ אֲחַשְׁוֵרֹ֔שׁ וַיַּחְתֹּ֖ם בְּטַבַּ֣עַת הַמֶּ֑לֶךְ וַיִּשְׁלַ֣ח סְפָרִים֮ בְּיַ֣ד

Marginal masora notes (right/left margins):
ב | יב . ב . ל | ד חס למער | ל | ביהודים ק | ל | ל . ג . בסיפ | ג | ג | ל חס בסיפ | ד חס

‎. וטובה ב֗ וטובה לא ראה . וטובה אני ‏o: [6] ‏ברעה ב֗ וסימנהון אשר ימצא‎
‎. ואבינה ברעה ‏o: [9] ‏שבע ועשרים ומאה ג֗ ויהי בימי אחשורוש . ויקראו תיני֗ . וישלח‎
‎ספרים ‏o:

5 מַחֲשֶׁ֣בֶת הָמָ֣ן בֶּֽן־הַמְּדָ֗תָא הָאֲגָגִי֙ (T^R) | ἀπὸ ʼΑμάν G (abbr) | > G^{AT} (abbr) | *Aman (litterae) insidiatoris et hostis Iudaeorum* V (substit) | ܡܚܫܒܬܐ ܕܗܡܢ S (abbr) | מחשבתא דהמן בר המדת׳ T^{Sh} (abbr) ⁖ • הַיְּהוּדִ֔ים M^L M^{L34} G (V) | + כל M^Y La S T^R (ampl) | > G^{AT} (abbr) ⁖ • **6** יִמְצָ֖א (S) (T^{Sh}) | > G G^{AT} V (facil-styl) | וְֽרָאִ֙יתִי֙² (S) | σωθῆναι G (substit) | > G^{AT} V (facil-styl) | דתינדן T^R (interp) ⁖ • **7** וּֽלְמָרְדֳּכַ֖י הַיְּהוּדִ֑י V T^R | > G G^{AT} S (abbr) • ולמחמי T^R (interp) ⁖ • **8** בְּטַבַּ֣עַת הַמֶּ֑לֶךְ¹ S (T^R) | τῷ δακτυλίῳ μου G V (lib-seman) | > G^{AT} (abbr) • **9** הַשְּׁלִישִׁ֜י V S T^R | τῷ πρώτῳ G (harm-ctext) | > G^{AT} (abbr) • סִיוָ֗ן (V) (S) T^{Sh} | Νισά G (substit) | > G^{AT} T^R (abbr) • אֶל־הַיְּהוּדִ֔ים (G) V (T^R) (T^{Sh}) | > G^{AT} (abbr) | ܠܗܘܢ S (assim-ctext) ⁖ • **10** וַיִּכְתֹּ֗ב T^R | ἐγράφη G S (lib-seman) | > G^{AT} V (abbr) • בְּיַ֣ד הָרָצִים֮ בַּסּוּסִים T^{Sh} | διὰ βιβλιαφόρων G (abbr) | > G^{AT} (abbr) | *per librarios currentes in equis* La (lib-seman) | *per veredarios* V S (abbr) | בידא דרהטונין רהטי סוסוון T^R (ampl) •

11 הָרָצִים בַּסּוּסִים רֹכְבֵי הָרֶ֫כֶשׁ הָאֲחַשְׁתְּרָנִים בְּנֵי הָרַמָּכִֽים: אֲשֶׁר֩
נָתַ֨ן הַמֶּ֜לֶךְ לַיְּהוּדִ֣ים ׀ אֲשֶׁ֣ר בְּכָל־עִיר־וָעִ֗יר לְהִקָּהֵל֮ וְלַעֲמֹ֣ד
עַל־נַפְשָׁם֒ לְהַשְׁמִיד֩ וְלַהֲרֹ֨ג וּלְאַבֵּ֜ד אֶת־כָּל־חֵ֨יל עַ֤ם וּמְדִינָה֙
12 הַצָּרִ֣ים אֹתָ֔ם טַ֖ף וְנָשִׁ֑ים וּשְׁלָלָ֖ם לָבֽוֹז: בְּי֣וֹם אֶחָ֗ד בְּכָל־מְדִינ֛וֹת
הַמֶּ֥לֶךְ אֲחַשְׁוֵר֖וֹשׁ בִּשְׁלוֹשָׁ֥ה עָשָׂ֛ר לְחֹ֥דֶשׁ שְׁנֵים־עָשָׂ֖ר הוּא־חֹ֥דֶשׁ
13 אֲדָֽר: פַּתְשֶׁ֣גֶן הַכְּתָ֗ב לְהִנָּ֤תֵֽן דָּת֙ בְּכָל־מְדִינָ֣ה וּמְדִינָ֔ה גָּל֖וּי לְכָל־
הָעַמִּ֑ים וְלִהְי֨וֹת הַיְּהוּדִ֤ים עֲתוּדִים֙ לַיּ֣וֹם הַזֶּ֔ה לְהִנָּקֵ֖ם מֵאֹיְבֵיהֶֽם:
14 הָרָצִ֞ים רֹכְבֵ֤י הָרֶ֙כֶשׁ֙ הָֽאֲחַשְׁתְּרָנִ֔ים יָֽצְא֛וּ מְבֹהָלִ֥ים וּדְחוּפִ֖ים בִּדְבַ֣ר
15 הַמֶּ֑לֶךְ וְהַדָּ֥ת נִתְּנָ֖ה בְּשׁוּשַׁ֥ן הַבִּירָֽה: וּמָרְדֳּכַ֞י יָצָ֣א ׀ מִלִּפְנֵ֣י
הַמֶּ֗לֶךְ בִּלְב֤וּשׁ מַלְכוּת֙ תְּכֵ֣לֶת וָח֔וּר וַעֲטֶ֤רֶת זָהָב֙ גְּדוֹלָ֔ה וְתַכְרִ֥יךְ
16 בּ֖וּץ וְאַרְגָּמָ֑ן וְהָעִ֣יר שׁוּשָׁ֔ן צָהֲלָ֖ה וְשָׂמֵֽחָה: לַיְּהוּדִ֕ים הָֽיְתָ֥ה אוֹרָ֖ה
17 וְשִׂמְחָ֑ה וְשָׂשֹׂ֖ן וִיקָֽר: וּבְכָל־מְדִינָ֨ה וּמְדִינָ֜ה וּבְכָל־עִ֣יר וָעִ֗יר מְקוֹם֙
אֲשֶׁ֨ר דְּבַר־הַמֶּ֤לֶךְ וְדָתוֹ֙ מַגִּ֔יעַ שִׂמְחָ֤ה וְשָׂשׂוֹן֙ לַיְּהוּדִ֔ים מִשְׁתֶּ֖ה וְי֣וֹם

Mp

ג . ל

ג

ל

ג

ג . ב .   הַיְהוּדִים ב . עתידים ק   ק

ב . ל ומל

ב ראש פס

ל . ל

ל . ל . ל   ל חס . ב . ה   פסוק אית בהון ובכל ובכל

[10] האחשתרנים ב וסימ ויכתב שם . הרצים ס: [11] ולעמד ג וסימנהון לפני העדה .
בבקר בבקר . להקהל ולעמד ס: [13] ולהיות ב וסימנה ולהיות לו משרתים
ומקטרים . ולהיות היהודים עתידים ס: [16] ו דברים עשו אבותינו באילו ימים אבל
גדול וצום ובכי ומספד שק ואפר: חילוף להם המקום ברוך הוא ששה דברים תחת ששה
אורה ושמחה וששן ויקר משתה ויום טוב ומשלוח־מנות איש לרעהו ס: ויקר ב וסימנה
וששן ויקר . חסן ויקר יקחו . וכל לשון ארמית דכות ס:

10 הָאֲחַשְׁתְּרָנִים | > G G^AT V (abbr) | (מבד) ܐܣܦܘܣ S (lib-synt) | ערטולייני T^R • בְּנֵי הָרַמָּכִים: (S) (T^Sh) | > G G^AT V (abbr) | (lib-seman) | ערטילאי T^Sh (lib-seman) ÷ • **11** אֲשֶׁר¹ T^R | ὡς G (lib) | > G^AT (abbr) | רמכין T^R (lib-seman) • לְהַשְׁמִיד | ܐܬܐ ܘ(ܠܡܚܒ)ܕ S (explic) • quaecunque La (lib) | quibus V (lib) | וְלַהֲרֹג וּלְאַבֵּד (S) T^R | > G G^AT (abbr) | interficerent atque delerent V (facil-styl) | כָּל־חֵיל (T^R) | τοῖς ἀντιδίκοις G (lib-seman) | > G^AT (abbr) | omnes V (facil-styl) | הַצָּרִים אֹתָם T^R | τοῖς ἀντικειμένοις αὐτῶν G (lib-seman) | > G^AT (abbr) | inimicos suos V (facil-styl) | ܠܒܥܠܕ(ܒܒ)ܝܗܘܢ S (lib-seman) • **12** אֲדָר: V S T^R | foll E 1-24 G (lit) | foll 7:22-32 G^AT (lit) | **13** וְלִהְיוֹת G | > G^AT (abbr) | esse V S T^R (facil-styl) ÷ • עֲתוּדִים | עֲתוּדִים M^L(ket) עֲתִידִים M^Y M^S1 | G G^AT V S T^R T^Sh (indet) • **14** הָאֲחַשְׁתְּרָנִים | > G G^AT V T^R (abbr) | ܐܣܦܘܣܐ S (lib-synt) | שלטוני T^Sh (substit) ÷ • **15** וְתַכְרִיךְ V T^R | καὶ διάδημα G G^AT (ign-lex?) | ܘܟܠܝܠܐ S (substit) ÷ •

ו . ל טֽוֹב וְרַבִּ֞ים מֵעַמֵּ֤י הָאָ֙רֶץ֙ מִתְיַהֲדִ֔ים כִּֽי־נָפַ֥ל פַּֽחַד־הַיְּהוּדִ֖ים

עֲלֵיהֶֽם: וּבִשְׁנֵים֩ עָשָׂ֨ר חֹ֜דֶשׁ הוּא־חֹ֣דֶשׁ אֲדָ֗ר בִּשְׁלוֹשָׁ֨ה עָשָׂ֥ר יוֹם֙ בּ֔וֹ **9**

ב ומל אֲשֶׁ֨ר הִגִּ֧יעַ דְּבַר־הַמֶּ֛לֶךְ וְדָת֖וֹ לְהֵעָשׂ֑וֹת בַּיּ֗וֹם אֲשֶׁ֨ר שִׂבְּר֜וּ אֹיְבֵ֤י

ל ומל הַיְּהוּדִים֙ לִשְׁל֣וֹט בָּהֶ֔ם וְנַהֲפ֣וֹךְ ה֔וּא אֲשֶׁ֨ר יִשְׁלְט֧וּ הַיְּהוּדִ֛ים הֵ֖מָּה

ל בְּשֹׂנְאֵיהֶֽם: נִקְהֲל֤וּ הַיְּהוּדִים֙ בְּעָ֣רֵיהֶ֔ם בְּכָל־מְדִינ֖וֹת הַמֶּ֣לֶךְ 2

ל אֲחַשְׁוֵר֔וֹשׁ לִשְׁלֹ֣חַ יָ֔ד בִּמְבַקְשֵׁ֖י רָֽעָתָ֑ם וְאִישׁ֙ לֹא־עָמַ֣ד לִפְנֵיהֶ֔ם כִּֽי־

ז . ג מילין נָפַ֥ל פַּחְדָּ֖ם עַל־כָּל־הָעַמִּֽים: וְכָל־שָׂרֵ֨י הַמְּדִינ֜וֹת וְהָאֲחַשְׁדַּרְפְּנִ֣ים 3
בקר דמ̇ין

ג וְהַפַּח֗וֹת וְעֹשֵׂ֤י הַמְּלָאכָה֙ אֲשֶׁ֣ר לַמֶּ֔לֶךְ מְנַשְּׂאִ֖ים אֶת־הַיְּהוּדִ֑ים כִּֽי־

ל נָפַ֥ל פַּֽחַד־מָרְדֳּכַ֖י עֲלֵיהֶֽם: כִּֽי־גָ֤דוֹל מָרְדֳּכַי֙ בְּבֵ֣ית הַמֶּ֔לֶךְ וְשָׁמְע֖וֹ 4

ב מל בס̇ . ח הוֹלֵ֣ךְ בְּכָל־הַמְּדִינ֑וֹת כִּֽי־הָאִ֤ישׁ מָרְדֳּכַי֙ הוֹלֵ֥ךְ וְגָדֽוֹל: פ

ל וַיַּכּ֤וּ הַיְּהוּדִים֙ בְּכָל־אֹ֣יְבֵיהֶ֔ם מַכַּת־חֶ֥רֶב וְהֶ֖רֶג וְאַבְדָ֑ן וַיַּֽעֲשׂ֧וּ 5

ל בְּשֹׂנְאֵיהֶ֖ם כִּרְצוֹנָֽם: וּבְשׁוּשַׁ֣ן הַבִּירָ֗ה הָרְג֤וּ הַיְּהוּדִים֙ וְאַבֵּ֔ד חֲמֵ֥שׁ 6

מֵא֖וֹת אִֽישׁ: וְאֵ֧ת | 7

ל פַּרְשַׁנְדָּ֖תָא וְאֵ֧ת |

ל דַּֽלְפ֖וֹן וְאֵ֧ת |

ל אַסְפָּ֑תָא: וְאֵ֧ת | 8

ל פּוֹרָ֖תָא וְאֵ֧ת |

[9:3] ג מילין בקר מן̇ כל חדא י̇א אותיות וסימנהון וכעלילותיכם . ובתועבותיהן .
והאחשדרפנים ס̇: עשי יו̇ כ̇ת יוד וסימנה מלא אתם . שכר . מאשרים . ועמך . ועל
ידם . ויתנו תינינה דפסוק . ויתיכו . ויעשו . לעבדת . דברו . רצונו . במים .
אמונה . מניות . אשקול . מנשאים . ומן ויהי בשנת עשרים ושלוש עד סיף דסיפ
דכות ס̇:

17 מֵעַמֵּ֤י הָאָ֙רֶץ֙ S T^R | τῶν ἐθνῶν G (abbr) | τῶν Ἰουδαίων G^AT (shift) | *alterius
gentis et sectae* V (shift) • מִתְיַהֲדִ֔ים S | περιετέμοντο καὶ ἰουδαΐζον G (exeg) |
περιετέμοντο G^AT (substit) | *eorum religioni et caerimoniis iungerentur* V
(exeg) | מתגיירין T^R (lib-seman) ✢ • **9:1** אֲשֶׁ֨ר בַּיּ֗וֹם V T^R | ἐν αὐτῇ τῇ ἡμέρᾳ G
(transp) | > G^AT S (abbr) ✢ • **3** וְעֹשֵׂ֤י הַמְּלָאכָה֙ (S) T^R | οἱ (βασιλικοὶ)
γραμματεῖς G G^AT (lib-seman) | *omnisque dignitas quae singulis locis et operibus
praeerat* V (ampl) ✢ • מְנַשְּׂאִ֖ים (G) (G^AT) V (S) (T^Sh) | *honorificabant* La (lib-
seman) | ممنن T^R (paraphr) ✢ • פַּֽחַד־מָרְדֳּכַ֖י G G^AT V T^R | ܕܚܠܬܐ ܕܡܪܕܟܝ S
(substit) • **4** וְשָׁמְע֖וֹ S T^Sh | > G (abbr) | *fama quoque nominis eius* V (ampl)
• ומטבעיה T^R (midr) • **7** vv 7-9 ✢ •

אֲדַלְיָ֖א וְאֵ֣ת ׀ ל

אֲרִידָ֑תָא וְאֵ֣ת ׀ ל 9

פַּרְמַ֖שְׁתָּא וְאֵ֣ת ׀ ל

אֲרִיסַ֖י וְאֵ֣ת ׀ ל

אֲרִדַ֖י וְאֵ֣ת ׀ ל

וַיְזָֽתָא׃ עֲשֶׂ֖רֶת ל 10

בְּנֵ֨י הָמָ֧ן בֶּֽן־הַמְּדָ֛תָא צֹרֵ֥ר הַיְּהוּדִ֖ים הָרָ֑גוּ וּבַ֨בִּזָּ֔ה לֹ֥א שָׁלְח֖וּ אֶת־

יָדָֽם׃ בַּיּ֣וֹם הַה֗וּא בָּ֣א מִסְפַּ֧ר הַֽהֲרוּגִ֛ים בְּשׁוּשַׁ֥ן הַבִּירָ֖ה לִפְנֵ֥י 11

הַמֶּֽלֶךְ׃ ס   וַיֹּ֨אמֶר הַמֶּ֜לֶךְ לְאֶסְתֵּ֣ר הַמַּלְכָּ֗ה בְּשׁוּשַׁ֣ן הַבִּירָ֡ה 12 יד

הָרְגוּ֩ הַיְּהוּדִ֨ים וְאַבֵּ֜ד חֲמֵ֧שׁ מֵא֣וֹת אִ֗ישׁ וְאֵת֙ עֲשֶׂ֣רֶת בְּנֵֽי־הָמָ֔ן בִּשְׁאָ֖ר

מְדִינ֣וֹת הַמֶּ֔לֶךְ מֶ֣ה עָשׂ֔וּ וּמַה־שְּׁאֵֽלָתֵ֖ךְ וְיִנָּ֣תֵֽן לָ֑ךְ וּמַה־בַּקָּשָׁתֵ֥ךְ ל נסיבֿ

ע֖וֹד וְתֵעָֽשׂ׃ וַתֹּ֤אמֶר אֶסְתֵּר֙ אִם־עַל־הַמֶּ֣לֶךְ ט֔וֹב יִנָּתֵ֣ן גַּם־מָחָ֗ר 13

לַיְּהוּדִים֙ אֲשֶׁ֣ר בְּשׁוּשָׁ֔ן לַעֲשׂ֖וֹת כְּדָ֣ת הַיּ֑וֹם וְאֵ֛ת עֲשֶׂ֥רֶת בְּנֵֽי־הָמָ֖ן

יִתְל֣וּ עַל־הָעֵֽץ׃ וַיֹּ֤אמֶר הַמֶּ֨לֶךְ֙ לְהֵֽעָשׂ֣וֹת כֵּ֔ן וַתִּנָּתֵ֥ן דָּ֖ת בְּשׁוּשָׁ֑ן וְאֵ֛ת 14 ב. ל

עֲשֶׂ֥רֶת בְּנֵֽי־הָמָ֖ן תָּלֽוּ׃ וַיִּקָּהֲל֞וּ הַיְּהוּדִ֣ים אֲשֶׁר־בְּשׁוּשָׁ֗ן גַּ֠ם בְּי֣וֹם 15 דים ק

אַרְבָּעָ֤ה עָשָׂר֙ לְחֹ֣דֶשׁ אֲדָ֔ר וַיַּֽהַרְג֣וּ בְשׁוּשָׁ֔ן שְׁלֹ֥שׁ מֵא֖וֹת אִ֑ישׁ וּבַ֨בִּזָּ֔ה

לֹ֥א שָׁלְח֖וּ אֶת־יָדָֽם׃ וּשְׁאָ֣ר הַיְּהוּדִ֡ים אֲשֶׁר֩ בִּמְדִינ֨וֹת הַמֶּ֜לֶךְ נִקְהֲל֣וּ׀ 16 ל וחד שרתי במדינות

וְעָמֹ֣ד עַל־נַפְשָׁ֗ם וְנ֨וֹחַ֙ מֵאֹ֣יְבֵיהֶ֔ם וְהָרֹג֙ בְּשֹׂ֣נְאֵיהֶ֔ם חֲמִשָּׁ֥ה וְשִׁבְעִ֖ים ל חס

אָ֑לֶף וּבַ֨בִּזָּ֔ה לֹ֥א שָׁלְח֖וּ אֶת־יָדָֽם׃ בְּיֽוֹם־שְׁלֹשָׁ֥ה עָשָׂ֖ר לְחֹ֣דֶשׁ אֲדָ֑ר 17

10 בֶּֽן־הַמְּדָ֛תָא T[R] | Ἀμαδάθου Βουγαίου G (G[AT]) (lib-seman) | > V (abbr) | **✻ •** וּבַבִּזָּ֔ה לֹ֥א שָׁלְח֖וּ אֶת־יָדָֽם: (S) T[R] | καὶ διήρπασαν G (assim-3:13?) | καὶ διήρπασαν πάντα τὰ αὐτῶν G[AT] (assim-3:13?) | *praedas de substantiis eorum agere noluerunt* V (ampl) **✻ • 12** וּמַה־¹ | τί οὖν G V S T[R] | > G[AT] (abbr) **✻ • 13** אִם־עַל־הַמֶּ֣לֶךְ ט֔וֹב יִנָּתֵ֣ן V T[R] T[Sh] | > G[AT] S (abbr) **• 14** תָּלֽוּ V S T[R] | κρεμάσαι G (assim-styl) | + ἐπὶ ξύλου G[Ms] T[Sh] (harm-ctext) | > G[AT] (abbr) **✻ • 15** וּבַבִּזָּ֔ה לֹ֥א שָׁלְח֖וּ אֶת־יָדָֽם: (G) S T[R] | > G[AT] (abbr) | *nec eorum ab illis direpta substantia est* V (ampl) **✻ • 16** בִּמְדִינ֨וֹת (S) (T[R]) | ἐν τῇ βασιλείᾳ G (lib-seman) | > G[AT] (abbr) | *per omnes provincias* V (assim-ctext) **•** וְנ֨וֹחַ G S (T[R]) T[Sh] | > G[AT] V (abbr) **✻ •** חֲמִשָּׁ֥ה וְשִׁבְעִ֖ים אָ֑לֶף V S T[R] | μυρίους πεντακισχιλίους G (substit) | μυριάδας ἑπτὰ καὶ ἑκατόν G[AT] (substit) **✻ • •** וּבַבִּזָּ֔ה לֹ֥א שָׁלְח֖וּ אֶת־יָדָֽם: (G) S T[R] | > G[AT] (abbr) | *et nullus de substantiis eorum quicquam contingeret* V (ampl) **✻ •**

וְנֹ֗וחַ בְּאַרְבָּעָ֤ה עָשָׂר֙ בֹּ֔ו וְעָשֹׂ֣ה אֹת֔וֹ י֖וֹם מִשְׁתֶּ֣ה וְשִׂמְחָֽה׃ וְהַיְּהוּדִ֣ים 18   ג . וְהַיהודים ק
אֲשֶׁר־בְּשׁוּשָׁ֗ן נִקְהֲלוּ֙ בִּשְׁלֹשָׁ֤ה עָשָׂר֙ בֹּ֔ו וּבְאַרְבָּעָ֥ה עָשָׂ֖ר בֹּ֑ו וְנֹ֗וחַ
בַּחֲמִשָּׁ֤ה עָשָׂר֙ בֹּ֔ו וְעָשֹׂ֣ה אֹת֔וֹ י֖וֹם מִשְׁתֶּ֣ה וְשִׂמְחָֽה׃ עַל־כֵּ֞ן הַיְּהוּדִ֣ים 19   הפרזים ק
הַפְּרָזִ֗ים הַיֹּשְׁבִים֮ בְּעָרֵ֣י הַפְּרָזוֹת֒ עֹשִׂ֗ים אֵ֠ת י֣וֹם אַרְבָּעָ֤ה עָשָׂר֙
לְחֹ֣דֶשׁ אֲדָ֔ר שִׂמְחָ֥ה וּמִשְׁתֶּ֖ה וְי֣וֹם ט֑וֹב וּמִשְׁלֹ֥וחַ מָנ֖וֹת אִ֥ישׁ   ב וחס
לְרֵעֵֽהוּ׃   פ   וַיִּכְתֹּ֣ב מָרְדֳּכַ֔י אֶת־הַדְּבָרִ֖ים הָאֵ֑לֶּה וַיִּשְׁלַ֣ח 20
סְפָרִ֗ים אֶל־כָּל־הַיְּהוּדִ֔ים אֲשֶׁר֙ בְּכָל־מְדִינ֔וֹת הַמֶּ֖לֶךְ אֲחַשְׁוֵר֑וֹשׁ
הַקְּרוֹבִ֖ים וְהָרְחוֹקִֽים׃ לְקַיֵּם֙ עֲלֵיהֶ֔ם לִהְי֣וֹת עֹשִׂ֗ים אֵ֠ת י֣וֹם אַרְבָּעָ֤ה 21   ה מל . ז מל
עָשָׂר֙ לְחֹ֣דֶשׁ אֲדָ֔ר וְאֵ֛ת יוֹם־חֲמִשָּׁ֥ה עָשָׂ֖ר בֹּ֑ו בְּכָל־שָׁנָ֥ה וְשָׁנָֽה׃
כַּיָּמִ֗ים אֲשֶׁר־נָ֨חוּ בָהֶ֤ם הַיְּהוּדִים֙ מֵא֣וֹיְבֵיהֶ֔ם וְהַחֹ֗דֶשׁ אֲשֶׁר֩ נֶהְפַּ֨ךְ 22   ד
לָהֶ֤ם מִיָּגוֹן֙ לְשִׂמְחָ֔ה וּמֵאֵ֖בֶל לְי֣וֹם ט֑וֹב לַעֲשֹׂ֣ות אוֹתָ֗ם יְמֵ֤י מִשְׁתֶּה֙   ל . ד מל בכתי
וְשִׂמְחָ֔ה וּמִשְׁלֹ֤וחַ מָנוֹת֙ אִ֣ישׁ לְרֵעֵ֔הוּ וּמַתָּנ֖וֹת לָֽאֶבְיוֹנִֽים׃ וְקִבֵּל֙ 23   ב וחס . ג חס
הַיְּהוּדִ֔ים אֵ֥ת אֲשֶׁר־הֵחֵ֖לּוּ לַעֲשֹׂ֑ות וְאֵ֛ת אֲשֶׁר־כָּתַ֥ב מָרְדֳּכַ֖י
אֲלֵיהֶֽם׃ כִּי֩ הָמָ֨ן בֶּֽן־הַמְּדָ֜תָא הָֽאֲגָגִ֗י צֹרֵר֙ כָּל־הַיְּהוּדִ֔ים חָשַׁ֥ב עַל־ 24   ב
הַיְּהוּדִ֖ים לְאַבְּדָ֑ם וְהִפִּ֥יל פּוּר֙ ה֣וּא הַגּוֹרָ֔ל לְהֻמָּ֖ם וּֽלְאַבְּדָֽם׃

[17] ועשה ג וסימנֹ ועשה תעשינה . כזמתכנה . ועשה אתו יום משתה ושמחה .
וחבירו ‏o‏: [20] רחוקים ז מל וסימנהון רחוקים אנחנו . ורחוקים המה . שמעו
הרחוקים מצדקה . ורחוקים יבאו . הקרובים . רחוקים איש מאחיו ‏o‏: [22] כימים ד
וסימנהון ותשבו בקדש . הראשנים . הראשנים . אשר נחו בהם ‏o‏:

18 v 18 (G) V T^R | > G^{Mss} G^{AT} S (homtel) • וְעָשֹׂ֣ה אֹת֔וֹ י֖וֹם מִשְׁתֶּ֣ה וְשִׂמְחָֽה׃ (T^R) |
μετὰ χαρᾶς καὶ εὐφροσύνης G (abbr) | > G^{AT} | *diem constituere sollemnem
epularum atque laetitiae* V (ampl) • **19** הַפְּרָזִ֗ים | הפרוזים M^{ket} | הַפְּרָזִים M^{qere} |
οἱ διεσπαρμένοι G S (explic) | > G^{AT} (abbr) | *qui in oppidis non muratis (ac
villis morabantur)* V (lib-seman) | פצחאי T^R (explic) ✧ • **20** הַדְּבָרִ֖ים הָאֵ֑לֶּה S
T^R | τοὺς λόγους τούτους εἰς βιβλίον G G^{AT} (explic) | *omnia haec* V T^{Sh}
(lib-seman) • **22** כַּיָּמִ֗ים S T^{Sh} | ἐν γὰρ ταύταις ταῖς ἡμέραις G (lib-seman) |
> G^{AT} (abbr) | *quia in ipsis diebus* V (ampl) | כזמן יומין T^R (ampl) ✧ • **23** וְקִבֵּל֙
| καὶ προσεδέξαντο G G^{AT} V S T^R (assim-ctext) ✧ • אֲשֶׁר־הֵחֵ֖לּוּ לַעֲשֹׂ֑ות וְאֵ֛ת (V)
(S) T^R | > G G^{AT} (abbr) | *et posuerunt in memoratione, et* La (shift) • **24**
הָֽאֲגָגִ֗י
S T^{Sh} | ὁ Μακεδών G (substit) | > G^{AT} (abbr) | *stirpis Agag* V (lib-seman) |
דמן ייחוס אגג T^R (paraphr) ✧ • כָּל־ S T^R | > G G^{AT} V (abbr) ✧ •

בְּרֹא פסוק

²⁵ וּבְבֹאָהּ לִפְנֵי הַמֶּלֶךְ אָמַר עִם־הַסֵּפֶר יָשׁוּב מַחֲשַׁבְתּוֹ הָרָעָה
אֲשֶׁר־חָשַׁב עַל־הַיְּהוּדִים עַל־רֹאשׁוֹ וְתָלוּ אֹתוֹ וְאֶת־בָּנָיו עַל־

ה בטע ברא
פסוק . ה

²⁶ הָעֵץ: עַל־כֵּן קָרְאוּ לַיָּמִים הָאֵלֶּה פוּרִים עַל־שֵׁם הַפּוּר עַל־כֵּן

ל

עַל־כָּל־דִּבְרֵי הָאִגֶּרֶת הַזֹּאת וּמָה־רָאוּ עַל־כָּכָה וּמָה הִגִּיעַ

וקבלו
ק

²⁷ אֲלֵיהֶם: קִיְּמוּ וְקִבְּל הַיְּהוּדִים | עֲלֵיהֶם | וְעַל־זַרְעָם וְעַל כָּל־

גׁמל

הַנִּלְוִים עֲלֵיהֶם וְלֹא יַעֲבוֹר לִהְיוֹת עֹשִׂים אֵת שְׁנֵי הַיָּמִים הָאֵלֶּה

ל . ל

²⁸ כִּכְתָבָם וְכִזְמַנָּם בְּכָל־שָׁנָה וְשָׁנָה: וְהַיָּמִים הָאֵלֶּה נִזְכָּרִים וְנַעֲשִׂים

ל . ב

בְּכָל־דּוֹר וָדוֹר מִשְׁפָּחָה וּמִשְׁפָּחָה מְדִינָה וּמְדִינָה וְעִיר וָעִיר וִימֵי

הַפּוּרִים הָאֵלֶּה לֹא יַעַבְרוּ מִתּוֹךְ הַיְּהוּדִים וְזִכְרָם לֹא־יָסוּף

²⁹ מִזַּרְעָם: ס וַתִּכְתֹּב אֶסְתֵּר הַמַּלְכָּה בַת־אֲבִיחַיִל וּמָרְדֳּכַי

ל . ל

הַיְּהוּדִי אֶת־כָּל־תֹּקֶף לְקַיֵּם אֵת אִגֶּרֶת הַפּוּרִים הַזֹּאת הַשֵּׁנִית:

ג

³⁰ וַיִּשְׁלַח סְפָרִים אֶל־כָּל־הַיְּהוּדִים אֶל־שֶׁבַע וְעֶשְׂרִים וּמֵאָה מְדִינָה

³¹ מַלְכוּת אֲחַשְׁוֵרוֹשׁ דִּבְרֵי שָׁלוֹם וֶאֱמֶת: לְקַיֵּם אֶת־יְמֵי הַפֻּרִים

[26] לֹא יֹאכְלוּ . יִדְרְכוּ . חָרָה . אֲבָכָה . קָרְאוּ :ס לְיָמִים ה וְסִימָנְהוֹן וְעֶרֶךְ בְּגָדִים
וּמְחִיתֵךְ . וּבְגַלְחוֹ אֶת . הַיְעַמֵד . וּבָאתִי . עַל כֵּן :ס [28] וִימֵי ב לְמַעַן יִרְבּוּ יְמֵיכֶם וִימֵי
בְּנֵיכֶם . וִימֵי הַפּוּרִים הָאֵלֶּה :ס [29] מִן וַתִּכְתֹּב אֶסְתֵּר הַמַּלְכָּה עַד סוֹפֵהּ דְּסִיפָה הַפָּרִים
חַס וּשְׁאָר מל :ס [30] אֶל כָּל הַיְּהוּדִים ג וְסִימָנְהוֹן הַדָּבָר אֲשֶׁר הָיָה דִירְמִ' . וַיִּשְׁלַח
סְפָרִים . וַחֲבֵירוֹ :ס

25 וּבְבֹאָהּ I καὶ ὡς εἰσῆλθεν G (assim-ctext) I > G^AT (abbr) I *et postea ingressa
est Hester* V S T^R (explic) ✢ • עִם־הַסֵּפֶר I > G G^AT T^R (abbr) I *litteris regis* V
(lib-seman) I ܣܦܪܐ S (lib-seman) I מַה דְּכַת' בְּסִיפְרָא T^Sh (lib-seman) ✢ •
26 פוּרִים V S T^R I Φρουραί G (facil-lex) I Φουραια G^AT (facil-lex) ✢ • עַל־כֵּן²
(V) T^R I διά G (facil-styl) I > G^AT (abbr) I ܘܓܠ S (facil-styl) ✢ • **27** וְקִבֵּל I
וקבל M^L(ket) M^L34 M^Y (V) I וְקִבְּלוּ M^L(qere) G S T^R (assim-ctext) I > G^AT (abbr) ‖
pref וְקִבֵּל M^L(ket) M^Y M^L34 (V) ✢ • וְלֹא יַעֲבוֹר (S) T^R (T^Sh) I οὐδὲ μὴν ἄλλως
χρήσονται G (lib-seman) I > G^AT (abbr) I *ut nulli liceat* V (lib-seman) ✢ •
וְכִזְמַנָּם (T^R) T^Sh I > G G^AT (abbr) I *et certa expetunt tempora* V (lib-seman) I
(ܕܚܠܒܐ) ܚܘܒܚܕܘ S (lib-seman) • **29** וַתִּכְתֹּב G S T^R I > G^AT (abbr) I
scripseruntque V (assim-ctext) ✢ • אֶת־כָּל־תֹּקֶף (S) T^Sh I > G G^AT (abbr) I
firmamentum La (substit) I *ut omni studio* V (lib-seman) I יָת כָּל מְגִלָּאתָא הָדָא T^R (paraphr) ✢ • הַשֵּׁנִית: I > G G^AT S (abbr) I *secundam* V
(transl) I תִּנְיֵיתָא T^R (substit) • **30** וַיִּשְׁלַח S T^R I > G G^AT (abbr) I *et miserunt* V
(assim-ctext) ✢ • מַלְכוּת T^R I > G G^AT (abbr) I *regis* V (harm-ctext) I ܕܡܠܟܘܬܐ
S (harm-ctext) I דְּמַלְכוּת' T^Sh (harm-ctext) •

בַּ הָאֵ֙לֶּה֙ בִּזְמַנֵּיהֶ֔ם כַּאֲשֶׁר֩ קִיַּ֨ם עֲלֵיהֶ֜ם מָרְדֳּכַ֤י הַיְּהוּדִי֙ וְאֶסְתֵּ֣ר

לַ הַמַּלְכָּ֔ה וְכַאֲשֶׁ֛ר קִיְּמ֥וּ עַל־נַפְשָׁ֖ם וְעַל־זַרְעָ֑ם דִּבְרֵ֥י הַצֹּמ֖וֹת

לַ 32 וְזַעֲקָתָֽם׃ וּמַאֲמַר֙ אֶסְתֵּ֔ר קִיַּ֕ם דִּבְרֵ֥י הַפֻּרִ֖ים הָאֵ֑לֶּה וְנִכְתָּ֖ב

גַ בסיפ . ק   אחשורוש   בַּסֵּֽפֶר׃ פ   וַיָּ֩שֶׂם֩ הַמֶּ֨לֶךְ אֲחַשְׁוֵרֹ֧שׁ ׀ מַ֛ס עַל־הָאָ֖רֶץ וְאִיֵּ֥י הַיָּֽם׃ 0

גַ.ל.ל.בּ 2 וְכָל־מַעֲשֵׂ֤ה תָקְפּוֹ֙ וּגְב֣וּרָת֔וֹ וּפָרָשַׁת֙ גְּדֻלַּ֣ת מָרְדֳּכַ֔י אֲשֶׁ֥ר גִּדְּל֖וֹ

ט מל בכת הַמֶּ֑לֶךְ הֲלוֹא־הֵ֣ם כְּתוּבִ֗ים עַל־סֵ֙פֶר֙ דִּבְרֵ֣י הַיָּמִ֔ים לְמַלְכֵ֖י מָדַ֥י

חַ 3 וּפָרָ֑ס כִּ֣י ׀ מָרְדֳּכַ֣י הַיְּהוּדִ֗י מִשְׁנֶה֙ לַמֶּ֣לֶךְ אֲחַשְׁוֵר֔וֹשׁ וְגָדוֹל֙

לַ.ל.ה לַיְּהוּדִ֔ים וְרָצ֖וּי לְרֹ֣ב אֶחָ֑יו דֹּרֵ֥שׁ טוֹב֙ לְעַמּ֔וֹ וְדֹבֵ֥ר שָׁל֖וֹם

לְכָל־זַרְעֽוֹ׃

קְסֹח

[10:2] וכל מעשה ג וסימנ וכל בגד וכל כלי עור . וישתמר חקות עמרי וכל מעשה בית
אחאב . וכל מעשה תקפו וגבורתו ופרשת :o

31 וְאֶסְתֵּ֥ר הַמַּלְכָּ֖ה G S T^R | > G^AT (abbr) | *et Hester* V (abbr) ⋮ •
דִּבְרֵ֥י הַצֹּמ֖וֹת וְזַעֲקָתָֽם׃ (T^R) | > G G^AT (abbr) | *ieiunia atque clamores* V (lib-
seman) | מילי דצומי[ן]א ודתעניתא S (lib-seman) | ܟܐ̈ܡܬܣ ܟܝ̈ܬܥܬ܇ ܐܬܣܐܟ T^Sh (lib-seman) ⋮ • **10:1** וַיָּ֩שֶׂם֩ V S T^R | ἔγραψεν δέ G (assim-cultur) | καὶ
ἔγραψεν G^AT (assim-ctext) • | אֲחַשְׁוֵרֹ֧שׁ (V) S T^R | > G G^AT (abbr) ⋮ • **2** מָרְדֳּכַ֔י
La S T^R | > G G^AT (abbr) | *Mardocheum* V (lib-seman) ⋮ • מָדַ֥י וּפָרָ֑ס V S T^R |
Περσῶν καὶ Μήδων G G^AT (transp) | *Medorum* La (abbr) • **3** וְגָדוֹל֙ לַיְּהוּדִ֔ים |
καὶ μέγας ἦν ἐν τῇ βασιλείᾳ καὶ δεδοξασμένος ὑπὸ τῶν Ἰουδαίων G (ampl) |
καὶ μέγας ἦν ἐν τῇ βασιλείᾳ καὶ φιλούμενος ὑπὸ πάντων τῶν Ἰουδαίων G^AT
(ampl) | *et magnus inter Iudaeos* V (differ-gram) | ܟܠ ܒ̈ܢܝ ܝܗܘܕܐ S (T^R)
(lib-seman) | וסבא דיהודאי T^Sh (lib-seman) ⋮ • וְרָצ֖וּי לְרֹ֣ב אֶחָ֑יו (V) | καὶ
φιλούμενος διηγεῖτο τὴν ἀγωγὴν παντὶ τῷ ἔθνει αὐτοῦ G (ampl) | καὶ ἡγεῖτο
αὐτῶν καὶ δόξαν παντὶ τῷ ἔθνει αὐτοῦ περιετίθει G^AT (ampl) | > S (abbr) |
ורעי בסגיעתהון T^R (paraphr) | ומתרעי לסגי אחוי דמן שבטא דבנימן T^Sh (paraphr)
⋮ • זַרְעֽוֹ׃ S T^R | foll F 1-11 G (lit) | foll 8:53-59 G^AT (lit) | foll 10:4-13
(= F 1-10); 11:1 (= F 11); 11:2-13 (= A 1-11); 12:1-6 (= A 12-17); 13:1-7
(= B 1-7); 13:8-18 (= C 1-11); 14:1-19 (= C 12-30); 15:1-3 (= 4:8); 15:4-19
(= D 1-16); 16:1-24 (= E 1-24) V (lit) ⋮ •